Actively

Activities that are tied to each skill level offer students multiple opportunities to interact with the reading and receive immediate feedback.

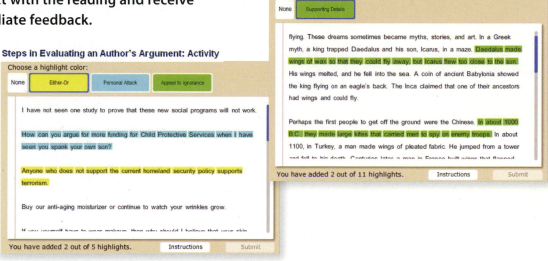

Steps in Evaluating an Author's Argument: Activity

Choose a highlight color:

None | Either-Or | Personal Attack | Appeal to ignorance

I have not seen one study to prove that these new social programs will not work.

How can you argue for more funding for Child Protective Services when I have seen you spank your own son?

Anyone who does not support the current homeland security policy supports terrorism.

Buy our anti-aging moisturizer or continue to watch your wrinkles grow.

You have added 2 out of 5 highlights. | Instructions | Submit

Identifying, Marking, and Annotating Supporting Details: Activity

Choose a highlight color:

None | Supporting Details

flying. These dreams sometimes became myths, stories, and art. In a Greek myth, a king trapped Daedalus and his son, Icarus, in a maze. Daedalus made wings of wax so that they could fly away, but Icarus flew too close to the sun. His wings melted, and he fell into the sea. A coin of ancient Babylonia showed the king flying on an eagle's back. The Inca claimed that one of their ancestors had wings and could fly.

Perhaps the first people to get off the ground were the Chinese. In about 1000 B.C. they made large kites that carried men to spy on enemy troops. In about 1100, in Turkey, a man made wings of pleated fabric. He jumped from a tower

You have added 2 out of 11 highlights. | Instructions | Submit

"Connect Reading gives [students] more study options and a fresh perspective to listen and learn from."
–Yvette Daniel, Central Georgia Tech.

Critically

LiveInk, a research-based technology, increases the reader's comprehension, which leads to improved synthesis and understanding of information, the foundation of critical thinking.

When Not Asking for Directions Is Dangerous to Your Health

by Deborah Tannen

If conversational-style
differences
lead to troublesome outcomes
in work
as well as private settings,
there are some work settings
where
the outcomes of style
are a matter
of life and death.

Health-care professionals
are often
in such situations.

So are airline pilots.
Of all the examples
of women's and men's
characteristic styles
that I discussed
in You Just Don't Understand,
the one that
(to my surprise)
attracted the most attention

"When Not Asking for Directions Is Dangerous to Your Health," Deborah Tannen

Click to Read in Live Ink® for a better grade
Learn More about Live Ink

If conversational-style differences lead to troublesome outcomes in work as well as private settings, there are some work settings where the outcomes of style are a matter of life and death. Health-care professionals are often in such situations. So are airline pilots.

Of all the examples of women's and men's characteristic styles that I discussed in You Just Don't Understand, the one that (to my surprise) attracted the most attention was the question "Why don't men like to stop and ask for directions?" Again and again, in the responses of audiences, talk-show hosts, letter writers, journalists, and conversationalists, this question seemed to crystallize the frustration many people had experienced in their own lives. And my explanation seems to have rung true: that men are more likely to be aware that asking for directions, or for any kind of help, puts them in a one-down position.

With regard to asking directions, women and men are keenly aware of the advantages of their own style. Women frequently observe how much time they would save if their husbands simply stopped and asked someone instead of driving around in vain to find a destination themselves. But I have also been told by men that it makes sense not to ask directions because you learn a lot about a neighborhood, as well as about navigation, by driving around and finding your own way.

2

Experience Reading

Suzanne Liff
Nassau Community College

Joyce Stern
Nassau Community College

Mc
Graw
Hill

Connect
Learn
Succeed™

The McGraw·Hill Companies

Connect
Learn
Succeed™

Published by McGraw-Hill, an imprint of The McGraw-Hill Companies, Inc., 1221 Avenue of the Americas, New York, NY 10020. Copyright © 2012. All rights reserved. No part of this publication may be reproduced or distributed in any form or by any means, or stored in a database or retrieval system, without the prior written consent of The McGraw-Hill Companies, Inc., including, but not limited to, in any network or other electronic storage or transmission, or broadcast for distance learning.

This book is printed on acid-free paper.

1 2 3 4 5 6 7 8 9 0 RJE/RJE 10 9 8 7 6 5 4 3 2 1

ISBN: 978-0-07-340715-9 (Student's Edition)
MHID: 0-07-340715-1 (Student's Edition)
ISBN: 978-0-07-329239-7 (Instructor's Edition)
MHID: 0-07-329239-7 (Instructor's Edition)

Sponsoring Editor: *John Kindler*
Marketing Manager: *Jaclyn Elkins*
Developmental Editors: *Anne Leung and Deborah Kopka*
Production Editor: *Rachel J. Castillo*
Supplements Editor: *Sarah Colwell*
Manuscript Editor: *Barbara Hacha*
Cover Designer and Design Manager: *Jeanne Schreiber*
Text Designer: *Amanda Kavanagh, Ark Design*
Illustrator: *Ayelet Arbel*
Photo Researcher: *Sonia Brown*
Buyer: *Louis Swaim*
Composition: *11/13 Sabon by Laserwords Private Limited*
Printing: *45# New Era Matte Thin, R. R. Donnelley & Sons/Jefferson City, MO*

Vice President Editorial: *Michael Ryan*
Publisher: *David S. Patterson*
Director of Development: *Dawn Groundwater*

Cover: © James Balog/Stone/Getty Images

Credits: The credits appear at the end of the book and are considered an extension of the copyright page.

Library of Congress Cataloging-in-Publication Data

Liff, Suzanne.
 Experience reading. Book 2/Suzanne Liff, Joyce Stern. — 1st ed.
  p. cm.
 Includes bibliographical references.
 ISBN-13: 978-0-07-340715-9 (alk. paper)
 ISBN-10: 0-07-340715-1 (alk. paper)
 ISBN-13: 978-0-07-329239-7 (alk. paper)
 ISBN-10: 0-07-329239-7 (alk. paper)
 1.   College readers.   I. Stern, Joyce D.   II. Title.
 PE1417.L524   2011
 808'.0427—dc22

2010052881

The Internet addresses listed in the text were accurate at the time of publication. The inclusion of a website does not indicate an endorsement by the authors or McGraw-Hill, and McGraw-Hill does not guarantee the accuracy of the information presented at these sites.

www.mhhe.com

To my father, Nathan Brandell. For six years, he never wavered in his query, "How's the book coming?" inspiring perseverance and kindling love. Here it is, Dad.

– Suzanne Liff

To my children, Eric and Robyn, for their love, support, and encouragement.

– Joyce Stern

Brief Table of Contents

Table of Contents

Chapter 3
Lost in Translation: *Developing College-Level Vocabulary 50*

Chapter 4
What's the Big Idea? *Identifying the Main Idea in College Reading 78*

part three Modules: Theme-Based Reading Selections 278

Module 1
Readings About Food and Nutrition 278

Module 5
Readings About the Job Market   398

Module 6
Readings About the Media   428

Module 7
Readings About Social Networks   458

Module 8
Readings About the Environment 494

Take the Leap with
Experience Reading!

Experience Reading engages students personally, actively, and critically through an integrated print and digital program designed to prepare them for college—and lifelong—reading. Here's how:

Personally

Experience Reading invites students to make the connection between their lives and reading.

Scaffolded modules help students move from guided to independent reading with selections that are personal and relevant to their lives. By helping students move from practicing to applying, the modules meet a program's goals of making students independent readers.

Self-Monitored Reading
Reading Selection 2

Adolescents' TV Watching Is Linked to Violent Behavior
By Rosie Mestel

This newspaper article appeared as a feature selection in the Health Section of the Los Angeles Times. It reports on a long-term study of young people that was designed to find out how watching television might relate to future acts of aggression.

connect

Powered by Connect, Video Scenarios demonstrate how course concepts apply to the student's everyday life. In this video about inferences and drawing conclusions, students are asked to identify each concept in action. The students will have the opportunity to see what they caught and missed.

Making Inferences and Drawing Conclusions

Click to View

Experience Reading!

Actively

Experience Reading makes students active participants in their learning. Students are provided with hands-on experience in testing their knowledge and applying it to their lives.

try it and apply it activities get students to think about what they've learned. Being aware of how one learns (metacognition) enables students to actively and critically understand "What did I learn, how did I learn it, and how can I use it in the future."

Utilizing symbols such as this pause button, students are given a visual cue as to what they should be doing. In this case they are to pause and think about what they have learned. ▼

try it and apply it! 7-4   **Detecting Negative Connotation**

Directions: For each set of words, underline the word or words that you think have a negative connotation. Discuss your answers with your classmates. You may discover that perceptions of words differ depending on your background and culture.

Answers may vary.

1. boss, supervisor, superior
2. housewife, homemaker, stay-at-home mom
3. vagrant, bum, homeless
4. senior citizen, old-timer, geezer
5. fired, dismissed, canned
6. unmarried woman, spinster, single girl
7. skinny, slender, bony
8. steadfast, stubborn, inflexible
9. finicky, careful, picky
10. lady, broad, woman

connect

Powered by Connect, activities allow students multiple opportunities to interact with the reading skills and receive immediate feedback.

In this activity students are asked to read some text and then highlight those sentences that offer inferences and those that do not.

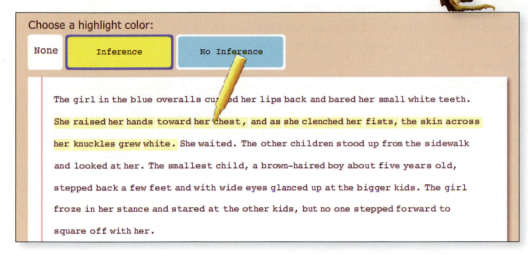

Choose a highlight color:

| None | Inference | No Inference |

The girl in the blue overalls curled her lips back and bared her small white teeth. She raised her hands toward her chest, and as she clenched her fists, the skin across her knuckles grew white. She waited. The other children stood up from the sidewalk and looked at her. The smallest child, a brown-haired boy about five years old, stepped back a few feet and with wide eyes glanced up at the bigger kids. The girl froze in her stance and stared at the other kids, but no one stepped forward to square off with her.

Collaborative learning experiences are stimulating learning experiences. Opportunities to discuss and respond to reading material with peers and in small groups fosters personal confidence and social skill growth, while developing a sense of community and belonging. Collaborative learning opportunities are found throughout the text, identified by the following icon: . Many exercises are structured so that they can be completed individually, in pairs, or in small groups.

Experience Reading!

Critically

Experience Reading encourages students to think critically, to question what they know and don't know, and then to use their insight to read and learn more effectively.

Each **scaffolded module** is arranged from least to most challenging, taking students from Guided Reading to Self-Monitored Reading, to Independent Reading. Students build on skills previously learned and apply them to future concepts.

Guided Reading
Reading Selection 1

The Green Mirage
By Rick Newman

In this selection from U.S. News & World Report, *Rick Newman interviews the president of Yankelovich, a market research firm, about what American consumers say about the environment.*

Self-Monitored Reading
Reading Selection 2

The Green Campus: How to Teach New Respect for the Environment?
The 3 R's: Reduce Your Carbon Footprint, Reuse, and Recycle
By Anne Underwood

In this article from Newsweek, *the author explains in what ways colleges are getting involved with environmental issues.*

Independent Reading
Textbook Reading Selection: Environmental Science

What Can Individuals Do?
"Green Washing" Can Mislead Consumers
By William P. Cunningham and Mary Ann Cunningham

This selection is from an environmental science textbook chapter titled "What Can Individuals Do?" The excerpt focuses on the impact of business and marketing on the consumer.

connect™

Comprehension is improved with Connect. *Experience Reading* uses the research-based LiveInk technology to increase the student's reading comprehension, which leads to improved synthesis of information, the foundation of critical thinking.

Check out the Live Ink Video at http://www.liveink.com/learnmore.php

Check out a Connect Reading demonstration at http://marcomm.mhhe.com/Connect/features/connectreading.php

"A Letter to My Teacher,"
    Kate Boyes

Dear Professor,
  I didn't belong in college.

I should have told you that.

My father
  dropped out of school
    after third grade.

My mother
  went through twelfth grade,
  but her family thought
    she was a little uppity
      for doing so.

Like my mother,
  I finished high school,
  and immediately got married
    and started having babies.

Critically

DIAGNOSTIC SCORE	COMPLETE YOUR TEST	CORRECT	PERCENTAGE
1. The Main Idea		--	--
2. Supporting Details		--	--
3. The Author's Purpose		--	--
4. The Author's Tone		--	--
5. Figurative Language		--	--
6. Patterns of Organization		--	--
7. Making Inferences and Drawing Conclusions		--	--
8. Bias		--	--
9. Fact and Opinion		--	--
10. Evaluating Author's Reasoning and Evidence		--	--
11. Scanning, Skimming, and Speed-Reading		--	--
12. Reading Textbooks		--	--
13. Vocabulary		--	--
14. Study Skills		--	--
AVERAGE		--	--

connect

Powered by Connect, Individual Learning Plans are targeted to each student's specific needs, and offer a systematic examination of all aspects of reading, from the author's purpose and tone to making inferences and drawing conclusions.

Previewing is taught as skill to successful reading.

Using the acronym THIEVES (Title, Headings, Introduction, Every first sentence in every paragraph, Vocabulary and visuals, End of chapter questions, Summary) students are aided in learning and synthesizing the skills they need to be successful, critical readers.

T Title—*The title identifies the topic, theme, or author's thesis, or argument.* Think about the title. What do you already know about it? Turn the title into a question that you can look for an answer to as you read.

H Headings—*Headings are the gateways into each section of the chapter or selection.* Like the title, they can be turned into questions that give you a reason for reading that section of the text. When you make a question out of a heading, try to connect it to the title. Notice the subheadings as well. They can often provide the answers to questions you make from the headings.

I Introduction—*The introduction to a chapter can fill you in on a subject by providing important background information.* Make sure you read it. If you are reading a selection, read the first paragraph to find out what is going to be discussed.

E Every first sentence in every paragraph—*The first sentences in textbook paragraphs are often the topic sentences or main ideas of the paragraphs.* Thus, you will gain a lot of information about the subject by reading them. You will also encounter selections without any headings, so the first sentences of the paragraphs will be your entry into the content. They will help you predict what the author will discuss.

V Vocabulary and Visuals—*The language of the discipline in which you are reading will probably be new and unfamiliar, so get ready to increase your vocabulary every time you read.* If you take a moment to look at new words ahead of time, it will help you to move through the selection more smoothly when you are reading. Notice the words, often given with their definitions, at the beginning of a chapter, boldface within the text, written in the margin, or reviewed at the end. Highlight these words. Say them aloud. Read their definitions.

Visuals—*Textbooks provide pictures, or visuals, that explain and illustrate what is being taught,* so be sure to look at them before you read the text. Read the captions, titles, descriptions, and keys. Many people remember and understand best when they can "see" a visual presentation of an idea. Common visuals include: photographs, drawings, graphs, figures, charts and tables, cartoons, and maps.

E End-of-Chapter Questions—*Reading these questions will give you a good idea of what the author believes it is important to know.* You also establish a purpose for reading: to find the answers to these questions or to gain enough knowledge from the chapter to apply the information and develop a thoughtful response to them. Reading and answering end-of-chapter questions can also help you prepare for exams.

S Summary—*Reading the summary first means you will have a lot of background knowledge and information already in your head when you read the chapter, which makes it easier to understand.* Be sure to check out the chapter to see if a summary exists.

Jump in and Teach with
Experience Reading!

Resources available for use with this text support both new and veteran instructors, whether they favor traditional text-based instruction or a blend of traditional and electronic media. The First Edition text and support materials provide complementary experiences for instructors and students. All of these components are built around the core concepts articulated in the text to promote a deeper understanding of reading. This type of integration gives instructors the flexibility to use any of the text-specific electronic or print materials knowing they are completely compatible with one another. Please see your McGraw-Hill sales representative for information on policy, price, and availability of the following supplements.

Online Learning Center for Instructors. The password-protected instructor side of the Online Learning Center (www.mhhe.com/experience_reading) contains the Instructor's Manual, Test Bank files, PowerPoint Presentations, and other valuable material to help you design and enhance your course. See more information about specific assets below. Ask your local McGraw-Hill sales representative for password information.

Instructor's Manual, by Jim Bernarducci of Middlesex Community College. This comprehensive guide provides all the tools and resources instructors need to present and enhance their developmental reading course. The Instructor's Manual contains suggested activities and best practices for teaching the course, learning objectives, interesting lecture and media presentation ideas, student assignments and handouts. The many tips and activities in this manual can be used with any class, regardless of size or teaching approach.

Test Bank, by Nicole Williams of Community College of Baltimore County. The test bank contains more than 400 multiple-choice items and 60 short-answer questions, classified by cognitive type and level of difficulty, and keyed to the appropriate key concept and page in the textbook. All questions are compatible with EZ Test, McGraw-Hill's Computerized Test Bank program.

PowerPoint Presentations, by Pamela Huntington and Lenice Wilson of Merced College. These presentations cover the key points of each chapter. They can be used as is, or you may modify them to meet your specific needs.

Ways to Experience Reading!

Create

Craft your teaching resources to match the way you teach! With McGraw-Hill Create, you can easily rearrange chapters, combine material from other content sources, and quickly upload content you have written, such as your course syllabus or teaching notes. Find the content you need in Create by searching through thousands of leading McGraw-Hill textbooks. Arrange your book to fit your teaching style. Create even allows you to personalize your book's appearance by selecting the cover and adding your name, school, and course information. Order a Create book and you'll receive a complimentary print review copy in 3–5 business days or a complimentary electronic review copy (eComp) via email in about one hour. Go to www.mcgrawhillcreate.com today and register. Experience how McGraw-Hill Create empowers you to teach your students your way.

CourseSmart This text is available as an eTextbook at www.CourseSmart.com. At CourseSmart your students can take advantage of significant savings off the cost of a print textbook, reduce their impact on the environment, and gain access to powerful web tools for learning. CourseSmart eTextbooks can be viewed online or downloaded to a computer. The eTextbooks allow students to do full text searches, add highlighting and notes, and share notes with classmates. CourseSmart has the largest selection of eTextbooks available anywhere. Visit www.CourseSmart.com to learn more and to try a sample chapter.

Tegrity

Tegrity Campus is a service that makes class time available all the time by automatically capturing every lecture in a searchable format for students to review when they study and complete assignments. With a simple one-click start and stop process, users capture all computer screens and corresponding audio. Students replay any part of any class with easy-to-use browser-based viewing on a PC or Mac. Educators know that the more students can see, hear, and experience class resources, the better they learn. With Tegrity Campus, students quickly recall key moments by using Tegrity Campus's unique search feature. This search helps students efficiently find what they need, when they need it, across an entire semester of class recordings. Help turn all your students' study time into learning moments immediately supported by your lecture.

Professional Acknowledgments

We are tremendously grateful to the following instructors whose insightful contributions during the development and production of *Experience Reading* have improved it immeasurably.

Manuscript Reviewers

Albany Technical College
Tomekia Cooper

Anne Arundel Community College
Kerry Taylor

Baltimore City Community College
Carol Anne Ritter

Bowling Green Community College
Brenda Miller
Jeanette Prerost

Brevard Community College–Melbourne
Kathleen Carlson

Bronx Community College
Joseph Todaro

Broward College–South
Gary Kay

Camden County College
Donna Armstrong
Christine Webster

Catawba Valley Community College
Kay Gregory

Community College of Baltimore County–Catonsville
Rachele Lawton
Nicole Willams

Community College of Baltimore County–Essex
Sharon Hayes

Cedar Valley College
Janet Brotherton

Central Georgia Technical College
Yvette Daniel

Central Piedmont Community College
Patricia Hill-Miller

Citrus College
Beverly Van Citters

Community College of Denver
Marta Brown
Yvonne Frye

Delaware Technical Community College–Dover
Martha Hofstetter

El Camino College
Inna Newbury

Florence-Darlington Technical College
Hattie Pinckney

Fullerton College
Amy Garcia

Gloucester County College
Birdena Brookins

Gray's Harbor College
Kathy Barker

Greenville Technical College
Toi Graham
Mahalia Johnson

Harold Washington College
Amelia Lopez

Henry Ford Community College
Pamela Kaminski

Hillsboro Community College
Aimee Alexander-Shea

Houston Community College–Southeast
Patricia Dennis-Jones

Illinois Central College
Nikki Aitken

Imperial Valley College
Deirdre Rowley

JS Reynolds Community College
Eric Hibbison
Nancy Morrison

Jackson State Community College
Letitia Hudlow

Lansing Community College
Leslie Lacy

Lone Star College–North Harris
Wei Li

Merced College
Pamela Huntington
Lenice Wilson

Miami Dade College–Kendall
Billy Jones

Miami Dade College–Wolfson
Jessica Carroll

Middlesex County College
James Bernarducci
Gertrude Coleman

Minneapolis Community and Technical College
Kim Zernechel

Navarro College
Shari Waldrop

Niagara County Community College–Sanborn
Joan Mooney

Normandale Community College
Denise Chambers

North Lake College
Tamera Ardrey

Northwest Vista College
Sharla Jones

Owens Community College
Margaret Bartelt

Palm Beach Community College–Lake Worth
Catherine Seyler

"This is going to be my next textbook–it is exciting, energetic, presents basic skills in an excellent format and in a logical sequence!!"

– Bonnie Arnett, Washtenaw Community College

Passaic County Community College
Linda Bakian

Prince George's Community College
Marcia Dawson
Gwendalina McClain-Digby
Mirian Torain

Pulaski Technical College
Lynetta Doye
Betty Raper

Richard J Daley College
Shirley Carpenter

St John's River Community College–Palatka
Linda Black
Julie Kelly
Theresa Kleinpoppen

St. Petersburg College
Patricia Windon

Saint Philips College
Raymond Elliot

South Texas College
Florinda Rodriguez

Tacoma Community College
Lydia Lynn Lewellen
John Sandin

Tallahassee Community College
Laura Girtman

Tarrant County College–Northeast
Karen Harrel

Tidewater Community College–Norfolk
Wanda Stewart

University of Texas at Brownsville
Herman Pena

University of Texas at El Paso
Cheryl Baker Heller
Andrea Berta

Valencia Community College–West
Karen Cowden
Tracy Harrison
Dawn Sedik

Wake Technical Community College
Cheryl Burk

Washtenaw Community College
Bonnie Arnett

Design Reviewers

Albany Technical College
Tomekia Cooper

Baltimore City Community College
Carol Ann Ritter

Brevard Community College–Melbourne
Kathleen Carlson

Catawba Valley Community College
Kay Gregory

Central Georgia Technical College
Yvette Daniel

Community College of Baltimore County–Catonsville
Rachele Lawton
Nicole Williams

Community College of Baltimore County–Essex
Sharon Hayes

Community College of Denver
Marta Brown

Greenville Technical College
Toi Graham

Harold Washington College
Amelia Lopez

Illinois Central College
Nikki Aitken

Imperial Valley College
Deirdre Rowley

Jackson State Community College
Letitia Hudlow

Merced College
Pamela Huntington

Miami Dade College–Kendall
Billy Jones

Middlesex County College
James Bernarducci

Normandale Community College
Denise Chambers

Prince George's Community College
Gwendalina McClain-Digby
Mirian Torain

Pulaski Technical College
Lynetta Doye

St John's River Community College–Palatka
Linda Black
Julie Kelly

St. Petersburg College
Patricia Windon

Saint Philips College
Raymond Elliott

South Texas College
Florinda Rodriguez

Tallahassee Community College
Laura Girtman

Tarrant County College–Northeast
Karen Harrel

University of Texas at Brownsville
Herman Pena

University of Texas at El Paso
Cheryl Baker Heller
Andrea Berta

Wake Technical Community College
Cheryl Burk

Washtenaw Community College
Bonnie Arnett

Cover Reviewers

Anne Arundel Community College
Kerry Taylor

Central Georgia Technical College
Yvette Daniel

Central Piedmont Community College
Patricia Hill-Miller

Citrus College
Beverly Van Citters

Commonwealth School of Western Kentucky University
Jeanette Prerost

Community College of Baltimore County
Sharon Hayes
Nicole Williams

Delaware Technical and Community College
Martha Hofstetter

El Camino College
Inna Newbury

Grays Harbor College
Kathy Barker

Harold Washington College
Jennifer Meresman

Illinois Central College
Shari Dinkins

Imperial Valley College
Michael Heumann

J. Sargeant Reynolds Community College
Eric Hibbison
Nancy Morrison

Jackson State Community College
Letitia Hudlow

Merced College
Pamela Huntington

Miami Dade College
Jessica Carroll

Minneapolis Community & Technical College
Kim Zernechel

Niagara County Community College
Joan Mooney

Normandale Community College
Denise Chambers

North Lake College
Tamara Ardrey

Northwest Vista College
Sharla Jones

Owens Community College
Marge Bartelt

Prince George's Community College
Marcia Dawson
Gwendalina McClain-Digby
Mirian Torain

Pulaski Technical College
Betty Rape

Richard J. Daley College
Shirley Carpenter

St. Johns River Community College
Terrie Kleinpoppen

"An interesting way of teaching students the strategies required to understand reading. Finally something I don't have to work at creating."

– Florinda Rodriguez, South Texas College

St. Petersburg College
Patricia Windon

Tacoma Community College
Lydia Lynn Lewellen
John Sandin

Tallahassee Community College
Laurie Girtman

Tarrant County College
Karen Harrel

University of Texas at Brownsville
Herman Pena

University of Texas at El Paso
Cheryl Baker Heller

Valencia Community College
Dawn Sedick

Developmental Reading Symposia Attendees

Every year, McGraw-Hill conducts several Developmental Reading Symposia that are attended by instructors from across the country. These events are an opportunity for editors from McGraw-Hill to gather information about the needs and challenges of instructors teaching the course. They also offer a forum for the attendees to exchange ideas and experiences with colleagues whom they might not otherwise have met. The feedback we have received has been invaluable and has contributed—directly or indirectly—to the development of *Experience Reading*.

Borough of Manhattan Community College
Mark Hoffman

Broward Community College
James Rogge

Cedar Valley College
Janet Brotherton

Central Texas College
Phyllis Sisson

Chattanooga State Community College
Sarah Kuhn

Cincinnati State Technical & Community College
Sandi Buschmann

College of the Desert
Gary Bergstrom

Daytona State College
Sandra Offiah-Hawkins

Delaware Technical Community College–Dover
Ted Legates

El Camino College
Cynthia Silverman

Fullerton College
Amy Garcia

Greenville Technical College
Mahalia Johnson

Guilford Technical Community College
Bart Trescott

Harper College
Judy Kulchawik

Jackson State Community College
Letitia Hudlow

Lonestar College North Harris
Wei Li

Miami Dade College–Kendall
Sylvia Orozco

Miami Dade College–North
Leighton Spence

Miami Dade College–Wolfson
Majorie Sussman

Moraine Valley Community College
Joe Chaloka

Mountain View College
Julie Sepulveda

Navarro College
Shari Waldrop

Normandale Community College
Denise Chambers

Northeast Lakeview College
Wendy Crader

Prince George's Community College
Gwendalina McClain-Digby

Pulaski Technical College
Betty Raper

Saint Phillips College
Janet Flores

St. Petersburg College
Diane Reese

San Jacinto College South
Joanie DeForest

Santa Fe College
Laurel Severino

South Texas College
Romaldo Dominguez

Suffolk Community College
Nancy Gerli

Tallahassee Community College
Christine Barrileaux

Valencia Community College–West
Tracy Harrison

Westchester Community College
Lori Murphy

Personal Acknowledgments

We would like to extend our deepest appreciation to the many energetic individuals who help make *Experience Reading* possible. At McGraw-Hill, we'd like to thank John Kindler, Dawn Groundwater, Rachel Castillo, Sonia Brown, Jeanne Schreiber, and Marty Moga for all their efforts. Thanks also to Gillian Cook, Deborak Kopka, Barbara Hacha, and Anne Leung for their fine manuscript work. Finally, we would like to thank our students at Nassau Community College for providing us with inspiration.

About the Authors

Suzanne Liff is an Associate Professor in the Department of Reading and Basic Education at Nassau Community College. A former district-wide chairperson of secondary Special Education, Suzanne holds advanced degrees in Special Education and in Educational Administration and Supervision. She has taught preschoolers through adult learners, focusing on the learning, affective, behavioral, and metacognitive needs of students. She has presented to parents and colleagues, locally and nationally, on topics including cognitive and learning style differences, college reading and study strategies, effective classroom management, successful transition from high school to college, developmental learning communities, and social and emotional intelligence and the developmental learner. Her original works have been published for college-wide distribution as well as in professional juried journals. Professor Liff's work always links affective components with learning theory to yield academic success and scholarly joy. She teaches several developmental college reading classes, holds leadership positions on developmental reading and faculty development committees in higher education, and maintains a private practice for psycho-educational evaluation and intervention. She coordinates a unique initiative called IDEAS, which integrates basic academic skill development within all disciplines of college study. Professor Liff is an honorary life member of SEPTA. She is the recipient of the 2003 Faculty Distinguished Achievement Award for outstanding scholarly and professional accomplishment and the SUNY Chancellor's Award for Excellence in Teaching, 2007.

Joyce Stern is an Associate Professor in the Department of Reading and Basic Education at Nassau Community College. An educator for over thirty-five years, Professor Stern holds an advanced degree in TESOL from Hunter College. She is currently serving as the coordinator of her college's Learning Community Program and is involved in the design, implementation, and assessment of learning communities for liberal arts, career and technical education, ESL, and developmental students. She also wrote the curriculum for the English Language Institute, a language immersion program for entry-level second language learners. For her work at the college, she has been recognized by the college's Center for Students with Disabilities for her dedication to student learning and was the recipient of the 2008 NISOD Award in recognition for her achievement of excellence in teaching and leadership. She has also been awarded several Perkins Grants to develop learning communities for career and technical education students and recently participated in the STAR Grant to support nursing students in their professional studies.

chapter

1

It's Up to You
Taking Ownership of College Learning

In this chapter

you will learn to

- Become a successful student
- Set goals
- Manage your time effectively
- Control your concentration
- Monitor your progress
- Discover your learning style

Being a Successful College
Student

What does it take to be a success in college? While hard work and commitment, intelligence, good fortune, and an interesting, kind professor can surely make a difference, experts in the field of education know that several other factors are critical for college success. Ask any "A" students and they are likely to tell you that setting goals, putting aside enough time to complete assignments, studying for exams, knowing how to study effectively, and keeping track of how they are doing in each course really helps them succeed. Goal setting, time management, concentration, monitoring one's progress, and understanding one's learning strengths and style are among the most important keys to academic success. We'll take a look at each in this chapter. First, consider the importance of *choosing* to be successful.

Choosing Success

"Nothing meaningful or lasting comes without working hard at it, whether it's in your own life, or with people you're trying to influence."

What is your response to that statement? Do you agree? Think about a time in your life when you were successful. How did your success come about? Did it involve hard work and commitment on your part?

People experience and define success in different ways. In the following reading selection, basketball coach Rick Pitino shares his philosophy of success as it applies not only to his sport, but also to life in general. The earlier quotation comes from his article.

As you will see in all your future reading experiences, your personal response and connection to a reading selection is what will make it interesting, meaningful, and relevant to you. As you come across statements in the following reading that touch you personally, highlight them to share with your classmates in a discussion after you read.

Please read and enjoy the following selection. Take a look at the questions following the selection *before you read*. Keep them in mind as you read.

Success Is a Choice

By Rick Pitino

Rick Pitino is currently the head basketball coach at the University of Louisville. He also served as the head coach at the University of Kentucky, leading his team to the NCAA championship in 1966. The following excerpt is taken from his book, Success Is a Choice: Ten Steps to Overachieving in Business and Life, *Broadway Books, 1998, 1–3.*

(1) Winston Churchill *served as Prime Minister to the United Kingdom during WW II. He led his country in the war effort against the countries opposed to the Allies.*
(2) denominator— *something shared or held in common*
(3) fool's gold– *relatively worthless (Origin: reference to pyrite, a metal which resembled gold because of its yellowish hue, but was actually a "worthless" mineral.)*

(1) Winston Churchill's rallying cry for the British people during WW II was simple and succinct: hoping and praying for victory was fine, but deserving it was what really mattered.

What does it mean to "deserve victory"?

According to Churchill, victory comes only to those who work long and hard, who are willing to pay the price in blood, sweat, and tears. Hard work is also the building block of every kind of achievement: Without it, everything else is pointless. You can start with a dream or an idea or a goal, but before any of your hopes can be realized, you truly must deserve your success. This may sound old-fashioned in this age of self-gratification, but from the Sistine Chapel to the first transcontinental railroad to today's space shuttle, there's no mystery as to how these things of wonder were created. They were created by people who worked incredibly hard over a long period of time.

If you look closely at all great organizations, all great teams, all great people, the (2) one common denominator that runs through them is a second-to-none work ethic. The intense effort to achieve is always there. This is the one given if you want to be successful. When it comes to work ethic, there can be no compromises. Any other (3) promise of achievement is fool's gold.

We can see the evidence of fool's gold around us every day. It's the people looking for a quick fix. The easy way to lose weight. The no pain way to have a greater body. The instant way to get rich. The easy, no-assembly-required way to feel better about yourself, as if all you have to do is follow some simple directions and your problems will disappear like frost in the noonday sun.

But shortcuts fail.

The bottom line: Nothing meaningful or lasting comes without working hard at it, whether it's in your life or with the people you are trying to influence.

Take our basketball program at the University of Kentucky: We see ourselves as the hardest-working team in America. That is our standard, the yardstick by which we measure ourselves. We try to live up to it every day.

Are we the hardest-working team in America?

Who knows?

And who cares.

The important thing is we believe it. That's our edge. In close games, when the pressure intensifies and the margin between who wins and who loses can be as thin as an eggshell, we believe that all our hard work, all the long hours, all the perspiration will enable us to come out on top. Why? Because we deserve it. We deserve our victory; we feel we've sweated more blood than our opponents and will earn it the old-fashioned way.

In my years of coaching, I have worked with many players and seen a variety of attitude problems. Some players were selfish. Some doubted what we were trying to do. Some weren't as committed to the team concept as they should have been. I can live with all that. What I can't live with is a player who won't work hard. If players are willing to give the effort, they have no problem with me.

And you know what?

What's true on the basketball court is true in business and in life. You want to succeed? Okay, then succeed. Deserve it. How? Outwork everybody in sight. Sweat the small stuff. Go the extra mile. But whatever it takes, put your heart and soul into everything you do. Leave it all out on the open court.

But that won't happen unless you choose to make it happen. Success is not a lucky break. It's not a divine right. It's not an accident of birth.

Success is a choice.

Refer to the reading as you respond in complete sentences to the following questions.

1. What is Rick Pitino's philosophy of success?
    Rick Pitino believes success is earned and deserved. It is the result of "choosing" to work hard in order to reach your goals. Nothing meaningful or lasting comes without hard work and effort.

2. How does the author's philosophy of success compare with your own?
    Answers will vary.

3. What messages from this selection can you apply to yourself as a student in college?
    Answers will vary.

Set Goals

It may come as a surprise to learn that the simple act of stating a goal is the first step to achieving it. Just as you wouldn't get into your car and begin driving down the road without a destination, it makes little sense to begin your college experience or start any course without considering your goals. Goals may be developed for long-term, short-term, or even intermediate periods of time. For example, as a freshman in college, you might set passing this reading course as a **short-term goal,** completing your degree as your **intermediate goal,** and getting a job in your chosen career as a **long-term goal.**

Short-term, long-term, and intermediate goals can also be applied to smaller time periods. For instance, your long-term goal for this semester may be to pass all your classes. A short-term goal could include purchasing all the required texts and materials by the end of the first week. An intermediate goal might be to complete all your assignments on time. The more specifically you can state your goals, the more meaningful they become. For example, instead of stating that you intend to pass this class, you might say, "I will earn a B or better in this class."

try it and apply it! 1-1   Setting Goals for the Year

Directions: Give it a try! Identify at least one short-term, one intermediate, and one long-term goal for yourself for this academic year.

Time Frame	Goal(s) for This Year
Short-term	
Intermediate	
Long-term	

try it and apply it! 1-2   Setting Goals for a Class

Directions: Now be more specific. Identify goals, as described previously, for this or another class you are taking this semester.

Class: _____

Time Frame	Goals for This Class
Short-Term	
Intermediate	
Long-Term	

Keep in mind that it is important to review your goals periodically to be sure you are on the right track and that they are realistic and manageable. You might decide to revise them along the way. For example, you might need to limit the number of classes you originally set out to take in order to make room for more hours at work. Rather than take on more course work than is realistically manageable and compromising the quality of your work inside and out of school, adjust your intentions in one area to make time for both. Make your goals realistic enough to attain, but flexible enough to allow you to achieve success.

Commitment to your goals will affect other decisions you make in life. For example, if your goal is to get an "A" on your history exam, you are likely to study and prepare rather than decide to go out the night before the test.

Setting Goals

Problems with Setting Goals

- Being too vague in stating goals.
- Setting goals that are unrealistic and too demanding.
- Not allotting enough time to achieve goals successfully.
- Being impatient.
- Not being willing to make the effort to obtain goals.

Advantages of Setting Goals

- Provides a clear direction and motivation to succeed
- Puts you in control of your plans
- Helps you set priorities in your life
- Builds character

Manage Your Time Effectively

How am I ever going to get everything done? This is a very important question. In fact, the inability to manage their time in college is the number one reason why students don't succeed. The average high school student spends about 30 hours in class each week. Although college students spend about half as many hours in school, they are expected to study a great deal more outside of class. In fact, it is recommended that college students allot two hours of study time for each contact hour. For 15 contact hours (time spent in the classroom), this adds up to 30 additional hours of independent work, for a total of 45 hours a week. For some students, managing time effectively means finding a comfortable balance between their academic life and social activities; for many others, this balance also includes a job or family responsibilities.

Have you encountered any problems with time management this semester? Complete this brief survey to see how well you plan your time. For each statement, write the number that best describes you in the space provided.

Time Management Survey

Scale:	Never 1	Seldom 2	Sometimes 3	Often 4	Always 5

1. _____ I submit my assignments and projects on time.
2. _____ I remember important test and assignment due dates.
3. _____ I record my assignments and test dates in a planner.
4. _____ I complete my assignments before I go out and have fun.
5. _____ I allot sufficient time to complete each assignment.
6. _____ I review class material each day.
7. _____ I keep my schedule flexible so that I can have more time to study before midterms and finals.
8. _____ I arrive before the class session begins.

_____ **Total Score**

If you scored 40, you have **excellent** time management skills.
If you scored 30–39, you have **above average** time management skills.
If you scored 20–29, you have **average** time management skills.
If you scored 10–19, you have **below average** time management skills.
If you scored 1–9, you have **poor** time management skills.

Each item on the survey represents a key element in time management for college students. Are you pleased with your score? Is there room to improve your time management skills? Most students will probably say a resounding YES.

A simple purchase of a college planner is one of the best ways to improve your time management skills. Along with your textbooks, it's also one of the most important investments you can make at the beginning of each semester. And as American Express says in its advertising: "Don't leave home without it." Because college students have so many assignments to complete, papers to write, presentations to make, quizzes and tests to take, family obligations to meet, and work schedules to juggle, it's impossible to remember everything. Your college planner serves as a central organizer. Numerous planners are available at the campus bookstore, so you can select the one that best suits your needs.

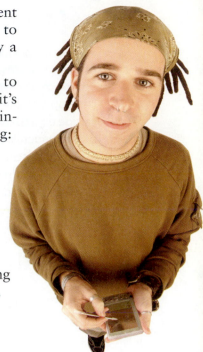

The acronym ORGANIZE stands for a system, detailed in the following box, that will help you use your planner to schedule your time effectively.

ORGANIZE Your Planner

O **O**rder a planner online or purchase a planner when you buy your textbooks.

R **R**eview your course syllabi at the beginning of the semester and highlight your assignments, research papers, presentations, quizzes, and exams.

G **G**et the due dates for assignments from your syllabi and write them in your planner.

A **A**llocate enough time to complete your work. Some assignments will require more time on task than others.

N **N**ote the due dates and work backward in planning your time. Give yourself more time than you think you may need. Don't forget to hand in completed assignments on time to avoid losing points.

I **I**nclude the dates of personal, social, or work-related commitments.

Z **Z**ero in on the instructions for your assignments to be sure you are meeting requirements and not wasting your time.

E **E**merge from this process with a sense that you have planned ahead and that you have used your time effectively and efficiently.

Note: Arriving on time for classes is another indication of effective time management. Paste a copy of your schedule in the front of your planner and refer to it regularly. Set your alarm clock, arrange for transportation, and arrive in class early if possible.

Tips for successful time management

- Set specific personal and academic goals.
- Attend all classes and arrive on time.
- Review course syllabi and create a semester plan.
- Develop a weekly schedule.
- Decide on a specific time to work on each course.
- Do not underestimate the time needed to complete tasks.
- Modify your schedule if necessary.
- Set up leisure time periods as a reward—*after* completing studies.
- Make time for yourself!

try it and apply it! 1-3   Time-Management Scenarios

Directions: Practice finding solutions to time-management problems. Break up into groups. You have 15 minutes to discuss your assigned scenario. As a group, you need to identify the poor time-management skills outlined in your scenario and develop a better plan for the characters involved. Assign a director to lead the discussion, a note-taker to complete the form on page 11, and a timekeeper/taskmaster to make sure the group adheres to the time limits and stays on task. The note-taker is responsible for reporting back to the class.

Scenario 1

Carlos was meeting in the Academic Advisement Center. It was the last day to register for the fall semester. Carlos told his advisor that he worked all day, but he could begin evening classes at 5:30 p.m. The advisor was able to schedule three classes for him even though these were not the classes he had wanted to take. Contrary to the advisor's advice, Carlos also insisted on adding one more class to his schedule so that he would be a full-time student. Now he will be attending classes four nights a week. What should Carlos have done?

Scenario 2

On the first day of class, Maya's history professor distributes the course syllabus. The first response journal is due on Friday. She hasn't bought the book yet and is not sure when her financial aid will come through. She also has to buy textbooks for three other classes. How could she complete the journal assignment?

Scenario 3

CSI is on tonight, and Coleisha just has to watch this program. She has never missed an episode, but she has two more chapters to read in history for class tomorrow. She has about twenty minutes before the show begins. What should she do?

Scenario 4

It's Thursday afternoon. Mustafa has a midterm in psychology next Monday, and his best friend is having a party tomorrow night. On Saturday, he will be working all day, and on Sunday he has tickets to a hockey game. What is the best way to manage his time so that he can do well on this test?

Scenario 5

It's the third week of classes, and Brian has already been late three times for his Friday morning English class. On Thursday evenings, he meets up with some high school friends and plays pool. On Friday mornings, he usually staggers in 15 minutes after the session has begun. Most of the time, he has forgotten his textbook, so he has to share with another classmate. What should he do differently if he wants to pass this course?

Scenario # _____

Brainstorm a list of possible ways to avoid the situation.

1. _____
2. _____
3. _____
4. _____
5. _____

Now use your list to generate a solution.

_____
_____
_____
_____
_____

Time Management

Outcomes of Poor Time Management

- Being late for class
- Always feeling stressed
- Making mistakes because of pressure
- Never having enough time to finish assignments or exams
- Forgetting test and assignment due dates
- Not having time to relax and have fun

Advantages of Effective Time Management

- Reduces anxiety
- Eliminates procrastination
- Promotes good study habits
- Eliminates cramming
- Leaves time for revision and review
- Leads to better academic success

Control Your Concentration

"Concentration is the secret of strength in politics, in war, in trade, in short in all management of human affairs."

—Ralph Waldo Emerson

According to Emerson, **concentration,** or focused thinking, is the vehicle for success in everything we try to accomplish in life. College freshmen identify difficulty with focusing as a major cause of study problems and poor academic performance. How can you control your concentration and make yourself a stronger student? To enhance your listening, reading, and studying skills, it is important to recognize what things distract you and interfere with your concentration.

try it and apply it! 1-4   Identifying What Distracts You

Directions: Following is a list of common distractions. Check off the statements that apply to you. You may want to add other statements that do not appear on this list. Then discuss your choices with other classmates and recommend ways to eliminate or minimize any of these distractions.

Common Distractions Checklist

___ 1. I am worried about paying for college.

___ 2. I am worried about paying off my loans.

___ 3. I am worried about meeting my expenses.

___ 4. I am working full time.

___ 5. I am helping in my family's business.

___ 6. I am worried about finding a place to live.

___ 7. I am worried about taking care of my siblings, children, or parents.

___ 8. I am worried about flunking out.

___ 9. I don't want to lose my financial aid.

___ 10. I am worried about making new friends in college.

___ 11. I miss my high school friends.

___ 12. I miss my parents.

___ 13. I want to go back to my country. I miss my family and friends.

___ 14. I am suffering from migraines.

___ 15. I always get hungry when I do my work.

___ 16. My little brother/sister always comes into my room and bothers me.

___ 17. My cell phone keeps ringing.

___ 18. My neighbors play loud music.

___ 19. The TV is always blasting in the den.

___ 20. I listen to music while I am studying.

___ 21. I fall asleep while I am studying.

___ 22. I daydream a lot.

___ 23. I like to sit in the back of the classroom.

___ 24. I go out to drink a beverage, eat a snack, or smoke a cigarette during the lecture.

___ 25. I finish my assignments while I am in another class.

___ 26. _____

___ 27. _____

___ 28. _____

___ 29. _____

___ 30. _____

The art of concentration, no matter if you are studying psychology or playing pool, is to reduce or eliminate distractions and focus on the task at hand. Following are some helpful hints:

Hints for Enhancing Concentration

Outside of Class

Study in a quiet and comfortable environment. Select a place that is designated for reading and studying. The college library provides large tables or individual desks. On a nice day, a quiet place on campus might be just the right spot for you. Even your dorm room, when your roommate is out, might be an ideal location to study.

Create your own study area. At home, find a comfortable working space where you will not be bothered by others. Gather all your study materials, make sure there is adequate lighting, and turn off your cell phone, music (unless background music helps you concentrate), and TV. Minimize visual distractions, such as pictures, your computer, and outside activities.

Establish a regular weekly schedule. Find the best time to read and study. Most people are more alert and able to concentrate during the day and early evening. However, if you have other responsibilities, such as work or family, you might have to plan to work early in the morning or later at night.

Set reading and study goals, and be positive and realistic. Some college reading may be challenging or uninteresting; however, to pass your class and meet graduation requirements, you will need to do the work. In addition, if you know you have difficulty concentrating, begin with short study periods and increase them gradually over time.

Take breaks. Divide assignments into manageable chunks. Reward yourself with a small break. Step away from your studies and do something different.

In Class

Before lectures, look over notes from the previous session. This will remind you what you have learned and assist you in predicting what will be discussed in the current lecture.

Read ahead. It is always a good idea to read the chapters in your textbook that pertain to what is going to be covered in the next lecture. By doing so, you will become an active listener who can participate in discussions and ask questions.

Show interest during lectures. Sitting in the back of the room, putting your head on the desk, or looking out the window will make it more difficult to concentrate. In contrast, an attentive expression and posture will help you concentrate. It will also show the instructor that you are actively listening and participating in class.

Be active and take notes. Focus on the instructor's lesson by asking questions and taking notes.

Resist distractions. Turn off your cell phone and put it away so you will not be tempted to view your messages. Sit in front of the classroom and position yourself away from disruptive classmates.

Minimize taking breaks in the middle of lectures. Students who leave class to answer calls or to get a drink miss valuable material. Instructors generally schedule breaks when classes meet for long blocks of time, so wait for a break.

Monitor Your Progress

Before you entered college, probably many people in your life kept track of how you were doing in school. Can you name a few? No doubt parents, guardians, teachers, guidance counselors, and supervisors were among those who not only kept an eye on your progress, but also had a right to know how you were doing. If you ran into difficulty, someone was likely to step in and offer support or guidance.

In college, it all changes. When you enroll, the school makes a contract with you, and no one else. Your grades, transcripts, accomplishments, and transgressions are shared with no one, unless you give your permission. Yes, privacy. How wonderful! But with that privacy comes a new level of responsibility.

To be a successful college student, you track your own journey, judge how things are going, and make adjustments when they are needed. You need to know how you are doing in each class, at all times. You need to know when you are truly in command of the material you are studying for an exam, rather than simply stopping when you have turned the last page of a reading assignment or spent the amount of time you have allocated for studying. Last, you also must be honest with yourself. If you realize that you are not performing optimally, or are not coming close to meeting the goals you have set out to attain, you must make some changes.

The good news is that by monitoring yourself within classes and keeping track of your performance, you will do better in school. You will become more self-aware and pay closer attention to your own behavior. You will make judgments about yourself and change the behaviors that are blocking your success. If you ever answer the question "How are you doing?" with "I have no idea," it's time to learn some self-monitoring skills.

Tips for monitoring your progress

- Buy and use a planner!
- Preview all course outlines and enter important due dates in your planner.
- Keep track of all your grades and your attendance in all classes. (You can do this in your planner.)
- Force yourself to recite or write without looking at notes or the text in the final phases of your studying. (See Chapter 9.)
- Anticipate test questions, and don't stop studying until you can answer them. (See Chapter 11.)

try it and apply it! 1-5   Monitoring Your Progress

Directions: The following checklist of questions will help you monitor your behavior and progress in school. Read each question carefully and check *Always*, *Sometimes*, or *Never* as it applies to you. Then read the comments that follow.

"How Am I Doing" Checklist

Task	Always	Sometimes	Never
1. Do I plan my schedule to include time during the week to complete all of my course work?			
2. Do I review all of my course outlines at the start of each semester so that I know where I am headed in each class?			
3. Do I enter important due dates from the syllabus into my own planner at the beginning of the semester?			
4. Do I break long assignments into manageable parts and assign these to myself on a weekly basis?			
5. Do I check off assignments after I have completed them?			
6. Do I make sure I never miss a class?			
7. Do I arrive on time to all of my classes?			
8. Do I ask questions in or after class when I need to clarify something that has been said in class?			
9. Do I prepare well for exams?			
10. Do I record all my grades on exams and assignments as I receive them so I have a running record?			
11. Do I make appointments to meet with my professors when I am unclear about an assignment or confused by a topic?			
12. Do I find out in a timely manner what I may have missed in class because of an unavoidable absence?			
13. Do I schedule personal and social events around the completion of my assignments?			
Total Number of Checks in Each Column			

- **If you identified between 10 and 13 items in the *Always* column,** you are already doing a fine job of self-monitoring. Notice any items where you selected *Sometimes* or *Never* and try including them this semester.

- **If you scored between 6 and 9 items in the *Always* column,** you are doing fairly well in self-monitoring, but should set goals in three or four areas to get even better.

■ **If you scored five or fewer items in the *Always* column**, you need to take much better charge of your self-monitoring. Consider ways to incorporate the behaviors into your regular college routine. Focus on the items you checked as Never and start including them in your college routine. Set personal goals in these areas for the semester. Meet with an advisor or counselor to get support.

try it and apply it! 1-6   Monitoring Your Progress

Directions: Look at the items on the checklist that you do only *Sometimes* or *Never*. Select one of these tasks and write it below. Then indicate how you will approach this task to be more successful this semester.

Answers will vary.

A self-monitoring task I need to improve on this semester is _____

_____

To address this task I will _____

_____

_____

Monitoring Your Progress

Outcomes of Poor Self-Monitoring

- Feeling unsure about responsibilities
- Being unaware of your level of performance
- Fooling yourself about potential outcomes
- Being surprised by the results of quizzes and exams
- Missing information or assignments
- Experiencing stress about how you are doing in college

Advantages of Monitoring Your Progress

- Puts you in control of your own destiny
- Allows you to make appropriate adjustments
- Helps you to identify when to seek additional support
- Improves preparation for exams
- Offers a sense of well-being when prepared

Discover Your Learning Style

Do all your friends wear their hair the same way, enjoy the same music, or drive at the same speed? Of course not. We all have our own preferences about many aspects of our lives: the kinds of food we eat, how we spend our leisure time, and the types of books or movies we choose to read and watch. The list goes on.

As individuals, we also have preferences in the way we learn. Many educators and theorists have spent a good deal of time researching the different learning styles people use to complete tasks or acquire new knowledge. Think about it. Suppose you and three of your friends purchase the same computer system and desk that require assembly.

First thing in the morning, after a hearty breakfast, Robyn rips open the package and, through trial and error, manipulates the parts until everything fits and is in place. She doesn't stop until she is finished, even though it takes her two hours. On the other hand, Jeremy decides to begin the project at 3 a.m. Listening to his tape of the latest Mets game, he lays out each part, reads the directions to himself, and begins assembling the equipment, rereading the directions along the way until the setup is complete. Benny chooses to work with his sister Tali in the basement of their house where it is cool. Tali reads the directions out loud to Benny, and he hooks up the computer and assembles the desk according to the directions he hears. Finally, you might choose to look at the picture of the items on the box cover, all the diagrams included in the directions, and read the instructions aloud to yourself, as you complete the assembly independently. You snack on chips as you work and make sure the room is very bright so you can concentrate easily.

You and your friends were each successful in assembling the computer and desk, but used different methods, often in different environments. Next to each person's name, identify the different ways or preferences each person used to complete the same task, as noted in the paragraph.

Robyn: *hands-on, tactile, trial and error, persevering*

Jeremy: *works at night, listens to tapes or background sounds while working, follows written directions in a sequence, reads silently*

Benny: *works with a companion, listens to directions*

"You": *Possible answers include works independently, munches a snack while working, looks at visuals, reads aloud, prefers to work in very bright light*

The differences you noted are differences in learning style. We apply our individual learning style preferences to our everyday life, and our academic life. Research in this field has shown that when students study and learn in a way that is compatible with their preferred style, they do better. So it is important to identify learning styles, and especially your own.

Learning style is the way that a person concentrates, processes, internalizes, and remembers new and difficult information (Dunn and Dunn 1992, 1993, 1999). It relates to biological and developmental, or acquired, characteristics, and differs from person to person.

The web article that follows includes information from the research of Professors Ken and Rita Dunn, who have identified twenty-one elements of learning style that are grouped into five major categories, or "stimuli." As you read the article, stop to note your style in each element on the lines provided.

Pay particular attention to your perceptual preferences in the "Physiological Stimuli" section. It is very important for you to learn study strategies that work with the perceptual preferences you identify here.

Dunn and Dunn Learning Style Model

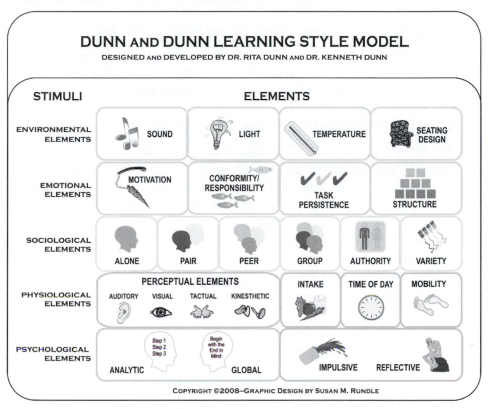

The 21 elements are grouped across five "stimuli" that include environmental, emotional, sociological, physiological, and psychological (cognitive processing) preferences. Each of the 21 elements is described below. Think about *your* preference for each, and indicate it on the line provided.

Environmental Stimulus *(The surroundings in which you prefer to learn.)*

Sound: This element refers to a student's preference for background sound while learning. To what extent do you prefer silence or background noise or music while concentrating or studying?

My preference: _____

Light: Light refers to the level of illumination that is preferred while studying and learning. This element explores the extent to which a student prefers soft, dim, or bright light while concentrating.

My preference: _____

Temperature: What level of temperature do you prefer while involved in studying and/or other learning activities? Preferences for this element may vary from a cool room to a warm room, while studying or engaged in various instructional activities.

My preference: _____

Design: Design refers to the room and furniture arrangements that each student prefers while learning. Do you prefer to study sitting at a traditional desk and chair? Or do you like a more informal arrangement with different types of furniture, such as a couch, a recliner, or pillows and carpet on the floor?

My preference: _____

Emotional Stimulus *(The internal feelings and mood behind your learning)*

Motivation: This element deals with the level and/or type of motivation the student has for academic learning—that is, the extent to which a student is interested in learning. Are you self-motivated (intrinsic), motivated through interest in a topic or contact with peers, or are you primarily motivated by feedback and reinforcement from others?

My preference: _____

Persistence: This element relates to each student's persistence on learning or instructional tasks. Persistence relates to the student's attention span and ability to stay on task. Do you have a preference for working on one task until it is finished, or do you prefer to work on a variety of tasks simultaneously?

My preference: _____

Responsibility: To what extent do you prefer to take responsibility for your own academic learning? This element involves the preference to work independently on assignments with little supervision, guidance, or feedback. Do you prefer to work independently without another person telling you how to proceed? Or do you prefer to have frequent feedback and guidance?

My preference: _____

Structure: This element focuses on the student's preference, or lack of preference, for structured learning activities and tasks. Do you prefer being told exactly what the learning task is, how you should proceed, and what is expected of you? Or do you prefer to be given an objective and then be left alone to decide which procedures or options you use to reach the objective?

My preference: _____

Sociological Stimulus *(The extent to which you prefer to interact with others)*

Self: Self relates to your preference for working on a learning task by yourself. When working on an assignment, do you prefer to work alone or do you prefer working as a member of a group? Some students prefer working independently. Others may prefer working with someone else.

My preference: _____

Pair: This element relates to working with one other student. Do you prefer working with one other person rather than working as a member of a group? Some students may prefer working with others but not in a small group or alone.

My preference: _____

Peers and Team: Do you like working as a member of a team, or do you prefer to complete a task by yourself? This element helps determine a student's preference for working with a small group with interaction, discussion, and completion of the task as a team member, rather than independently.

My preference: _____

Adult/Authority Figure: How do you react to working with an authority figure? Do you like to work together with a supervisor and/or instructor, or do you react negatively to directed or supervised interaction during a task? This element relates to preference for interaction and guidance from an authority figure.

My preference: _____

Variety Versus Concentrating in Routines or Patterns: This element refers to a preference for involvement in a variety of tasks while learning. Do you like routines or patterns, or do you prefer many different procedures or activities while concentrating on new or difficult academic tasks?

My preference: _____

Physiological Stimulus *(The various physical aspects related to your learning style.)*

Perceptual: Learning by listening, viewing, experiencing, or touching is the focus of this element. Do you prefer instruction and retain more information when the activities involve *visual* materials (viewing pictures, maps, or reading), *auditory* activities (listening to tapes, lectures, music), or *tactile and kinesthetic* involvement, such as note taking, and/or working on projects that involve making things (i.e., science projects, storybooks, diaries, model building, etc.)?

My preference: _____

Intake: Intake is concerned with the need to eat, drink, or chew while engaged in learning activities. Do you prefer to drink something while studying, such as a soft drink or coffee? Do you prefer to chew gum? Does munching on snacks help you concentrate?

My preference:_____

Time: This element is related to the concept of energy levels at different times during the day. Do you prefer to work on a task that needs concentration in the early morning, late morning, early afternoon, late afternoon, or evening?

My preference: _____

Mobility: Can you sit still for a long period of time as long as your are interested in what you are doing, or do you prefer to move constantly—standing, walking, changing body positions? Mobility is concerned with the extent to which you prefer to be moving, even unconsciously, while involved in concentration.

My preference: _____

Psychological Stimulus: *(The elements related to the way in which you think.)*

Global-Analytic: This element determines whether a student learns best when considering the total topic of study, or when approaching the task sequentially, one aspect at a time. Students who have a preference for global learning are concerned with the whole meaning and the end results. They need to start with an overview of the *big picture* before they deal with details and facts. Students who prefer an analytic style of learning prefer to learn one detail at a time in a meaningful sequence. After they know all the parts, they put them together and comprehend the *big picture.*

My preference: _____

Hemisphericity: Hemisphericity is associated with left-brain or right-brain processing. Left-brain individuals tend to be more analytic or sequential learners, whereas right-brain dominance (strength) tends to be associated with simultaneous or global learners. This preference overlaps the Global/Analytic.

My preference: _____

Impulsive-Reflective: This element relates to the tempo of thinking. Do you draw conclusions and make decisions quickly, or do you think about the various options and evaluate each before making a decision?

My preference: _____

(Adapted from: http://www.learningstyles.net/2004/l_ls_model.html)

try it and apply it! 1-7   Identifying Your Learning Style

Directions: Write a paragraph in which you describe your learning style, based on your responses in the Dunn and Dunn model. Discuss and compare your style with a classmate.

_____

_____

_____

_____

_____

Personalize Your Learning Strategies

After you identify your learning style preferences, it is very helpful to use study strategies that match your style. It is especially important to pay attention to the perceptual preferences you identified under "Psychological Stimulus" in the article.

Following are several strategies you can use to study, based on your perceptual preferences. Check off the strategies you already use as part of your study routine. Then add any strategies you will begin to use or think could be helpful. Discuss your responses with your classmates.

Visual Learning Strategies

_____ Pay attention to diagrams, sketches, semantic maps, photographs, charts and other visual representations of your course material. Look at these during your studying and use them to help you recall the information.

_____ Transfer your lecture notes or information from reading selections into visual representations of your own. Create your own word maps, flow charts, and diagrams from which to learn your material.

_____ Watch video recordings about the subjects you are studying.

_____ Color code your notes or portions of your textbook, using different highlighters to designate different kinds of information. For example, highlight main ideas in blue and examples in yellow.

_____ Create symbols to represent key information you are learning.

_____ Sit in class where you can easily see the board, screen, or other visual representations of the instruction.

_____ Other: _____

Auditory Learning Strategies

_____ Use your class notes to recite the day's lecture aloud.

_____ Read important points aloud from your textbook while studying.

_____ Listen to audio recordings about the subjects you are studying and listen to them.

_____ Discuss your subjects with friends after class.

_____ Be part of a study group that meets regularly.

_____ Other _____

Tactile/Kinesthetic Learning Strategies

_____ Participate in classes where you can move about and/or be actively involved, such as laboratory classes, hands-on art classes, or physical education classes.

_____ Take a lot of notes; keep busy in class.

_____ Move around as you study. It's OK to recite the information you are learning as you walk.

_____ Study while you exercise or power walk.

_____ Make your own recordings for study.

_____ Create flash cards or study cards that you can manipulate or maneuver while reviewing.

_____ Other: _____

You're on Your Way

As you have probably concluded by now, being successful in college is the result of a combination of many factors and certainly does not depend only on how smart you are. Intelligence and your past achievements are important, but just as valuable are the ways in which you conduct yourself: you need to work hard, set goals, manage your time, concentrate when you study, monitor your progress, make changes when you are not as successful as you would like to be, and know yourself as a student.

The following article is from a magazine called *Campus Life*. It was written to provide students with some guidelines for how to attain success in college. Read it, and see what you think. Mark the portions of the text that seem most relevant to you and complete the exercise that follows.

Have a great semester!

This Is Not Your High School English Class

By Mark Moring

Wondering what to expect from college classes? Check out these six steps for a head start.

Your alarm buzzes, jarring you from much-needed sleep. You hit the snooze button and roll back over. Then suddenly you realize your mom's not around to shake you awake and force you out the door. For the first time in your life, you're on your own. You've got to get yourself moving for that early 8:00 class. As you stumble toward the bathroom for your morning wake-up shower, questions dart through your mind:

Will I be able to handle my class load this semester?

Will I be able to keep up with the required reading?

Will I understand anything the prof says?

Welcome to the world of college studies! No doubt about it. You'll definitely find college academics different from high school. How different? For one thing, you'll learn at a faster pace, trying to grasp more information in a shorter amount of time. Subjects are covered in more depth, so you'll need to understand concepts, not just facts and figures.

You'll do a lot more reading than you've done in high school. And with more material to cover, you just can't cram it all in the night before an exam. You'll need to pace yourself and commit to doing the work even when you don't want to.

Sound overwhelming? It doesn't have to be. Sure, college studies will be different from high school. And for many, it will be more difficult. But you can do a lot to assure success by following these six important guidelines:

1. **Realize your schedule will be drastically different**. As a high school student, you're probably busy most of the day, from about 7:00 in the morning till at least 3:00 in the afternoon. If you're involved in after school activities, or if you've got a part-time job, your typical high school day probably lasts much later than 3 p.m. You might not even get home till 9 p.m. or later on many nights. And that's when you typically start studying—at night. You put in a couple hours a night, and next thing you know, it's bedtime.

    That won't be the case in college. You'll probably have a lot more free time during the day. In high school, you might spend 30 hours or more per week in classes; in college, you'll spend about half that.

2. **Take advantage of daytime free time**. You'll have to get out of the mindset that studying is something that's only done at night. If you look for every opportunity to study during the day, you won't have to study so much in the evening. And as a result, your weekends will end up relatively free.

    So when will you study? Well, between classes is as good a time as any. Don't think you need a big 3- or 4-hour gap to study. An hour here and 30 minutes there will help a lot.

    And use your Friday afternoons well. Once the week's last class is over, it's tempting to slow down and welcome the weekend. But if your last Friday class ends at 1 or 2 p.m., take advantage of the rest of the afternoon. Study for a few hours and you might not have to hit the books again all weekend. If you've got a Monday quiz, you can study hard for it on Friday afternoon and just review the material on Sunday night.

    Also, use all your afternoons. Next to Fridays, late afternoons are usually the most wasted time for college students. What you do from 3 to 6 p.m. determines whether you'll be studying late that night or not. The more you do during the day, the more free time you'll have at night. At the same time, don't think you have to study every afternoon. If a friend suggests a bike ride or a tennis match on a gorgeous sunny day, go for it. Just don't do it every day.

3. **Find a place to study**. No, the dining room table won't be available anymore. As for studying in your dorm room, that may not always be a great idea. Dorms can be busy, noisy places. If you can concentrate under these circumstances, great. If not, you'll want to look for a quiet place—and the library is a good place to start.

4. **Know your workload and keep up with assignments**. Avoid last-minute cramming for tests and exams. Don't put off term papers till the last couple of days. The things you got away with in high school aren't going to work in college. You can't fall behind and expect to catch up. So keep up all along.

5. **Attend classes.** Yeah, it sounds obvious. But in college, it's pretty easy to cut classes. Nobody's gonna send you to the principal's office. Professors rarely take roll, except on the first day. It's tempting to turn off the alarm clock and sleep through that 8 a.m. Spanish class. It's hard to pass up a sunny afternoon at the lake when your best friends are going, even though it conflicts with your chemistry lab. But it's even harder to catch up when you miss. Sure, you can get lecture notes from someone else in the class, but the prof just might explain something critical that day. Something that will end up being on your final exam—and worth 40 percent of your grade.

6. **Get a study buddy or join a study group.** Studying alone can be difficult, especially if you're putting in some 20–30 hours a week doing it. Studying with classmates can make it more interesting. They'll have ideas you won't have, and you'll have ideas they won't have. They'll understand things you didn't understand, and vice versa. Everybody benefits.

And another benefit . . . Sure, college will be hard work. But it will be worth all the effort you put into it. After all, you'll learn more than just facts and figures. You'll learn how to "do" life. College classes will help you develop other, nonacademic skills as well. Along with teaching you the expected stuff in the course, professors want you to learn to speak, write, and think clearly and thoughtfully—great "life" skills to have long after college graduation.

So follow these six guidelines, apply those good study habits you've developed in high school, and get ready for an exciting new adventure.

try it and apply it! 1-8   **Guidelines for Attaining Success in College**

Directions: List six guidelines identified by Mark Moring for achieving success in college, and answer the questions that follow.

1. *Realize your schedule will be different and make adjustments.*

2. *Use your free time to study.*

3. *Find a good place to study, where you can easily concentrate.*

4. *Keep up with assignments on a regular basis; don't fall behind or cram.*

5. *Make sure you go to all your classes. Don't cut!*

6. *Become part of a study group or study with a companion when possible.* _____

_____

7. Which of these strategies do you already use? _____

_____

_____

_____

8. Which new strategies do you plan to start using? _____

_____

_____

_____

9. What other strategies have you learned so far from reading this text or discussing the information in it? _____

_____

_____

_____

_____

It's Up to You: Taking Ownership of College Learning

- Choose to be successful!
- Set realistic short- and long-term goals.
- Manage your time.
- Leave time for rest, relaxation, and personal interests.
- Control your concentration by eliminating distractions.
- Ask for and get support when you need it.
- Monitor your progress regularly and honestly.
- Understand your own learning needs and styles.
- Value and honor your commitment to yourself and your education.

Key Terms

auditory learning	kinesthetic learning	short-term goal
concentration	learning style	tactile learning
distractions	long-term goal	time management
intermediate goal	monitor	visual learning

chapter

2

Are You Ready to Read?

Active Reading Strategies for Managing College Texts

In this chapter

you will learn to

- Become an active reader
- Survey your textbook
- Access prior knowledge
- Preview a reading selection
- Read for a purpose
- Manage your textbook

Studying
Sociology

Introductory courses in sociology cover broad topics concerning societies, such as marriage and family; age, race, gender, and class; religion, government, education, health and medicine. They look at the impact of media and crime on societies, the social norms of different cultures, the ways governments work, and how social movements develop and change societies.

Sociology in the Workplace

A degree in sociology opens the door to many jobs in state and local government. It can prepare you for a career working in a nonprofit organization as a social worker, substance abuse or family planning counselor, or case manager. Training in sociology may also lead to work within the criminal justice system as a probation officer or in health care, perhaps as a caseworker for the elderly or abused children.

Become an Active Reader

Effectively reading a textbook is a dynamic process. It requires far more than turning to page one, sitting back, and moving your eyes across the page. Successful readers are **active readers**: They engage with the textbook before, during, and after reading.

Active readers check out the entire textbook to discover the book's features before reading a specific section. Before reading, active readers think about what they already know about a subject, and what they would like to learn. They look over individual chapters in a systematic way to preview the main points and predict what will be discussed.

As they read, active readers are always thinking about what they are reading, often visualizing the material. They ask questions about the material, establishing a purpose for reading it—to discover the answers to their questions. They monitor their progress along the way. They recognize when something is unclear or confusing to them, and stop to reread or question the material in order to understand it, allowing them to move on to the next section.

Active readers read with a pen, pencil, and/or highlighter in hand. They mark up their textbooks; highlighting or underlining key points, writing notes in the margin, and identifying key vocabulary terms.

Active readers "talk" with the author—not literally, but in their minds. They question, challenge, or even disagree with the author. They show this by writing comments in the places where they question an author's argument, disagree with a point, find an answer to a question they developed during previewing, or want to note information from their own experience that relates to the text.

Active readers adjust how quickly they read, based on the purpose or difficulty of the assignment.

Active readers are thinkers!

Metacognition

Being aware of what you do and do not understand as you read is part of a process known as metacognition. **Metacognition** is the capacity to think about your own thinking. It comes from the term *meta,* meaning going beyond, transcending, or being more comprehensive, and *cognition,* referring to thought and mental processes. Active readers use metacognition constantly. They think about how well they are learning and what they can do to best meet their learning goals.

It is very important to have metacognitive skills: to be aware of your own level of comprehension while you are reading, and to be mindful of how your new learning fits into your broader understanding of a topic. Metacognition helps you remember what you are reading. Your analysis of your thinking makes what you read meaningful, personal, and relevant to you. It helps you take different steps and try different strategies until you are satisfied that you understand the material. When you understand, your ability to use and remember the new information is greatest.

Throughout this textbook, activities have been created to help you use metacognition. At places where it is most important, you will see the symbol shown at the beginning of this section. It is a reminder to you to think about your thinking—to be especially aware of your own learning process and to take responsibility for your learning.

In the pages that follow, you will learn and practice important strategies to help you become an active and purposeful reader.

Survey Your Textbook

Let's imagine you have just purchased a car. You're in the automobile dealership, and the salesperson hands you the keys. You go out to the lot, eager to drive away, but before you head out, it's quite likely that you will take some time to familiarize yourself with your new vehicle. You will want to be clear about the location of all the features: how they work and how to access them. It would be a shame to have had seat warmers included and not even know it. You want to get all you can out of your new car, and be in control at all times.

Though perhaps not as much fun, you can apply this scenario to your textbooks. Your texts are important vehicles for your studies. You need to know what each offers, how it is organized, and what features it includes. If you do, you will use your textbook efficiently and effectively as a study tool and a resource. You'll have a smoother and more enjoyable ride. Surveying a textbook means checking it out and familiarizing yourself with it thoroughly before actually reading or referring to it. Take off that shrink wrap, write your name on the inside cover, and take a peek.

try it and apply it! 2-1   Identifying Textbook Features

Directions: The following features are common to most textbooks, although each is not necessarily found in every book. You are undoubtedly familiar with many. Try matching each feature with its correct definition from the following list. Write your answers on the lines provided.

_b_ 1. Title Page
_d_ 2. Table of Contents
_f_ 3. Preface
_e_ 4. Index
_a_ 5. Glossary
_g_ 6. Appendix
_h_ 7. Bibliography
_i_ 8. Webliography
_c_ 9. Acknowledgments

a. An alphabetical listing of terms and their definitions used within the textbook. Generally found in the back of the book.

b. A page at the front of the text with the name of the book, author, and publisher.

(continued)

(continued)

c.   A page in the text in which the author expresses appreciation or gratitude to those who have supported the writing of the text.

d.   A sequential or chronological listing of the sections, units, chapter names, and chapter parts, as well as their page numbers, found at the beginning of the book. Looking this feature over will give you a good overview of the topics you will be studying.

e.   At the end of a book, an alphabetical listing of the topics, subjects, ideas, terms, and names mentioned in the text, and the page(s) on which each is located.

f.   A brief essay, at the beginning of the book in which the author presents a personal message to the reader. This may include his or her reasons for writing, a related anecdote, aims, hopes, or expectations. Sometimes the organization of the chapters is reviewed.

g.   Usually at the end of the text, a compilation of various charts, graphs, tables, lists, maps, or documents to which reference is made throughout the text. Sometimes answer keys are found here as well.

h.   An alphabetical listing, by author, of printed sources used in the creation of, or cited in, the text. Textbook writers may obtain information from other texts or articles and give credit to those sources, just as you would in writing a paper.

i.   An alphabetical listing of electronic sources used in the creation of, or cited in, the text.

try it and apply it! 2-2   Surveying This Textbook

Directions: Now check out this textbook. What features does it include? List five of them in the table that follows, along with the page numbers on which they are found. What information about the text does each one help you to understand?

Answers will vary.

	Feature	Page No.	What I Learned About This Text
1.			
2.			
3.			
4.			
5.			

Access Prior Knowledge

Most students believe that opening their text to the assigned pages and immediately beginning to read is the way to handle assignments. However, educational research shows that *before* reading an assignment, students can take several steps that will enable them to better understand and remember the material.

People understand and learn best when they attach new material to information that they already know. Think about it. If you know a lot about clothing trends, reading a magazine on designers and style will make a lot of sense to you. You will connect any new information to your prior knowledge about fashion. If you are familiar with the law and the correctional system, an introductory text on criminal justice will be generally comprehensible to you.

Before you read *anything*, it is important to think about what you already know about the subject. Surprisingly, you probably know *something* about most topics or issues that will come your way in college reading. Before you read, ask yourself, "What do I already know about this?" and recite the answer.

For the readings in this textbook, you will be asked to think actively about what you already know about the topic, and then list that information or write a short paragraph about it before you read.

try it and apply it! 2-3   Accessing Prior Knowledge

Directions: The following are actual titles of chapters or sections from a sociology textbook. Beside each title, write *anything* you may know related to the titles. The last title is that of a complete chapter in the appendix of this book, which you will be applying active reading skills to later in this chapter. Compare your responses with your classmates.

Answers will vary.

Racial and Ethnic Inequality _____
_____

The Mass Media _____
_____

Crime _____
_____

Stratification by Social Class _____
_____

The Lingering Impact of Divorce _____
_____

A Culture of Cheating _____
_____

(*continued*)

(continued)

Binge Drinking _____

_____

Does Hard Work Lead to Better Grades? _____

_____

Domestic Violence _____

_____

The "Graying of America" _____

_____

Groups and Organizations _____

_____

Keep this in mind

- Get acquainted with every textbook you use each semester. The more you know about each one, the better you can use it to support your success in class.
- Always think about what you already know about a topic before you begin reading about it. You will learn new information more efficiently if you can connect it to knowledge you already have about a subject.

Preview the Chapter or Selection

Another important strategy you can use to prepare yourself for textbook reading is to preview the material you have been assigned. As the word parts imply, previewing means to look over a reading assignment before you actually read it. Just as the previews, or coming attractions, for movies give you an overview of what they are all about and what you might expect when you actually watch them, previewing a selection or chapter will do the same for your reading experience.

Previewing will accomplish the following:

- **Familiarize you with the subject matter you are about to read.** This helps to get you ready for your reading, serving as a "warm-up." It will help you ease your way into the material.

■ **Supply you with additional prior knowledge about a topic.** As mentioned earlier, prior knowledge is important, especially when you will be reading about a new or challenging topic.

■ **Help you establish a purpose for your reading.** You may think that your only reason for reading is to complete an assignment—to answer questions posed by your instructor or questions in the text. Well, yes, in part. But even if you don't have a specific written assignment, by previewing a selection you can anticipate important questions that will be addressed in it. Developing these questions yourself, before you read, will help focus and guide you. Your purpose for reading, then, is so that you can answer questions *you* have created based on the text and other questions that occur to you as you read. You'll come to understand this process in greater depth as we move along.

Apply THIEVES

What should you look at ahead of time to give you all this information? An **acronym** (a word made from the first letters of several words) that can help you remember the parts of a selection you should preview is **THIEVES**. Think about "stealing" information from a text before you read it. Be greedy! Take a look at page 36 as you preview a chapter or reading.

try it and apply it! 2-4   Previewing a Selection

Directions: Take out your highlighter and turn to the complete textbook chapter in the appendix of this text, titled "Groups and Organizations" (page A-26). Preview the chapter by applying the THIEVES method. Carefully and thoughtfully move through the chapter, highlighting the items you preview. The first section has been modeled for you. Review this as part of your preview, and continue on your own until you come to the last page of the chapter.

Referring only to what you have previewed, you should be able to answer the following questions:

1. What is the topic of the chapter? *groups and organizations*

2. Why is it important to study groups? *They play a key role in transmitting cultures.*

3. Based on the headings on text pages 130–133, what are six types of groups? *primary, secondary, in groups, out groups, focus groups, and reference groups*

4. Based on your preview of Table 6-1, what are three differences between primary and secondary groups?

   Primary groups are smaller, last for a longer period of time, and are more cooperative and

   friendly than secondary groups.

(*continued on page 37*)

Title—*The title identifies the topic, theme, or author's thesis, or argument.* Think about the title. What do you already know about it? Turn the title into a question that you can look for an answer to as you read.

Headings—*Headings are the gateways into each section of the chapter or selection.* Like the title, they can be turned into questions that give you a reason for reading that section of the text. When you make a question out of a heading, try to connect it to the title. Notice the subheadings as well. They can often provide the answers to questions you make from the headings.

Introduction—*The introduction to a chapter can fill you in on a subject by providing important background information.* Make sure you read it. If you are reading a selection, read the first paragraph to find out what is going to be discussed.

Every first sentence in every paragraph—*The first sentences in textbook paragraphs are often the topic sentences or main ideas of the paragraphs.* Thus, you will gain a lot of information about the subject by reading them. You will also encounter selections without any headings, so the first sentences of the paragraphs will be your entry into the content. They will help you predict what the author will discuss.

Vocabulary—*The language of the discipline in which you are reading will probably be new and unfamiliar, so get ready to increase your vocabulary every time you read.* If you take a moment to look at new words ahead of time, it will help you to move through the selection more smoothly when you are reading. Notice the words, often given with their definitions, at the beginning of a chapter, in boldface within the text, written in the margin, or reviewed at the end. Highlight these words. Say them aloud. Read their definitions.

Visuals—*Textbooks provide pictures, or visuals, that explain and illustrate what is being taught, so be sure to look at them before you read the text.* Read the captions, titles, descriptions, and keys. Many people remember and understand best when they can "see" a visual presentation of an idea. Common visuals include the following: photographs, drawings, graphs, figures, charts and tables, cartoons, and maps.

End of chapter questions—*Reading these questions will give you a good idea of what the author believes it is important to know.* You also establish a purpose for reading: to find the answers to these questions or to gain enough knowledge from the chapter to apply the information and develop a thoughtful response to them. Reading and answering end-of-chapter questions can also help you prepare for exams.

Summary—*Reading the summary first means you then read the chapter with a lot of background knowledge and information already in your head, which makes it easier to understand.* Be sure to check out the chapter to see if it has a summary.

5. Based on your reading of the first sentences in the paragraphs of the "Focus Group" section, why were focus groups first developed? What do they have to do with the photo of George Clooney?

   They were first developed to evaluate radio advertisements. Members of a focus group were

   negative about the original ending of the movie "The Perfect Storm," which George Clooney

   starred in, so it was changed.

6. Previewing some of the vocabulary on page 134, what is the difference between a dyad and a triad?

   A dyad is a two member group, and a triad has three people.

7. What is a bureaucracy?

   It is a part of a formal organization that uses rules and hierarchical ranking to achieve efficiency.

8. Using your subheadings, list five characteristics of a bureaucracy.

   It has a division of labor, hierarchy of authority, written rules and regulations, impersonality,

   and employment based on technical qualifications.

9. What is an oligarchy?

   It is when only a few people control the government or a group.

10. What is a synonym for the classical theory of formal organization?

    scientific management approach

11. According to this theory, what motivates workers? *economic rewards*

12. What does the pie graph in Figure 6-1 show? What is one statistic you learn?

    It shows the membership of voluntary organizations in the U.S.A. 26% of the people belong

    to at least one voluntary group.

13. What two "teams" are depicted in the photographs on pages 142 and 143?

    The team to reconstruct the space shuttle Columbia, and a work team

14. Using the headings and subheadings, what are three primary ways in which today's workplace is changing?

    Restructuring of organizations, more telemarketing, and more electronic communication

15. What is collective decision making?

    It is the active involvement of employee problem-solving groups in corporate management.

16. List six reasons to explain the decline in union membership.

    changes in the kinds of industry we have, growth in part-time jobs, the legal system gets in

    the way of forming unions, globalization, hostile employers, the rigidity of unions and their

    resistance to change and growth

17. Look at Figure 6-2, page 145, and name a state with the following:

    a. high union membership *California*

    b. average union membership *Montana*

    c. low union membership *Texas*

(continued)

(continued)

18. Write three important points made in the summary. Try to put them in your own words.

1. The group you identify with the most is your primary group. Less personal groups you are part of are secondary groups. 2. A bureaucracy, according to Weber, has five characteristics: division of labor, hierarchical authority, rules and regulations in writing, impersonality, and employment based on qualifications. 3. Because of economic changes, labor unions are declining.

19. What textbook feature is provided on page 148? *a glossary of terms used in the chapter*

20. What technical resources are provided on the last page of the chapter?
URLs related to groups and organizations and a CD-ROM about understanding groups

It's amazing, but all the information you provided was available from previewing the text. Do you think you are better prepared to read and understand the chapter now that you have previewed it? Why or why not? Write your response on the following lines.

Answers will vary.

_____

_____

_____

In reality, you will adapt your previewing to meet the needs of each assignment. When the reading is new and unfamiliar, an extensive preview will help you gain background knowledge, provide you with the motivation to read, and prepare you for reading the assignment in depth.

Keep this in mind

Previewing doesn't take *that* long, and it can make a huge difference in your capacity to understand a reading. Try not to skip it as a first step, especially when you are going to read about a topic that is new or unfamiliar to you.

Read for a Purpose: Asking and Answering Your Own Questions

Do you remember your homework assignments in high school, or even elementary school? Usually, when you were asked to read, you were also asked to answer questions. If you were a savvy student, you would certainly have looked at the questions ahead of time, so that these questions were in your mind while you read. You might have even stopped to write the answers down when you came upon them. Maybe you simply scanned your reading selection, looking for the answers, and didn't bother reading the rest of the selection at all.

In college, you will be assigned to read chapters or selections and be expected to know and use the content. Sometimes your professor will assign questions for you to answer. Whether or not you are given questions doesn't matter: **Assign yourself the questions**.

Creating your own questions, before and while you read, is one of the best ways to keep active and connected to your reading. If you formulate questions, you will have them in your mind, and they will give you a purpose for reading: to find out the answers. As you read, you will also be *thinking*.

You can create four kinds of questions to help you become an active, thoughtful reader.

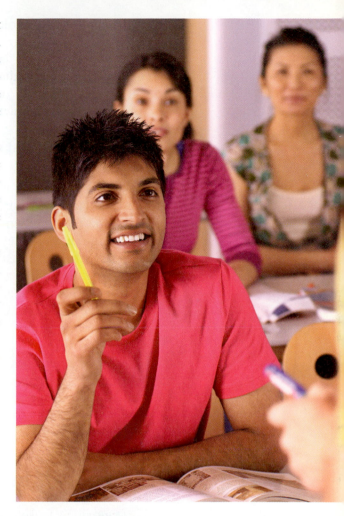

- preview questions
- guide questions
- monitoring questions
- study questions

Preview Questions

Preview questions are the general questions you create when you read the title, headings, and subheadings of your text. You make them into questions by attaching words such as *what, how, where, why, who*, and *when*, to the heading.

For example, in "Groups and Organizations," the sociology textbook chapter you previewed earlier, there is a heading titled "Understanding Groups." You might ask yourself, "What are groups, in sociological terms? Why should we understand them? How can we understand them?" The first subheading in this section is "Types of Groups." You might think, "What are the various types of groups?" Seeing the next subheading, "Primary and Secondary Groups," you could ask, "What is a primary group? What is a secondary group? How are they alike? What are their differences?" By creating these questions from the headings, before you read, you can look for the answers to them when you begin to read.

Guide Questions

Guide questions involve taking important sentences, often the first ones in textbook paragraphs, and turning them into questions to guide your reading. Your intention is to find the answers to these questions as you read. For example, one paragraph in the sociology chapter begins with the sentence "Primary groups play a pivotal role in the socialization process." You might think, "What is the important role primary groups play in socialization?" and read to discover the answer. In a later portion of the text, a paragraph starts, "Another concern about the media is that television distorts the political process." Here you might ask, "How does TV manipulate or change the political process?" You would then read with the purpose of finding the answer to this question.

Monitoring Questions

How many times have you read a section of a text, only to realize that you just didn't get any of it? What a waste of your precious time. **Monitoring questions** are questions you ask yourself to find out how you are doing *as you read*. You use them to check your understanding of what you are reading along the way. They help ensure that you are reading with real comprehension rather than just moving your eyes along the page.

When you monitor your comprehension, you stop, reflect, and recite. You do this at the conclusion of each paragraph. Do you know the answer to your guide question? Can you think it, recite it, or even write it? (See the next section on annotation.) Can you state the most important point about what you just read?

A more general way to monitor yourself is to stop a moment at the end of a paragraph or section and ask yourself if you understood what you just read. If you didn't, you will need to go back and reread, probably more slowly. A good way to challenge yourself here is to see if you can paraphrase the passage, or put it into your own words.

Keep this in mind

Many students like to place a check at the conclusion of each text passage to indicate that they have stopped and asked and answered monitoring questions to their satisfaction. The check means they have given themselves "permission" to move on.

Study Questions

Study questions are created by you after you complete an assigned reading. You may want to review the material or actually start preparing for an exam. Here is your opportunity to be the professor. In order to ask intelligent, meaningful questions, you must have at least a fairly good understanding of the subject the question is about. Good study questions show that you understand the subject and recognize the important topics and their relationship to one another. Anticipate the questions your professor would ask on an exam. Sometimes these will be the very same questions you created as preview or guide questions.

For example, in the sociology chapter you previewed, "Groups and Organizations," when you came upon the subheading "Characteristics of a

Bureaucracy," you likely asked the preview question, "What are the characteristics of a bureaucracy?" Because that is an important aspect of the chapter, that very same question would be an excellent study question to use for review and preparation for a test on the chapter. By reading this section and looking at the chart, you learn that there are five characteristics of bureaucracy; a more specific study question you could ask is, "What are the five characteristics of a bureaucracy?" Sometimes you will need to create larger, broader questions that tap your understanding of the language and material and require you to demonstrate your ability to apply the content to other situations—for example, "What is a bureaucracy and how does my college reflect the characteristics of a bureaucracy?"

There are two types of study questions for you to create that are very important: *discipline terminology questions* and *essay questions*.

Discipline Terminology Questions   Expanding your knowledge of words, concepts, and processes—the terminology specifically related to the subjects you are studying—is an important part of college learning. In your textbooks, important words may be referred to as **vocabulary words** or **key terms.** When you study, you should always create questions that ask you to identify the meaning of these important terms. In addition, your courses will include important **concepts** and **processes.** These are ideas and procedures or systems related to a particular discipline. They involve a more extensive explanation. Key terms, vocabulary words, concepts, and processes are likely to be in bold type or highlighted in your texts. You should consider these as important when creating study questions. For example, when creating study questions for the chapter "Groups and Organizations," you would ask yourself to define and explain the following:

Key terms, such as *dyad* and *coalition*
   Example: What is a dyad?
   Example: Define a coalition.

Concepts, such as *formal organization* and *focus group*
   Example: Explain the elements in a formal organization.
   Example: What is a focus group and what does it do?

Processes, such as the *Peter Principle* and *McDonaldization*
   Example: How does the Peter Principle work?
   Example: What is McDonaldization?

Keep this in mind

To improve your general understanding of a reading, circle or highlight *any* words in the text that you do not understand, even if they aren't directly related to your topic of study. You can look these up in a dictionary or use context clues to help your comprehension and strengthen your vocabulary in general.

Essay Questions   Essay questions require you to go further in demonstrating your understanding of what you have read. They ask you to think about, analyze, and even apply your broader knowledge of the material in your writing. This may take several sentences, a paragraph, or many paragraphs.

With practice, you can become very good at predicting the essay questions that will appear on an exam. Based on your reading, and using the headings and subheadings to guide you, try to make up significant essay type questions for yourself. For example, if a subheading in a sociology chapter is titled "Social Networks and Technology," a good essay question might be

Define the meaning of social networks, and explain how they are influenced by changes in technology.

Reread the portions of the text that will help you answer your own questions. In doing so, you will challenge yourself in a very meaningful way, and you may even come up with the exact test questions you will see on your next exam. Important essay questions based on a student's reading of "Groups and Organizations" might include the following:

- Identify and describe the five characteristics of a bureaucracy.
- Compare and contrast primary groups and secondary groups.
- Explain the purpose and importance of voluntary organizations. Cite examples of some in your own neighborhood.

Essay questions often begin with, or may include, one of the terms listed in the next section. It is important to know the difference between them to respond accurately to a question. The following exercise will help you learn what specific terms mean when they are used in test questions.

try it and apply it! 2-5   **Matching Study Terms and Definitions**

Directions: Match the following terms with their definitions. Write the letters of the correct definitions on the lines provided. Make sure you understand the meaning of each term.

_b_ 1. Analyze

_c_ 2. Compare

_g_ 3. Contrast

_j_ 4. Discuss

_i_ 5. Evaluate

_h_ 6. Explain

_e_ 7. Identify

_a_ 8. Justify

_f_ 9. Prove

_d_ 10. Summarize

_k_ 11. Trace

a. Argue in support of a decision, concept, or action by giving reasons or evidence in favor of it.

b. Break something into its component parts to understand it and its working and patterns.

c. Show similarities and differences between things or ideas.

d. Provide information briefly, covering all important major points but omitting details and examples.

e. Name or list features, elements, or characteristics.

f. Provide logical and convincing arguments or support for an idea, action, or situation.

g. Show how things or ideas are different.

h. Examine something in a broad, thorough way, providing key questions, issues, evidence and information from a multifaceted perspective.

i. Discuss the strengths and weaknesses of something; its value and benefits.

j. Make something clear or meaningful; clarify something by discussing how it works or why it does.

k. List and describe the steps or stages in the development of an idea or process.

try it and apply it! 2-6 Asking Questions for Active Reading

Directions: Use the guidelines below to preview and read the following excerpt, "Privacy and Censorship in a Global Village," on social change and technology from the college textbook _Sociology: A Brief Introduction_ by Richard Schaefer. Read it actively by asking and answering your own questions. You can enter your questions and responses in several places provided in the margins and in the space below the text. Place a check in the box after each paragraph when you feel that you have understood it and are ready to move on.

1. **Create Preview Questions**

   Before you read the text, preview it. On the lines provided, write three preview questions based on the title and the headings. Keep these questions in mind when you read.

2. **Make Guide Questions**

   Now start to read the selection. STOP after you read the first sentence of each paragraph. Underline it. Think of a specific question that the sentence makes you think will be answered in the paragraph. Write this

(continued)

(*continued*)

in the space provided in the margin next to the opening sentence. Then read the paragraph. As you read, CIRCLE any terms that are unfamiliar to you, or that you think are important words connected to the topic of privacy and censorship. When you get to the end of the paragraph, STOP and write an answer to the question you wrote in the margin.

3. **Ask Yourself Monitoring Questions**

   As you finish each paragraph, ask yourself, "Did I understand what I just read? Should I continue?" If the answer is *yes*, go on. **Place a check in the box at the end of the paragraph to indicate you are comfortable with your understanding of the material.** If your answer is *no*, go back and reread the paragraph more slowly.

4. **Design Study Questions**

   At the conclusion of your reading, list at least three terms you believe are important to know in order to understand this selection. Next, write three essay-type questions that cover the most important points made by the author. Then challenge yourself to write answers to them.

5. **Peer Discussion**

   Compare your responses with those of another student and discuss any differences between them.

Privacy and Censorship in a Global Village

Preview Question(s): *What are the privacy issues in the world today? What censorship is there?*

We Are Being Watched!

Preview Question(s): *Who is being watched? Who is watching? How?*

According to the BBC News, the average city dweller is seen on closed-circuit TV about 300 times a day. Preposterous, you say? Look around you. In train stations and lobbies, on street corners and in elevators, the electronic eye is watching you. In some places, digital cameras may be snapping your picture and sending it to a computer that compares it to the photos of known criminals. You may not want to know about it, but your phone calls, e-mails, credit card purchases, and other forms of electronic communication are all being monitored in some way or other. (Rheinbold 2003). ☐

Question:
How is this possible?

Answer:

Not all these means of surveillance are used for crime prevention. Much of the data organizations gather about you is used for marketing purposes, or compiled for resale to other organizations or individuals. While many people consider such activities an invasion of privacy, at this point in the United States, privacy laws have so many loop-holes, it is often difficult to distinguish between legally and illegally gathered data. The other side of this coin is censorship—the fear that in an attempt to protect citizens' privacy, government will restrict the flow of electronic information too much. Not everyone is worried about censorship, however; many people think the government should be allowed to ban pornography on the Internet. ☐

Question:
What else do they use surveillance for?

Answer:

Issues with Computer Technology

Preview Question(s) *What are the issues with computer technology?*

The typical consumer in the United States is included in dozens of marketing data-bases. These lists may seem innocent enough at first. Does it really matter if companies can buy lists of our names, addresses, and telephone numbers? Part of the problem is that computer technology has made it increasingly easy for any individual, business firm, or government agency to retrieve and store more and more information about any of us. ☐

Question:
What is a marketing database?

Answer:

For the average U.S. citizen, the question of how much free expression should be permitted on the Internet relates to the issue of pornography. Pornographic websites have proliferated especially since the Supreme Court struck down federal legislation to regulate "indecent" works and images in 1997. Some of the X-rated material is perfectly legal, if inappropriate for children. Some sites are clearly illegal, such as those that serve the needs of pedophiles who prey on young children. Others are morally and legally ambiguous, such as the sites that post images taken by cameras aimed up the skirts of unsuspecting women in public places. ☐

Question:
What is the relationship between free expression and pornography?

Answer:

In what countries is censorship of the Internet an issue? For instance, the People's Republic of China bans independent reporting in online discussion groups that are not approved by the government. Also prohibited are discussion of sensitive issues, such as economic failures, and web postings that challenge the Communist party (Magnier 2004). ☐

Question:
How so?

Answer:

Now that you have completed the reading, write three study questions on the following lines that you predict a professor would ask students about the selection.
1. How are people being monitored? 2. What is a marketing database and what does it have to do with privacy? 3. How do other countries deal with censorship on the Internet?

How did it feel to read actively and with purpose? Hopefully, it felt pretty good. Yes, you spend more time thinking about your reading, but you are also putting that additional time to very good use if you come away with a complete understanding of what you have read.

Keep this in mind

- Don't continue reading for very long without checking your understanding of the material. You don't want to come to the conclusion of a chapter and wonder what you just read. Monitor yourself by stopping periodically, paragraph by paragraph, to check your understanding.
- Re-read sections that are difficult or confusing.
- Give yourself permission to continue when you are satisfied that you have understood the content.
- When you have focused for long periods, especially on difficult material, you might want to take a break before continuing.

Manage Your Textbook: Highlight, Annotate, and Take Marginal Notes

So many differences exist between high school and college. One of the best is that in college you can write in your books—not only *can*, but *should*.

Your textbooks contain a lot of information. As you read, you want to think about and identify the important content and have it stand out from the rest. That way, when you go back to review the material, to write about it or study it, you will need to focus only upon the information you identified as being most important. It's a real time saver. Highlighting, annotating, and writing marginal notes are three active reading strategies that ask you to think and make decisions as you read. Using these techniques together, you can turn your textbook into a user-friendly review book.

Highlighting

Highlighting involves using markers to make important information stand out. The dilemma with highlighting, however, is that many students end up with multicolored pages. They highlight so much that it is impossible to tell what information is significant. The remedy for this is: *Do not highlight as you read*. Wait. When you have completed reading a paragraph, decide on the most important information, probably the topic sentence and major supporting details, and then go back and highlight them. Read and highlight all the boldface information as well, including chapter titles, headings, subheadings and key vocabulary words. You might ask, "Why should I highlight these if they are already in bold type?" They are boldface because they are important information, and highlighting them when you reread enables you to capture them in your net of important information.

Annotating and Marginal Notes

Annotating is a more in-depth method of identifying main ideas, important details, and key vocabulary terms that you use in combination with highlighting. When you annotate, you still underline important points, but you also write notes and use symbols to explain why you have done so and to identify important types of information. You can annotate *within the text*, and/or *in the margin*s of the pages (marginal notes). For example, within the text you might circle important vocabulary words and underline their definitions. When you come upon a list of related points in the text, number the items directly in the text. Place stars next to important points and question marks next to statements you doubt or find confusing.

Use the margin to label the topics and subtopics discussed in each paragraph. Words such as *definition, causes, effects, goals, problems, reasons,* or *examples* can indicate that a list is to follow, which would be useful to number. For example, the word *causes* in an article on disappearing animal species might be followed by a list of reasons (causes) for their disappearance. You can also respond personally to the text in the margin by writing comments like *I disagree, No way, Amazing, Yes!* or *Check this later.*

Develop your own list of annotation symbols, and get in the habit of using them regularly as you read. After a while, you will never be able to read textbook material without a pen or pencil in your hand.

Here is an example of one student's system of annotation. You might choose to use some of these ideas, or develop your own.

Main or key point ☆, _____

Important supporting detail ✓, _____

Word to know or define word , word

Definition of a word Defn.→, ～～～

Numbering of points or examples ①,2,3

Question or confusion ?

Marginal notes: Ex., Def, Cz (Cause), Ef (Effects or Results) Topic, Prob.

Reread this portion for better understanding RR →

Definitely a test question TestQ.

I like this idea ☺, Yes!

I disagree ☹, No!

try it and apply it! 2-7   **Highlighting and Annotating**

Directions: Turn to the first section, "Understanding Groups," of "Groups and Organizations" in Appendix 3, page A-20. Actively read the section from the beginning through the heading "Primary and Secondary Groups." Stop at the end of each paragraph to highlight and annotate. Then compare your work to the excerpt that follows. Make modifications or additions in your own annotation based on your review of the model below.

How can we understand groups?

What are the different types of groups?

■ UNDERSTANDING GROUPS

Grps.

Most of us use the term *group* loosely to describe any collection of individuals, whether three strangers sharing an elevator or hundreds attending a rock concert. However, in sociological terms a *group* is any number of people with similar norms, values, and expectations who interact with one another on a regular basis. College sororities and fraternities, dance companies, tenants' associations, and chess clubs are all considered examples of groups. The important point is that members of a group share some sense of belonging. This characteristic distinguishes groups from mere *aggregates* of people, such as passengers who happen to be together on an airplane flight, or from *categories* of people—those who share a common feature (such as being retired) but otherwise do not act together.

defn.

Examples

defn.

Characteristics of Groups

Consider the case of a college a cappella singing group. It has ① agreed-on values and social norms. All members want to improve their singing skills and schedule lots of performances. In addition, like many groups, the singing ensemble has both ② a formal and an informal structure. The members meet regularly to rehearse; they choose leaders to run the rehearsals and manage their affairs. At the same time, some group members may take on ③ unofficial leadership roles by coaching new members in singing techniques and performing skills.

The study of groups has become an important part of sociological investigation because they play such a key role in the transmission of culture. As we interact with others, we pass on our ways of thinking and acting—from language and values to ways of dressing and leisure activities.

Types of Groups

Sociologists have made a number of useful distinctions between types of groups—primary and secondary groups, in-groups and out-groups, and reference groups.

What's the difference?

Primary and Secondary Groups

What are these? How are they different?

Charles Horton Cooley (1902) coined the term *primary group* to refer to a small group characterized by intimate, face-to-face association and cooperation. The members of a street gang constitute a primary group; so do members of a family living in the same household as do a group of "sisters" in a college sorority.

Primary Ex.

Examples

Primary groups play a pivotal role both in the socialization process (see Chapter 4) and in the development of roles and statuses (see Chapter 5). Indeed, primary groups can be instrumental in a person's day-to-day existence. When we find ourselves identifying closely with a group, it is probably a primary group.

We also participate in many groups that are not characterized by close bonds of friendship, such as large college classes and business associations. The term *secondary group* refers to a formal, impersonal group in which there is little social intimacy or mutual understanding. (see Table 6-1, page 132) The distinction between primary and secondary groups is not always clear-cut. Some social clubs may become so large and impersonal that they no longer function as primary groups.

Secondary Group defn.

Secondary groups often emerge in the workplace among those who share special understandings about their occupation. Almost all of us have come into contact with people who deliver pizzas. Using observation research…

In workplace

Keep this in mind

- Be prepared! Read with your highlighter and pen and pencil in hand. Be ready to mark important information in your text.
- Don't over highlight! Be selective. Read the entire paragraph before deciding what matters most and is important to note.
- Develop a personal system of annotating that you apply to all your reading. Be creative, and enjoy the process.

Are You Ready to Read? Active Reading Strategies for Managing College Texts

Remember that reading is a *process* that includes all the activities before, during, and after you read.

- Before you begin using your textbooks, survey them all to learn their organization and features.
- Think about what you already know about a topic before you start to read about it.
- Preview selections by applying THIEVES .
- Establish your purpose for reading portions of your textbook by creating your own guide questions based on titles, headings, and introductory sentences in paragraphs.
- Periodically stop and reflect upon your understanding. Reread portions when you are unsure.
- Always read with a pen, pencil, or highlighter in hand. Interact with the content of your textbooks. Note important information, terms, or ideas by annotating, highlighting, and writing marginal notes.
- Check your understanding of the material by asking and answering your own questions based on the most important points in a chapter.

Key Terms

acknowledgments
acronym
active reading
annotating
appendix
bibliography
essay questions
glossary
guide questions

highlighting
index
key terms
metacognition
monitoring questions
preface
preview
preview questions
prior knowledge

processes
study questions
survey a textbook
table of contents
THIEVES
title page
webliography

chapter

3

Lost in Translation
Developing College-Level Vocabulary

In this chapter

you will learn about

- Discipline-specific vocabulary
- Academic vocabulary
- Context clues
- Figurative language
- Techniques for learning vocabulary

Studying
Psychology

The discipline of psychology is concerned with how human beings function emotionally, behaviorally, interpersonally, and cognitively. It also involves research into the causes of behavior and the development of treatment options, such as counseling, therapy, and medication. Introductory courses in psychology focus on the history of psychology, the biological foundations of behavior, learning and adaptation, memory, language and thinking, motivation and emotion, and intelligence.

Psychology in the Workplace

Many entry-level positions in the fields of human services, social work, criminal justice, and even business and marketing are open to people with a background in psychology and good "people" skills. For example, there are jobs such as employment counselor, residential youth counselor, social service director, store manager, sales representative, admissions counselor, or newspaper reporter. More advanced degrees, including a master's or doctorate, can lead to work as a clinical psychologist, treating people with psychiatric problems; as a school psychologist, testing and counseling children; or as an art or music therapist, as well as jobs in sports, industry, health and forensics. A psychology degree can also open the door to performing research in a wide range of areas, including child development and learning, abnormal behavior, and brain functioning.

51

The Importance of Having a Good Vocabulary

Depending on the environment you are in at any given time, you use different kinds and levels of communication.

Spoken language is typically less formal than written language. It varies, too, based on the setting in which you find yourself and with whom you are communicating. Certainly, your conversation with a friend about the dream you had last night will sound different from your oral presentation about dream theories in your psychology class. Your research paper on the same topic would probably include an even higher level of academic vocabulary. The published sources, from which you may have gathered your information, such as *The Journal of Sleep and Sleep Disorders Research* or your psychology textbook, have been written at the highest level of all.

How does this impact you now? It means that you need to take your audience and purpose into account when you communicate. The language you use when you speak and write in college should reflect your academic environment. Using the right language, and having a broad vocabulary that includes the keywords of the disciplines you are studying, will significantly affect how successful you are in college. Your ability to understand what you hear in lectures or discussions and your capacity to understand college-level material is directly related to your knowledge of vocabulary. Research has shown that even when only *two* percent of words are unfamiliar in a textbook, students will have difficulty comprehending the material on their own (Carver 1994).

An improved vocabulary will also lead to benefits in other areas of your life. It will impact your future career opportunities and your capacity to succeed in your work. Your ability to communicate effectively will go a long way in establishing good first impressions when you meet new people, whether they are friends, employers, or colleagues.

Discipline-Specific Vocabulary

As you will discover in college, each area of study, or discipline, has its own **discipline-specific vocabulary**—terminology, or technical words specific to the subject.

For example, students who study psychology will encounter words such as *agoraphobia*, *cognition*, and *neuromodulators*. These words will often appear in bold or italic type in the body of the text. They are typically followed by definitions, explanations, and examples, because authors realize you are learning a new subject and want to support you in this process. They may also appear in the margins, in text boxes, or in the introduction or summary section of the chapter. Discipline-specific terms are usually defined in the glossary of a textbook as well. It is your responsibility to master these new terms. Your active involvement in class discussions and activities will give you an opportunity to use and learn these new words.

You should also pay close attention to the possibility of terms having more than one meaning. For example, you know that the meaning of the word *drive* relates to the action of controlling the motion of a car. However, in psychology, the term *drive* is defined *as a state of internal tension that motivates an organism to behave in ways that reduce tension:* Quite a different meaning. To recognize differences in meaning such as this, it is necessary to think about the content of the selection you are reading.

Read the following excerpt from the psychology text *Psychology: The Science of Mind and Behavior*, by Passer and Smith. Notice how many of the vocabulary terms, especially in the second paragraph, are related to the field of psychology. Circle these in the text.

Escape and Avoidance Conditioning

Behavior often involves escaping from or avoiding aversive situations. Escape occurs when we take medications to relieve pain or put on clothes when we are cold. Avoidance occurs when we put on sunscreen to prevent sunburn or obey traffic laws to avoid tickets. You can probably think of many more examples.

In escape conditioning, the organism learns a response to terminate an aversive stimulus. Escape behaviors are acquired and maintained through negative reinforcement. If you're cold, putting on a sweater is negatively reinforced by the desired consequence that you no longer shiver. Taking a pain reliever is negatively reinforced by the reduction of pain. In avoidance conditioning, the organism learns a response to an aversive stimulus. We learn to dress warmly to avoid feeling the cold in the first place.

(Passer & Smith 2007)

How many of these terms did you circle? _____

- escape conditioning
- avoidance conditioning
- organism
- response
- stimulus
- aversive situations
- escape behaviors
- negative reinforcement

Notice that the word **response** has a meaning specific to the discipline of psychology. Rather than the familiar meaning that a response is an answer to a question, it is used to describe *behavior in reaction to a particular stimulus.*

Can you imagine how difficult it would be to understand this excerpt without knowing the meaning of these terms? Throughout this chapter, you will learn strategies to help identify the meaning of these terms as you read.

Academic Vocabulary

In addition to discipline-specific vocabulary, all college textbooks include words known as **academic vocabulary**. Compiled in *The Academic Word List* (Coxhead 2000) are 570 word families that have been identified as commonly appearing throughout academic writing. In fact, a recent study determined that in community college textbooks, one out of every six words, about 16 percent, are academic vocabulary words (Santos 2000). In the reading modules in Part 3 of this textbook, the academic words found in all the selections are identified and used in practice exercises. As you read, you will see how important it is to know the meanings of these words in order to understand assigned readings.

try it and apply it! 3-1   Practicing with Academic Vocabulary

Following are eleven words taken from the Academic Word List. They appear in bold in the selection that follows.

Directions: Read the selection. Then write definitions of the words you think you can define on the lines provided. Look up the remaining words and write their definitions.

1. acquire *to achieve native or native-like command of*
2. aspects *characteristics*
3. complex *higher order*
4. consists *is made up of*
5. foundation *a basis such as a principle*
6. generate *result in*
7. infinite *immeasurable amount, an unlimited amount*
8. involves *relates the use of*
9. intelligent *high degree of mental capacity*
10. psychological *mental, pertaining to the mind*
11. symbols *arbitrary signs*

Language

Language has been called "the jewel in the crown of cognition" (Pinker 2000) and "the human essence" (Chomsky 1972). Much of our thinking, reasoning, and problem solving **involves** the use of language. In turn, these advanced cognitive processes build on the large store of knowledge that resides in the memory, and they provide a **foundation** for **intelligent** behavior.

Language **consists** of **symbols** and rules for combining these symbols in ways that **generate** an **infinite** number of possible messages and meanings. To most

of us, using our native language comes as naturally as breathing, and we give as much thought. Yet using language actually involves a host of **complex** skills. Psycholinguists is the scientific study of the **psychological aspects** of the language, such as how people understand, produce and **acquire** language.

(*Psychology: The Science of Mind and Behavior,* Third Edition, by Passer and Smith, 2007.)

You were probably familiar with many of the words in bold in the excerpt. However, some of the words you may still need to learn. Sometimes you will be able to determine their meaning using the surrounding words. Other times, you will need to consult a dictionary. You will find it helpful to keep a running list of the new academic vocabulary words you encounter in the reading selections in this text. List them with their definitions and different word forms. For example, *acquire, acquires, acquired, acquisition, complex,* and *complexity.* Study them. You will find them used across the disciplines in textbooks and lectures. They will also be useful for college writing assignments.

Using Context Clues to Learn the Meaning of Words

On the first day of class, a professor asks her students to tell her about all the courses they are taking. Students repeatedly mention psychology, sociology, business, mathematics, and English composition. The professor tells the students they will be learning the skills they need to read in all these disciplines in her course.

"What does **discipline** mean?" she asks.

One student replies, "Discipline means *behavior* or *how we are punished*."

"Yes, but what does the word mean in the context of our discussion?"

"Does *being punished* really make sense here?" she asks again.

Finally, a clever student in the back of room says, "A discipline means *a course*, like sociology or history."

This scenario shows how students often rely on the familiar meaning of a word instead of using the context in which it appears to figure out whether it has a different, more specific meaning. Ignoring context can often lead to confusion and poor comprehension.

What does this have to do with college reading? As you read across the disciplines, you will encounter many new and unfamiliar words and terms. If you rely only on your prior experience with a word, you may or may not understand its specific meaning in material you are reading. If you stop to look up every new word you encounter, you will also waste a lot of time. However, if you use the **context clues**, words or phrases embedded in the text that hint at the meaning of words, you will probably be able to guess what a word means or understand enough to be able to continue to read efficiently and effectively. A good strategy is to circle new words or those used in an unfamiliar way as you encounter them, use context clues to get a general understanding of their meaning, complete the reading, and then look the words up in a dictionary.

The five most common context clues are

- definition clues
- synonym clues
- contrast and antonyms clues
- example clues
- inference clues

Definition Clues

A definition may be the most obvious way an author helps you to understand new words, especially discipline-specific terminology. Often the term is in bold or italic type and the definition follows immediately after it. Signal words and punctuation are also used to indicate that a definition in being given.

Signal words, words and phrases such as *is, means, can be defined as, refers to, involves, that is,* and *in other words* indicate that a definition of a term is about to be provided. The following examples show how signal words and punctuation can help you understand new words or terminology by providing definitions of them.

> **Memory** refers to the process that allows you to recall previous experiences or information.
>
> (From *Psychology,* Passer and Smith)

The signal word *refers* tells the reader that a definition of the term in bold type will follow. Therefore, **memory** means *a process that allows you to recall previous experiences or information.*

Storage involves remembering information over time.

(From Psychology, Passer and Smith)

The signal word *involves* tells the reader that a definition of the word in bold type will follow. Therefore, **storage** means *the ability to remember information over time.*

The definition of a word or term may also be set off by **punctuation cues,** such as parentheses, commas, and dashes, or it may simply follow a comma or dash. Note the way punctuation is used in the sentences that follow:

Through selective attention, some information enters **short-term memory**, a memory store that temporarily holds a small amount of information.

(From Psychology, Passer and Smith)

The comma after the word in bold type indicates that a definition will follow, so **short-term memory** means *a memory store that temporarily holds a limited amount of information.*

Memory experts recommend using the method of **loci** (Latin for "places"), a memory aid that associates information with mental images of physical locations.

(From Psychology, Passer and Smith)

In this example, the information in parentheses provides the reader with information about the boldface word; that is, the word **loci** comes from Latin and means *place*. In addition, the comma after **loci** precedes additional information about the meaning of the term. Specifically, the definition of **loci** is *a memory aid that associates information with mental images of physical locations.*

In some textbooks, **special font clues** are used to signal that a definition of a term is being presented; for example, words are presented in *italic*, **bold,** or colored font.

Schema *is an organized pattern of thought that is used to provide a framework in understanding new information.*

(From Psychology, Passer and Smith)

In this example, the word being defined, *schema*, is in bold, and the words in italic that follow it tell the reader the meaning of the term. So **schema** can be defined as an organized pattern of thought that is used to provide a framework for understanding new information.

try it and apply it! 3-2 Using Definition Clues

Directions: Underline the definition clues used in these sentences. Then on the lines provided, write the clues and the meanings of the boldface words.

1. People often forget **traumatic** events, experiences that are disturbing and stressful.

   Clue: *comma*

   Meaning: *experiences that are disturbing and stressful*

(continued)

(*continued*)

2. German psychologist Hermann Ebbinghaus created over 2,000 **nonsense syllables** (meaningless letter combinations) to study how memory works when there is very little influence from past learning.

   Clue: *parentheses*

   Meaning: *meaningless letter combinations*

3. One early explanation for why people forget information was the **decay theory,** which proposed that with time and disuse, the long-term memory trace in the nervous system fades away.

   Clue: *commas*

   Meaning: *It proposed that with time and disuse, the long-term memory trace fades away.*

4. **Repression** is *a motivational process that protects us by blocking the conscious recall of bad and painful memories.*

   Clue: *italic and the word "is"*

   Meaning: *a motivational process that protects us by blocking the conscious recall of bad and painful memories*

5. Almost all of us have had the retrieval experience called the **tip-of-the-tongue:** that is, we cannot recall something but we feel that we are on the verge of remembering it.

   Clue: *that is*

   Meaning: *we cannot recall something but we are on the verge of remembering it*

6. In laboratory experiments, older adults generally display poorer **prospective memory**—remembering to perform an activity in the future.

   Clue: *dash*

   Meaning: *remembering to perform an activity in the future*

7. The most dramatic occurrences of forgetfulness occur in **amnesia,** which refers to memory loss due to a special condition.

   Clue: *comma, refers to*

   Meaning: *the memory loss due to a special condition*

8. After a brain operation, one patient experienced **anterograde amnesia.** In other words, he was no longer able to recall new facts and experiences after amnesia had occurred.

   Clue: *in other words*

   Meaning: *a condition in which a person can no longer recall new facts and experiences after the onset of amnesia*

9. Almost all of us encounter **infantile amnesia,** also known as childhood amnesia.

   Clue: *comma, also known as*

   Meaning: *childhood amnesia*

10. There are more than a dozen types of **dementia,** which can be defined as a progressive brain disorder in adults over 65 years of age.

    Clue: *comma, can be defined as*

    Meaning: *progressive brain disorder in adults over 65*

    (Sentences 2–10 adapted from *Psychology*, Passer and Smith)

Synonym Clues

Another way an author can tell you what a word means is by providing a synonym for it. A **synonym** is a word that has the same or a similar meaning as the targeted term.

Signal words such as *and* and *or* are used to indicate that a synonym is being provided. Punctuation cues, such as commas, dashes, or parentheses, may also be used to signal a synonym for an unfamiliar term.

> The most famous mnemonist, Shereshevski, had an **extraordinary** and outstanding memory.

> (From *Mosaic Two: A Reading Skills Book*, Wegmann, Knezevic and Bernstein, 5th Edition)

The term in bold type is followed by *and*. The word *and* signals a synonym of the target word will follow, so another word for **extraordinary** is outstanding.

> However, Shereshevski was often frustrated by the abundance of **trivial** or meaningless information he remembered because he had stored too much information in his memory.

> (From *Mosaic Two*, Wegmann, Knezevic and Bernstein)

The term in bold type is followed by *or,* a signal word that tells the reader a synonym will follow. A similar meaning for **trivial** is *meaningless information.*

try it and apply it! 3-3 Using Synonym Clues

Directions: Underline the clue words or punctuation used to signal a synonym for a word is being provided. Then on the lines provided, write the clues and the meanings of the words in boldface type.

1. A perfect memory can **deprive** or take way our ability to forget unpleasant thoughts.

   Clue: *or*

   Meaning: *take away*

   (continued)

(*continued*)

2. **Rote** learning—sheer memorization—is not helpful when you are pre-paring for an exam that requires you to apply a concept or analyze information.

   Clue: *dashes*

   Meaning: *sheer memorization*

3. Having a good memory is not just an **innate** quality or something you are born with; you can improve it by reviewing the material that you need to learn.

   Clue: *or*

   Meaning: *something you are born with*

4. There are no **enigmatic** or mysterious ways to improve your memory.

   Clue: *or*

   Meaning: *mysterious*

5. Memory aids can **enhance** and improve your memory.

   Clue: *and*

   Meaning: *improve*

6. If you have difficulty recalling all the dates for your history course, try to create a **mnemonic** or memory trick.

   Clue: *or*

   Meaning: *memory trick*

7. A student in an art course used **acronyms** (word associations) to recall the colors of the rainbow (ROY G. BIV for red, orange, yellow, green, indigo and violet.)

   Clue: *parentheses*

   Meaning: *word association*

8. Using **imagery** and visualization can help you retain information and remember it.

   Clue: *and*

   Meaning: *visualization*

9. **Motivation,** the desire to want to push yourself to improve your memory, is probably the most significant factor in actually remembering more.

   Clue: *commas*

   Meaning: *the desire to want to push yourself*

10. Another factor in achieving a better memory is the **incentive** or reward that an individual can gain.

    Clue: *or*

    Meaning: *reward*

(Sentences 1–4 and 7–9 are adapted from *Psychology*, Passer and Smith)

Contrast and Antonym Clues

You can also determine the meaning of an unfamiliar word by noting a word or phrase in the context that means just the opposite of it (an antonym).

Signal Words That Show Contrast

different from	although (though)
differ	even though
but	nevertheless
yet	while
however	whereas

In the following sentences, contrast clues will give you hints about the words in bold type:

> While some psychological researchers believe intelligence is **inborn**, others suggest it is a result of our upbringing.
>
> (From *Psychology*, Passer and Smith)

The word *while* shows a contrast, so **inborn** means the opposite of upbringing or some quality with which you are born.

> Although scientists agree that genetics and heredity contribute to intelligence, the impact of **nurture** cannot be ignored.
>
> (From *Psychology*, Passer and Smith)

The word *although* also indicates a contrast. In other words, **nurture** means the opposite of genetics and hereditary. It means some quality you acquire through your upbringing or environment.

try it and apply it! 3-4   Using Contrast and Antonym Clues

Directions: Underline the signal words for contrast/antonym clues that are included in the following sentences. Then in the spaces provided, write the clues and the meanings of the words in boldface type.

1. Researchers thought there would be **discrepancies** between the scores of men and women on ability test scores, <u>but</u> in fact the results were similar.

    Clue: *but*

    Meaning: *differences*

(continued)

(*continued*)

2. **Although** some educators believe IQ tests are a sufficient way to measure intelligence, psychological research shows that these tests are **inadequate.**

   Clue: *although*

   Meaning: *not sufficient*

3. **Even though** many experts **concur** with these findings, colleges do not agree, and so they continue to administer the SAT as an entry requirement.

   Clue: *even though*

   Meaning: *agree with*

4. One report showed that some students scored poorly on their SATs, yet they **excelled** in their college course work.

   Clue: *yet*

   Meaning: *not poorly or to do extremely well*

5. If parents tell their preschoolers exactly how to perform certain tasks, they can **hamper** the development of their children's intelligence; however, if they encourage their children to think about a problem and act independently, they can encourage their children's intellectual growth.

   Clue: *however*

   Meaning: *not encourage or to hold back from doing something*

6. There are also extremes of intelligence. At the upper end are the intellectually gifted whose IQ scores are 130 or higher, whereas the mean score of the **cognitively disabled** is 103.

   Clue: *whereas*

   Meaning: *not intellectually gifted or not smart*

7. Social and emotional **deprivation** causes a decrease in IQ scores, but those children who are introduced to an enriched environment show a gradual increase in IQ.

   Clue: *but*

   Meaning: *not an enriched environment or an environment that is lacking in stimulation*

8. In **affluent** families, the caregiver is able to afford to send his or her child to a choice of preschool programs, whereas in families with limited finances, there are fewer options.

   Clue: *whereas*

   Meaning: *not with limited finances, rich*

9. Some parents of disadvantaged youth confuse day-care centers with preschool programs. While many preschool programs are **accredited,** many childcare facilities are not given official recognition because they do not comply with certain standards, such as having an educational curriculum.

   Clue: *while*

   Meaning: *having official recognition*

10. In the past, cognitively disabled children were **segregated** into special education classes, <u>but</u> these children are now required by federal law to attend school in regular classrooms in their neighborhoods along with their peers.

    Clue: *but*

    Meaning: *separated from others*

    (Sentences adapted from *Psychology*, Passer and Smith)

Example Clues

Sometimes, authors provide examples to illustrate the meaning of unfamiliar words.

> ### Signal Words That Indicate Examples are Being Used
>
> | | |
> |---|---|
> | *for example* | *like* |
> | *for instance* | *consist* |
> | *such as* | *including* |

Read the following sentences to see how the examples provide information that clarifies the meanings of the words in bold type.

Nonverbal communication includes communicating messages through body language, facial expressions, and gestures.

The three examples indicate that **nonverbal communication** must be some way of sending a message that does not include the spoken word.

Proxemics is another type of nonverbal communication; for example, Americans are most comfortable standing about 18 inches to 4 feet from each other when they speak.

(From *Communicating Effectively*, 9th Edition, Hybels and Weaver II)

The example indicates that **proxemics** refers to a measurable distance between speakers.

try it and apply it! 3-5   Using Example Clues

Directions: Underline the example clues in the following sentences. Then on the lines provided, write the clues and the meanings of the words in boldface type.

1. Examples of **hyperboles** include "I read a million books over the vacation," "I eat tons of junk while I am watching TV," and "It's so hot in here that I'm boiling."

   Clue: *include*

   Meaning: *words used to show exaggeration*

2. You are probably familiar with some common **euphemisms** like "departed" (for dead), "bathroom" (for toilet) and "lame" (for not meeting expectations).

   Clue: *like*

   Meaning: *substitution of a mild or vague term for an offensive one*

3. In **psycholinguistics,** social scientists study aspects of language, including how people understand, produce, and acquire language.

   Clue: *including*

   Meaning: *the study of language that includes how people understand, produce and acquire language*

4. Research in psycholinguistics suggests that the ability to learn a language **diminishes** over time; for instance, it is much more difficult for an adult to learn a second language than for a young child to do so.

   Clue: *for instance*

   Meaning: *lessens*

5. **Phonemes** are speech sounds; for example, the phoneme *d* creates a different meaning from the phoneme *l* when it comes before *og* (like *dog* versus *log*).

   Clue: *for example*

   Meaning: *They are individual sounds that have meaning only when they are attached to other sounds.*

6. **Morphemes** are the basic units of meaning in a language, <u>such as</u> pre-fixes found at the beginning of words (un-, im-, il-) and suffixes found at the end of a words (-ist, -or, -er).

   Clue: *such as*

   Meaning: *smallest unit of meaning, but not a word by itself*

7. Each language has its own **grammar,** which <u>consists</u> of sounds, the combi-nation of sounds into words, and how words are combined into sentences.

   Clue: *consists*

   Meaning: *rules of a language*

8. Spoken language varies according to the **setting,** <u>such as</u> what you say at the dinner table, in a courtroom, in a classroom, in a car, or at a foot-ball game.

   Clue: *such as*

   Meaning: *places or locations*

9. It takes more than a good vocabulary to understand language and com-municate effectively; it also involves **pragmatics,** <u>like</u> understanding a social situation and knowing the rules for how to respond to others.

   Clue: *like*

   Meaning: *understanding a social situation and knowing how to respond to others*

10. One type of nonverbal communication is **haptics,** which could <u>include</u> handshakes, kissing, giving high fives, or putting your hands on some-one's shoulder.

    Clue: *include*

    Meaning: *touching as nonverbal communication*

   (Sentences 3–9 are adapted from *Psychology*, Passer and Smith. Sentence 10 is adapted from *Communicating Effectively*, Hybels and Weaver II)

Inference Clues

Sometimes there are no definitions, synonyms, antonyms, or examples to give you a clue to the meaning of an unfamiliar word. But don't give up. Continue to read the passage to see if you can get a general sense of the meaning of the word by drawing conclusions from the information the author provides.

   Look at the following example:

> Students who don't get enough sleep often feel **lethargic** in class. They can't seem to concentrate on lectures and even doze off.

From these sentences, we can conclude that feeling **lethargic** may result from lack of sleep. This lack of sleep causes students to experience difficulty in concentration and sleepiness. **Lethargic** probably means not being alert and feeling drowsy.

> **Somnambulism** is a common disorder among children. They usually get up while asleep, and wander around the house.

(From *Psychology*, Passer and Smith)

From these two sentences, we learn that **somnambulism** is a sleep problem that children often experience. While they are asleep, they engage in activities that are usually associated with being awake. **Somnambulism** must mean sleepwalking.

try it and apply it! 3-6   Using Inference Clues

Directions: Try to figure out the meanings of the words in boldface type by using inference clues from the surrounding text. Then write the clues and the meanings of the boldface words on the lines provided.

1. Not getting enough sleep is a way of life for many college students and other adults. The results of 19 studies showed that all types of **sleep deprivation** affected functioning, mood, and cognitive and physical performance.

    Clue: *not getting enough sleep, the effects . . . functioning, mood, cognitive and physical performance*

    Meaning: *any type of situation that prevents sleep (could be insomnia, staying up late to study, being out late with friends, working late).*

2. People who suffer from **insomnia** will also have problems during the day. They may experience excessive sleepiness, have trouble thinking clearly, or feel depressed or irritable.

    Clue: *a disorder that occurs at night and results in excessive sleepiness, trouble thinking clearly, and feeling depressed and irritable*

    Meaning: *a sleep disorder, sleeplessness*

3. About 1 out of 2,000 people suffers not from an inability to sleep but from an inability to stay awake. No matter how much they rest at night, individuals with **narcolepsy** may experience sleep attacks at any time.

    Clue: *inability to stay awake*

    Meaning: *a sleep disorder that results in falling asleep at any time*

4. Narcolepsy can be **devastating.** People with narcolepsy are more likely to have accidents, feel their quality of life has suffered, and may be misdiagnosed by doctors as having a mental disorder rather than a sleep disorder.

    Clue: *more likely to have accidents, feel their quality of life has suffered*

    Meaning: *overwhelming*

5. Some people may be genetically **predisposed** toward developing narcolepsy. In humans, if one identical twin has narcolepsy, the other twin has a 30 percent chance **of** developing it.

Clue: *identical twin . . . chance of developing it*

Meaning: *have a tendency, likely to, inclined*

6. What do we dream about? Given the stereotype of "**blissful** dreaming," it may surprise you that most dreams are not happy and pleasant but contain negative content.

    Clue: *surprise . . . not happy and pleasant (contrast)*

    Meaning: *utter and complete happiness*

7. One reason that dreams appear to be **bizarre** is because their content shifts rapidly. "I was dreaming about an exam and all of a sudden, the next thing I knew, I was in Hawaii on the beach."

    Clue: *I was dreaming about an exam . . . the next thing I knew I was in Hawaii.*

    Meaning: *strange, weird*

8. Drugs and alcohol can **alter** consciousness by changing brain chemistry.

    Clue: *by changing*

    Meaning: *change*

9. When alcohol is used repeatedly, a **tolerance** may result. The person must consume greater amounts of alcohol to achieve the same physical and emotional effects.

    Clue: *The person must consume greater amounts to feel the same effects.*

    Meaning: *able to endure or handle*

10. When tolerance develops, and a person suddenly stops drinking, **withdrawal** can be experienced. As a result, in the absence of alcohol's relaxing effects, the drinker may feel tense.

    Clue: *a tense feeling that occurs when a person stops drinking suddenly*

    Meaning: *a distressing feeling associated with stopping a dependent habit, such as drinking*

(Sentences adapted from *Psychology*, Passer and Smith)

Using Context Clues

Clues	Look For	Example
Definition	is, means, can be defined as, refers to, involves, that is, in other words	**Psychology** *is* formally *defined* as the scientific study of the behavior of individuals and their mental processes.

(*continued*)

(*continued*)

Clues	Look For	Example
Definition	dashes, commas, parentheses	As the field of psychology has developed, it has become clear that psychologists cannot directly investigate **mental processes,** *the workings of the human mind.*
Definition	italics, boldface, different colors	The **scientific method** *is a process used to analyze and solve problems.*
Synonym	and, or	Our **perceptions** or *observations* may be influenced by many factors, including experience, emotions, abilities and attitudes.
Contrast/ Antonym	different from, differ, but, yet, however, although (though), nevertheless, while, whereas	Some psychological researchers believe intelligence is a product of our upbringing, *while* others feel it is **innate.**
Example	for example, for instance, such as, like, to illustrate	People who have had a stroke may develop an **aphasia,** for they may experience partial or total loss of the ability to understand or produce speech.
Inference	another sentence before or after the unfamiliar word that may provide additional information	It is much more difficult to learn a second language in adulthood. Children younger than 10 years of age are much more successful at achieving native **proficiency.**

Figurative Language

Your college textbooks are typically written in a straightforward manner. Because their purpose is to inform and instruct, authors tend to use literal language, so as to be as clear and concise as possible.

However, even within textbooks, and certainly in many other genres of college writing, you will come upon words and phrases that are not meant to impart their literal meaning. Rather, writers will use words in a symbolic way, to represent feelings or ideas that are not stated directly. This is called *figurative language*. Figurative language creates an interesting and enriched form of speaking or writing. It is especially effective when the author wants to make a comparison between ideas or objects. For example, using direct, straightforward language about the weather, a sentence might state:

> It was sunny and warm last Sunday.

Using figurative language, the author can express a more creative and enriched reading experience:

> Last Sunday, the sun was a glistening fireball in the sky. The air embraced us. It was like being wrapped in warm blankets and sitting before a fire after coming in from a snowstorm.

There are many forms of figurative language, often referred to as figures of speech. Four of the most commonly used figures of speech are metaphor, simile, personification, and hyperbole.

Metaphors

A **metaphor** is a figure of speech that makes a direct comparison between two dissimilar objects or ideas. They help readers use their imaginations to visualize something or to understand an object or idea by relating it to something they already know or have experienced. Writers usually use a form of the verb *to be*, saying something *is* or *was* something else, to make a strong and clear comparison in the minds of readers. For example:

> *Bill was an erupting volcano last week* after learning the results of his company's sales.

> Bill was very angry and upset.

> Aunt Bertha *is the clasp on our family bracelet,* making sure we all stay close and connected.

> Aunt Bertha keeps our family together.

Similes

A **simile** also makes a comparison between two unlike objects or ideas, but slightly less directly. Here authors use the words *like* or *as* to compare objects or ideas or to point out the similarities between people or things. The previous examples of metaphors would be similes if they were rewritten in the following ways:

> Bill was <u>*like*</u> *an erupting volcano* last week after learning the results of his company's sales.

> Aunt Bertha holds our family together <u>*like*</u> *the clasp on a bracelet,* making sure we all stay close and connected.

Some similes are used so often that they have become part of our everyday conversation or writing:

> She is light as a feather.
>
> Mary is as sweet as sugar.
>
> The soldier was as tough as nails.
>
> He is as gentle as a lamb.
>
> I'm hungry as a horse.
>
> She's as stubborn as a mule.

Notice how metaphors and similes enrich writing and make it more interesting. Of course, the meaning is not literal. Aunt Bertha is not really a clasp on a bracelet, the soldier is not actually made of metal, and Mary doesn't taste like sugar. But, by using metaphors and similes, authors create vivid images for their readers.

When interpreting the meaning of a metaphor or simile, always be sure you identify what items or things are being compared, and how the author sees them as being alike or related.

Personification

When authors use **personification,** they attribute human qualities to non-human beings or inanimate objects. When you read the *roar of the ocean* or *the whisper of the wind*, you are experiencing personification. Oceans don't have the capacity to really roar, and the wind certainly cannot whisper. Neither one has vocal chords! But describing actions in this manner is creative and imaginative, and often more powerful than simply saying that the ocean was loud or the wind was blowing softly. Here are some other examples of personification:

> The *buildings stared* at us steadfastly as we approached the city.
>
> The buildings were tall and imposing.
>
> The *wind chimes giggled and frolicked* in the breeze.
>
> The wind chimes clanked and moved about in the breeze.

Hyperbole

Hyperbole is the use of exaggerated language to make a strong point or to provide emphasis. It is commonly used in spoken language—for example, "I told you a million times!" Of course, the million mark is not likely to have been reached, but by using an expression that exaggerates the facts, the speaker emphasizes a degree of concern or frustration and makes a strong statement. It is the same in written language. A writer may exaggerate, especially when he or she is expressing a strong opinion and attempting to enhance an argument or emphasize a point of view. Sometimes a hyperbole is amusing, but watch out for the use of hyperbole in argumentative essays and advertisements. It may be used to persuade you to believe something that is incorrect or to entice you to buy something you do not need.

Here are some examples of hyperbole:

Leaving the restaurant, I felt like I had gained a hundred pounds!

I ate a lot in the restaurant, but a one hundred pound gain is impossible.

Earn more money than you ever dreamed of!

This may be true, but it might just be an exaggeration to get you involved with an activity or program that will cost *you* money.

try it and apply it! 3-7   Using Figurative Speech

Directions: Figurative language is found in all kinds of writing. Many statements that are considered wise or inspirational include figures of speech. They are meant to teach us about life or about ourselves. Following are several such statements. Work out the meaning of the figurative language used in each statement. Then write it on the line provided, using your own words.

Metaphors

1. Do not go where the path may lead, go instead where there is no path and leave a trail.

—Ralph Waldo Emerson

Don't go along with the crowd or what has been established. Create your own ideas and act on them, so that others may adopt them or follow you.

(*continued*)

(continued)

2. It's hard for an empty bag to stand up straight.

—Benjamin Franklin

Be a person of substance, filled with ideas and good qualities. It's difficult to be proud of

yourself if you are not.

3. Our truest life is when we are in our dreams awake.

—Henry David Thoreau

We are most real and satisfied with our lives when we live the desires and hopes we

have, rather than think about them.

4. In the confrontation between the stream and the rock, the stream always wins, not through strength, but by perseverance.

—H. Jackson Brown, quoted in H. Jackson Brown, Jr.,
A Father's Book of Wisdom, p. 103. Thomas Nelson, Inc., 1999.

In life, strength is not achieved by holding steadfast to a position, but through movement

and persistence to carry on.

Similes

5. Minds are like parachutes; they only function when open.

—Sir Thomas Dewar

It is important to have an open mind and be willing to take in new ideas. That is the only

way in which we can think.

6. Marriage resembles a pair of shears, so joined that they cannot be separated; often moving in opposite directions, yet always punishing any one who comes between them.

—Sydney Smith

The relationship in marriage is like scissors. People in marriage are connected and cannot

be separated; yet sometimes move in opposite directions. Anyone who comes in between

the partners will be punished.

Personification

7. The heart has its reasons which reason knows not of.

—Blaise Pascal

Our emotions, especially when it comes to love, do not always have a logical explanation.

8. Misery loves company.

—Old English proverb

When we are unhappy it often helps us to know that we are not alone, or the only person

experiencing that pain or suffering.

9. Love is blind, but friendship closes its eyes.

—Anonymous

When in love, we often are unable to see the flaws in others. With our friends, we are able
to see the problems, but choose to not look at or focus on them.

Hyperbole

10. One loyal friend is worth ten thousand relatives.

—Euripides

A true friend is very valuable, even more so than many family members.

11. A true friend will give you the shirt off his back.

—old saying

A real friend will give up things of their own on your behalf.

12. I can't eat another bite. I ate a million pieces of candy last night.
I can't eat anything more because I ate way too much candy last night.

What do you think of each of the statements? Do you agree with them? Discuss your opinions with a partner or in groups.

Idioms

Midway through their first semester in college, freshmen may be heard saying:

I'd better *hit the books,* or else I'm going to get an F in psychology.

I *worked like a dog* to get my English paper in on time.

I *burned the midnight oil* last night. I was up until 2:00 a.m. studying for my psych midterm.

These expressions or **idioms** often add interest and sometimes a dash of humor to spoken English. Most native speakers are familiar with many of them and use them often in conversations. Nonnative speakers, however, may struggle with idioms because they are not easily translated and may not be found in standard dictionaries. Idioms are not commonly used in college textbooks because they are informal, but may be used in anecdotes, fiction, and nonacademic articles To help understand this kind of figurative language, both native and nonnative speakers of English should use the context of the sentence or sentences in which they appear.

try it and apply it! 3-8   Using Idioms

Directions: Idiomatic expressions are used to describe emotions and behaviors. How many of the following expressions, which relate to feelings or behavior, do you recognize? Work out the meanings of the idioms in bold print and rewrite them using your own words. Use the context clues in the sentences to help you.

Answers may vary.

1. Jim's **blood boiled** as the police officer wrote him a ticket for going five miles an hour beyond the speed limit.

    Jim became very angry.

2. Knowing she would disappoint someone based on her decision, Janet was **stuck between a rock and a hard place** in attempting to make her vacation plans.

    Janet was unable to make a decision, feeling that either solution would be a problem.

3. Having just finished cleaning it moments earlier, Bob **saw red** when he entered his living room and it was filled with candy wrappers and soda cans.

    Bob was very angry.

4. Wishing she could go on a world tour just like her sister, Karen was **green with envy** when she heard the plans for the trip.

    Karen was jealous or envious.

5. Morgan was so **spent** that he **couldn't see straight.** He had worked on his computer system all day, but still was not able to access the program he needed for his project.

    He was so exhausted and fatigued that he couldn't focus or pay attention . . .

6. "Are you **off your rocker?** Have you **lost your marbles,** or are you just completely **out of your mind!**" shouted Trevor. He was shocked at the behavior of his friend who ostensibly, was on a diet, but had just eaten two gallons of chocolate chip ice cream followed by a vanilla milk shake.

    All these expressions mean, crazy and mentally unbalanced.

7. Rachel **didn't have a leg to stand on.** There really was no conceivable explanation that would justify cheating on the exam.

    Rachel had no excuses or acceptable reasons.

8. By criticizing his paper so harshly, Professor Levin really **ruffled the feathers** of his student who had **run himself ragged** to complete it.

    Prof. Levin angered and annoyed the student who had worked so hard.

9. The book's portrayal of abused children **got under her skin** and Mary decided to volunteer her time at the shelter for battered teens.

    The book had a meaningful impact on Mary.

10. Bob didn't mean to brag, but he couldn't help but **toot his own horn** and **pat himself on the back** after **acing** the biology exam.

    Bob bragged about himself and spoke of his accomplishments in getting an A on the exam.

11. Mitch knew that he had to **cough up** the money for his mortgage payment or the bank would begin foreclosure proceedings on his house.

    Mitch had to come up with the money to make a payment on the loan.

12. By the expression on her father's face, Tali knew that she had **crossed the line** when she had asked him for even more money to buy video games.

    Tali went beyond what was acceptable to her father.

13. Working as a nurse at the hospital during the day and at collecting tickets at the movie theater in the evening, Shana was really **burning the candle at both ends** in order to **make ends meet.**

    Shana was working long hours throughout the day in order to pay for her expenses.

14. After dating her for several months, when Josh gave Naomi the **cold shoulder** at the football game, she felt that her **heart had broken.**

    Josh ignored Naomi, and she felt very hurt.

Using Figurative Language

Figure of Speech	Definition	Example
Metaphor	A direct comparison between two dissimilar objects or ideas	. . . raindrops are tears from the sky . . . jazz is a colorful garden of rhythm and soul
Simile	A comparison between two unlike objects or ideas, using "like" or "as"	. . . happy as sunshine . . . hopeful as a rainbow
Personification	Attributing human qualities to nonhuman beings or inanimate objects	. . . the rustling leaves waved good-bye . . . nature called us to her heart

(continued)

(continued)

Figure of Speech	Definition	Example
Hyperbole	Exaggerated language to make a point or provide emphasis	. . . I'm losing my mind. . . . He's drowning in paper work.
Idioms	A figurative expression whose meaning has evolved within a particular language or people. The origin may be obscure.	. . . . I saw red! (was very angry) . . . He's quick on the trigger. (overreacts)

Lost in Translation: Developing College-Level Vocabulary

wrap it Up

- Do not rely on *familiar* meanings of words when reading college material.

- Don't look up every new word in the dictionary. It slows down your reading process and makes you lose concentration.

- Use context clues to guess the meaning of unfamiliar words *while* reading.

- Remember that authors will use figurative language and idioms to express ideas and feelings. Use context clues to help you determine their meaning as these are often not found in the dictionary.

- Look up new words in a dictionary or thesaurus *after* you read, and use context clues to help you select their correct meanings.

- Break words up into their word parts and use the meanings of the word parts to help you understand the meaning of the whole word. See Appendix 1.

- Read marginal notes, and use glossaries to find the meaning of discipline-specific terms.

- Do not hesitate to ask your professor to help you understand new words and terminology.

Key Terms

academic vocabulary

context clues

discipline-specific vocabulary

figurative language

hyperbole

idioms

memory

metaphor

personification

signal words

simile

special font clues

storage

synonym

chapter

4

What's the Big Idea?

Identifying the Main Idea in College Reading

In this chapter

you will learn about

- Steps for identifying the main idea
- Identifying the topic of selections
- Finding stated main ideas or topic sentences
- Determining unstated or implied main ideas in paragraphs and longer selections
- Determining the thesis of a selection

Studying
Health

Traditionally, health has been thought of as the state of physical well-being and focused on the cure and prevention of illness. Today, health is viewed as multidimensional and so is the study of health, which includes understanding our bodies, focusing on issues such as physical fitness, healthy weight, diet and nutrition, and the prevention and treatment of disease. Health studies address stress management and mental illness, drug abuse and additions, sexuality and reproduction, and consumer and safety issues related to health-care services and the environment at home, work, and in the community. Introductory college courses in health often survey these topics, whereas others focus on specific areas. For example, colleges offer standalone courses in dying and death, human sexuality, cardiovascular health and disease, family planning, and health care.

Health in the Workplace (Part One)

According to the *Occupational Outlook Handbook*, the number of job opportunities related to health and health care will increase over the next decade. Occupations range from entry-level positions that require simple certification in a specific skill, such as drawing blood, to the most sophisticated careers in medicine and research requiring years of preparation and study. Some of the fastest growing occupations in health-related fields include personal and home care aides, medical assistants, skin care specialists, physical therapists, and dental hygienists.

The Main Idea

It's Saturday night and you are walking out of the movie theater with your friends. You have just seen the latest and greatest thriller. It was two hours long. Your cell phone rings. It's Bob, who had to stay home to finish his final paper in sociology. "What was it about?" he asks. You certainly would not want to spend another two hours telling him, nor would you want to waste all your valuable airtime going into great detail. What you need to do is very much like a task you are often confronted with in the reading process; that is, you want to relay the central message, gist or main point; you want to simply state the main idea.

College reading requires you to identify and understand the key concept or major point an author is making, the **main idea**. Whether you are reading a paragraph, an essay, an article, or a textbook chapter, your ability to understand and express the central thought expressed by the author is critical.

In a longer reading selection, the main idea is called the **thesis**, or **thesis statement**, and it usually appears near the end of the introductory paragraph. This is the main point the author discusses throughout the course of the essay, article, or textbook chapter. Each paragraph in a reading contains a key point or main idea, often expressed in a sentence called the **topic sentence**. Topic sentences frequently appear at the beginning of a paragraph, but can also be found in the middle or at the end of a paragraph. The main ideas in each paragraph support the point made in the thesis statement. In class discussion, you may hear the main idea referred to as

- the gist
- the key point
- the central idea
- the thesis

Being able to identify the main idea of a paragraph or longer reading can help you because it will

- give you the BIG picture; you will have a frame of reference so that all the details within a paragraph or reading will come together and have meaning.
- tell you the most important point the author wants you to understand.
- establish a *purpose* for your reading; the main idea is always an important goal for any reader.
- enable you to take good notes while you read.
- prepare you to write a summary or create an outline after you read.
- prepare you to convey the gist of the reading to a professor or classmate.

Two Steps for Identifying the Main Idea

Being able to identify the main idea of what you are reading is a critical skill for you as a college student. However, the task doesn't need to be very complicated. In fact, you need to complete only two important steps. The first is to identify the topic of the reading selection. The second is to determine the most important, overall point the author is making about the topic throughout the selection or portion you have read. When you combine the main point with the topic in a complete sentence, you will have identified the main idea.

Step 1: Identify the Topic

Whether you are reading a paragraph or a chapter, the first step in identifying the main idea is to recognize or identify the **topic** of the selection. The topic is the subject. It is a broad term or idea. The rest of the paragraph or chapter tells more about it. Even individual sentences have topics. They are usually referred to as the subject of the sentence.

When looking for the topic, ask yourself, "Who or what is this about?" Some students find it helpful to think of the topic as the title of their reading selection.

The topic

- can be a single word, a few words, or a phrase.
- is *not* a sentence.
- is often repeated several times within a paragraph or selection.
- can be the same term or phrase or different words that mean the same thing.
- is often seen in the title or heading.
- may appear in boldface or italic type.
- is sometimes never actually stated, but may be identified through reasoning.

Even a list has a topic. You can use the same thinking that you use to identify the topic of a list to identify the topic of a reading. Look at the following list of terms related to health:

> sore throat
>
> runny nose
>
> cold symptoms
>
> watery eyes
>
> general fatigue

Do you notice that one item in the list seems to cover or describe all the others? That item is the subject or topic of the list. Which item is the topic?
cold symptoms _____

Following is a list of items, *without a topic*. To identify the topic on your own, think about a heading that would work as a title for the list. You will use the same thinking in your reading when an author does not directly state the topic.

> jogging
>
> running

weight training

bicycling

swimming

What is the subject of the items in the list? That subject is the topic. What is the topic? What heading could you put at the top of the list? *ways to exercise*

Now look back at the second paragraph at the opening of this chapter that begins with the words "College reading . . ." What word or words appear throughout the paragraph? Circle the words in the paragraph that help you identify the topic. You should have circled *main idea, key concept, major point, central thought*. Now what is the topic of the paragraph? *the main idea*

try it and apply it! 4-1   Identifying Topics in Lists and Sentences

Directions: Read the following lists of terms related to issues in health. One of the words in each list is the topic, the word that includes all of the other items. Underline the topic of each list.

1. opium, <u>narcotics</u>, heroin, morphine, codeine
2. bulimia, binging, purging, <u>eating disorders</u>, anorexia
3. <u>fast food chains</u>, Wendy's, Hardee's, McDonald's, Burger King
4. traffic, test anxiety, <u>causes of stress</u>, relationship problems, lack of sleep
5. weight reduction, physical activity, <u>high blood pressure reducers</u>, salt restriction, limited intake of alcohol

Now read the following sentences. Underline the subject, or topic, of each one. Ask yourself, "Who or what is the sentence about?"

6. <u>Remedies for stress</u> include exercise, meditation, proper nutrition, and getting enough sleep.
7. Runny nose, watery eyes, aches and pains, and a listless feeling are all <u>symptoms of a cold</u>.
8. <u>Hepatitis</u> is an inflammatory process in the liver that can be caused by viruses.
9. There are <u>many reasons people choose to be celibate</u> rather than engage in a sexually intimate relationship.
10. Health programming on cable television stations, stories in lifestyle sections of newspapers, health-care correspondents appearing on national network news shows, and the growing number of health-oriented magazines are all sources of <u>health information in the mass media</u>. (Hahn et al. 2007)

try it and apply it! 4-2   Identifying Topics in Paragraphs

Directions: Read the following paragraphs from the textbook *Focus on Health*. Identify the topic of each paragraph by looking for the term or the form of the term that is repeated throughout the paragraph. Synonyms, or words with similar meanings, may be used. Underline the term and synonyms for the term. Then write the topic of each paragraph on the line provided.

Paragraph 1

Hint: In this paragraph, the same term is used repeatedly.

Exercise is another physical aspect of stress management. Exercising aerobically at least three times a week for 20 to 30 minutes has been found to manage stress effectively for several reasons. First, exercising requires you to focus on your breathing and to breathe deeply, the key to stress management. By tensing and releasing the muscles through exercise, you are allowing your body to relax and unwind. Second, active movement can alleviate stress through the release of endorphins, naturally occurring chemicals in the brain. Endorphins help to counter stress, subdue pain, and increase pleasure, which is the reason people talk about the runner's high. Hitting a racquetball against the wall or playing basketball can be a great way to release the frustrations of the day and let go of tensions and stress. Aerobic exercise includes walking briskly, running, bicycling, skating, and dancing.

(Adapted from Hahn et al. 2007)

What is the topic of the paragraph?

exercise

Paragraph 2

Hint: In the following paragraph, different terms refer to the same topic or subject.

What are some positive, effective methods for coping with stress? Different strategies and methods for stress management involve the physical, social, environmental, and psychological aspects of your stress. We will review techniques and strategies with each of these dimensions, and you will need to practice and experiment to find the stress management techniques that are right for you.

(Adapted from Hahn et al. 2007)

What is the topic of the paragraph?

strategies for dealing with stress

(continued)

(continued)

Paragraph 3

The cause of heart disease, where the illness is present at birth or congenital, is not clearly understood. One cause, rubella, has been identified. The fetuses of mothers who contract the rubella virus during the first 3 months of pregnancy are at greater risk of developing a wide variety of effects, including heart defects, deafness, cataracts, and mental retardation. Other hypotheses about the development of congenital heart disease implicate environmental pollutants; maternal use of drugs, including alcohol during pregnancy; and unknown genetic factors.

(Adapted from Hahn et al. 2007)

What is the topic of the paragraph?

the causes of congenital heart disease

Paragraph 4

Besides the cardiovascular illnesses already discussed, the heart and blood vessels are also subject to other pathological conditions, or disease. Tumors of the heart, although rare, occur. Infections, conditions involving the pericardial sac that surrounds the heart (*pericarditis*) and the innermost layer of the heart (*endocarditis*) are more commonly seen. In addition, inflammation of the veins, (*phlebitis*) is troubling to some people. The heart and blood vessels are subject to a variety of diseases.

(Adapted from Hahn et al. 2007)

What is the topic of the paragraph?

pathological conditions or diseases of the heart and blood vessels

Paragraph 5

Because tobacco use is a learned behavior, it is reasonable to accept that modeling stimulates or triggers experimental smoking. Modeling suggests that susceptible people smoke to emulate, or model their behavior after smokers whom they admire or with whom they share other types of social or emotional bonds. Particularly for young adolescents (ages 14 to 17), smoking behavior corresponds with the smoking behavior of slightly older peers, and very young adults (ages 18–22), older brothers or sisters, and, most important, parents.

(Adapted from Hahn et al. 2007)

What is the topic of the paragraph?

modeling and its impact on smoking

Notice that the term *modeling*, by itself, does not have meaning as a topic. It must be connected to the context of the paragraph, that is, smoking.

try it and apply it! 4-3   Identifying Topics in Longer Passages

Directions: Read the following passages adapted from a health textbook. Apply similar strategies to identify the topic of longer readings. Ask yourself, "What is the overall subject of the paragraphs included in the selection?" Each paragraph will highlight a component or example of the broader topic being discussed. Consider a good title to cover all the information presented. Often the topic is introduced or indicated in the first paragraph. Underline terms that are repeated or presented more than once in different ways. Determine the topic and write it on the lines that follow.

Selection 1

We will look at health in a holistic way. Health has several aspects, so we must recognize it as multidimensional. We will examine six components, or dimensions, of health, all interacting in a synergistic manner, allowing us to engage in the wide array of life experiences.

Most of us have a number of physiological and structural characteristics we can rely on to aid us in accomplishing the variety of activities in our days. Among these physical characteristics are our body weight, visual ability, strength, coordination, endurance, susceptibility to disease, and powers of recuperation. In certain situations, the physical dimensions of health may be the most important.

We also possess certain emotional characteristics that can help us through the demands of daily living. The emotional dimension of health encompasses our ability to see the world in a realistic manner, cope with stress, remain flexible, and compromise to resolve conflict.

A third dimension of health includes social skills and cultural sensitivity. Initially, family interactions, school experiences and peer group interactions foster development of these areas, but future social interactions will demand additional development and refinement of skills, as well as new insights as people move into adulthood. Interactions in college enhance the social dimensions of health for both traditional and non-traditional aged students.

The ability to process and act on information, clarify values and beliefs, and exercise decision-making rank among the most important aspects of total health. For many college-educated persons, the intellectual components of health may prove to be most satisfying of all the dimensions.

Other dimensions of health are also considered. The spiritual dimension encompasses religion and a more diverse belief system, including relationship with other living things in the universe, the nature of human behavior, and the need and willingness to serve others. The occupational dimension defines the importance of the workplace to people's well-being. Lastly, some academics would add an environmental dimension, defined on the basis of land, air, and water quality.

(Adapted from Hahn et al. 2007)

What is the topic of the entire selection?

the many dimensions or components of health

(continued)

(continued)

Selection 2

Managing your time effectively can help you cope with your stress by feeling more in control, having a sense of accomplishment, and having a sense of purpose in your life. Establishing good time management habits can take two to three weeks. By using specific systems, even the most disorganized people can make their lives less chaotic and stressful.

The first step is to analyze how you are spending your time. What are your most productive and least productive times of day and night? Do you underestimate how long something will take you to complete? Do you waste time or allow interruptions to take you off task? Carrying a notebook with you for a week and writing down how you spend your time might provide you with some insight into the answers. Be honest about your study habits.

Keeping a daily planner to schedule your time is the next step in managing your time more effectively. First, block out all the activities that are consistent, regular, weekly activities, such as attending classes, eating meals, sleeping, going to meetings, exercising, and working. Then look at the time remaining. Schedule regular study time, relaxation time, and free time. Schedule study time when you are most productive. Be realistic about what you can accomplish in every hour.

Set goals for the week as well as for each day. If something unexpected interferes with your time schedule, modify your plans but don't throw out the entire schedule. Making a to-do list can be helpful, but it is only the first step. Break large tasks into smaller, more manageable pieces and then prioritize them. Try the ABC method. The A tasks are the most urgent and must be done today. The B tasks are important but could wait 24 hours. The C tasks are activities that can easily wait a few days to a week. Don't fall into the C trap of doing the less important tasks because they are quick and can be checked off your list with ease. This can lead to putting off the important A activities, leaving them until you feel stressed and overwhelmed. Procrastination is the enemy of time management.

(Adapted from Hahn et al. 2007)

What is the topic of the entire selection?

time management

Step 2: Determine the Main Idea

After you have determined the topic, ask yourself, "What is the most important point the author is making about the topic in the selection?" That is the main idea. The *main idea* is a statement that includes the topic and the author's most important or general idea about the topic.

The main idea

- must be a complete sentence.
- must include the topic of the paragraph or selection.
- may be stated directly in the text.
- may not be stated directly but implied.

Finding the Stated Main Idea in Paragraphs: Topic Sentences The main idea is the most important point the author wants to make about the topic. When the main idea is stated directly in a paragraph, it is called the **topic sentence**. In college textbooks, topic sentences appear most frequently as the *first* sentences of paragraphs. However, be aware that the topic sentence may appear anywhere in a paragraph: at the beginning, in the middle, or at the end. Sometimes, to restate or emphasize the main point, an author will open and close with the main idea.

The following paragraphs are all about alcoholism. Each paragraph has a point to make about that topic. That point, or main idea, is expressed in the topic sentence. The rest of the paragraph adds information or details to tell about that main idea. Notice the location of the topic sentence.

Example 1: Topic Sentence as the Beginning

- *TOPIC SENTENCE*
- _____
- _____
- _____

Here the author states the topic sentence at the beginning and then adds more specific information, often including examples, to explain more about the main point.

> **Recently, the unusually high prevalence of alcoholism among adult children of alcoholics has been identified**. It is estimated that these children are about four times more likely to develop alcoholism than children whose parents are not alcoholics. Even those who do not become alcoholics may have a difficult time adjusting to everyday living.
>
> (Adapted from Hahn et al. 2007)

Example 2: Topic Sentence in the Middle

- _____
- _____
- *TOPIC SENTENCE*
- _____
- _____

If an author is continuing a discussion from a previous paragraph, or wants to provide some background information to lead into the next point, the topic sentence of the new paragraph may not appear until the middle. More supportive information or examples will follow.

> In response to this concern, support groups have been formed to help prevent the adult sons and daughters of alcoholics from developing the condition that afflicted their parents. **Support groups for children of alcoholics play a very strong role in the prevention of the alcoholism continuum.** These include Al-Anon and Adult Children of Alcoholics. Experts agree that adult children of alcoholics who believe they have come to terms with their feelings can sometimes face lingering problems.
>
> (Adapted from Hahn et al. 2007)

Example 3: Topic Sentence at the End

- ■ _____
- ■ _____
- ■ _____

■ *TOPIC SENTENCE*

An author may want to build up to the main point, providing related and background information that leads to the topic sentence, which is finally stated at the very end of the paragraph.

> For decades, women have consumed less alcohol and had fewer alcohol-related problems than men. At present, evidence is mounting that a greater percentage of women are choosing to drink and that some subgroups of women, especially young women, are drinking more heavily. An increased number of admissions of women to treatment centers may also reflect that alcohol consumption among women is on the rise. **Studies indicate that drinking among women is, indeed, on the rise and currently there are almost as many female alcoholics as male alcoholics.**
>
> (Adapted from Hahn et al. 2007)

Example 4: Topic Sentence at the Beginning and the End

- ■ *TOPIC SENTENCE*
- ■ _____
- ■ _____

■ *TOPIC SENTENCE RESTATED*

When an author wants to emphasize the main point, you may find a topic sentence both at the beginning and the conclusion of a paragraph. The initial main idea will be restated using different words.

> **The absorption of alcohol is influenced by several factors, most of which can be controlled by the individual**. The strength of the beverage matters. The stronger the drink, the greater the amount of alcohol that is absorbed. The greater the number of drinks consumed, the more alcohol is absorbed. The speed of consumption should also be considered. Consumed rapidly, even relatively few drinks will result in a larger concentration of blood alcohol. The presence of food also makes a difference. Food can compete with alcohol for passage into the bloodstream, slowing the absorption of the alcohol. A person's body chemistry and even their race or ethnicity impacts their ability to tolerate alcohol in the blood. Finally, gender is a factor, in that women absorb about 30 percent more alcohol into the bloodstream than men, despite an identical number of drinks and equal body weight. **With the exception of a person's body chemistry, race/ethnicity, and gender, all the various factors that influence absorption can be moderated by the alcohol user.**
>
> (Adapted from Hahn et al. 2007)

Keep this in mind

How can you be sure you have identified the topic sentence in a paragraph? Here are some important tips:

- The sentence must include the topic of the paragraph.
- The sentence must include the main idea about the topic.
- The sentence must be broad or general enough to encompass the key points or details in the rest of the paragraph.
- The sentence is *not* a detail that supports the main idea.
- The sentence is *not* an example.

try it and apply it! 4-4   Identifying Topic Sentences in Paragraphs

Directions: The following paragraphs discuss aspects of stress and stress management. Read each paragraph. Determine the topic and consider the most important overall point the author is making about it. Then go back and underline the topic sentence in each paragraph. Beneath each paragraph identify the topic and write the topic sentence on the line provided. The topic sentence is the stated main idea of the paragraph.

Paragraph 1

A number of negative ways of dealing with stress are quite common and often quite harmful. Some people turn to alcohol and drugs to avoid their problems and numb their feelings, and cigarettes are also cited as a way of relieving stress. Many people use food to comfort themselves. Putting off distasteful tasks and avoiding stressful situations is another way of coping with stress. Some people use sleep as a way of escaping their problems, and certainly depression has been associated with not having the ability to effectively manage stress.

(Adapted from Hahn et al. 2007)

The topic of the paragraph is *negative ways of dealing with stress*

The stated main idea is *A number of negative ways of dealing with stress are quite common and often quite harmful.*

Paragraph 2

You have studied for the test you are about to take and are well prepared. You look at the first test question and suddenly your mind goes blank. The harder you try to think, the more nervous and stressed you feel. You just can't think clearly and feel as though you have some sort of mental block—what is happening? One-fifth of students

(continued)

(*continued*)

experience these feelings, referred to as test anxiety. Test anxiety is a form of performance anxiety—people anticipate that they will perform poorly on the test. Exams are one of the greatest sources of stress for college students. The physical sensations associated with test anxiety are similar to those of general anxiety, such as fidgeting; having feelings of butterflies in your stomach; rapid heart rate; difficulty breathing; nausea; tension in your neck, back, jaw and shoulders; headaches; sweaty palms, and feeling shaky. People suffering from test anxiety make more mistakes on their tests, don't read tests accurately, and tend to make simple mistakes, such as spelling errors or adding something incorrectly. Many don't pace themselves well and have a hard time finishing exams.

(Adapted from Hahn et al. 2007)

The topic of the paragraph is *test anxiety*

The stated main idea is *Test anxiety is a form of performance anxiety—people anticipate that they will perform poorly on the test.*

Paragraph 3

To try this technique, take a moment to focus on your breathing: in for a count of four and out for four. After doing so for a few times, tighten your body, clench your hands, teeth, and jaw, close your eyes tightly, and pull your shoulders up while you are still breathing deeply. Are you able to do so? It is virtually impossible to tense your body and breathe deeply, because they are mutually exclusive activities. Thus, the relaxation response is the foundation of most of the stress-management techniques described in this chapter. Relaxation and deep breathing are the fundamental aspects of stress management.

(Adapted from Hahn et al. 2007)

The topic of the paragraph is *relaxation and deep breathing*

The stated main idea is *Relaxation and deep breathing are the fundamental aspects of stress management.*

Paragraph 4

To manage stress effectively, you must also make time for fun, play, and friends. Like exercise, laughter increases the release of endorphins and requires you to breathe deeply, and so having humor in your life is an essential part of stress management. Research has shown that stress can be related to having inadequate social interactions. Hugging and human contact have also been demonstrated as having a significant effect in reducing the harmful physical effects of stress. Participating in social activities, such as social organizations, sports or just talking with friends can give you the break you need to reset your mind and focus on something other than work. Having social interaction is an important stress reducer.

(Adapted from Hahn et al. 2007)

The topic of the paragraph is *the social aspects of managing stress*

The stated main idea is *To manage stress effectively, you must also make time for fun, play, and friends. Having social interaction is an important stress reducer.*

Paragraph 5

Studies have shown that just petting an animal produces calming effects such as lowered blood pressure and decreased heart rate. Cardiac patients who own pets tend to live much longer than those who have no pets. Actually, you don't even need human contact to reduce stress—just owning a pet can make a difference.

(Adapted from Hahn et al. 2007)

The topic of the paragraph is *pets and stress reduction*

The stated main idea is *Actually, you don't even need human contact to reduce stress—just owning a pet can make a difference.*

Paragraph 6

If you go away to college, it can be beneficial to have your friends visit you (rather than you going home) so they can interact with you in your new environment and meet your new friends. Often students feel as though they live in two worlds, home and school, and it can be stressful to negotiate going from one to the other. The more you can connect home and school while you are in college, the less stress you will experience. So it can be helpful to share what you are doing in your day activities around campus, with your family and friends. Discuss the details of your classes or even who you ate lunch with. Find out what your family has been doing as well.

(Adapted from Hahn et al. 2007)

The topic of the paragraph is *going away to college and stress*

The stated main idea is *The more you can connect home and school while you are in college, the less stress you will experience.*

Finding the Stated Main Idea in Readings: Thesis Statements   A thesis **statement** is the main idea of a longer selection. You can think of it very much like the topic sentence of a paragraph. It is the most general point the author is making or discussing throughout the entire selection. In some way, all the paragraphs within the selection support, or tell about, that main point or thesis. Often the thesis of the selection is stated in the first, or introductory, paragraph. As an active college reader, you will want to keep the thesis in mind as you identify the more specific points of each paragraph that explain or provide details about it. Like a topic sentence, the thesis must be a complete sentence. It includes the topic of the selection and the most important point the author is making about the topic.

Let's take another look at a passage you read when learning to identify the topic of a selection on page 85 (reprinted next). Reread it. This time write the topic of each paragraph in the margin. Underline the topic sentence in each paragraph. Then think about which sentence in the selection includes the topic and the most important, yet general point, the author is making. That sentence is the thesis statement.

The Dimensions of Health

the six dimensions of health

We will look at health in a holistic way. Health has several aspects, so we must recognize it as multidimensional. We will examine six components, or dimensions, of health, all interacting in a synergistic manner, allowing us to engage in the wide array of life experiences.

physical dimensions of health

Most of us have a number of physiological and structural characteristics we can rely on to aid us in accomplishing the variety of activities in our days. Among these physical characteristics are our body weight, visual ability, strength, coordination, endurance, susceptibility to disease, and powers of recuperation. In certain situations, the physical dimensions of health may be the most important.

emotional dimension of health

We also possess certain emotional characteristics that can help us through the demands of daily living. The emotional dimension of health encompasses our ability to see the world in a realistic manner, cope with stress, remain flexible, and compromise to resolve conflict.

social dimension of health

A third dimension of health includes social skills and cultural sensitivity. Initially, family interactions, school experiences and peer group interactions foster development of these areas, but future social interactions will demand additional development and refinement of skills, as well as new insights as people move into adulthood. Interactions in college enhance the social dimensions of health for both traditional and nontraditional aged students.

intellectual dimension of health

The ability to process and act on information, clarify values and beliefs, and exercise decision making rank among the most important aspects of total health. For many college-educated persons, the intellectual components of health may prove to be most satisfying of all the dimensions.

other dimensions of health: spiritual, occupational, environmental

Other dimensions of health are also considered. The spiritual dimension encompasses religion and a more diverse belief system, including relationship with other living things in the universe, the nature of human behavior, and the need and willingness to serve others. The <u>occupational dimension</u> defines the importance of the workplace to people's well-being. Lastly, some academics would add <u>an environmental dimension</u>, defined on the basis of land, air, and water quality.

(Adapted from Hahn et al. 2007)

As you may recall, the topic of this selection was *the many dimensions or aspects of health*. The thesis statement is in the first paragraph: *Health has several aspects, so we must recognize it as multidimensional*. Notice how the thesis statement includes the topic and how all the paragraphs discuss an aspect of the thesis

If you were using this selection as a source to write a paper, you might want to paraphrase, or put the thesis statement in your own words. You might choose to expand the thesis statement by including the various dimensions, which you identified as the topics of the paragraphs. Thus, you could restate the thesis in your own words as: *There are several aspects to our health, including physical, emotional, cultural, intellectual, spiritual, occupational, and environmental dimensions*.

Keep this in mind

How can you be sure you have identified the thesis of a selection? Here are some important tips:

- The thesis must include the overall topic of the selection and the most important, general point the author is making about it.
- It must be a complete sentence.
- It is likely to be located in an introductory paragraph in a textbook selection.
- It must be broad or general enough to encompass the key points or major details of the entire selection.
- It is *not* an example.
- Remember that just because a statement is true, that does not make it the thesis!

try it and apply it! 4-5   Identifying Main Ideas and the Thesis Statement

Directions: Actively read the following longer selections adapted from the text, *Focus on Health*. For each selection, write the topic of each paragraph in the margin. Underline the topic sentence of each paragraph. Then review this information to select the best thesis statement for each selection from the list of options that follow it. Be careful—all the answer choices are true, but only one in each set is the thesis statement of the entire selection.

(continued)

(continued)

A. Time Management

managing time

Finding methods to manage your time effectively can help you cope with your stress by feeling more in control, having a sense of accomplishment, and having a sense of purpose in your life. Establishing good time management habits can take two to three weeks. By using specific systems, even the most disorganized people can make their lives less chaotic and stressful.

analyze how you spend time

The first step is to analyze how you are spending your time. What are your most productive and least productive times of day and night. Do you underestimate how long something will take you to complete? Do you waste time or allow interruptions to take you off task? Carrying a notebook with you for a week and writing down how you spend your time might provide you with some insight into the answers. Be honest about your study habits.

using daily planners/ scheduling

Keeping a daily planner to schedule your time is the next step in managing your time more effectively. First, block out all the activities that are consistent, regular, weekly activities, such as attending classes, eating meals, sleeping, going to meetings, exercising, and working. Then look at the time remaining. Schedule regular study time, relaxation time, and free time. Schedule study time when you are most productive. Be realistic about what you can accomplish in every hour.

weekly and daily goals

Set goals for the week as well as for each day. If something unexpected interferes with your time schedule, modify your plans but don't throw out the entire schedule. Making a to-do list can be helpful, but it is only the first step. Break large tasks into smaller, more manageable pieces, and then prioritize them. Try the ABC method. The A tasks are the most urgent and must be done today. The B tasks are important but could wait 24 hours. The C tasks are activities that can easily wait a few days to a week. Don't fall into the C trap of doing the less important tasks because they are quick and can be checked off your list with ease. This can lead to putting off the important A activities, leaving them until you feel stressed and overwhelmed. Procrastination is the enemy of time management.

(Adapted from Hahn et al. 2007)

The thesis statement of the selection is: ____*c*____

a.   Use a daily planner to effectively manage your time.

b.   Setting goals and analyzing your time are important elements of time management.

c.   Finding methods to manage your time effectively can help you cope with your stress by feeling more in control, having a sense of accomplishment, and having a sense of purpose in your life

d.   Students should apply time management strategies to get their work done and be successful in college.

B. The Environmental Aspects of Stress Management

environmental factors that cause stress

Stress has been linked to being exposed to prolonged daily noise, such as that in a factory. We know that depression can be related to the amount of light to which you are exposed, and this can also affect your circadian rhythms. Natural light tends to elevate your mood, whereas prolonged exposure to artificial lighting can increase your stress level. Research also suggests that different colors can raise or lower your stress and energy level. Some people associate the color red with feelings of anger or hostility and blue with feeling depressed. Having plants or photos of friends around your living or workspace can also alleviate stress. To effectively manage your stress, you should consider adjusting various environmental factors such as the noise in which you operate, the amount of light available to you, and the aesthetic quality of the space you inhabit.

Other factors can play a significant role in managing stress. As the saying goes, "Stop and smell the roses." Studies have shown that aromatherapy, using different aromas or odors therapeutically, can lower stress levels. When you breathe in these oils, they send a direct message to your brain via your olfactory nerves, where they can affect the endocrine and the hormonal systems via the hypothalamus. Odors have an amazing effect on our emotional states because they hook into the emotional or primitive parts of our brains. Aromatherapy has been used to relieve pain, enhance relaxation and stress relief, unknot tense muscles, soften dry skin, and enhance immunity. So it is wise to pay attention to your aromatic surroundings, because they affect you much more than you realize.

aromatherapy and stress

Spending time with negative, pessimistic people can increase your stress level rather than decrease it. It is obviously more advantageous to surround yourself with positive, optimistic friends. Feeling crowded in a room and not having enough personal space can also lead to an increase in stress. Interestingly, it is not being in crowds itself but how familiar you are with the people, the activity that is taking place, and how much control you feel over your personal space that makes the difference. In other words, being in a crowded room with your friends during a party feels different than feeling trapped in a crowded restaurant filled with strangers. Thus, while social interaction has been shown to have positive results on lessening the effects of stress, the beneficial effect depends on the types of friends with whom you surround yourself.

social interaction and stress

Another important aspect of managing stress in your environment includes having a meaningful job. Having work that is stimulating but not beyond your abilities helps to keep your response at a moderate, optimal level for performance. Feeling content in the workplace minimizes the amount of stress in one's life.

contentment on the job and stress

(Adapted from Hahn et al. 2007)

The thesis statement for this selection is: _____ *b* _____

a. The environmental aspects of stress management include stressors such as noise, light, and space.

b. The management of stress is clearly related to components of a person's environment.

c. Social interactions have positive effects in lowering stress.

d. Having meaningful work will help you manage stress.

Implied Main Ideas

Every paragraph contains a main idea. However, it is not always stated directly in a topic sentence. Nevertheless, the content of the paragraph supports an overall point or key thought. This key point or thought is called the **implied** or **unstated main idea.**

Just as when you are speaking with someone who does not state a point directly in the conversation but you conclude it by thinking about all the information the person did share, so you can find the implied main ideas in your reading material.

Finding the Implied (Unstated) Main Idea in Paragraphs

As an active reader, you can work out the main idea of a paragraph by first identifying the topic and then noting the information, or details, the author provides to tell about it. You use this information to determine the most important, overall point the author wants you to know. After you have understood the implied or unstated main idea of a paragraph, you can express it using your own words. You will learn more about working with the details of a paragraph in Chapter 5.

Following is a sample paragraph that contains an unstated main idea. As you read it, circle repeated words or phrases that indicate the topic of the paragraph. Then underline the important points of information that tell more about that topic. Think about how they may be related. Ask yourself, "What overall point does the information help me understand about the topic?"

What events or situations trigger stress for you? For some it is financial worries, for others it may be a relationship conflict, and for still others it is work-related stress. Even positive events, such as getting married, starting a new job, or moving to a new place can be stressors. Going on vacation can be stressful as you get things done ahead of time to prepare for being away, pack your belongings, spend money on the trip, and completely change your routine.

(Adapted from Hahn et al. 2007)

So, who or what is the paragraph about? Perhaps, you circled these words: *stressors, stressful,* or *trigger stress*. The topic then is *the causes of stress*. Now review the paragraph and the sentences you underlined.

What is the most important point about stress that the author is making in this paragraph? The answer is that *both positive and negative events can trigger stress*. If you combine the answers to the two questions, "Who or what is the paragraph about (the topic)?" and "What is the most important point about stress the author is making in this paragraph?" The implied main idea of the paragraph is:

> *Stress is triggered by both positive and negative events or situations in everyday life.*

This is the unstated main idea of the paragraph.

Sometimes the implied, or unstated, main idea is formulated by combining two sentences in a paragraph. Both are important, but individually each does not tell the whole point. Together they do.

Read the following paragraph on cold remedies. Notice the two sentences in italic within the paragraph. These could be connected to cover the major points expressed. Restate them as a single sentence to identify the implied main idea. Write it on the line provided.

> *At this time there is no effective way to prevent colds.* In 1999 a medication, pleconaril, appeared to be effective in reducing the extent and duration of colds after the initial symptoms had developed. However, in 2002 the FDA denied approval of pleconaril in part due to adverse reactions in some women using the drug and oral contraceptives. *There are, however, some over-the-counter cold remedies that can help you manage a cold.* They will not cure your cold, but may lessen the discomfort associated with it.

(Adapted from Hahn et al. 2007)

Implied main idea: *At this time there is no effective way to prevent colds, but there are some over-the-counter cold remedies that can help you manage a cold.*

The most important points of the paragraph are that we do not currently have an effective way to prevent colds, but that remedies sold in stores can help us manage cold symptoms. You may have written: *At this time there is no effective way to prevent colds, but there are some over-the-counter cold remedies that can help you manage a cold.*

Keep this in mind

How can you be sure you have formulated a main idea statement that works for your selection?

- It must be a complete sentence.
- It must include the general topic or topics of the paragraph or selection.
- It must state the most important overall point the author is making about the topic.
- It may *not* be a specific detail or example.
- It would work well as the first sentence of the paragraph if you were to add it.

try it and apply it! 4-6   **Identifying Implied Main Ideas in Paragraphs**

Directions: Now apply the preceding strategy to the following paragraphs, which relate to the discipline of health and to sexual harassment. For each paragraph, circle the repeated words and phrases that indicate the topic. Underline the portions that indicate the main point the author is making. Write the topic on the line provided. Then formulate the implied main idea and write it on the line below the paragraph. Remember to mention the topic and the most important point the writer is making about it in the thesis statement.

Paragraph 1

It is estimated that about two-thirds of students work while going to college, and more students are working full-time to pay for the costs of tuition. It is estimated that between 5 and 10 percent of college students also have children. This, of course, adds stress to a student's life in balancing time for school, children, work, and household responsibilities. The increase in the number of students who have children is partly a result of a nationwide trend of more women in their mid-20s or older starting or returning to college. In fact, a nationwide study by the University of Michigan showed that the number of full-time female students over 25 years old grew by 500 percent over recent years. While some campuses offer support, many do not have child care services, which leaves students having to coordinate schedules and juggle responsibilities, causing even more stress. Also, the cost of child care can be exorbitant for some and can certainly add to financial worries. Managing time well and having a strong support system are essential for students with children, particularly single parents. Often there is little to no time available for relaxation, socialization, or exercising, and so employing stress relief strategies can be challenging.

(Adapted from Hahn et al. 2007)

Topic: *the stress of college students who are parents*

Implied main idea: *College students who are also parents experience a great deal of stress.*

Paragraph 2

Examples of sexual harassment include unwanted physical contact, excessive pressure for dates, and sexually explicit humor. It also includes the making of sexual innuendos or remarks, offers of job advancement based on sexual favors, and outward sexual assault. Sexual harassment may be applied in a subtle manner and can, in some cases, go unnoticed by co-workers and fellow students. Both men and women can be victims of unwanted attention of a sexual nature, creating embarrassment or stress.

(Adapted from Hahn et al. 2007)

Topic: *sexual harassment*

Implied main idea: *Sexual harassment comes in many forms, affecting both men and women.*

Paragraph 3

Sexual harassment is a form of illegal sex discrimination. On campus, sexual harassment may be primarily in terms of the offer of sex for grades. If this occurs to you, think carefully about the situation and document specific times, events, and places where the harassment took place. Consult your college's policy concerning sexual harassment. Next, you could report these events to the appropriate administrative office. In the workplace, the victim should document the occurrences and report them to the management or personnel officials. Sexual harassment workshops and educational seminars are available to educate men and women about the problem.

(Adapted from Hahn et al. 2007)

Topic: *sexual harassment*

Implied main idea: *There are steps that should be taken to report incidences of sexual harassment, both in school and on the job.*

Paragraph 4

Signs of the common cold include a runny nose, watery eyes, general aches and pains, a listless feeling, and a slight fever. These are the most pervasive symptoms of acute rhinitis, in its early stages. Eventually, the nasal passages swell, and the inflammation may spread to the throat. Stuffy nose, sore throat, and coughing are symptoms that may follow. The senses of taste and smell are also often blocked and appetite declines.

(Adapted from Hahn et al. 2007)

Topic: *cold symptoms*

Implied main idea: *Several signs or symptoms are indicative of a cold, also known as acute rhinitis.*

Paragraph 5

Most young adults can cope with the milder strains of influenza that appear each winter or spring. However, pregnant women and older people—especially older people with additional health complications, such as heart disease, kidney disease, emphysema, and chronic bronchitis—are not as capable of handling this viral attack. People who regularly come into contact with the general public, such as teachers, should also consider annual flu shots.

(Adapted from Hahn et al. 2007)

(continued)

(*continued*)

> **Topic:** *how different people deal with influenza*
>
> **Implied main idea:** *People can cope with the flu in different ways and should take precautions based on their situation.*

try it and apply it! 4-7   Identifying Stated and Implied Main Ideas in a Longer Selection

Directions: Read the following excerpt from a chapter on managing stress. Identify the main idea of each paragraph by locating the topic sentence *or* by identifying the topic, noting important content, and formulating the implied main idea. Underline any topic sentences and circle repeated words that indicate the topic. Then, write the main idea for each paragraph on the line that follows it. Finally, select the most general or *overall main point* of the entire selection. This will be the thesis of the selection. It is not stated completely, but is implied by combining the topic and main ideas.

Procrastination

Procrastination means postponing doing something that is necessary to reach a goal. Putting things off, or procrastination, is a common problem that plagues students and can cause stress. A survey of college students found that approximately 23 percent of students said they procrastinated about half the time, and 27 percent of students said they procrastinated most of the time. Procrastination has been viewed as a time-management problem, but it is really more than that, and so time-management strategies tend to be ineffective in resolving this problem. Procrastination is also different from indecision, because people can make a decision but have trouble implementing it.

(Hahn et al. 2007, p. 66)

1. Main Idea: *Putting things off, or procrastination, is a common problem that plagues students and causes stress.*

Typically there is a psychological aspect to procrastination, because we tend to delay things we don't want to do. Emotions such as anxiety, guilt, and dread often accompany thinking about the task. By putting the dreaded activity off, you can temporarily alleviate the anxiety and discomfort, which is a reinforcing aspect of procrastination. In the short term, procrastination seems to be a good solution and helps you feel better. However, in the long run, procrastination usually leads to bigger problems and more work. For example, putting off paying your bills may feel good at the moment, but when your electricity is turned off and you have to pay late fees, and your roommates are upset with you because they thought you had paid the bill, your pleasurable feeling soon turns sour.

(Adapted from Hahn et al. 2007, p. 66)

2. Main Idea: *Typically there is a psychological aspect to procrastination, because we tend to delay things we don't want to do.*

Many people who procrastinate report feeling overwhelmed and highly anxious. They have difficulty tuning out external stimulation and concentrating on the task at hand. They also worry about how their performance will be judged by others and have perfectionist standards for themselves. Students who procrastinate tend to perform less well and retain less than students who do not. Procrastination impacts the way people perform.

(Adapted from Hahn et al. 2007)

3. Main Idea: *Procrastination impacts the way people perform.*

One technique for combating procrastination involves time-management. Procrastinators tend to both over- and underestimate how much time a task will take. When they underestimate the time, they feel justified in procrastinating because they erroneously believe they have plenty of time to complete the task. When they overestimate the time needed, they feel intimidated by the magnitude of the job, feel anxious, and so have trouble getting started. Most students explain that their anxiety stems from a fear of failure or of being evaluated in any way. As a result, they delay completing their tasks. Sometimes their anxiety manifests itself because they don't understand the material or what the instructor wants but are afraid to ask for clarification, further putting off their assignments. Learning and using time-management strategies, especially to help create realistic judgments about the time needed to complete tasks, can be very helpful to procrastinators.

(Adapted from Hahn et al. 2007)

4. Main Idea: *Learning and using time-management strategies, especially to help create realistic judgments about the time needed to complete tasks, can be very helpful to procrastinators.*

People also report procrastinating when they feel forced or pressured to do something they don't want to do and cannot assert their real feelings. Rather than communicating assertively, they rebel by agreeing to do something but then constantly put

(continued)

(continued)

it off, which can be a passive-aggressive way of behaving. They fear the consequences of saying no or of not fulfilling their obligation but are also angry about what they perceive as unfair expectations and demands on them. This is when some assertiveness training may be helpful.

(Adapted from Hahn et al. 2007)

5. Main Idea (Implied): *Weakness in being assertive increases procrastination, so assertiveness training may be useful.*

Finally, increasing self-esteem can solve problems with procrastination because feeling better about yourself relieves you of worrying about what others might think of you and having constantly to prove yourself to them. Some people procrastinate because they think they need to do everything perfectly or not at all. With increased self-esteem, you are more accepting of mistakes and don't expect to perform perfectly.

(Adapted from Hahn et al. 2007)

6. Main Idea: *Poor self-esteem can also cause procrastination, so finding ways to increase self-esteem can effect a change.*

Overall Main Idea or Thesis: *Procrastination is a problem that causes stress and impacts our performance, but can be helped by strategies including time management, assertiveness training, and improving self-esteem.*

Keep this in mind

Getting the main idea will help you discover the most important points of textbook paragraphs, reading selection, or textbook chapters. Remember the following points:

- Just because a statement is factual or accurate doesn't necessarily mean it is the main point.
- Don't be distracted by familiar or amusing statements. These may be interesting but may not reflect the author's most important point.
- Stay focused on the text and not on your own opinions on the topic. Remember, the main idea is what the author *says or implies about* the subject. It's not your viewpoint.
- Don't assume the first sentence will be the topic sentence. It can be located anywhere within a paragraph.
- Identifying and writing the main ideas of your assigned reading is a simple and effective way to take notes and prepare for exams. You will learn more about this in Chapter 11.
- Identifying and writing the main ideas will help you write summaries of your reading. You will learn more about this in Chapter 9.

What's the Big Idea?
Identifying the Main Idea
in College Reading

wrap it Up

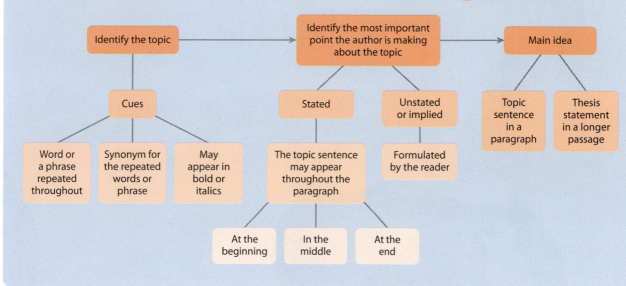

Key Terms

implied

main idea

thesis

thesis statement

topic

topic sentence

unstated main idea

5

Backing Up the Big Idea

Finding and Using Important Details in College Reading

In this chapter

you will learn about

- Identifying major and minor supporting details in text
- The different types of transitions used by authors
- Using transitions to locate supporting details
- Using details to aid your studying

Studying
Health

Health in the Workplace (Part Two)

Careers in the field of health are numerous, varied, and increasing in today's society. Broad areas of occupation include geriatric care for the elderly; pediatric care for children; heath information and communication, including jobs as medical illustrators, photographers, or health educators; and technological positions in areas such as radiology, biomedicine, ultrasound, and surgical technology. Careers in health also include working as an audiologist, occupational therapist, physical therapist, respiratory therapist, or speech language pathologist. Those interested in vision care can work as an optician, optometrist, or, with a medical degree, as an ophthalmologist. Nursing credentials and physician assistant positions can be achieved with either a two- or four-year degree. Becoming a physician, dentist, veterinarian, or medical researcher requires advanced degrees and extensive education. For students who have an interest in health, employment opportunities are likely at every level of educational preparation.

Finding and Using the Important Details

There isn't just one type of college student. Take a moment to look around at your classmates, and notice the many different types of students. Some are recent high school graduates. Others are older and returning to college, perhaps after having been in the workplace or raising a family. Students from many different cultures may be part of your class.

Readers notice main ideas and details in a similar way. First, they get the big idea or the main idea (there are many different types of college students). Then, they notice examples (there are recent high school graduates, older students, students from different cultures).

In college reading, understanding the main idea by itself does not provide enough information. In fact, you need details to help you understand better and learn more. These details tell you the *how, what, when, where, why,* and *how much* information you need to know about the main point. Specifically, **supporting details** provide you with examples, facts and statistics, explanations, or reasons for the author's point or show you how ideas are related to one another.

As you will learn in this chapter, not all details are created equal; that is, some will help you understand the material, whereas others will simply make your reading more interesting. Becoming an effective college reader requires you to learn how to locate supporting details and separate important details from less important ones.

Identifying Supporting Details

As you learned in Chapter 4, all paragraphs contain a topic and main idea. To identify the topic, ask yourself: What is the whole paragraph about? To recognize the main idea, you ask yourself: What does the author say about the topic? Now, you will learn about another element in a paragraph, called the *supporting details*. These details help explain the author's main point. To identify the supporting details, ask yourself: How does the author explain, develop, or prove his or her main point?

To see the relationship between all the parts in a paragraph, look at the following basic outline.

> **Topic**
> > **Main Idea**
> > > Supporting Detail 1
> > > Supporting Detail 2
> > > Supporting Detail 3

Now read the following paragraph, adapted from *Focus on Health*. Notice how supporting details work in this passage. You will see that the author uses examples and statistics to explain his main point and tell about the number of diverse students who attend college. Then look at the explanation and the basic outline that follows.

Today's College Students

(1) Today, there is no one type of student on U.S. college campuses. (2) In fact, in most institutions of higher learning, you will discover a student body that is a rich tapestry of age, color, culture, language and ability. (3) Sixty-two percent of all undergraduates are traditional age students, between the ages of 18–25. (4) In 2001, nearly 38.5 percent of U.S. undergraduate college students were classified as nontraditional age students. (5) Most of these students are 25–40 years old. (6) Included in this vast overlapping group are part-time students, military veterans, students returning to college, single parents, older adults, and evening students. (7) Although enrollment patterns at colleges and universities vary, the overall number of minority students is increasing. (8) In 2001, approximately 25 percent of all college students were minority students, with African Americans, Hispanic Americans and Asian Americans representing the largest number of minority students. (9) People with disabilities are yet another rapidly growing student population, currently constituting 9.3 percent of all undergraduates.

(Adapted from Hahn et al. 2007)

Applying the strategies you learned in Chapter 4, you can determine that the topic of the passage, stated in the heading, is *college students today*. The main idea (or topic sentence), located in sentence 1, is *Today, there is no one type of student on U.S. college campuses*. Sentence 2 provides more information on how the author will talk about the main idea; that is, the author will describe the diversity of the student body in terms of age, color, culture, language, and ability. The remainder of the paragraph provides specific information about the types of students who attend college today. The information in these sentences provides the supporting details.

Following is a basic outline of the paragraph, "Today's College Students." It includes the topic, main idea, and supporting details.

Topic: College Students Today

> **Main Idea:** Today, there is no one type of student on U.S. college campuses.

>> **Supporting Detail 1:** traditional age students

>> **Supporting Detail 2:** nontraditional age students

>> **Supporting Detail 3:** minority students

>> **Supporting Detail 4:** students with disabilities

Notice how all the supporting details in this paragraph relate back to the main idea. There are no unrelated or random sentences. A paragraph is like an *umbrella*. The topic is the tip of the umbrella, the main idea is the canopy of the umbrella and covers the entire surface, and the supporting details are the ribs, all of which fall under the umbrella. See the illustration that follows.

The supporting details listed in the outline are called *major* **supporting details** because they explain the main idea. Other details that further explain the major supporting details are called *minor* **supporting details.** For example, in sentence 3, the writer tells you about a type of college student (traditional age students), their age range (18–25), and what percentage (62%) they are of the whole. In sentence 6, he identifies groups of nontraditional students, such as part-time, military veterans, returning students, single students, older students, and evening students. Some of the sentences contain both major and minor details.

The following visual representation will help you distinguish between major and minor supporting details.

> Topic
>> **Main Idea**
>>> **Major Supporting Detail 1**
>>>> Minor Supporting Detail 1
>>>> Minor Supporting Detail 2
>>> **Major Supporting Detail 2**
>>>> Minor Supporting Detail 1
>>> **Major Supporting Detail 3**

A list of major and minor supporting details from the paragraph on today's college students looks like this:

Today's College Students

Major Supporting Detail 1: traditional age students
   Minor Supporting Detail 1: ages 18–25
   Minor Supporting Detail 2: 62%

Major Supporting Detail 2: non-traditional age students in 2001
   Minor Supporting Detail 1: 38.5%
   Minor Supporting Detail 2: most ages 25–40
   Minor Supporting Detail 3: part-time students, military veterans, students returning to college, single parents, older adults, evening students

Major Supporting Detail 3: minority students
   Minor Supporting Detail 1: 25%
   Minor Supporting Detail 2: African Americans, Hispanic Americans, Asian Americans

Major Supporting Detail 3: people with disabilities
   Minor Supporting Detail 1: rapidly growing student population
   Minor Supporting Detail 2: 9.3% of all undergraduates

You can also visualize or see the relationship of main ideas to supporting details in the following diagram:

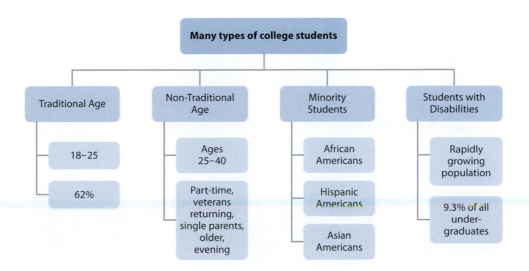

try it and apply it! 5-1   **Identifying Major and Minor Supporting Details**

Directions: Read the passage. Then complete the outline that follows. Parts of it have been completed for you.

Developmental Tasks of Young Adulthood

Because most of today's undergraduate college students range between the ages of 18 and 40, we address five areas of growth and development (defined as developmental tasks) that characterize the lives of people in this age group. One task is forming an adult identity. By achieving an adult identity, young adults become capable of answering the question: "Who am I?" Another task is establishing independence, which involves moving away from the dependent relationships provided by the family, school, and peer groups. The next developmental task is that traditional-age college students are expected to progress to increasing levels of responsibility. Broadening appropriate social skills, including communication, listening, and conflict management, is also a task. The last task is the nurturing of intimacy, which begins in young adulthood and continues through midlife. When people feel they are making progress in some or all of these areas, they are likely to report a sense of life satisfaction or a sense of well-being.

(Adapted from Hahn et al. 2007)

Main Idea: Five areas of growth characterize undergraduate college students age 18–40 today.

Major Supporting Detail 1: forming an adult identity

Minor Supporting Detail 1: Young people can answer the question, Who am I?

Major Supporting Detail 2: establishing independence

Minor Supporting Detail 1: moving away from dependent relationships: family, school, peer groups

Major Supporting Detail 3: *progressing to increasing levels of responsibility*

Major Supporting Detail 4: *broadening appropriate social skills*

Minor Supporting Detail 1: *communication, listening, conflict management*

Major Supporting Detail 5: *nurturing of intimacy*

Minor Supporting Detail 1: *continues through midlife*

try it and apply it! 5-2

Identifying Major and Minor Supporting Details

Directions: Read the following passage and complete the outline that follows it.

Establishing Independence

In today's society, the primary responsibility for socialization begins at home and later shifts to experiences that help a person become independent. During childhood and adolescence, learning how to adapt to social needs is assigned to family and school, and less formally to the peer group. For nearly two decades, these groups function as the primary contributors to a young person's knowledge, values, and behaviors. By young adulthood, however, students of traditional college age should be demonstrating the desire to move away from the dependent relationships that have existed between them and the socializing agents. Travel, new relationships, marriage, military service, and, of course, college have been traditional avenues to detach from the family. Generally, the ability and willingness to follow one or more of these paths helps a young adult establish independence.

(Adapted Hahn et al. 2007)

Main Idea: In today's society, the primary responsibility for socialization begins at home and later shifts to experiences that help a person become independent.

Major Supporting Detail 1: During childhood and adolescence, learning how to adapt to social needs is assigned to family and school, and less formally to the peer group.

Minor supporting Detail 1: For nearly two decades, these groups function as the primary contributors to a person's knowledge, values, and behaviors.

Major Supporting Detail 2: *By adulthood, however, students of traditional college age should be demonstrating the desire to move away from the dependent relationships that have existed between them and the socializing agents.*

Minor Supporting Detail 1: *Travel, new relationships, marriage, military service, and, of course, college have been traditional avenues to detach from the family.*

Minor Supporting Detail 2: *The ability and willingness to follow one or more of these paths helps a young adult establish independence.*

Using Transitions to Locate Supporting Details

Often, a writer will introduce supporting details by using **transitional words.** These are words or phrases that help you to anticipate what is coming next and tell you what kind of information will be presented. Look for words that signal the relationship between the supporting details and the main idea. In the passage, "Developmental Tasks of Young Adulthood," the author lists five tasks that emerging adults must accomplish to some degree in order to experience a sense of life satisfaction. He uses the transitional words *one, another, next, also* and *last* as signposts to each detail.

Types of Transitions Used in College Reading

Addition	Example	Reasons	Sequence	Comparison	Contrast
and	for example	as a result	after, afterward	just as, just like	however
also	for instance	because	before	like, likewise	in contrast
another	including	consequently	by the time	similarly	on the other hand
besides	specifically	for this reason	during	in the same way	unlike
finally	such as	since	first, second, etc.		but
furthermore	to illustrate	therefore	finally		conversely
in addition	namely	thus	later		otherwise
first, first of all, last			next		on the contrary
moreover, next			then		nonetheless
other			meanwhile		instead
too			eventually		whereas

Now read the following paragraph titled "Assuming Responsibility." Notice how the words *such as* and *for instance* signal that the author will be providing examples as details.

Assuming Responsibility

(1) Traditional-age college students assume different types of responsibility through a variety of opportunities. (2) College-age young adults may accept responsibility voluntarily, for instance, when they join a campus organization or establish a new friendship. (3) Other responsibilities are placed on them, such as when professors

assign term papers, when dating partners exert pressure on them to conform to their expectations, or when employers require consistently productive work. (4) They may also accept responsibility for doing a particular task not for themselves but for the benefit of others; for example, serving as a peer mentor for incoming freshmen.

(Adapted Hahn et al. 2007)

The first sentence in the passage is the main idea or topic sentence. It tells you the topic (traditional-age students) and the main point the writer wants to make about it (they assume different types of responsibility through a variety of opportunities). You probably want to know what kinds of responsibilities these students have and also examples of these opportunities, so you will have a better understanding of the author's main point. Sentence 2 provides you with one type of responsibility: a voluntary one. The **transition** phrase *such as* tells you that an example will follow. In fact, the author provides you with two examples (join a campus organization or establish a friendship). Sentence 3 begins with a transition (*Other* responsibilities), which indicates the writer will discuss an additional responsibility. These responsibilities are placed on students by others. Here the writer uses *such as* to indicate that an example will follow (assignment of papers, expectations of dating partners and employers). In sentence 4, the transition *also* indicates one more type of responsibility is being listed: doing a task for another's benefit, not for your own advantage. The transition *for example* gives an example of this kind of responsibility (peer mentor of incoming freshmen).

Types of Transitions

Different types of transitional words and phrases are used to indicate that an author is going to provide certain types of supporting details, such as additional items, examples, explanations and reasons, sequences of events, or comparison and contrast.

Additional Items

In the paragraph "Assuming Responsibility," the writer used transitions that signal additional items (*other, also*) to indicate that he is going to provide details that support the main idea. Some of the most commonly used transitions in college reading are words that signal additional items. Specifically, these words indicate that an author is continuing with the same idea and is going to provide more supporting details.

Common Addition Transitions

and	besides
also	another
another	other
in addition	last
furthermore	finally

try it and apply it! 5-3   Additional Item Transitions

Directions: Read the following passage and underline the transition words. Then complete the outline that follows.

Changing for the Better: The Importance of Risk Reduction

Although some risk factors cannot be reduced, such as gender, race, age, and genetic predisposition, focusing on good health can reduce health problems. Refrain from using tobacco in any form. In addition, if you drink alcohol, do so in moderation. You should also engage in regular exercise designed to develop the cardiorespiratory system as well as maintain muscle strength. Another important action is to familiarize yourself with the newly adopted Dietary Guidelines for Americans. Strong emphasis is now being placed on controlling portion size and increasing the amounts of fruits and vegetables in our diets to maintain normal body weight. It is also recommended that you develop coping techniques for use in moderating the effects of stress. Finally, receive regular preventive health care from competent professionals. This should include routine screening and risk-reducing lifestyle management, early diagnosis, and effective treatment if needed.

(Adapted from Hahn et al. 2007)

Main Idea: Although some risk factors cannot be reduced, such as gender, race, age, and genetic predisposition, focusing on good health can reduce health problems.

Major Supporting Detail 1: Refrain from using tobacco in any form.

Major Supporting Detail 2: If you drink alcohol, do so in moderation.

Major Supporting Detail 3: *You should engage in regular exercise designed to train the cardiorespiratory system as well as maintain muscle strength.*

Major Supporting Detail 4: *Familiarize yourself with the newly adopted Dietary Guidelines for Americans.*

Minor Supporting Detail 1: Strong emphasis is now being placed on controlling portion size and increasing the amounts of fruits and vegetables in our diets to maintain normal body weight.

Major Supporting Detail 5: *It is recommended that you develop coping techniques for use in moderating the effects of stress.*

Major Supporting Detail 6: *Receive regular preventive health care from competent professionals.*

Minor Supporting Detail 1: *This should include screening and risk-reducing lifestyle management, early diagnosis, and effective treatment if needed.*

Examples

In college textbooks, examples are used to help students understand concepts (health promotion, social and emotional intelligence, and body image), problems (mood disorders, body dysmorphic disorder, and obesity), or processes (achieving psychological health, maintaining a healthy weight, or preventing infectious diseases).

Common Example Transitions

for example	to illustrate
for instance	including
such as	specifically

try it and apply it! 5-4   Example Transitions

Directions: In the following section, underline the transitions that signal examples and then complete the outline that follows.

Health Promotion

Throughout the United States, there are many health-sponsored programs to promote healthy living. Unlike the approaches used by those employed in preventive medicine, these non-physician health facilities attempt to guide their clients toward activities and behaviors that will lower their risk of chronic illness. For instance, the YMCA/YWCA-sponsored wellness programs, commercial fitness clubs, and corporate fitness centers offer risk-reduction programs under the direction of qualified instructors. Another example is church congregations or neighborhood associations that provide local programs for individuals and groups that traditionally have been underserved by the health care system.

(Adapted from Hahn et al. 2007)

Main Idea: Throughout the United States, there are many health-sponsored programs to promote healthy living.

Major Supporting Detail 1: *For instance, the YMCA/YWCA-sponsored wellness programs, commercial fitness clubs, and corporate fitness centers offer risk-reduction programs under the direction of qualified instructors.*

Major Supporting Detail 2: *Another example is church congregations or neighborhood associations that provide local programs for individual groups that traditionally have been underserved by the health care system.*

Explanations and Reasons

Writers of textbooks often provide explanations or reasons to support their main point. You will often find supporting details that offer explanations in persuasive or argumentative writing. Authors support their opinions by providing reasons for their ideas, beliefs, or actions.

Common Explanation and Reason Transitions

because	consequently
since	as a result
therefore	so
thus	if

---

try it and apply it! 5-5   Explanation and Reason Transitions

Directions: In the following paragraph, notice how reasons are provided to help you understand why many health problems may be caused by the unwillingness or inability of people to change certain aspects of their behavior. Look for the transitional words in the preceding box that signal reasoning or explanation. Underline them in the passage, and complete the outline below.

Why Behavior Change Is Often Difficult

People's desire to change high health-risk behaviors may be based on unwillingness or lack of ability. They may find it difficult to change their behavior because they do not recognize it as a health problem. They might not believe they are at risk since they have not developed any serious health problems. They may not know about risk-reduction intervention strategies; consequently, they believe there is no support to help them change. People may not feel that the change in behavior will provide relief; therefore, they continue with the same behavior. They may not feel that a significant other in their life cares whether they alter their high-risk health behavior. Thus, they persist with the same behavior without making any proactive changes. When one or more of these conditions are in place, the likelihood that people will be successful in reducing health-risk behaviors is greatly diminished.

(Adapted from Hahn et al. 2007)

Main Idea: People's desire to change high health-risk behaviors may be based on unwillingness or lack of ability.

> **Major Supporting Detail 1:** People may find it difficult to change their behavior because they do not recognize it as a health problem.
>
> **Major Supporting Detail 2:** People might not believe they are at risk since they have not developed any serious health problems.
>
> **Major Supporting Detail 3:** *People may not know about risk-reduction intervention strategies; consequently, they believe there is no support to help them change.*
>
> **Major Supporting Detail 4:** *People may not feel changes in behavior will provide relief; therefore, they continue with the same behavior.*
>
> **Major Supporting Detail 5:** *People may not feel that a significant other in their life cares whether they alter their high-risk behavior. Thus, they persist in the same behavior without making proactive changes.*

Sequence

When writers want to explain the order in which events occurred or the steps in a process, concept, or theory, they use sequential transitions.

Common Sequence Transitions

later	after
next	when
finally	during

try it and apply it! 5-6   Sequence Transitions

Directions: In the following section, you will learn about the sequential order of the steps involved in making changes in one's behavior. Underline the words that signal sequence, and then complete the outline that follows.

Stages of Change

The process of behavioral change unfolds over time and progresses through defined stages. The <u>first</u> stage is called precontemplation, during which a person might think about making a change but ultimately finds it too difficult and avoids doing it. For many, however, progress toward change begins as they move into the <u>second</u> stage, the contemplation stage,

(continued)

(continued)

during which they might have the desire to change but have little understanding about how to go about it. Typically, they see themselves taking action within the next six months. In the third stage, a preparation stage begins when change begins to appear not only desirable but also possible. Plans for implementing the change occur in the fourth stage, the action stage. The fifth stage is the maintenance stage, during which new habits are consolidated and practiced for an additional six months. The sixth and final stage is called termination, which refers to the point at which new habits are well established, and so efforts to change are complete.

(Adapted Hahn et al. 2007)

Main Idea: The process of behavior changes over time and progresses through defined stages.

Major Supporting Detail 1: Stage 1—Precontemplation

Minor Supporting Detail 1: *A person might think about making a change but ultimately finds it too difficult and avoids doing it.*

Major Supporting Detail 2: *Stage 2—Contemplation*

Minor Supporting Detail 1: Progress begins, and a person might have the desire to change but has little understanding of how to do it.

Minor Supporting Detail 2: *The person sees himself taking action within six months.*

Major Supporting Detail 3: Stage 3—Preparation

Minor Supporting Detail 1: *Change seems desirable and possible.*

Major Supporting Detail 4: *Stage 4—Action*

Minor Supporting Detail 1: *Plans for action take place.*

Major Supporting Detail 5: Stage 5—Maintenance

Minor Supporting Detail 1: *New habits are consolidated and practiced for an additional six months.*

Major Supporting Detail 6: *Stage 6—Termination*

Minor Supporting Detail 1: *New habits are well established.*

Comparison and Contrast

If writers want to show how a previous idea is similar to one that follows, they will use transitions such as *like* or *similarly*. If they want to talk about the differences between items or ideas, they will use transitions such as *unlike* or *in contrast*.

Common Comparison and Contrast Transitions

Comparison: like, likewise, similarly, in the same manner, also, too
Contrast: unlike, but, yet, however, nevertheless, still, while, whereas, although, even though, on the other hand, in contrast

try it and apply it! 5-7   Contrast Transitions

Directions: Read the following passage from *Eye on the Media* to learn about the variety of media sources that provide health information, some of which are more reliable than others. Underline the transition words that signal the contrast of major supporting details. Then complete the chart using details from the selection.

Where Does Our Health Information Come from? Radio

When you think of the radio, the first thing that might come to mind is your favorite song. However, two areas are especially important for news and information about today's health issues: talk radio and public radio. Public radio includes the National Public Radio (NPR) and Public Radio International (PRI) networks. On talk radio, questions are raised by the host, whose point of view may be harsh and strong. Viewers call in and offer their own points of view, which may not be based on authoritative information. This is certainly not a good source for making your health decisions. In contrast, public radio takes a more scholarly approach to the news. Whereas talk radio gets its information from listeners, public radio features experts who do not always agree on an issue. In general, unlike talk radio, public radio presents a more in-depth, balanced treatment of health-related topics and provides a better source for your health decisions.

(Adapted from Hahn et al. 2007)

Sources of Health Information

	Talk Radio	Public Radio
How is the information presented?	Host asks questions, listeners call in	*Scholarly presentation, Experts are invited to discuss the issues*
Who presents the information?	*Host—harsh, strong* *Listeners offer own points of view, which may not come from authoritative sources*	Features experts who do not always agree or have the same point of view on the issue
Is it a good source of health information?	Not a good source for making health decisions	*An in-depth, balanced treatment of health-related topics; better source of information for making health decisions*

try it and apply it! 5-8   Comparison Transitions

Directions: Read the following paragraph. In this excerpt from *Eye on the Media*, we learn about the variety of media sources that provide health information, some of which are more reliable than others. Underline the transition words that signal the comparison of supporting details. Then complete the chart.

Professional Journals and Government Documents

Other sources of health information are professional journals and government documents. Your college library offers a broad selection of professional and academic journals. These publications contain articles written by members of different academic disciplines who share the latest developments, issues, and research in their field. Because most of these journals are peer-reviewed, and the articles in them will not be published unless the information is from a reliable source, we can learn a lot about our health from them. Similarly, government documents are a reliable source of information. The Department of Health and Human Services releases the results of research being done under the oversight of its many divisions and agencies. These publications can be purchased through the U.S. Printing Office, and just like academic journals, they can be found at large university libraries.

(Adapted from Hahn et al. 2007)

Sources of Health Information

	Professional Journals	**Government Documents**
Who provides this information?	*Members of academic disciplines*	Dept. of Health and Human Services
What kind of information is presented?	Latest developments, issues and research in health field	*Current research conducted by other governmental agencies and divisions*
How is it published or printed?	*Peer-reviewed*	*Printed by U.S. Printing Office—official*
Is it a good source of health information?	*Good source of health information*	*Good source of health information*

Studying Supporting Details

You borrow a friend's college textbook and discover that everything is highlighted in yellow. You are impressed that your friend has read the chapter for homework; however, you realize that because everything is highlighted, it is difficult for you to decide which information is important.

Because college textbooks contain so much information, it is virtually impossible to learn and remember everything. So, how can you know what is really important? After studying Chapter 4, you know it's important to understand the main ideas of a selection. In this chapter, you have learned that major and minor supporting details also provide significant information to help in comprehension. So now what's important?

As you read, you should use the major supporting details to understand the main ideas, and use the minor supporting details to get more information about the corresponding major details. When you mark your textbook, it's usually best to focus only on the major supporting details; otherwise, nothing will stand out as important. These are the details you should remember for test taking.

Sometimes, you will have to make decisions about the value of minor supporting details. In the following passage, "Food Safety," you will see how the major and minor supporting details together provide a better understanding of the main idea

Food Safety

(1) Technological advances in food processing have done much to assure that the food we eat is fresh and safe; however, there is a growing concern that recent developments may also produce harmful effects. (2) One example is irradiation.

(3) This lowers the levels of bacteria in meats, but it does not kill all bacteria. (4) In fact, proper cooking kills more bacteria. (5) Some fear that irradiation will lull consumers into a false sense of security so that they won't believe they need to take proper precautions for food handling and preparation. (6) Another technological advance is the genetic engineering of foods. This process increases crops, lowers cost production, and introduces new food characteristics. (7) Scientists believe we need to conduct more studies to determine the long-term safety issues with these food products. (8) Without these measures, consumers may be at risk for unrecognized problems.

(Adapted from Hahn et al. 2007)

Sentence 1 is the main idea of the passage. It is a general statement and does not identify the technological advances or the growing concerns. It is of little value to have this information without the important examples that let you know how food is being produced today and why the public should be concerned about it. Sentence 2 provides the reader with an example of an advance in food technology—irradiation. Sentences 3–5 explain the problems with this process: Irradiation does not kill all bacteria, and the public may think it does, so they might be less careful in the preparation and handling of food. Sentence 6 introduces a second technological advance, called genetic technology. Sentences 7 and 8 describe the serious concern of scientists who say we will need to conduct extensive studies to determine the long-term safety of genetically engineered food.

try it and apply it! 5-9   Studying Supporting Details

Directions: In the following paragraph, the author discusses how to avoid food poisoning through the safe handling of food. Read the passage. Underline the transition words that help you locate the supporting details. Then complete the outline that follows.

Safe Handling of Food

It is important to handle food properly to avoid food poisoning. First, frequent hand washing is at the top of the list of food safety tips. Bacteria live and multiply on warm, moist hands, and hands can inadvertently transport germs from one surface to another. Second, it is important to clean surfaces with hot, soapy water and keep nonfood items such as the mail, newspapers, and purses, off the countertops. Some people advocate the use of antibacterial products, whereas others maintain that if they are overused, these products can lose their effectiveness, and bacteria can become resistant to them. Finally, utensils, dishes, cutting boards, cookware, towels, and sponges need to be washed in hot soapy water and rinsed well.

(Adapted from Hahn et al. 2007)

Main Idea: It is important to handle food properly to avoid food poisoning.

Supporting Detail 1: *Wash your hands frequently.*

Supporting Detail 2: *Clean surfaces with hot, soapy water.*

Supporting Detail 3: *Utensils, dishes, cutting boards, cookware, towels, and sponges must be washed in hot soapy water and rinsed well.*

try it and apply it! 5-10   Studying Supporting Details

Directions: Read the following passage and underline the transition words that help you locate the supporting details. Then answer the questions about the major and minor supporting details.

Foodborne Illness

Foodborne illness is the result of eating contaminated food. Salmonella is the most common cause of food poisoning. It is found mostly in raw or undercooked poultry, meat, eggs, fish, and unpasteurized milk. Another cause is clostridium perfringens, also called the "buffet germ," which grows where there is little to no oxygen and grows fast in large portions held at low or room temperatures. For this reason, buffet table servings should be replaced often and leftovers should be refrigerated quickly. Refrigerated leftovers may become harmful to eat after three days. The old adage "if in doubt, throw it out" applies to any questionable leftovers. A final cause of food poisoning is botulism, which is rare and often fatal. It occurs when home-canned or commercially canned food has not been processed or stored properly. Some warning signs are swollen or dented cans or lids, cracked jars, loose lids, and clear liquids turning milky.

(Adapted from Hahn et al. 2007)

_a_ 1. The three types of foodborne illnesses are
- a. salmonella, the "buffet germ," and botulism
- b. botulism, the "buffet germ" and clostridium pefringens
- c. botulism, pefringens clostridium and food poisoning
- d. the "buffet" table, unpasteurized milk and commercially canned food

_d_ 2. Where can salmonella be found?
- a. in swollen or dented cans
- b. on buffet tables
- c. in leftovers
- d. in unpasteurized milk

(*continued*)

(*continued*)

_b_ 3. What condition contributes to the growth of clostridium perfringens?

    a. undercooked or raw poultry
    b. little or no oxygen
    c. food not stored properly
    d. buffet table servings

_c_ 4. How can contracting the "buffet germ" be avoided?

    a. Don't throw out any leftovers.
    b. Don't eat from a buffet.
    c. Replace buffet food often.
    d. Store leftovers properly.

_b_ 5. How can you prevent contracting botulism?

    a. Cook meat thoroughly, especially poultry.
    b. Check canned goods for warning signs.
    c. Refrigerate canned goods.
    d. Loosen the lids of jarred foods.

try it and apply it! 5-11 Studying Supporting Details

Directions: Read the following passage. Underline the transition words that help you locate the supporting details. Then complete the exercise.

International Nutritional Concerns

    Nutritional concerns in the United States are centered on over-nutrition, including fat density and excessive caloric intake. In contrast, in many areas around the world the main problem is the limited intake and quality of food. Reasons for these problems are many, including the weather, the availability of arable land, religious practices, political unrest, social infrastructure, and material and technical shortages. Underlying all these factors, however, is unabated population growth.

    To increase the availability of food to countries whose demand for food outweighs their ability to produce it, a number of steps have been suggested. First, these countries can increase the yield of land currently under cultivation. Second, they can use water (seas, lakes, and ponds) more efficiently for the production of food. Third, they can develop unconventional foods through the use of technology. Finally, they can improve nutritional practices through education.

In some regions of the world, little progress is being made in spite of technological breakthroughs in agriculture and food technology, the efforts of governmental programs, and the support of the Food and Agricultural Organization of the United Nations, and the U.S. Department of Agriculture.

For example, in many third-world countries, where fertility rates are two to four times higher than those of the United States, annual food production needs to be increased between 2.7 percent and 3.9 percent to keep up with their population needs.

The world population is now at 6.6 billion. It is projected to reach 9 billion by 2070 before it levels off to 8.4 billion in 2100. As a result, food production in the coming decades may need to be increased beyond current estimates.

(Adapted from Hahn et al. 2007)

_c_ 1. In the United States, nutritional concerns deal with
    a. the increasing population
    b. foods high in caloric content
    c. over-nutrition
    d. the limited intake of food

_c_ 2. The main reason for nutritional concerns in regions outside of the United States is
    a. the lack of resources and important technology
    b. political unrest
    c. the growing population
    d. unsuitable land for growing crops

(*continued*)

(continued)

_d_ 3. Several important steps can be taken to yield more food in these countries. They include all of the following *except*
   a. increasing annual food production
   b. more efficient use of ponds, lakes, and seas
   c. the development of new foods with the help of technology
   d. educating populations about fertility

_b_ 4. Third-world countries are not making very much progress with nutrition because of
   a. technological barriers in agriculture and food technology
   b. increasing fertility rates
   c. poor educational practices
   d. lack of support by the U.S. Department of Agriculture

_d_ 5. The projected increase in global population may result in
   a. the need for more water resources
   b. greater governmental efforts
   c. higher caloric intake
   d. increased food production

Backing Up the Big Idea:
Finding and Using Important Details
in College Reading

wrap it Up

Understanding the supporting details in a paragraph will help you make more sense of the main idea, so when you read you should do the following:

- **Distinguish between main ideas and supporting details**. The main idea states the overall message of the paragraph, while the supporting details help explain what an author is saying in his or her main point.

- **Distinguish between major and minor supporting details**. The major details give evidence about the main idea, whereas the minor supporting details tell you more about the major supporting details. Minor supporting details follow the major detail they describe.

- **Look for transition words or expressions that signal different types of details**.

- **If there are no transition words, see how the information relates to the main idea**. Does it add information, provide examples, describe a time order of events, describe a process, or explain why the author is making his or her main point?

- **Remember that in college reading, the major supporting details provide specific information about the main idea, so you should read them carefully**. Not only will they help you understand better, but they will also be important for studying.

Key Terms

sequence

supporting details:

major supporting details

minor supporting details

transitional words

transition

6

What Is the Author's Plan of Action?

Identifying and Integrating Writing Patterns

In this chapter

you will learn to

- Recognize organizational patterns in textbook writing
- Use organizational patterns to improve your comprehension

Studying
Criminology

Criminology focuses on the study of the law, criminals, the reason for criminal acts, and methods of punishment. Issues studied in this field are very current: identity theft, terrorism, drug trafficking, immigration law, global crime and justice, juvenile crime, and organized crime.

Courses in criminology introduce students to the concepts of crime and justice and their impact on society, law enforcement, the courts, and correctional systems, including prisons and alternative methods of punishment such as probation, house arrest, and electronic monitoring.

Criminology in the Workplace

Many interesting and varied occupations are available to those who study criminology. These include jobs in law enforcement and security, such as police officer, forensic scientist, criminal profiler, or deputy sheriff. Within the court or legal system, one might work as a bailiff, court reporter, paralegal, or even as an attorney or Judge. A range of positions also exist in corrections or rehabilitation, including chaplain, case manager, sex offender therapist, job placement officer, substance abuse counselor, or warden.

Organizational Writing Patterns

This chapter teaches you how to recognize and identify the organizational writing patterns used by authors. Learning how the details are arranged, or **organizational patterns,** will help you become a stronger reader. You will be better able to identify main ideas, predict where the author is going, organize the information you are learning, and recall it later on. These are important tools for a college-level reader!

To understand organizational patterns in writing, consider the strategies people use every day to manage their lives or to communicate information. After class, you might ask your professor to explain the meaning of, or *define,* a term she has used in a lecture. We make *lists* to remind us of what we need at the supermarket. You give your friend directions to your apartment by explaining the series of streets and turns she needs to take in order, or *sequence,* to get there. Most of us prepare our laundry by separating, or *classifying,* fabrics into piles of delicate fabrics and machine washables. You are likely to visit several stores and *compare* the features and prices of flat screen televisions before choosing the one to buy. When you get stuck in unexpected traffic on your way to school, you may wonder about the *cause,* and try to calm yourself as you experience its *effect* on your nerves, especially when you realize that you will be late for class.

Writers use strategies just like these to organize the information they present in textbooks. To do so, an author will explain and discuss a subject thoroughly from different perspectives, presenting the material in various ways, or patterns. Following is a list of the most common writing patterns, and their purpose:

Common Patterns of Organization

Definition: The author explains the meaning of new terms or concepts.

Listing or Enumeration: The author presents a list of items or concepts for which the order is not important.

Sequence: The author presents a series of events, items, or ideas in a particular order or time frame.

Classification: The writer breaks larger groups or topics into subgroups or categories.

Comparison and Contrast: The author shows how items or ideas are similar to one another and/or different from one another.

Cause and Effect: The author presents reasons for an event or condition and/or outcomes and results of an event.

You use these same patterns in your everyday life when you think and communicate, so they should be fairly easy to understand and remember. Look at the preceding list to help you complete the scenario that follows. Then check your answers.

> You have become very energy conscious and believe it would benefit the environment if everyone drove hybrid cars. You want to convince your friend, in the market for a new auto, to buy a hybrid. You first want to explain what a hybrid car is. To do so, you would use a 1. ___*definition*___ pattern of organization. If you wanted to help your friend understand how hybrid manufacturing has developed gradually from the 1980s until today, you would use a 2. ___*sequence*___ pattern. Because you would like your friend to understand how much more fuel efficient a hybrid car is than a standard gasoline engine car, you would attempt to convince him or her using a pattern of 3. ___*comparison/contrast*___. To note how much money you are saving on gasoline by using a hybrid car, you would use the 4. ___*cause and effect*___ pattern. To help your buddy become familiar with the different types of hybrids, you would likely explain them using a 5. ___*classification*___ pattern. Finally, if you chose to conclude your argument by naming all the benefits of driving hybrid automobiles, you would likely use a/an 6. ___*listing/enumeration*___ pattern of organization.

(Answers: 1. definition, 2. sequence, 3. comparison/contrast, 4. cause and effect, 5. classification, 6. listing)

Now that you have the general idea, you can apply this knowledge of writing patterns to textbook reading. It will help you formulate the main idea of paragraphs and chapter sections and enhance your overall comprehension of the material. As you learn about each pattern, you will also come to recognize **signal words,** also called **clue words,** that suggest a particular writing pattern is being used.

The excerpts that follow are taken from a freshman college textbook, *Introduction to Criminal Justice,* by Robert Bohm and Keith Haley.

Definition Pattern

As a college reader, you will come across many new terms. Authors of textbooks know their readers are likely to be unfamiliar with the language they use and the concepts they discuss. Therefore, they often define the meaning of these terms and ideas, both in the context of the writing as well as in sidebars and lists. Entire paragraphs may be devoted to defining a term or identifying a concept or idea. Thus, the main idea of an entire paragraph might, in fact, be a definition.

Signal Words for Definitions

Signal words often used by authors to let you know a term is being defined include:

is

means

refers to

can be defined as

is called

also known as

which states that

or (followed by a synonym for the less familiar term)

Notice the signal words in the following sentences.

- The term **parole** *can refer to* a being released from prison before an entire sentence has been served.
- **Parole** *can also mean* a period of community supervision following early release.
- We are concerned with the **former**, *or* first, meaning.
- **Commutation**, *also known as* a reduction of the original sentence, is a way to be released from prison.

Punctuation is often used to signal that a definition is being provided. Notice how different punctuation marks are used to set off the definitions of the term *recidivism* in the following examples.

- **Commas:** Reasons for the high rate of recidivism, *the return to illegal activity after serving time in prison*, can be identified.
- **Dashes:** We shall conclude this chapter by considering recidivism—*the return to illegal activity after release.*
- **Parentheses:** The most recent national study of recidivism (*the return of inmates to criminal activity after release from prison*) found that 67.5% of nearly 300,000 inmates in 1994 were rearrested for a new offense within 3 years of their release.
- **Colon:** A problem facing the correctional institution today is the increasing rate of recidivism: *the return of prisoners to crime after they are released from prison.*

try it and apply it! 6-1   Practicing with Definition

Directions: Read the following paragraphs. Keep in mind that the author wants to help you understand the meaning of new terms or concepts related to the prison system. Underline any signal words or clues to the pattern of organization. Then answer the questions that follow.

A.   In his classic book *Asylums*, sociologist Erving Goffman described prisons as total institutions. Goffman defined a total institution as a place of residence and work where a large number of like-situated individuals, cut off from the wider society for an appreciable period of time, together lead an enclosed, formally administered round of life. . . . A prison represents a miniature, self-contained society.

(Bohm and Haley 2007)

1. What is the organizational pattern of the paragraph? *definition*

2. What term is defined? *total institution*

3. What is the meaning of the term? *a place of working and living where people who are in a similar situation live together, are closed off from the rest of society, and follow a formally governed life*

B.   Central to the inmate society of traditional men's prisons in the United States is the convict code. The convict code refers to a constellation of values, norms, and roles that regulate the way inmates interact with one another and with prison staff. For example, a principle of the convict code is that individual inmates should mind their own affairs and do their own time. Others are that inmates should not inform the staff about illicit, or not legally permitted, activities of other prisoners and that inmates' overall attitude and behavior should be indifferent to the staff and loyal to the other convicts.

(Adapted from Bohm and Haley 2007)

4. What is the organizational pattern of the paragraph? *definition*

5. What concept is defined? *convict code*

6. What is the definition of the concept? *A grouping of values, norms, and roles that controls the way prisoners in jail relate to each other and to the prison staff*

7. What is the main idea of the paragraph? *The main idea is that the convict code is a constellation of values, norms, and roles that controls the way inmates relate to one another and to the staff when in prison.*

Note: To identify the main idea of the paragraph, combine the key term that is being defined with its definition. Just like in a math text, **examples** are provided to help you better understand the term being defined. Be careful. Do not confuse the example with the definition and or/the main idea itself.

(continued)

Now continue on your own. Focus on the list that is generated in each paragraph. Number the items within the paragraphs.

A.   Furthermore, what we know about violent crime in general suggests that much prison violence is probably spontaneous, motivated by particular circumstances. Some common perpetrator motives for physical violence in prison are to demonstrate power and dominance over others; to retaliate against a perceived wrong, such as the failure of another inmate to pay a gambling debt; and to prevent the perpetrator from being victimized (for example, raped) in the future.

(Bohm and Haley 2007)

1. What is the organizational pattern of the paragraph? *listing or enumeration*
2. What is the topic of the paragraph? *spontaneous motives for prison violence*
3. What is the main idea? *There are three common perpetrator motives for physical violence in prison.*
4. Complete the following notes to identify the list embedded in the paragraph.

Common Motives for Perpetrator Violence in Prison

  a. *demonstrate power and dominance over others*
  b. *get back at another inmate*
  c. *prevent future victimization*

B.   Correctional officers face a number of conflicts in their work. Criminologists Richard Hawkins and Geoffrey Alpert observe that the job is characterized by both boredom and stimulus overload; officers assigned to the towers may experience the former, whereas officers assigned to work in the cell blocks may experience the latter. Much has also been written about the role ambiguity and role strain resulting from conflict between custody and treatment objectives. How does an officer supervise and discipline inmates and at the same time attempt to counsel and help them? . . . In addition, a series of court decisions has given many officers the perception that they have lost power while inmates have gained it.

(Bohm and Haley 2007)

5. What is the organizational pattern of the paragraph? *listing or enumeration*
6. What is the topic of the paragraph? *conflicts of correctional officers*
7. What is the main idea? *Correctional officers experience a number of conflicts on the job.*
8. Complete the following notes to identify the list embedded in the paragraph.

Conflicts Faced by Correctional Officers

a. *boredom and stimulus overload*
b. *conflicts between custody objectives and treatment objectives*
c. *feeling that inmates have gained power while officers have lost it*

Sequence Pattern

As you read your college texts, you will come upon lists embedded in the paragraphs or selections *in which the order of the items in that list does matter very much*. In that case, you would identify the writing pattern as one of sequence. The order of items, or their sequence, can be arranged in several ways: chronological order, process order, spatial order, or order of importance.

Chronological Order

When events are listed according to the time when they occurred, the writer is using a chronological, or time, order. You will encounter this pattern in all college texts, particularly when the author wants you to understand the background or development of an event or concept. For example, the events leading up to WWII or the history of the advancements in health care in third-world nations would likely be presented in chronological order.

Signal Words for Chronological Order

Signal words often used by authors to indicate that a list is being presented include the following:

date

times

lasting for . . .

beginning in

since

until

during

soon after

formerly

currently

presently

try it and apply it! 6-3   Practicing with Chronological Order   ⏸

Directions: Read the following paragraph about structured fines, or day fines. These are fines for crimes that are based, in part, on a defendant's daily income. Notice the chronological order that is included. Underline signal words that indicate information is being listed chronologically. This will help you to formulate the main idea of the paragraph. Answer the questions that follow.

A.   Structured fines, or day fines, were first introduced in the 1920s in Sweden and soon thereafter were adopted by other Scandinavian countries. West Germany began employing them in the early 1970s. Since then, the western European nations have made day fines the sanction of choice in a large proportion of criminal cases, including many involving serious offenses . . . The first structured-fine program in the United States began in 1988 in Richmond County Staten Island, New York, as a demonstration project. Other structured-fine demonstration projects have been established in Arizona,

Connecticut, Iowa, and Oregon. An evaluation of the Richmond County project . . . showed promising results.

(Bohm and Haley 2007)

1. What is the organizational pattern of the paragraph? *sequence/chronological order*

2. What is the topic of the paragraph? *structured fines*

3. What is the main idea of the paragraph? *Since the 1920s, structured fines have been used as punishments; first in Sweden, then in Europe, and most recently, in the United States.*

Now read the following paragraph about halfway houses, community-based residential facilities that are an alternative to confinement in jail or prison. Notice the chronology that is included. It will help you formulate the main idea. Underline signal words and dates. Then answer the questions that follow.

B.   Halfway houses have existed in the United States since the mid-1800s and, prior to the 1960s, were used primarily for persons coming out of prison and making the transition back into the community. During the 1960s, the number and functions of halfway houses programs in the nation expanded. In addition to providing services for parolees and prereleases (prisoners nearing their release date), houses began to service probationers, pretrial detainees, and persons on furlough from prison. More recently, in the 1980s, halfway houses became an integral part of the intermediate-sanction movement. They are now sometimes used in conjunction with other intermediate sanctions. For example, as part of a probation sentence, an offender may complete a stay in a halfway house before being discharged, or a person who has violated a home confinement order may be placed in a halfway house program to give authoritative added control.

(Bohm and Haley 2007)

Did you recognize that the predominant organizational pattern is sequence, and in particular, chronological sequence? Write four phrases that signaled the chronological order to you.

1. *Since the mid-1800s*

2. *prior to the 1960s*

3. *During the 1060s*

4. *More recently, in the 1980s*

Notice how you can use time order to help you find and state the main idea.

1. What is the topic? *halfway houses*

2. What is the most important point the author is making; that is, what is the main idea? *The main idea is that the use of halfway houses in the criminal justice system has changed since its development in the mid-1800s.*

Process Order

When the process order pattern is used in listing, the steps followed for an event or process to unfold are identified. You see this often in the life sciences, where there are stages of development, or in government, where there are procedures to follow in order for an event to occur. For example, the fetal development of a human, or the steps one follows to become a candidate for president, represent processes.

Signal Words for Process Order

Signal words often used by authors to indicate that steps in a process are being listed include the following:

first	after that	stages
second	subsequently	progressions
third	following	sequence
then	lastly	series
next	finally	continuum
finally	steps	

try it and apply it! 6-4   Practicing with Process Order

Directions: Read the following paragraph, which briefly explains the process, titled "From Arrest Through Initial Appearance," when a person is charged with a crime. Notice the procedure. Draw a box around the signal words that help you pay attention to the process. Annotate and number the steps in the process within the text. Answer the questions that follow.

Soon after most suspects are arrested, they are taken to the police station to be "booked." Booking is the process in which suspects' names, the charges for which they were arrested, and perhaps their fingerprints or photographs are entered on the police blotter. Following booking, a prosecutor is asked to review the facts of the case and, considering the available evidence, to decide whether a suspect should be charged with a crime or crimes. Sometimes prosecutors may review a case prior to the arrest. As a result of the review, the prosecutor may tell the police that they do not have a case or that the case is weak, requiring further investigation and additional evidence.

However, if the prosecutor decides that a suspect is "charge-able," the prosecutor (then) prepares a charging document. The crime or crimes with which the suspect is charged may or may not be the same crime or crimes for which the suspect is originally arrested. (An arrest warrant, ordering law enforcement persons to arrest the person, may be written. Charges are specified in the warrant.) (After) the charge or charges have been filed, suspects, who are now defendants, are brought before a lower court judge for an initial appearance, where they are given formal notice of the charges against them and advised of their constitutional rights.

(Adapted from Bohm and Haley 2007)

Recognizing that the predominant pattern here is sequential, with a focus on process, will help you formulate the main idea. The topic of the paragraph is the steps taken from a person's arrest to his or her first appearance in court. Thus, the main idea of the excerpt is that several steps are followed from arrest through an initial court appearance.

Next, briefly paraphrase the steps. Use your annotations to help you.

The Process from Arrest to Initial Court Appearance

Step 1. *arrest*
Step 2. *booking*
Step 3. *prosecutor reviews the case*
Step 4. *charging document is prepared*
Step 5. *charges filed*
Step 6. *defendant brought to court for initial appearance*
Step 7. *formal notice of charges and advisement of constitutional rights*

Spatial Order

This order reflects position in space. It occurs when an author describes the location of objects or items in relation to one another. It is often used in descriptive writing so that the reader can visualize a setting. Here is an example:

Just behind the tree, off to the left, sat a small child. To the right of the child, next to the brook, was a rosebush.

Spatial order is used in textbooks as well. For example, spatial description might be used in a biology textbook to identify the parts of the heart or locations of the different lobes of the brain.

Signal Words for Spatial Order

Signal words often used by authors to indicate that spatial order is being used include the following:

above	lined up
below	linear
beneath	circular
to the left	separated by
to the right	leading to
behind	leading away from
adjacent to	next to
aligned	in a row

try it and apply it! 6-5   Practicing with Spatial Order

Directions: Read the paragraph that follows about "first generation" prisons, dating back to the eighteenth century. See if you can get a sense of their architectural design from the description. How did the prisons look? What was the layout? Underline signal words that help you "see" items in their place or in relation to one another.

> The earliest jails . . . were built in a linear design. These first-generation jails have inmates live together in cells, dormitories, or "tanks." The cells line corridors, which makes the supervision of the inmates difficult. Guards, at regular intervals walk up and down the corridors and observe inmates in their cells. To observe inmates in the dormitories or tanks, guards periodically walk through the dormitories or along a perimeter catwalk, which separates them from the inmates by bars. A "48 man tank," for example, is a large cage that might have six inner cells, each with eight bunks that open into a "dayroom" or "bullpen" equipped with two long metal picnic-like tables attached to the floor and, perhaps, one television for the entire tank. In the cells, beds, sinks, and toilets are made of reinforced metal and are bolted to the floor or wall. . . .The first generation jail is often a separate building or set of buildings surrounded by walls of reinforced concrete topped with razor wire.

> (Adapted from Bohm and Haley 2007)

Were you able to visualize the first-generation prison based on the author's description?

If so, then the writer did a good job creating a paragraph with spatial organization.

Order of Importance

Sometimes items, reasons, or causes are listed in a reading selection, but they vary in their degree of significance. Authors want you to get a sense of what is the most important item and which are of lesser importance. This happens often in essays or persuasive writing, as well as in textbooks. For example, there may be three reasons why teens start to smoke, but one is the most important. There may be four causes for students dropping out of college, but one may occur the most often, another may be infrequent, and two others may be somewhere in the middle. Authors generally present items in order of importance in the following two ways:

Descending order refers to moving from most important to least important.

Ascending order refers to moving from least important to most important.

Signal Words for Order of Importance

Signal words often used by authors to indicate that items are being presented in order of importance include the following:

most important

least important

primary

secondary

minor

major

most significant

least significant

try it and apply it! 6-6   Practicing with Order of Importance

Directions: Following is a paragraph that discusses the qualities of a successful police officer. Based on the author's use of order of importance to arrange details, can you rank the qualities of a good police officer from most important to least important? Read the paragraph, underline the signal words, number the qualities as you come upon them, and then complete the chart that follows.

> Given the complexity of the role of the police officer, it comes as no surprise that deciding what qualities the successful police officer needs is not easy. Indeed, police officers require a combination of qualities and abilities that are rare in any pool of applicants. . . . Three qualities seem to be of paramount

(continued)

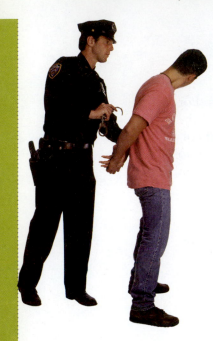

(continued)

importance. One commentator refers to them as the three I's of police selection. <u>First</u> is intelligence, <u>next</u> integrity, and <u>then</u> interaction skills. In short, police officers need to be bright enough to resist—and have a lifestyle that allows them to resist—the temptation of corrupting influences in law enforcement. They should also be able to communicate clearly and get along with people of diverse backgrounds.

<u>Nearly as important</u> as the three I's, however, are common sense and compassion. In resolving conflicts and solving problems they encounter, police officers must often choose a course of action without much time to think about it . . . Police agencies also seek to employ officers with the core value of compassion. Without a genuine concern for serving one's fellow human beings, a police officer is not likely to sustain a high level of motivation over a long period of time. . . .

<u>Other qualities</u>, such as physical strength, endurance, and appearance, seem <u>less important</u>. If you were the one who needed to be dragged from a burning automobile, however, the physical strength of the police officer might be important to you.

(Adapted from Bohm and Haley 2007)

Now compile your list. Notice that some room exists for variability in certain places. For example, the qualities listed in the last paragraph are enumerated in no particular order.

Important Qualities in a Police Officer

1. *appearance*
2. *endurance*
3. *strength*
4. *compassion*
5. *common sense*
6. *interaction skills*
7. *integrity*
8. *intelligence*

Classification Pattern

In many college subjects, you will find yourself learning the material by breaking larger topics into subtopics or categories. Think of it like a menu at a restaurant. When you look at the menu to order, you see that the items prepared by the restaurant are not listed in random order, but rather they are subdivided into categories such as appetizers, salads, entrees, and desserts. Even the entrees may be further classified or subdivided as seafood, meats, and poultry.

Indeed, all subject areas include classification or categorization systems. Think about it: Consider the three branches of the federal government, the animal and plant kingdoms in biology, the kinds of diseases you may learn about in health, the different levels of crime and punishment in our society, or types of art in the twentieth century.

When an author identifies the categories or subsets of a larger entity, the author is using the writing pattern of classification. Recognizing that the larger group is viewed or organized into subgroups is a key component in your understanding and identifying the main point an author is making. Typically, what follows are the salient points, or distinguishing characteristics, of each type or group.

Be careful. Although an author may list the categories, it is important for you to understand that the key pattern is classification, and the list has been used to present categories and subcategories of the topic.

Signal Words for Classification

Signal words often used by authors to indicate that classification is occurring include

groups

levels

kinds

categories

type

subsets

divided into

broken into

Introductory phrases used to indicate that classification is forthcoming include

This can be divided into three categories . . .

There are four types of . . .

We can break this down into two major groups.

Charts are often used to explain classification and categories.

try it and apply it! 6-7   Practicing with Classification

Directions: Read the following paragraphs. Underline any classification signal words. Annotate the major categories or groups by underlining and/or numbering them within the paragraph. Notice that the method of classification being used is usually found in the topic sentence of the paragraph, which may not always be the first sentence. Use your sense of the categories or groupings that are presented to formulate the main idea.

(continued)

(continued)

Example

Categories of prison sex

A good deal of prison violence—but not all—has sexual overtones. It is important to realize that not all instances of sex in prison are violent; that not all instances are homosexual in nature, and that sexual encounters can involve both inmates and staff. Instances of prison sex can further be divided into three basic categories: 1 consensual sex for gratification, 2 prostitution, and 3 sexual assault. In the first category, both participants are willing partners. The third category obviously involves violence, and the first two sometimes have indirect links to violence. For example, a consensual sexual relationship between two inmates may have started out as a forced one. Likewise, an inmate who is vulnerable to sexual assault may perform sexual favors for an aggressive, well-respected prisoner in exchange for protection from other inmates. . . .

(Bohm and Haley, 2007, p. 399)

This paragraph begins by listing some general information about instances of sex in prison. It then moves on to the major focus, or main idea, that prison sex can be divided into three basic categories: consensual, prostitution, and assault. It provides details about each in the sentences that follow by making some comparisons and contrast among the categories.

Now continue reading about another topic from the criminal justice textbook. Pay attention to the classification of the broader subject set forth in the paragraphs. Number or mark each subcategory of the larger topic, rehabilitation programs, as you come upon it. Annotate important details so you understand the category better. Then answer the questions that follow.

Inmate Rehabilitation Programs

Main idea

Inmates hoping to better themselves during their incarceration normally have the opportunity to participate in a number of rehabilitation programs. The particular programs offered vary across jurisdictions and institutions. One type of rehabilitation is a 1 self-improvement program. Religious and civic groups offer these. Examples include Alcoholics Anonymous, the Jaycees, and a Bible club.

1—self-improvement

*2—work variations among programs and type of work:
-running institution
-industrial
-agricultural*

Another kind of rehabilitation program is a 2 work program. Since the creation of the first houses of correction in Europe, there has been the belief that the imprisonment experience should improve inmates' work habits. Today, there is tremendous variation among institutions regarding work programs. In some, all inmates who are physically able are required to work. In other institutions, the inmates who work are those who choose to do so. Likewise, there is great variation in the types of work inmates perform. Some inmates are employed to help in the daily running of the institution and work in such areas as food services, maintenance and repair, laundry, health care, and clerical services. Other inmates work in factories at industrial tasks, such as wood or metal manufacturing. Still other inmates perform agricultural work. Institutions also vary in the degree to which the private sector is involved.

A third type of rehabilitation is [3] educational and vocational training. It has long been assumed that rehabilitation can be facilitated by improving inmates' academic skills and providing them with job skills. Many offenders enter prison with deficits in their education. It is not at all uncommon to encounter adult inmates who are reading, writing, and performing math operations at an elementary school level. Therefore, much prison education amounts to remedial schooling designed to prepare inmates to obtain their GEDs. Though there is some availability, low educational levels render college courses inappropriate for many inmates. Some prison vocational programs operate as part of job assignments, on-the-job training, and others are separate from job assignments . . .

3—Ed and rehab.

Finally, a wide range of [4] counseling techniques and therapy modalities are used in prisons across the nation. . . . The techniques and modalities used at a given institution ordinarily reflect the training and professional orientation of the treatment staff—caseworkers, religious counselors, social workers, psychologists, and psychiatrists. . . . Group counseling is more popular than individual counseling in institutional settings, primarily because it is more economical and because there are large numbers of inmates who share similar backgrounds and problems.

4—Counseling and therapy

group counseling

(Adapted from Bohm and Haley 2007)

1. What is the overall writing pattern used in these paragraphs? *classification*
2. What is the overall topic of this excerpt? *rehabilitation programs for inmates*
3. Did you see how the broader topic of rehabilitation programs was broken down into four different kinds? What are they?

Kinds of Rehabilitation Programs

a. *self-improvement*

b. *work*

c. *educational and vocational training*

d. *counseling and therapy*

4. What is the main idea of the passage? *prison rehabilitation programs can be categorized into four main types: self-improvement, work programs, educational and vocational training, and counseling and therapeutic programs.*

Classification and Graphics

Graphics, such as tables, charts, and semantic maps, are often used to depict the organization, or classification system, of large bureaucracies. The images clearly and simply present the key categories, subcategories, and important components or details.

try it and apply it! 6-8   **Practicing Classification with Graphics**

Directions: Use the following chart to learn about the organization of the Dallas Police Department. Refer to the chart to answer the questions that follow.

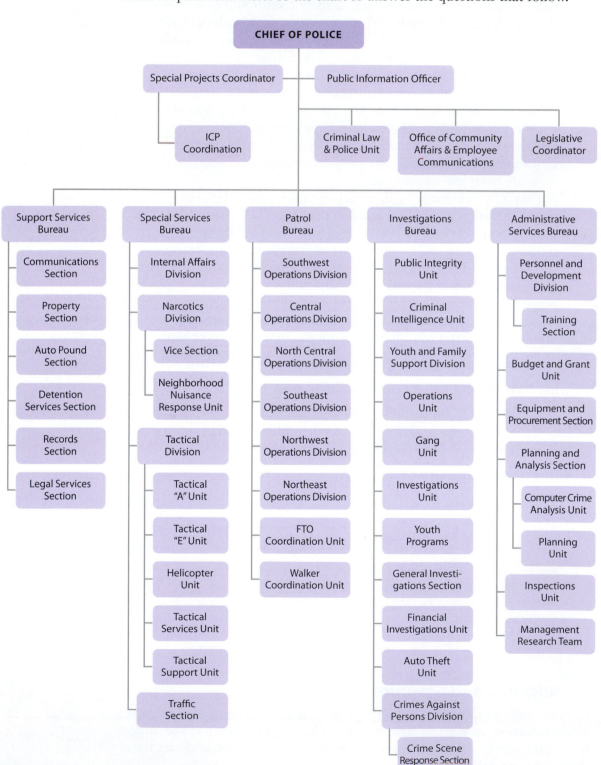

CHIEF OF POLICE

Special Projects Coordinator   Public Information Officer

ICP Coordination

Criminal Law & Police Unit   Office of Community Affairs & Employee Communications   Legislative Coordinator

Support Services Bureau
- Communications Section
- Property Section
- Auto Pound Section
- Detention Services Section
- Records Section
- Legal Services Section

Special Services Bureau
- Internal Affairs Division
- Narcotics Division
  - Vice Section
  - Neighborhood Nuisance Response Unit
- Tactical Division
  - Tactical "A" Unit
  - Tactical "E" Unit
  - Helicopter Unit
  - Tactical Services Unit
  - Tactical Support Unit
- Traffic Section

Patrol Bureau
- Southwest Operations Division
- Central Operations Division
- North Central Operations Division
- Southeast Operations Division
- Northwest Operations Division
- Northeast Operations Division
- FTO Coordination Unit
- Walker Coordination Unit

Investigations Bureau
- Public Integrity Unit
- Criminal Intelligence Unit
- Youth and Family Support Division
- Operations Unit
- Gang Unit
- Investigations Unit
- Youth Programs
- General Investigations Section
- Financial Investigations Unit
- Auto Theft Unit
- Crimes Against Persons Division
  - Crime Scene Response Section

Administrative Services Bureau
- Personnel and Development Division
  - Training Section
- Budget and Grant Unit
- Equipment and Procurement Section
- Planning and Analysis Section
  - Computer Crime Analysis Unit
  - Planning Unit
- Inspections Unit
- Management Research Team

1. How many bureaus fall under the Chief of Police? _5_____
2. What bureau has the largest number of units? _investigation_____
3. What two positions report directly to the chief? _Special Projects Coordinator and Public Information Officer_____

Comparison and Contrast Pattern

Textbook authors often want you to understand the relationships among topics and ideas. One way they do this is by highlighting comparisons and contrasts.

Comparisons are similarities or likenesses. **Contrasts** show differences. Thus, the comparison and contrast pattern in writing emphasizes likenesses and differences between two or more concepts, events, or ideas. If only similarities are noted, you might say the pattern is entirely comparison. If only differences are discussed, the pattern is more specifically contrast.

For example, an anthropology text might point out how cultures, in two different parts of the world, are, surprisingly, very much alike. A government textbook discussing political parties may discuss their differences in ideology, thus focusing on the contrasts between them.

Signal Words for Comparison

Signal words often used by authors to let you know a comparison is being made include the following:

similarly	both	less than
likewise	same	more important
along the same vein	more than	less important

Comparisons are also indicated by adding endings to descriptive words, such as happ*ier*, bigg*er* than, small*er* than, the wis*est,* and so on.

Signal Words for Contrast

Signal words often used by authors to let you know a contrast is being shown include the following:

on the contrary	whereas	unlike
in contrast	although	opposite
in opposition	on the other hand	opposed
however	while	different
nevertheless		

Contrasts may also be signaled by word opposites:

pro and con	advantages and disadvantages	benefits and problems
support and refute	strengths and weaknesses	

try it and apply it! 6-9   **Practicing with Comparison and Contrast**

Directions: Read the following paragraph, which discusses the degree of confidence minorities feel about the ethics of police officers. Try to identify the main idea by noting the comparison and contrast pattern in the writing. Underline comparison and contrast signal words to help you focus.

A.   Among minorities, however, confidence in the police is much lower than in the majority of the population. On every measure of performance, blacks and Hispanics rate the police lower than whites. . . . When asked to rate the honesty and ethical standards of the police, 14 percent of the general public rate the police as "very high" on this measure, 45 percent rate them as "high," 35 percent rate them as "average," 4 percent rate them as "low," and 2 percent rate them as "very low." In contrast, Blacks rate the honesty and ethical standards of police lower: Only 6 percent rate the police as "very high," 26 percent rate them as "high," 52 percent rate them as "average," 12 percent rate them as "low," and 3 percent rate them as "very low."

(Adapted from Bohm and Haley 2007)

1. What is being compared and contrasted in this paragraph?
    The differences in the degree of confidence in police ethics among minority ethnic groups and the white majority are being compared and contrasted.

2. After you can see what is being compared and contrasted, you should be able to formulate the most important overall point of the passage. Write it here.

Answers may vary.

_____

_____

_____

The next paragraph is about correctional officers. Read it to identify the more specific topic and the overall point. Underline the writing pattern signal words and notice the predominant organizational pattern. This will help you formulate the main idea and answer the questions that follow.

B.   How do correctional officers respond to their roles and their work conditions? According to Hawkins and Alpert, some officers become alienated and cynical and withdrawn from their work. Withdrawal can be figurative: an officer may minimize his or her commitment to the job and may establish a safe and comfortable niche in the prison, such as prolonged tower duty. Withdrawal can also be literal: turnover and absenteeism are high in many prison systems. Other officers become overly authoritarian

and confrontational in a quest to control inmates by intimidation. Those officers put up a tough façade similar to that displayed by some inmates. Still other officers respond by becoming corrupt. (For example, selling drugs to inmates in response to a low salary). Finally, in contrast, a number of officers respond by adopting a human-service orientation toward their work. Those officers seek to make prison a constructive place for themselves and for inmates. They try to deliver goods and services to inmates in a regular and responsive manner, to advocate and make referrals on behalf of inmates when appropriate, and to assist inmates in coping with prison by providing protection and counseling. . . .

(Bohm and Haley 2007)

1. What is the organizational pattern of the paragraph? *comparison and contrast*

2. What is the topic of the paragraph? *how correctional officers respond to their work conditions*

3. What is the main idea of the paragraph?
The main idea is that correctional officers respond to their roles and work conditions very differently.

(continued)

(continued)

You might be tempted to say that the author is simply listing the ways officers respond. There is some truth to that, but the more thoughtful response would be to see the comparison and contrast nature of the list and identify the organization based on the author's purpose.

Comparison and Contrast with Graphics

Graphics, such as charts, tables, and graphs, are often used to visually illustrate how factors compare and contrast.

try it and apply it! 6-10   **Practicing Comparison and Contrast with Graphics**

Directions: Look at the two pie graphs that show Characteristics of Sheriff's Personnel, 2000. Refer to them to answer the questions that follow.

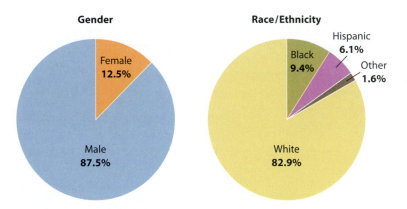

1. What aspects of the personnel in a sheriff's office are being compared?
   ethnicity and race

2. What conclusions can you draw from reading the charts?
   There are a far greater number of men employed in the sheriff's office than women; most people working in the sheriff's department are white.

The following bar graph compares and contrasts the incarceration rates of nations. Look at it carefully and then answer the questions that follow.

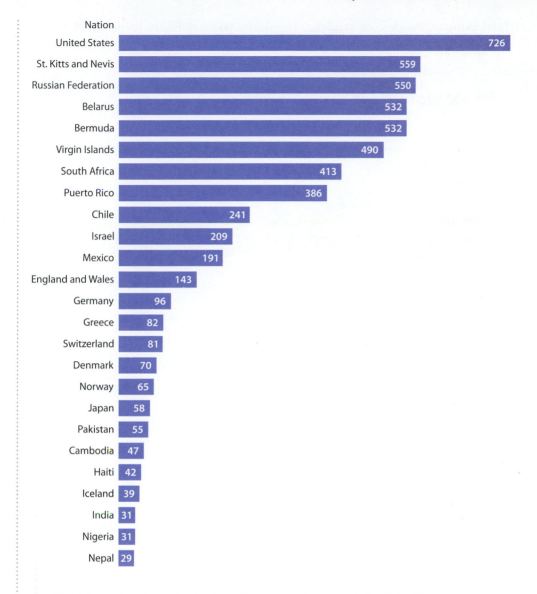

3. Which nation has the highest incarceration rate? *the United States*
4. Which has the lowest? *Nepal*

Source: Roy Walmsley, www.prisonstudies.org. Published by the International Centre for Prison Studies.

Cause and Effect Pattern

When a writer wants to help you understand the reasons something happened or the results of an event, he or she will use a cause and effect writing pattern. When you read about the events leading to World War II, global warming, poverty in the inner city, or the results of eating foods with trans fats, using pesticides, or studying regularly, you are likely to be reading text that is using a cause and effect organization pattern.

Signal Words for Cause

Signal words often used by authors to let you know a cause is being discussed include the following:

reason(s)

cause(s)

creates

because

. . . is due to

. . . results from

. . . leads to

Signal Words for Effect

Signal words often used by authors to let you know an effect is being discussed include the following:

the effect	resulted in or from
the results	created . . .
the outcome	thus
the responses	therefore
the consequences	consequently
leads or led to	as a result

try it and apply it! 6-11   Practicing with Cause and Effect

Directions: Read the following paragraph. It has been annotated for you. The general topic is violence in prison. Notice that, more specifically, the purpose of the author is to explain the reasons for physical violence in men's prisons.

Reasons for high rates of prison violence

A.   . . . It is generally agreed that there is more physical violence by inmates in today's men's prisons than there was in earlier periods. . . . Commonly cited reasons for high rates of prison violence include [1] improper management and classification practices by staff, [2] high levels of crowding and [3] competition over resources, the [4] young age of most inmates in prisons, and [5] increases in racial tensions and prison gang activity.

(Adapted from Bohm and Haley)

The author cites the reasons for the high rate of prison violence. Do you see that as the topic? Notice the five reasons that have been numbered in the annotation, even though the author did not number them in the paragraph. Now answer the following questions:

1. What is the organizational pattern of the paragraph? *cause and effect*

2. What is the topic of the paragraph? *causes of prison violence*

3. What is the main idea of the paragraph? *There are several reasons for the high rate of prison violence today.*

4. What are the reasons, or causes, of prison violence cited by the author?

   a. *poor management and practices of prison staff*

   b. *prison crowding*

   c. *competition among prisons for resources*

   d. *the young age of inmates*

   e. *increased racial tension and gang activity*

Now read the following paragraph, which discusses an aspect of criminal behavior. Keep in mind the author's purpose. Pay attention to signal words as you read. Respond to the questions that follow.

B.   In a more recent book, Michael Gottfredson and Travis Hirschi argue that the principal cause of many deviant behaviors, including crime and delinquency, is ineffective child-rearing, which produces people with low self-control. Low self-control impairs a person's ability to accurately calculate the consequences of his or her actions and is characterized by impulsivity, insensitivity, physical risk taking, shortsightedness, and lack of verbal skills. The theory posits that everyone has a predisposition toward criminality; therefore, low self-control makes it difficult to resist.

(Bohm and Haley 2007)

1. What is the topic of the paragraph? *the cause of crime and delinquency*

2. What do authors Gottfredson and Hirschi argue is the cause of most deviant behaviors? *ineffective child-rearing*

3. What do they say is the result of ineffective child-rearing? *low self-control*

4. What is the effect of low self-control? *an impaired ability to accurately perceive the consequences of one's own actions*

5. What is the overall main idea of the paragraph? *The main idea is that many deviant behaviors, including crime and delinquency, are caused by poor parenting that results in people having low self-control.*

Mixed Patterns

Look at paragraph B in the last section on the cause and effect writing pattern. Notice the enumeration of the characteristics of low self-control. This information is a valuable part of the paragraph, though it doesn't exactly fit

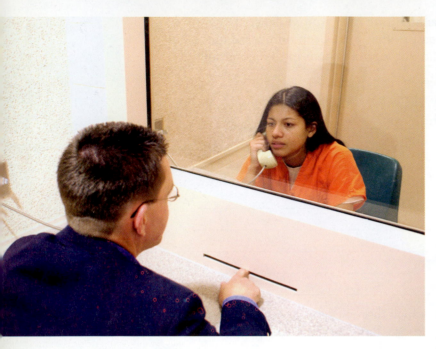

into the cause and effect pattern. It is a list. Thus, we see that paragraphs will often have more than one writing pattern. Just as textbooks use different writing patterns based on the purpose of the author and the information that is being shared, you will often come across paragraphs that include more than a single pattern, although one may be dominant.

Read the following paragraph about life in women's prisons. It is a good example of a paragraph that *primarily* uses the compare and contrast pattern. It explains how life in women's prisons is similar to life in men's prisons, but also different. This is stated as the main idea in the first, or topic, sentence. However, the author's concluding sentence offers a result of the different environments in women's prisons. So, you could say that the paragraph also uses cause and effect to present its point.

> Life in women's prisons is similar to life in men's prisons in some respects, but there are also important differences. For example, both female and male inmates must cope with the deprivations, stress, depersonalization, and authoritarian atmosphere of prison life. However, women's prisons are usually not characterized by the levels of violence, interpersonal conflict, and interracial tension found in men's institutions. Consequently, the environments of women's prisons are often less oppressive.

> (Bohm and Haley 2007)

1. Can you identify how life in men and women's prisons is similar?
   Both must cope with the deprivations, stress, depersonalization, and authoritarian atmosphere of prison life.

2. Can you identify how they differ or contrast? *Men deal with a greater amount of violence, one-on-one conflict, and racial tension.*

3. Can you identify which prison situation results in less oppression?
   women's prisons

try it and apply it! 6-12   Practicing with Mixed Patterns

Directions: The following paragraph continues the discussion about inmates and the structure of prisons. The *primary* organizational pattern is comparison and contrast. (You can anticipate that from the heading at the beginning.) But other patterns are used as well. Recognizing each will help you identify the most important points of the paragraph. Read the paragraph and respond to the questions that follow.

Custody Level vs. Security Level

Custody level should be distinguished from security level. Whereas institutions are classified by security level (super maximum-security, maximum-security, medium-security, minimum-security), individual inmates are classified by custody level. An inmate's custody level indicates the degree of precaution that needs to be taken when working with that inmate. Confusion arises because custody levels are sometimes designated by the same terms used to designate institutional security levels. However, the two levels are independent of one another. For example, some inmates with medium or minimum custody levels may be housed in maximum-security prisons.

(Adapted from Bohm and Haley 2007)

1. The author uses the comparison and contrast pattern to distinguish _custody level_ from _security level_.

2. The author uses definition to explain the meaning of custody level. What is the definition of custody level? _Custody level is the degree of precaution that is needed to be taken when working with a prisoner._

3. Within the prison system, what is the difference between custody level and security level? _Custody level refers to the classification given to an inmate, based on the degree of precaution that is needed to work with that inmate, whereas security level is the classification of the institutions or prisons themselves._

4. Within the paragraph, the author lists the levels of prison security. What are the levels? _The levels of prison security are super-maximum, maximum, medium, and minimum._

The paragraph is a good example of one with mixed writing patterns. It includes comparison and contrast, definition, classification, and listing.

Keep this in mind

- **Recognizing writing patterns will help you discover the author's purpose for writing**: to provide the meaning of terms, list items, sequence items or events in a particular order, classify information, compare and contrast ideas or items, explain causes and/or results.
- **Knowing the patterns will support your comprehension and help you formulate the main ideas of your reading.**
- **Keep in mind that authors will often provide examples to help explain the information they are discussing**. Sometimes the examples are key details for you to learn. More often, the examples are there to help you understand the key points or new terms.
- **Do not assume that a paragraph or selection is primarily organized in a listing pattern just because it includes lists or because points of information are presented one after the other.** Try to dig deeper, to recognize the qualities and purpose of the writing. Think about what is really going on in the writing and what an author is helping you know.

What Is the Author's Plan of Action? Identifying and Integrating Writing Patterns

Pattern	Purpose	Signal Words	Helpful Hints
Definition	Explores the meaning of new terms or concepts	*is, means, refers to, is defined as, is called, is known as, or, which states, that*	Terms in textbooks are often in boldface, italicized, or set apart by punctuation.
Listing or Enumeration	Presents a list of items or ideas for which the order is not important	*and, also, another, further, furthermore, additionally, firstly, next, last in conclusion*	Items may be numbered, although the numbers do not signify a specific order. Writers also often use bullets or letters to enumerate.
Sequence	Presents a series of events, items, or ideas in a particular order		1. Some signal words are interchangeable and may indicate more than one type of sequence.
■ **Chronological**	Organized according to time	dates, times: *lasting for, since, beginning in, until, during, soon after, formerly, currently, presently*	2. Knowing the actual sequence of details is critical to understanding the main idea of a piece.
■ **Process**	Organized according to the steps or stages followed	*first, second, third, then, now, after that, subsequently, following, lastly, steps, stages, progressions, sequence, series, continuum*	3. Numbering items within your annotation of text is very helpful.
■ **Spatial**	Organized according to position "in space" to show location or objects in relation to one another	*above, below, beneath, next to, adjacent to, to the left/right, aligned, behind, circular, separated by, leading away, in a row*	
■ **Order of Importance**	organized according to value from most important to least important, or vice versa	*most/least important, most/least significant, minimal/maximum value*	
Classification	Breaks larger groups or topics into subgroups or categories.	*several groups, many types, kinds, sub-sets, categories, families*	For studying, it helps to transfer narrative text of classification to a graph or other visual organizer.

Comparison	Show how items or ideas are similar to one another	*similarly, likewise, along the same lines, both, this, too*	"Opposite" listings signal contrast, i.e., *pro and con, advantages and disadvantages, support and refute, positives and negatives, in favor of and opposed to*
Contrast	and different from one another	*on the contrary, however, in contrast, in opposition, unlike, although, however, whereas, on the other hand, unlike*	
Cause	Identify reasons or motives for an event or condition and/or the	*reasons, causes, because, is due to, leads to, creates, motivates, because of, is due to*	Causes and effects may be "listed"; be aware of the more important pattern that focuses on causes and/or effects.
Effect	Outcomes and results of an action or event	*results from, the effect, the results, the responses, the outcomes, the findings, the consequences*	

Key Terms

cause
clue words
comparison
contrast
define
effect

enumerate
examples
list
organizational patterns
sequence
signal words

Let's Get Critical
Making Inferences and Incorporating Critical Reading Skills

In this chapter

you will learn about

- Making inferences
- Determining the author's purpose for writing
- Considering the audience
- Distinguishing between facts and opinions
- Detecting the tone
- Recognizing bias
- Evaluating the author's argument

Studying
Communications

As an academic discipline, communications examines a wide body of knowledge. We often think of communications in terms of learning how to speak clearly and effectively. For sure, there are classes on public speaking, debating, and oral communications. Today, however, courses in communications emphasize other aspects as well, such as media and telecommunications, interpersonal and group interaction, and business, intercultural, and global communications.

Working in Communications

Career choices for those interested in communications are varied. In business you can work as a personnel recruiter, sales representative, or media planner in advertising. In the entertainment industry, you might work as an actor, disc jockey, or comedy writer. Journalism positions in both print and electronic media include that of reporter, newscaster, editor, and writer. Within the educational arena, positions such as teacher, drama director, guidance counselor, audio-visual specialist, and speech-language pathologist all benefit from studies in communications.

161

Critical Reading

One of the most valuable tools you can have in college, and in life for that matter, is the ability to read critically. We often connect the word *critical* with being negative or finding fault. At times, it does mean this. But critical reading is much more. Critical readers are thinking readers. They go beyond understanding the literal meaning of a selection to develop their own conclusions about the subject, insights about the author's attitudes and purpose, and judgments about the quality of the work.

In this chapter you will explore the various components of critical reading. Critical reading involves drawing conclusions and evaluating the content of the text. It includes recognizing the author's reason for writing and noting differences between the use of facts and opinion. A critical reader determines the mood or feeling of the writing by considering the language used by the author.

Although these components are presented separately so you can learn about each, be aware that they are all related and impact one another. When you discuss a work in a critical way, you will consider any or all of the concepts together.

For example, when you determine an author's tone, it will help you identify the author's point of view on an issue and even the underlying purpose for writing.

Reading critically is very stimulating. It allows you to be an active participant in the reading process by thinking, reacting, deciding, and concluding as you read. When you are actively engaged in this way, your reading experience is more meaningful, interesting, and well remembered! Ultimately, being a savvy, critical reader will help you develop your own views and ideas on different issues.

You will learn about and practice critical reading using excerpts from the textbook *Introduction to Mass Communication: Media Literacy and Culture* by Stanley J. Baran.

Determine the author's purpose

Consider the audience

Make inferences

Critical Reading

Evaluate the author's argument

Distinguish facts and opinions

Recognize bias and points of view

Detect the tone

Making Inferences

An **inference** is a conclusion you draw based on information or data that is presented to you. You make inferences all the time in your daily life. If your friend leaves an exam with a big smile on her face while giving you a thumb's up signal, you would likely infer that she was successful on the test. If, as you walk out onto campus, the sky darkens and you hear rumbling in the distance, you are likely to predict that a storm is on the way.

Making inferences based on your reading utilizes a similar reasoning process. You attempt to conclude, or reason, based on the information that is presented, but what you infer is not stated or written directly. In a sense, you "read between the lines" when you make inferences. You have already used inferential thinking in Chapter 3, where you formulated the unstated main idea in a paragraph or reading selection based on the details provided.

Apply the following thinking strategies to make accurate inferences as you read:

- Be sure to understand the literal meaning of the text.
- Notice the author's choice of details and examples.
- Think about what the details and examples "add up to."
- Consider what may have been omitted, or left out.
- Draw a conclusion based on the information or data that is presented. Don't "jump to conclusions" without that evidence!
- Check the accuracy of your inference by reviewing the material. Think about the logic of your conclusion based on the information that is presented.

Read the following passage, which introduces the topic of mass media, technology such as radio, television, movies, and computer networks that carry messages to large numbers of people. Think about the inferences, or conclusions, you can draw about the author's view of the media based on the information included. Write as many inferences as you can on the lines that follow.

What Is Mass Communication?

"Does a fish know it's wet?" influential cultural and media critic Marshall McLuhan would often ask. The answer, he would say, is "No." The fish's existence is so dominated by water that only when water is absent is the fish aware of its condition.

So it is with people and mass media. The media so fully saturate our everyday lives that we are often unconscious of their presence, not to mention their influence. Media inform us, entertain us, delight us, and annoy us. They move our emotions, challenge our intellects, and insult our intelligence. Media often reduce us to mere commodities for sale to the highest bidder. Media help define us; they shape our realities.

(Baran 2008)

_____

_____

_____

_____

Based on the content of the passage, you might have inferred the following:

- Marshall McLuhan is an important writer about media and culture.
- Media are all around us.
- Media influence our lives tremendously.
- We have grown very accustomed to having media around us.
- We are not always even aware of the impact media have on us.
- Sometimes the media are a positive force; sometimes they are negative.
- We need to be aware of the impact media has on our lives and our behavior.
- The media are used by big business to make money.
- Media are important and worth studying and understanding.

When making inferences, be careful not to go beyond what is stated. If you do, you will be making an assumption. For example, based on what is written, it would be *inaccurate* to infer the following:

- The author believes all media are bad.
- Marshall McLuhan is close-minded and anti–free speech.
- The media are insulting.

Keep this in mind

- Remember to draw conclusions and make inferences *based on what is stated*.
- Be careful not to include your own opinions or attitudes.
- Check back in the text to verify or locate information that will support your conclusions. Ask yourself if your inference is logical and reasonable. When you do this, your inferences are more likely to be accurate and, therefore, valid.

try it and apply It! 7-1   Practicing with Inferences

Directions: Read the following excerpts. Several *possible inferences* are listed after each one. Underline the inferences that are valid based on the information that is stated.

What Is Culture?

A.   *Culture* is the learned behavior of members of a given social group. Many writers and thinkers have offered interesting expansions of this definition. Here are four examples, all from anthropologists. These definitions highlight not only what culture *is* but also what culture *does*.

1. Culture is learned, socially acquired traditions and lifestyles of the members of a society, including their patterned, repetitive ways of thinking, feeling and acting. (M. Harris 1983)

2. Culture lends significance to human experience by selecting from and organizing it. It refers broadly to the forms through which people make sense of their lives, rather than more narrowly to the opera or art of museums. (R. Rosaldo 1989)

3. Culture is the medium evolved by humans to survive. Nothing is free from cultural influences. It is the keystone in civilization's arch and is the medium through which all of life's events must flow. We are culture. (E.T. Hall 1976)

4. Culture is a historically transmitted pattern of meanings embodied in symbolic forms by means of which people communicate, perpetuate, and develop their knowledge about and attitudes toward life. (C. Gertz, as cited in Taylor 1991)

(From Baran 2008)

Possible Inferences

1. We are born having a culture.
2. Culture is behavior that is learned by the members of society.
3. Anthropologists study culture.
4. According to Hall, all the occurrences of our lives are part of our culture.
5. Culture is primarily the idea of music and art.
6. Everyone defines culture in the exact same way.
7. At least one anthropologist believes culture is needed for survival.

Culture and Behavior

B.   A culture's learned traditions and values can be seen as patterned, repetitive ways of thinking, feeling, and acting. Culture limits our options and provides useful guidelines for behaviors. For example, when conversing, you do not consciously consider, "Now, how far away should I stand? Am I too close?" You simply stand where you stand. After a hearty meal with a friend's family, you do not engage in mental self-debate, "Should I burp? Yes! No! Arghhh . . ." Culture provides information that helps us make meaningful distinctions about right and wrong, appropriate and

(continued)

(continued)

inappropriate, good and bad, attractive and unattractive, and so on.

(Baran 2008)

Possible Inferences

1. Our behavior in day-to-day situations is often governed by our culture.
2. Our culture is limiting and controlling.
3. Culture gives us information that helps shape our values and decisions.
4. Burping after a meal is seen as a complimentary sign to the host or hostess.
5. The traditions and values of a culture are intermittent and isolated.
6. The traditions and values of a culture repeat themselves historically within a culture.

The Origins of Paperback Books

C.   Dime novels were "paperback books" because they were produced with paper covers. But publisher Allen Lane invented what we now recognize as the paperback in the midst of the Great Depression in London when he founded Penguin Books in 1935. Four years later, publisher Robert de Graff introduced the idea to the United States. His Pocket Books were small, inexpensive (25 cents) reissues of books that had already become successful as hardcovers. They were sold just about everywhere—newsstands, bookstores, train stations, shipping terminals, and drug and department stores. Within weeks of their introduction, de Graff was fielding orders of up to 15,000 copies a day. (Tebbel, 1987) Soon, new and existing publishers joined the paperback boom. Traditionalists had some concern about the "cheapening of the book," but that was more than offset by the huge popularity of paperbacks and the willingness of publishers to take chances. For example, in the 1950s and '60s, African American writers such as Richard Wright and Ralph Ellison were published, as were controversial works such as *Catcher in the Rye*. Eventually, paperback books became the norm, surpassing hardcover book sales for the first time in 1960. Today, more than 60% of all books sold in the United States are paperbacks.

Paperbacks are no longer limited to reprints of successful hardbacks. Many books now begin life as paperbacks. The John Jakes books, *The Americans* and *The Titans*, for example, were initially issued as paperbacks and later reissued in hardcover. Paperback sales today top 1 million volumes a day, and bookstores generate half their revenue from these sales.

(From Baran 2008)

Possible Inferences

1. In its day, the idea of the paperback book was revolutionary.
2. Like many new ideas, the paperback book had its critics.
3. Before paperback books, one would probably have had to go specifically to a bookstore to purchase a hardcover book.
4. Approximately 50% of book sales today are from paperback books.
5. There was a time when it was considered risky to publish a book by an African American author.
6. The paperback book industry has grown over the years.
7. A book must first be published in hardcover to be considered for paperback publication.
8. Paperback books may have been introduced in order to boost book sales during a time when many people were low on funds.

Determining an Author's Purpose for Writing

As you read critically, consider the author's purpose, or reason, for writing. It will give you greater insight into what you are reading. Generally speaking, the **four primary purposes** for writing are to

- inform
- instruct
- entertain
- persuade

Based on their purpose, authors use different kinds of language to express their thoughts. They may choose to include or omit information. The tone, or mood, of their writing will also vary. Good questions to ask yourself to determine an author's purpose for writing are: Why did the author write this? To inform me about something? To teach me how to do something? To amuse or entertain me? To persuade or convince me about an action or an issue?

Writing to Inform

Most textbooks are written with the intention of **informing** the reader about a given subject—to provide information or explanations about a topic of study within a particular discipline. Other material is also written to inform, such as newspaper or magazine articles, articles in scholarly journals, and material in reference books. Most nonfiction writing is generated to familiarize the reader with information.

Information is best presented in an unbiased, objective manner. Thus, if an issue is discussed, all points of view should be presented. An author will generally not express his or her opinion in a piece of informative writing.

Following are two examples of informative writing. The first is from a news article on the influence of media on clothing sales. The second, from a textbook on mass media, describes the scope of the newspaper industry. Notice how each article presents factual information in a straightforward manner.

> Time spent watching TV continues to increase. During the fourth quarter of 2005, Bridge Ratings found that adults, ages 25 to 49, watched TV an average of 4.5 hours daily. This is a 25 percent increase from the fourth quarter of 2004. J. C. Penney has begun a more aggressive marketing campaign to attract fashionable customers . . .

> (Adapted from Cecily Hall and Emily Kaiser, "The Power of Persuasion,"
> *WWD,* Thursday, January 19, 2006.)

> Today there are more than 9,800 newspapers operating in the United States. Of these, about 1,500 (15%) are dailies, and the rest are weeklies (77%) and semiweeklies (8%). The dailies have a combined circulation of 56 million, the weeklies more than 70 million. The average weekly has a circulation of just over 9,000. Pass-along readership—readers who did not originally purchase the paper—brings 132 million people a day in touch with a daily and 200 million a week in touch with a weekly. However, overall circulation has remained stagnant despite a growing population. Therefore, to maintain their success and to ensure their future, newspapers have had to diversify.

> (From Baran 2008)

Writing to Instruct

In college, you are likely to encounter material written with the purpose of teaching or **instructing** you in how to do something. A biology or chemistry laboratory manual will guide you through a process of study or experimentation. Similar writing is found in cookbooks, "how-to" magazine articles, your driver's manual, or on any exams or assignments with directions on how to complete a task. In instructional writing, the sequence of steps involved in a process is often important, so it is advisable to read through all of them before beginning a specific task.

Following is an excerpt from an online tutorial from the Indiana University website on how to use library databases. It teaches students how to use keyword searches for research. Its purpose is to instruct.

> **Keyword Searching:** Searching for information by keyword permits greater flexibility. You do not need to know authors or subject headings to perform a keyword search. When you search by keyword, every field will be searched for the term(s) you have entered. However, this type of searching will also generally return more records, as well as some records that are not relevant to your topic. Keyword searching allows you to combine terms and concepts to retrieve records for the most relevant articles, books, videos, etc. You can combine terms using Boolean Operators and Nesting.

Boolean Operators can be used to combine words or terms when you search, to make a better defined search. See the examples below.

AND	*Example:* **teenage pregnancy AND prevention** will retrieve records that contain both the word teenager as well as the word prevention.
OR	*Example:* **adolescent OR teen** will retrieve records that contain either the word adolescent or the word teen or both of the words.
NOT	*Example:* **prevention NOT abortion** will retrieve records that contain the word prevention only if the word abortion is not in the record.

Nesting is the use of parentheses to put your keywords into sets. It preserves the "logic" of your keyword search.

Example: pregnancy and (adolescent or teen)

This keyword search will retrieve records that contain the word pregnancy and the record must also contain either the word adolescent or the word teen or both of these words. Nesting is often used when search terms have similar meanings.

Writing to Entertain

Do you enjoy reading for pleasure? If so, you have probably read books whose purpose was, indeed, to entertain you. Much fiction is written for this purpose. Fiction can be a wonderful way to escape everyday life, stimulating your imagination and making you laugh or even cry. Even newspaper and magazine articles or columns seemingly written on a "serious" topic may use language intended to amuse the reader. Sometimes in writing that is intended to amuse or entertain you, the writer is making a serious point. So be on the lookout for meaning that may be hidden in humor or wit.

Exploratory or personal essays are viewed as "entertaining" as well. They share personal observations, life experiences, or reflections. They are often written in a creative way that stimulates and encourages the reader to think about the author's thoughts and consider their own. Following is the introduction to a personal essay about the writer's recollection of her mother.

> Even though my mom was a dance instructor, I never had the urge to "shake a rug." From the time I can remember, mother was always pirouetting around the house, in front of both my friends and my dates. Or maybe it was because my idea of shaking my booty was to wipe my rubber clad feet when I came in from the rain.

Does the humor in the conversation make you want to read more? Do you think that writing in an entertaining way is a good idea to introduce more serious material? Why or why not?

Writing to Persuade

Very often authors use writing to express their points of view on issues, with the purpose of convincing or **persuading** the reader to go along with them. Effective persuasive writers usually support their viewpoint with data, statistics, and related material so their writing appears to be primarily informative. But be careful, and be critical. Although persuasive writing may include accurate information, it may also be one sided and opinionated. It is important to acknowledge that, even if you happen to agree with the author! A critical reader should always be able to see the difference between informative and persuasive writing.

Think about infomercials you have seen on television. They appear to alert you to the latest breakthroughs in losing weight, getting rid of headaches, or becoming a homeowner. However, their real goal is to convince you to buy a product or invest your money. In the same way, print advertisements may seem to be informative reports about a product or opportunity, but there is always a hidden agenda to convince you to buy, join, or commit your time or money in some way to the product or organization being advertised.

Following are two examples of persuasive writing. The first is an advertisement for an investment company. The second appears as part of a magazine article about the media's contribution to creating stress. What does each passage want to convince you about?

Many investment firms call themselves low cost. But, the truth is, many of them charge about six times as much as Vanguard®. This can cost you thousands of dollars. For instance, over twenty years, if you invest $10,000 a year with an average return of 8% before expenses, you would keep about $58,000 more with the Vanguard fund! And the longer you invest, the greater the savings. It's your money. Keep more of it. Vanguard. That's the simple truth about investing.

(© 2009 The Vanguard Group, Inc. All rights reserved. Used with permission.)

Media overkill causes unnecessary trauma and makes bad situations worse. It may be that more psychiatrists are diagnosing bipolar disorder in children, but a cover story in a newsmagazine repeated in daily newspapers and news broadcasts simply makes anxious parents with active and often belligerent kids scared to death that their child has a serious mental illness. ("Bi-polar Youth" replacing the "Hyperactive Youth" of yesterday's headlines.) When we read and hear that "Anxiety—It's up, way up . . ." and "Are you too Anxious?" a nation of fearful people that is told regularly that terrorists are going to blow up their neighborhoods floods HMO offices crying for a pill to ease their woes.

(Joe Saltzman, "Media Overkill Is More Frightening than the Real Thing," *USA Today* magazine, November 2002)

Considering the Audience

The **audience,** or readership, for whom an author is writing, impacts how the author writes. The textbooks you read are intended for an audience of college students. Over-the-counter magazines focused on cars, dogs, or housekeeping are intended for segments of the general population who have a specific interest in these topics. They might include articles designed to inform, entertain, or even instruct. Scholarly journals such as the *New England Journal of Medicine* or the *Law Review* are written for professionals in the fields of medicine and law, respectively, and are likely to be informative or perhaps persuasive.

Being aware of an author's intended audience can provide you with greater insight into the author's purpose. Books and articles have been the inspiration for many significant political and social changes in our society, because they have been written to empower particular segments of the population. For example, in his textbook on mass communication, author Stanley Baran tells us about a book written for women called *Our Bodies, Ourselves,* created by the Women's Health Book Collective of Boston. He states that it is credited with creating greater awareness among women and girls of issues such as health care, aging, racism, hunger, and contraception. The famous novel *Uncle Tom's Cabin,* written by Harriet Beecher Stowe in 1852, helped people learn of the horrors of slavery and increased support for the efforts of abolitionists. *Dr. Spock's Baby and Child Care*, written for new parents in the 1950s has influenced child rearing ever since. Furthermore, based on an author's intended readership, you will notice differences in the language used in writings about the same topic. The word choices used in a popular magazine article on sleep disorders or on a Googled Internet website will be simpler than that in your college biology textbook. Likewise, the language in your biology text will not be nearly as challenging as the medical jargon used in the text of someone studying neurology. The writer of an article on study skills for college students wants to make it friendly and accessible and will use less-formal language than if writing a journal article for college professors.

Think about your own writing and how it might change depending on your audience. Suppose you want to sell your 10-year-old car and you place ads in both the college newspaper, *Cool Times*, and in the senior citizen newsletter, *Old Times*. Compose the ad for each paper, choosing what you would address and how you would phrase it for each publication based on your intended audience.

Share your ads with a partner. How do they compare?

Cool Times	*Old Times*
_____	_____
_____	_____
_____	_____
_____	_____
_____	_____

try it and apply it! 7-2   **Determining the Author's Purpose for Writing and Intended Audience**

Directions: Read the following paragraphs, which are all about an aspect of the book-making industry. (They appear in the mass communication textbook used throughout this chapter, so college students like you are one intended audience.) See if you can detect a difference in the purpose for each, as well as the audiences for which the writing could be intended. Answer the questions that follow each passage.

A. The earliest colonists came to America primarily for two reasons—to escape religious persecution and to find economic opportunities unavailable to them in Europe. Most of the books they carried with them to the New World were religiously oriented. Moreover, they brought very few books at all. Those willing to make the dangerous journey tended to be poor, uneducated, and largely illiterate.

(Baran 2008)

1. **What is the purpose of the paragraph?** *to inform readers about the reasons colonists came to America and what kind of books they brought with them*

2. **Who is the intended audience?** *students of history or communications*

B. The mystery and miracle of a book is . . . that it is a solitary voice penetrating time and space to go beyond time and space, and to alight for a moment in that place within each of us which is also beyond time and space . . . Books are the royal road that enables us to enter the realm of the imaginative. . . . to experience what it is to be someone else. . . . Through books we recognize who we are and who we might become . . . Books require that we temporarily put our egos in a box by the door and take on the spirit of others . . . Deep within the solitary wonder in which we sit alone with a book, we confess and recognize what we would be too ashamed to tell another—and sometimes we are as ashamed of joy and delight and success as we are of embarrassment and failure.

(Julius Lester, "Carved Runes in a Clearing: The Place of the Book in Our Lives," UMassMag, Spring 2002)

3. **What is the author's purpose?** *to entertain, to stimulate the reader to think about books and their experience in reading them in a new and different way*

4. **Who is the author's intended audience?** *anyone who reads books, students, writers*

C. Book publishers must confront censorship by recognizing that their obligation to their industry and to themselves demands that they resist censorship. The book publishing industry and the publisher's role in it is fundamental to the operation and maintenance of our democratic society. Rather than accepting the censor's argument that certain voices require silencing for the good of the culture, publishers in a democracy have an obligation to make the stronger argument that free speech be protected and encouraged. . . . The power of ideas must be protected. A list of frequently censored titles, including *Harry Potter*, *Of Mice and Men,* and *The Catcher in the Rye*, should immediately make it evident why the power of ideas is worth fighting for.

(Adapted from Baran 2008)

5. **What is the author's purpose?** *to persuade or convince readers that censorship should not be allowed in a democracy, and that the publishing industry should do everything they can to resist it*

6. **What words signal this purpose?** *publishers must confront, demand, resist, have an obligation, ideas must be protected, should make it evident, worth fighting for*

7. **Who is the intended audience?** *public, students, publishers, government officials*

Distinguishing Between Facts and Opinions

When evaluating or reacting to reading material, it's important to think about an author's use of facts and opinions. Both have value, if used appropriately and with integrity.

Facts

A **fact** is something that has been proven to be true through observation or experience. Facts are statements that can be proved; that is, you can find sources that will verify they are true. Facts are used in informative writing in textbooks and in persuasive writing to back up or support an author's argument or point of view.

Signal Words and Phrases for Facts

Writers use words and phrases to introduce factual information such as the following: *according to, as reported in the…, cited in…, as documented in…,* and *as published in…*

Look at the following list of statements of facts. They report data or are commonly known truths and can be verified. Can you add some statements of fact about two topics that interest you to complete the list?

1. More than 195,000 new titles and editions (of books) were issued in the United States in 2004. (Baran 2008)

2. If you mix red and blue paints together you will get the color purple.

3. According to a survey by NCH Marketing Services, 75 percent of all consumers still use coupons. (Adapted from Cecily Hall and Emily Kaiser, "The Power of Persuasion," *WWD*, Thursday, January 19, 2006.)

4. _____

5. _____

Opinions

Opinions represent the *belief* or *point of view* of a writer or of the source a writer is quoting. Opinions can be valid and worth consideration, especially if the persons expressing them have experience and knowledge in that area and/or support opinion with facts. When this is the case, they are called *informed* opinions.

It is important to recognize when an opinion is inaccurate or even misleading. This can be tricky, as some writers present their opinions as though they were facts. There is nothing to prevent a writer or speaker from using the phrase, "The fact is . . ." and then go on to present an opinion.

However, most authors want to make it clear that they are expressing an opinion. When this is the case, they use qualifying signal words and phrases.

Signal Words and Phrases for Opinions

I think, feel, believe, suspect, conclude, assume, hope, wish
We must, should, need to, have to
It is important, imperative, necessary
The only way, the best way, the most important way
Maybe, hopefully, probably, apparently, seemingly, likely

Look at the following list of sentences. Each reflects an opinion or personal point of view. Remember, just because something is in print does not mean it is true or factual. Furthermore, because something is an opinion doesn't mean it is wrong. Add some statements of opinion of your own to complete the list.

1. To improve economic conditions, it is imperative that we raise interest rates right now.
2. Colleges should provide free parking for all students who request it.
3. Violence shown in the media has increased the number of acts of violence in our country.
4. _____
5. _____

Facts and Opinions

Although textbooks contain many facts, they also include the opinions of the author as well as those of the authorities quoted. Read the excerpt that follows. It focuses on shielding children from pornography on the World Wide Web. Notice how the content includes both facts and opinions.

> The Child Pornography Prevention Act of 1996 forbade online transmission of any image that "appears to be of a minor engaging in sexually explicit conduct." (FACT) Proponents argued that the impact of child porn on the children involved, as well as on society, warranted this legislation. (OPINION) Opponents argued that child pornography per se was already illegal, regardless of the medium. Therefore, they said this law was an unnecessary and overly broad intrusion into freedom of

expression on the Net. (OPINION) In April 2002, the Supreme Court sided with the act's opponents. (FACT) They said its effect would be too damaging to freedom of expression. (OPINION) "Few legitimate movie producers or book publishers, or few other speakers in any capacity, would risk distributing images in or near the uncertain reach of this law," wrote Justice Anthony Kennedy. (FACT THAT HE WROTE THIS EXPRESSION OF HIS OPINION) . . . Kennedy cited the anti-drug film *Traffic*, Academy Award-winning *American Beauty*, and Shakespeare's *Romeo and Juliet*, all works containing scenes of minors engaged in sexual activity, as examples of expression that would disappear from the Net. (FACT)

(From Baran 2008)

From reading this passage, you can see how an author can be factual when directly reporting someone else's opinions. In the passage, the signal words *proponents* (those in favor of something), *opponents* (those against something), and *argued* indicate statements of belief or opinion are being made, as do the phrases implying judgment, such as *say it is unnecessary*, *overly broad*, and *too damaging*.

try it and apply it! 7-3   Distinguishing Facts from Opinions

Directions: Read the following passage. It continues the preceding discussion of whether censorship should be used on the Web to protect children from pornography. Look for the signal words for both facts and opinions and underline them. Fill in the parentheses following the various statements to indicate whether you have just read a FACT or an OPINION. Then respond to the questions that follow.

1   Proponents of stricter control of the Net liken the availability of smut on the Internet to a bookstore or library that allows porn to sit side by side with books that children should be reading. (*opinion*_____) In actual, real-world bookstores and libraries, professionals, whether book retailers or librarians, apply their judgment in selecting and locating material, ideally striving for appropriateness and balance. Children are the beneficiaries of their professional judgment. No such selection or evaluation is applied to the Internet. (*fact*_____) Opponents of control accept the bookstore/library analogy but argue that, as troubling as the online proximity of all types of content may be, it is a true example of the freedom guaranteed by the First Amendment. (*opinion*_____)

2   The solution seems to be in technology. (*opinion*_____) Filtering software, such as Net Nanny (www.netnanny.com), can be set to block access to websites by title and by the presence of specific words and images (*fact*_____) . . . Few free speech advocates are troubled by filters on home computers, but they do see them as

(continued)

(continued)

problematic when used on more public machines, for example, in schools and libraries. They argue that software that can filter sexual content can also be set to screen out birth control information, religious sites, and discussions of racism. Virtually any content can be blocked. (*opinion*_____) This, they claim, denies other users—adults and mature teenagers, for example—their freedoms. (*opinion*_____)

3   Congress weighed in on the filtering debate by passing the Children's Internet Protection Act in 2000, requiring schools and libraries to install filtering software (*fact*_____). . . . Then, a federal appeals court ruled in June 2002 that requiring these institutions to install filters changes their nature from places that provide information to places that unconstitutionally restrict it. (*fact*_____) Nonetheless, in June 2003 a sharply divided Supreme Court upheld the Children's Internet Protection Act, declaring that Congress did indeed have the power to require libraries to install filters. (*fact*_____)

4   But then, in June 2004 . . . the same Court, again in a sharply divided opinion, rejected the 1998 Child Online Protection Act, which would have fined commercial pornographic websites $50,000 a day if people younger than 17 could access their content. (*fact*_____) Filters, not criminal penalties, said the Court, were the "least restrictive means" of achieving the "compelling government interest" of protecting children from harmful Net material (Greenhouse, 2004). (*opinion*_____)

(From Baran 2008)

1. In paragraph 1, what comparison is made in the discussion of the presence of pornography on the Web?
    It is compared to the availability of smut and porn sitting right next to important literature for children in bookstores and libraries.

2. What is the opinion of the supporters of stricter Internet control?
    As in bookstores or libraries, there should be some "authority" with good judgement available to help children make good selections.

3. What do the opponents of control have to say?
    Even though it may be troubling to have porn online and easily accessible, it is an example of First Amendment freedom of free speech and should be protected.

4. What aspect of technology is introduced in paragraph 2 as a means of solving the problem?
    filtering software

5. What is the concern of the free speech advocates?

    They don't mind the use of filters in private homes, but think they will create censorship in schools and libraries and restrict the freedom of other more mature users to view and read what they like.

6. Based on the facts in paragraphs 3 and 4, list the series of congressional and Court decisions, by date, that reflects changing views on filtering and the Children's Internet Protection Act.

    2000: Congress passed the Children's Internet Protection Act, requiring schools and libraries to install filter software.

    2002: Federal appeals court ruled that requiring this was unconstitutional, making schools and libraries restrictors of information, rather than providers of information.

    2003: A sharply divided Supreme Court upheld the Children's Internet Protection Act and said Congress had the power to require libraries to install filters.

    2004: The Supreme Court rejected the 1998 Child Online Protection Act, which would have fined pornographic websites $50,000 a day if people under 17 were able to access them. They supported the use of filters, rather than criminal regulation.

7. Based on the various opinions expressed in this passage, and the facts reported about the changing governmental view, what can you infer about the issue of censorship on the Web and First Amendment rights?

    It seems it is very difficult to balance the desire to protect people, especially children, from things that are thought to be harmful or inappropriate with the rights that are guaranteed to all citizens, including free speech, in the First Amendment of the Constitution.

Detecting the Tone

Another important component of critical reading is to detect the tone of the writing. **Tone** refers to the mood, attitude, or feeling that is conveyed in the text. In spoken English, we use many cues to detect how a person feels about a subject. We can hear emotion in a speaker's voice or observe it through facial expressions and body language. The speaker may also use words or expressions that reflect his or her attitude.

Below is a dialogue about television. The speakers are having a conversation about *Family Guy*, a popular TV program on the Fox network. Read it to see if you can detect the mood or feelings—that is, the tone of the participants.

Jeremy: Did you watch TV last night?

Robyn: Nope. I was studying, and when I wasn't studying, I was working on my history paper.

Jeremy: You missed a great *Family Guy*. Stewie decides to find his roots and . . .

Robyn: Saw it.

Jeremy: No way. They said it was an all-new episode.

Robyn: Saw it.

Jeremy: Stop being so smug. So, if you didn't watch TV, how'd you see it? Download it on your computer? That still counts as watching TV. A video screen is a video screen.

Robyn: Nope. I saw it four months ago on DVD.

Jeremy: No way.

Robyn: Way. Television is changing, my friend, more than you realize.

(Adapted from Baran 2008)

In the dialogue, Jeremy has picked up on Robyn's smug attitude from her curt or brief responses. Robyn continues with her smugness when she calls her buddy, "My friend." After Jeremy hears how Robyn managed to watch the new episode before it was aired, he responds in a surprised and astonished way by saying, "No way."

In written English, you can also discern the mood or attitude of the writer. However, because you cannot *hear* the author's voice or *observe* his or her body language, you have to rely on the language and the author's choice of words to detect the tone. A writer may use neutral words or emotional words. Through their use of language, writers convey positive or negative attitudes, neutrality, anger, elation, joy, sadness, criticism, stress, disappointment, hope, and so on. In fact, they can convey every attitude they feel.

Detecting tone can also be helpful in determining an author's purpose. In the box below, words that describe tone are listed according to the *possible* purposes an author would have for using a particular tone.

Tone and Purpose

Purpose: Inform and Instruct

factual: based on fact

formal: written using academic conventions; not casual

neutral: not supporting a particular side or position, unbiased

objective: not influenced by personal feelings; based on fact

straightforward: direct, honest

Purpose: Entertain

amused: pleasing in a light-hearted way

carefree: playful

comical: causing laughter

dramatic: filled with emotion

humorous: funny, witty

ironic: mocking; conveying a humorous or angry meaning

joyful: happy

laughable: comical, amusingly ridiculous

light-hearted: free from care

ridiculous: suggests extreme foolishness

romantic: marked by emotional and imaginative appeal

sentimental: influenced more by emotion than by reason

witty: using words in a clever and funny way

uplifting: offering or providing hope

Purpose: Persuasive

accusing: charging of wrongdoing

angry: extremely upset

blaming: accusing

compassionate: having or showing concern for feelings of another

condemning: blaming

critical: inclined to find fault

cynical: bitter, distrustful

disapproving: passing unfavorable judgment

distressed: upset

frustrated: displaying feelings of discouragement

impassioned: strongly emotional

judgmental: authoritative and often having critical opinions

negative: disagreeable, marked by features of opposition, hostility or pessimism

opinionated: stubborn, biased, prejudiced

outraged: angry, extremely offended

pessimistic: no hope, seeing the worst side of things

sarcastic: bitter, making fun of things

subjective: placing emphasis on one's own attitudes and opinions

supportive: promoting the interests of a particular idea

upbeat: cheerful and happy

worried: concerned

Now read the following two excerpts that illustrate how detecting tone helps you to understand an author's purpose.

A Short History of Television

After the printing press, the most important invention in communication technology to date has been television. Television has changed the ways teachers teach, governments govern, and religious leaders preach. . . . In 1952, 108 stations were broadcasting to 17 million television homes. By the end of the decade, there were 559 stations, and nearly 90% of U.S. households had televisions. In the 1950s more television sets were sold in the United States (70 million) than there were children born (40.5 million).

(Baran 2008)

In this example, the writer's tone is straightforward, neutral, factual, and informative. The writer mentions facts, such as dates and statistics, and provides details that can be verified or proven to be true. The purpose is to inform.

A direct, straightforward, neutral tone is fairly typical of college textbooks. However, sometimes, when the author includes quotations from authorities or experts, you may detect a less objective tone on the part of those being quoted. In the following example, the author includes the response of a member of the public about the advent of radio in the last century. What tone is conveyed by the speaker?

> "Is radio to become the chief arm of education? Will the classroom be abolished, and the child of the future stuffed with facts as he sits home or even as he walks about the streets with his portable receiving set in his pocket?"
>
> *(Century,* June 1924:149 in Baran 2008)

When new technology is introduced, it is not unusual for some people to be afraid about how it will impact society. In this case, the speaker is fearful that radio will put an end to traditional ways of teaching, including classroom instruction and teacher-student interaction. Clearly, the speaker has a concerned, alarmed, almost fearful tone. The examples he uses are somewhat exaggerated and are used to alert the American public to his opinion about the negative effects of this new media. The speaker's purpose is to persuade his readers to turn away from the radio. Keep in mind that the purpose of the textbook author is to inform students that there were many concerns about radio as a new technology. These concerns do not necessarily reflect the textbook author's opinion about radio.

Here's another example from a section titled "Television and Its Audiences." The author of the textbook provides a portion of Newton Minow's 1961 landmark speech about the medium of TV. Minow, the Chairperson of the Federal Communications Commission, said the following to broadcasters:

> "Sit down in front of your television set when your station goes on the air and stay there without a book, magazine, newspaper, profit and loss sheet, or ratings book, and keep your eyes glued to that set until the station signs off. I assure that you will observe a vast wasteland . . ."
>
> (Baran 2008)

When Minow referred to television as a *vast wasteland*, he was telling the broadcasters that commercial TV was not doing enough to serve the public's interest. A wasteland is barren, lacking value or substance. Minow was displeased with the current programming. He found it worthless. The tone is critical. It reflects the views of Minow and not those of the textbook author.

Sometimes, the inclusion of negative words in a section of text can confuse you about the overall tone of the material. In the paragraph that follows, you will read about a dispute between television networks and Nielson, a TV ratings company.

Can't Find Them or They Aren't There?

Just as the radio networks questioned the rating system they had long embraced when television began to erode their audiences, today's television networks are at war with Nielson, blaming the ratings-taker for precipitous or steep declines in viewers, especially young men and minorities . . . Broadcasters and Nielson feud often—whenever there are declines in ownership.

(Baran 2008)

The words *at war, blame, blaming,* and *feud* are negative; however, the overall tone is informative and straightforward.

Denotation and Connotation

Tone can also be understood by thinking about the meaning of words. Most words have two levels of meaning. The **denotation** is the literal meaning, the one you find in a dictionary. The **connotation** of a word is the secondary meaning associated with it, which often has emotional overtones. For example, the words *selective* and *picky* have the same denotation, yet how we perceive the meaning of these words or their connotation is quite different.

> Shawn is *selective* about the TV shows he lets his children watch. Shawn chooses from educational broadcasts, news programming, and all the programs shown on Channel 13.

> Shawn is *picky* about the TV shows he lets his children watch. Shawn only allows his children to watch shows that air before 8 p.m. In addition, he does not permit them to watch any cartoons or sitcoms about single parents or divorced couples.

In the first example, the tone of the term *selective* is positive. Shawn is a caring parent who monitors what his children watch on television. In the second example, the use of the word *picky* indicates that Shawn is overly choosy in what he allows his children to watch on TV. He eliminates many programs and restricts his children's viewing beyond what most would consider necessary.

Some words have more definite positive or negative connotations. For example, consider the following group of words: *television, the box,* and *boob tube*, or *newspaper, tabloid,* and *rag sheet*. Only the first word in each group has a positive connotation. The latter two in each group clearly indicate a negative feeling about the subject. A good reader carefully considers the connotations of words both positive and negative in order to determine the tone of a reading selection.

try it and apply it! 7-4   Detecting Negative Connotation

Directions: For each set of words, underline the word or words that you think have a negative connotation. Discuss your answers with your classmates. You may discover that perceptions of words differ depending on your background and culture.

Answers may vary.

1. boss, supervisor, superior
2. housewife, homemaker, stay-at-home mom
3. vagrant, bum, homeless
4. senior citizen, old-timer, geezer
5. fired, dismissed, canned
6. unmarried woman, spinster, single girl
7. skinny, slender, bony
8. steadfast, stubborn, inflexible
9. finicky, careful, picky
10. lady, broad, woman

try it and apply it! 7-5   Detecting Tone

Directions: Read each of the following statements about different types of mass media. Pay particular attention to the author's choice of words and their connotations. Select the answer that best describes the tone of each statement.

_a_ 1. In the 1950s, two new formats appeared in television: feature films and talk shows. Talk shows were instrumental in introducing radio personalities to the television audience, which could see its favorites for the first time . . .

    a. straightforward
    b. objective
    c. nostalgic
    d. judgmental

_b_ 2. When I watch the old *Father Knows Best* clips from the 1960s, I can smell dinner cooking on the stove.

    a. uplifting
    b. nostalgic
    c. carefree
    d. positive

_c_ 3. In 1969, after much research into producing a quality children's television show and studying the best instructional method for teaching preschool audiences, the Children's Television Workshop (CTW) unveiled *Sesame Street*.

    a. instructional
    b. optimistic
    c. straightforward
    d. positive

_c_ 4. The zooming popularity of *Sesame Street* created a sensation in U.S. television.

    a. ironic
    b. outraged
    c. uplifting
    d. critical

_a_ 5. Now parents, too busy to spend time with their kids, plop them in front of the boob tube for hours on end.

    a. judgmental
    b. angry
    c. dramatic
    d. objective

_d_ 6. Seeing constant brutality, vicious-ness, and unsocial acts results in hardness, intense selfishness, even mercilessness, proportionate to the amount of exposure and its play on the temperament of the child.

   a. informative
   b. playful
   c. laughable
   d. outraged

_a_ 7. And what happens when people finally make it to their seats? Chatty neighbors, rude cell phone users, crying babies, and antsy children watching inappropriate movies.

   a. annoyed
   b. witty
   c. angry
   d. dramatic

_c_ 8. The newest way to receive and view television is on a mobile device, either a cell phone or other portable video player.

   a. critical
   b. instructive
   c. objective
   d. carefree

_d_ 9. No one would think of putting a newspaper on television. Why would you put television on a cell phone?

   a. formal
   b. happy
   c. ridiculous
   d. critical

_a_ 10. Will the promise of the Web be drowned by a sea of commercials?

   a. cynical
   b. upbeat
   c. informative
   d. objective

(Sentences 1–4 and 6–10 adapted from Baran 2008)

The author's tone and the connotation of words can influence your personal reaction to a piece of writing. How do you react when a friend rants and raves compared to when he or she speaks gently and kindly? It's often easier to listen to someone who speaks in a mild manner than someone who yells. However, if you know your friend is worried, you won't simply dismiss him; you'll understand that he is stressed out and think about what is really important. The same is true when you read. As a critical reader, you will sometimes have to separate the "feelings" a writer evokes in you and look past the tone. Then you can evaluate the ideas and viewpoints more objectively.

Keep this in mind

- Pay attention to the author's language and choice of words.
- Determine how the author feels about his or her subject.
- Evaluate how the connotations of words affect your response to what you read.

Recognizing Bias

Bias is an author's tendency to believe in a particular viewpoint and not consider alternative viewpoints as valid. Bias can lead to an author being prejudiced about an issue and unable to be objective about it. Bias often reveals an author's political preferences and beliefs. To recognize bias, a critical reader must be aware of how language is used and consider its effect on meaning. Tone and connotation can also reveal bias. For example, if your sociology professor announces that cell phones must be turned off at the beginning of the session because they are distracting, she is stating a fact and setting a reasonable rule. On the other hand, if she states the cell phone is a technological invention that has ruined the quality of everyday life, she is expressing her opinion and not taking into account the many advantages of mobile phones when used in other situations.

Bias is not always bad. A writer may have a strong bias in favor of a particular point of view, but provide a well-grounded argument for his or her opinion that is supported by facts and takes into account and addresses alternative views. However, this is not always the case, and it is important to always be on the lookout for signs of prejudice when you read.

It is especially important to look for bias when a writer addresses a controversial issue. All issues can be looked at in a variety of ways. If a writer presents only one perspective and does not discuss and evaluate other points of view, at least briefly, then he or she is probably biased. If a writer includes more than one side of an issue, he or she is being more objective. In the following example, from the chapter "Theories and Effects of Mass Communication," the author presents some different viewpoints on the effects of the media. The inclusion of an argument and counterarguments on the effects of the media help make it more objective and less biased.

The Effects of Media

If media have any effects at all, they are only on the unimportant things in our lives, like fads and fashions. The counterpoint arguments: (a) Fads and fashion are not unimportant to us. The car we drive, the clothes we wear, and the way we look help define us; they characterize us to others. In fact, it is media that have helped make fads and fashion so central to our self-definition and happiness. Kids don't kill other kids for their $150 basketball shoes because their mothers told them that Air Jordans were cool. (b) If media influence only the unimportant things in our lives, why are billions of dollars spent on media efforts to sway opinion about social issues, such as universal health care, nuclear power, and global warming?

(Adapted from Baran 2008)

Scholarly texts, newspapers, journals, and magazines are filled with articles that address controversies, such as the effects of television. As a college student, you may be asked to research this important topic or others to find opposing viewpoints.

To recognize bias, it is helpful to ask yourself the following questions:

- What is the author's purpose?
- Does the author present all sides of an issue?
- Does the author offer discussion and evaluation of opposing viewpoints?
- Do the facts and opinions presented represent various points of views?
- What is the tone of the selection and what are the connotations of the language used?

try it and apply it! 7-6   Recognizing Bias in Writing

Directions: Read this article that discusses violence on television. Then answer the questions that follow.

TV Violence

Bashing, crashing overwhelms children

Here's what they say: "Viewing entertainment violence can lead to increases in aggressive attitudes, values and behaviors, particularly in children."

Here's who says it: the American Medical Association, the American Academy of Pediatrics, the American Psychological Association and the American Academy of Child and Adolescent Psychiatry.

Here's what to expect as a result of their efforts: Nothing. The sleazy brotherhood of blood-and-guts peddlers in the entertainment industry will just keep rolling their twisted version of life downhill to all of us, adults and children alike.

You think you can protect your child from murder and sadism glorified, magnified and brought to life on TV, in the movies and in video games? Think again. Unless you homestead in the remotest patch of Bush Alaska and forswear all modern "entertainment," you might as well resign yourself to violence in one form or another rubbed in your face almost daily. If not at your house, at your child's playmate's. Or on the playground, where other children act out what they've seen.

Parents with no scruples bring children too young to go to the bathroom by themselves to R-rated movies with one terrifying death scene after another. They buy video

(*continued*)

(continued)

games based on torture and killing for kids whose feet don't touch the floor when they sit down.

. . . Some experts hope for the entertainment industry to develop and live by a code of conduct. Dream on. The only code of conduct is "Whatever it takes to line my pockets." It doesn't speak well for those who pay for it, it doesn't speak well for those who profit from it, and it doesn't bode well for a generation raised on it.

(Anchorage Daily News, August 2, 2000)

1. What is the issue being discussed?
   the effects of media violence

2. What is the author's point of view on the issue?
   Media violence leads to aggressive behavior.

3. What is the overall tone? List the words that reveal the tone.
   The tone is critical, angry, and frustrated. (bashing, crashing, sleazy brotherhood, blood-and-guts peddlers, twisted version, nothing, think again)

4. Is the author biased? Explain.
   Yes. The author uses a lot of negative connotative language. The writer's tone is negative. The author does not give opposing viewpoints.

5. How did this article make you think or feel?
   Answers will vary.

6. Would you use this article for a college paper, or would you search for other articles that present a less biased viewpoint?
   Answers will vary.

Did you view the author as being critical and sounding angry? He expresses his criticism through the use of name-calling and accuses parents, the media, and society for being complicit in promoting violence. He is also concerned about how TV promotes violence. He is frustrated because he believes medical experts who might be able to do something about curbing violence are doing *nothing*. This is also a wake-up call. He's hoping that if you agree with his opinion, you might do something about it.

What is the effect of recognizing bias? As a critical reader, you should read texts carefully so that you can make your *own* judgments. Much of what you read does have somewhat of a slant. However, this should not stop you from exploring your own viewpoints, which may be different. A strongly prejudiced or biased piece can draw a reader into an author's perspective. The reader may begin to "feel" instead of "think" about the subject. For a critical reader, such bias may also make the author's argument appear weaker. A good reader may decide to search for additional readings to evaluate the arguments.

Evaluating the Author's Argument

When reading a selection that presents an author's point of view, you not only want to identify the viewpoint but also evaluate the author's development of it. Assessing the quality of the author's argument is an important tool for a critical reader. Here are some factors to consider:

- **Adequacy of coverage:** There should be enough information to support the argument. Writers need to offer a sufficient amount of details and reasons to back up their position.
- **Relevancy:** All the information must directly relate to the issue being discussed.
- **Objectivity:** The author presents material in an unbiased, nonsubjective manner. If the author overly personalizes, this will distract the reader from the real issue.
- **Currency:** Authors should present information that is up-to-date. The writer must take into account the latest findings, research, and news.
- **Authority:** The author has qualifications or their own expertise in the field that he or she is discussing. This adds a degree of authority to the argument.
- **Strength of the Evidence:** The author offers many kinds of support for the argument. These include

  - Personal experiences
  - Expert or informed opinions
  - Citations
  - Historical documentation
  - Statistical data
  - Research

Keep this in mind

- Determine whether the author has any political beliefs that may affect his or her objectivity.
- Notice details that are included or overemphasized, and think about details that have been omitted.
- Observe the author's language for evidence of bias.
- Look for statements of opposing viewpoints that are expressed in a fair manner.
- Assess the quality of a writer's argument If you personally agree with the writer's viewpoint.

try it and apply it! 7-7   Practicing Critical Reading

Directions: Read this essay and in the spaces provided, answer the critical thinking questions that follow.

"TV Can Be a Good Parent"

Ariel Gore

1   Let me get this straight.

2   The corporations have shipped all the living-wage jobs off to the developing world, the federal government has "ended welfare" and sent poor women into sub-minimum wage "training programs" while offering virtually no child-care assistance, the rent on my one-bedroom apartment just went up to $850 a month, the newspapers have convinced us that our kids can't play outside by themselves until they're 21 and now the American Academy of Pediatrics wants my television?

3   I don't think so.

4   Earlier this month, the AAP released new guidelines for parents recommending that kids under the age of 2 not watch TV. They say the box is bad for babies' brains and not much better for older kids. Well, no duh.

5   When I was a young mom on welfare, sometimes I needed a break. I needed time to myself. I needed to mellow out to avoid killing my daughter for pouring bleach on the Salvation Army couch. And when I was at my wits' end, Barney the Dinosaur and Big Bird were better parents than I was. My daughter knows that I went to college when she was a baby and preschooler. She knows that I work. And, truth be told, our television set has been a helpful co-parent on rainy days when I've been on deadline. Because I'm the mother of a fourth-grader, Nickelodeon is my trusted friend.

6   There was no TV in our house when I was a kid. My mother called them "boob tubes." But that was in the 1970s. My mother and all of her friends were poor—they were artists—but the rent she paid for our house on the Monterey (Calif.) Peninsula was $175 a month and my mother and her friends helped each other with the kids. The child care was communal. So they could afford to be poor, to stay home, to kill their televisions. I, on the other hand, cannot.

7   Now the AAP is saying I'm doing my daughter an injustice every time I let her watch TV. The official policy states that "Although certain television programs may be promoted to [young children], research on early brain development shows that babies and toddlers have a critical need for direct interactions with parents and other significant caregivers for healthy brain growth and the development of appropriate social, emotional, and cognitive skills. Therefore, exposing such young children to television programs should be discouraged."

8   Maybe my brain has been warped by all my post-childhood TV watching, but I'm having a little trouble getting from point A to point B here. Babies and toddlers

have a critical need for direct interactions with actual people. I'm with them on this. "Therefore, exposing such young children to television programs should be discouraged." This is where they lose me. I can see "Therefore, sticking them in front of the TV all day and all night should be discouraged." But the assumption that TV-watching kids don't interact with their parents or caregivers is silly. Watching TV and having one-on-one interactions with our kids aren't mutually exclusive.

9   I've been careful to teach my daughter critical thinking in my one-woman "mind over media" campaign. It started with fairy tales: "What's make-believe?" and "How would you like to stay home and cook for all those dwarves?" Later we moved on to the news: "Why was it presented in this way?" and "What's a stereotype?" But if you think I was reading *Winnie the Pooh* to my toddler when I thought up these questions, think again. I was relaxing with a cup of coffee and a book on feminist theory while Maia was riveted to PBS.

10   I read to my daughter when she was little. We still read together. But even a thoughtful mama needs an electronic babysitter every now and again. Maybe *especially* a thoughtful mama.

11   Not surprisingly, the television executives feel there's plenty of innocuous programming on television to entertain young kids without frying their brains. "It's a bunch of malarkey," said Kenn Viselman, president of the itsy bitsy Entertainment Co., about the new policy. Itsy bitsy distributes the British show *Teletubbies,* which is broadcast on PBS. While I prefer Big Bird to Tinky Winky, I have to agree with him when he says, "Instead of attacking shows that try to help children, the pediatricians should warn parents that they shouldn't watch the Jerry Springer show when kids are in the room."

12   The AAP's policy refers to all television, of course, but it's hard not to feel like they're picking on PBS. *Teletubbies* is the only program currently shown on non-cable television marketed toward babies and toddlers. Just two weeks ago, the station announced a $40 million investment to develop six animated programs for preschoolers. The timing of the AAP's report is unfortunate.

13   Cable stations offer a wider variety of kid programming. Take for example Nick Jr., an offshoot of the popular Nickelodeon channel. On weekdays from 9 a.m. to 2 p.m., the programming is geared specifically toward the preschool set. "Our slogan for Nick Jr. is 'Play to Learn'," Nickelodeon's New York publicity manager, Karen Reynolds, told me. "A child is using cognitive skills in a fun setting. It's interactive. With something like *Blue's Clues,* kids are talking back to the TV. They are not just sitting there."

14   Still, the station has no beef with the new AAP policy on toddlers. "Nick Jr. programs to preschool children ages 2 to 5, but we are aware that children younger than 2 may be watching television," said Brown Johnson, senior vice president of Nick Jr. "We welcome a study of this kind because it encourages parents to spend more time bonding and playing with their children."

15   In addition to telling parents that young children shouldn't watch television at all and that older kids shouldn't have sets in their bedrooms, the AAP is

(continued)

(*continued*)

recommending that pediatricians ask questions about media consumption at annual checkups. The difference between recommending less TV-watching and actually mandating that it be monitored by the medical community is where this could become a game of hardball with parents. What would this "media file" compiled by our doctors be used for? Maybe television placement in the home will become grounds for deciding child custody. ("I'm sorry, your honor, I'll move the set into the bathroom immediately.") Or maybe two decades from now Harvard will add TV abstention to their ideal candidate profile. ("'Teletubbies' viewers need not apply.") Better yet, Kaiser could just imprint "Poor White Trash" directly onto my family's medical ID cards. Not that those cards work at the moment. I'm a little behind on my bill.

16   I called around, but I was hard-pressed to find a pediatrician who disagreed with the academy's new policy. Instead, doctors seemed to want their kids to watch *less* TV, and they're glad to have the AAP's perhaps over-the-top guidelines behind them. "If all your kids did was an hour of *Barney* and *Sesame Street* a day, I don't think that the academy would have come out with that statement," said a pediatrician at La Clinica de la Raza in Oakland, Calif., who asked not to be named. "It's not the best learning tool." And he scoffs at the notion of "interactive" TV. "It's not a real human interaction. When you're dealing with babies and toddlers, this screen is an integral part of their reality. You want kids to be able to understand interaction as an interaction. It's like the Internet. We're getting to a place where all of your relationships are virtual relationships."

17   Fair enough.

18   I'm not going to say that TV is the greatest thing in the world for little kids—or for anyone. I'm not especially proud of the hours I spend watching *Xena: Warrior Princess, The Awful Truth* and *Ally McBeal.* Mostly I think American television is a string of insipid shows aired for the sole purpose of rounding up an audience to buy tennis shoes made in Indonesian sweatshops.

19   But it seems that there is a heavy middle-class assumption at work in the AAP's new policy—that all of us can be stay-at-home moms, or at least that we all have partners or other supportive people who will come in and nurture our kids when we can't.

20   I say that before we need a policy like this one, we need more—and better—educational programming on TV. We need to end the culture of war and the media's glorification of violence. We need living-wage jobs. We need government salaries for stay-at-home moms so that all women have a real career choice. We do not need "media files" in our pediatricians' offices or more guilt about being bad parents. Give me a $175 a month house on the Monterey Peninsula and a commune of artists to share parenting responsibilities, and I'll kill my TV without any provocation from the AAP at all. Until then, long live Big Bird, *The Brady Bunch* and all their very special friends!

1. **What is the issue being discussed?**

   The AAP has released new guidelines for parents suggesting that children under the age of two not watch television. Moreover, they are recommending that pediatricians ask children about TV consumption at annual checkups.

2. **What is the author's point of view on the issue?**

   Although TV should not be the only interaction for children under the age of two, it can be beneficial and helpful for parenting.

3. **How does the author support her opinion? Is the material mostly fact or opinion?**

   She supports her opinion by relating personal experiences about TV viewing and pointing to societal issues. As a mother on welfare who was putting herself through college, she felt that television was a "helpful co-parent" and a "trusted friend." She used TV viewing as an opportunity to promote interaction, and develop critical thinking skills, important life skills. She explains how she believes this policy does not address the needs of lower socioeconomic groups and single parents and provides factual information about these flaws.

4. **What authorities does the author cite in supporting her opinion? Is her selection of authorities biased?**

   She cites Kenn Visel, President of the itsy bitsy Entertainment Co., Karen Reynolds, New York Publicity Manager of Nickelodeon, and Brown Johnson, Senior V. P. of Nick Jr. All of these people are involved in the same industry, the educational TV industry, and are likely to support children viewers.

5. **What is the author's purpose?**

   To persuade people that other issues need to be addressed before TV viewing for children under the age of 2 is curtailed, and that these policies do not address the needs of all of society.

6. **Who is the intended audience?**

   the general public

7. **What is the tone? Underline some words or phrases in the text that support your answer. How do you think her tone and use of language impacts her argument?**   *Answers will vary.*

   The tone is critical, sarcastic, and mocking. Her informal tone and slang diminishes the seriousness of the issue and the strength of her argument.

8. **Is the author biased?**

   Yes, for the most part she has her own slant. A critical reader will recognize the author's personal situation and reflections that lead to her views about American society.

9. **What is the author's credential or qualifications to write this article? Do you think they are substantial?**   *Answers will vary.*

   mother of a 4th grader

(*continued*)

(*continued*)

Answers will vary.

10. **How did this article make you feel? Do you agree with the author? Do you find her points convincing? Explain.**

_____

_____

_____

_____

_____

Let's Get Critical:
Making Inferences and Incorporating
Critical Reading Skills

wrap It Up

Throughout this chapter, you have learned about concepts that will help you be a more critical reader. The chart below lists questions you should ask yourself as you read to go beyond the literal meaning of the text to read critically.

Questions to Ask Yourself	Critical Reading Concept
■ Based on what the author states, what can I conclude? ■ What does the writer imply by omitting certain points? ■ What does he or she mean or suggest here?	This is **inference.**
■ Are there statements that are introduced by phrases like *according to, as reported in the . . . , cited in . . . , as documented in . . . ,* and *as published in . . . ?* ■ Can the information be verified or checked out in a reliable source?	These are **facts.**
■ Are there statements that start with words or phrases like *I think, feel, believe, suspect, conclude, assume, hope, wish . . . We must, should, need to, have to . . . It is important, imperative, necessary . . . The only way, the best way, the most important way . . . apparently, presumably, this suggests, possible, can, may,* and *might?*	These are **opinions.**
■ Why is the author writing this selection? ■ Does the author want to *inform* me about the topic, *teach* me how to do something, *entertain* me, or *persuade* me to go along with his or her opinion?	This is the **author's purpose.**

(*continued*)

■ For whom is the article or text intended? ■ Does the author write in a way that will appeal to a certain group or readership, or is it for the general population?	This is the writer's **intended audience.**
■ What mood or feeling is conveyed by the author's writing? ■ How do the writer's choice of words and the connotation of those words reflect his or her point of view about a topic or issue?	This is the **tone** of the writing.
■ What is the effect of the tone? ■ Does the author use a lot of positive words to describe his or her own viewpoint? ■ Does the author present opposing viewpoints? ■ Does the author use a lot of negative words to describe opposing viewpoints? ■ What impression does this language make? ■ Does the author include, omit or emphasize details?	These questions will help you discover **bias.**
■ Is there adequate information? ■ Is all the information relevant? ■ Is the author objective? ■ Does the author present updated information and current research? ■ Does the author have credentials in the field in which he/she is writing? ■ Does the author provide strong evidence to back up his/her point of view?	This will help you evaluate the **author's arguments.**

Key Terms

authority
bias
connotation
currency
denotation

fact
inference
intended audience
objectivity
opinion

purpose
relevancy
tone

chapter
8

What About the Web?
Evaluating Web Resources

In this chapter

you will learn to

- Use keywords for research
- Craft your thesis
- Evaluate web resources

Studying
Business

Businesses use resources (money, owners and managers, workers, locations, and facilities) to buy, make trades, and sell goods and services to make a profit. (Adapted from Jones 2007.) The study of business begins with an overview of what makes a business or organization function well. In subsequent course work, management skills, marketing strategies, financial analysis and statistics, business law, and accounting are studied. Additional courses in economics, international business, and business ethics are also important to take as students prepare for the world of work. As a business student, you should also have the ability to communicate concise written and verbal information.

Business in the Workplace

This is a very broad area of study, so someone with a degree in business can pursue a career in a variety of occupations ranging from finance, management, human resources, marketing, and information systems to hotel administration. Some of the jobs available in the field include salesperson, manager, human resource manager, market researcher, public relations representative, financial analyst, customer service representative, or real estate broker.

Using the Internet for Research

The Internet provides a wealth of information on just about anything you can possibly imagine. Do you want to find out what's happening on your favorite soap opera, learn how to repair your DVD player, locate the best price for an iPod, or read a review on a new movie release? Just type in your subject on Google, or your favorite search engine, and everything you want to know will be at your fingertips. And if you are like most college students, you will also rely heavily on the Internet for your research.

Before You Start: Select a Topic

Before you sit down in front of your computer and begin your research, you should think about the topic you want to explore. In most college course work, your professors provide you with a list of recommended topics related to the disciplines you are studying. Your job is to develop these subjects, explore your own thinking, and draw your own conclusions.

Starting Your Research: Use Keywords

Suppose you've been thinking about researching the topic *sexual harassment in the workplace* for a final paper you will be submitting in your business course. If you begin with this broad topic, the results from the Internet will be too general, and you will have to sift through all the hits to find relevant information. If you add other words or phrases to the general topic, your results will get smaller and get you to the sites that have more specific information: These words are called keywords.

Let's see what happens as you narrow down your search and use keywords. Here are the results of a keyword Google Search:

- *sexual harassment, workplace*: 1,940,000 hits. Wow!
- *sexual harassment, workplace, prevention*: 1,040,000 hits. Whoa!
- *sexual harassment, workplace, prevention, employer's role*: 48,100 hits. Whew!
- *sexual harassment, same-sex, workplace, employer's role, prevention, liability*: 36,000 hits. Getting Better!

That's still a lot of information to sort through. But at least it's a better starting point.

If you need some assistance finding just the right keywords to conduct your search, ask your college librarian. He or she can direct you to an Advanced Search. In an Advanced Search you can identify specific words or phrases to be included or omitted from your search, as well as domains you would like to access.

Crafting a Thesis Statement

Now you can begin to craft a good thesis statement. As you recall from Chapter 3, a thesis statement is the topic and what *you* think about the topic; it shows your conclusion about the subject and requires you to take a stand or present a viewpoint. Because Internet research can be quite over-whelming, starting with a strong thesis statement will also help you man-age your research and save you a lot of time. From your research on your narrowed-down topic, you may decide to craft the following thesis statement:

> It's the employer's responsibility to investigate sexual harassment in the workplace.

Evaluating Web Resources

After you've created a thesis, you are ready to use the Web for your research. But wait—not only do you need to know how to locate information on the Web—you also have to evaluate it.

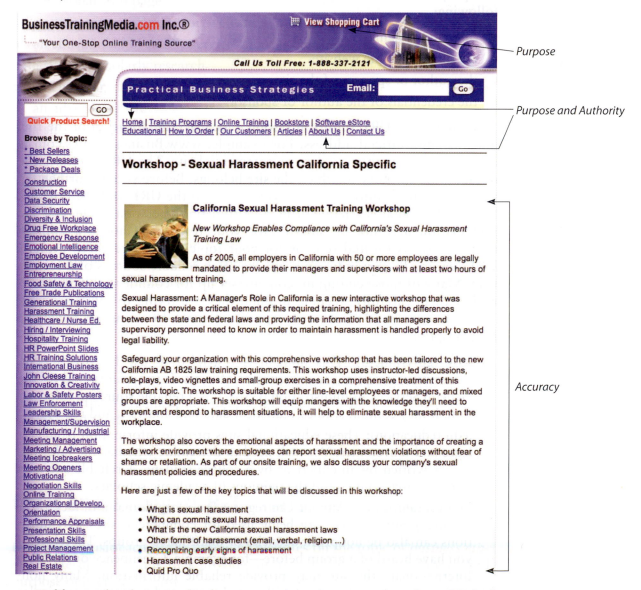

Unlike textbooks, periodicals, or magazines that are written by published authors or experts, anyone can post material on the Web, so it is essential

(continued)

Answers will vary.

1. www.web-miner.com/businessethics.htm

   dead link, site cannot be found

2. www.business-ethics.com

   online magazine, formally available in print media, does not mention individual authors but is linked to reputable online sources such as Bloomberg.com, inform

3. www.wikipedia.org/wikiBusiness-ethics

   online encyclopedia, no credentials required to make submissions and modifications can be made daily, inform

4. www.management.about.com/od/businessethics

   part of New York Times, network experts, requires professional experience and advanced education, inform

5. www.societyforbusinessethics.org

   international organization, provides a forum for research and teaching, contains a mission statement, board members are all college faculty, inform

Currency

Currency refers to the date on which information was posted or to the last time a web page was updated. Evaluate the currency of a website by checking out the following:

- the date on the website
- the date the page was revised
- the status of the links

You should also check to see if links on the page work; this will let you know if the author or sponsor is still maintaining the page. If a link leads to an *error message,* then be cautious about the quality of the information on the original page. Depending on your subject, it may be important to have current information. You certainly don't want to include outdated details on a current issue or evolving topic from the news.

try it and apply it! 8-2   Checking Out Currency

Directions: Visit each of the following websites that contain information about the topic of *sexual harassment.* Locate the details that will provide information about the currency of the website, and write them below.

1. www.eeoc.gov:

   U.S. Equal Employment Opportunity Commission March 4, 2008.

2. www.employer-employee.com:

   Sells business software and books, only a copyright date—1997–2007, but no indication of

   recent updates

3. www.lawguru.com:

   free advice from a network of lawyers, only a copyright date—1996–2007, but no

   recent updates

4. www.abanet.org:

   American Bar Association, provides law school accreditation, current references to news

   developments and upcoming meetings and conferences

5. www.oeo.od.nih.gov:

   The Office of Equal Opportunity and Diversity Management, contains current documents and

   reports of current news developments

Accuracy

Here are guide questions you can use to help you evaluate the accuracy of a website.

1. How does the information compare to what you already know?
2. Are opinions or facts offered?
3. What is the tone of the text? Do you detect bias?
4. Does the author include a list of works cited?
5. Are there any spelling or grammatical errors?

Unlike printed resources, web resources are less likely to have editors or fact-checkers, so it is a good idea to compare what you've already studied in your textbooks, learned from your lectures, or read about in periodicals or newspapers to the information on the Web. If information on the site does not match information obtained from other sources, it may be inaccurate. You should also evaluate the material in the same way you learned to evaluate printed material in Chapter 7: distinguish between fact and opinion, identify the tone, be alert to connotations of the language used, and look for signs of bias. You should also check for grammatical or spelling errors, which can indicate that a site is a less-reliable source. If the information meets all the preceding criteria, then you can feel comfortable about including it in your research. Otherwise, explore other Internet sites and evaluate them in the same way.

Checklist for Evaluating Websites

1. Does the URL contain any information that gives you a clue to its source?

Check the ones that apply.

_____ An individual's name

_____ The name of a familiar company, organization or institution

_____ No/cannot find information on site

2. What is the domain? Check all that apply.

_____ .gov

_____ .edu

_____ .com

_____ .org

_____ Other _____

3. Do you think another domain would provide you with better information?

_____ Yes   Which one(s)? _____

_____ No   Why? _____

4. What is the purpose of the website? Check all those that apply.

_____ Personal page

_____ Forum for an organization

_____ Forum for ideas or opinions

_____ To sell a product or provide a service

_____ Entertainment

Other _____

5. Is the author of the page mentioned?

_____ Yes

_____ No

6. Are the qualifications of the author or group listed?

_____ Yes

_____ No

7. Do they indicate the author is an expert?

_____ Yes   What are his/her qualifications? _____

_____ No   _____

8. Is there a date on the page, or has the page been updated?

_____ Yes _____

_____ No

9. Are the links broken?

_____ Yes

_____ No

10. Is the article related to your topic?

_____ Yes

_____ No

11. Does the information appear to be similar to what you have read on other sites?

_____ Yes

_____ No

12. Does the information match what you already know?

_____ Yes

_____ No

13. Are opinions or facts offered?

_____ Yes

_____ No

14. Can you discern tone or connotations that indicate bias?

_____ Yes

_____ No

15. Are there any spelling or grammatical mistakes?

_____ Yes

_____ No

16. Does the author include a list of works cited?

_____ Yes

_____ No

17. Based on your responses to this survey, is this a good source for your college research?

_____ Yes

_____ No

Why?

_____

_____

_____

try it and apply it! 8-3   Evaluating Websites

Directions: Evaluate each of the web pages listed below that deal with the topic of *how employers can prevent sexual harassment in the workplace*, using the Checklist for Evaluating Websites. Then, based on your evaluation, answer the following question: Which site(s) is the most appropriate for a college research project?

(continued)

(*continued*)

1. www.usual.com/article4.htm
2. www.internet.freedom.org
3. www.rense.com/general67/FRED
4. www.fcc/gov/mediagoals
5. www.andrew.cmu.edu/user/jmrobins/milieux/index2.htm

The Value of the Internet

Internet material can be valuable for academic research. The number of resources on the World Wide Web continues to grow. Academic and scholarly journals and articles, news organizations offering up-to-date developments, and online encyclopedias are being added daily. However, effective evaluation of online resources must be part of your college research; otherwise, you may include unreliable or inaccurate information. You also shouldn't limit your research to digitized sources. Print sources are still lining the shelves of your college library. In fact, some of them may be more relevant to your research. More importantly, a trip to your library can help you enlist research specialists and college librarians, who can help guide you to all kinds of valid resources, including the Web.

What About the Web?
Evaluating Web Resources

- Remember, not all resources on the Internet are created equal.
- Great variations exist in the quality of the Web resources.
- Evaluate the strengths and weaknesses of the resources.
- Check the purpose and authority, currency, and accuracy of each site.
- When in doubt, leave it out.
- Avoid plagiarism.

Key Terms

accuracy	credentials	purpose
author	currency	sponsor
authority	domain	

Lights, Camera, and Action!

Rehearsing the Information

In this chapter

you will learn to

- Paraphrase
- Outline
- Summarize
- Use visuals to organize information

Studying
Anthropology

Anthropology is the study of how human beings have evolved through time. It traces the biological, cultural, and linguistic (language) development of humans from their most primitive ancestors up to the modern day. Anthropology explores the roles of men and women, family structures, child-rearing practices, kinship, marriage, and aging in cultures around the world. The study of human behavior helps students gain a broad understanding of cultural diversity.

Anthropology in the Workplace

Students who complete a degree in anthropology acquire an appreciation of other cultures and learn the importance of record keeping, paying attention to details, and clear thinking. As a result, they are prepared for many career paths. In the field of education, a graduate may seek a job as an ESL teacher, a bilingual program specialist, an academic advisor, a career or family service counselor, or a librarian. In today's global market, many opportunities exist in international trade. Many companies are looking for people who can help them learn how their products will be perceived abroad. A foundation in anthropology can also be a springboard to more advanced studies that lead to an MBA (Masters in Business Administration) or to a career in medicine or the law.

207

Rehearsing Information

Before a performance, whether it's the opening night of a play, an important business presentation, or an apology to a friend or colleague, it's important to remember what you want to say. In college, your performance in class or on tests always requires a strategy to recall important details you have read in your textbooks and other academic resources. Three important ways to **rehearse** or review information from college reading are outlining, mapping, and summarizing. The method you select will often depend upon the nature of the reading material, the purpose for reviewing textbook information, or your preference for a particular strategy. All three strategies require you to paraphrase.

Paraphrasing

Paraphrasing is restating an author's material using your own words. It shows your understanding of the reading material and helps you to recall important information for exams. In fact, according to research, putting material into your own words actually helps you remember it better.

Here are some tips for writing a paraphrase.

Writing a Paraphrase

1. Read through the entire section or paragraph you want to paraphrase so that you understand the context.
2. Read the sentence you will be paraphrasing to get a general understanding of it.
3. Identify the main idea of the sentence.
4. Note key details that support the main idea of the sentence.
5. Use synonyms or phrases that have the same meaning as the word you are paraphrasing.
6. Note the grammatical structure of the original sentence and consider rearranging it while maintaining the author's meaning.
7. Look away from the text and try paraphrasing what you have just read.
8. Check the accuracy of your paraphrase by substituting it for the sentence in the text. It should make sense and fit in with the rest of the ideas.
9. Do not add your own opinion.
10. Acknowledge the source of your paraphrase.

Here's an excerpt from the opening paragraph of Chapter 1 in *Anthropology: The Exploration of Human Diversity,* followed by a sample paraphrase.

What Is Anthropology?

Anthropologists study human beings wherever and whenever they find them—in Northern Kenya, a Turkish café, a Mesopotamian tomb, or a North American shopping mall. Anthropology is the exploration of human diversity in time and space. Anthropology studies the whole of the human condition: past, present, and future: biology, society, language, and culture.

(From Kottak 2008)

Example of Paraphrase

Experts in anthropology study people from all over the world, under a variety of circumstances, and throughout history. The study of anthropology examines how humans react to and cope with life events and the differences among people in terms of their biological, sociological, linguistic, and cultural attributes.

You can see how the main ideas were included, some repetitious examples were excluded, and the language was simplified and restructured.

try it and apply it! 9-1   Paraphrasing

Directions: Read the following excerpt. Then reread each numbered sentence and write a paraphrase of it in the space provided.

What Makes Us Human?

Bipedalism

(1) . . . Bipedalism—upright, two-legged locomotion—is the key feature differentiating early homonins (all human species that ever existed) from the apes. African fossil discoveries suggest that homonin bipedalism is more than five million years old.

(continued)

(continued)

(2) Bipedalism is considered to be the adaptation to an open grassland or savanna habitat (grassland with scattered trees). (3) Scientists have suggested several advantages of bipedalism in such an environment: the ability to see over long grass, to carry items back to home base, and to reduce the body's exposure to solar radiation. (4) The fossil and archaeological records confirm that upright bipedal locomotion preceded stone tool manufacture and expansion of the homonin brain. (5) However, although the earliest homonins could move bipedally through open country during the day, they also preserved enough of an apelike anatomy to make them good climbers. They could take to the trees to sleep at night and to escape terrestrial predators.

(Adapted from Kottak 2008)

1. Bipedalism—upright two-legged locomotion—is the key feature differentiating early homonins (all human species that ever existed, except chimps and gorillas) from the apes.

   The main characteristic that distinguishes the human species from apes is that humans walk on two legs and apes do not.

2. Bipedalism is considered to be an adaptation to an open grassland or savanna habitat.

   One explanation for walking upright is a changed need that required humans to learn how to live in open environments.

3. Scientists have suggested several advantages of bipedalism in such an environment: the ability to see over long grass, to carry items back to home base, and to reduce the body's exposure to solar radiation.

   Based on research, scientists believe that the benefits of bipedalism include navigating through high grass, transporting material back home, and protecting the body from the sun's heat.

4. The fossil and archaeological records confirm that upright bipedal locomotion preceded stone tool manufacture and the expansion of the homonin brain.

   According to findings, bipedalism occurred before homonins learned how to make tools and prior to the increase in brain size.

5. However, although the earliest homonins could move bipedally through open country during the day, they also preserved enough of an apelike anatomy to make them good climbers. They could take to the trees to sleep at night and to escape terrestrial predators.

   During the day, the homonins walked upright through the open plains, and at night because of their apelike framework, they were still able to climb up the trees, where they slept safe from wild animals.

Keep this in mind

- Always refer back to the selection.
- Do not use paraphrasing to express your opinion on the topic.
- Focus on explaining what the author says or means using your own words rather than merely rearranging the existing words of the author.
- Use paraphrasing when you take notes, outline, map, and summarize.

Outlining

Outlining is a writing technique that shows the hierarchy of main ideas and supporting details in a piece of writing. In other words, it shows the importance of details and how one idea is related to another. This strategy helps you organize information from textbooks and assists you in studying and recalling what is most important to know. It is also a good way to synthesize information from several reading sources or from your lecture notes and textbook. This method works well for students who learn material in an orderly and sequential manner. Outlines are a good way to organize information from disciplines that focus on process, time order, or classification.

The outline should be simple. The best way to do this is to focus on the main ideas and corresponding details. Include only what you think you will be required to remember. Don't forget to paraphrase or use your own words. To create an effective outline, follow these guidelines.

Creating an Outline

1. Read the text carefully, and then annotate it.
2. Create an outline title that reflects the overall topic of the selection.
3. List the main ideas you highlighted or annotated.
4. List the major supporting details for each main idea.
5. Include minor supporting details (facts, dates, or examples) the author uses to provide support for major supporting details. Remember your outline should show the importance and relationship among ideas.
6. Indicate the connection between main ideas and the details that support them using Roman numerals (I, II, III), capital letters (A, B, C), Arabic numbers (1, 2, 3), and lowercase letters (a, b, c).

Here is an example of the outline format:

Title

I. First Major Topic

   A. First Main Idea

      1. First Major Supporting Detail

         a. First Minor Supporting Detail

         b. Second Minor Supporting Detail

      2. Second Major Supporting Detail

   B. Second Main Idea

II. Second Major Topic

try it and apply it! 9-2   Outlining

Directions: Knowing the meaning of these words will help you understand the following selection on bipedalism.

- **arboreal**—pertaining to trees
- **arid**—extremely dry
- **gait**—a manner of stepping, walking or running
- **Miocene**—the geologic time period that began about 25 million years ago (and lasted approximately 18 million years) when grazing mammals became widespread
- **savanna**—grassland area with scattered trees

Answers may vary.

Now read the selection and annotate it as suggested in Chapter 2. Then complete the outline that follows.

What Makes Us Human?

Bipedalism

. . . Bipedalism—upright two-legged locomotion—is the key feature differentiating early homonins (all human species that ever existed) from the apes. African fossil discoveries suggest that homonin bipedalism is more than five million years old.

One explanation for bipedalism centers on environmental changes that swept Africa more than five million years ago. During the late Miocene, as the global climate became cooler and drier, grasslands in sub-Saharan Africa expanded. The rain forests contracted, shrinking the habitat available to the arboreal primates (Wilford 1995). Also, at the very same time, a geological shift deepened the Rift valley, which runs through Ethiopia, Kenya, and Tanzania. The sinking of the valley thrust up mountains.

This left the land west of the valley more humid and arboreal, while the east became more arid and dominated by the savannas. The common ancestors of homonins and chimpanzees were divided as a result. Those adapting to the humid west became the chimpanzee family. Those in the east had to forge a new life in an open environment (Coppens 1994).

At least one branch of the eastern primates—those that became homonins—ventured more and more into open country seeking food, but retreating into the trees to escape predators and to sleep at night. To move about more efficiently and perhaps also to keep a lookout above the grasses for food or predators, these primates started standing upright and walking on two legs. Presumably, this adaptation enhanced their chances of surviving and passing on genes that favored this stance and gait, leading eventually to bipedal homonins (Wilford 1995).

Yet another factor may have contributed to bipedalism. Early homonins may have found the intense tropical heat of the savannas very stressful. Most savanna-dwelling animals have built-in ways of protecting their brains from over-heating as their body temperature rises during the day. This isn't true of humans, nor is it likely to have been true of early homonins. The only way we can protect our brains is by keeping our bodies cool. Could it be true that early homonins stood up to cool off? Studies with scale models of primates suggest that quadrapedalism exposes the body to 60 percent more solar radiation than does bipedalism. The upright body could catch the cooler breeze above the ground (Wilford 1995).

(Adapted from Kottak 2008)

(continued)

(*continued*)

Outline Topic: What Makes Us Human?

I. Bipedalism—upright two-legged locomotion

   A. Key feature distinguishing homonins from apes

   B. *Fossil discoveries suggest bipedelism dates back to 5,000,000 years ago.*

II. Factors that may have led to bipedalism

   A. *environmental changes in Africa*

      1. Rain forests contracted, so primates who lived in trees had no place to live.

      2. Geological shift changed climate to humid or dry and caused split.

         a. *Chimpanzee family adapted to humid climate.*

         b. *Homonins adapted to open and dry environment.*

      3. Homonins began to stand upright.

         a. *to move about better to get food or look out for predators*

         b. *to improve chances of survival*

   B. Tropical heat caused stress for early homonins.

      1. *needed to protect brains by cooling off bodies*

      2. May have stood up to lower body temperature

         a. *Four-legged animals are exposed to more sun.*

         b. *upright body exposed to cooler breezes above the ground*

try it and apply it! 9-3   Outlining

Directions: The following excerpt is about other clues about the development of our human ancestors. Annotate the reading and complete the outline that follows.

Teeth

One example of an early homonin trait that has been lost during subsequent human evolution is the big back teeth. (Indeed a pattern of overall dental reduction has characterized human evolution.) As they adapted to the savanna, with its gritty tough and fibrous vegetation, it was adaptively advantageous for early homonins to have large back teeth and thick tooth enamel. This permitted thorough chewing of fibrous

vegetation and mixture with salivary enzymes to permit digestion of foods that otherwise would not have been digestible.
The churning, rotary motion, associated with such chewing also favored reduction of the canines and first premolars
(bicuspids). These front teeth are much sharper and longer
in the apes than in early homonins. The apes use their sharp
self-honing teeth to pierce fruits. Males also flash their sharp
canines to intimidate and impress others, including potential
mates. Although bipedalism seems to have characterized the
human lineage since its split from the line leading to African
apes, many other "human" features came later. Yet other early
homonin features, such as large back teeth and thick enamel—
which we don't have now—offer clues about who was a
human ancestor back then.

(Adapted from Kottak 2008)

Outline Topic: Evolution of Teeth

I. Back teeth and thick tooth enamel—early homonin trait that has
disappeared.
   A. *used for chewing of thick and fibrous vegetation found in the savanna*
   B. *used with salivary enzymes to assist in digestion*
II. Front teeth
   A. *Churning and rotary motion used in eating of fibrous foods led to the reduction
      of canines and the development of first premolars*
   B. Sharper front teeth in apes
      1. *used to pierce fruits*
      2. *Males used canines to intimidate others and to attract potential mates.*

Keep this in mind

- Write an outline after you have read and annotated the material.
- Read over the highlighted sections and marginal notes, and then select
  the main ideas of each section.
- Use phrases or sentences, whichever you prefer, for each line in your outline.
- Use your *own* words.

Summarizing

Writing a summary is an important way to organize information after you've
finished an assigned textbook reading. It demonstrates your overall comprehension of what you've read. Textbook writers often include a concise

overview at the beginning of a chapter, and a summary section at the conclusion of a chapter. **Summaries** are shorter or condensed versions of important points in a longer passage and contain limited details. Writing brief summaries like these can be helpful when you are preparing for essay exams or when you need to write the key points of case studies, lab reports, or articles. However, your study summaries should be more comprehensive. Here are some tips for writing an effective summary.

Writing a Summary

1. Limit your summary to no more than one-quarter of the entire portion of the reading selection. Include the details that are important to help you remember the material. Like outlining, summarizing requires you to paraphrase an author's ideas.
2. After you've identified the topic, main idea, and supporting details from the highlighted and annotated portions of the reading, you are ready to write a summary.
3. Begin by writing a sentence that restates the overall main idea. This is called the thesis statement.
4. Then briefly state each major supporting detail.
5. Use transition words that show you understand the relationships between the details you are including.
6. Add minor supporting details that help explain each of the major supporting details.
7. If the author presents an opinion about one of the main points, you may want to include this in your summary; however, *do not include your own opinions*.
8. End your summary with a concluding sentence that restates the overall main idea.
9. Generally, your summary should follow the order of details presented by the author.

Here is a sample summary of *What Makes Us Human?* on pages 212–213.

Sample Summary

Bipedalism is the most significant distinguishing feature between humans and apes. Some anthropologists believe that environmental changes that caused the land in Africa to become cooler and drier contributed to a division between the early homonins and the chimpanzee family. The homonins moved into more open land. To protect themselves and seek nourishment in this new region, they began to stand upright. Another factor that may have led to bipedalism was the need of early humans to cool their bodies during the tropical heat of the savanna days. According to studies, standing upright exposes the body to less heat than moving on all fours.

In college, you may be asked to research news articles and write summaries of them. The details of a general news article answer *wh-* questions (who, what, when, where, why). The answers to these questions form the content of news stories that follow *journalistic style*.

To write a summary of a news article, answer the following *wh-* questions:

> ## Writing a Summary of a News Article
>
> **Who** is the article about?
> **What** happened?
> **When** did the event happen?
> **Where** did it occur?
> **Why** did it happen?
> **How** did it happen?

Your summary of the article will be a synthesis of the answers to these questions.

try it and apply it! 9-4   Creating a Summary of a News Article

Directions: Read this news article on bipedalism. Answer the *Wh-* questions, and then write a summary.   *Answers may vary.*

Humans Walk Upright to Conserve Energy

Randolph E. Shmid

Why did humans evolve to walk upright? Perhaps because it's just plain easier.

Make that "energetically less costly," in science-speak, and you have the conclusion of researchers who are proposing a likely reason for our modern gait.

Bipedalism—walking on two feet—is one of the defining characteristics of being human, and scientists have debated for years how it came about.

So, in the latest attempt to find an explanation, researchers trained five chimpanzees to walk on a treadmill while wearing masks that allowed measurement of their oxygen consumption. The chimps were measured both while walking upright and while moving on their legs and knuckles.

That measurement of the energy needed to move around was compared with similar tests on humans, and the results are published in this week's online edition of Proceedings of the National Academy of Sciences.

It turns out that humans walking on two legs use only one-quarter of the energy that chimpanzees use while knuckle-walking on four limbs. And the chimps, on average, use as much energy using two legs as they did when they used all four limbs.

There was, however, variability among chimpanzees in how much energy they used, and this difference corresponded to their different gaits and anatomy.

One of the chimps used less energy on two legs, one used about the same and the others used more, said David Raichlen, assistant professor of anthropology at the University of Arizona.

(continued)

(*continued*)

"What we were surprised at was the variation," he said in a telephone interview. "That was pretty exciting, because when you talk about how evolution works, variation is the bottom line. Without variation there is no evolution."

If an individual can save energy moving around and hunting and spend more of it on reproduction, "that's how you end up getting new species," he added.

Walking on two legs freed our arms, opening the door to manipulating the world, Raichlen said. "We think about the evolution of bipedalism as one of the first events that led hominids down the path to being human."

Theirs is the latest of several explanations for walking upright. Among the others have been the need to use the arms in food-gathering, the need to use the upper limbs to bring food to a mate and offspring, and raising the body higher to dissipate heat in the breeze.

Who: *researchers*

What: *found that efficiency may have led to bipedalism*

Where: *(doesn't say)*

When: *recently*

How: *conducted a study and tests*

Why: *to look for additional reasons for why humans walk upright*

Summary: *According to a July 16, 2007 Associated Press article,* Humans Walk Upright to Conserve Energy, *another factor may have led to bipedalism. Researchers have discovered that humans expend less energy walking on two legs than chimps do when they walk using both their hands and feet. The result of this research indicates that humans may have opted for walking upright because it was a much more efficient modality for hunting and mating.*

Keep this in mind

- Keep your summary simple, concise, and complete.
- Use the highlighted and annotated sections of your reading to identify key ideas and major supporting details.
- Add the minor supporting details that are the most important.
- Avoid adding your personal opinions or details not in the text.
- Use transition words to make your summary easy to understand.

Using Visuals to Organize Information

In addition to outlining and summarizing, you can also use visuals to organize information for study. Concept maps are especially helpful to map the relationships of ideas. Graphic organizers, such as tables, timelines, process diagrams, and Venn diagrams, illustrate specific organizational patterns.

Concept Maps

Creating a **concept map** is another way to show the relationship among ideas and concepts and to organize information from your textbooks. Maps are especially useful for visual learners and students with a creative flair. You can use different colored markers and draw pictures or symbols to help you remember what is important to learn. Unlike an outline, an entire textbook chapter can be mapped on *one* page. You can even add details from other sources, including supplementary reading materials, information you gleaned from a film or fieldtrip, and your class notes. Here are some simple steps for creating a map.

Creating a Concept Map

1. Begin with a page that has plenty of room.
2. Write the topic in the center of your page. You can use circles, squares, or rectangles to add details.
3. Select the main ideas and the major and minor supporting details from your reading, and arrange them so they radiate from the topic at the center.
4. There is no standard method, but lines or arrows are often used. Just make sure the minor supporting details are connected to the major supporting details, and the major supporting details to main ideas.

Here is a commonly used format for maps.

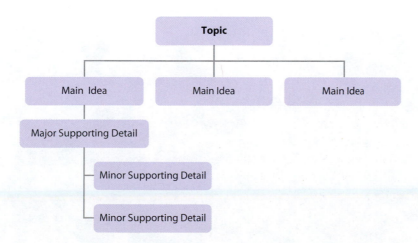

Here is a map for the passage *What Makes Us Human?*

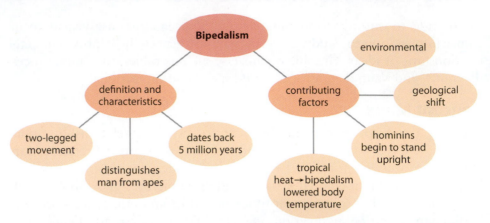

try it and apply it! 9-5   Creating a Concept Map

Directions: Knowing the meaning of the words below will help you understand the following selection on nuclear families.

- **authority**—control or influence
- **precedence**—priority

Nuclear Families

A nuclear family lasts as long as the parents and children remain together. Most people belong to at least two nuclear families at different times in their lives. They are born into

a family consisting of their parents and siblings. When they reach adulthood, they may marry and establish a nuclear family that includes the spouse and eventually the children. Since most societies permit divorce, some people establish more than one family through marriage.

Anthropologists distinguish between the *family of orientation* (the family in which one is born and grows up) and the *family of procreation* (formed when one marries and has children). From the individual's point of view, the critical relationships are with parents and siblings in the family of orientation and with spouse and children in the family of procreation.

In most societies, relations with nuclear members (parents, siblings and children) take precedence over relationships with other kin. Nuclear family organization is widespread but not universal, and its significance in society differs greatly from one place to another. In a few societies, such as the classic Nayar case, nuclear families are rare or nonexistent. In others, the nuclear family plays no special role in social life. The nuclear family is not always the basis of residence or authority . . .

(Adapted from Kottak 2008)

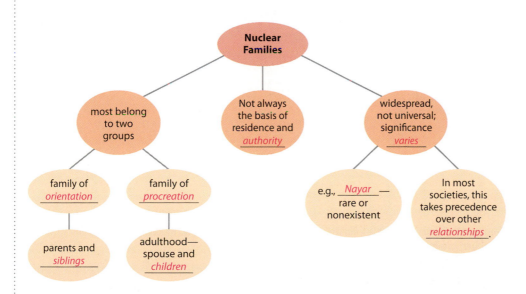

Tables

Tables are used to organize large amounts of information into an easy-to-read format; they are ideal for summarizing. They are often used at the end of textbook chapters to put all the information that has been discussed in an easy-to-read format. You can also use tables to compare and contrast. The following table compares and contrasts New World and Old World monkeys.

Knowing the meaning of the following terms will help you understand this table:

- **arboreal**—live in trees
- **frugivorous**—fruit-eating
- **monogamous**—having one mate during a period of time
- **prehensile**—adapted for grasping
- **semibrachiation**—arms rotate at the shoulder, as when pitching a baseball

	New World Monkeys	Old World Monkeys
Habitat	arboreal	arboreal terrestrial
Dental Formula	2–1–3–3	2–1–2–3
Nose Shape	flat	downward-facing
Locomotion	quadrupedal semibrachiation vertical clinging-leaping prehensile tail	quadrupedal semibrachiation
Diet	frugivorous insectivorous leaves	omnivorous leaf-eaters
Social Organization	multisex-multiage groups monogamous pairs plus offspring extended family groups mated pair and offspring female, male mates and offspring	multisex-multiage groups monogamous pairs plus offspring

Source: D. Applegate, CAL Learning Strategies Database, www.muskingum.edu/~cal/database/general/organization.html.

Timelines

Textbook authors use **timelines** to highlight dates or to show a sequence of events that has been discussed in the text. You can use timelines to rehearse information you learned in a chapter. For example, in psychology, you may be reading about the development of modern psychology. In history, you might be learning about the events that led up to World War I.

In the timeline that follows, you can see the chronology, or order of the events, of the development of cultural anthropology theory.

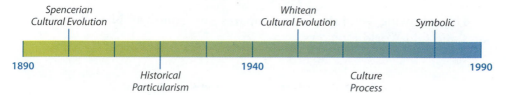

100 Years of Cultural Anthropology Theory

Spencerian Cultural Evolution — *Whitean Cultural Evolution* — *Symbolic*

1890 — 1940 — 1990

Historical Particularism — *Culture Process*

Source: D. Applegate, CAL Learning Strategies Database, www.muskingum.edu/~cal/database/general/organization.html.

Process Diagram or Flow Chart

A **process diagram,** or **flow chart,** helps you to visualize the steps in a process. Understanding processes is part of every college discipline. For example, in political science, you may learn how a bill becomes a law; in biology, you might study how the body digests food; and in criminal justice, you could find out what happens when a person is charged with a crime.

Here is a process diagram, or flow chart, showing the steps in the fall of the Aztec Empire during the early 1500s.

**Fall of the Aztec
1519–1521**

Legends and mysterious omens

↓

Arrival of Cortés

↓

Spanish unite with Aztec enemies

↓

Motecuhzoma killed by Spanish

↓

Two-year battle

↓

Aztec capital falls

Source: D. Applegate, CAL Learning Strategies Database, www.muskingum.edu/~cal/database/general/organization.html.

Venn Diagrams

A **Venn diagram** is an effective way to show comparison and contrast. Information is arranged within two large intersecting circles, each one labeled with the name of the concepts you are comparing. In the intersecting, or overlapping, part you write the similar attributes or characteristics of each and in the nonintersecting parts of the circles, you write the differences between them.

The following Venn diagram compares and contrasts New World monkeys and Old World monkeys.

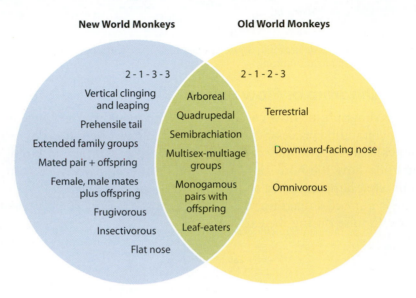

New World Monkeys

2 - 1 - 3 - 3

Vertical clinging and leaping

Prehensile tail

Extended family groups

Mated pair + offspring

Female, male mates plus offspring

Frugivorous

Insectivorous

Flat nose

Arboreal

Quadrupedal

Semibrachiation

Multisex-multiage groups

Monogamous pairs with offspring

Leaf-eaters

Old World Monkeys

2 - 1 - 2 - 3

Terrestrial

Downward-facing nose

Omnivorous

Source: D. Applegate, CAL Learning Strategies Database, www.muskingum.edu/~cal/database/general/organization.html.

Keep this in mind

- Create your graphic organizers after reading and annotating a selection.
- Select the type of organizer that best suits your purpose.
- Allow enough space for details.
- Use any shapes you want. Be creative and have some fun.
- Use colored ink, special print, or illustrations to enhance retention of the material.

try it and apply it! 9-6   Using Graphic Organizers

Directions: Read each of the following passages about Native Americans. Complete the graphic organizer for each reading selection.

1. A Chronology of North American Archaeology

Ever since the discovery of the New World, discoverers, colonists and members of European society all began to ponder the history of the Native American and the nature of their culture. This gave rise to the fields of anthropology and archaeology. The beginning of these fields is one in which discovery was accidental and answers to questions were almost always speculative.

In 1589, Jose de Acosta published *Historia Natural y Moral de las Indias*. He concluded that Native Americans had arrived on this continent by means of a land route from Asia. In the 1780s, Thomas Jefferson conducted the first systematic excavation of mounds of land in which he discovered an ancient Indian burial place. During the next ten years as colonists moved westward, many more land sites were uncovered, revealing remnants of stone weapons used by Native Americans. In the early 1800s, conflicting research was published concerning the origin of the mounds. First, Caleb Atwater theorized that some of the excavations were not built by the current Native Americans or by their ancestors. Then in 1817, Dr. McCollah stated that it was, in fact, the Native Americans who created the mounds.

(www.mnsu.edu/emuseum/archaeology/archaeology/timeline/history.html)

Directions: Complete the following timeline.

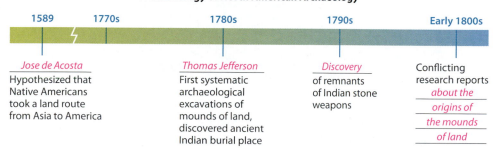

A Chronology of North American Archaeology

1589	1770s	1780s	1790s	Early 1800s
Jose de Acosta		*Thomas Jefferson*	*Discovery*	Conflicting research reports
Hypothesized that Native Americans took a land route from Asia to America		First systematic archaeological excavations of mounds of land, discovered ancient Indian burial place	of remnants of Indian stone weapons	*about the origins of the mounds of land*

2. Rites of Passage

All rites of passage, the customs associated with the transition from one stage of life to another, have three stages: separation, liminality, and incorporation. The liminal state is a transitional stage, which is characterized by uncertainty, disorientation, and openness. The traditional vision quests of Native Americans, particularly the Plain Indians,

(*continued*)

(*continued*)

illustrate the rites of passage for young men. When the youth moves from boyhood to adulthood, he temporarily separates himself from his community. After a period of isolation in the wilderness, often involving (or featuring) fasting and drug consumption, the young man sees a vision, which becomes his guardian spirit. He then returns to his community as an adult. In contemporary cultures, the rites of passage may include confirmations, baptisms, and bar and bat mitzvahs.

(Adapted from Kottak 2008)

Directions: Complete the following process diagram.

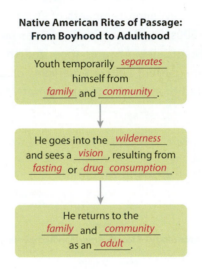

Native American Rites of Passage: From Boyhood to Adulthood

Youth temporarily _separates_ himself from _family_ and _community_.

↓

He goes into the _wilderness_ and sees a _vision_, resulting from _fasting_ or _drug consumption_.

↓

He returns to the _family_ and _community_ as an _adult_.

3. Recurrent Gender Patterns

According to the cross-cultural data from 185 randomly selected societies on the division of labor, male activities tended to include activities such as hunting, fishing, clearing land, preparing the soil, and the building of boats and homes. Women, on the other hand, generally gathered firewood and wild vegetables, made dairy products, spun clothing, did the laundry, fetched water and cooked meals. In some cultures, women engaged in activities that were more often relegated to men. That is, although there is a general tendency for men to build boats, in one Native American group, known as the Hidatsa, it was the women who made the boats to cross the Missouri River. Another exception is the Pawnee women, who worked wood. This was the only Native American group that assigned this activity to women.

(Adapted from Kottak 2008)

Directions: Complete the following table.

Generalities in the Division of Labor by Gender, Based on Data from 185 Societies

Generally Male Activities	Male and Female "Swing" Activities	Generally Female Activities
• Hunting • _Fishing_ • Clearing _land_ • Preparing _the soil_ • Building of _boats_ and _homes_	• Making _boats_ • Working with _wood_	• Gathering firewood and _wild vegetables_ • Making _dairy_ products • _Spinning_ clothes • Doing _laundry_ • Fetching _water_ • Cooking _meals_

4. Marital Rights and Same-Sex Marriages

Legal same-sex marriages could easily give each spouse rights to the other spouse's labor and products. Some societies have allowed marriage between members of the same biological sex, who may, however, be considered to belong to a different, socially constructed gender. Several Native American groups had figures known as *berdaches,* representing a third gender (Murray and Roscoe 1998). These were biological men who assumed many of the mannerisms, behavior patterns, and tasks of women. Sometimes *berdaches* married men, who shared the products of their labor from hunting and traditional male roles, as the *berdaches* fulfilled the traditional wifely role. Also, in some Native American cultures, a marriage of a "manly hearted woman" (a third or fourth gender) to another woman brought traditional male-female division of the labor to the household. The manly woman hunted and did other male tasks, while the wife played the traditional female role.

(Adapted from Kottak 2008)

Directions: Complete the following Venn diagram.

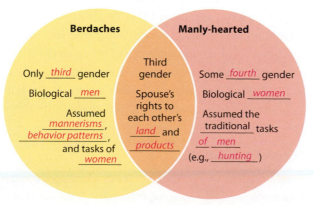

Marital Rights and Same-Sex Marriages Among Native Americans

Berdaches

Only _third_ gender

Biological _men_

Assumed _mannerisms_, _behavior patterns_, and tasks of _women_

Third gender

Spouse's rights to each other's _land_ and _products_

Manly-hearted

Some _fourth_ gender

Biological _women_

Assumed the traditional tasks _of_ _men_ (e.g., _hunting_)

try it and apply it! 9-7   Rehearsing the Information

Directions: In the following passages, the author examines the diversity of types of communication, including call systems, sign language, nonverbal communication, and spoken language. After you read each excerpt, decide on the best way to organize the information in it. Create an outline, draw a concept map, or write a summary for each on separate sheets of paper.

Answers will vary.

1. Call Systems

Only humans speak. No other animal has the complexity of language. The natural communication systems of other primates (monkeys and apes) are *call systems.* These vocal systems consist of a limited number of sounds—*calls*—that are produced only when particular environmental stimuli are encountered. Such calls may be varied in intensity and duration, but they are much less flexible than language because they are automatic and can't be combined. When primates encounter food and danger simultaneously, they can make only one call. They can't combine the calls for food and danger into a single utterance, indicating that both are present. At some point in human evolution, however, our ancestors began to combine calls and to understand the combinations. The number of calls also expanded, eventually becoming too great to be transmitted even partly through genes. Communication came to rely on learning. . . .

2. Sign Language

More recent experiments have shown that apes can learn to use, if not speak, true language (Miles 1983). Several apes have learned to converse with people through other means than speech. One such communication is American Sign Language, or ASL, which is widely used by deaf and mute Americans. ASL uses a limited number of basic gesture units that are analogous to sounds in spoken language. These units combine to form words and larger units of meaning.

The first chimpanzee to learn ASL was Washoe, a female. Captured in West Africa, Washoe was acquired by R. Allen Gardner and Beatrice Gardner, scientists at the University of Nevada in Reno, in 1966, when she was a year old. Four years later, she moved to Norman, Oklahoma, to a converted farm that had become the Institute for Primate Studies. Washoe revolutionized the discussion of language-learning of apes. At first she lived in a trailer and heard no spoken language. The researchers always used ASL to communicate with each other in her presence. The chimp gradually acquired a vocabulary of more than 100 signs representing English words. At the age of two, Washoe began to combine as many as five signs into rudimentary sentences such as "you, me, go out, hurry."

3. Nonverbal Communication

Language is the principal means of human communication, but it isn't the only one we use. We communicate when we transmit information about ourselves to others and receive information from them. Our facial expressions, bodily stances, gestures, and

movements, even if unconscious, convey information and are part of our communi-cation styles. Deborah Tannen (1990) discusses the differences in the communication styles of American men and women, and her comments go beyond language. She notes that American girls and women tend to look directly at each other when they talk, whereas American boys and men do not. Males are more likely to look straight ahead rather than turn and make eye contact with someone, especially another man, seated beside them. Also, in conversational groups, American men tend to relax and sprawl out. American women may adapt a similar relaxed posture in all-female groups, but when they are with men, they tend to draw in their limbs and adopt a tighter stance. . . .

4. The Structure of Language

The scientific study of spoken language (descriptive linguistics) involves several interrelated areas of analysis: phonology, morphology, lexicon, and syntax. *Phonol-ogy*, the study of speech sounds, considers which sounds are present and significant in a given language. *Morphology* studies the forms in which sounds combine to form morphemes—words and their meaningful parts. Thus, the word *cats* would be analyzed as containing two morphemes: *cat*, the name for a kind of animal, and *–s*, a morpheme indicating plurality. A language's *lexicon* is a dictionary containing all its morphemes

(continued)

chapter 10

Searching Other Sources:
Reading Across the Genres

In this chapter

you will learn how to read efficiently and effectively across the genres

- Newspaper articles
- Essays
- Academic journals
- Primary resources
- Novels

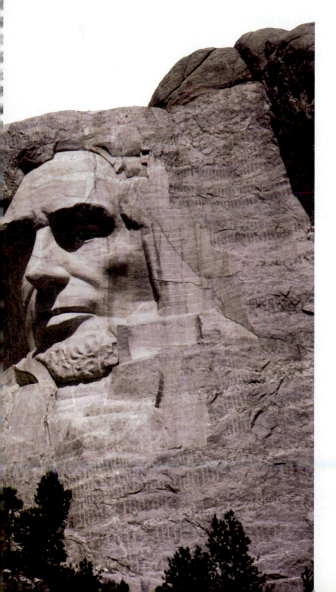

Studying
History

History involves study and research into major social, political, cultural, and economic events of the past and provides a perspective on events that have shaped the contemporary world. It includes the broad study of our own Western civilization—its birth, growth, and expansion. It also explores non-Western cultures, helping students to develop a global awareness and understanding of what has shaped our world today. Students who major in history may elect to take courses in the foundations of modern Western civilization in the ancient and medieval world, the historical forces, events, and movements that shaped the world in the nineteenth and twentieth centuries, the history of the United States, Native American history, African American history, the role of women in history, the history of diverse ethnic groups, and even the history of sports.

History in the Workplace

Options for a person with a BA in history include educator, researcher, communicator or editor, information manager, advocate, businessperson, consultant, congressional aide, editor, foreign service officer, foundation staffer, information specialist, intelligence agent, journalist, legal assistant, lobbyist, personnel manager, public relations staffer, researcher, or teacher.

233

Reading Across the Genres

Although understanding textbooks is an essential part of your college course work, it is also important to develop reading strategies to aid in understanding and learning from other reading genres. Searching other sources or categories of reading material, such as news articles, essays, academic journals, primary sources, and literature can help you learn more about your course work and provide important opportunities for enriching your knowledge on a topic, concept, or issue.

- **Newspaper articles** furnish up-to-date information.
- **Essays** offer different viewpoints and perspectives.
- **Academic journals** discuss current research.
- **Primary sources** give first-hand accounts of events.
- **Literature,** especially novels, provides a window into a time period, including specific aspects of society, culture, economics, and politics.

In this chapter, you will find some helpful reading tips to assist you in understanding and using additional sources of information to enhance your reading and study. Start by reading the following textbook excerpt taken from *A Survey: American History* (Brinkley 2007). It discusses McDonald's place in American history and its impact throughout the world.

Fast Food

The automobile also transformed the landscape of retailing. It encouraged the creation of fast-food chains, many of which began with drive-in restaurants, where customers could be served and eat in their cars. The first drive-in restaurant (Royce Hailey's Pig Stand) opened in Dallas in 1921, followed later in the decade by White Tower, the first fast-food company to create franchises. Ray Kroc's McDonald's opened its first outlets in Des Plaines, Illinois, and southern California in 1955. Five years later, there were 228 McDonald's outlets; and over the decades that followed, McDonald's franchises spread throughout the nation and abroad—making the "golden arches" the most recognizable symbol of food in the world.

(Adapted from Brinkley 2007)

From this paragraph, you learned how the automobile-centered landscape of post-war America changed many patterns of life, including eating. McDonald's was originally established as a drive-in restaurant and later developed into a national franchise that was eventually introduced into the global market.

Now explore other genres to learn more about McDonald's, its marketing strategies (from a news article), opposing viewpoints (from an essay), its history (from an academic journal article), and first-hand accounts (from primary sources).

Reading Newspaper Articles

If you are looking for the most current developments in your area of study, you might choose to read a newspaper. News articles are generally reliable, up-to-date sources on topics of current interest. A newspaper is a current periodical that is published usually daily. You will find that newspapers are written on different levels and for different audiences. Generally, for college research, select more fact-based ones, such as *The New York Times, The Wall Street Journal,* or *The Washington Post.*

Following are some tips for reading and understanding newspaper articles.

Tips for Understanding Newspaper Articles

- Newspaper articles are written for the general public.

- The author's purpose for writing a news article is to inform.

- The most important information is presented first. This can be found in the headline and the lead (first and/or second) paragraph(s). They provide objective information about the news event.

- The remainder of the article is designed to provide details to help the reader understand more specifically what happened.

- Sometimes, the writer will include details from an interview. This provides the reader with subjective information. A critical reader has to distinguish between fact and opinion, detect the tone of the speaker, and recognize the speaker's point of view or bias.

Here is a graphic representation of a news article. It illustrates journalistic style, which goes from the main point to specific details.

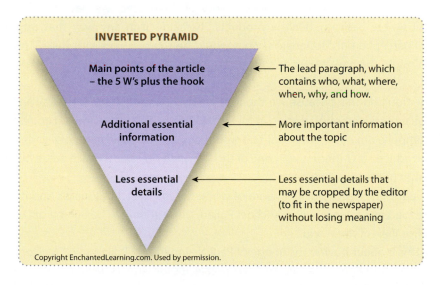

INVERTED PYRAMID

Main points of the article – the 5 W's plus the hook ← The lead paragraph, which contains who, what, where, when, why, and how.

Additional essential information ← More important information about the topic

Less essential details ← Less essential details that may be cropped by the editor (to fit in the newspaper) without losing meaning

Copyright EnchantedLearning.com. Used by permission.

Use these questions to guide you in understanding news articles.

1. *Who* is the article about?
2. *What* happened?
3. *When* did it happen?
4. *Where* did it happen?
5. *Why* did it happen?
6. *How* did it happen?

try it and apply it! 10-1 **Reading and Understanding a News Article**

Directions: Read this newspaper article about McDonald's. Then answer the questions that follow. Write your answers in the spaces provided.

"McDonald's Tries to Bottle Paul Newman"

By Marian Burros

In an effort to burnish its tarnished image on Wall Street and Main Street, McDonald's has formed a partnership with the blue-eyed elder statesman of Hollywood and Broadway, Paul Newman.

Mr. Newman will not be a spokesman for the fast-food chain, though his picture will appear in its restaurants. Instead, he has agreed to sell McDonald's a line of salad dressing, similar to the bottled dressing made by his company, Newman's Own. Under the same philanthropic principle that guides Newman's Own, Mr. Newman said, all after-tax profits from the deal will be given to charity.

Some see the partnership as a brilliant marketing move by McDonald's; others say it's too little too late. Mr. Newman said he is unconcerned. He has no problem with the chain's efforts to improve its image through association with his company. "We get to give a lot more money to charity, and whatever we have to do with—the salads—are basically healthy products," he said. "If in any way that upgraded people's perception of McDonald's, what would be the problem with that?" The partnership might increase Newman's Own charitable giving by as much as 25 percent, he said.

"We didn't do this because we thought we had a lousy image," said Kay Napier, a senior vice president for marketing at McDonald's. "Salads have increasing appeal."

If compelled to eat at McDonald's, I would choose the new menu of salads, which were introduced on Monday, with one of the Newman dressings, which are tastier than most other packaged versions.

The partnership does give an aura of wholesomeness to McDonald's and its food, said the food and science writer Michael Pollan, the author of "The Botany of Desire: A Plant's-Eye View of the World."

"All this is about buying the image of Paul Newman," Mr. Pollan said. "McDonald's is in the hole. It is trying to freshen and go upscale. It's redoing its flavor profile and making it more sophisticated and giving it an aura of health-consciousness and virtue, and this is a way to connect with virtue."

Or as Michael Pertschuk, a former Federal Trade Commission chairman and a co-director of the Advocacy Institute, which monitors public health issues, said: "Innocence by association. It's really pushing the limits of public interest entrepreneurship."

But leave aside the philosophical questions, said Phil Lempert, who runs a website devoted to food and health news, www.supermarketguru.com, and is the Today Show's food trends editor. The real test of the partnership will be in the marketplace, where McDonald's has come late to the premium salad game, behind Burger King and Wendy's. "I think people will snicker," Mr. Lempert said. "I don't think what they have done appeals to McDonald's current consumer. If they wanted to capture new customers they should have had an organic salad and Newman's Own Organic dressing, and all those aging baby boomers who haven't been going to McDonald's for years would have returned."

Nell Newman, Mr. Newman's daughter, a co-founder of Newman's Own Organics, once part of her father's company but now independent, likes the idea: "That would have been wonderful, but no one asked me."

"It's a grand idea," her father said. "Just think: we'll change the fast-food industry into nothing but salad bars."

A book by Ms. Newman, *The Newman's Own Organics Guide to a Good Life*, has just been published by Villard. Mr. Newman is on the cover with his daughter, and according to the book, he does eat organic from time to time. The book says nothing about eating at McDonald's.

"If McDonald's did what was politically correct, humanely correct and nutritionally correct and sophisticated," Mr. Pollan said, "if they did all those things, they wouldn't be McDonald's."

1. **Who is the article about?** *McDonald's and Newman's Own, the company owned by famous actor Paul Newman*

2. **What happened?** *McDonald's formed a partnership with Newman's Own. Newman's Own agreed to sell them a line of its dressings.*

3. **When did it happen?** *March 11, 2003*

4. **Where did it happen?** *NA*

5. **Why did it happen?** *McDonald's wanted to improve its image, so it thought it was a good marketing strategy to align itself with a company that sells healthy products and also donates after-tax profits to charities.*

6. **How did it happen?** *McDonald's will be using Newman's salad dressings, which have a picture of Paul Newman on each bottle.*

Reading Essays

Essays generally provide an author's perspective or point of view on a topic or issue. They can reflect a personal point of view or the opinions of a group and can attempt to persuade a reader to change his or her beliefs and/or take action. Here are some tips for reading and understanding essays.

Tips for Understanding Essays

- Essays can be written for all types of audiences. Sometimes, the source in which the essay appears may suggest the audience.

- In an essay, the author's primary purpose for writing varies. Sometimes the author is writing to persuade the reader to adopt a particular point of view. Other times, essayists are reflecting upon their own observations, opinions, or life experiences. The author may state his or her viewpoint in a thesis statement at the beginning of the essay, or state the overall point in the conclusion. At times, the reader will have to discern the author's point of view from the supporting details. The supporting details will explain the author's thesis by providing examples, personal experiences, causes and effects, or by making comparisons or contrasts. Transition words help the reader find the details and understand the relationships among ideas.

- The writer's tone may be serious or funny. He or she may argue openly or attempt to convince the reader subtly by using irony or sarcasm.

- A critical reader should try to answer the following questions about the essay:

  a. What is the author's thesis?

  b. Is the thesis convincing?

  c. Why did the author write the essay and for whom? (Who is the intended audience?)

  d. What is the author's tone?

  e. Is it possible to distinguish between facts and the author's opinions?

  f. Is there bias?

  g. Is the author persuasive?

try it and apply it! 10-2   Reading and Understanding an Essay

An understanding of these words will help you understand the following essay:

- **festooned**—decorated, garlanded
- **cognitive dissonance**—internal conflict or anxiety relating to inconsistency between one's beliefs and one's actions
- **vexing**—puzzling

Read the following excerpt from an essay on food and nutrition that appeared in the magazine section of *The New York Times*. Then, answer the questions that follow to check your understanding of this portion of the essay. To read the essay in its entirety, log onto www.nytimes.com.

Unhappy Meals

By Michael Pollan

Eat food. Not too much. Mostly plants.

That, more or less, is the short answer to the supposedly incredibly complicated and confusing question of what we humans should eat in order to be maximally healthy. I hate to give away the game right here at the beginning of a long essay, and I confess that I'm tempted to complicate matters in the interest of keeping things going for a few thousand more words. I'll try to resist but will go ahead and add a couple more details to flesh out the advice. Like: A little meat won't kill you, though it's better approached as a side dish than as a main. And you're much better off eating whole fresh foods than processed food products. That's what I mean by the recommendation to eat "food." Once, food was all you could eat, but today there are lots of other edible food-like substances in the supermarket. These novel products of food science often come in packages festooned with health claims, which brings me to a related rule of thumb: if you're concerned about your health, you should probably avoid food products that make health claims. Why? Because a health claim on a food product is a good indication that it's not really food, and food is what you want to eat.

Uh-oh. Things are suddenly sounding a little more complicated, aren't they? Sorry. But that's how it goes as soon as you try to get to the bottom of the whole vexing question of food and health. Before long, a dense cloud bank of confusion moves in. Sooner or later, everything solid you thought you knew about the links between diet and health gets blown away in the gust of the latest study.

Last winter came the news that a low-fat diet, long believed to protect against breast cancer, may do no such thing—this from the monumental, federally financed Women's Health Initiative, which has also found no link between a low-fat diet and rates of coronary disease. The year before we learned that dietary fiber might not, as we had been confidently told, help prevent colon cancer. Just last fall two prestigious studies on omega-3 fats published at the same time presented us with strikingly different conclusions. While the Institute of Medicine stated that "it is uncertain how much these omega-3s contribute to improving health" (and they might do the opposite if you get them from mercury-contaminated fish), a Harvard study declared that simply by eating a couple of servings of fish each week (or by downing enough fish oil), you could cut your risk of dying from a heart attack by more than a third—a stunningly hopeful piece of news. It's no wonder that omega-3 fatty acids are poised to become the oat bran of 2007, as food scientists micro-encapsulate fish oil and algae oil and blast them into such formerly all-terrestrial foods as bread and tortillas, milk and yogurt and cheese, all of which will soon, you can be sure, sprout fishy new health claims. (Remember the rule?)

By now you're probably registering the cognitive dissonance of the supermarket shopper or science-section reader, as well as some nostalgia for the simplicity and solidity of the first few sentences of this essay. Which I'm still prepared to defend against the

(continued)

(continued)

shifting winds of nutritional science and food-industry marketing. But before I do that, it might be useful to figure out how we arrived at our present state of nutritional confusion and anxiety.

The story of how the most basic questions about what to eat ever got so complicated reveals a great deal about the institutional imperatives of the food industry, nutritional science and—ahem—journalism, three parties that stand to gain much from widespread confusion surrounding what is, after all, the most elemental question an omnivore confronts. Humans deciding what to eat without expert help—something they have been doing with notable success since coming down out of the trees—is seriously unprofitable if you're a food company, distinctly risky if you're a nutritionist and just plain boring if you're a newspaper editor or journalist. (Or, for that matter, an eater. Who wants to hear, yet again, "Eat more fruits and vegetables"?) And so, like a large gray fog, a great Conspiracy of Confusion has gathered around the simplest questions of nutrition—much to the advantage of everybody involved. Except perhaps the ostensible beneficiary of all this nutritional expertise and advice: us, and our health and happiness as eaters.

(The New York Times Magazine, Jan. 28, 2007)

1. What is the thesis of this essay?

Eat food products that don't make health claims.

2. Is the author's thesis convincing? Explain.

Yes. He provides support using a variety of research studies that have presented contradictory claims.

3. Why did he write it and for whom?

He is writing for the general public. He wants to inform the public that the food industry, nutritional scientists, and journalists are presenting contradictory findings and reports. He also believes that the food industry and journalists have ulterior motives in publicizing this confusing information. He suggests that the public listen to its own intuition about what is healthy, as they have successfully done since the beginning of time.

4. What is the author's tone?

The tone is humorous and lighthearted, but also very critical.

5. Can you distinguish between facts and opinions?

Yes. The author uses words and expressions such as should, that's what I mean, and a number of adjectives to express his opinion. When he presents facts, he cites his sources—for example, the federally financed Women's Health Initiative, the Institute of Medicine, and a Harvard study.

6. Do you recognize bias?

Yes. While the author presents facts, he criticizes each by focusing on the contradictory reports and claims about them, which he feels only contributes to the "Conspiracy of Confusion." However, he does not present studies that have made significant and valid claims.

7. Is the author persuasive?

No. The author does not discuss the value of scientific and nutritional research as consumers try to determine which foods may be contributing to serious diseases such as breast and colon cancer and heart disease. He also criticizes foodlike substances and the value of food science, which may be necessary to address the demands of an ever-increasing global population.

Reading Academic Journals

Academic journals contain the latest scholarly research in both academic and professional areas. You may already be familiar with *The Journal of the American Medical Association* or *The New England Journal of Medicine* because these journals are often cited in newspaper articles. As a college student, you may be required to use academic journals as a source for your own research and writing. For example, in researching the discipline of history, you might come across scholarly articles taken from *The American Historical Review* or *The Journal of American History*. Following are some tips for reading and understanding academic journals.

Tips for Understanding Academic Journals

- An academic journal is a periodical or magazine in which researchers, experts, or professionals publish information and reports about their work.
- Journal articles are written for experts or students who specialize in a particular field of study.
- The authors' purpose is to inform their readership about current research findings.
- The information is presented in an objective manner. The tone is serious.
- The level of vocabulary is high. It contains a lot of technical words and language from specialized areas.

Features of Academic Journal Articles

Journal articles may contain the following features or parts:

Abstract—a summary of the article

Literature Review—a discussion of all previous work on the topic

Methods and Data—explanation of the process(es) by which the research was conducted

Analysis and Results—the outcomes of experiments or research and the meaning and significance of the research data

Discussion and Conclusion—explanation of the implications of this new research and the researcher's theory or opinions about it

Illustrations—tables, graphs, maps, or other visuals that illustrate and explain the data

References—a complete listing of sources or works cited

Journal articles are generally lengthy, so a comprehensive preview of an article will assist you in understanding it. Here are some previewing tips.

Tips for Previewing Journal Articles

1. First, read the entire abstract. It will contain enough information to let you know the basis of the article. Some journal articles list keywords, without definitions, pertaining to the article. These are further clues to understanding the information you will read in the article.

2. Then read the first paragraph or two from the introduction, discussion, and conclusion. These sections will inform you about the thesis of the article and the main findings of the research.

3. You may also want to skim the methods section. This will tell you how the research was done.

4. Look over the charts and illustrations to gather information about the results or findings of the research.

5. Finally, read the first paragraphs in the sections on analysis and results to determine the importance and impact of the research.

After your preview, you will be prepared to read the article more carefully to understand more details about the research and it findings.

try it and apply it! 10-3   **Reading and Understanding an Academic Journal Article**

Directions: Read this article about McDonald's taken from The *Journal of Business Strategy.* (HINT: Preview the title, the abstract, and the first and last paragraphs before reading the entire article.) Then write the answers to the questions that follow in the spaces provided.

Ray Kroc (1902–1984):

Flipping over Efficiency

Meryl Davids

Abstract

Ray Kroc was already 53 years old when he opened his first McDonald's in suburban Chicago. It was a replica of the McDonald brothers' San Bernardino, California, restaurant. Ultimately, what Kroc did best was to position his McChain as a family-friendly value eatery, and to ensure that each eating experience was identical, so a customer from New York vacationing in Florida would know exactly what he was in for.

Full Text

Often, it's not the person who invents the better mousetrap, but the person who has the vision to set that mousetrap where all the critters are.

Ray Kroc was already 53 years old when he opened his first McDonald's in sub-urban Chicago. It was a replica of the McDonald brothers' San Bernardino, California, restaurant, based on siblings Maurice ("Mac") and Richard's ("Dick") sizzling concept of producing a limited menu of burgers, fries, and shakes in assembly-line fashion. The brothers even developed McDonald's famed symbol, the golden arches. Business was brisk, but the men gave no thought to adding locations. That brainstorm came from Kroc, who recognized America's growing desire for a quick, inexpensive, and dependable place to eat out.

Of course, Kroc's expansion of McDonald's to its current place as the world's No. 1 fast-food chain with 25,000 restaurants in 115 countries and revenues of $12.4 billion, is now the stuff of legends. Ultimately, what Kroc did best was to position his McChain as a family-friendly value eatery, and to ensure that each eating experience was identical, so a customer from New York vacationing in Florida would know exactly what he was in for. He accomplished these objectives by carefully controlling franchisees, giving them little freedom to experiment with menu items, pricing, or decor (that stranglehold would cause problems for the chain in later years, but during Kroc's reign it worked masterfully). In many ways, his operation was perfect for the times, when a post-war America, still searching for its footing, was eager to embrace the sense of confidence that came from conformity.

Ray Kroc had put his fingers into numerous lines of work before he came across McDonald's. After a stint as an ambulance driver during WWI, he was a musical director for a radio station, a salesman of Florida real estate, and a sales manager for a cup company. In 1937, in what would be a pattern he'd repeat with McDonald's, he learned of a customer who was buying cups by the truckload. It turned out that Earl Prince

(continued)

(continued)

had invented a five-spindle "Multimixer" to make numerous shakes at once. Showing his entrepreneurial mettle, four years later Kroc mortgaged his home and invested his entire life savings to become an exclusive distributor for the product.

For the next 17 years, Kroc crossed the country peddling his mixer. Then he again learned of a customer buying vast quantities of his product, this time the multimixer. Perplexed how such a small restaurant could be selling so many shakes, Kroc stopped in at the McDonalds brothers' store. He wasted no time pitching the franchise idea to the brothers. "Who could we get to open them for us?" they wondered aloud. "Well, what about me?" Kroc famously responded.

Ironically, Kroc's first McDonald's outlet was closer to home cooking than the growing chain would soon become. Potatoes were peeled right in the restaurant, and fresh hamburger meat came from local suppliers. Ever eager to expand, Kroc opened two more stores in his first year.

Because quality and cleanliness were near obsessions with Kroc (his oft-quoted motto: "If you have time to lean, you have time to clean"), he automated as many operations as possible and instituted rigid training programs at "Hamburger University" for franchise owners, whom he required to manage their own stores. Many who came in contact with Kroc over the years complained of his abrasive manner and large ego, but his insistence on absolute conformity to his ideas was largely the reason for the chain's success.

In the same way that Henry Ford realized that by keeping selections limited (e.g., color choice: black) he could mass-produce economical cars, Kroc kept the menu simple and the standardization high, to mass-produce economical meals. Each patty, for example, had to weigh exactly 1.6 ounces and be exactly 0.221 inches thick. Manuals documented to the second how to make a shake. Then, through massive advertising, Kroc enticed Americans to recognize their need for his product. As Kroc once cleverly said, "The definition of salesmanship is the gentle art of letting the customer have it your way."

Kroc couldn't pull off that same feat in some of his later ventures, however. He had little success with an upscale hamburger restaurant, pie shops, a theme park, or even the San Diego Padres, which he purchased in the mid-1970s but gave up operating control of after just a few years.

But of course he had that golden touch with McDonald's. Customers flocked to his outlets in such numbers, he sold his billionth burger in 1963, two years after he had bought out the brothers for what in retrospect was a meager $2.7 million. During the next 21 years, until his death in 1984, he sold billions and billions more, thanks to a worldwide empire that, at his death, numbered a remarkable 7,500 stores.

(*The Journal of Business Strategy,* Boston: Sep/Oct 1999. Vol 20, Iss. 5; pg. 34)

1. How did Kroc get the idea to start a McDonald's franchise?

When he was peddling his multimixer, he noticed a customer was buying large amounts of his appliances to distribute or sell to other stores.

2. **List *three* business practices of Kroc's franchises that led to his chain's success.**

   He automated many operations. He instituted a rigid training program, and required owners to manage their own franchises. He insisted on quality and cleanliness. He kept the menu simple and the standardization high. He adopted a massive advertising campaign to get Americans to recognize the need for his product.

3. **What contributed to Kroc's idea of creating McDonald's?**

   He recognized America's growing need for a quick, inexpensive, and dependable place to eat.

4. **Why did Kroc create identical fast-food establishments?**

   He wanted travelers to be assured that wherever they went, they would find the same menu in the same friendly atmosphere.

5. **What historical event set the stage for the success of McDonald's?**

   Following World War II, Americans were happy to find an eating establishment that was welcoming, imbued confidence, and embraced a sense of conformity.

Understanding Primary Sources

A primary source is a first-hand account of an event. It may have been written by an eyewitness or a participant. Primary sources can include any of the following: laws, public records, judicial cases, personal letters, journals or memoirs, photographs or illustrations, and artifacts. They provide the reader with a special glimpse into the thoughts and ideas of people from the past.

Textbooks are secondary sources because the authors have interpreted or analyzed information for the reader. Textbooks are written for students; however, not all primary sources have a specific audience in mind. The purpose of a textbook is to *tell* students what is important to know and learn. Students have to determine the purpose of a primary resource on their *own*.

Tips for Reading Primary Sources

To interpret and evaluate a primary source, ask yourself some of the following general questions:

- What do you already know about the topic or event depicted in the primary source from your personal experiences, textbook reading, or class lectures?
- What type of source is it?
- What is its date of origin?
- Who is the author or creator?
- What is the purpose of the primary source?
- What did you learn about the topic from the primary source? Does it agree with what you have already read about the topic?

try it and apply it! 10-4   Interpreting a Primary Resource

Directions: A photograph of a hamburger that you might buy at McDonald's is shown next. Look at the picture and then answer the following questions.

*Answers may vary.
Sample answers
provided.*

This image shows a juicy double-decker cheeseburger, dressed with lettuce, tomato, and onions. During the 1980s, advertisements for fast-food restaurants depicted huge portions of meals, including this example of a hamburger, encouraging Americans to eat larger portions. Simultaneously, studies showed that Americans were suffering increasingly from eating disorders, such as anorexia, bulimia, and bigorexia—a desire in men to be as strong and defined as possible. Men all over the United States began taking nutritional supplements to promote muscle growth and athletic performance, while admitting to depression and dissatisfaction with their body images. For Americans, it was a frustrating juxtaposition between advertising images of larger portions of fast food, enticing them to eat more, and models who were becoming increasingly smaller, encouraging both women and men to eat less.

Source: Caption and questions below from *Primary Source Investigator* CD accompanying Alan Brinkley, *American History: A Survey,* 12e. McGraw-Hill, 2007.

1. Describe the hamburger—what makes this burger particularly appetizing?

   It shows a super-sized cheeseburger on a sesame bun. It looks juicy, and it is dressed with lettuce, tomato, and onions. It makes me hungry.

2. How do you think this image was used?

   It may have been used as a magazine advertisement for McDonald's or another fast-food chain.

3. How does this image help us understand late twentieth-century history and culture?

   Both men and women worked outside the home. Home-cooked meals were replaced by fast food or food that required no preparation.

4. What can images such as this one tell you about changing ideas of body image in American history?

   This image shows a huge quantity of food. As an advertisement, it serves to encourage Americans to eat larger portions. It might suggest that bigger is better. That is, don't just eat one hamburger, but have two. From what I know about body image in American culture, there is actually a confusing message here because other forms of the media are telling teenagers to eat less so they can look like their favorite model or movie star. These confusing images can lead to tremendous stress and dissatisfaction.

try it and apply it! 10-5

Understanding and Reading a Primary Resource

Directions: Read the following excerpt found in *A Survey: American History*. The chapter is titled "The Affluent Society (1946–1969)." Read and examine the primary source that follows, and answer the questions in the spaces provided.

The Landscape and the Automobile

The success of Disneyland depended largely on the ease of highway access and the dense urban areas around it, as well as the vast parking lots that surrounded the parks. It was, in short, a symbol of overwhelming influence of automobiles on American life and on the American landscape in the postwar era. Between 1950 and 1980, the nation's population increased by 50 percent, but the numbers of automobiles owned by Americans increased by 400 percent.

The Federal-Aid Highway Act of 1956, which appropriated $25 million for highway construction, was one of the most important alterations of the national landscape in modern history. Great ribbons of concrete—40,000 miles of them—spread across the nation, spanning rivers and valleys, traversing every state and providing links to every major city (and between cities and their suburbs). These highways dramatically reduced the time necessary to travel from one place to another. They also made trucking a more economical way than railroads to transport goods to markets. They made travel by automobile and bus faster than travel by passenger trains, resulting in the long, steady decline of railroads.

Highways also encouraged the movement of economic activities . . . out of cities and into suburban and rural areas where land was cheaper . . . The proliferation of automobiles and the spread of automobiles also made it easier for families to move into homes that were significant distances from where they worked . . . The shift of travel from train to automobile helped spawn a tremendous proliferation of motels, drive-in theaters, and fast-food chains. Ray Kroc's McDonald's opened its first outlets in Des Plaines, Illinois, and southern California in 1955 . . .

(Adapted from Brinkley 2007)

Primary Source

Federal Highway Act (1956)

To amend and supplement the Federal-Aid Road Act approved July 11, 1916, to authorize appropriations for continuing the construction of highways; to amend the Internal Revenue Code

(*continued*)

- **Uncover the plot** The action of a story is called the **plot**. The plot is not always revealed in chronological order. Sometimes, authors use **flashbacks** that tell about actions that occurred at an earlier point in time. At other times, they use **foreshadowing,** a technique that allows them to provide readers with a glimpse into future events in the story, which can help readers predict actions that are about to occur. A traditional plot includes a *conflict*, a problem or a change; a *complication*, an introduction of a character or action that makes the initial problem worse; the *climax*, a crisis or turning point in the story that leads to the conclusion of the story; and the *resolution*, a real or potential resolution to the conflict. In some stories, the conflict is never resolved.

- **Examine the symbolism** In some novels, certain characters, actions or places symbolize or stand for something more abstract or general.

- **Evaluate the author's tone.** Just as in nonfiction, an author's tone in a novel is revealed through his or her choice of words, the connotations of words, and figurative language. The tone varies depending on the type of novel and the point the author is conveying. (See Chapter 7, "Let's Get Critical.")

- **Discover the theme(s).** The theme is the central idea of a story that the reader can infer from the plot or characters. It is broader than the main idea found in other genres mentioned in this chapter in that it often teaches a life lesson.

try it and apply it! 10-6   Previewing a Novel

Directions: Below you will find information taken from the book jacket of the popular novel *The Kite Runner* by Khaled Hosseini. Read it through and see what you can learn about the setting, characters, conflicts, themes, or tone of the novel. Underline these points of information, and then answer the questions in the spaces provided.

Answers may vary.

From the Jacket

An epic tale of fathers and sons, of friendship and betrayal, that takes us from Afghanistan in the final days of the monarchy to the atrocities of the present.

The unforgettable, heartbreaking story of the unlikely friendship between a wealthy boy and the son of his father's servant, *The Kite Runner* is a beautifully crafted novel set in a country that is in the process of being destroyed. It is about the power of reading, the price of betrayal, and the possibility of redemption, and it is also about the power of fathers over sons—their love, their sacrifices, their lies.

The first Afghan novel to be written in English, *The Kite Runner* tells a sweeping story of family, love, and friendship against a backdrop of history that has not been told in fiction before, bringing to mind the large canvases of the Russian writers of the nineteenth century. But just as it is old-fashioned in its narration, it is contemporary in its subject—the devastating history of Afghanistan over the last thirty years. As emotionally gripping as it is tender, *The Kite Runner* is an unusual and powerful debut.

1. What is the setting?
   Afghanistan, end of monarchy through the present time—over a period of thirty years

2. Who are the characters?
   father, son, son of father's servant

3. What is the conflict?
   struggle between father and son and/or unlikely relationship between classes

4. What is the theme?
   power of reading, power of fathers over sons—their love, sacrifices, their lies; price of betrayal; possibility of redemption

5. What is the tone?
   heartbreaking, emotionally gripping

   Now that you have read the details on the book jacket, you should also explore your own experiences about the subject of the novel. What do you know about Afghanistan's history? What have you read about Afghanistan in the newspaper? Do you know anything about life in Afghanistan, its people, and its culture?

Answers will vary.

_____

_____

_____

_____

_____

try it and apply it! 10-7   Reading and Understanding a Novel

Directions: Read the first chapter from *The Kite Runner*. Write notes in the margins about what the author reveals about the point of view, setting, characters, symbolism, and plot. Then use your notes to answer the questions in the spaces provided.

Answers will vary.

One

December 2001

I became what I am today at the age of twelve, on a frigid overcast day in the winter of 1975. I remember the precise moment, crouching behind a crumbling mud wall, peeking into the alley near the frozen creek. That was a long time ago, but it's wrong what they say about the past, I've learned, about how you can bury it. Because the past claws its way

(continued)

(continued)

out. Looking back now, I realize I have been peeking into that deserted alley for the last twenty-six years.

One day last summer, my friend Rahim Khan called from Pakistan. He asked me to come see him. Standing in the kitchen with the receiver to my ear, I knew it wasn't just Rahim Khan on the line. It was my past of unatoned sins. After I hung up, I went for a walk along Spreckels Lake on the northern edge of Golden Gate Park. The early-afternoon sun sparkled on the water where dozens of miniature boats sailed, propelled by a crisp breeze. Then I glanced up and saw a pair of kites, red with long blue tails, soaring in the sky. They danced high above the trees on the west end of the park, over the windmills, floating side by side like a pair of eyes looking down on San Francisco, the city I now call home. And suddenly Hassan's voice whispered in my head: *For you, a thousand times over.* Hassan the harelipped kite runner.

I sat on a park bench near a willow tree. I thought about something Rahim Khan said just before he hung up, almost as an afterthought. *There is a way to be good again.* I looked up at those twin kites. I thought about Hassan. Thought about Baba. Ali. Kabul. I thought of the life I had lived until the winter of 1975 came along and changed everything. And made me what I am today.

Point of View: *First person. The narrator is telling the story.*

Setting: *2001, San Francisco, CA*

Characters: *Rahim Khan, someone from the narrator's past; Hassan, a harelipped kite runner; Baba and Ali from Kabul*

Symbolism: *The title of the book refers to kite running. The first chapter mentions kite running. Hassan was a kite runner. Kite running might be a symbol.*

Figurative language: *Because the past claws its way out. They (the kites) danced high above the trees on the west end of the park, over the windmills, floating side by side like a pair of eyes looking down on San Francisco.*

Plot: *Whatever happened in 1975 must have been painful to the narrator; he is still suffering from that past event. He feels guilty. Rahim Khan tells him there is a way to be good again.*

Answers will vary. Predicting action will help you understand the novel. Examine the foreshadowing provided by the author in Chapter 1. What do you think will happen next?

_____

_____

_____

_____

_____

Adjusting Your Reading Rate to Meet Your Needs

There is so much to read and so little time. Between attending classes, completing written assignments and projects, working, and taking care of family concerns, how can you read efficiently and effectively? First, find a quiet place to read. Perhaps your room, the library, or a bookstore might be a good spot. Then eliminate distractors. Turn off your cell phone. Finally, plan your time. Leave yourself enough time to complete the assignment. Remember, it's always a good idea to overestimate how much time you will need.

Several factors determine how much time you should allot for college reading assignments. It's not a one-size-fits-all-assignments situation. Following are some tips to help you decide how much time to set aside for an assignment.

Tips for Determining Reading Times

■ **Consider the nature and difficulty of the material.** Because college reading is made up of different genres, you need to take into account the nature and complexity of the material. For example, a newspaper or magazine article can be read fairly quickly. However, reading textbooks, academic journals, or primary sources can require a much slower pace because the material is more complex and often new and unfamiliar.

■ **Consider how familiar you are with the subject or discipline.** Reading in the health sciences may be easier for some students than reading in the physical or biological sciences. Reading on a topic that is difficult for you will require a slower pace, whereas material you find easier will permit a more rapid rate.

■ **Consider your purpose for reading.** Your purpose for reading determines how fast or slow you read material. If you are previewing a chapter in your textbook, you can read quickly. If you are trying to analyze an essay, you might want to read more slowly.

Remember to *slow down* when you

- ■ have very little prior knowledge on a subject
- ■ encounter new words
- ■ find many long and complex sentences
- ■ need to learn new concepts
- ■ read technical material

Read *faster* when you

- ■ are familiar with the subject
- ■ can easily grasp concepts
- ■ read newspaper and magazine articles

try it and apply it! 10-8   Determining Your Reading Rate

Directions: Read each of the following scenarios. Write what your purpose would be for reading each one and what you think your approximate reading rate (fast or slow) would be.

Answers will vary.

1. You are reading an academic journal article in *The Journal of Educational Psychology*. You are an education major.

    Purpose _____

    Rate _____

2. You are reading an article from *Time Magazine* on parenting. You have two teenage daughters.

    Purpose _____

    Rate _____

3. You are reading the first chapter in your sociology textbook. You're not even sure what sociology means.

    Purpose _____

    Rate _____

4. You are reading a chapter in your math textbook. You've already studied this topic in high school.

    Purpose _____

    Rate _____

5. You are reading a critical essay on *Macbeth*. You are taking a course on Shakespearean literature.

    Purpose _____

    Rate _____

6. You are reading a section of your chemistry textbook. You did not take chemistry in high school.

    Purpose _____

    Rate _____

7. You are reading parts of *The Declaration of Independence*. You are enrolled in an American History course.

    Purpose _____

    Rate _____

8. You are reading case studies in marketing and business. You will be writing a term project.

    Purpose _____

    Rate _____

Keep this in mind

- Find a quiet place to read.
- Plan your time.
- Determine the nature and difficulty of the material.
- Consider the general complexity of the subject or discipline.
- Establish a purpose.
- Adjust your reading rate.

Searching Other Sources: Reading Across the Genres

Types of Sources	Audience	Purpose	Tone
Textbooks	College students	Inform, instruct	Objective, straightforward
News Articles	General public	Inform	Objective
Essays	Varies	Persuade	Varies: serious, ironic, sarcastic, humorous, etc.
Academic Journals	Professionals, experts in the area or discipline	Inform	Objective
Primary Sources	Varies	Varies	Varies
Novels	General public	Varies	Varies

Key Terms

academic journals

essays

flashbacks

foreshadowing

literature

newspaper articles

plot

primary sources

11

Show What You Know:
Become an Effective Test Taker

In this chapter
you will learn to

- Prepare for exams
- Understand the different kinds of exam formats
- Reduce test anxiety

Taking
Exams

Studying for Exams

There are several ways in which your achievement in college courses is evaluated. Research projects and papers, writing assignments, laboratory activities, presentations, and classroom participation may all be used to determine your grade. One of the most common methods of evaluating a student's performance is through the written examination.

The information and techniques you will learn in this chapter are applicable across all the academic disciplines. Select those that feel most comfortable to you, match your learning style, and fit the demands of each class and exam you take. Several strategies here are helpful in preparing for standardized exams you may be required to take and pass in college, including academic proficiency exams and exit exams, and for entry exams for graduate education. The more you know about studying for and taking exams, the more confident you will feel on test day. Prepare well and increase your capacity to become an effective test taker.

Exams in the Workplace

You may be surprised to learn that test taking continues into the world of work. In order to find the best candidate for a position, many employers use selection testing to evaluate job applicants on their technical skill and knowledge, reading and writing abilities, aptitude, physical ability, work-related personality, and psychological characteristics (Rieschi 2009). Although many governmental jobs are no longer filled through written examination, specific careers, such as law enforcement, administrative support in public schools, and air traffic controllers are required to take and pass a comprehensive entrance exam. The majority of postal workers, about 80 percent, must also take an entrance exam (http://federaljobs.net). Indeed, certain professions, including those of teacher, physician, lawyer, or even information security manager, require the passing of an exam, beyond a college degree, in order to be certified to practice in the field.

Prepare for Exams

Probably no other aspect of college life creates the amount of anxiety and concern that tests do—especially midterms and finals. Wouldn't it be great to be able to deal more comfortably and effectively with these stressful, yet inevitable, college experiences? This chapter discusses how you can effectively prepare for exams, reviews the most common types of test formats and the best strategies to use in responding to each, and provides methods to help you reduce your anxiety about taking exams.

Though it may sound simple, the best way to ready yourself for an exam is to realize that *you should start preparing the minute you enter your class . . . on day one!* Your ongoing, active involvement in class is probably the most important way to prepare for your exams. Regular attendance, steady completion of assignments throughout the semester, good note-taking, active participation in discussions and lectures, active reading of the assigned material, and asking questions during or after class will provide you with a strong foundation of knowledge and understanding on which to build and ready yourself for test day. Not only will you benefit from being a productive and responsible student, but you will also be in a position of control and preparedness when you begin to review material for an exam.

Review is the operative word. Studying for an exam should not be the first time you encounter the content being tested! At its best, it should be a time for relearning material you have already learned and applied. Keep this in mind as you plan your weekly studies and schedule tasks throughout the semester.

So what are some specific techniques you can use to keep yourself actively engaged in learning and preparing for exams? The following selection, "I Got My B.A. by Sheer Luck, or How Study Skills Saved the Student," is a lighthearted, fictional reflection written by educator Walter Pauk. In the retelling of "his college experience in an Egyptian History class," Dr. Pauk imbeds several study strategies that all college students can use to prepare for exams. His audience is you, and his purpose is to share these very important methods.

try it and apply it! 11-1   Identifying Study Strategies

Directions: Read and annotate the following selection to identify as many study strategies as you can. Paraphrase Dr. Pauk's suggestions, and list them on the lines following the selection. Then answer the questions. Knowing the meaning of the following references to ancient Egypt will be helpful:

King Tut, short for Tutankhamun, was an Egyptian Pharaoh whose burial mask is well-known today as an icon of ancient Egyptian culture

Osiris—Egyptian god of life, death, and fertility

Ra—ancient Egyptian sun god

Sarcophagus—a stone coffin

Hieroglyphics—ancient Egyptian picture writing

I Got My B.A. By Sheer Luck, or How Study Skills Saved the Student

By Walter Pauk

In this selection, Professor Pauk tells about on experience he had when he was an undergraduate. The abbreviation "B.A." stands for "Bachelor of Arts," an undergraduate college degree.

Now it can be told: I got my B.A. by sheer luck. I say sheer luck because, if events were ordinary, I would have failed almost every course. Instead, when things looked impossible, some "chance" idea pulled me out. Here is my story.

Professor Kolb (the students called him "King Tut") was especially rough that year. Some said that an editor had turned down his manuscript; others said that he was just tired of students. But whatever it was, exactly 63.6 percent of the class failed Egyptian History. And if it were not for sheer luck, I'd have raised the percentage to 65.4.

I remember most vividly the frightening pace of the lectures. No one could take notes as fast as "King Tut" talked, especially when he became excited. My frantic scribbling and almost indecipherable abbreviating were so slow that I missed more than half. Without complete notes, it was impossible to study. I was lucky to have gotten even the 38 on one exam. As the fellows used to say, the "handwriting on the 'sarcophagus'" was clear for me. I knew that my only chance for survival was to get fuller notes.

That night after the exam grades came out, I tried to fall asleep—to forget my devastating grade for even awhile—but words like "hieroglyphics" and "rosetta stone" kept kaleidoscoping and rolling through my mind. As I mulled over my missing more than half of each lecture, I suddenly hit upon an idea: Why not leave every other line on my note paper blank? Then during the following period I could recall the lecture and fill in the missing portions. In deference to the ancients, I called this the "Osiris Plan."

The next day I tried the "Osiris Plan," and it worked! What luck! At first it was difficult to recall the lecture, but as days passed, it became sort of a game. Often, in the privacy of my room I would, in softer voice, imitate the old professor and try to redeliver the lecture as best as I could without looking at my notes. This mimicry almost got me into trouble, when, on a rare occasion, the professor called on me to answer a question. Stunned by being called, I jumped to my feet and for the first two sentences, before I caught myself, the fellows said I sounded "exactly like Old Tut."

(continued)

(continued)

One evening while quietly reciting the day's lecture to myself, I made an important discovery. In trying to make my presentation as smooth as possible (about this time I had begun imagining that I was a lecturer), I used the transitional words "Now that we have discussed the major reason for the phenomenal success of Pharaoh Hophra, let us look at the subsidiary reasons." At that moment I stopped still, for at no time did the professor seem to cut up the lecture into topics and subtopics; nevertheless, the topics and subtopics were neatly packaged and embedded into the seeming onrush of words, waiting to be perceived by the student. With this secret in mind, I found that I could take better notes during the lecture, and during the periods after class I could very easily supply the missing portions, filling in the blank every-other-line.

I tried to share this find with other students, but they'd always say, "You're foolish to take all those notes. Just sit back and listen." Although this sounded too easy to be good advice, I was struck by the great intelligence of my fellow students who could remember the main ideas of lecture after lecture, just by listening. I knew I couldn't; so to hide my inferior intelligence, I continued taking notes, completing them directly after class, categorizing the ideas, supplying the titles and subtitles, and reciting the lectures.

Another incident finally convinced me of my intellectual inferiority when I found that the other students just "flipped the pages" of the textbook. But poor me, I had to work on each chapter for hours. It was only luck that I wasn't found out, because the professor never quizzed us on our reading; everything depended on the final exam. I was luckier still when, looking in the library stacks for a book on Egyptian religion, I ran across an entire shelf filled with books on Egypt. I spent the rest of the day until 10:00 P.M. (closing time) perusing this lucky find. I finally picked out three books which were written in a style easy enough for me to understand, and I took these back to my room. By first reading these extra books, I found I could come back to the assigned chapter in the textbook and understand it better. I noticed that the author of our textbook frequently referred by footnote to these library books. So with luck I solved the textbook problem.

Well, all of this simply led up to the final examination. There I was with a notebook, about two inches thick, filled with lecture notes. Now, was I to memorize all these notes for the exam? And the textbook? Realizing that I didn't have the brains to memorize everything in my notes, I decided (this time without Osiris's help) to read each lecture bearing one focusing thought in mind: "What is the really important idea here?" As I found the answer, I'd jot this central point on separate sheets which I called "Summary Sheets." When I finished, I had "boiled" down inches of lecture notes to just twelve pages of "main issues." I then did the same with my textbook.

Thus armed, I aligned the "Summary Sheets" so that the main issues for both the lecture and textbook synchronized. I learned these main issues by first reading them over, thinking about them, reflecting on them, then without looking at my notes, by trying to recite them in my own words. I went through my summary sheets in the same way, issue by issue.

I guess that I had played the role of the professor too long, because after having mastered these main issues, I composed ten questions—questions that I'd ask if I were the professor. Still having some time left, I pretended that I was in the examination room; and I spent the next four hours rapidly answering my own ten questions. I then corrected my answers by referring to the lecture and textbook notes, and much to my delight, I had discussed all the facts and ideas accurately. For the first time I felt that I had achieved something. I felt almost adequate. But the warm glow was short-lived. What if the professor didn't ask what I had staked my life on? Well, I thought, "It is too late to change." With the feeling that my luck had really run out, I half-heartedly studied for six more hours. I went to bed at 10:00 for a good night's sleep, having refused to go to the second show of a "relaxing" movie with the rest of the boys.

On the way to the examination room the next morning. I knew without quesition that my luck had run out when I met Jack, who sat next to me. He had not taken a single note all semester; he had not even gone through the motions of "flipping" the textbook pages. When I asked why he wasn't nervous, he answered, "This is the semester for Examination Set #4, the one dealing with dates, names of pharaohs, dynasties, battles, and so forth."

"What's Examination Set #4?"

Everybody on campus except me, I guess, knew that old "King Tut" had five sets of examinations (ten questions in every set), which he rotated over a five-year period. Though "King Tut" collected the exam questions from each student, he did not reckon with the organizing ability of fraternity students. The plan worked like this: Specific students were given the mission to memorize question #1, another group to memorize #2, and so forth. When the students left the examination room, they jotted down these questions quickly from memory and put them into the fraternity hopper. In this clever way all five sets of the examination found their way into the files of numerous students.

I knew then that even Osiris and Ra, put together, couldn't help me. I had studied relationships.

The room was hot, yet others complained of the cold. My mind reeled. I knew my luck had run out. Dimly, as the examination sheets were passed up each row, I heard successive moans of various kinds: "Oh, No!" "No!" and occasional uncontrolled, almost hysterical laughter. I thought that perhaps the professor had by mistake given out Exam #5 instead of the anticipated #4.

By the time the sheets reached me (I always sat in the rear corner of the room where it was quieter) I, too, involuntarily gasped, "Oh! It can't be." I closed my eyes and waited for my vision to clear so that I could read the ten questions. They were the same ten questions that I had made up only yesterday—not in the same order, but nevertheless, the same ten questions. How could that be? One chance in a million, I'm sure. How lucky can one get? I recovered my composure and wrote and wrote and wrote.

"Old Tut" gave me a 100 plus. He penned a note saying, "Thank goodness for one good scholar in all my years of teaching." But he didn't know the long line of luck that I had, and I never told him.

Now that twenty years have passed, I think that it is safe to reveal that here is one fellow who got his B.A. just by sheer luck.

Source: Pauk, Walter (1965, October). "I Got My B.A. by Sheer Luck, or How Study Skills Saved the Student." *Journal of Reading,* 9(1), 37–40. Used with permission of the International Reading Association, www.reading.org.

(continued)

(continued)

Dr. Pauk's Suggestions

_____   _____
_____   _____
_____   _____
_____   _____
_____   _____
_____   _____

1. Now compare your list to the one that follows. How many of these strategies did you identify?

Strategies for Effective Studying

1. Leave every other line on your paper blank when you take notes. Then, following the class or lecture, add to these and fill in any missing portions.
2. Imitate your professor and redeliver lectures with and without looking at your notes.
3. Categorize ideas in a lecture. Pay attention to and identify the topics and subtopics within an entire lecture. Organize and take notes with this categorization in mind.
4. Read your textbooks, rather than just flipping through them.
5. Find and read additional books on subjects you are studying. Use the footnotes of your textbook's author to find titles.
6. Create summary sheets identifying the most important points of each lecture. Read them, think about them, and recite the key points without looking at the summary sheets.
7. Compose test questions you believe the professor would ask, answer them, and correct your answers by referring to your lecture and textbook notes.
8. Spend a lot of time studying!
9. Get a good night's rest before an exam.

2. Can you state the thesis, or most important overall message Dr. Pauk wants students to understand about studying in college?
Knowing and applying good study strategies, not luck, is responsible for being successful on exams in college.

Additional Ways to Prepare for an Exam

In addition to Dr. Pauk's recommendations, here are several other strategies to help you get ready for exams.

- **Speak with your professor.** Be sure you know what material will be covered on an exam and the format of the test. You will need to adjust your study based on this information.

- **Understand the material you are learning, rather than simply memorizing it.** Focusing on the meaning of information enhances your ability to process, learn, and remember it. (Benjamin & Bjork 2000, in Passer and Smith.)

- **Intend to remember!** Although this may seem obvious, it is important to be conscious of your goal to learn or commit something to memory. It will make a difference in accomplishing your objective.

- **Seek support if you are having difficulty understanding the material.** Your professors are usually available to help you. Your college may provide tutorial services designed to lend you this assistance. Don't hesitate to take it!

- **Read simpler versions of the material presented in your textbook.** This can help you gain background knowledge that will help you later in learning the material at a higher level.

- **Rehearse for the specific type of exam you will be taking.** Challenge yourself as you study in the way you will be challenged on your exam. For example, for essay exams, *plan* and *write out* essays based on the questions you anticipate will be asked. If you know your exam will have a "fill in the blank" portion and your professor will be providing a list from which to choose your answer, study with a list of choices. If on a math exam you need to "show your work," you should do so as you solve practice problems to prepare for the test. If "spelling counts," particularly on foreign language exams, be sure to write and correctly spell all your terms as you study.

- **Organize your information.** Whenever possible, break large amounts of information into categories and subcategories so that you are not just remembering one unrelated fact after another. For example, if you were studying the history of World War II, you might first divide the events you need to learn into those that occurred prior to the war, during the war, and after the war. Or you might review aspects of the conflict according to the different countries involved (America, England, Germany, France, and so on) and the political, economic, and social events that took place in and between them. The point is to cluster your information into related areas of study, and then organize it into major and minor points.

- **Study over a longer period of time than you think you need.** Start studying further in advance of the exam than you might normally. This way you can study for shorter periods of time, covering less content at each session, but doing a meaningful job with it. Organize the material you have to study by breaking large units of information into smaller, more manageable parts. After you have organized the information, use your planner to assign yourself specific areas to study at specific times before the exam. Make sure you review previously studied information briefly each time before you move on to the next unit.

- **Create mnemonic (memory) devices.** Devise *your own* acronyms, acrostics, and simple graphic aids to help you to recall items, sequences, or processes.

  - An **acronym** is a word formed from the initial letters of each component of a list, organization, or process. For example, THIEVES is an acronym for recalling the steps for previewing a reading selection. Can you recite them? (Look back to page 36.)

    Psychology students formulated the acronym WIRES to recall the different types of memory: Working, Implicit, Remote, Episodic, and Semantic (Di Spezio 1996). Many acronyms have become commonly used words themselves. Did you know that LASER is actually an acronym for Light Amplification by Stimulated Emission of Radiation, and SCUBA is an acronym for Self-contained Underwater Breathing Apparatus?

  - An **acrostic** is a memorable phrase or sentence in which the first letter of each word triggers a memory of a part of a list or series. Sometimes these are nonsensical, making them easier to remember. Music students use the acrostic "Every good boy does fine" to recall the order of line notes on the G clef staff, EGBDF. Students of biology have created acrostics to remember the classification hierarchy. "King Philip Came Over For Great Spaghetti" has helped many students remember Kingdom, Phylum, Class, Order, Family, Genus, Species.

  - Using **graphic aids** can be very helpful, if you tend to recall things visually. Making simple charts or graphs showing the key elements of a model, system, or process can help you recall them and trigger your memory for the related details.

It is usually allowed, assuming you are permitted to write notes on your test paper, to jot down your mnemonics, so you have them available to you during an exam.

■ **Study According to Your Learning Style.** Maximize the impact of your studies by knowing how you learn best. Then integrate techniques that tap into your strongest areas; visual, auditory, tactile-kinesthetic. (See pp. 18–23.) If you are good with language and remember what you hear, you should recite information aloud. Pauk's suggestion of reciting a lecture is a good one for you. If you are more of a visual learner, writing out information and drawing charts, semantic maps, and simple outlines should be helpful. Create "pictures" in your mind on which you can attach information. If your attention span is a little short, take frequent breaks and study for shorter periods, but set aside enough time to cover all the material. If you like movement, move around while you study. If you are social, form a study group with friends and meet regularly. Let the process of studying be personal and meaningful to you.

Understand Exam Formats

Generally, in-class exams include two types of questions: objective questions and essay questions. Find out the format of the test in advance from your professor so you can better prepare for it.

Objective Questions

Objective questions generally tap your knowledge of specific information, although they may also ask you to apply and synthesize your understanding of information. Usually there is only one correct response to an objective question. The most commonly used kinds of objective questions are multiple-choice, fill-in-the-blank (also known as cloze when included within paragraphs or reading selections), true/false, and matching.

Multiple-Choice Questions   Because college classes can be very large, professors often choose a **multiple-choice format** for exams. Four to five possible responses to a question are provided, and you are asked to select the best answer. You might be asked to enter your responses on a grid sheet so that grading can be done mechanically. Following are some tips for responding to multiple-choice questions.

Tips for Responding to Multiple-Choice Questions

■ **Read each question carefully.** Pay close attention to words that may change the answer you choose, particularly if the question asks you to identify the response that is *not* accurate. For example:

Which of the following is not an example of a violent crime?

a. robbery

b. larceny

c. manslaughter

d. kidnapping

The correct response is larceny. As you work through this question, you may think to yourself, "Which *are* violent crimes?" As you note that robbery, manslaughter, and kidnapping are violent, you will conclude that the answer to the question is choice b.

Another way the question could be phrased is this:

> All of the following are examples of violent crimes *except:*

Again, the answer is choice b. This is another way of asking you to identify the item that is *not* something.

- **When multiple-choice questions use the cloze technique, be sure to read past the blank until the end of the sentence or paragraph.** The context will help you identify the correct answer.

- **Anticipate the answer first, without looking at the choices.** Then see if your response, or a version of it, is presented as a possible option. If it is, you are likely to be correct.

- **Read all the possible choices to be sure you choose the *best* possible answer.**

- **Use the process of elimination to narrow down your choices.** Cross out answers you know are incorrect. The odds are more in your favor if you are selecting one out of two or three options, rather than one out of four.

- **When unsure, eliminate choices that present an all-or-nothing response.** Life tends not to exist in absolutes. Thus, consider passing over choices that include *always, all, never, only,* or *no one.* However, bear in mind that, indeed, this could be the case. This strategy doesn't *always* work!

- **Mark and come back to questions of which you are unsure.** Sometimes, by working your way through the rest of the exam, you will pick up, or even recall, information that is helpful to you.

- **If you are *sure* that more than one response is correct, even if you are not sure of the others, selecting "all of the above" if it is given as a choice is a good idea.**

Cloze Questions   Many standardized tests used for college placement or to measure competence use a **cloze** format. Blanks, representing sections of missing information, are included in sentences, paragraphs, or longer selections, and possible answers for completing them are presented in a multiple-choice format.

Tips for Responding to Cloze or Fill-in-the-Blank Questions

- **Whether or not choices are provided, always try to complete the response on your own first.** Actually say the word "blank" aloud as you read through to the end of the sentence(s) so that you can "hear" how something sounds. If choices are provided, find the one that most closely matches your prediction. For example, consider the following sentence on a criminal justice exam:

> The unlawful taking and carrying away of another person's property, called _____, includes the intention of depriving the owner of that property.

You might think "stealing" or "theft" could fit in the blank. Suppose you are provided with the following word bank from which to choose your response:

| burglary | larceny | arson | embezzlement | fraud |

You would look for the choice that most closely corresponds to your idea. In this case, the term *larceny* is the correct response.

- **If you have no idea what the answer is, reread the sentence, substituting different choices in the blank.** Decide which seems to work best. You can use the process of elimination here as well.

- **If you are provided with choices, mark these as you use them.** Check to see if you are provided with more options than will be actually used, so that you won't be concerned if you have some left over.

True/False Questions   In true or false questions, you are asked to decide if a statement is accurate or inaccurate.

Tips for Responding to True/False Questions

If any part of the statement is false, then the statement is probably false.

- If you are unsure, and a statement contains terms such as *all, always, everyone* or *never, nothing,* or *no one,* you may do best to mark it false. Likewise, statements that are more qualified, that is they contain words like *perhaps, may, some,* or *might,* are more likely to be true.

- **Read statements with two or more parts closely.** Even though one part of the statement may be true, if the second part is not, then the statement must be considered false.

Matching Questions   This format generally presents two lists, and you must pair or match the items.

Tips for Responding to Matching Questions

- Read all the items first before responding.

- Complete matches of which you are sure first. This will narrow your choices for the remaining items.

- Track your responses. Check off or circle items you use so the "pool" of remaining choices narrows as you move along. Be sure not to completely cross out items you have used so that you can no longer read them! You may need to rethink items and return to previously selected matches.

Essay Questions

Essay questions ask you to respond to a question or series of questions in a narrative written format. You should expect to write answers that are from one paragraph to several in length, depending on the nature of the questions.

This type of question not only taps your understanding and recall of facts and information but also your ability to explain, integrate, and apply that knowledge.

Essay questions are posed in a variety of ways. It is important to understand what each question asks you to do. The terms in the following box are often used in essay questions. Be sure you understand the meaning of each.

Terms Used in Essay Questions

Term	What the Term Is Asking You to Do
Describe	Provide details about a given place, time, or situation. **Describe** the political climate in the United States during the years prior to the Civil War.
Identify	Name or list something. In an essay question, it is often combined with another task. **Identify** the signs and symptoms of HIV Infection and **describe** three methods of treatment currently in use.
Summarize	Identify the key points or elements of an issue, event, process, etc. and tell about each briefly. **Summarize** the characteristics that scientists have used to differentiate the earliest humans from their animal ancestors.
Explain	Provide the reasons, rationale, or process behind a behavior. **Explain** how the release of stress hormones in the body can impact the immune system.
Compare	Show how things are similar. **Compare** the impact of mass media on children today with the impact of mass media on children in the 1950s.
Contrast	Show how things are different. **Contrast** the conditions of maximum-security prisons today with those at the turn of the century. Often, comparison and contrast are included in the same question. **Compare** and **contrast** the similarities and differences between humans and nonhuman primates.
Justify	Provide the reasons or causes for an action or behavior. **Justify** the use of force by the colonists in the acts of rebellion prior to the Revolutionary War.
Discuss	Explain and describe the issue or topic. Include different perspectives and viewpoints. **Discuss** the feelings of educators regarding the issue of year-round schooling.
Evaluate/ Assess	State your opinion or make a judgment about a situation or actions related to it. Back up your view with information or facts. **Assess** the effectiveness of the Salk vaccine in combating polio during the 1950s and 60s.
Trace	Provide a sequential or chronological overview that identifies key elements in the development of a concept, object, or living creature. **Trace** the evolution of homonins from their first appearance through the Paleolithic era.

Tips for Responding to Essay Questions

- **Read all the essay questions first as part of your exam preview.** This way you can jot down any ideas related to the questions that may be triggered as you complete other portions of the test.

- **Annotate the essay questions.** Number the various tasks or criteria that may be part of a question. Underline keywords in the directions or content of the question.

- **Create a quick graphic organizer of your ideas before you begin writing.** A simple outline, chart, or semantic map may help you recall your ideas, organize your essay ahead of time, and provide a guide to which you can refer after you begin composing your essay.

- **Pay attention to your time.** Be sure you allocate enough time to complete your written responses. Also, consider dividing up the time so you can complete the following tasks:

  - *Plan and organize your information before you actually begin to write.* (10–25% of your time) Create a brief outline or map in which you identify your key points and important supporting details. Realize that this planning time is not wasted time, but an important part of your composing process. *Write your response.* (60–80% of your time) Write as legibly as you can, so you won't need to use your revision time to repair messy handwriting!

  - *Proofread, edit, and revise.* (10–20%) Here is your time to check word use, capitalization, punctuation, spelling, and perform a quick content review. Try not to make major adjustments here. Your preplanning should help avoid major organizational pitfalls. Polish and add any additional relevant thoughts that make your work stronger or clearer.

    For example, if you have an hour to complete one essay, you might devote 6 to 15 minutes planning it, 36–48 minutes actually writing it, and 6–12 minutes proofreading, editing, and revising it.

- **It is often best to begin with a thesis statement that states the main idea or point of your response.** Generating a thesis statement helps bring clarity to your response and helps you stay focused on your key points and purpose.

- **Follow the same strategies you have learned for writing a good composition.** Include an introduction that includes brief background information and states your thesis, create body paragraphs that explain and support your thesis, develop clear topic sentences, use transitions, and provide a conclusion in which you summarize your key points.

Reducing Test Anxiety

It would be great if we could just wish away our nervousness about taking exams. Because that's not possible, at least for most of us, let's consider some strategies to lessen the anxiety. Which do you do already? Which might you attempt this semester?

Tips for Reducing Test Anxiety

1. **First and foremost, be prepared for the exam.** Even though you may still have the jitters on test day (which is quite normal), you will be far less stressed out if you know you have done your best to prepare. There's no getting around preparation.

2. **Study for the exam over several days, rather than the night before.** Review your class material on a daily basis and complete your homework assignments on time. *Studying the night before a test should not be the first time you attempt to learn material.* In other words, avoid cramming! The nature of cramming for a test at the last minute lends itself to stress.

   You are likely to feel overwhelmed by the sheer quantity of material you attempt to learn or review in too a short period of time. If the process keeps you up late the night before test day, it has done even greater damage because you need your rest.

3. **Get a good night's sleep before an exam.** Avoid the rationalization that you can relax by going out late and partying! Save that for the night after the exam. You should enter an exam rested, not exhausted.

4. **Eat a light meal before your test.** Don't go into a test hungry. This can impact your energy level and ability to focus and even cause headaches.

5. **Try to arrive at class a little early the day of an exam.** You don't want rushing or worry over being late to be yet another avenue of stress. Leave yourself enough time so you can exhale and relax a bit before the exam is distributed.

6. **Plan on being the last person to leave the exam room.** Take all the time that is afforded to you.

7. **Allow yourself a few minutes at the beginning to preview your exam.** Look over the entire test first. This will help you know what's in store and allow you to pace yourself. You might choose to take care of portions you find easiest first. Previewing the test may also trigger recall of certain ideas or terms you will need for questions at the beginning of the test.

8. **Read all directions slowly and carefully.** In a question with multiple tasks, you might number them to be sure you answer them all. Check off each portion as you complete it.

9. **Write down mnemonics, keywords, simple lists, or formulas that you expect will be needed in the margin or on paper provided.** That way you won't be concerned about forgetting them.

10. **If needed, take a minute "breather" mid-way.** Literally take a deep breath or two, and stretch your hands if you have been writing intensely.

11. **Ask questions.** If this isn't permitted, you will be told. But if it is permissible, you should ask any questions you have.

12. **Some students find it relaxing to chew gum, suck on a candy, or sip a soft drink during an exam.**

13. **Try to remove the notion that any one test or assignment will "make or break" your grade.** Your grades are usually determined using several measures of your achievement. Try to keep this in mind if you find yourself getting very nervous about a particular exam.

14. **Believe in yourself!** If you have prepared and studied for your exam, then wish yourself well, trust in your capabilities, and feel empowered.

In the following box is an article from the Penn State Learning Website that focuses on how you can relieve the physical tension that can be brought on by test anxiety. You might want to incorporate these into your daily life to help cope with stress in general.

Dealing with Physical Tension

Here are a few exercises you can use to help relieve tension in your body. They can also help you relax and boost your energy level.

Focal Breathing

Often, stress is a result of a lack of oxygen. This exercise focuses on breathing and optimizing oxygen intake during every breath.

1. **Start by exhaling all the air in your lungs**. Exhale slowly for 10 seconds. Then, keep exhaling until you feel your lungs are completely empty.
2. **Breathe in through your nose to a count of eight**. Keep your shoulders down and focus on filling your rib cage. As you feel it expand, start to push down into your abdomen. You should feel your lower body expand and near the end of the breath experience pressure in your lower back as your diaphragm moves down.
3. **Exhale slowly, focusing your breathing by shaping your lips in an ooh position**. Pretend there is a candle in front of your mouth that you are trying to blow out. Focusing on this type of breathing will help to focus your mind as well as work to reoxygenate your blood and reenergize your body.

Body Check

Sit down someplace comfortable and close your eyes. Focus on the muscles in your feet and notice if there is any tension. Tell the muscles in your feet that they can relax.

Do the same with your ankles, then move up to your calves, thighs, and buttocks. Tell each group of muscles to relax. Work slowly being sure to scout out any tension that may be hiding in obscure places.

Do the same for your lower back, diaphragm, chest, upper back, neck, shoulders, jaw, face, upper arms, lower arms, fingers, and scalp. Pretend you are tracking an electrical current through your body that is starting at your toes and escaping from your fingertips and scalp. You may have to do this twice to be sure not to overlook any tension spots; be thorough in your search.

Tense and Relax

When scanning your body, you will find tense muscles or groups of muscles. This method will help you to relax specific areas of your body. Focus on the tense muscles and increase the tension. If your shoulders are tense, flex them and pull them back. Arch your back to make them even tenser and hold that position for a count of five.

Then, relax the muscles slowly and keep relaxing them until all the tension is gone. In this way, you can consciously purge an area of all stress.

Exercise Aerobically

This is more of a lifestyle choice than a practical onsite method. Still, it can help to reduce general stress and even improve your health. Do some form of exercise that elevates your heart rate and keeps it beating at a higher rate for 20 to 30 minutes. It should be something you enjoy, and that you can do at least three times a week. Aerobic exercise includes cycling, basketball, running, swimming, walking, and tennis, just to name a few.

Penn State Learning Website: www.PennStateLearning.psu.edu. The Pennsylvania State University, 220 Boucke Building, University Park, PA 16802; ph. 814-865-1841 http://pennstatelearning.psu.edu/resources/ study-tips/test-anxiety/anxiety#tension/07/23/10

Keep this in mind

- Arrive to exams ahead of time with all needed materials.
- Look over the entire test before you begin.
- Keep track of your time.
- Apply strategies to best respond to the various types of questions.
- Use your mnemonic devices and graphic organizers to trigger your memory and organize responses.
- Use extra time to edit and revise your work as needed.
- Apply strategies to stay focused and relaxed.

Show What You Know: Become an Effective Test Taker

In this chapter, you learned how to prepare for exams, understand exam formats, and reduce test anxiety. Key points for each of these skills are shown on the graphics below.

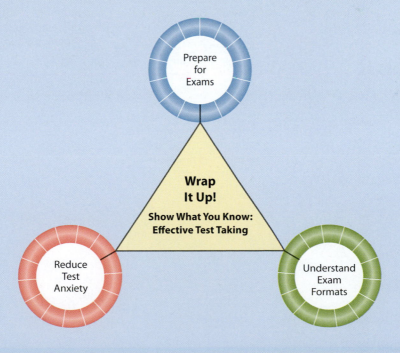

(continued)

(continued)

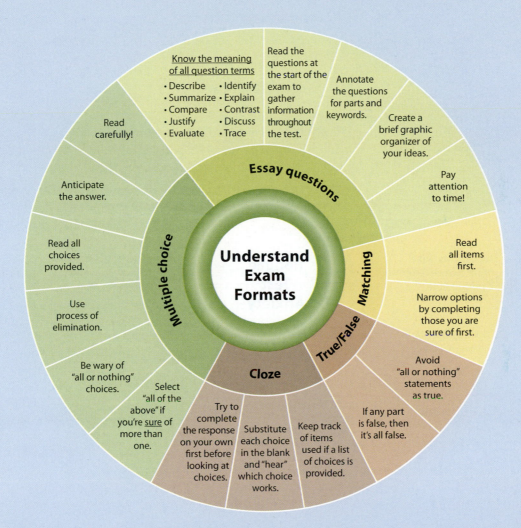

Know the meaning of all question terms
- Describe
- Summarize
- Compare
- Justify
- Evaluate
- Identify
- Explain
- Contrast
- Discuss
- Trace

Read carefully!

Anticipate the answer.

Read all choices provided.

Use process of elimination.

Be wary of "all or nothing" choices.

Select "all of the above" if you're sure of more than one.

Multiple choice

Essay questions

Read the questions at the start of the exam to gather information throughout the test.

Annotate the questions for parts and keywords.

Create a brief graphic organizer of your ideas.

Pay attention to time!

Understand Exam Formats

Matching

Read all items first.

Narrow options by completing those you are sure of first.

True/False

Avoid "all or nothing" statements as true.

If any part is false, then it's all false.

Cloze

Try to complete the response on your own first before looking at choices.

Substitute each choice in the blank and "hear" which choice works.

Keep track of items used if a list of choices is provided.

(*continued*)

(continued)

Reduce Test Anxiety

- Believe in your success.
- Study over several days, not just the night before.
- Get a good night's sleep.
- Exercise and learn breathing strategies for stress reduction.
- Eat a light meal, don't be hungry.
- Arrive a little early—rather than late!
- Plan to stay for all the time allotted.
- Preview your exam to know where you're headed and feel in control.
- Read directions slowly and carefully—annotate to note multiple steps.
- Write down key-words or mnemonics at the start to refer to throughout.
- Take mini "breaks" if time permits.
- If permitted, ask any questions you may have.
- Chew gum, suck candy, sip a drink to relieve tension, if permissible.
- Realize that typically no one measure will constitute your grade.
- Come into the test prepared!

Key Terms

assess

acronym

acrostic

cloze format

compare

contrast

describe

discuss

essay questions

evaluate

explain

graphic organizer

identify

justify

mnemonic device

multiple-choice format

objective questions

summarize

test anxiety

trace

module

Readings About Food and Nutrition

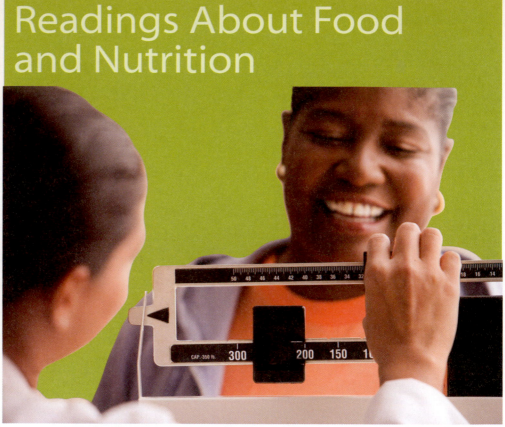

Get Acquainted with the Issue

"You are what you eat."

To be fit and healthy, you need to eat food that is good for you. For many Americans, food has become an obsession. We watch celebrity chefs on television, try to get into the best restaurants, and shop in gourmet super-markets and at health food chains. We teach our children what foods they should and should not eat and pack healthy snacks in their school lunch-boxes. Ironically, researchers have noted an increase in obesity and Type II diabetes, and food safety fears are on the rise. Who's to blame? What can we do? What are other countries doing about trying to stay healthy?

In "A Plateful of Myths," Katherine Hobson asks sociologist Barry Glassner about many food myths. Glassner claims that we pay too much attention to food warnings and nutritional guidance and says we should enjoy what we eat even if it is not always good for our health. In "Japanese Food Pyramid Revised . . ." Stephen Clapp discusses new dietary guidelines that were designed to account for the many young, single people who eat out or bring in prepared foods. In an excerpt from a health textbook, titled "The New Dietary Guidelines for Americans 2005," we learn about the new face of the food pyramid and how scientific research has called for modifications in health and nutrition.

You will encounter the topics of food and nutrition in various academic disciplines. In addition to health, you are likely to read about these subjects in biology, nutrition, nursing, sociology, psychology, media and communications, and business and marketing.

Guided Reading
Reading Selection 1

A Plateful of Myths
By Katherine Hobson

In this selection from U.S. News & World Report *sociologist Barry Glassner, the author of* The Gospel of Food, *answers some important questions about food and nutrition.*

⏪ **before you read**

It's important to review what you may already know about a topic before you read about it. In this way, you will attach your new learning to your background knowledge and more easily understand the new information. (See the section "Access Prior Knowledge" in Chapter 2, page 33.)

Answer the following questions about food and *your* eating habits.

- How would you describe your eating habits?
- Do you think fast foods are to blame for widespread obesity?
- Are you a vegetarian?
- Do you eat organic food?
- Do you think a healthy diet will help you live longer?

Prepare to Read

Preview the selection "A Plateful of Myths," using the THIEVES strategy on page 37.

Exercise 1   **Previewing**

Directions: Complete the following items.

1. Take a look at the selection and check off the items that are available for you to preview.

   _X_ Title
   ___ Headings
   _X_ Introduction
   _X_ Every first sentence in each paragraph
   _X_ Visuals/vocabulary
   ___ End of chapter questions
   _X_ Summary/concluding paragraph

2. Read and highlight to preview the selection.

3. Based on your preview, what do you anticipate the reading will be about?
   The article will discuss food myths, such as that McDonald's is responsible for all the problems related to poor nutrition and obesity. He believes that all eating establishments serve food high in calories. People must be responsible for their own good health and nutrition.

Check Out the Vocabulary

The words in the following section appear in boldface type in the reading. Are you already familiar with them? Knowing what these terms mean will help you better understand the reading.

| **Exercise 2** | **Checking Out the Vocabulary** |

Directions: Complete the matching exercise below *before, during,* or *after* reading. Be sure to review each word in the context of the selection.

_j_	1. acknowledge*	a. part of something larger
_i_	2. anonymously	b. nothing
_l_	3. compromised	c. firmly fixed
_f_	4. condemn	d. commonly repeated word or phrase
_a_	5. component*	e. idea or opinion
_h_	6. demonized	f. to show strong disapproval
_k_	7. dictates	g. distorted; impaired in quality
_c_	8. entrenched	h. to turn into a demon or a bad influence
_d_	9. mantra	i. not named or identified
_b_	10. naught	j. admit as true
_e_	11. notion*	k. governing principles or requirements
_g_	12. warped	l. unable to function well because of a disease

*from the Academic Word List

▶ as you read

Establish Your Purpose

Now, read and annotate the selection. Focus on major points of information about Glassner's discussion of food myths.

Actively Process While You Read

Stop and process information as you read.

| **Exercise 3** | **Processing While You Read** |

Directions: Answer the following questions at the conclusion of each paragraph. This will help you monitor your reading process and understand the material.

Paragraph 1

1. What is the topic of this paragraph?
   Americans' distorted relationship with food

2. What does Barry Glassner tell us about the topic?
   We should spend less time worrying about food and more time enjoying it.

Paragraph 3

3. How does Glassner describe Americans' attitude toward food consumption?
   Americans believe that if they eat foods that are lower in fats, calories, or preservatives, the food will be more nutritious.

Paragraph 5

4. Glassner discovers *two* myths about food and nutrition. List them and explain each one.

1. Restaurant Reviewers: Restaurant owners can identify reviewers, so they prepare food especially for them. As a result, the public cannot count on reviewers for an unbiased opinion. 2.Nutrition: Fresh food is not always the best tasting or the most nutritious. Glassner provides examples of long pasta (better dried), tomato sauces and salsas (more flavorful days or weeks later), and flash-frozen foods (retain more nutrients).

Paragraph 7

5. According to Glassner, what is McDonald's role in the obesity epidemic?

There is no clear evidence that McDonald's has contributed to the increase in obesity because the fast-food industry developed long before obesity became a widespread health problem.

Paragraph 9

6. How would you compare the caloric value of food in fast-food chains and expensive restaurants?

The food in both establishments is just as high in calories.

Paragraph 11

7. Who benefits the most when research tells us a certain food is bad for our health?

the food industry

8. What does the term *functional food* mean?

These are ingredients in foods that claim to promote good health because they have been enhanced through the addition of vitamins and other substances.

Paragraph 13

9. According to Glassner, what are the benefits of eating organic foods?

They provide a benefit only for young children or people who are sick and have weak immune systems.

Paragraph 15

10. What did Glassner learn about the causes of obesity?

The antismoking campaign may have played a role in obesity; when people quit smoking, they ate more.

Paragraph 17

11. Paraphrase Glassner's answer to the following question: Is being obese as bad as we think?

If you are just a little bit overweight, you shouldn't have to worry about becoming obese.

Paragraph 19

12. According to Glassner, what is the relationship between diet and living longer?

Studies do not show a strong correlation between diet and longevity.

Paragraph 21

13. What impact has Glassner's research had on his own philosophy on diet?

He eats what he likes and enjoys, but eats in moderation.

Paragraph 23

14. In the final paragraph, Glassner describes the best meal he ate since he began his research. What can you infer about his diet?

He enjoys eating in expensive restaurants, which may very likely serve food high in calories.
He also does not always eat moderately.

A Plateful of Myths

By Katherine Hobson

1   Sociologist Barry Glassner thinks Americans have a **warped** relationship with food. We simultaneously obsess over celebrity chefs and consider cutting out entire nutrient categories—like fat or carbohydrates—because we think doing so is more healthful. Glassner takes on some of our **entrenched** beliefs about nutrition, restaurants, and health in his new book, *The Gospel of Food,* and wonders what would happen if we spent a little less time torturing ourselves about what we eat and a little more time enjoying a good meal.

2   What's wrong with Americans' relationship with food?

3   Many people believe in a "gospel of **naught**." This is the view that the worth of a meal lies not in what it contains but in what it lacks; the fewer calories, less sugar, less fat, less carbs, fewer preservatives, the better the food. It's an oddly self-depriving notion.

4   What things did you believe about food until you looked into them?

5   One [myth] is that you can rely on restaurant reviewers to know where to eat. Reviewers think they're dining **anonymously**, [but] when I went behind the scenes, most successful restaurateurs know what most of the reviewers look like—as well as how they dress, what disguises they use, and what they tend to order—and they cater to them. On the nutrition side, I certainly subscribed to the **notion** that fresh is best. But fresh isn't always best. Long pastas actually taste better dried; the full flavor of tomato sauces and salsas emerges days or weeks after being prepared. And flash-frozen foods tend to retain more of their nutrients than fresh.

6   McDonald's gets quite a beating in the media. Is it deserved?

7   I neither praise nor **condemn** McDonald's, but the notion that fast-food chains are responsible for all the world's ills just goes way too far. One writer blamed McDonald's for Asian children not being able to use chopsticks as well as their parents' generation. And it's not clear at all that fast food is responsible for the obesity epidemic: The fast-food industry exploded way before the upsurge in obesity. At the same time, a regular

diet of fast food would be unhealthy and unsatisfying, and the critics of chains have done a great service in raising questions about their treatment of workers and animals.

8   The fast-food chains get a lot more criticism than higher-end restaurants. Is there a class issue at work here?

9   Foods at the expensive restaurants in any community are likely to be at least as high in calories, fat, and the substances we're supposed to watch out for as in fast-food restaurants. If you go to Starbucks and buy a Frappuccino, you're going to be getting a tremendous number of calories, too.

10   So what do you think about the new trans-fat ban in New York City?

11   We certainly want to protect our food supply, but when we get hung up on a particular **component**, like refined carbs or a certain type of fat, we can oversimplify it and go too far. Whenever a category of food gets **demonized**, there's a huge opportunity for the food industry; when you condemn one kind of supersizing, you open up the door to another kind. For example, no one would defend the nutritional benefits of supersizing soft drinks, but what about the supersizing in the functional-food market, where omega-3 oils are in everything? Are we overdosing?

12   Did you find any good reason to eat organic foods?

13   Except for special populations, like those with **compromised** immune systems or young children, I found little evidence for the health benefits relative to the additional costs.

14   What did you learn about obesity?

15   What I found out is that there are many causes. The notion that it's just people eating more is simplistic. For example, antismoking campaigns [may have played a role]. When people's weight increased, smoking was going down.

16   Is being obese not as bad as we think it is?

17   There's no question that truly obese people face health dangers. But it's a far cry from **acknowledging** that reality to saying that people who are a few pounds overweight should be worried about it and condemned to eating meals that don't satisfy them.

18   Did you see any evidence that diet can make us live longer?

19   The deeper I looked into the studies, the clearer it became that while my diet partly doesn't meet the current recommendations from the preachers of the gospel of naught, I probably wouldn't live any longer—or maybe only a little bit longer—if I followed their **dictates.**

20   So how do you eat?

21   The moral of the story for me, and what has become my own **mantra,** is to eat well and enjoyably and moderately over the long haul rather than according to any of these pathological patterns that have been common.

22   What's the best meal you ate in your five years of researching the book?

23   It was at Daniel [in New York City]. I had a terrine of foie gras with pheasant. Then tuna tartare with fresh wasabi followed by a Meyer lemon coulis. I had Nantucket Bay scallops served with wild mushrooms and bacon in a rosemary-infused lentil broth and, finally, whole roasted squab with crispy spinach and seared foie gras.

(Hobson, Katherine. "A Plateful of Myths." *U.S. News & World Report* 142.3 [Jan 22, 2007]: 28)

 after you read

Review Important Points

Going over major points immediately after you read, while the information is fresh in your mind, will help you to recall the content and record key ideas.

Exercise 4   **Answering Study Questions**

Directions: Answer the following questions based on the information provided in the selection. You may need to go back to the text and reread certain portions to check that your responses are verifiable and textually based.

1. What is Glassner's personal philosophy about food consumption?
    eat well, enjoyably, and moderately

2. What is the overall tone of the selection? Choose words from the article that support your choice.
    The overall tone is critical. Words from the article that indicate tone include warped, obsess, torturing, self-depriving, goes too far, hung up, demonized, simplistic, a far cry, preachers of the gospel of naught, pathological concern.

3. According to Glassner, what is the impact of food myths on society?
    They create unnecessary and sometimes misplaced fear and anxiety about food, as well as provide simple answers that don't always get to the core of eating problems.

Organize the Information

Organizing the information you have learned from a reading selection shows you have understood it and can restate the material in a different way. You can use this reorganized material to help you study for exams and prepare for written assignments. (See Chapter 9.)

Exercise 5   **Organizing the Information**

Directions: Make a list of food myths that Glassner claims are false or that he debunks in this article.

1. *Fresh food is the most nutritious.*
2. *Fast-food chains are responsible for obesity.*
3. *Only fast-food establishments serve food that is not nutritious.*
4. *If you listen to restaurant reviewers, you will know where to go to eat healthy food.*

Integrate the Vocabulary

Make new vocabulary presented in the reading *your* vocabulary. Using terms in other contexts will help you make them a part of your own spoken and written language.

| Exercise 6 | Integrating the Vocabulary |

Answers will vary. Sample answers provided.

Directions: Replace the italicized, boldfaced phrase in each of the following sentences with a word, or alternate form of the word, from the vocabulary list at the beginning of the selection on page 281. Then, rewrite or paraphrase the sentence using the new word.

1. We learned about the *parts* of healthy nutrition, found in the *New Dietary Guidelines for 2005.*

   *In my health course, we studied the **components** of good nutrition, outlined in the New Dietary Guidelines for 2005.*

2. The college administrator *strongly disagreed with* the fraternity joke that harmed a group of students.

   *The Dean of Student Affairs **condemned** the fraternity prank that had caused injuries to several students.*

3. Incoming freshmen were told to write down only the last four digits of their social security number on the survey so they would remain *unidentified.*

   *The students were asked to not put their names on the survey so that they could remain **anonymous.***

4. My freshman seminar professor always tells us that if you expect *nothing,* you'll get *nothing,* so we have to set goals.

   *Professor Green, who teaches my freshman seminar class, says: "If you expect **naught,** you get **naught,** so you must establish short-term and long-term goals."*

5. Departments such as business, marketing and retailing, and criminal justice now *require* their students to take more course work in English, the social sciences, and humanities.

   *The departments that serve career and technical students now **dictate** more academic course work and liberal arts electives.*

6. The instructor in my criminal justice class has a *distorted* way of being funny; he often makes himself the brunt of his jokes and laughs at them, too.

   *My criminal justice instructor has a **warped** sense of humor; he is constantly laughing at his own jokes and often makes fun of himself.*

7. Each session, my history professor *repeats the same phrase:* Don't forget in the new millennium, it's critical to get a college education. It is because of his strong words that I plan to complete my associate's degree.

   *My history professor's **mantra** about the importance of a liberal arts education inspired me to stay in college and get my associate's degree.*

8. Since the television and newspapers *have indicated* that fast food has *a bad impact* on your health, the college food vendors have begun offering more salads and healthier snacks.

   *Now that the media has **demonized** the fast-food industry, the food court has begun to serve healthier snacks.*

9. Since I read the New Dietary Guidelines, I *recognize* that I have to change my eating habits and exercise routines.

   *After reviewing the New Dietary Guidelines, I can **acknowledge** that my food intake and exercise regimen need to be modified.*

10. Charles was so *involved* in gathering the material, revising the paper, and typing the final draft that he almost forgot to hand it in.

    *Charles was so **entrenched** in his research project that he nearly missed the due date.*

11. Our health professor told us that *ideas* of food and nutrition differ from culture to culture.

    *In health, we learned that **notions** of food and nutrition are culturally determined.*

12. Because the young woman suffers from lupus, and her weak immune system sometimes *makes it difficult for her to function*, she is absent a lot.

    *Since the young lady has lupus, and she has a **compromised** immune system, she misses a lot of classes.*

Exercise 7   **Defining Compound Words**

Directions: Use your knowledge of word parts to define each of the following words. Then write a sentence for each one that uses the word.   *Sentences will vary.*

1. oversimplify (11) *to make so much more simple that errors may be introduced*

2. self-depriving (3) *something that you deprive yourself of*

3. supersizing (11) *increase by a considerable amount or size; to make something larger*

4. upsurge (7) *a rapid increase*

Exercise 8   **Integrating Idiomatic Language**

Directions: Study the meanings of these unusual phrases. The number of the paragraph is indicated in parentheses. Then complete the sentences that follow.

1. **a far cry:** very different from (17)
2. **go too far:** to do something that is extreme (7)
3. **hung up:** to have excessive interest in (11)
4. **over the long haul:** over a long period of time (21)
5. **take on:** to accept as a challenge (1)

1. In your first semester in college, _____*don't take on*_____ more courses than you can handle.

2. If you _____*go too far*_____ with extracurricular activities, you may risk not having enough time to complete your course work.

3. After completing my freshman year of college, I can finally see that the workload is _____*a far cry*_____ from high school.

4. Although I complete all my assignments and prepare for all my exams, I try not to get too _____*hung up*_____ on grades.

5. _____*Over the long haul*_____, I would like to transfer to a four-year college after I get my associate's degree.

Make Personal Connections Through Writing and Discussion

When you make your new learning relevant to yourself in some way, it becomes more meaningful and long lasting. Whenever you read, try to connect to the content on a personal level. How does it relate to you? How can you apply what you have read to other situations? What else would you like to know?

| **Exercise 9** | **Making Personal Connections** |

Directions: Think about yourself in relation to the article you have just read. Apply information you learned from reading it to respond to the following questions.

Answers will vary.

1. When you go to the supermarket, which of these products do you buy? Do you read nutritional labels, or do you buy what you like and enjoy regardless of what you've heard on TV or read in the newspaper or on the Internet?

- trans fat-free products
- organic foods
- farm-fed beef
- free-range chicken
- fish
- low-cholesterol foods
- low-calorie snacks
- fresh fruit
- hormone-free turkey
- nonfat milk

2. According to Dr. Joyce Brothers, psychologist and advice columnist, America's great food obsession has been driven by fear. Since 9/11, the public has been concerned about the upsurge in Type II diabetes. Do you agree or disagree with this statement?

3. In 2001, there was an outbreak of mad cow disease, and most recently, in 2006, an e-coli outbreak at several Taco Bell fast-food establishments. Have any of these incidents impacted your eating habits? If so, how?

Self-Monitored Reading
Reading Selection 2

Japanese Food Pyramid Revised to Take Account of Eating Out

By Stephen Clapp

This selection from Food Chemical News *reports on the new Japanese dietary guidelines.*

 **before you read**

It's important to review what you may already know about a topic before you read about it. In this way, you will attach your new learning to your background knowledge and more easily understand the new information. (See the section "Access Prior Knowledge" in Chapter 2, page 33.)

Answer the following questions about your own experiences before you begin to read.

- Do you prepare your own meals?
- Do you cook from scratch, or do you use canned or frozen foods?
- Do you order take-out or delivery?
- Do you eat out a lot? At fast-food chains? At restaurants?

Prepare to Read

Preview the reading selection by applying the THIEVES strategy on page 37.

Exercise 1	**Previewing**

Directions: Based on your preview, respond to the following questions:

1. Why has the Japanese Food Pyramid been revised?
   to account for the widespread practice of young Japanese eating out at restaurants or buy take-out food

2. How is the new pyramid promoted?
   annual nutrition education convention, food labeling policy, cell phone straps, stickers, and other gadgets that display information about the new food pyramid, revision of textbooks to include these new concepts of nutrition

3. Who will be especially impacted by this new pyramid?
   U.S. exporters to Japan

Check Out the Vocabulary

The following words appear in bold type in the reading. Are you familiar with them? Knowing the meaning of all these terms will increase your comprehension of the material.

Exercise 2	**Checking Out the Vocabulary**

Directions: Complete the matching exercise *before, during,* or *after* your reading. Be sure to review the words in the context of the selection.

_c_	1. consumption*	a.	encourage the sale of
_f_	2. fundamental*	b.	aims at, shoots for
_h_	3. incorporated*	c.	process of eating or drinking
_i_	4. mainstream	d.	meet the needs of
_a_	5. promote*	e.	places where action takes place

_j_ 6. revision*   f. basic, essential

_d_ 7. suit   g. symptoms that are characteristic of a
                                     disease

_g_ 8. syndrome   h. to include as a part of something

_b_ 9. targets   i. belong to a widely accepted group

_e_ 10. venues   j. the process of making changes

*from the Academic Word List

 ## as you read

Establish Your Purpose

Read and annotate the selection as you focus on major points of information. Identify the changes in the new Japanese pyramid. In addition, note how the nutritional guidelines will be promoted.

Actively Process While You Read

Monitor your comprehension as you read. (See the "Monitoring Questions" section in Chapter 2, page 40.) Be sure to stop to reflect at the conclusion of each paragraph, and ask yourself the following questions:

- Did I understand the paragraph?
- What is the main idea?
- Am I ready to continue?

Highlight the most important points. Write your notes in the margins and move on.

Japanese Food Pyramid Revised to Take Account of Eating Out

By Stephen Clapp

---

1   The Japanese Food Pyramid has been significantly revised to take account of the widespread practice of young Japanese to eat out at restaurants or buy take-out food, according to a report by the U.S. embassy's agricultural attache in Tokyo.

2   The previous pyramid resembled an upside-down version of the USDA pyramid, after which it was modeled. Japan's Shokuiku (Food Education) Committee borrowed the **fundamental** dietary principles from the USDA pyramid but altered the design to **suit** the Japanese diet and emphasize best food choices when dining outside the home, the report said. The Japanese pyramid outlines five food groups (grains, vegetables, meats, dairy products, and fruits) and the quantities to be consumed to

The Japanese Food Pyramid

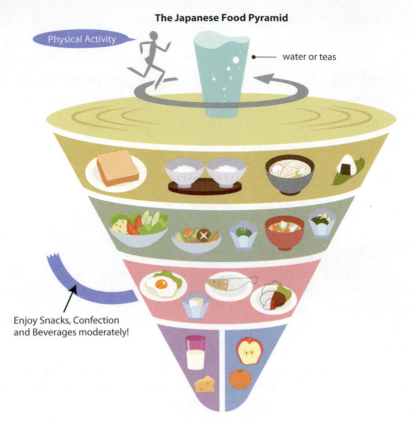

Physical Activity

water or teas

Enjoy Snacks, Confection
and Beverages moderately!

maintain a daily balanced diet. The Japanese pyramid emphasizes **consumption** of locally produced Japanese foods and use of traditional cooking practices. The text warns that failure to follow the recommendations could lead to diabetes, metabolic **syndrome** and other health complications.

3   The upside-down pyramid resembles a child's spinning top, a traditional Japanese toy, with a man running on the surface to symbolize the need to supplement a balanced diet with exercise. The string tab on the side of the pyramid suggests consumption of two servings of Japanese beer.

4   A major difference from the USDA version is that the Japanese pyramid consists of prepared dishes, whereas the American graphic consists of ingredients. Japan wants the advice to be easier to understand by single people who usually dine out or buy take-out foods.

5   The Shokuiku Committee specifically **targets** individuals aged 18–49 with advice to order foods at restaurants according to amounts needed to maintain a daily balanced diet. By displaying prepared foods instead of ingredients, the committee hopes to:

■   Show restaurant chefs what dishes to prepare to fulfill the balanced diet requirements, and

■   Allow individuals to quickly visualize whether or not they consumed an adequate amount of each food group.

The American dietary plan, on the other hand, makes special recommendations for special population groups, such as people over 50, women of child-bearing age, and older adults (Hahn 2007).

6   A third major difference is that the meat groups of the Japanese and USDA pyramids reflect different amounts of red meats and fish. Whereas the Japanese pyramid features mostly fish in its meat group, the USDA pyramid consists almost entirely of red meats. The substitution of rice for grains in the Japanese Food Pyramid is another noticeable difference.

7   The Shokuiku Committee promotes the Japanese pyramid through three **venues:** school systems, households, and food policy. The Ministry of Agriculture, Forestry and Fisheries plans to rely on mass communication channels, such as an annual nutrition education convention and food labeling policy, as the primary promotion methods for introducing the new pyramid.

8   In addition, Japanese nutrition educator Yukio Hattori is proposing the production and marketing of cell phone straps, stickers and other gadgets as a subtle way to introduce the pyramid's five food groups into **mainstream** consciousness.

9   The Ministry of Education, Sports and Arts is currently discussing a **revision** of textbooks used by public elementary and middle schools to include these new concepts of nutrition education. Officials were scheduled to meet this month to decide whether to officially insert shokuiku content into elementary and middle school textbooks.

10   As a result of the Shokuiku Committee's efforts to **promote** concepts in the pyramid, American exporters can expect a possible increase in preference for traditional Japanese agricultural products, the attaché's report said. However, shokuiku proponents don't seem to be going so far as to say that locally produced goods are superior to those that are imported from the U.S. and other countries, nor does it assert that U.S. agricultural products can't be **incorporated** into a Japanese healthy lifestyle.

11   According to Hattori, the manner in which U.S. agricultural imports are prepared is the key to determining their health properties. Japanese businesses and consumers could purchase U.S. agricultural products and prepare them using traditional Japanese cooking styles. Thus, U.S. exporters and Japanese consumers could benefit each in a healthful way, the attaché's report said.

(Adapted from *Food Chemical News* 47.32 [Sept 19, 2005]: 20.)

■ ■ ■

▶ after you read

Review Important Points

Going over major points immediately after you have read, while the information is fresh in your mind, will help you to recall the content and record key ideas.

Exercise 3   **Reviewing Important Points**

Directions: Complete the following exercise using information from the selection. You may need to go back to the text and reread certain sections to be sure your responses are accurate and textually based.

_b_ 1. **The overall topic is:**
   a. the USDA Pyramid.
   b. the Japanese Food Pyramid.
   c. the traditional Japanese toy.
   d. Japanese nutrition.

_c_ 2. **The Japanese Food Pyramid is modeled after:**
   a. a child's spinning toy.
   b. the Japanese school system.
   c. the USDA Pyramid.
   d. individuals aged 18–49.

_d_ 3. **In paragraph 2, the author states that the Japanese Food Pyramid has been revised to account for:**
   a. the five food groups.
   b. a balanced diet.
   c. enjoying home cooked meals.
   d. eating out.

_d_ 4. **Unlike the USDA Pyramid, the Japanese Food Pyramid consists of:**
   a. ingredients.
   b. the five food groups.
   c. take-out foods.
   d. prepared dishes.

_b_ 5. **In paragraph 6, the transition word that indicates a comparison between the Japanese Food Pyramid and the USDA version is:**
   a. major.
   b. whereas.
   c. easier.
   d. or.

_d_ 6. **From paragraph 5, we can infer that a second major difference of the Japanese Food Pyramid is that it:**
   a. is a quick and easy visual.
   b. targets restaurant chefs.
   c. displays fast food.
   d. singles out individuals aged 18–49.

_c_ 7. **The third difference in the Japanese food pyramid can be found in:**
   a. the meat group.
   b. the fish group.
   c. both the grains and meat groups.
   d. the amounts of food.

_d_ 8. **The Shokuiko Committee is going to promote the new pyramid through:**
   a. food labeling.
   b. printed gadgets.
   c. school curriculum.
   d. all of the above.

_a_ 9. **As a result of the revised Japanese Food Pyramid:**
   a. Japan may be using more traditional home-grown products.
   b. Japan will no longer import products from the United States.
   c. America will only be exporting Japanese agricultural products.
   d. The United States will have to be vigilant about the health prop-
      erties of agricultural products.

_c_ 10. **Select the best paraphrase of the following sentence: "According to
      Hattori, the manner in which U.S. agricultural imports are prepared
      is the key to determining their health properties."**
   a. Hattori will determine the nutritional value of food.
   b. Both U.S. and Japanese agricultural products are prepared in a
      healthy way.
   c. U.S. agricultural exports can be incorporated into Japanese
      healthy lifestyle if they are prepared properly.
   d. If the Japanese are going to continue to import agricultural prod-
      ucts from the United States, exporters will need to prepare them
      according to the guidelines in the new Japanese pyramid.

Organize the Information

Organizing information shows that you have understood it and provides
you with a useful study tool. (See Chapter 9.)

Exercise 4   **Organizing the Information**

Directions: Complete the following tasks.

1. Using your notes, complete this table to show the differences between
   the Japanese Food Pyramid and the USDA version.

Japanese Food Pyramid	USDA Food Pyramid
1. Focuses on _____ *prepared* _____ dishes.	1. Focuses on _____ *ingredients* _____.
2. Targets individuals _____ *18–49* _____.	2. Makes special recommendations for special population groups, such as the _____ *elderly* _____, _____ *adults over 50* _____, and _____ *women of child-bearing age* _____.
3. Mostly _____ *fish* _____ in meat group.	3. Almost entirely _____ *red meat* _____ in meat group.
4. Rice _____ *substituted* _____ for grains.	4. Rice is _____ *included* _____ among other grains.

2. Complete the following concept map using details from the selection about how the Shokuiku Committee plans to promote the Japanese pyramid.

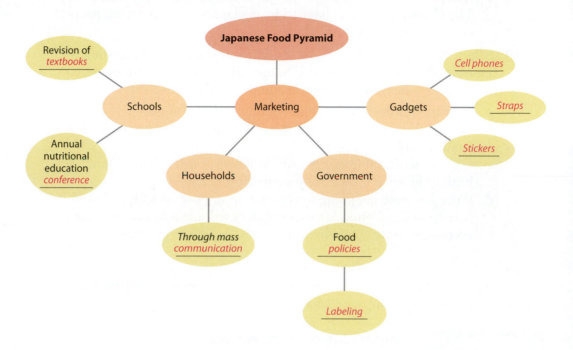

Integrate the Vocabulary

Make the new vocabulary *your* vocabulary.

Exercise 5   **Integrating the Vocabulary**

Answers will vary. Sample answers provided.

Directions: Replace the italicized, boldfaced word or phrase in each sentence with a word, or form of the word, from the vocabulary list at the beginning of the selection. Then paraphrase and rewrite the sentence using the new word.

1. Flyers were hung up throughout the campus to *encourage* students to purchase tickets for the theater class's production of *Hamlet*.
   *To **promote** the sale of tickets for the student performance of Hamlet, flyers were posted all around the campus.*

2. Completing a college degree enables students to become part of *a widely accepted group* of society.
   *The successful completion of a college degree should provide access to **mainstream** society.*

3. In spite of Prof. Green's opposition to Jane's support of gun control, he could not deny her *basic* right to say how she felt.
   *Although Prof. Green was opposed to Jane's position in support of gun control, he could not deny her **fundamental** rights to freedom of speech.*

4. Instructors need to learn how to change their teaching styles to *meet the needs* of different ways that students learn.
   *Instructors must learn to adapt their teaching strategies to **suit** varying learning styles.*

5. Being tired and irritable can be *symptomatic* of a *stress disorder* from which incoming students may suffer.
   *Fatigue and irritability can be signs of a freshman **syndrome**.*

6. One of the roles of a community college is to *aim at* students who want to switch to a four-year college, get a two-year degree, get a vocational certificate, obtain an associate's degree, or get a certificate in a career and technology program.
   *Community colleges **target** students who want to transfer to a four-year college, obtain an associate's degree, or pursue a certificate in a career and technology program.*

7. Colleges often promote their degree and certificate programs through various *places where things happen,* such as open houses, college fairs, and local high schools.
   *The marketing of colleges is often promoted through **venues** such as open houses, college fairs, and local high schools.*

8. Research has shown that **the** *drinking* of soda and *eating* **of** sugary snacks lead to poor grades in young children.
   *A body of research has indicated that the **consumption** of carbonated beverages and sugary snacks contributes to poor academic performance among young children.*

9. It's essential that you *build* enough time for studying into your daily activity plan; otherwise, you will find yourself studying at the last minute for tests.
   *It's critical that you **incorporate** a sufficient amount of time into your schedule so that you will not find yourself cramming for exams.*

10. The Writing Center helped me *make changes in* the final draft of my English term paper before I turned it in for a grade.
    *The Writing Center assisted me in **revising** my English paper before I submitted it for a final grade.*

Make Personal Connections Through Writing and Discussion

| **Exercise 6** | **Making Personal Connections** |

Directions: Think about yourself in relation to the article you just read. Apply the information you learned from reading it to respond to the following questions. *Answers will vary.*

1. Do you believe that Americans would also benefit from dietary guidelines that focus on prepared foods?

2. What information is available to Americans who eat out? Discuss one of the means of conveying that information, or a venue from the following list where this information is available, or mention one of your own ideas.

   ■ healthy menus
   ■ health food restaurants
   ■ listed dietary amounts and values

3. Take a look at the following Mediterranean and Latin American food pyramids. How do they compare to the Japanese food pyramid discussed in the article? Do any of these pyramids reflect the way you eat? Explain.

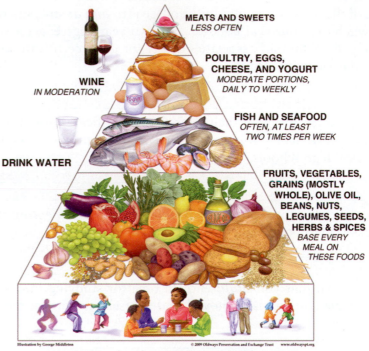

Mediterranean Diet Pyramid
A contemporary approach to delicious, healthy eating

MEATS AND SWEETS
LESS OFTEN

**POULTRY, EGGS,
CHEESE, AND YOGURT**
*MODERATE PORTIONS,
DAILY TO WEEKLY*

WINE
IN MODERATION

FISH AND SEAFOOD
*OFTEN, AT LEAST
TWO TIMES PER WEEK*

DRINK WATER

**FRUITS, VEGETABLES,
GRAINS (MOSTLY
WHOLE), OLIVE OIL,
BEANS, NUTS,
LEGUMES, SEEDS,
HERBS & SPICES**
*BASE EVERY
MEAL ON
THESE FOODS*

Illustration by George Middleton   © 2009 Oldways Preservation and Exchange Trust   www.oldwayspt.org

BE PHYSICALLY ACTIVE; ENJOY MEALS WITH OTHERS

**The Traditional Healthy
Latin American Diet Pyramid**

Daily Beverage
Recommendations:

6 Glasses of Water

Alcohol in
moderation

MEAT
SWEETS
& EGGS

WEEKLY

PLANT OILS

FISH
& SHELLFISH

DAIRY

POULTRY

DAILY

WHOLE GRAINS, TUBERS,
PASTA, BEANS & NUTS

AT EVERY
MEAL

FRUITS

VEGETABLES

Daily Physical Activity

© 2000 Oldways Preservation & Exchange Trust   www.oldwayspt.org

Independent Reading
Textbook Reading Selection: Health

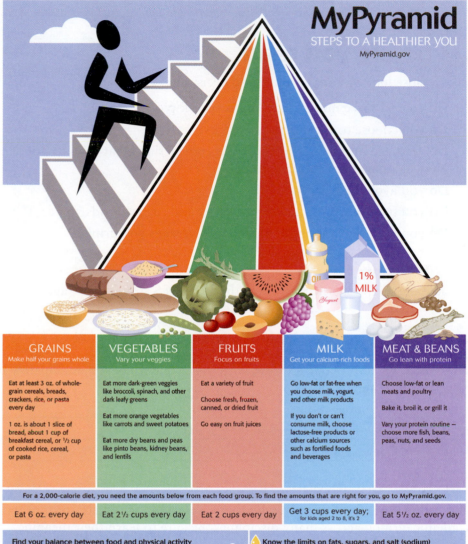

The New Dietary Guidelines for Americans 2005
By Dale B. Hahn, Wayne A. Payne, and Ellen B. Lucas

This selection is excerpted from a health textbook chapter titled "Understanding Nutrition and Your Diet." The chapter discusses the USDA Food Pyramid and provides important dietary guidelines for a healthy diet. Current recommendations focus on the role of trans fat, saturated fat, sodium, and physical activity in health and disease. (Note: As of December 2010, new dietary guidelines are being established.)

◀◀ **before** you read

Take a close look at your current food decisions:

- Do you eat three meals a day, or do you skip one?
- Do you choose to eat nutritious snacks?
- Do you read nutritional labels before considering what food to buy? Now examine your eating patterns.
- Do you avoid high-fat foods?
- Do you try to curb the amount of sweet and sugary foods you eat?
- Do you limit the amount of alcoholic beverages you drink?

Prepare to Read

Preview the textbook selection using the THIEVES strategy on page 36.

Exercise 1   **Developing Preview Questions**

Answers will vary. Sample answers provided.

Directions: Based on your preview, write *three* questions you anticipate will be answered in the selection.

1. *What are the new dietary guidelines for Americans?*
2. *How do the revised guidelines compare with the previous ones?*
3. *What are the new guidelines for sodium and alcohol?*

Check Out the Vocabulary

The following words from this textbook selection are likely to appear in academic writing across many disciplines. Be sure to learn their meanings.

Academic Word List

aspect	part, feature
assess	evaluate
emphasis	indicates importance of something
emphasize	to single out as important, to stress
formulate	to develop as a system or method
linked	a logical connection or relationship (cause and effect)
signify	to make known by actions, signs or speech

| **Exercise 2** | **Checking Out the Vocabulary** |

Directions: Complete each of the following sentences using a word from the Academic Word List.

1. At the beginning of each semester, I try _____*to formulate*_____ an effective schedule that allows time for class and test preparation, as well as work.

2. During the freshman orientation, advisors _____*signified*_____ the importance of reading the college catalog.

3. The _____*aspect*_____ of college I like best is the opportunity to select the courses I want to take.

4. COMM 101, Oral Communications, _____*emphasizes*_____ the study of the historical and contemporary principles and concepts of human communication.

5. According to research, being a successful college student *is* _____*linked*_____ to effective time management.

6. My health professor _____*assesses*_____ my written assignments based on content, organization, use of health terminology, grammar, and word usage.

▶ as you read

Establish Your Purpose

Read and annotate the selection, and focus on the major points of information. Identify the aspects of the new dietary guidelines. See how they differ from the ones established in 1992.

Actively Process While You Read

Highlight the most important points, and annotate within the paragraph and in the margins.

The New Dietary Guidelines for Americans 2005

By Dale B. Hahn, Wayne A. Payne, and Ellen B. Lucas

---

1   The Dietary Guidelines for Americans is science based and summarizes the analysis of new scientific information regarding nutrition, health, physical activity, and food safety. The goal of these guidelines is to lower the risk of **chronic** disease.

2   The United States Department of Agriculture (USDA) releases a revision of their dietary guidelines every five years. However, the food pyramid has not undergone a revision since it was created in 1992. The most recent revision, announced in 2005, has some significant changes to the food pyramid, including its name. It's now called MyPyramid to reflect a personalized approach to healthy eating. The changes are

based on findings that Americans are consuming too many calories and yet are not meeting the recommended intake for some nutrients. It was determined that some Americans have too much saturated and trans fats, cholesterol, and added sugar and salt in their diets and not enough calcium, potassium, fiber, magnesium, and vitamins A, C, and E. There are also some special recommendations for specific population groups. For people over 50, consuming vitamin B12 in its crystalline form (such as **fortified** foods or supplements) is recommended. Women of child-bearing age need to eat iron-rich plant food or iron-**fortified** food with an **enhancer** for iron absorption, such as vitamin-C-rich foods. Taking in adequate amounts of folic acid daily from **fortified** foods or supplements is important for pregnant women or women who may become pregnant. Older adults, people with dark skin, and those not exposed to enough sunlight need to consume extra vitamin-D-fortified foods and/or supplements.

3   These findings were used to **formulate** the new USDA Food Guide for Americans, which focuses on overall caloric intake rather than on one particular food group, such as fats or carbohydrates. Portion sizes are **emphasized**, and the recommendations are made in cups rather than serving size, to help people have better portion control. There is also an increased **emphasis** on consuming nutrient-dense foods, which provide substantial amounts of vitamins and minerals and comparatively few calories. Junk foods typically are not nutrient dense, because they are high in sugar and saturated and trans fats, high in calories, and low in vitamins and minerals.

4   Americans are advised to consume more whole grains, milk products, fruits, and vegetables as well. Another key **aspect** is the focus on daily exercise, with 60 to 90 minutes of **moderate** exercise as the recommended amount. Restricting salt, alcohol, and trans fat are other important aspects of the dietary guidelines.

5   The new food pyramid, MyPyramid, takes a more personalized approach to health eating (see Figure A). The pyramid has been tipped on its side, and the colors and the size of the bands reflect the proportion of each food group people generally need to consume each day. The steps **signify** the importance of daily exercise. The food pyramid acknowledges that people have different dietary needs based on age, **gender,** and physical activity level. There are 12 different recommendations based on these factors, and you can find the one that best fits you through the USDA's website at www.mypyramid.gov. People can also **assess** their activity level and food intake through www.mypyramidtracker.gov.

Sodium Intake

6   Something new to the USDA guidelines is the limitation on salt intake. They advise consuming less than 2,300 mg, or 1 teaspoon, of sodium each day and to choose and prepare foods with little salt. Most of our salt intake comes from processed or prepared foods. Many people are unaware of the high sodium content in prepared food, sauces, soups, and canned foods, and so reading the labels for ingredients is extremely important. You might be surprised by some of the foods that contain salt—cookies, minute rice, canned green beans, soft drinks, and cereal. It is also difficult to know how to make healthy choices when eating out if you don't know the sodium content in the menu items. Too much sodium is **linked** to hypertension, and about 30 percent of Americans have sodium-sensitive high blood pressure, which can lead to heart attack or stroke. It is estimated that about 150,000 deaths each year are caused by too much salt.

Alcohol Consumption

7   Another difference in the new dietary guidelines is the recommendation regarding alcohol consumption. The USDA states that "those who choose to drink alcoholic beverages should do so sensibly and in **moderation**." **Moderation** is defined as the consumption of up to 1 drink per day for women and up to 2 drinks per day for men. One drink is defined as either 12 fluid ounces of regular beer, 5 fluid ounces of wine, or 1 ½ fluid ounces of 80-proof distilled spirits. Since alcoholic beverages tend to contribute calories but little nutrition, they are **counterproductive** to taking in sufficient nutrients while not going over the daily caloric allotment. However, there are some indications that **moderate** alcohol consumption, such as having a glass of red wine each day, assists in decreasing the risk of coronary heart disease.

(Adapted from Hahn 2007)

after you read

Think back to the questions you posed after previewing the selection but before you actually read. Now that you have read the selection, can you answer your initial questions?

| **Exercise 3** | **Answering Your Preview Questions** |

Directions: If you have discovered the answers to your preview questions, *Answers will vary.*
write the answers on the lines provided.

1. _____

2. _____

3. _____

| **Exercise 4** | **Reviewing Important Points** |

Directions: Choose the best answer for each of the following questions using information provided in the selection.

_c_ 1. The design of the food pyramid is based on:
    a. current food safety findings.
    b. physical activity requirements.
    c. scientific evidence or findings.
    d. nutritional needs of a particular age group.

_a_ 2. The main idea of paragraph 2 is that:
    a. The new pyramid reflects the need to decrease the intake of calories and increase the intake of certain vitamins.
    b. The dietary guidelines are revised every five years.
    c. The new guidelines are focused on certain age groups, but mostly on younger people.
    d. Women of child-bearing age require a special diet to be healthy.

<u>d</u>   3. **The 2005 pyramid reflects the following changes:**
a. focuses on overall caloric intake instead of one food group.
b. portion sizes emphasized in cups rather than serving size.
c. emphasis on increased consumption of nutrient-dense foods high in minerals and vitamins but lower in calories.
d. All of the above

<u>c</u>   4. **Another important change to the guidelines is the emphasis on:**
a. occasional exercise.
b. rigorous exercise.
c. daily exercise.
d. aerobics.

<u>a</u>   5. **The main idea of paragraph 5 is:**
a. located in the first sentence.
b. located in the last sentence.
c. stated and restated in the first and last sentences.
d. unstated.

<u>d</u>   6. **The personalized approach to healthy eating is evident in all of the following except:**
a. the personal steps.
b. the slogan and URL.
c. the acknowledgment of different dietary needs.
d. the five food groups.

<u>d</u>   7. **From Figure A, we can infer that daily physical activity is represented by:**
a. the colors and sizes of the bands.
b. the slogan, "Steps to a Healthier You."
c. the website.
d. the steps and the person climbing them.

<u>c</u>   8. **To limit your intake of salt, you should:**
a. Eat foods cooked at home.
b. Consume more processed or prepared foods.
c. Check labels for ingredients.
d. Avoid adding salt to food.

<u>c</u>   9. **High sodium intake can lead to:**
a. an increase in weight.
b. low blood pressure.
c. coronary heart disease.
d. diabetes.

<u>d</u>   10. **Drinking a glass of red wine a day may:**
a. increase the chance of coronary heart disease.
b. lower caloric allotment.
c. provide sufficient daily nutrients.
d. lower the risk of a heart attack.

| Exercise 5 | **Organizing the Information** |

Directions: The USDA Nutritional Guidelines have been modified to reflect the current scientific research in health and nutrition. Using the sections of the reading you highlighted and your annotations, complete the following table with details from the 2005 food pyramid.

The *New* Food Pyramid

	Modification	**Significance**
Name	MyPyramid	personalizes approach
Design	*turned on its side*	*does not show a hierarchy of foods to eat*
	color and size of bands	*shows proportion for each food group in cup size*
	steps	*emphasizes the importance of daily exercise or activities*
	website	*Gives more information and provides an opportunity to see which recommendation suits you (personal assessment).*
Food intake	cup size	*allows for better portion control*
	Focuses on overall caloric intake	Not focused on one food group, such as fats or carbohydrates
Food selections	Emphasizes more nutrient-dense food	*Provides more vitamins and minerals, fewer calories*
	sodium	*Limits salt intake to one teaspoon daily to lower risk of hypertension.*
	alcohol	Alert public to drink in moderation because alcohol adds a lot of calories to the diet but little nutrition

| Exercise 6 | **Using Context Clues** |

Directions: Use context clues in the reading selection to discern the meaning of the following words in bold print. The paragraph in which each sentence appears is indicated in parentheses. A second sentence shows the word used in another context. Underline any clue words that help you define the bold-face words or terms. Then write a definition for each.

1. • The goal of these guidelines is to lower the risk of **chronic** disease and promote health through diet and physical activity. (1)
   • The consumption of too much salt in your diet can lead to hypertension and other **chronic** diseases.

The word **chronic** means *a serious illness of long or ongoing duration, such as hypertension*

2. • Women of child-bearing age need to eat iron-rich plant food or an iron-fortified food including an **enhancer**, such as vitamin C, for iron absorption. (2)
   • People who suffer from certain eating disorders may require medications to reduce anxiety and **enhancers** to stimulate their appetite.

The word **enhancer** means *something taken to supplement and increase the desired effect of another substance* .

3. • Consuming adequate amounts of folic acid daily from **fortified** foods or supplements is important for pregnant women or women who may become pregnant. (2)
   • Prior to the **fortification** of milk with vitamin D, it was not uncommon for children to suffer from rickets, a bone disease.

The word **fortified** means *to increase effectiveness by adding ingredients.*

4. • The food pyramid acknowledges that people have different dietary needs based on age, **gender,** and physical activity level. (5)
   • Courses in Women's Studies emphasize the roles of women in a cross-cultural context, introducing students to **gender** bias in the workplace, in professions, and in the arts.

The word **gender** means *the condition of being male or female* .

5. • Another key aspect is to focus on daily exercise, with 60 to 90 minutes of **moderate** exercise as the recommended amount. (4)
   • A **moderate** consumption of alcohol might be considered one glass of red wine.

The word **moderate** means *not an excessive amount* .

6. • Since alcoholic beverages tend to contribute calories but little nutrition, they are counterproductive to taking in sufficient nutrients while not going over the daily caloric **allotment.** (7)
   • The **allotment** of student scholarships is usually based on the amount of funds that were raised during the year.

The word **allotment** means *the amount set aside for a specific purpose* .

Exercise 7	**Defining Compound Words**

Directions: Use your knowledge of word parts to define the following words. Then write a sentence that uses the word.

Sentences will vary.

1. counterproductive (7) *tending to defeat the purpose instead of serving the purpose*

2. hypertension (6) *high blood pressure*

3. intake (6) *taking in of food, consumption*

4. iron-fortified (2) *iron is added* _____

_____

5. iron-rich (2) *abundance of iron* _____

_____

6. nutrient-dense (3) *contains a lot of nutritional value but is low in calories* _____

_____

7. sodium-sensitive (6) *sensitive to the effects of sodium or salt* _____

_____

Exercise 8   **Make Personal Connections Through Writing and Discussion**

Directions: Think about yourself in relation to the article you just read. Apply the information you learned from reading it to respond to the following questions.

Answers will vary.

1. Recommend additional ways to maintain a healthy lifestyle, which include physical activities.

2. Make a list of *smart* supermarket tips. These tips will help you buy more nutritious food and maintain a healthy diet.

   Example: Read food labels and check for the percentages of fat, sodium, and sugar in each product.

3. A vegetarian diet consists of food mostly obtained from plant sources. Modify the food pyramid to provide a substitute for meat. Survey your classmates to see if there are any vegetarians to help you with your suggestions.

4. Considering that people from many cultures live in the United States and still choose to eat their traditional foods, do you think the new pyramid accounts for their choices? How can the pyramid be designed to include multicultural eating habits?

Synthesizing Your Reading: Reflective Journal Writing

Food and Nutrition

Having read these three selections on the topic of food and nutrition, you now have a broader, more scholarly understanding of the subject matter.

Write a reflective journal entry on the topic of food and nutrition, demonstrating both your knowledge of the content in the selections and your own viewpoints on the issues. You should write at least one page.

In your first section, briefly summarize each selection. Include a thesis and a few key points for each.

In the second section, reflect on the topic. Consider your own experience with food and nutrition. What ideas from the readings do you feel are most valuable personally? What new insights from the readings do you value the most? How else can society support good eating habits? Explain your thinking.

Readings About Stress

Get Acquainted with the Issue

"I'm so stressed out!"

Even if you have never uttered these words, you have probably felt this way. Stress is a reaction experienced by us all. It is a human response to our thoughts, our environment, or both. Sometimes stress can actually help us. It moves us into action. But stress can also have negative effects, both physically and psychologically.

In "Taming the Stress Monster," you will read about how stress works in our bodies, ways to recognize your own stress, and personalized strategies for coping with it. "The Aftermath of Disaster" discusses the long-term, emotional impact of surviving a disastrous event. Last, in an excerpt titled "Job Stress," from a criminal justice textbook, you will learn of the extraordinary work-related stressors experienced by police officers, and stress management techniques they use that may be applicable to us all.

You will encounter the topic of stress in various academic disciplines. In addition to criminal justice, you are likely to read about stress in social sciences, such as sociology, psychology, and anthropology, and in life sciences such as biology, health, and anatomy. Study in communications and business and marketing are also likely to include a discussion of this topic.

Guided Reading
Reading Selection 1

Taming the Stress Monster
By Terri D'Arrigo

This selection, from the journal Diabetes Forecast, *discusses several aspects of stress, including how it develops in our bodies and how we can cope with it.*

◀◀ before you read

It's important to think about what you may already know about a topic before you read. In this way, you will attach your new learning to your background knowledge and more easily understand the new information. (See Chapter 2, "Access Prior Knowledge," page 33.)

Answer the following questions about stress. Think about your own experiences with stressful events in your life.

- What kinds of events create stress in your life?
- How does your body physically react to stress?
- What are some ways you cope with stress?

Prepare to Read

Preview the selection "Taming the Stress Monster," using the THIEVES strategy on page 36.

Exercise 1   **Previewing**

Directions: Complete the following items.

1. Take a look at the selection and check off the items that are available to you for preview.

   _X_ Title
   _X_ Headings
   _X_ Introduction
   _X_ Every first sentence in each paragraph
   _X_ Visuals/vocabulary
   ___ End of chapter questions
   _X_ Summary/concluding paragraph

2. Read and highlight to preview the selection.

3. Based on your preview, what do you anticipate the reading will be about?
   It will discuss the meaning of stress; how it works and affects our body. It will also discuss how to respond to stress and how to cope with it.

Answers will vary. Sample answers provided.

Check Out the Vocabulary

The words in the following section appear in boldface type in the reading. Are you already familiar with some of them? Knowing the meaning of all these terms will increase your understanding of the material.

Exercise 2   **Checking Out the Vocabulary**

Directions: Complete the matching exercise below *before, during, or after* reading. Be sure to review each word in the context of the selection.

_a_	1. chronic	a. continuing over a long time or recurring frequently
_b_	2. complementary*	b. going well with, making perfect in combination with
_k_	3. deliberately	c. fine or delicate; not strong or direct
_d_	4. deviating*	d. turning aside from the normal course of action
_j_	5. gauge	e. soothing, contemplative thinking or mind relaxation
_f_	6. glucose	f. sugar occurring in the body
_h_	7. inadvertently	g. characterized by unexpected or seemingly contrary outcomes
_i_	8. involuntary	h. unintentionally or thoughtlessly

_g_   9. ironically   i. occurring without conscious choice; unintentional

_e_   10. meditation   j. measure; determine the exact dimensions, capacity, quantity or force

_c_   11. subtle   k. done with intent or purpose

*Academic Word List

 as you read

Establish Your Purpose

Now, read and annotate the selection. Focus on major points of information. Identify ways to recognize stress and strategies you can use to cope with stress.

Actively Process While You Read

Stop and process information as you read.

| Exercise 3 | **Processing While You Read** |

Directions: Answer the following questions at the conclusion of each paragraph. This will help you monitor your reading process and understand the material.

Paragraph 1

1. What is the topic of this paragraph?
   stress

2. What is the main idea of the paragraph?
   If left unchecked, stress can have many negative physical effects on us.

Paragraph 2

3. What are the two forms of stress discussed in the paragraph?
   The author discusses the stress of major life events, both good and bad, and the smaller stresses that sneak up on us and build up to cause tension more subtly.

Paragraph 4

4. According to the author, what is the key to conquering stress?
   The key is to learn your body's subtle reactions to the things that cause stress and then use techniques to cope with them before the stress gets out of control.

Paragraphs 5–6

5. What happens in the body when it is confronted with danger?
   It releases hormones, such as epinephrine and cortisol, that raise blood pressure, increase heart rate, and make you more alert and sensitive to your environment. The liver releases glycogen, which converts to glucose to give the body energy.

6. When is your body's stress response most helpful to you?

It helps when you are in danger, especially if you need to run away quickly or fight.

Paragraph 7

7. How can this response be harmful, especially to people with diabetes?

People with diabetes can be left with high blood sugar. People can get tension headaches. If they deal with constant stress, their bodies don't have time to recover. This can lead to raised blood pressure and cholesterol, a weakened immune system, and an upset digestive system.

Paragraph 9

8. What is the irony that the author identifies about learning how to relax?

*The irony is that by discovering what it feels like to be relaxed, it easier to identify when one is **not** relaxed and when tension is taking over.*

Paragraphs 9–14

9. Identify three methods suggested by the author to help you recognize signs of stress, and briefly describe each.

1. Progressive muscle relaxation—tighten and release muscles one group at a time, forcing muscles to relax. Knowing how they feel relaxed can help you know when they are tense. 2. Keep a journal. Record all negative events and note the intensity of your reactions and how you felt. 3. Biofeedback—instruments measure involuntary physical responses to stress so you can recognize what they feel like.

Paragraphs 15–24

10. What is the author listing in this paragraph?

The author is listing different strategies for coping with stress.

Paragraph 25

11. Paraphrase the meaning of this paragraph.

Everyone experiences stress.

Paragraph 26

12. In this paragraph, what two categories are used to review additional signs of stress?

physical signs and psychological signs

Taming the Stress Monster
By Terri D'Arrigo

Taming the stress monster: Here's the lowdown on stress—how it works, how to recognize it, and how to beat it.

1   It's a soft word for something so rough on your health. Studies have shown that stress can affect everything from your blood glucose to your digestion to your ability to get a good night's sleep. If it's not managed, stress can even shorten your life by raising your blood pressure and cholesterol and damaging your heart.

2   Stress can take two forms. First there is the stress of major life events, like getting married or divorced, having a child, mourning the loss of a loved one, changing jobs,

moving, or caring for a chronic disease like diabetes. All of these events cause stress, even the happy ones.

3   But stress can sneak up on you, too. When it does, it's usually negative stress. Little things like traffic jams, computer glitches, and rude salespeople can build tension with only the subtlest of clues until—WHAM!—seemingly out of nowhere your head is pounding and you feel like you've just gone a few rounds with Mike Tyson.

4   There are ways to conquer stress, however. The key lies in learning your body's **subtle** reactions to the things that set you on edge, then applying techniques for coping that don't involve blowing your stack.

How Stress Works

5   Your body's stress response is geared toward keeping you alive. When confronted with danger, your body releases stress hormones like epinephrine (adrenaline) and cortisol, which raise your blood pressure, speed your heart rate, and make you more alert and sensitive to your environment. The liver releases a burst of glycogen that is converted into glucose to give your muscles quick energy.

6   "This is all fine if you have to run away, or engage in a battle, but if you are in an office and someone is screaming at you, you have all of that extra glucose in your blood," says Angele McGrady, PhD, MEd, LPCC, professor in the department of psychiatry and director of the **Complementary** Medicine Center at the Medical University of Ohio in Toledo. In people without diabetes, the body releases more insulin to counteract the extra glucose in the blood. If you have diabetes, however, you may be left with high blood glucose. If you're having an argument with someone, the stress response will be obvious. You'll feel your heart pounding and the sweat beading on your brow. Eventually you'll calm down again and your body will recover.

7   But what about the little stressors of daily life—the traffic jams and long lines? Other than feeling annoyed, your reactions to those things may be so subtle that you miss them entirely—until they all come together and give you that killer tension headache. What's more, if you're constantly dealing with low-grade stress, your body doesn't have a chance to recover. This can put your health at risk by raising your blood pressure and cholesterol, weakening your immune system, and upsetting your digestive system. The trick, then, is to handle stress before it becomes **chronic.**

Recognizing the Signs

8   There are several ways to learn how you respond to stress.

9   *Learn to relax.* **Ironically**, learning how to relax can help you recognize when you're stressed, says Richard Surwit, PhD, professor and vice chairman for research, psychiatry, and behavioral sciences and chief of the division of medical psychology at the Duke University Medical Center in Durham. "Once you know what relaxation feels like, it's easier to tell when you're **deviating** from that and tension is taking over," he says. He suggests a technique called progressive muscle relaxation in which you tighten and release your muscles one group at a time in sequence. **Deliberately** tensing and releasing your muscles forces them to relax. Knowing how your muscles feel

when relaxed will make it easier to tell when you're **inadvertently** tensing them in response to stress. Often this technique begins with one foot or hand, then moves to the other foot or hand, then progresses through the body. As you work each group, tense the muscles of that group as tightly as you can for 8 to 10 seconds, then suddenly release.

10   Your local community center, hospital, or university may offer classes in progressive muscle relaxation, either by itself or as part of a stress management course.

11   *Keep a journal.* Experts at the multicenter Mayo Clinic suggest keeping a stress journal for a week. Record any events or interactions that led to negative feelings or physical reactions, including who was involved, where you were, what time of day it happened, and what you said or did at the time. Note the intensity of your reactions as well. Were you merely irritated, or were you very angry? Were you a little bit rattled afterwards, or did you feel nauseated?

12   *Biofeedback.* Biofeedback is a procedure in which an instrument **gauges** subtle, **involuntary** physical reactions to stress so you can learn what they feel like. Electrodes are placed on your face and various places on your body and a therapist guides you through exercises designed to inspire either a stress response or relaxation. During the exercises, a machine records changes in your skin temperature or how tense the muscles of your face are. The therapist—usually a psychologist, counselor, nurse, or social worker—alerts you to those changes as they happen so you can become aware of them.

13   "After a while, you'll no longer need the machine," says McGrady. "You'll know when you're clenching your teeth or scrunching your face up."

14   You can ask your doctor for a referral for biofeedback or enroll yourself in a stress management program that offers it.

Taming the Beast

15   Once you know the signs of stress, it's time to work on your coping.

16   *Start small.* One cause of stress is feeling like things are beyond your control, so empowering yourself by approaching a small, manageable task can help, says William H. Polonsky, PhD, CDE, president of the Behavioral Diabetes Institute in San Diego. It doesn't matter how small the task is, he adds. "If you can't think of anything else, rearrange your silverware or sock drawer."

17   *Exercise.* Studies have shown that exercise helps you burn off "nervous energy" and relieve muscle tension. "If you've been having trouble sleeping because your body is wired, that might be the kind of stress you can work out by getting regular physical activity like brisk walking," says Polonsky.

18   *Meditate.* On the other hand, if you can't sleep because you can't turn your mind off, **meditation** might be more effective, says Polonsky. You might consider seeking formal instruction in meditation if you have no experience with it.

19   *Avoid stress eating.* When you're feeling stressed, you might be tempted to snack, and "comfort" foods high in carbohydrate like cake, pasta, or mashed potatoes might be particularly appealing. This can leave you feeling more anxious as your blood **glucose** skyrockets, however.

20   *Talk it out.* Sometimes just talking about what's causing stress is enough to relieve some of the tension. Talk to people who will listen and offer support instead of those

who will feed your stress by venting along with you or blaming you for your problems, says Polonsky.

21   *Remove stressors from your environment.* One way of coping is to resolve the issues that are causing the stress. This is called "problem-focused coping." Say your commute requires sitting in bumper-to-bumper traffic for at least an hour each way. With problem-focused coping, you might research options in public transportation, map out a new route involving side roads that are less clogged, or ask your boss if you can telecommute.

22   *Rethink your response.* Sometimes there's nothing you can do to change a situation. That's when it's useful to use "emotion-focused coping" in which you change how you react to a stressor, says Polonsky. Say your job and location leave you no choice but to commute in traffic. Rather than sit in your car stewing, you might instead view the time as an opportunity to listen to new music or a chance to think quietly without interruption from co-workers or family.

23   *Take a class.* Many hospitals, community health centers, and employers offer stress management courses or seminars. These classes can include several different techniques ranging from progressive muscle relaxation to meditation.

24   *Know when to seek psychiatric help.* "Self-help is a legitimate thing to do, but if, at the end of 6 or 8 weeks you're not getting anywhere, consider getting professional psychiatric help," says Surwit. If you start to feel overwhelmed, don't be afraid to ask your doctor for a referral to a mental health professional.

25   *When you're confronted with stress, remember that you're not alone.* It strikes everyone in varying degrees at different times in their lives. "Show me someone who doesn't have stress and I'll show you someone in massive denial," says Surwit.

26   In the interest of your health and peace of mind it's best to subdue the stress monster, however. Your head, heart, stomach, and blood glucose will thank you for it.

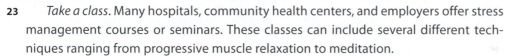

Recognizing the Signs of Stress

Physical Signs of Stress

back pain	diarrhea	racing heart
chest pain	headaches	shortness of breath
cold hands	indigestion	changes in blood glucose
constipation	muscle tension	

If these symptoms are sudden or severe, or if they persist despite attempts to cope with stress, contact your doctor.

Psychological Signs of Stress

anxiety	frustration	irritability
difficulty thinking clearly	indecisiveness	nervousness
forgetfulness	insomnia	

Some of these signs are similar to signs of low blood glucose. If you experience them, check your blood glucose.

A Word About Lows

27   Several symptoms of low blood glucose overlap with signs of stress, including headaches, a racing heart, anxiety, and irritability. When you experience these symptoms, check your blood glucose.

28   If you use techniques like progressive muscle relaxation, don't worry about relaxing so much that you miss a low, says Angele McGrady, PhD, MEd, LPCC, professor in the department of psychiatry and director of the Complementary Medicine Center at the Medical University of Ohio in Toledo.

29   "You can't relax away symptoms that are really from low blood glucose," she says. "The anxiety caused by the brain's need for sugar is a survival drive, and it won't go away through relaxation."

30   She adds that not knowing what you are experiencing—stress or a low—is anxiety-provoking itself, so checking your blood glucose will not only ensure that you catch any lows in time to treat them, but will ease your mind as well.

Adapted from "Stress and Diabetes," by Terri D'Arrigo, appearing in the April 2000 issue of *Diabetes Forecast*.

■ ■ ■

after you read

Review Important Points

Going over major points immediately after you read, while the information is fresh in your mind, will help you to recall the content and record key ideas.

Exercise 4   **Reviewing Important Points**

Directions: Answer the following questions based on the information provided in the selection. You may need to go back to the text and reread certain portions to be sure your responses are correct and can be supported by information in the text.

1.   What is the author's overall message in this selection?

Stress can have many negative effects on one's physical and mental health. It is important for people to recognize when they are stressed and learn strategies to cope with stress.

2.   What is the difference between "problem-focused" coping and "emotion-focused" coping of stress? Provide an example for each.

Problem-focused coping involves resolving the issues that are causing stress. For example, if you get stressed driving to work every day in traffic, change your route or take public transportation. In emotion-focused coping, you try to change your reaction to a situation. If you must commute, try to turn it into a time for thinking and listening to pleasant music.

3.   Explain how biofeedback works as a method to recognize stress.

It measures involuntary physical reactions to stress by hooking a person up to electrodes while they are going through exercises that create either a stress response or relaxation. A machine records changes in skin temperature or muscle tension. A therapist tells the person of the changes so he/she can become aware of them. Over time, the person won't need the machine to let him/her know when his/her body is showing tension.

Organize the Information

Organizing the information you have discovered in a reading selection shows you have understood it and can restate the material in a different way. You may use this reorganized material to help you study for exams and prepare for written assignments. (See Chapter 9.)

| **Exercise 5** | **Organizing the Information** |

Directions: The following outline covers a section of the article "Taming the Stress Monster." Notice how the heading of the section "Discovering Your Stress" is used as the title of the outline. Use your annotations of major topics and important details to guide you in completing this outline.

Discovering Your Stress

I. **Learn to Relax**

    A. Relaxing can help you recognize when you are stressed.

    B. Relaxing makes it easier to tell when you are *deviating from relaxation* and tension is taking over.

    C. Try the technique called *progressive muscle relaxation*.

        1. Tighten and release muscles one group at a time.

        2. It forces muscles to *relax*.

        3. Knowing the relaxed sensation helps you recognize *when you are inadvertently tensing them in response to stress*.

        4. The technique begins with *one foot or hand* and moves to the rest of the body.

II. *Keep a Journal*

    A. Suggested by *the Mayo Clinic*.

    B. Record events or interactions that led to *negative feelings or physical reactions*.

    C. Note the *intensity* of your reactions.

III. *Use Biofeedback*

    A. Instruments gauge subtle, involuntary, *physical reactions to stress*.

    B. Procedure

        1. *Electrodes* placed on face and body

        2. Therapist guides exercises to *inspire a stress response or relaxation*.

        3. Machine records *changes in skin temperature or facial muscles*.

        4. Therapist alerts you to *changes so you can become aware of them*.

    C. Long-term results

        1. *No longer need the machine*.

        2. *You will know when your body is feeling stress*.

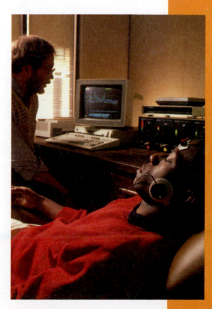

Integrate the Vocabulary

Make the new vocabulary presented in the reading *your* vocabulary. Using the terms in other contexts will help you make them a part of your own spoken and written language.

Exercise 6   **Integrating the Vocabulary**

Directions: Replace the italicized, boldfaced phrase in each of the following sentences with a word, or alternate form of the word, from the vocabulary list at the beginning of the selection. Then, rewrite and paraphrase the sentence using the new word.

Example

Bob was in ***imminent danger*** of failing biology because he had not completed two important assignments.

Answers will vary. Sample answers provided.

<u>*Because Bob had not finished two important assignments, he was in **peril** of failing biology.*</u>

1. Because Randi had not kept a running record of her grades on projects and exams in Chemistry 203, it was difficult for her to ***realistically measure*** how she was doing in the class.
   *Because she had not kept track of her grades, it was difficult for Rand to **gauge** how she was doing in Chemistry class.*

2. The professor didn't accept Jana's excuse for being late this time, because she had been absent ***on an ongoing and regular basis*** throughout the semester.
   *Because she had been **chronically** absent the whole semester, her professor didn't accept Jana's latest excuse for being tardy.*

3. Much to his dismay, Jason **automatically** ducked when the basketball came toward him, rather than intercepting it to make the final shot of the game.
   *Jason **involuntarily** ducked when the ball came at him, instead of going for it to take the final shot of the basketball game.*

4. To try to relax before her final exams, Michelle ***sits quietly and contemplatively to clear her mind*** in a quiet corner of her room for at least 15 minutes every day for a week.
   *Michelle **meditates** regularly every day for 15 minutes before final exams.*

5. The advisor ***intentionally*** omitted two classes when planning John's program for the spring semester so that he would select them himself.
   *John's advisor **deliberately** left out two classes in his schedule so that he would choose them on his own.*

6. ***Without thinking***, she ***accidentally*** marked the Scantron sheet with a pen instead of a pencil, and got a 0% as her first quiz grade.
   *She **inadvertently** used a pen instead of a pencil on the Scantron and got a 0 on the quiz.*

7. *In a strange twist of events*, I took the ice cream out of the freezer and took it to the picnic, and my roommate came home that day with syrup and whipped cream for sundaes!

   Ironically, my roommate brought home ingredients to make sundaes with the ice cream that I had taken to the picnic that afternoon.

8. Her reactions are so *mild or even guarded*, that it is often difficult to detect just what my sister is really feeling.

   My sister's reactions are so subtle that it is often tough to figure out how she really feels.

9. All the parties and social activities on campus are so enticing that it would be really easy to *go off track from* my study plan and just hang with my friends!

   Because there are so many parties and social activities at the college, it would be very easy to deviate from my study plan and just have fun!

10. The members of our study group *really work well with one another*; we all have different strengths, so that by the time we are finished discussing and reviewing the subject, we have covered it completely.

    The members of the study group complement one another very well; because of our different strengths, we help each other cover all of our material completely.

11. It is important to limit the amount of sweets you eat. Too much *sugar in your system* converts to fat and is a major cause of obesity.

    You should limit your intake of sweets and candy. Glucose in your body turns into fat and contributes to problems with weight gain.

Making Personal Connections Through Writing and Discussion

When you make your new learning relevant to yourself in some way, it becomes more meaningful and long lasting. Whenever you read, try to connect to the content on a personal level. How does it relate to you? How can you apply what you have read to other situations? What else would you like to know?

Exercise 7   **Making Personal Connections**

Directions: Think about yourself in relation to the article you just read. Apply the information you learned from reading it to respond to the following questions.

Responses will vary.

1. Which three recommendations to help cope with stress do you think would work best for you? Identify them and explain why you believe they could help you cope. Do you already use any of the strategies suggested? If so, how?

2. Could the methods identified in "Discovering Your Stress" be applied to other areas of our behavior? How do you see the techniques impacting or helping other issues of the human condition?

3. Do you have any suggestions for coping with stress that were not already identified? Please describe and explain it.

Self-Monitored Reading
Reading Selection 2

The Aftermath of Disaster
By Dale B. Hahn, Wayne A. Payne, and Ellen B. Lucas

This selection, from a health textbook chapter on managing stress, discusses the lasting emotional impact of disasters, such as Hurricane Katrina, on the survivors. After the reporting or coverage of a disaster has subsided, survivors often continue to suffer. They feel stress and psychological upset as they rebuild their lives, and they emotionally relive the trauma they experienced during the event.

 before you read

It's important to think about what you may already know about a topic before you read. In this way, you will attach your new learning to your background knowledge and more easily understand the new information. (See Chapter 2, "Access Prior Knowledge," page 33.)

Answer the following questions before you read the selection.

■ What do you know or recall about Hurricane Katrina (2005), the tsunami in Indonesia (2005), or the earthquake in Haiti (2010)? Were you or any of your friends or school involved in activities that lent support to the survivors? How so?

- Aside from the physical loss and devastation, what do you think are some of the long-term emotional problems experienced by survivors?

- Have you ever lived through a devastating event? What happened? What might be some stressors you continue to feel, even though the disaster has passed?

Prepare to Read

Preview the article by applying the THIEVES strategy on page 36.

| Exercise 1 | **Previewing** |

Directions: Based on your preview, respond to the following questions.

Answers will vary. Sample answers provided.

1. What were some of the devastating effects of Hurricane Katrina?
   More than 100 people died. Homes, businesses, schools, churches, and personal belongings were destroyed. People lost their jobs and property. They experienced vulnerability and helplessness.

2. What is the term used to describe the long-term, emotional impact felt after a disaster like Hurricane Katrina?
   posttraumatic stress disorder

3. What is a common first response to surviving a disaster?
   feeling numb, as if the event didn't even happen

Check Out the Vocabulary

The following words appear in bold type in the reading. Are you familiar with some of them? Knowing the meaning of all these terms will increase your comprehension of the material.

| Exercise 2 | **Checking Out the Vocabulary** |

Directions: Complete the following matching exercise *before, during,* or *after* your reading. Be sure to review each word in the context of the selection.

_k_	1. adversity	a.	the period following a problematic event, the result
_a_	2. aftermath	b.	approximated, determined roughly
_d_	3. coping	c.	the capacity to be hurt or wounded
_i_	4. dissipated	d.	dealing with, in an attempt to overcome problems
_b_	5. estimated*	e.	psychological reaction after experiencing a stressful event
_f_	6. flashbacks	f.	vivid remembrances of a past time or event
_h_	7. logistics	g.	a grievous or ruinous price or cost
_e_	8. posttraumatic	h.	the handling of the details of an activity or operation
_j_	9. resilient	i.	dissolved, lessened, degenerated

_l_	10. stability*	j. capable of withstanding shock, able to recover or adjust
_g_	11. toll	k. a state of continued difficulty or misfortune
_c_	12. vulnerability	l. the quality of being stable, enduring, and firm

*from the Academic Word List

 ## as you read

Establish Your Purpose

Now read and annotate the article. Focus on the major points of information. Read to discover the long-term, emotional impact of surviving a natural disaster. Consider the strategies and interventions that are suggested to help people manage their lives after living through devastation and trauma.

Actively Process While You Read

Monitor your comprehension as you read. (See page 40.) Be sure to stop to reflect at the conclusion of each paragraph, and ask yourself the following questions:

- Did I understand that paragraph?
- What is the main idea?
- Am I ready to continue?

Highlight the most important points. Write notes in the margin, and move on.

The Aftermath of Disaster

By Dale B. Hahn, Wayne A. Payne, and Ellen B. Lucas

1   The **aftermath** of a natural disaster, such as Hurricane Katrina, which hit Louisiana, Alabama, and Mississippi in 2005 can have long-lasting effects. Hurricane Katrina cost over 1,000 people their lives as well as destroying homes, businesses, schools, churches, and personal belongings. The **estimated** cost from this disaster was over $100 billion, making Katrina the most costly storm in U.S. history. Over 400,000 people became jobless, and 150,000 properties were lost because of Katrina. People often experience feelings of **vulnerability**, confusion, loss, and helplessness when faced with such widespread devastation.

2   Many people suffer from posttraumatic stress disorder after experiencing this type of natural disaster. Individuals are faced with rebuilding their lives, some starting completely from scratch with little or no resources. It can take years to recover from such trauma; people need positive, effective **coping** skills to get through an extended recovery period. Sights, sounds, and smells associated with hurricanes, such as rain, wind, and thunder, can create a great deal of distress in hurricane survivors. Seeing

images of hurricanes on television or any similar reminders can bring back feelings of fear, powerlessness, and exposure. Merely hearing a loud noise, such as a pan dropping on the kitchen floor, can trigger a strong, negative emotional response. Survivors may also experience nightmares and **flashbacks** in addition to extreme startle responses to any kind of unexpected sound. People with **posttraumatic** stress disorder may experience clinical depression and severe anxiety for months and even years after the event.

3   Losing one's pets and significant places such as home, church, school, and work can leave people feeling lost and without their usual coping strategies. . . . Talking to friends and family members is a helpful way to express feelings associated with stress and to gain support. However, some people may be separated from their support group or have lost family and friends to the disaster. With the familiar, comfortable surroundings now gone, it may be extremely hard to connect to places and environments that help people to feel safe and secure. Some people may also experience survivor guilt—guilt associated with having escaped harm or one's home being untouched while others were destroyed.

4   Initially, many people respond to this type of disaster by feeling numb, as if the event didn't occur or couldn't have really happened. As the reality of what did occur sinks in, individuals may begin to feel a range of emotions—depression, anxiety, anger, and hopelessness. Helpers need to instill hope, the belief that people do survive these types of tragedies and can rebuild their lives again. They should encourage survivors to express their feelings and reassure them that these feelings are normal. This type of encouragement can bring a sense of **stability** and calmness to people's lives. Helpers should also remember that people have good days and bad days and remind survivors that soon the good days will outnumber the bad ones. Providing opportunities for survivors to share feelings appropriately with others who can understand and relate to how they are feeling is also helpful. Focusing on what one can control rather than what one cannot control is another positive coping strategy. Connecting with community resources and statewide efforts to assist survivors can also help. Knowing that people are there to help and that people don't have to rebuild their lives alone makes a tremendous difference in the recovery process.

5   Sometimes people are so focused on the **logistics** of what they need to do to get food, shelter, and clothing that they don't have time or energy to really process what has happened to them until after these basic needs are met. So it may be months later that the emotional **toll** becomes apparent. Often, assistance is plentiful when a disaster first hits, but later, when the psychological distress is worsening, the rescue efforts and relief efforts have **dissipated** and people are not getting the aid they need at that time. Having ongoing community support groups and mental health care services available is essential. It is also helpful to reestablish a routine as soon as possible. Returning to work, school, or just having a schedule can help people to feel safe, secure, and normal.

6   People also respond in individual ways to disaster, with some people being more **resilient** than others. Those who are experienced in coping with change, crisis, and **adversity** may recover more quickly than those who are unaccustomed to these problems. Most human beings are geared to survival, and so people eventually will

rebuild their lives—one hopes to an equal or improved quality of living. Some people might find a "silver lining" and even find some positive outcomes in the aftermath of such disasters—for example, taking the chance to start over and reconsidering what is important to them in their lives.

(Adapted from *Focus on Health*, 8th ed., Hayn, Payne, and Lucus, p. 76.)

after you read

Review Important Points

Going over the major points immediately after you have read, while the information is fresh in your mind, will help you to recall content and record key ideas.

Exercise 3   **Reviewing Important Points**

Directions: Choose the best answer for each of the following questions using information provided in the selection. You may need to go back to the text and reread certain portions to be sure your responses are correct and can be supported by information in the text.

_c_ 1. The overall main idea of the selection is:
   a. Hurricane Katrina cost more than any other storm in the history of America.
   b. Survivors of Hurricane Katrina experienced physical stress.
   c. Many people who survive a catastrophic event, such as a natural disaster, experience long-term emotional trauma.
   d. All people respond to catastrophic events in the same way.

_b_ 2. The long-lasting toll of Hurricane Katrina included all of the following *except:*
   a. more than 150,000 homes.
   b. more than $100 billion in medical costs.
   c. more than 1,000 lives.
   d. more than 400,000 jobs.

_b_ 3. In paragraph 2, an example of a sight associated with the aftermath of a hurricane may be:
   a. a pan dropping on the floor.
   b. scenes of a hurricane on television.
   c. flashbacks or nightmares.
   d. a startling response.

_a_ 4. From paragraph 2, we can infer that posttraumatic stress disorder can be defined as:
   a. an anxiety disorder that can develop after exposure to a terrifying event.
   b. a physical disorder that results from a natural disaster.

c. a disorder that makes a person afraid of loud noises.

d. an emotional problem that results in sleep deprivation, nightmares, and flashbacks.

_c_ 5. **Why is it often difficult to reach out to friends or family members in the aftermath of a natural disaster?**

    a. They may be out of town.

    b. They may be afraid to speak with you.

    c. They may have lost family and friends in the disaster.

    d. They may be estranged from you.

_d_ 6. **What is the unstated main idea in paragraph 4?**

    a. People who have experienced a disaster may try to deny it ever happened.

    b. Those who survived a disaster may feel depressed.

    c. Getting in contact with community resources is a good way to deal with anxiety, depression, and anger.

    d. Survivors of a catastrophe should reach out for support in order to ease the recovery process.

_a_ 7. **Why is ongoing help necessary for those who have experienced a catastrophic event?**

    a. The emotional effects may linger for a long time afterward.

    b. Physiological distress may worsen.

    c. Community and mental health resources may not be available where you live.

    d. People need to be reminded daily about what they have experienced.

_b_ 8. **According to the text, what can help make survivors feel safe and sound?**

    a. ongoing community support

    b. resuming school or work

    c. creating a schedule for life activities

    d. all of the above

_c_ 9. **In paragraph 6, what does the author say contributes to faster recovery?**

    a. having survived a similar experience

    b. thinking about what good can come out of your experience

    c. possessing good coping skills and resilience

    d. wanting a better lifestyle

_d_ 10. **What is the overall pattern of organization of this selection?**

    a. comparison and contrast

    b. definition

    c. chronological order

    d. cause and effect

Organize the Information

Organizing information shows that you have understood it and provides you with a useful study tool. (See Chapter 9.)

Organizing the Information

Directions: Use your notes to answer the questions about the selection and complete the right side of the table below.

Posttraumatic Stress Disorder

Questions	Answers
What is posttraumatic stress disorder, or PTSD?	An *anxiety* disorder that can develop after exposure to a *terrifying event*.
What causes PTSD?	The *aftermath* of a natural disaster or a *catastrophic* event, such as the loss of a pet, a home, *church*, *school*, or *job* that leaves people without coping strategies.
What are the effects?	Inability to cope with current situation, long-term stress, clinical *depression*, severe *anxiety*, psychological *distress*, sensitivity to feelings that remind survivor of event, feelings of being alone, *nightmares*, flashbacks.
How can people cope?	Find a *helper*, return to work or *school*.
Where can people get help?	*Community support groups*, *mental health care services*.

Integrate the Vocabulary

Make the new vocabulary presented in the reading *your* vocabulary.

Integrating the Vocabulary

Answers will vary. Sample answers provided.

Directions: Replace the italicized, boldfaced word or phrase in each of the following sentences with a word, or alternate form of the word, from the vocabulary list at the beginning of the selection on pages 321–322. Paraphrase and rewrite the sentence on the line provided, using the new term.

1. Having been involved in several romantic relationships over the last few years, Rhonda longed for *the quality of endurance and groundedness* in her recent connection with James.

   Rhonda was hoping that her new relationship with James would have stability.

2. After the car accident, Jennifer was gripped regularly throughout the day with *visions of all the events leading up to and after* the crash.

   Jennifer had flashbacks of her automobile accident several times throughout the day.

3. The town was unrecognizable in the *time just following* the touchdown of the tornado.

   During the aftermath of the tornado, we couldn't recognize the town.

4. Being a new mother presented a challenge to Jenna's capacity to *deal with the many problems of* raising a baby as a single parent.

   A single mom, Jenna had to cope with raising a baby on her own.

5. We couldn't say exactly, but we *approximated* the cost of a year's tuition to be about $15,000.

   The cost of the tuition was estimated at $15,000.

6. Although the pain of breaking his leg was intense, it eventually *dissolved and became less severe* as time went by.

   The pain of breaking his leg dissipated over time.

7.–8. Perhaps because Wayne had experienced *many difficulties and disappointments* throughout his young life, he showed a great *capacity to withstand and recover from* the loss of his home in the fire.

   Maybe because Wayne had dealt with so much adversity in his life, he showed great resilience when the fire burned down his house.

9. Wendy had no idea that her wedding preparations would involve so many different *plans, activities, and details*.

   Many logistics were involved in preparing for Wendy's wedding.

10.–11. Living with *extreme psychological distress* after the contentious divorce of his parents left Michael *open to upset or hurt* by the slightest disagreement in his marriage.

   Michael experienced posttraumatic stress after his parents got divorced and was vulnerable to the smallest discord in his own marriage.

12. Years of marathon running had *long-lasting and damaging effects* on Robert's ankles, knees, and hips.

   Running in marathons for so many years took its toll on Robert's ankle, knees, and hips.

Exercise 6 **Making Personal Connections**

Directions: Think about yourself in relation to the article you just read. Apply the information you learned from reading it to respond to the following questions.

Answers will vary.

1. Catastrophic events, other than natural disasters, can lead to posttraumatic stress disorder. These include being involved in a fire or car accident, serving in the military during war, being physically or verbally abused, or being the victim of a violent crime. Consider one of these events and describe what you think the long-term emotional effects might be.

2. What interventions do you think would be most effective in addressing these problems? Refer back to the selection to review some of the recommended supports.

3. The author alludes to the possibility of a "silver lining" in the aftermath of a disaster. What positive outcome might emerge as a result of any of the events listed above?

Independent Reading
Textbook Reading Selection: Criminal Justice

Job Stress
By Robert M. Bohm and Keith N. Haley

This selection is from a criminal justice textbook chapter titled, "Policing America: Issues and Ethics" (Bohm and Haley, 2007).

We all experience stress—at home, at school, at work. Certainly, some careers are laden with more stress than others. The nature of a police officer's work is very complex, and, as we might expect, very stressful. Read to learn about the stresses connected to police work. Not only will you come away with a new understanding of police officers, but perhaps with a greater empathy for them as well.

Answer the following questions before you read the textbook selection "Job Stress."

■ Think about the kinds of stressors you encounter in your life, and, if you work, on the job. How do they impact you? How do you manage the stress?

■ Consider the occupation of a police officer. Do you believe it to be stressful? What do you believe may cause the greatest stress in this role?

Prepare to Read

Preview the textbook selection using the THIEVES strategy on page 36.

Exercise 1	**Developing Preview Questions**

Directions: Based on your preview, write *three* questions you anticipate will be answered in the selection.

Answers will vary. Sample answers provided.

1. *What are the sources and effects of stress for police officers?*
2. *What is copicide?*
3. *What are the ways to manage and reduce stress without leaving police work?*

Check Out the Vocabulary

The following words from this textbook selection are likely to appear in academic writing across many disciplines. Be sure you learn their meaning.

> ### Academic Word List
>
> | | |
> | --- | --- |
> | **attributed** | regarded as caused by, created by, or belonging to |
> | **discretion** | the quality of being tactful, judicious, and reflective, in conduct or speech |
> | **enforcement** | compelling obedience to |
> | **intervene** | to come between, as in action; to occur between events or periods |
> | **paradigm** | an example serving as a model |
> | **phenomenon** | an observed fact or circumstance, something that impresses as extraordinary |
> | **scheme** | a plan or program of action to be followed |
> | **source** | any thing or place from which something comes or is obtained |

Exercise 2   Checking Out the Vocabulary

Directions: Complete each of the following sentences using a word from the Academic Word List.

1. Although George was very upset about the grade he received on his research paper, he used _____discretion_____ when sharing his feelings with his professor.

2. It is the job of campus security officers to ensure the _____enforcement_____ of the parking regulations collegewide.

3. To help us understand the organizational requirements for the final thesis, Professor Morgan distributed a _____paradigm_____ for us to follow in planning our paper.

4. Richard was extremely agitated the other day in class, but he was very quiet and did not reveal the _____source_____ of his anger.

5. Roger _____attributed_____ his success on the exam to six hours of active studying, which included reciting his class notes aloud, formulating his own test questions and answering them, and rereading portions of his textbook.

6. In history class, we discussed the _____schemes_____ Hitler developed to meet his despicable objectives during the Holocaust.

7. I enlisted the support of my advisor to _____intervene_____ when I wasn't assigned the classes I registered for.

8. Some educators think it is an interesting _____phenomenon_____ that students who fail a course often want to retake it with the same professor.

 **as you read**

Establish Your Purpose

Read and annotate the selection. Focus on the major points of information. Consider the unique causes and effects of stress for police officers. Note the methods in place to reduce and manage the stress in police work.

 ## Actively Process While You Read

Highlight the most important points. Annotate within the paragraph and in the margin and move on.

Job Stress
By Robert M. Bohm and Keith N. Haley

1   Stress in the workplace is common today. A recent survey revealed that 80 percent of responding workers reported at least some degree of stress. Given the nature of police work, no one is surprised to discover that a law **enforcement** officer's job is stressful. Police officers **intervene** in life's personal emergencies and great tragedies. Working extended shifts, for example, at the scene of the bombing of the federal building in Oklahoma City or of the World Trade Center disaster would tax the resources of even the most resourceful police officer. Who would deny the stress involved in working deep undercover on a narcotics investigation over a period of several months? Some officers are able to manage stress on the job better than others.

2   **Job stress** is defined as the harmful physical and emotional outcomes that occur when the requirements of a job do not match the capabilities, resources, or needs of the worker. Poor health and injury are possible results of prolonged job stress. Police work has long been identified as one of the most stressful of all occupations, and many police officers suffer each year from the deleterious effects of a job that tests their physical and emotional limits.

Sources and Effects of Stress

3   A number of conditions can lead to stress: (1) design of tasks—heavy lifting, long hours without breaks, and monotonous repetition of dangerous maneuvers; (2) management style—lack of participation by workers in decision making, poor communication, lack of family-friendly policies; (3) interpersonal relationships—poor social environment and lack of support from co-workers and supervisors; (4) work roles—conflicting or uncertain job expectations, wearing too many hats, too much responsibility. The signs that stress is becoming a problem with an officer are frequent headaches, difficulty in concentrating, short temper, upset stomach, job dissatisfaction, abuse of alcohol and drugs, and low morale. Individually and collectively these symptoms can have other origins, but job stress is often the **source**.

Copicide

4   As if the work of confronting dangerous suspects and preserving the peace were not stressful enough, "copicide" or "death by cop" has entered the work life of some police officers. Copicide is a form of suicide in which a person gets fatally shot after intentionally provoking police officers. A recent study of police shootings resulting in the death of a citizen in Los Angeles found that 10 percent could be **attributed**

to copicide. One commentator believes that "dozens of times each year during jittery hostage dramas and routine traffic stops, desperate people lure police officers into shooting them in a **phenomenon** known in law enforcement circles as 'suicide by cop.'" The truth is that no one knows exactly how many times copicide incidents occur each year. Most police officers require a lot of time to emotionally recover from a fatal shooting in circumstances where they were fully authorized to use deadly force. To later discover that they were provoked into killing people who simply used police as a tool in a suicide **scheme** creates an extra emotional burden to bear.

Stress Management and Reduction

5   Fortunately, there are ways to manage and reduce stress without leaving police work. The "fixes" for stress come in two general categories. Stress management now encompasses a variety of programs and procedures that include discussing stressful events with colleagues and mental health professionals, regular exercise, relaxation techniques such as structured visualization, a healthy diet that also eliminates caffeine and nicotine, enriched family support, religious support, prayer, meditation, and stress management classes that often involve spouses.

6   Organizational change can also reduce the potential for stress in the police work environment. Officers, for example, may be given **discretion** in determining their work hours and shifts as long as the police agency is able to respond effectively to the workload requirements of the community. Flattening the organizational structure can help reduce stress by giving officers more discretion in carrying out the responsibilities of their job. Community policing is an effective **paradigm** for increasing officers' ability to control their work and perhaps minimize stress. Job redesign can assist by assigning the right number and type of tasks to a police position when one job requires too much of an officer to maintain emotional stability and good health. Finally, excellent public safety equipment can minimize stress. Proper police weaponry, dependable vehicles, and the best of protective equipment such as high-grade body armor can not only protect officers but can also put their minds a little more at ease on those important concerns.

(From *Introduction to Criminal Justice,* 4th ed., Bohm and Haley, pp. 251–253)

after you read

Think back to the questions you posed after previewing the selection but before you actually read. Now that you have read the selection, can you answer your initial questions?

Exercise 3	**Answering Your Preview Questions**

Directions: If you have discovered the answers to the preview questions you created earlier, write them on the lines provided.

Answers will vary.

1. _____

2. _____

3. _____

Exercise 4	**Reviewing Important Points**

Directions: Choose the best answer for each of the following questions using information provided in the selection.

_d_ 1. The overall topic of the selection is:

    a. job stress.

    b. the criminal justice system.

    c. ways to manage stress in police work.

    d. the job stress of police officers.

_c_ 2. The main idea of introductory paragraphs 1 and 2 is that stress:

    a. is very common in all occupations.

    b. is greatest when working extended shifts.

    c. is found in all occupations, but particularly in police work.

    d. is the harmful physical and emotional outcome that occurs when working too hard.

_a_ 3. The author presents two lists in paragraph 3 which:

    a. identify the causes and effects of stress.

    b. define job stress in police work.

    c. compare and contrast kinds of stress.

    d. compare and contrast management style with interpersonal relationships.

_d_ 4. All of the following are identified as conditions that may lead to stress for a police officer *except:*

    a. difficult design of tasks.

    b. poor management styles.

    c. conflicting or uncertain job expectations.

    d. positive interpersonal relationships.

_a_ 5. The last sentence in paragraph 3 can be paraphrased as:

    a. Although the behaviors listed could have various causes, stress is the most likely one.

    b. The behaviors listed have various causes related to the individual and the workplace.

     c. Signs of stress in the police force are manifested individually and collectively.

     d. Stress is a problem with many sources and it is hard to tell which is the most important.

b 6. **The topic of paragraph 4 is clearly copicide. The topic sentence is the _____ sentence in the paragraph.**

     a. first
     b. second
     c. third
     d. last

a 7. **In paragraphs 5 and 6, the two major categories the author identifies to classify "fixes" for stress are:**

     a. stress management programs and organizational changes.
     b. relaxation techniques and stress management classes.
     c. community policing and job redesign.
     d. effective body armor, weaponry, and vehicles.

b 8. **In discussing organizational change as a means of reducing stress in police work, the writing pattern used is a combination of:**

     a. definition and enumeration.
     b. listing and cause and effect.
     c. sequence and cause and effect.
     d. enumeration and comparison and contrast.

c 9. **From the selection, the reader may infer that law enforcement agencies:**

     a. don't really consider the emotional needs of officers.
     b. expect officers to have the ability to deal with stress better than the rest of us.
     c. consider the emotional needs and stresses of officers.
     d. do not consider management style and interpersonal relationships important.

b 10. **The overall tone of the selection is:**

     a. critical, negative, and sarcastic.
     b. straightforward, informational, and objective.
     c. sad, depressed, and discouraging.
     d. biased, subjective, and opinionated.

Exercise 5 **Organizing the Information**

Directions: Using your notes, complete the following concept maps to review two important topics covered in the selection.

Job Stress of Police Officers

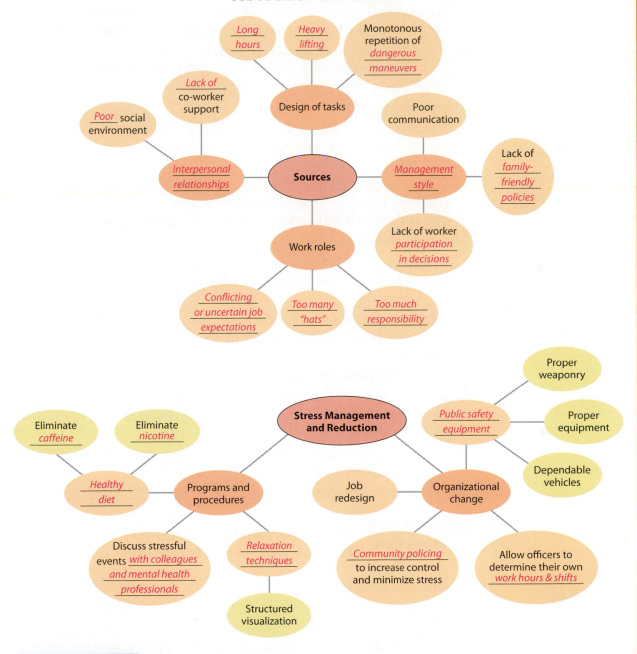

Exercise 6   Using Context Clues

Directions: Use the context clues in the following sentences to discern the meaning of the words in bold type. Underline any clue words that help you define these words or terms. The first sentence is from the text. The paragraph in which the sentence appears has been indicated for you in parentheses.

1. a. Police work has long been identified as one of the most stressful of all occupations, and many police officers suffer each year from the **deleterious** effects of a job that tests their physical and emotional limits. (2)

   b. The **deleterious** consequences of long-term sleep deprivation have been documented; these include chronic fatigue, anxiety, lowered metabolism, and an impaired immune system.

   The word **deleterious** means *injurious to health, hurtful or harmful*   .

2. a. A number of conditions can lead to stress: (1) Design of tasks—heavy lifting, long hours without breaks, and **monotonous** repetition of dangerous maneuvers. (3)

   b. Voters complained that the governor's speech was so **monotonous**, repeating the same ideas over and over, that they wondered whether or not she had a real understanding of the important issues.

   The word **monotonous** means *repetitive, tirelessly uniform, boring, dull, tedious* .

3. a. A number of conditions can lead to stress: . . . **Interpersonal** relationships—poor social environment and lack of support from co-workers and supervisors. (3)

   b. Developing **interpersonal** skills, to create friendships and find study partners, can enhance the quality of the college experience for most students.

   The word **interpersonal** means *pertaining to the relationship between people*   .

4. a. To later discover that they were **provoked** into killing people who simply used police as a tool in a suicide scheme creates an extra emotional burden to bear.

   b. The customer's loud complaints and use of profanity **provoked** the store manager to step in on the salesperson's behalf.

   The word **provoke** means *to stir up anger or action, to arouse feelings or activity* .

| **E x e r c i s e   7** | **Making Personal Connections Through Writing and Discussion** |

Answers will vary.

Directions: Think about yourself in relation to the article you just read. Apply the information you learned from reading it to respond to the following questions.

1. The selection discusses the sources and effects of stress on police officers. What are the sources and effects of stress for other occupations. Following the organizational plan used by the author in paragraph 3, discuss or write about these.

2. What is your reaction to the phenomenon of copicide? Can you think of other situations in which a person provokes another purposefully to create a hurtful retaliation?

3. Consider the programs, procedures, and organizational changes that were discussed to manage stress for police officers. Are these applicable to other workplaces? Have you had personal experience with any of them? Which do you believe would be most effective? Why?

Synthesizing Your Reading: Reflective Journal Writing

Stress

Having read these three reading selections on the topic of stress, you now have a broader, more scholarly understanding of the subject matter.

Write a reflective journal entry on the topic of stress, demonstrating both your knowledge of the content in the selections and your own viewpoints on the issue.

In your first section, briefly summarize each selection. Include the thesis and a few key points for each.

In the second section, reflect on the topic. Consider your own experience with stress: Where, when, and how have you experienced it? What strategies do you use to manage your stress? What ideas from the readings do you feel are most valuable to you personally? What new insights from the readings do you respond to the most? Explain your thinking.

Readings About Medical Ethics

Get Acquainted with the Issue

Do you think that advances in medicine ever cross moral boundaries? Are there medical procedures that you might consider wrong, even if there is a rationale or benefit behind the intervention?

Advancements in medicine have improved the quality of our lives, lessened our suffering, and increased our longevity. Diseases that have caused worldwide epidemics and deaths, such as tuberculosis and polio, are now cured or prevented through the use of medications or vaccines. Surgical implants replace ailing organs and lost limbs are replaced with prostheses, or artificial limbs. We can get rid of our headaches, sleep better, and even grow hair with the help of over-the-counter pharmaceuticals.

However, some medical advances also come with dilemmas. Are certain procedures morally wrong? Do they infringe on the rights of individuals or other living creatures? Do they contradict religious beliefs? Is it right to keep someone alive, only for them to live like a "vegetable"? Do doctors ever do too much?

Questions such as these are raised in the following selections. The magazine article "Pillow Angel Ethics" reviews a case in which doctors stunt the growth of a disabled child and sterilize her in order to make it easier for her family to care for her as she ages. In the essay "A Question of Ethics," the author asks us to consider the ethics of using animals in medical research.

Lastly, in an excerpt from a biology textbook chapter on gene technology, you will read about ethical issues raised in medicine by genetic engineering and how the scientific community addresses them.

Ethical questions—questions about whether something is morally "right" or "wrong"—find their way into many aspects of our lives as well as many academic disciplines. Views on how people behave, and the choices they make, are topics of interest not only in the sciences and medicine but also particularly in business, economics, politics, and law. By considering the ethical aspects of actions, we often engage in interesting reflection, discussion, and even argument. Think about your ethical views, and the views of others, as you read the following selections.

Guided Reading
Reading Selection 1

Pillow Angel Ethics
By Nancy Gibbs

This article from Time Magazine *discusses "The Ashley Case," in which the parents of a brain injured girl asked doctors to "keep her small." With such treatment, it was said that the quality of her life and their ability to care for her would be enhanced. What do you think?*

◀◀ before you read

It's important to think about what you may already know about a topic before you read. In this way, you will attach your new learning to your background knowledge and more easily understand the new information. (See Chapter 2, "Access Prior Knowledge," page 33.)

Answer the following questions related to medical ethics involving care for individuals who have disabilities.

- Do you know of any cases in the news in which the rights of an impaired individual were violated?

- Do parents always have the right to make decisions about medical interventions that might change the quality of their child's life? Under what circumstances?

- Do you think that if a person is incapable of raising a child, their biological capacity to reproduce should be removed? Under what circumstances?

Prepare to Read

Preview the selection "Pillow Angel Ethics" using the THIEVES strategy on page 36.

Exercise 1   **Previewing**

Directions: Complete the following items.

1. Take a look at the selection and check off the items that are available to you for preview.

   X Title

   ___ Headings

   X Introduction

   X Every first sentence in each paragraph

   X Visuals/vocabulary

   ___ End of chapter questions

   X Summary/concluding paragraph

2. Read and highlight to preview the selection.

3. Based on your preview, what do you anticipate the selection will be about?
   The reading will describe the controversial Ashley case in which doctors took steps to stunt the growth of a six-year-old girl so that her parents could care for her more easily. It will tell about other parts of the treatment, including removing her uterus and breast tissue. It will talk about the ethics committee involved and different sides of the issue from the doctors' and parents' point of view.

Check Out the Vocabulary

The words in the following section appear in boldface type in the reading. Are you already familiar with some of them? Knowing the meaning of all these terms will increase your understanding of the material.

| **Exercise 2** | **Checking Out the Vocabulary** |

Directions: Complete the matching exercise below *before, during or after* your reading. Be sure to review each word in the context of the selection.

<u>e</u> 1. ethics*   a. intrusive, infringing, causing change or harm by altering

<u>j</u> 2. humility   b. first

<u>b</u> 3. initial*   c. ungracefully tall, thin, bony

<u>a</u> 4. invasive   d. able to be carried or easily moved

<u>c</u> 5. lanky   e. system of moral principles, dealing with right and wrong and/or good and bad of certain actions

<u>l</u> 6. pediatric   f. capability of coming into actuality or realization

<u>d</u> 7. portable   g. likely to happen or to become

<u>f</u> 8. potential*   h. a gut feeling, an instinctive reaction felt within the body

<u>g</u> 9. prospective*   i. an idiom referring to the notion that one action or thought will lead to another and another

<u>i</u> 10. slippery slope   j. the quality of being humble, courteous, and respectful

<u>k</u> 11. sterilize   k. to make incapable of bearing children

<u>h</u> 12. visceral   l. the branch of medicine dealing with the care of children

*from the Academic Word List

▶ as you read

Establish Your Purpose

Now, read and annotate the selection. Focus on the major points of information. Identify Ashley's situation, the concerns and desires of her parents, and the views of those opposed to the treatment.

Actively Process While You Read

Stop to process information as you read.

| **Exercise 3** | **Processing While You Read** |

Directions: Answer the following questions at the conclusion of each paragraph. This will help you monitor your reading process and understand the material.

Paragraph 1

1. What treatments can you infer that doctors performed on the disabled child?

   They sterilized her and took steps to stop her from growing.

2. Based on the metaphor of the "steaming message boards," what issue can you infer will be discussed in the article?

   People are questioning whether doing such procedures is right or wrong.

Paragraph 2

3. What two doctors are involved? *Dr. Gunther and Dr. Diekema*
   What is their concern?

   that people who are critical of them don't really understand the nature of the case

4. What important challenge does the author believe is raised when considering the Ashley case?

   The challenge is deciding how to evaluate what medicine can do versus what it should do, what is right or wrong to do.

Paragraph 3

5. What medical intervention is the topic of this paragraph?

   giving Ashley high doses of estrogen to close her growth plates and reduce her prospective height, to keep her small and lightweight

6. According to Ashley's parents, what would be the benefit of the procedure?

   Her smaller and lighter size would make it more possible for her to be cared for and to participate in family life activities.

Paragraph 4

7. List two additional procedures, and their potential benefits, that are cited in the paragraph?

   1. Removal of Ashley's uterus to prevent menstrual cramps and pregnancy in case she is raped. 2. Removal of her breast tissue to prevent disease and discomfort.

Answers will vary.   8. What is *your* reaction to these procedures thus far?

   _____

   _____

Paragraphs 5–6

9. What is the topic of these paragraphs?

   the concerns of the doctors and the bioethics committee; the medical risks involved in the procedures

Paragraph 7

10. What does the bioethics committee conclude?

    They determine that the benefits outweigh the risks, both medically and emotionally.

11. What three medical benefits of being able to move Ashley are listed?

improved circulation, digestion and muscle condition, fewer sores and infections

Paragraph 8

12. What does Diekema imply when he says, "Humility is important in a case like this"?

He means that one should always be thoughtful and considerate, not arrogant or self-assured, in decisions such as these. There are no easy answers, and all views are important to consider.

Paragraph 9

13. Gunther says, "This is a girl who was never going to grow up. . . . she was only going to grow bigger." What does he mean?

Ashley was so disabled that although her body could develop, her mind never would. She could never mature and function as adult.

Paragraph 10

14. How is the idea of a "slippery slope" used to build a case against the Ashley treatment?

The idea of a slippery slope means that there will be no end to what medical treatments could be imposed to make it easier to take care of a disabled child.

15. Paraphrase Dr. Gunther's response to that argument.

All medicine has the potential of being misused. Being overly cautious, however, would lead to hardly ever using any important medical treatments.

Pillow Angel Ethics
By Nancy Gibbs

from the pages of

1   What kind of doctors would agree to intentionally shorten and **sterilize** a disabled six-year-old girl to make it easier for her parents to take care of her? The question has had message boards steaming for days, but the answers are in no way easy.

2   Dr. Daniel Gunther and Dr. Douglas Diekema, who first revealed the details of "The Ashley Case" in the *Archives of **Pediatric** and Adolescent Medicine*, think that many of their critics don't understand the nature of this case. Talk to them, and you confront every modern challenge in weighing what medicine can do versus what it should.

3   The case: Ashley is a brain-damaged girl whose parents feared that as she got bigger, it would be much harder to care for her; so they set out to keep her small. Through high-dose estrogen treatment over the past two years, her growth plates were closed and her **prospective** height reduced by about 13 inches, to 4'5". "Ashley's smaller and lighter size," her parents write on their blog "makes it more possible to include her in the typical family life and activities that provide her with needed comfort, closeness, security and love: meal time, car trips, touch, snuggles, etc." They stress that the treatment's goal was "to improve our daughter's quality of life and not to convenience her caregivers."

4   But the treatment went further: doctors removed her uterus to prevent **potential** discomfort from menstrual cramps or pregnancy in the event of rape; and also her breast tissue, because of a family history of cancer and fibrocystic disease. Not having breasts would also make the harness straps that hold her upright more comfortable. "Ashley has no need for developed breasts since she will not breast feed," her parents argue, "and their presence would only be a source of discomfort to her."

5   The parents say that the decision to proceed with "The Ashley Treatment" was not a hard one for them, but the same cannot be said for the doctors. "This was something people hadn't thought about being a possibility, much less being done," says Diekema, who chairs the bioethics committee of the American Academy of Pediatrics and was brought in to consult on this case. For the **ethics** committee of Seattle Children's Hospital, which reviewed the proposed treatment, "it took time to get past the **initial** response—'wow, this is bizarre'—and think seriously about the reasons for the parents' request," says Diekema.

6   First they had to be sure there would be no medical harm: removing breast buds, Gunther says, is a much less **invasive** procedure than a mastectomy. The hormone treatment was commonly used 40 years ago on **lanky** teenage girls who didn't want to get any taller. "The main risk," Gunther says, "is of thrombosis or blood clot, which is a risk in anybody taking estrogen. It's hard to assess in a young child because no one this young has been treated with estrogen." There were very few reports of thrombosis among the teenage patients, he says, "So I suspect the risk is fairly low. After treatment is finished, I don't see any long-term risk, and we've eliminated the risk of uterine and breast cancer."

7   The ethics committee essentially did a cost-benefit analysis and concluded that the rewards outweighed the risks. Keeping Ashley smaller and more **portable**, the doctors argue, has medical as well as emotional benefits: more movement means better circulation, digestion and muscle condition, and fewer sores and infections. "If you're going to be against this," Gunther says, "you have to argue why the benefits are not worth pursuing."

8   They knew that the treatment would be controversial, though they did not quite foresee the media storm that would erupt when they decided to publish the case and invite their peers to weigh in. "I felt we were doing the right thing for this little girl—but that didn't keep me from feeling a bit of unease," admits Diekema. "And that's as it should be. **Humility** is important in a case like this."

9   Gunther also understands why the case has inspired such intense feelings—but notes that "**visceral** reactions are not an argument for or against." This was not a girl who was ever going to grow up, he says. She was only going to grow bigger. "Some disability advocates have suggested that this course of treatment is an abuse of Ashley's rights and an affront to her dignity. This is a mystery to me. Is there more dignity in having to hoist a full-grown body in harness and chains from bed to bath to wheelchair? Ashley will always have the mind of an infant, and now she will be able to stay where she belongs—in the arms of the family that loves her."

10   But how far would Drs. Gunther and Diekema take this argument? Would they agree to amputate a child's legs to keep her lighter and more portable? Hormone treatment is nowhere near as risky and disfiguring as amputation, Diekema retorts; it just accelerates a natural process by which the body stops growing. Parents of short children give them growth hormones for social more than medical reasons, he notes. How can it be O.K. to make someone "unnaturally" taller but not smaller? To warnings of a slippery slope, Gunther tilts the logic the other way: "The argument that a beneficial treatment should not be used because it might be misused is itself a **slippery slope**," he says. "If we did not use therapies available because they could be misused, we'd be practicing very little medicine."

■ ■ ■

 **after you read**

Review Important Points

Going over major points immediately after you have read, while the information is fresh in your mind, will help you to recall the content and record key ideas.

Exercise 4   **Reviewing Important Points**

Directions: Answer the following questions based on the information provided in the selection. You may need to go back to the text and re-read certain portions to be sure your responses are correct and can be supported by information in the text.

1. What is the overall controversy being discussed in this article?
    Whether it was morally right or wrong to subject Ashley to the medical procedures that changed her physically.

2. List the medical treatments received by Ashley and the purpose of each.
    - *removal of her breast buds—reduces chance of breast cancer and allows her to fit more easily into harness straps to sit upright*
    - *closing her growth plates through high-dose estrogen treatment—to stay small and portable enough to be part of family life*
    - *removal of her uterus to prevent pregnancy and discomfort from menstrual cramps*

Organize the Information

Organizing the information you have discovered in a reading selection shows you have understood it and can restate the material in a different way. You may use this reorganized material to help you study for exams and prepare for written assignments. (See Chapter 9.)

(See Chapter 9.)

Exercise 5   **Organizing the Information**

Directions: Complete the following concept map. Identify key ideas that reflect the different points of view of the parties involved in the Ashley case. Refer back to the selection to gather material for your map.

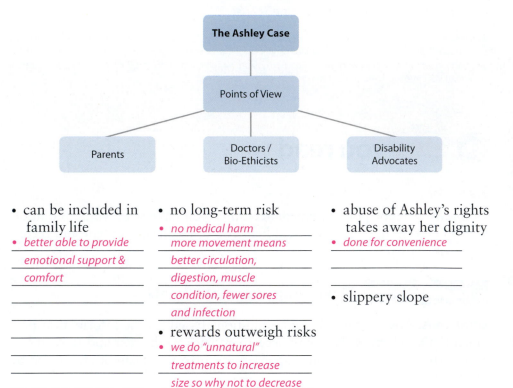

The Ashley Case

Points of View

Parents | Doctors / Bio-Ethicists | Disability Advocates

- can be included in family life
- *better able to provide emotional support & comfort*

- no long-term risk
- *no medical harm more movement means better circulation, digestion, muscle condition, fewer sores and infection*
- rewards outweigh risks
- *we do "unnatural" treatments to increase size so why not to decrease*

- abuse of Ashley's rights takes away her dignity
- *done for convenience*

- slippery slope

Integrate the Vocabulary

Make the new vocabulary presented in the reading *your* vocabulary. Using the terms in other contexts will help you make them part of your own spoken and written language.

Exercise 6   **Integrating the Vocabulary**

Answers will vary.

Directions: Replace the italicized, boldfaced phrase in each of the following sentences with a word, or alternative form of the word, from the vocabulary list at the beginning of the selection. Write the word in parentheses. Next, write a sentence of your own on the line provided in which you use the term in some aspect of your own life.

1. In my business class, we spend a great deal of time discussing *the moral principles and issues of right and wrong* that are part of the advertising world. (_____ethics_____)

   _____

2. Since Junaid loves kids so much, he plans to study *the field of medicine that deals with the health of children* when he enters medical school. (_____pediatrics_____)

   _____

3. Because I will be changing residences over the next several years, I am looking for a wall unit that is *easily moved around from place to place.* (_____portable_____)

   _____

4. Not considering himself exceptional or unique, Professor Jenkins accepted his award for outstanding teaching with *courtesy, respect, and a humble manner.* (_____humility_____)

   _____

5. The process of *surgically altering* cats and dogs *so that they are unable to reproduce* is common practice at pet adoption centers today. (_____sterilizing_____)

   _____

6. Although Caroline enjoys her work as a fashion model today, she hasn't forgotten her early teenage years when she felt very awkward being *extremely thin, tall, and not very graceful.* (_____lanky_____)

   _____

7. As soon as Peter took a bite of the chocolate cookie he felt his diet was over and that this single act would send him on *his way to one bad behavior after the next,* leading to weight gain. (_____slippery slope_____)

   _____

8. It seems as though Wanda's *likelihood for attaining* good grades has really improved since she increased her weekly study time. (_____potential for_____)

   _____

9. Do you go along with the adage that your *first* response to a multiple-choice question is usually correct? (_____initial_____)

   _____

10. After driving 10 miles over the speed limit, Phil had an *intense, gut* reaction when he heard the sound of sirens behind him. (_____visceral_____)

    _____

11. Maureen felt it was very *intrusive and impinged upon her privacy* when her parents came into her bedroom unannounced. (_____invasive_____)

    _____

12. The *likelihood of realizing his dream* to become a professional actor increased when Eric was selected to star in the freshman class drama series. (_____prospective_____)

    _____

Make Personal Connections Through Writing and Discussion

When you make your new learning relevant to yourself in some way, it becomes more meaningful and long lasting. Whenever you read, try to connect to the content on a personal level. How does it relate to you? How can you apply what you have read to other situations? What else would you like to know?

Exercise 7	**Making Personal Connections**

Directions: Think about your own views in relation to the article you just read. Apply the information you learned from reading it to respond to the following questions.

Answers will vary.

1. Do you believe it was ethical to perform the medical treatments Ashley received?

2. Have you, or anyone you have known, been in a similar situation, perhaps with an elderly loved one? Tell about this.

3. What recommendations would you make to a family facing a similar situation? What would you say to the medical community?

Self-Monitored Reading
Reading Selection 2

A Question of Ethics
By Jane Goodall

This essay, which appeared in Newsweek Magazine, *is written by well-known animal rights advocate and activist Jane Goodall. Perhaps you saw her story documented in the film* Gorillas in the Mist. *Famous for "living with" and establishing close relationships with chimps in Africa, Goodall discusses the morality of using animals in medical research.*

⏪ before you read

It's important to think about what you may already know about a topic before you read. In this way, you will attach new learning to your background knowledge and more easily understand the new information. (See Chapter 2, Access Prior Knowledge, page 33.)

Answer the following questions before you read the selection to find out what you already know about the topic.

- Have you ever heard of the author? What do you know of her work?
- Did you know that animals are used in medical research? For what purposes? In what ways?
- Do you know of any medical breakthroughs that have come about as the result of research on animals?
- Do you believe it is cruel to use animals in research for medical advancements that will help human beings? Why or why not?

Prepare to Read

Preview the reading selection by applying the THIEVES strategy on page 37. Notice that there are no section headings. In this case, the first sentence in each paragraph is an important part of your preview.

| Exercise 1 | **Previewing** |

Directions: Based on your preview, respond to the following questions.

1. Why have researchers used chimpanzees as test subjects for new drugs and vaccines?

   because they are thought to be physiologically close to humans

2. What key question does Goodall raise to challenge the use of animals in research?

   She asks if it is ethical to use animals in research if we think of them as caring, feeling creatures.

3. What do you learn that animal rights activists did in the past to protest the use of animals in medical experiments?

   They resorted to violence.

Check Out the Vocabulary

The following words appear in bold type in the reading. Are you familiar with some of them? Knowing the meaning of all these terms will increase your comprehension of the material.

| Exercise 2 | **Checking Out the Vocabulary** |

Directions: Complete the following matching exercise *before, during,* or *after* your reading. Be sure to review each word in the context of the selection.

a	1. alternative*	a.	a choice, another way or possibility
i	2. apathy	b.	to regard or treat as equal
j	3. assumption*	c.	recognition of difference
e	4. counterproductive	d.	to make or become smaller or less important

_d_ 5. diminish*   e. resulting in something contrary to what is intended

_c_ 6. distinction*   f. experiencing sensation, conscious

_b_ 7. equate*   g. alone, apart from others

_k_ 8. extremism   h. relating to the body or living organisms

_g_ 9. isolated*   i. absence of emotion; lack of interest or concern

_h_ 10. physiologically   j. the act of taking for granted or supposing without proof

_f_ 11. sentient   k. tendency to go beyond the ordinary, being radical

*from the Academic Word List

as you read

Establish Your Purpose

Now read and annotate the selection and focus on the major points of information. Identify the author's thesis. Number the points that serve to support that thesis, noting key details, as you read.

Actively Process While You Read

Monitor your comprehension as you read. (See Chapter 2, "Monitoring Questions," page 40.) Be sure to stop to reflect at the conclusion of each paragraph, and ask yourself the following questions:

- Did I understand that paragraph?
- What is the main idea?
- Am I ready to continue?

Highlight the most important points. Write your notes in the margins and then move on.

A Question of Ethics
By Jane Goodall

---

1   David Graybeard first showed me how fussy the **distinction** between animals and humans can be. Forty years ago I befriended David, a chimpanzee, during my first field trip to Gombe in Tanzania. One day I offered him a nut in my open palm. He looked directly into my eyes, took the nut out of my hand and dropped it. At the same moment he very gently squeezed my hand as if to say, I don't want it, but I understand your motives.

2   Since chimpanzees are thought to be **physiologically** close to humans, researchers use them as test subjects for new drugs and vaccines. In the labs, these very sociable creatures often live **isolated** from one another in 5-by-5 foot cages, where they grow surly and sometimes violent. Dogs, cats, and rats are also kept in poor conditions and subjected to painful procedures. Many people would find it hard to sympathize with rats, but dogs and cats are part of our lives. Ten or 15 years ago, when the use of animals in medical testing was first brought to my attention, I decided to visit the labs myself. Many people working there had forced themselves to believe that animal testing is the only way forward for medical research.

3   Once we accept that animals are **sentient** beings, is it ethical to use them in research? From the point of view of the animals, it is quite simply wrong. From our standpoint; it seems ridiculous to **equate** a rat with a human being. If we clearly and honestly believe that using animals in research will, in the end, reduce massive human suffering, it would be difficult to argue that doing so is unethical. How do we find a way out of the dilemma?

4   One thing we can do is change our mind-set. We can begin by questioning the **assumption** that animals are essential to medical research. Scientists have concluded that chimpanzees are not useful for AIDS research because, even though their genetic makeup differs from ours by about 1 percent, their immune systems deal much differently with the AIDS virus. Many scientists test drugs and vaccines on animals simply because they are required to by law rather than out of scientific merit. This is a shame, because our medical technology is beginning to provide **alternatives**. We can perform many tests on cell and tissue cultures without recourse to systemic testing on animals. Computer simulations can also cut down on the number of animal tests we need to run. We aren't exploring these alternatives vigorously enough.

5   Ten or 15 years ago animal-rights activists resorted to violence against humans in their efforts to break through the public's terrible **apathy** and lack of imagination on the issue. The **extremism** is **counterproductive**. I believe that more and more people are becoming aware that to use animals thoughtlessly, without any anguish or making an effort to find another way, **diminishes** us as human beings.

■ ■ ■

▶▶ after you read

Review Important Points

Going over major points immediately after you have read, while the information is fresh in your mind, will help you to recall the content and record key ideas.

| Exercise 3 | **Reviewing Important Points** |

Directions: Choose the best answer for each of the following questions using information provided in the selection. You may need to go back to the text and reread certain sections to be sure your responses are correct and can be supported by information in the text.

_c_ 1. **The topic of the reading selection is:**
   a. chimpanzees in Tanzania.
   b. seeing animals as sentient beings.
   c. the use of animals in medical research.
   d. the pros and cons of animal research.

_d_ 2. **The thesis of the selection is that:**
   a. Though people sympathize with cats and dogs, they do not feel the same way about rats.
   b. Chimps are not useful for AIDS research because their immune systems deal differently with the AIDS virus.
   c. Medical technology is finding alternative solutions to using animals in research.
   d. Using animals in medical research is wrong, and alternative methods should be explored.

_a_ 3. **In paragraph 1, Goodall recounts the story about David Graybeard to:**
   a. humanize the thoughts and emotions of a chimp.
   b. claim that chimps are smarter than humans.
   c. show her experience in working with animals.
   d. none of the above.

_b_ 4. **The overall topic of paragraph 2 is:**
   a. the change in animal treatment over the last fifteen years.
   b. the lab conditions of animals used in research.
   c. the feelings of animals.
   d. the cause of violence in animals.

_a_ 5. **What dilemma is raised in paragraph 3?**
   a. Since animals are feeling and caring beings, using them in medical research is unethical, *but* how can we not use them in research if it will reduce human suffering and cure disease?
   b. Since it is ridiculous to equate a rat and a human, how can we argue against using rats for research?
   c. Since using animals is the only way to do medical research effectively, how can we deny scientists the right to do so if it will save human lives?
   d. If we honestly believe that using animals in research will reduce human suffering, how can we say it would be ethical to do so?

_c_ 6. **What is the main idea of paragraph 4?**
   a. Scientists test drugs and vaccines on animals because they are required to by law.
   b. AIDS research on chimps is a waste of time because our immune systems are too different.
   c. Animals are not essential to medical research and we should look for alternatives.
   d. Computer simulations can cut down on the number of animal tests we run.

_c_ 7. **The statement, "This is a shame, because our medical technology is beginning to provide alternatives," primarily voices:**
   a. an assumption.
   b. a fact.
   c. an opinion.
   d. a topic.

_d_ 8. **By identifying various alternatives to using animals in medical research in paragraph 4, the author uses the organizational pattern of:**
   a. classification.
   b. definition.
   c. comparison and contrast.
   d. listing or enumeration.

_d_ 9. **The primary purpose of the selection is to:**
   a. instruct.
   b. entertain.
   c. inform.
   d. persuade.

_a_ 10. **We can infer that the author would be in favor of:**
   a. fundraising to support efforts to find alternative ways to do medical research.
   b. stopping medical research.
   c. using violence, when necessary, to protest the use of animals in medical research.
   d. arresting people who work in medical labs using animals.

_a_ 11. **At the end of the selection, the author concludes that:**
   a. If we continue to treat animals thoughtlessly, it lessens our value as people.
   b. To break through public apathy on this issue, we must resort to violence.
   c. The public will never change and lacks the imagination to come up with alternatives.
   d. Extremism is sometimes needed to create change.

Organize the Information

Organizing information shows that you have understood it and provides you with a useful study tool. (See Chapter 9.)

Exercise 4   **Organizing the Information**

Directions: Refer to your notes to complete the following table. Under the two headings, paraphrase the main points made by the author.

Using Animals for Medical Research Is Wrong

It's Unethical	It's Unnecessary
1. *Animals are social.*	1. *Chimps are not useful in AIDS research because their immune systems deal differently with the AIDS virus.*
2. *They are caring and have feelings.*	2. *Medical technology provides alternatives.*
3. *They are cramped and isolated in lab cages.*	3. *Tests can be performed on cells and tissue cultures, not animals.*
	4. *We can do simulations on computers, not animals.*

Integrate the Vocabulary

Make the new vocabulary *your* vocabulary.

Exercise 5   **Integrating the Vocabulary**

Directions: On the line provided, write a word or form of the word from the vocabulary list at the beginning of the selection that could replace the italicized, boldfaced phrase in each sentence.

1. Never having had a room of his own, Robert felt *alone and far away from everyone* when assigned to a private room in his dorm. _____isolated_____

2. Because she had seemed so intent on making her own decisions and taking charge of her life, I was very surprised by my sister's *lack of caring and involvement* when it came to selecting colleges to which she would apply. _____apathy_____

3. Although it was difficult to explain the *individual differences that made them unique,* I knew the pizza at Gino's was far better than at Ray's Restaurant. _____distinction_____

4. Partying all night before the math midterm would surely lead to results that were *undesirable and unwanted*. ___counterproductive___

5. Even many who opposed abortion were offended by the *outlandish and over-the-top behavior and acts of violence* of the right-to-life advocates who bombed clinics and murdered physicians. ___extremism___

6. Laurel and Hardy, an old-time comedy team, were very different *in their body types and shape;* Stan Laurel was thin and lanky, whereas Oliver Hardy was portly and round. ___physiologically___

7. When I initially began working out, my body was filled with aches and pains. However, after the first two weeks, the discomfort began *to lessen so that I could barely feel it*. ___diminish___

8. Although the statue was cold, hard marble, the look on its face was so *intelligent and full of feeling* that it was hard not to think it was listening to and understanding our conversation. ___sentient___

9. Environmentalists have long been concerned with developing *different options* for creating fuel and energy sources on our planet. ___alternatives___

10. Before he set out to car shop, Caleb's father warned him to not *consider* the salesperson's pitch *as being equal* to advice from a knowledgeable friend. ___equate___

11. After Jacob broke up with Serena, he was quick to advise, "Just because you may have a wonderful time on a first date, do not *jump to a quick conclusion* that you have found the love of your life!" ___assume___

Make Personal Connections Through Writing and Discussion

When you make your new learning relevant to yourself in some way, it becomes more meaningful and long lasting. Whenever you read, try to connect to the content on a personal level. How does it relate to you? How can you apply what you have read to other situations? What else would you like to know?

Exercise 6	**Making Personal Connections**

Directions: Think about yourself in relation to the article you just read. Apply the information you learned from reading it to respond to the following questions.

Answers will vary.

1. Is it ethical or unethical to use animals for medical research? Explain your point of view.

2. Do you agree with the statement, "it seems ridiculous to equate a rat with a human being." Do you draw that same distinction?

3. In our culture, one might say that the rights of animals are, and have always been, violated in a variety of ways. Humans have taken over the habitats of animals to settle and build cities. We kill animals for sport. We raise and hunt animals for food. We use the skins and fur of animals for our clothing, shoes, and suitcases. Animals have been slaughtered so that their body parts can be used in jewelry and as lucky charms. Animals have been used in research by cosmetic companies to test their products. We capture animals and put them in cages in zoos, so we can look at them. What are your thoughts about this? How does using animals for medical research fit into this picture?

Independent Reading
Textbook Reading Selection: Biology

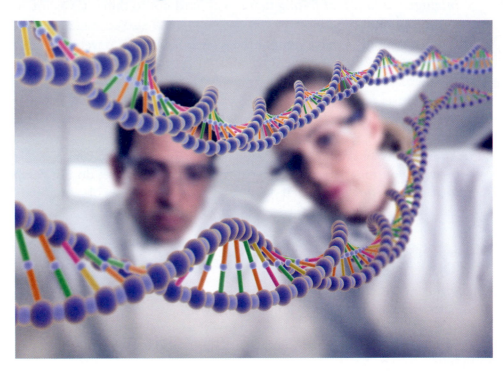

Ethical Issues Raised by Gene Therapy
By George Johnson and Jonathan Losos

The section that follows concludes a biology chapter titled "The Revolution in Cell Technology," from The Living World. *In the chapter, the authors discuss several developments in biologic science with which you may be familiar. These include reproductive animal cloning, using human embryonic stems cells to treat a wide range of diseases, and genetic engineering, or introducing "healthy" genes from one organism to another to cure disease.*

before you read

Answer the following questions before you read the textbook section on ethical issues of gene therapy.

- Do you know what gene therapy is or how it may be used?
- Do you think that medical science ever goes "too far"? How so?
- Look at the following list of medical advancements made over the last decades. Do any of these raise ethical issues for you? Can you add any others? Do you think the benefits of these breakthroughs raise moral concerns? Discuss these with your classmates.

- artificial insemination
- in vitro fertilization
- robotic surgery
- facial plastic surgery
- birth control pills
- medication for shortened menstrual cycles
- prosthetic limbs

- hair transplants
- heart transplants
- Magnetic Resonance Imaging (MRI)
- Viagra and other medication for erectile dysfunction
- Xanax and other medication to curb anxiety and depression

Prepare to Read

Preview the textbook selection using the THIEVES strategy on page 36.

| **Exercise 1** | **Developing Preview Questions** |

Directions: Based on your preview, write *three* questions you anticipate will be answered in the selection.   *Answers may vary.*

1. *What is gene intervention?*
2. *What is the difference between somatic tissue and germ-line tissue?*
3. *What is the beneficence principle? What is the respect-for-persons principle?*

Check Out the Vocabulary

The following words from this textbook selection appear in academic writing across many disciplines. Be sure you learn their meanings.

(A vector is a virus that is used to carry healthy genes to treat the disorder.) However, the trial was halted in 2005 after three other children in the trial developed cancer. The potential benefit was simply not worth the risk. Trials will resume with the new, safer vectors now available.

5   What about "enhancements" that seek to improve a person's genes? Are "designer babies" okay? How about non-lethal disorders like hypercholesterolemia, a gene mutation leading to too-high cholesterol (the most common human genetic disorder)? The risk would have to be very low before the beneficence principle would recommend such changes.

The Respect-for-Persons Principle

6   Ethicists apply a second principle, a test called the **respect-for-persons principle**, in trying to assess the desirability of gene intervention. The respect-for-persons principle states that the persons affected by the procedure have a right to make their own informed decisions. Prospective parents contemplating germ-line gene intervention have a right to a clear explanation of the risks, of possible benefits, and particularly of the alternative ways available to have healthy children before they make up their mind. Parents who know they carry a gene disorder might instead choose in vitro fertilization, for example, where the doctor can select a healthy embryo for implantation in the mother.

(Adapted from Johnson and Losos, 2008)

■ ■ ■

 **after you read**

Think back to the questions you posed after previewing the selection but before you actually read. Now that you have read the selection, can you answer your initial questions?

Exercise 3   **Answering Your Preview Questions**

Directions: If you have discovered the answers to the preview questions you created earlier, write them on the lines provided.

Answers will vary.

1. _____
   _____

2. _____
   _____

3. _____
   _____

Exercise 4   **Reviewing Important Points**

Directions: Choose the best answer for each of the following questions using information provided in the selection.

_b_ 1. The overall topic of this textbook excerpt is:
   a. medical ethicists and their dilemmas.
   b. ethics and gene therapy.
   c. gene intervention.
   d. the beneficence principle.

_c_ 2. The main idea of paragraph 1 is:
   a. stated in the first sentence.
   b. stated in the last sentence.
   c. a combination of the last two sentences.
   d. not stated directly but implied.

_a_ 3. The ethics of whether to perform gene interventions are generally determined by:
   a. whether changes will be hereditary or not.
   b. who is performing the intervention.
   c. the long-term effects of the therapy.
   d. the location at which the intervention is performed.

_d_ 4. The main difference between gene intervention related to somatic tissue and gene intervention related to germ-line tissue is that:
   a. Changes in somatic tissue are hereditary but they are not in germ-line tissue.
   b. In germ-line tissue, the changes are not passed on to offspring.
   c. In germ-line tissue, procedures attempt to correct problems by adding healthy tissue.
   d. Somatic tissue changes are not passed on to offspring but germ-line tissue changes are.

_b_ 5. The primary organizational pattern used to develop paragraph 2 is:
   a. listing or enumeration.
   b. comparison and contrast.
   c. cause and effect.
   d. sequence order.

_a_ 6. Based on the definition of the beneficence principle in paragraph 3, you can infer that:
   a. Most procedures have some risk.
   b. Benefits always outweigh risk.
   c. Risks most often outweigh benefits.
   d. Only patients suffering from a severe condition should ever be treated with gene interventions.

_c_ 7. As described in paragraph 4, the beneficence principle was used to justify the discontinuation of treatment for children with SCID because:
   a. There was no benefit to the treatment.
   b. Several children developed cancer.
   c. The risk of getting cancer outweighed the potential benefit of curing SCID.
   d. The risk of transmitting SCID was increased as the children got better.

_a_ 8. **The topic of paragraph 6 is:**
   a. the respect-for-persons principle.
   b. prospective parents wanting intervention.
   c. in vitro fertilization.
   d. plagiarism.

_d_ 9. **It can be inferred that an "informed" decision includes awareness of:**
   a. risks.
   b. benefits.
   c. alternatives.
   d. all of the above.

_b_ 10. **The overall main idea of this textbook section is that:**
   a. Medical ethicists have a difficult job to do when it comes to using gene interventions.
   b. Two major ethical principles are applied by the medical community to make decisions regarding the use of gene therapy.
   c. Risks generally outweigh the benefits when using gene interventions to treat serious illnesses.
   d. Gene interventions create controversy.

Exercise 5   **Organizing the Information**

Directions: Using your notes, complete the following outline to identify the major points and important details of the selection. You may want to rewrite the outline on a separate sheet of paper to practice the outline format.

Ethical Issues Raised by Gene Therapy

I. Gene Therapy

   A. Raises _serious medical issues_

   B. Referred to by ethicists as _"gene interventions"_

      1. Still largely _experimental_

      2. Any procedure that _deliberately alters a person's genes_

         a. by _modification of existing genes_

         b. by _contributing additional genes_

II. Draw Distinctions in Types of Changes Made by Gene Interventions

   A. Somatic Tissue

      1. Cells of the body _other than sperm or eggs_

      2. Procedures attempt to correct problems by _adding healthy genes to cells_

      3. Changes are not _hereditary_

B. *Germ-line Tissue*

   1. *Sperm* and *egg* cells

   2. Not yet attempted on *humans*

   3. Changes are passed on to offspring

      a. *alters the human genome*

      b. *possibility of unanticipated negative consequences*

III. The Beneficence Principle

A. Used by bioethicists to *assess ethical questions raised by gene interventions*

B. Carefully *weigh risks versus benefits*

C. Patient must *suffer from a condition sufficiently "bad" to justify the risk*

   1. Ex. *cystic fibrosis*

   2. Ex. *muscular dystrophy*

D. Role in halting *clinical trials of SCID*

E. Applied to "enhancements" of genes

   1. Ex. *designer babies, non-lethal disorders*

   2. Risk would have to be very *low* before beneficence principle would recommend such a change

IV. *The Respect -for-Persons Principle*

A. To *assess the desirability of gene intervention*

B. Persons have a right to *make their own informed decisions*

   1. clear explanation of risks

   2. *possible benefits*

   3. *alternative options*

Exercise 6   Using Context Clues

Directions: Use the context clues in the following sentences to figure out the meaning of the words in bold print. Underline any clue words that help you define these words or terms. The paragraph in which the sentence appears has been indicated for you in parentheses.

1. The recent **advent** of highly publicized clinical trials of gene therapy has raised serious ethical issues that are being widely discussed within the medical and scientific communities. (1)

   The word **advent** means *arrival of, start of, coming of, beginning of*

2. A gene intervention is any procedure that deliberately alters a person's genes, whether by **modification** of existing genes or by contributing additional genes. (1)

   The word **modification** means *change, adjustment, alteration*

3. Changes induced by gene interventions in somatic tissues are <u>not</u> **hereditary.** They are <u>not passed on to offspring.</u> (2)

    The word **hereditary** means *passed on to offspring from generation to generation*

4. How about **non-lethal** disorders like hypercholesterolemia, a gene mutation leading to too-high cholesterol (the most common human genetic disorder)? (5)

    The word **non-lethal** means *not deadly, not severe, not fatal*

5. Prospective parents **contemplating** germ-line gene intervention have a right to a clear explanation of the risks, of possible benefits, and particularly of the alternative ways available to have healthy children <u>before</u> <u>they make up their mind.</u> (6)

    The word **contemplating** means *thinking about, considering, pondering.*

| **E x e r c i s e   7** | **Making Personal Connections Through Writing and Discussion** |

Directions: Think about yourself in relation to the article you just read. Apply the information you learned from reading it to help you respond to the following questions.

Answers will vary.

1. What are some ethical issues that are faced by society outside of the medical arena? Can you identify ethical questions you face at school, at work, or at home? Tell about some of these, and the dilemmas they raise.

2. What do you think of the beneficence and respect-for-persons principles? Do they cover enough ground to lead to ethically sound medical decisions? Can you apply these principles to decisions you might confront in your personal life, outside of the medical arena? How?

Synthesizing Your Reading: Reflective Journal Writing

Medical Ethics

Having read these three selections on the topic of medical ethics, you now have a broader, more scholarly understanding of the subject matter.

Write a reflective journal entry on the topic of medical ethics, demonstrating both your knowledge of the content in the selections and your personal viewpoint on the issue. You should write at least one page.

In the first section of your entry, briefly summarize each selection. Include the thesis and a few key points for each.

In the second section, reflect on the topic. Consider any or all of the following: Have any of the readings in this section changed your views on a particular issue? Explain. What do you consider to be the most important ethical issue in medicine today? Why? What issue that you have read about has touched you the most? Tell about this.

Readings About Body Language

Get Acquainted with the Issue

Do actions speak louder than words?

Recently, as I entered my classroom, a female student called out, "Professor, are you angry?" I hadn't uttered a word, yet my body language had *spoken* volumes about how I felt. The wrinkles on my brow and the downward gaze of my eyes had revealed to her my true emotions. I was, in fact, still angry about an altercation that had taken place the session before.

Body language is the unspoken communication that takes place in every face-to-face encounter with another person. According to researchers in the field of body language, individuals use speech to convey information and nonverbal body language to communicate interpersonal attitudes and emotions. In fact, nonverbal communication constitutes between 60 and 80 percent of the information in a conversation.

In the first article, "Business Communication: How to Bridge the Gender Gap," Candy Tymson tells us how men and women send different messages through their nonverbal communication. In "Body Language Speaks: Reading and Responding More Effectively to Hidden Communication," you will learn about a framework for evaluating nonverbal cues. Finally, in an excerpt from a communications textbook chapter on nonverbal communication, you will learn how body language is used in everyday life in courtship, televised politics, and crime and punishment.

You will encounter the topic of body language in a number of college textbooks. The disciplines of linguistics, communications, sociology, psychology, criminal justice, business, and political science all deal with this topic.

Guided Reading
Reading Selection 1

Business Communication:
How to Bridge the Gender Gap
By Candy Tymson

In this selection, from The Journal of Banking and Financial Services, *Candy Tymson, an expert in business communication for more than 20 years, discusses the differences between men and women in the world of work.*

 before you read

It's important to think about what you already know about a topic before you read. In this way, you attach new learning to your background knowledge and more easily understand the new information. (See Chapter 2, "Access Prior Knowledge," page 33.)

Answer the following questions about body language.

- Do men and women talk differently?
- Do they use different body language?
- How would you categorize the following nonverbal communication cues?

Circle Male or Female.

1. Male/Female Making a thumbs up
2. Male/Female Winking with one eye
3. Male/Female Giggling softly
4. Male/Female Hugging a colleague
5. Male/Female Making a fist
6. Male/Female Offering a firm handshake
7. Male/Female Making direct eye contact
8. Male/Female Putting one's hands on one's hips

- Are females or males more likely to discuss issues or problems before they attempt to resolve them? Whose communication styles do you think are better? Explain.

Prepare to Read

Preview the textbook selection "Business Communications: How to Bridge the Gender Gap" using the THIEVES strategy on page 36.

Exercise 1   Previewing

Directions: Complete the following items.

1. Take a look at the selection and check off the items that are available to you for preview.

   _X_ Title

   _X_ Headings

   _X_ Introduction

   _X_ Every first sentence in each paragraph

   _X_ Visuals/vocabulary

   ___ End of chapter questions

   _X_ Summary/concluding paragraph

2. Read and highlight to preview the selection.

3. Based on your preview, what do you anticipate the reading will be about?
   Today, as women take more leadership roles and own their own businesses, it has become more important to understand gender differences in the workplace, especially to avoid clashes and improve communication.

Check Out the Vocabulary

The following words appear in bold font in the reading. Are you already familiar with them? Knowing the meaning of these terms will increase your understanding of the material.

Exercise 2   **Checking Out the Vocabulary**

Directions: Complete the following matching exercise *before*, *during*, or *after* your reading. Be sure to review the word in the context of the selection.

_d_	1. colleague	a.	condition of being male or female
_j_	2. consultation	b.	absolutely necessary, essential
_g_	3. dynamics*	c.	marked by agreement in feeling, attitude, or action; cooperative
_a_	4. gender*	d.	fellow member of a profession, an associate
_c_	5. harmonious	e.	to lower one's head in acknowledgment or agreement
_b_	6. imperative	f.	way of acting or doing
_f_	7. mode*	g.	social process by which people interact
_e_	8. nod	h.	relationship, especially one of trust
_i_	9. priority*	i.	order of importance, preference
_h_	10. rapport	j.	discussion where views are exchanged or advice given

*from the Academic Word List

as you read

Establish Your Purpose

Now, read and annotate the selection. Focus on major points of information about Tymson's discussion of business communication.

Actively Process While You Read

Stop and process information as you read.

Exercise 3   **Processing While You Read**

Directions: Answer the following questions at the conclusion of each paragraph. This will help you monitor your reading process and understand the material.

Paragraph 1

1. Why do men and women sometimes have difficulty understanding each other?

because they are motivated by different things and have different needs

Paragraph 2

2. Why is it especially important today to understand the gender gap in business communication?

There are many more women in senior positions.

Paragraph 3

3. Describe the frustrations experienced by men and women in executive positions because they problem solve in different ways.

Women talk about solutions to problems before they attempt to resolve them. Men don't discuss problems and proceed immediately to resolve them. These different approaches create frustration for both men and women. Men think women are not doing their jobs, and women think men are taking away their responsibility and authority.

Paragraph 4

4. In general, how do men and women differ in their use of language?

Men use language to maintain their independence and position in the group. In contrast, women use language to create intimacy and connection.

Paragraph 5

5. What are the two styles of communication? Describe each one.

Information style—talk is used to preserve independence, negotiate, and maintain status.
Relationship style—talk is used to make connections and negotiate relationships.

6. Which one is connected to men, and which one is associated with women?

The information style—men
The relationship style— women

Paragraph 6

7. How do men and women differ in terms of decision making?

Most women consult with others and get feedback before making a recommendation. They want others to feel part of the decision-making process so that they will support their ideas. On the other hand, most men do not consult anyone else and want others to see that they are the boss.

Paragraph 7

8. What do their different styles of decision making say about men and women's sense of priority?

Women's priority is relationship, whereas men's priority is status.

Paragraph 8

9. What different verbal and nonverbal signals do men and women give?

Women nod and say things like "Yes," "OK," and "I understand." They try to relate to a speaker. In contrast, men show no expressions, say nothing, and take notes, which indicates they focus on the task, not on relating to the speaker.

Paragraph 9

10. How does the meaning of *nodding* differ for men and women? In what way does this difference cause a gap in communication?

Women—nodding shows she understands what is being said. Men—nodding indicates agreement. A man can misinterpret a woman's body language and think her nodding means she is in agreement, when in fact she is just listening.

Paragraph 10

11. How can businesses benefit from understanding the gender differences in communication styles?

It can help them to create more productive and harmonious working environments.

Business Communication: How to Bridge the Gender Gap
By Candy Tymson

1   Since time began, men and women simply have not understood each other. We are motivated by different things and have quite different needs. It's got nothing to do with whether or not we are "equal," we simply communicate in different ways.

2   With so many women now in senior positions and running successful companies, the need to understand the **gender** differences in business communication has become **imperative**—for both men and women. While a host of popular books in recent times has helped us to understand each other in personal relationships, very little has been written to distinguish the differences in business circles.

3   Discussing the issue over dinner recently, I was interested to hear some of the frustrations expressed by CEOs about their senior female executives. The managing director of a large food importer was complaining that his senior women have a tendency to come into his office, "dump" all their problems and leave. "I pay them to solve problems, not give them back to me," he says, showing his frustration. This is a typical example of the different way men and women operate. The woman is simply discussing the issues with him. She knows she needs to find the answers, but talking about it helps her work out the solutions. Meanwhile, he has moved straight into solution **mode**: "Once I'm told about a problem I have to solve it." The result is he's feeling frustrated because he now thinks he's got to do her job. She's feeling frustrated because she thinks he is taking away her responsibility.

Status vs. Relationship

4   So what are the differences? Generally speaking—and of course there are always exceptions—men use language to preserve their independence and maintain their position in the group; women use language to create connection and intimacy.

5   Next time you are in a mixed business meeting notice the **dynamics**. Basically there seem to be two styles, the information style and the relationship style. The information style is often, but not always, associated with men. Talk is primarily a means to preserve independence and negotiate and maintain status. The relationship style is often, but not always, associated with women. Conversation is primarily a language of **rapport:** a way of establishing connections and negotiating relationships.

Differences in the Workplace

6   Think about the different styles of approach when a male and female manager are asked to make a decision. Usually the woman will discuss it with others, seek their input and feedback before making a recommendation to senior management. She thinks it is important that everyone feels they have contributed to the decision and therefore are more likely to support it. In contrast, the man usually makes the decision without any **consultation**, and makes the recommendation. He believes that seeking input is unnecessary. He's in charge so he needs to make the decision. Because of this, it is likely that he will think that she cannot make a decision on her own, and needs to check with others first.

7   These are very different approaches for very different reasons. The female's first **priority** is relationship. The male's is status.

Body Language

8   Even in body language, men and women can give off different signals. A female **colleague,** who is a director at a large financial company, expressed it well recently. She recalled a meeting of senior executives that morning, half men and half women. "To my horror I noticed that all the women were **nodding** and saying things like 'yes,' 'OK,' 'I understand,' while the men just sat straight faced and wrote the occasional note," she said. "The men were totally focused on the task at hand. The women were working hard to relate to the speaker, rather than focusing on what he was actually saying."

9   Women **nodding** during a conversation usually means "I understand what you are saying." Men **nodding** in a discussion usually means "I agree with you." Often problems arise when a man misinterprets a woman's automatic **rapport**-building **nodding** as a sign of agreement. She may not be agreeing at all.

Avoiding Communication Clashes

10   Understanding the gender differences in business communication makes for a more productive, **harmonious** workplace. People communicate in different ways. Another style is not wrong—it's just different! Both men and women can profit enormously by learning to understand the differences between them.

(*Journal of Banking and Financial Services,* June 2001)

■ ■ ■

 **after you read**

Review Important Points

Going over the major points immediately after you read, while the information is fresh in your mind, will help you to recall the content and record key ideas.

| Exercise 4 | **Reviewing Important Points** |

Directions: Answer the following questions based on the information provided in the selection. You may need to go back to the text and reread certain portions to be sure your responses are correct and can be supported by information in the text.

1. In which paragraph is the overall main idea stated? Paraphrase the main idea.

   Paragraph 2. As women take a much greater role in business, it has become critical for men and women to understand the differences in their communication styles.

2. Discuss the emotional impact of the gender gap on men.

   Men are often frustrated by the way women communicate.

3. Describe the emotional needs of women in senior positions.

   Women need to discuss ideas to help them work out solutions to business problems.

4. Differentiate between the ways men and women communicate in business in terms of the following:

   a. Use of language

      Women—use language to create connections and intimacy

      Men—use language to preserve independence and maintain their position in a group

   b. Dynamics

      Women—relationship style

      Men—information style

   c. Decision making

      Women—discuss, seek input and feedback before making decisions

      Men—no discussion; go straight to making recommendations

5. Using information from this article, what is one difference in the body language of male and female executives?

   Women nod to show understanding, whereas men nod to indicate agreement.

Organize the Information

Organizing the information you have learned from a reading shows that you have understood it and can restate the material in a different way. You may use this reorganized material to help you study for exams and prepare for written assignments. (See Chapter 9.)

Directions: First, list the words or transitions in the selection that indicate the overall organizational pattern. Next, write the name of the overall pattern of organization. Then complete the table using details from the selection.

Words: _while, different, differences, in contrast, rather than_____

Pattern: _comparison/contrast_____

Gender Gap: Business Circles

Topic	Women	Men
Problem-Solving	Talk about problems with others	_Solve problems_
Use of Language	Create connections and _intimacy_	Preserve _independence_ and maintain position in group
Dynamics	_Relationship style_	_Information style_
Decision-Making	_Discuss, seek input and feedback, make decision_	No discussion, make recommendations
Body Language	Nod means _Yes, OK, I understand._	Nod means _I agree._

Integrate the Vocabulary

Make new vocabulary presented in the reading _your_ vocabulary. Using the terms in other contexts will help you make them part of your own spoken and written language.

Answers will vary. Sample answers are provided.

Directions: Practice integrating vocabulary by replacing the italicized word or phrase in each of the following sentences with a word, or alternate form of the word, from the vocabulary list at the beginning of the selection on page 369. Paraphrase and rewrite the sentence on the line provided, using the new term.

1. Since there are a great number of nontraditional students at community colleges today, it is _absolutely necessary_ to understand what these students need to succeed.

    With so many nontraditional students attending two-year colleges nowadays, it is **imperative** _to recognize the needs of this diverse student population._

2. When you next sit in your biology course, note the _interaction_ between the students and your professor.

    The next time you are sitting in your biology class, notice the **dynamics** _between the instructor and the students._

3. I was dropped from history without having the opportunity to *discuss* my professor's decision.

   My history professor dropped me from class without any **consultation.**

4. In July and August, when classes are not in regular session, I always *act like I am on vacation.*

   During the summer months when I have no classes, I am in vacation **mode.**

5. Some students consider their jobs to be their *most important* task, whereas for me it's getting good grades in all my classes.

   While some students make their jobs a top **priority,** *mine is doing well in all my classes.*

6. In my nursing classes, I occasionally meet nursing assistants *with whom I work* at the hospital.

   It is not unusual to meet **colleagues** *from the hospital in my nursing classes.*

7. When the student *moved her head up and down*, the male philosophy professor mistakenly thought she was saying, "I agree with what you are saying."

   The philosophy professor observed the student **nodding** *during his lecture and assumed she agreed with what he was saying.*

8. Linked courses help students create *interpersonal relationships* with their instructors.

   Learning communities or linked courses provide important opportunities for students to develop a **rapport** *with their professors.*

9. When students work well in groups, there is an improved sense of *cooperation* in the class, which leads to better learning.

   Effective group work strategies can create a **harmonious** *environment that enhances learning and studying.*

10. When you understand that the ways men and women communicate are related to differences in *male and female characteristics*, you will be able to develop ways to accomplish tasks more efficiently at work.

    Understanding the **gender** *differences between men and women in business communication makes for a more productive workplace.*

Words with Multiple Meanings

As you know, a word can have more than one meaning. For example, the word *study* is commonly used as a verb meaning *to acquire knowledge through review, learning, and reflection*, but it can also refer to a room in a home set aside for reading and writing.

As discussed in Chapter 3, you should use the context in which you hear or read a word to help determine its meaning.

Exercise 7 **Using Context Clues**

Directions: The following words from the article have multiple meanings. Beside each word are four possible definitions. Locate each word in the selection (the paragraph it appears in is indicated in parentheses) and use context to determine the meaning of the word. Write the letter of the meaning as it is used in the article, and take note of its alternate definitions.

_a_ 1. **position** (2)

    a. a post of employment or job
    b. a point of view or opinion
    c. a place or location
    d. the area for which a player is responsible

_d_ 2. **host** (2)

    a. a person who receives guests
    b. a master of ceremonies
    c. an animal or plant on which another organism lives
    d. a number of things

_c_ 3. **issue** (3)

    a. a matter of public concern
    b. a single copy of a magazine or periodical
    c. the essential part
    d. a complaint

_c_ 4. **operate** (3)

    a. to perform surgery
    b. to manipulate something in an irregular or devious way
    c. to manage or work
    d. to use a machine

_d_ 5. **preserve** (4)

    a. to seek safety or protection
    b. to prepare food for future use
    c. to treat food to keep it fresh
    d. to keep up or maintain

_b_ 6. **negotiate** (5)

    a. to deal or bargain
    b. to manage
    c. to succeed by passing through
    d. to settle through discussion

_b_ 7. **profit** (10)

    a. to gain money
    b. to gain advantage or benefit
    c. to take advantage
    d. to make progress

Make Personal Connections Through Writing and Discussion

When you make your new learning relevant to yourself in some way, it becomes more meaningful and long lasting. Whenever you read, try to connect to the content on a personal level. How does it relate to you? How can you apply what you have read to other situations? What else would you like to know?

| Exercise 8 | **Making Personal Connections** |

Directions: Think about yourself in relation to the article you have just read. Apply the information you learned from reading it to respond to the following questions.

1. Read below to see what Deborah Tannen, writer of many academic publications on interpersonal communication, wrote about in her latest book, *Gender Games: Doing Business with the Opposite Sex*. Work with a partner and discuss whether you agree or disagree with each of her findings. Provide examples of contexts or situations to support your opinion.

   - Men tend to talk more than women in public situations, but women tend to talk more than men at home.

   - Females are more inclined to face each other and make eye contact when talking, whereas males are more likely to look away from each other.

   - Girls and women tend to jump from topic to topic, but boys and men tend to talk at length about one topic.

   - When listening, women make more noises such as "mm-hmm" and "uh-huh," whereas men are more likely to listen silently.

   - Women are inclined to express agreement and support, but men are more inclined to debate.

2. Observe the nonverbal communication of men and women on your college campus. You may want to select from one of the following locations: the library, the cafeteria, the advisement center, the quad, or a grassy area. Take notes about the activities people are engaged in and the body language they display. For example, in the library, you may observe students reading, studying, or working on a paper. You might see some students yawning, rubbing their eyes, or fidgeting with their pens. Then see if you notice any differences between male and female body language. Finally, share your findings with your classmates.

Self-Monitored Reading
Reading Selection 2

> # Body Language Speaks: Reading and Responding More Effectively to Hidden Communication
>
> ## By Anne E. Beall

In this article from Communication World, *the author explains how to read and use nonverbal communication more effectively in the world of business.*

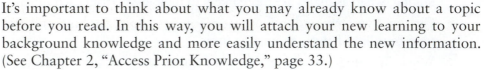

before you read

It's important to think about what you may already know about a topic before you read. In this way, you will attach your new learning to your background knowledge and more easily understand the new information. (See Chapter 2, "Access Prior Knowledge," page 33.)

Consider the following examples of nonverbal communication. Work with a partner and discuss the meaning of the following nonverbal cues that are mentioned in the article:

- Showing a quick expression of surprise
- Keeping distance between you and another person while talking to him or her
- Not facing a person directly
- Angling your body away
- Keeping your hands near to your body
- Using wild movement of your hands
- Playing with one's rings
- Touching one's hair

Prepare to Read

Preview the article by applying the THIEVES strategy on page 37.

Exercise 1   **Previewing**

Directions: Based on your preview, respond to the following questions.

1. According to research, what is the significance of nonverbal communication?

    Nonverbal communication accounts for about 2/3 or more of total communication.

2. List the eight factors that you should consider in evaluating body language.

   Proximity, expressions, relative orientation, contact, eyes, individual gestures, voice and
   existence of adapters.

Check Out the Vocabulary

The terms in the matching exercise that follows appear in bold type in the reading. Are you familiar with them? Knowing the meaning of all these terms will increase your comprehension of the material.

| **Exercise 2** | **Checking Out the Vocabulary** |

Directions: Complete the matching exercise *before*, *during*, or *after* your reading. Be sure to review the words in the context of the selection.

e	1. chaos	a.	how people position themselves
j	2. constitute*	b.	frenzied and wild movements
g	3. demoralized	c.	set into motion
d	4. dynamic	d.	charismatic and displaying energy
l	5. emerge*	e.	complete disorder
b	6. frenetic	f.	majority
n	7. gauge	g.	disheartened
j	8. havoc	h.	keep from being known
k	9. manipulative*	i.	compose, comprise, be a basic part of
m	10. monotonic	j.	disorder and confusion
a	11. orientation	k.	influence by cunning behavior
f	12. preponderance	l.	come into view
h	13. suppress	m.	unvarying tone
c	14. triggered*	n.	measure

*from the Academic Word List

▶ as you read

Establish Your Purpose

Now, read and annotate the selection. Focus on the major points of information. Read to discover what body language says about you and how people respond to your nonverbal communication. What are the implications for getting a job, keeping a job, and doing business?

Actively Process While You Read

Monitor your comprehension as you read. (See Chapter 2, "Monitoring Questions," page 40.) Be sure to stop to reflect at the conclusion of each paragraph. Ask yourself the following questions:

- Did I understand that paragraph?
- What is the main idea?
- Am I ready to continue?

Highlight the most important points. Write notes in the margin, and move on.

> ## Body Language Speaks: Reading and Responding More Effectively to Hidden Communication
> By Anne E. Beall

1   In a weekly status meeting with an employee, the director of communication observed that the employee began to gesture as he talked about a report he was preparing. He seemed to be putting things into "boxes" as he outlined various pieces of research. As the manager looked closer, she noticed that some of the areas he was gesturing to appeared disconnected. She asked him if he was having trouble figuring out how pieces of the research were connected, and he replied with amazement: "Yes, I am. How did you know?"

2   A manager at a large company did not attend to the body language of a new sales representative she was hiring, and her oversight became a costly mistake. When the manager gave the candidate the offer, he showed a quick expression of surprise. Because she did not want to read too much into his expression, she ignored it. Once on the job, however, the new sales rep's body language conveyed that he was often defensive in his interactions with his manager. He kept distance between them when talking, he often did not face her directly, and some of his expressions showed that he did not like her. The new hire also turned out to be a **manipulative** employee who liked to create **chaos** between staff members in the office. Before long, he proved not to be qualified for the job, which is why he showed the quick expression of surprise at the time of the initial offer. Ultimately, the company fired the sales rep, but not before he created **havoc** and wasted the company's valuable time and money.

Overlooking the Obvious

3   In this fast-paced world, the spoken and written word sometimes take center stage. It's possible to become so focused on what is being said that nonverbal communication—an equally important aspect of communication—is overlooked.

4   Research indicates that although people may strongly attend to what is said, nonverbal behavior may **constitute** two-thirds or more of total communication. And although people have the option not to speak, they can never be uncommunicative nonverbally. Nonverbal signals are a rich source of information, and one's own non-verbal behavior can be useful in responding to others, making stronger connections with clients and colleagues, and conveying certain impressions about oneself.

5   One common misconception is that specific behaviors indicate the same thoughts for all people. Unfortunately, nonverbal behavior is more complex. Using a framework is the most useful way to decode others, because a combination of behaviors tells a story. One such framework is PERCEIVE™, which stands for

- Proximity
- Expressions
- Relative **Orientation**
- Contact
- Eyes
- Individual Gestures
- Voice
- Existence of Adapters

6   Proximity and relative **orientation** are the building blocks. Proximity is the distance between individuals. Generally, people sit, stand and want to be near those they like. Increased proximity is an indication of feelings of liking and interest.

7   Relative **orientation** is the degree to which people face one another. A parallel **orientation** indicates that one is interested in and focused on the other person. As people become less interested in and less focused on another person, they tend to angle their bodies away. A good way to decode **orientation** is to observe where a person's feet are placed. Often people will point their feet in the direction they truly want to go.

8   Expressions are observed on the face and can last as little as 1/15 of a second. These very brief expressions are called micro-expressions, and they occur when people are trying to hide a feeling. Interestingly, when people begin to experience an emotion, their facial muscles are **triggered**. If they **suppress** the expression, it's shown for only 1/15 of a second. If they do not suppress it, the expression will appear prominently. The six universal expressions that all cultures recognize are happiness, sadness, anger, fear, surprise, and disgust.

9   Contact refers to physical contact. Generally, the amount and frequency of physical contact demonstrate closeness, familiarity and degree of liking. A lot of touching indicates strong liking for another person.

10   Eyes primarily show whom or what people are most interested in or like. One can **gauge** liking and interest by the frequency, duration and total amount of time spent looking.

11   Individual gestures can indicate an image in a person's mind that is sometimes not communicated with spoken language. Some typical gestures are ones in which

people indicate what refers to them and what refers to others (e.g., the hands come near the body or motion away), gestures that describe an emotion or experience (e.g., sobbing gesture or **frenetic** moving of the hands) or gestures that identify where objects are in relation to one another. Gestures can provide information about how things are organized in a person's mind. They can also reveal how people are feeling. People tend to gesture more when they are enthusiastic, excited and energized. People gesture less when they are **demoralized**, nervous or concerned about the impression they are making.

12   Voice, or speech, provides much information about the demographics of a speaker (e.g., gender, age, area of origin, social class). Voice can also reveal emotions, which are transmitted through the tone of the voice, accentuation of words, rapidity of speech and number of speech errors. Typically, speech errors indicate discomfort and anxiety. A person who begins to produce a lot of speech errors may be anxious and ill at ease.

13   Existence of Adapters is the last piece of PERCEIVE. Adapters are small behaviors that tend to occur when people are stressed or bored with a situation. Examples are playing with rings, twirling a pen or touching one's hair. As meetings extend, an increasing number of adapter behaviors tend to **emerge** among the people in the room.

14   Each aspect of body language provides an overall picture of what the other person is experiencing. If a person has close proximity, positive expressions (including micro-expressions), a parallel relative orientation, physical contact that is appropriate for the situation, eye contact about half the time, a small to moderate amount of gesturing, voice behaviors that do not include speech errors or emotional leaks, and very few adapters, then this person likes and is interested in what the other person has to say. Not all of these behaviors may be present, but a **preponderance** of them will tell a story.

Taking Personal Inventory

15   Reading people is tremendously important, but so is using one's own body language. Because nonverbal communication is not highly controlled, people can sometimes reveal their feelings without knowing it. Silent language can expose nervousness, anxiety, lack of interest, or dislike of another person. Using body language effectively means using nonverbal communication to present an image that is most effective for the situation.

16   One of the most common impressions that professionals want to convey is competence, or credibility. People appear most competent when they exhibit few speech errors, speak with slight rapidity (about 125 to 150 words per minute), face the listener directly, **sustain** eye contact about half of the time (do not look away while making a point), and assume an open and relaxed posture. These behaviors indicate that the speaker knows the subject and is confident and credible.

17   Another impression many people want to convey is likeability and dynamism. Persuasive communicators are often extremely likable because they are good at expressing their liking of others. Those who are **dynamic** are interesting to listen to

and observe when they're talking. The elements of likeability and dynamism are relatively close proximity (between 2 and 6 feet), positive facial expressions and micro-expressions, leaning toward others, a parallel **orientation,** moderate physical contact (as appropriate for the situation), eye contact about half the time, a moderate amount of gesturing (particularly to help the listener understand), a voice that is relaxed, not nasal or **monotonic** but vocally animated, and the absence of adapters. All of these behaviors increase perceptions of likeability and dynamism.

18   There are many useful business applications for nonverbal communication. One can use it to read others, detect deception, discern underlying emotions, determine interest in one's product or service, or ascertain degree of liking from another person. One can also use body language to convey certain impressions. But the most effective use of nonverbal communication is to read others and to respond to what one sees.

■ ■ ■

after you read

Review Important Points

Going over major points after you read, while the information is fresh in your mind, will help you to recall the content and record key ideas.

Exercise 3   **Reviewing Important Points**

Directions: Choose the best answer for each of the following questions using information provided in the selection. You may need to go back to the text and reread certain portions to be sure your responses are correct and can be supported by information in the text.

_a_ 1. The anecdote in paragraph 1 illustrates how:
     a. Nonverbal behavior can be useful in understanding others.
     b. Some people ignore body language completely.
     c. Employees can have difficulty understanding research material.
     d. People can use body language to reveal their inner feelings.

_a_ 2. From the second anecdote, we learn that:
     a. Overlooking body language, especially at the time of an interview, can result in future problems for a business.
     b. Some employees know how to use nonverbal communication to manipulate their employers.
     c. Body language conveys certain impressions about oneself.
     d. Keeping your distance from your manager and creating chaos among staff members is a reason to get fired from a job.

_b_   3. According to research, nonverbal behavior accounts for:
   a. total communication.
   b. almost 70% of communication.
   c. less than 2/3 of total communication.
   d. why people are uncommunicative.

_c_   4. The main idea of paragraph 5 is that:
   a. Nonverbal behavior is complex.
   b. PERCEIVE is a framework for verbal behavior.
   c. PERCEIVE can help us understand nonverbal behavior.
   d. The combinations of behaviors are different for everybody.

_a_   5. To understand nonverbal cues, we first look at:
   a. the distance between individuals and the degree to which people face each other.
   b. gestures and expressions.
   c. voice and physical contact.
   d. proximity and the distance between individuals.

_b_   6. The topic of paragraph 8 is:
   a. nonverbal behavior.
   b. micro-expressions.
   c. universal expressions.
   d. body language.

_b_   7. The main idea of paragraph 9 is:
   a. stated in sentence 1.
   b. stated in sentence 2.
   c. stated in the last sentence.
   d. unstated.

_c_   8. Which information about gestures in paragraph 11 relates to the anecdote in paragraph 1?
   a. Gestures describe an emotion or experience.
   b. People gesture more when they are enthusiastic.
   c. Gestures can provide information about how things are organized in your mind.
   d. People gesture less when they are demoralized, nervous, or concerned about the impression they are making.

_d_   9. The pattern of organization in paragraphs 5–15 is:
   a. comparison and contrast.
   b. cause and effect.
   c. listing or enumeration.
   d. definition.

_c_   10. What is the main idea of the section "Taking Personal Inventory"?
   a. Reading the nonverbal cues of others is very important in business communication.
   b. It is most important that professionals convey credibility.

    c. Monitoring your own body language is tremendously important at work.

    d. Another impression many people want to convey is likeability and dynamism.

_b_ **11. What is the overall main idea of the selection?**

    a. Body language conveys how people feel.

    b. Nonverbal communication is as important as verbal communication.

    c. People can use body language to convey emotions, understand how others are feeling, and relate to others.

    d. Nonverbal communication is often misunderstood.

_d_ **12. The tone of this selection is:**

    a. serious.

    b. formal.

    c. persuasive.

    d. informative.

Organize the Information

Organizing the information shows that you have understood it and provides you with a useful tool. (See Chapter 9.)

Exercise 4   **Organizing the Information**

Directions: In paragraphs 5–13, the author describes a framework for decoding nonverbal language. Use the details from the reading to complete the following table.

Framework for Decoding Nonverbal Communication

Term	Definition/Explanation	Significance
Proximity	_distance between individuals_	_Increased_ proximity is an indication of liking and interest.
Expressions	_emotions observed on the face_	Suppressed emotions—micro-expressions Not suppressed—_prominent expressions_
Relative orientation	Degree to which people face each other	_Parallel_—interested and focused _Angled away_—disinterested
Contact	_Physical contact_	Amount and frequency indicates _closeness_

(continued)

(continued)

Eyes	Amount and type of eye contact significant	*Shows whom or what people are interested in or like* Gauged by *frequency and duration*
Individual gestures	*Hand movements*	May indicate how things are *organized* in a person's mind, reveal emotions More frequent when a person is *enthusiastic* Less frequent when a person is *nervous*
Voice	Speech	Reveals *demographics*, emotions Speech errors indicate *anxiety*
Existence of adapters	Small behaviors like *playing with rings, twirling one's hair*	Used when *bored or stressed* Use of adapters *increases* if situation is prolonged or boring.

Integrate the Vocabulary

Make the vocabulary presented in the selection *your* vocabulary.

Exercise 5   **Integrating the Vocabulary**

Directions: On the lines provided, write a word or a form of the word from the vocabulary list at the beginning of the selection that could replace the italicized, boldfaced phrase in the sentence.

1. When Alyssa's phone rang in the middle of the class session, her ***frenzied and wild*** movements suggested something terrible had happened.
   frenetic

2. The cuts in the college budget and therefore spending caused ***disorder and confusion*** during registration because fewer advisors were on hand to assist students.
   havoc

3. John was ***completely destroyed*** when he received a D on his first essay in Creative Writing.
   demoralized

4. Jonathan ***came into view*** of the crowd of parents and guests wearing his medal of distinction for excellence in business studies.
   emerged

5. It is important for students to ***measure*** the amount of time they will need for reading and studying so they can manage their time effectively.
   gauge

6. When Jenna moved to the back of the classroom and angled her chair toward the window, the instructor interpreted her new *position* as showing disinterest in her course.
   orientation

7. Students should read through their syllabi at the beginning of the semester to determine what *makes up* a passing grade in each course.
   constitutes

8. Incoming students, especially freshmen, may find it difficult to *keep down* feelings of homesickness.
   suppress

9. College Security was alerted when a group of protesting students caused *massive disruption* as they demonstrated outside the Student Union building.
   chaos

10. When the student asked the professor to postpone her make-up exam because she was not feeling well again, the teacher realized that she was *trying to influence* him to give her yet another day to prepare for the test.
    manipulate

11. The college administration is still trying to figure out what *set in motion* the latest rash of thefts of student records from the registrar.
    triggered

12. The *overwhelming amount* of evidence, which included files from his hard drive and copies of students' pin numbers, indicated that the young man had, in fact, committed the theft of student IDs.
    preponderance

13. In my business communication course, we learned that using an *unvarying* tone in a business speech is a sure way to lose your audience.
    monotonic

14. A *charismatic* professor inspires, challenges, and interacts with his students.
    dynamic

Make Personal Connections Through Writing and Discussion

When you make new learning relevant to yourself in some way, it becomes more meaningful and long lasting. Whenever you read, try to connect to the content on a personal level. How does it relate to you? How can you apply what you have read to other situations? What else would you like to know?

Exercise 6　　**Making Personal Connections**

Directions: Think about yourself in relation to the article you have just read. Apply the information you learned from reading it to respond to the following questions.　　*Answers will vary.*

1. There are six universal expressions that all cultures recognize. They include the following: happiness, sadness, anger, fear, surprise, and disgust. Nevertheless, many cultures follow different rules about when each expression can and cannot be displayed. Write about how you use these expressions. Then compare your nonverbal behavior with that of another student, and note any cultural differences.

2. In the article, you learned that "a preponderance of nonverbal gestures can tell a story." During a break between classes, your lunch break, or free time, spend about an hour focusing on a small group of individuals. Observe their nonverbal communication, and then record all the body language (facial expressions, gestures, proximity, and eye contact) that you notice. Write the *story* of your observations.

3. If you work part- or full-time, see if you can detect any nonverbal behaviors among co-workers at your workplace that reveal the qualities of good employees. Share your findings with the members of your class.
    Look for some of the following positive characteristics:

    ■ likeability
    ■ dynamism
    ■ enthusiasm
    ■ honesty
    ■ empathy

4. For the next week, ask a member of your family to observe some of your nonverbal actions, and keep a list of what they notice. At the end of the week, you will find out if you are revealing emotions without knowing it or if you are exhibiting the *messages* that you want others to *know*. Discuss your findings with your classmates.

Independent Reading
Textbook Reading Selection: Communications

Nonverbal Communication in Everyday Life
By John Stewart

This selection is from a communications textbook titled Bridges Not Walls: A Book About Interpersonal Communication. *The chapter focuses on verbal and nonverbal contact. The excerpt from the chapter discusses nonverbal communication in everyday life.*

◀◀ before you read

Answer the following questions before you read the textbook selection on body language in everyday life.

- Think about body language in the classroom. What do each of these nonverbal cues suggest to you?
  - A student frantically waving his hand
  - A student avoiding eye contact with the professor
  - A student smiling as the instructor lectures
  - A student leaning forward as the professor speaks
  - A student checking his or her cell phone for messages in class
  - A student sending text messages during a lecture
  - An instructor glancing at his or her watch throughout class
  - An instructor standing up during the administration of a final exam
  - An instructor posing a question and a student gazing up and wrinkling his or her nose
- You've already read about the importance of nonverbal communication in business. What sort of body language may be involved in other situations in life? Consider some of the following areas and discuss your ideas with a partner.
  - music, dance, theater
  - crime and punishment
  - flirting and dating
  - TV and advertisements

Prepare to Read

Preview the textbook selection using the THIEVES strategy on page 37.

| Exercise 1 | **Developing Preview Questions** |

Directions: Based on your preview, write *three* questions you anticipate will be answered in the selection.

Answers will vary. Sample questions provided.

1. *What are some examples of nonverbal communication in courtship?*
2. *In what way do politicians use body language to generate support for themselves in an election?*
3. *How can criminals be identified through their nonverbal cues?*

Check Out the Vocabulary

The following words from this textbook selection are likely to appear in academic writing across many disciplines. Be sure you know their meaning.

Academic Word List

acknowledge	to take notice of
attributed, attributable	to regard as resulting from a specific cause
crucial	involving an extremely important result; vital, significant, or essential
core	basic
indicators	signals for attracting attention
subsequently	occurring or coming later or after, afterwards, following

---

Exercise 2   **Checking Out the Vocabulary**

Directions: Complete each of the following sentences with a word from the preceding Academic Word List.

1. It is _____ *crucial* _____ to hand in assignments on time; otherwise, your grade could be lowered.

2. Robert did not pass his first major exam in biology; _____ *subsequently* _____, his professor dropped him from the class roster.

3. Nonverbal _____ *indicators* _____ shown by students, such as glancing out of windows or fidgeting with pens, can demonstrate difficulty with concentration.

4. Professor Green _____ *attributed* _____ the high grades in his course to the establishment of study groups and the use of web-based materials.

5. The _____ *core* _____ of Professor Green's approach to teaching is getting his students to become active and independent learners.

▶ as you read

Establish Your Purpose

Now, read and annotate the selection. Focus on major points of information and important supporting details.

Actively Process While You Read

Highlight the most important points, and annotate within the paragraph and in the margins.

Nonverbal Communication in Everyday Life
By John Stewart

1   Clearly, nonverbal signals are a critical part of all our communication **endeavors** and efforts. Sometimes nonverbal signals are the most important part of our message. Understanding and effectively using nonverbal behavior is crucial in every sector of our society.

2   Consider the role of nonverbal signals in therapeutic situations. Therapists use non-verbal communication to build rapport with clients (Tickle-Degnen & Rosenthal 1994). Their ability to read nonverbal signals associated with client problems surely assists in diagnosis and treatment. A slight change in tone of voice or a glance away from the patient at the wrong time and a physician may communicate a message very different from what was intended (Buller & Street 1992). In situations where verbal communi-cation is often **constrained,** as in a nurse-physician interaction during an operation, effective nonverbal communication is literally the difference between life and death.

3   A list of all the situations where nonverbal communication plays an important role would be **interminable**. Therefore, we limit our discussion in this chapter to three areas that touch all our lives: courtship behavior, televised politics, and crime and punishment.

Courtship Behavior

4   One commentary on nonverbal courtship behavior is found in the following excerpts from the song "Something," written by George Harrison.

> *Something in the way she moves*
> *Attracts me like no other lover*
> *Something in the way she woos me …*
> *Somewhere in the smile she knows*
> *That I don't need no other lover*
> *Something in her style that shows me …*
> *You're asking me will my love grow …*
> *You stick around now it may show.*

As the song suggests, we know there is something highly influential in our nonverbal courtship behavior. We are, however, at an early stage in quantifying these patterns of behavior.

5   Studies involving flirtations between men and women in bars (singles bars, hotel cocktail lounges, bars with restaurants, etc.) provide some observational data on the role of nonverbal signals in the courtship process. Most of the early signaling seemed to be performed by women. In an effort to determine whether these behaviors were more likely to occur in a context where signaling interest in and attraction to others was expected, researchers observed the behavior of women and men in snack bars, meetings, and libraries. None of these contexts revealed anything close to the num-ber of flirting behaviors found in bars.

6   Does the courtship process proceed according to a sequence of steps? Perper (1985) describes courtship's "core sequence" like this: The *approach* involves getting two people in the same proximity; *acknowledging and turning toward the other* is the invitation to begin talking; during *talk,* there will be an increasing amount of fleeting, *nonintimate touching and a gradually increasing intensity in eye gaze;* finally, Perper says the two will exhibit *more and more* **synchrony** *in their movements.* Obviously, either person can short-circuit the sequence at any point.

Televised Politics

7   Politicians have long recognized the important role of nonverbal behavior . . . The tired, overweight, physically unappealing political bosses of yesteryear have been replaced by younger, good-looking, vigorous candidates who can capture the public's vote with an assist from their nonverbal attraction. The average American watches 30 to 40 hours of television each week. Television has certainly helped to structure some of the nonverbal perceptions, and more and more candidates recognize the tremendous influence perceptions may have on the eventual election outcome. Television seems especially suited to nonverbal signals that express positive relationship messages (e.g., facial expressions that communicate sincerity, body positions that suggest immediacy, or vocal tones that are perceived as caring. How have our presidential candidates fared?

8   An analysis of the 1976 Carter-Ford presidential debates argues that Gerald Ford's loss was attributable to less eye **gaze** with the camera, grimmer facial expressions, and less favorable camera angles (Tiemens 1978). Subsequently, Jimmy Carter's loss to Ronald Reagan in the 1980 debate was attributed to Carter's visible tension and his inability to "coordinate his nonverbal behavior with his verbal message." Effective leaders are often seen as people who confidently **take stock** of a situation, perform smoothly, and put those around them at ease. Many saw Reagan's nonverbal behavior in this way. In 1984 Reagan's expressiveness and physical attraction was evident, whereas his opponent, Walter Mondale, was perceived as low in expressiveness and attractiveness. Expressions of fear may be the biggest turnoff for voters. Looking down, hesitating, making rapid, jerky movements, or seeming to freeze as Dan Quayle did when Lloyd Bentsen told him in the vice presidential debate, "You're no Jack Kennedy."

Crime and Punishment

9   The desire to identify criminals has been the subject of study for centuries. Because it is unlikely that a person will tell you that he or she is a criminal or potential criminal, nonverbal indicators become especially important. At one time, some people thought criminals could be identified by their facial features or the patterns of bumps on their heads. In recent years, scientists have used the knowledge of nonverbal behavior to examine criminal acts . . .

10   One study analyzed the appearance and movements of people who walked through one of the highest assault areas in New York City (Grayson & Stein 1981). Then, prisoners who had the knowledge of such matters were asked to view the films of the potential victims and indicate the likelihood of assaults. In addition to finding that older people are the prime target, the researchers also found that potential victims tended

to move differently. They tended to take long or short strides (not medium); and their body parts did not seem to move in synchrony; that is, they seemed less graceful and fluid in their movement. Other studies have tried to examine nonverbal characteristics that rapists use to select their victims. Some rapists look for victims who exhibit passivity, a lack of confidence, and vulnerability; others prefer the exact opposite, wishing to "put an **uppity** woman in her place." The conclusion seems to recommend a public **demeanor** that is confident yet not aggressive (Myers, Templer, & Brown 1984).

11   Another study that assessed potentially aggressive acts focused on mothers who abused their children (Givens 1978). It was noted that even when playing with their children, these mothers communicated their dislike (turning away, not smiling, etc.) by their nonverbal behavior. Just as abusive and nonabusive mothers differ in their behavior, the children of abusive parents and nonabusive parents differ in their nonverbal behavior (Hecht, Foster, Dunn, Williams, Anderson, & Pulbratek 1986) . . .

(Adapted from *Bridges Not Walls, A Book About Interpersonal Communication*, 2009, ed. John Stewart, 174–79)

■ ■ ■

 **after you read**

Think back to the questions you posed after previewing the selection but before you read it. Now that you have read the selection, can you answer your initial questions?

Exercise 3   **Answering Your Preview Questions**

Directions: If you have discovered the answers to the preview questions you created earlier, write them on the lines provided.   *Answers will vary.*

1. _____
   _____

2. _____
   _____

3. _____
   _____

Exercise 4   **Reviewing Important Points**

Directions: Choose the best answer for each of the following questions using information provided in the selection.

_d_ 1. **What is the main idea of this selection?**
   a. It is important to understand the effects of nonverbal behavior.
   b. Nonverbal behavior is used in therapeutic situations, courtship behavior, televised politics, and by criminals to assess potential victims.
   c. Nonverbal behavior is apparent in every sector of society.
   d. It is important to understand and effectively use body language in all social interactions.

_b_ 2. According to the reading, in a therapeutic session, nonverbal communication is important in all of the following situations *except:*

    a. diagnosis and treatment.
    b. life and death.
    c. communication of messages.
    d. rapport building.

_c_ 3. In paragraph 4, the author includes the words to a song written by George Harrison to indicate that:

    a. George Harrison knew something about nonverbal communication.
    b. Nonverbal behavior is used in writing lyrics to songs.
    c. Nonverbal behavior is significant in courtship.
    d. Nonverbal behavior highly influences writers of music.

_a_ 4. In the excerpt from the song written by George Harrison, all of the following words are examples of body language *except:*

    a. love.
    b. smile.
    c. moves.
    d. woos.

_b_ 5. According to the studies about flirtation, researchers found that:

    a. Most flirting behaviors are conducted by women.
    b. Women seem to perform most of the early nonverbal behaviors in courtship.
    c. Women only flirt in singles bars, hotels, cocktail lounges, and bars with restaurants.
    d. Men in snack bars, meetings, and libraries perform most of the early nonverbal behaviors in courtship.

_c_ 6. The pattern of organization in paragraph 6 is:

    a. order of importance.
    b. listing or enumeration.
    c. sequence or process order.
    d. spatial order.

_c_ 7. Televised politics can convey positive relationship messages, such as:

    a. facial expressions which exhibit lack of sincerity.
    b. body positions that show the candidate is willing to take risks.
    c. a tone of voice that is warm and caring.
    d. vocal tones that express tension.

_d_ 8. What is the main idea of paragraph 8?

    a. Presidential candidates have always been careful to use effective nonverbal communication.
    b. Expression of fear is the biggest turnoff for voters.
    c. Voters do not pay attention to body language.
    d. Effective leaders display confident nonverbal behaviors.

_c_ 9. What is the topic of paragraph 9?

    a. crime and punishment
    b. scientific studies of criminal behavior

c. how to identify potential criminals

d. identification of nonverbal behavior

_d_ 10. **According to the second study in paragraph 10, the best way for women to avoid rape is to appear:**

    a. older and less graceful.

    b. different.

    c. confident and vulnerable.

    d. confident yet not aggressive.

_c_ 11. **One study showed that abusive mothers exhibited negativity toward their children:**

    a. by playing with them.

    b. by smiling at them.

    c. by turning away from them.

    d. by acting aggressively toward them.

_c_ 12. **The overall pattern of organization of the reading is:**

    a. comparison and contrast.

    b. cause and effect.

    c. definition.

    d. listing or enumeration.

Exercise 5   **Organizing the Information**

Directions: Complete the following concept map with details from the reading.

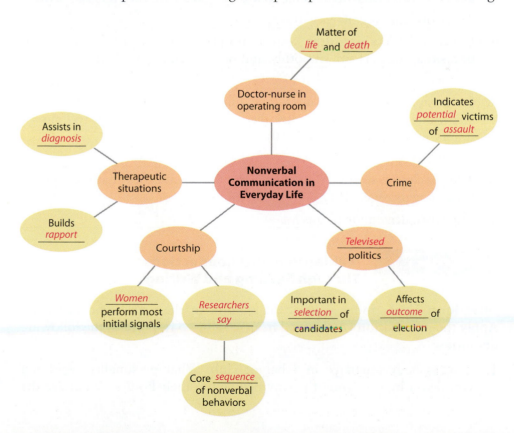

E x e r c i s e   6   **Using Context Clues**

Directions: Use context clues in the following sentences to figure out the meaning of the words in bold print. Underline any clue words that help you define the words or terms. The paragraph in which the sentence appears has been indicated for you in parentheses.

1. Clearly, nonverbal signals are a critical part of all our communication **endeavors** and efforts. (1)

   The word **endeavors** means *efforts*

2. In situations where verbal communication is **constrained,** as in nurse-physician interaction during an operation, effective nonverbal communication is literally the difference between life and death. (2)

   The word **constrained** means *close, confined*

3. A list of all situations where nonverbal communication plays an important role would be **interminable.** Therefore, we limit our discussion in this chapter to three areas that touch all our lives: courtship behavior, televised politics, and crime and punishment. (3)

   The word **interminable** means *endless*

4. Perper says that the two (a man and a woman) will exhibit more and more **synchrony** in their movements. (6)

   The word **synchrony** means *occurrence at the same time, simultaneous*

5. An analysis of the 1976 Carter-Ford presidential debates argues that Gerald Ford's loss was attributable to less eye **gaze** with the camera . . . (8)

   The word **gaze** means *steady, intent, attentive look*

6. Effective leaders are often seen as people who confidently **take stock** of a situation, perform smoothly, and put those around them at ease. (8)

   The words **take stock** mean *appraise, evaluate*

7. Some rapists look for victims who exhibit passivity, a lack of confidence, and vulnerability; others prefer the exact opposite, wishing to "put an **uppity** woman in her place." (10)

   The word **uppity** means *acting as though one is more important than others*

8. The conclusion seems to recommend a public **demeanor** that is confident yet not aggressive. (10)

   The word **demeanor** means *behavior*

E x e r c i s e   7   **Making Personal Connections Through Reading and Writing**

Directions: Think about yourself in relation to the article you just read. Apply the information you learned from reading to respond to the following questions.

Answers will vary.

1. Discuss body language in a bar or club. What personality types can you detect by observing the way people use their bodies? What are the

obvious behaviors of the flirt, the wallflower, the drunk, or the braggart? Consider nonverbal behaviors such as gestures, proximity, and eye contact.

2. Pick an election for political office. Check out your local TV listings for interviews and debates, and observe the body language of each of the candidates. Look at their facial expressions, movements, appearance, posture, eye contact, gestures, and listen to their tone of voice. Then write one paragraph describing their nonverbal communication and a second paragraph in which you draw conclusions about what you learned about the characteristics of these candidates. Have your observations impacted your choice of candidate? If so, for whom would you vote?

3. From this reading, you learned that criminals observe the body language of their potential victims. What will you do differently the next time you find yourself walking down a dark and lonely street at night? Make a list of safety tips.

Synthesizing Your Reading: Reflective Journal Writing

Body Language

Having read three selections on the topic of body language, you now have a broader, more scholarly understanding of the subject matter.

Write a reflective journal entry on the topic of body language demonstrating both your knowledge of the content in the selections and your personal viewpoint on the issue. You should write at least one page.

In the first section, briefly summarize each reading selection. Include the thesis and a few key points for each.

In the second portion, reflect on the topic. Consider what your body language reveals about you. What ideas from the readings do you feel are most valuable personally? What new insights from the readings do you value the most?

Readings About the Job Market

Get Acquainted with the Issue

What will the job market be like by the time I graduate from college?

Whether you are working while attending college or going to school full time, in the future your job will become a larger part of your life. Being familiar with issues and opportunities in the workplace will help you better prepare as you make decisions about building a career.

The first selection that follows, "They're So Vein: Tapping a Job Market," introduces you to a new career in health care that can be pursued by earning certification through classes in adult education. The excerpt from *The Occupational Outlook Handbook* provides predictions for occupational opportunities over the next decade. Finally, in the textbook portion, "The Interviewing Process," you will learn about interview formats and what to expect if you are offered a chance to interview for a position.

The more you know about the job market and aspects of searching for a job, the more likely you will be able to find employment that is meaningful to you and makes you happy. You are likely to find the topic of the job market discussed in business, economics, and communications college textbooks.

Guided Reading
Reading Selection 1

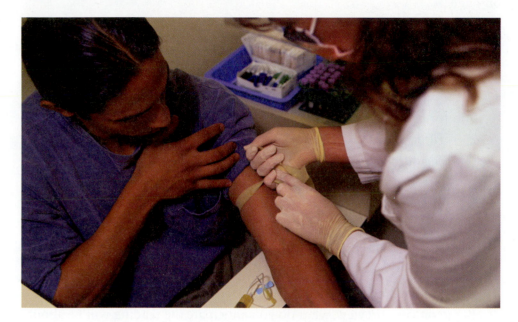

They're So Vein: Tapping a Job Market

By Gabe Opperheim

This feature article was originally published in the Washington Post *and then on the newspaper's website. Read it to learn about a unique opportunity in the health care profession that reflects both a need and a changing trend in the job market.*

⏪ before you read

It's important to think about what you may already know about a topic before you read. In this way, you will attach your new learning to your background knowledge and more easily understand the new information. (See Chapter 2, "Access Prior Knowledge," page 33.)

Answer the following questions related to the occupation discussed in this article:

- Have you or a relative ever had blood drawn for medical reasons? Where was this procedure completed? Who performed it?

- Do you know the credentials of the person who drew the blood? Did they have a medical license? Where and how were they trained?

■ Are you aware of occupations in the health care profession that allow you to perform simple medical procedures, even if you do not have an academic degree in that area?

Prepare to Read

Now, preview the selection, "They're So Vein," using the THIEVES strategy on page 36.

| **Exercise 1** | **Previewing** |

Directions: Complete the following items.

1. Take a look at the selection and check off the items that are available to you for preview.

    _X_ Title

    ___ Headings

    _X_ Introduction

    _X_ Every first sentence in each paragraph

    _X_ Visuals/vocabulary

    ___ End of chapter questions

    _X_ Summary/concluding paragraph

2. Read and highlight as you preview the selection.

3. Based on your preview, what do you anticipate the reading will be about?

    Answers will vary. Sample responses are provided.

    The selection will tell about a new career in phlebotomy. Phlebotomy is the collecting of blood for medical testing. There is an increasing need for people in this field. People from all different walks of life are being trained to perform the job.

Check Out the Vocabulary

The following words appear in bold font in the reading. Are you already familiar with some of them? Knowing the meaning of all these terms will increase your understanding of the material.

| **Exercise 2** | **Checking Out the Vocabulary** |

Directions: Complete the matching exercise below *before*, *during*, or *after* your reading. Be sure to review each word in the context of the selection.

_c_ 1. anticipation
_f_ 2. assessing*
_d_ 3. coagulated
_b_ 4. corporate
_e_ 5. derived
_i_ 6. economy*
_h_ 7. institutions*
_j_ 8. punditry

a. the act of breaking or bursting
b. belonging to a business organization
c. the act of looking forward to in advance
d. changed from a fluid into a thickened mass
e. originated or evolved from
f. evaluating or judging
g. a place from which something comes or is obtained
h. establishments devoted to the promotion of a particular object, often public, such as schools or hospitals

_a_   9. rupture   i. referring to the financial management of the
                             resources of a community or the country as a
                             whole

_g_   10. source*   j. discussion among learned persons, "those in the
                             know"

*from the Academic Word List

as you read

Establish Your Purpose

Now, read and annotate the selection. Focus on the major points of information. Identify the new job opportunity described in the selection, and the kind of training it requires. Notice how the author reveals information by reporting casual conversation among the students.

Actively Process While You Read

Stop and process information as you read.

Exercise 3   **Processing While You Read**

Directions: Answer the following questions at the conclusion as you complete each paragraph. This will help you monitor your reading process and understand the material.

Paragraph 1

1. What do the various ages and professions of people listed in the paragraph imply?

   That people of different ages and occupations are pursuing careers in phlebotomy.

2. What are they all trying to do? What does the phrase "tap a source of life" really *mean?*

   They are trying to puncture veins and take blood.

Paragraphs 2–5

3. What is the predominant tone of the paragraph? What language helps you determine it?

   The tone is relatively light-hearted and casual. Phrases like "Syringe draw!," and "Nice juicy red blood," and "Yum yum" create this mood.

4. Within this light tone, technical information is included. Why is it important to assess the firmness of a vein? What is the process called?

   Firmness is assessed to be sure the vein doesn't rupture. The process is called fishing.

   What kind of syringe is used?

   A 23-gauge needle of a plastic 3-cc syringe.

   What is the formal term for collecting blood?

   phlebotomy

Paragraphs 6–8

5. What is the main idea developed in these paragraphs?
    The main idea is that a class in phlebotomy, collecting blood for medical tests, is being offered in adult education to train "lower skilled" people for a career in a high demand, "growth industry."

Paragraph 9

6. Why is there a need for phlebotomists in the metropolitan area?
    The country is aging and more and more people are getting sick and needing medical tests. Seventy to 80 percent of medical decisions are based on lab tests, and we need professionals to administer them.

Paragraph 10

7. What is the length and cost of the training? What is the approximate salary?
    The course is 92 hours over 12 weeks, and costs about $1,900. The salary is close to $12 per hour.

Paragraphs 12–15

8. What is the mood of the class, as portrayed in the paragraphs?
    Again, it seems casual, and fun. People joke and tease one another.

Paragraph 16

9. What is the caduceus symbol? Why did the instructors have it tattooed under their left ear?
    It is the traditional symbol of medicine. They say it represents their dedication to help people by taking other people's blood.

Paragraph 17

10. What does the expression "The dummies are your peers" really mean?
    It means that, rather than practice on fruit or models, people in this class practice taking blood from one another.

Paragraphs 18–19

11. What is the main idea?
    The main idea is that phlebotomy is likely to become a popular job opportunity for people wanting to learn a profession in a short period of time.

Paragraphs 20–24

12. How do these paragraphs reinforce, or restate, the points made previously in the selection?
    They show how people with various backgrounds, often unskilled, can find a new career in a growth industry quickly through an adult education class.

Paragraphs 25–28

13. How is the potential of this job opportunity reinforced in the final paragraphs?
    A recruiter from Unity Health Care comes into the class to announce they are hiring, and the representative herself had attended Sanz College.

14. The expression "coup de grace" means a decisive or successful move or stroke. The author uses it to describe Cochran's final comment. Why?
    It supports the strength and confidence he feels in asking about a potential job and its starting salary.

They're So Vein: Tapping a Job Market

By Gabe Oppenheim

1   There's the 60-year-old math teacher from India and the 34-year-old medical assistant from Eritrea. A 52-year-old Dodge car salesman who left New Orleans after Katrina, and a 32-year-old bank teller who cared for two parents until both died. A 26-year-old college grad. All trying their best to puncture and penetrate—and, above all, to tap a **source** of life.

2   On this night in the milky white lab, students don blue scrubs for the first time. "Syringe draw!" announces instructor Shelly Chasteen, motioning the students to gather around as she extends her left arm. Another instructor in a backward baseball cap ties Chasteen's biceps with a tourniquet. He eyes a vein and strokes it, **assessing** its firmness. He doesn't want to **rupture** its walls. "What he's doing is called fishing," Chasteen tells the class.

3   And then he pierces her, plunging the 23-gauge needle of a plastic 3-cc syringe deep into her rich supply of cells. "Nice juicy red blooood," Chasteen coos, as her own trickles away. "Yum yum."

4   And 13 adults scurry to their stations, to begin practicing the art of phlebotomy.

5   On one another.

6   We hear a lot these days about classes like this, only we don't realize it. Politicians speak of unemployment and "low-skill work" that America lost, and the increasing number of openings in "growth industries." But rarely do they tender any details. What is a job of the future? How *does* one acquire skills for it? And where?

7   Answers may be writ in blood, on the stained counter of an adult education school. This phlebotomy class is at 17th and I streets NW, at Sanz College, which used to train government officials in foreign languages. Now it caters to those seeking a marketable skill in a rough market, who pass by the "No cash, please" sign in the reception area, past the bulletin board with the glittery blue words "First Step to a Better Future."

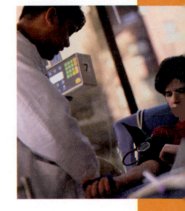

8   Since 1998, Sanz has offered medical courses, and since last December, due to increasing demand from local **institutions**, it has offered phlebotomy, or blood collection for medical tests. The word is **derived** from the Greek terms for "vein" and "cutting."

9   "We identified a market need of phlebotomists in the greater metropolitan area," says Ron Sandler, a **corporate** director at Sanz. "As our population in the country as a whole [gets] grayer and older, there's need for more and more testing as people get ill and need to get diagnosed."

10   Sanz students pay a little more than $1,900 for 92 hours of instruction in 12 weeks, during which they're supposed to complete 42 successful venipunctures. A 2005 survey showed that phlebotomists make an average of $11.74 an hour.

11   You want a peek into today's **economy**—beyond the business pages and TV **punditry**? Don a lab coat and latex gloves and wade into the gooey **coagulated** world of stick and prick. Doctors base 70 to 80 percent of their decisions on lab tests, according to industry experts, and someone needs to administer them.

12   In the class, a trio of instructors weaves between pairs of students, prodding and shouting. "You guys are groovy!" Chasteen says, tousling one older man's white hair. "You're not a virgin no more!" she says to a woman who has just been pricked. Tsigereda Fikak, who moved to Illinois from Eritrea in 1997, sits nearby. She holds her breath in **anticipation**. "Oh, I'm dying," she moans.

13   "Yes," Chasteen says, with a chuckle, "it's gonna hurt."

14   "Oh, Lord."

15   And then, *prick*, it's over—not with a bang but a whimper.

16   Instructors Chasteen, Bennett Fomen and Kesia Dixon call themselves the Caduceus Fans and threw a "tattoo party" in Largo a month ago at which they each got a little black caduceus—the winged staff of the Greek god Hermes wrapped in two snakes, a traditional symbol of medicine—under the left ear. They say it's a sign of their earnest desire to help people take other people's blood.

17   "We don't do no oranges or food up in here," Dixon says of the difference between the Caduceus Fans' classes and lesser programs that promise to teach students everything in a single day, and then have them practice on fruit or dummies. "The dummies," Dixon says of this class, "are your peers."

18   Tanita Moore, 32, isn't even enrolled in tonight's class, but came to get a jump on Saturday's session. "I actually got stuck six times Saturday," says the bank teller and mother of two. "I was loving it." She promised her dying mother earlier this year that she'd enter this field, which she hopes will lead to nursing. "Somebody always dies and someone's always being born and somebody always gets sick," she says. And in today's economy, that line of reasoning may become infectious.

19   "I expect to see a lot more interest among people . . . who are looking for extra income to take the short road to a quality profession," says Dennis Ernst, the director of the Center for Phlebotomy Education in Ramsey, Ind., and publisher of *Phlebotomy Today*. Northern Virginia Community College has already filled its 16 phlebotomy spots for the fall semester.

20   In the front of the lab, Hayden Cochran, 52, faces a dangling skeleton. His partner, attempting a microcapillary collection on Cochran's middle finger, bends over and botches the poke with his metal lancet. Cochran's hand, pocked with holes, begins to spurt blood. "You're talkin' about surgery!" Chasteen cries.

21   Cochran just shrugs. "I've been shot at," he had announced earlier, noting his years in Harlem and the 3rd Ward in New Orleans.

22   Now he tries to soothe his partner, a man squinting through small gold-framed glasses. "You did fine, you did fine," Cochran says, still leaking blood onto a pink cloth. "You did *great*."

23   A former tennis instructor and car salesman, Cochran moved to Washington in February, following his ill mother. He enrolled in the course "because all the skills that I have I don't have certificates for." He's an imposing man—he keeps popping the large latex gloves, prompting the instructors to call him "Big Daddy."

24   "I wanted a skill in an enclosed environment, in a growth field," he says. "The class is relatively short, the course is relatively inexpensive. . . . I'm told as you go up in continuing education courses, you can ask for money."

25   As it turns out, he gets the opportunity just an hour later, when a representative from Unity Health Care enters the class and says her company is hiring.

26   Students rush toward her, scribbling their numbers. But Cochran has a question: "How much do you start with?"

27   "It depends on your experience," says Unity's Tracie Washington, who attended Sanz herself. They go back and forth for a minute more, Cochran pushing for a figure and Washington demurring. Until finally he attempts a coup de grace.

28   "I'm very *confident*," he tells her. "Not cocky, but confident."

■ ■ ■

 **after you read**

Review Important Points

Going over major points immediately after you read, while the information is fresh in your mind, will help you to recall the content and record key ideas.

> **Exercise 4**   **Reviewing Important Points**

Directions: Answer the following questions based on the information provided in the selection. You may need to go back to the text and reread certain portions to be sure your responses are correct and can be supported by information in the text.

1. What is the author's overall message in this selection?
    A career in phlebotomy, or blood collection for medical tests, is a new opportunity in the job market.

2. What is both implied and stated regarding the background of potential students and the training involved?
    It is implied that the career is open to people with minimal medical experience and of a variety of ages and prior occupations. It is stated that certification can be obtained through courses in adult education in about three months.

3. Why is phlebotomy a "job of the future" and part of a "growth industry"? It is part of the health care system.
    More and more people in this country are aging and in need of medical testing to diagnose illnesses. There is a growing need for phlebotomists.

Organize the Information

Organizing the information you have learned from a reading selection shows you have understood it and can restate the material in a different way. You can use the reorganized information to help you study for exams and prepare for written assignments. (See Chapter 9.)

Organizing the Information

Directions: Using the reading selection, create a list of the potential benefits of planning for a career in phlebotomy. Then look over your list. Does the work interest *you?* Why or why not?

Benefits of a Career in Phlebotomy

1. *You can take courses locally through adult education.*

2. *You can be trained in only three months, while still working.*

3. *The training is relatively inexpensive.*

4. *The classes seem like fun.*

5. *You can be in the medical field, no matter your previous background.*

6. *There is good potential for obtaining a job because the demand is high.*

7. *As you go up in continuing education courses, you can ask for more money.*

Integrate the Vocabulary

Make the new vocabulary presented in the reading *your* vocabulary. Using the terms in other contexts will help you make them part of your own spoken and written language.

Exercise 6   **Integrating the Vocabulary**

Directions: Replace the italicized, boldface word or phrase in each of the following sentences with a word, or alternate form of the word, from the vocabulary list at the beginning of the selection on pages 400–401. Paraphrase and rewrite the sentence using the new word.

Example

Bob was in **imminent danger** of failing biology because he had not completed two important assignments.

*Bob was in **peril** of failing biology because he had not finished two assignments that were very important.*

Answers will vary. Sample answers are provided.

1. Carlos **reviewed the benefits and disadvantages** of working at the new pharmacy in order to make his decision to accept the job offer.
   *Carlos **assessed** whether or not to work at the new pharmacy to decide if he should take the job he was offered there.*

2. The mechanic was careful not to put too much air in the bicycle tire's inner tube so that it would not **burst open** as it expanded.
   *The mechanic took care not to pump too much air into the inner tube so that it wouldn't **rupture**.*

3. After graduating from the University of Pennsylvania, Edward decided to give up applying to law school and take a position with a **large company on Wall Street in the business sector.**

   *Ed decided to forgo law school and accept a job in the **corporate** world.*

4. Joann is such a good natured person. I want to know about **her background and early life experiences** to understand how that aspect of her personality developed.

   *Joann is so good natured. I want to learn the **source** of that aspect of her personality development.*

5. We all became concerned about the **financial and business resources of the country** when the stock market began to tumble and large corporations began to close.

   *We were worried about the **economy** when businesses began to fail and stock prices fell.*

6. During the months preceding an election, there is a great deal of discussion among **political analysts and those "experts" in the media** about the candidates.

   *Before an election there is a lot of discussion among political **pundits.***

7. The psychological term "narcissism" **comes from** an ancient myth about a young man who saw his image in a pond and fell in love with it.

   *The word "narcissism" is **derived** from a myth about a young man falling in love with his own image.*

8. Consuelo **looked forward with great excitement** to her mother's arrival in the United States because she had not seen her for two years.

   *Because she had not seen her Mom in two years, Consuelo eagerly **anticipated** her mother's arrival to this country.*

9. After remaining on the floor for days after the party, the soda that had been spilled on the floor **hardened into a thick, gooey mass,** making the clean-up even more difficult than we expected.

   *The soda spilled at the party **coagulated** and was very difficult to clean up.*

10. Our taxes go to running **the schools, hospitals, clinics, libraries, water and sanitation departments,** all of which provide services to the local community.

    *Our taxes are spent on the various **institutions** that provide local community services.*

Make Personal Connections Through Writing and Discussion

When you make your new learning relevant to yourself in some way, it becomes more meaningful and long lasting. Whenever you read, try to connect to the content on a personal level. How does it relate to you? How can you apply what you have read to other situations? What else would you like to know?

Exercise 7   **Making Personal Connections**

Directions: Think about yourself in relation to the article you just read. Apply the information you learned from reading it to respond to the following questions.

Answers will vary.

1. Would you ever consider a career in phlebotomy? Why or why not?

   _____

   _____

   _____

   _____

2. What do you think of obtaining certification to perform a medical procedure through adult continuing education? Should there be any prerequisites to be accepted into such a program?

   _____

   _____

   _____

   _____

3. What other positions in the health care profession might interest you?

   _____

   _____

   _____

   _____

Self-Monitored Reading
Reading Selection 2

Tomorrow's Jobs

This selection is edited and condensed from the U.S. Bureau of Labor Statistics Occupational Outlook Handbook, 2008–09 Edition. *The original appears both online and in hardcopy. The* Handbook, *published annually, is a resource to inform the public about trends in the job market and projections for future job opportunities.*

◀◀ before you read

Think about what you may already know about job opportunities. In this way, you will attach your new learning to your background knowledge and more easily understand the new information. (See Chapter 2, "Access Prior Knowledge," page 33.)

Answer the following questions before you read the selection.

- Think of the way jobs or careers have changed over the years. Can you identify any that existed in the past but do not exist any longer? Are there careers today that didn't exist a century ago? What accounts for the changes?

- For what job or career are you currently planning? Do you have a sense of your how good your prospects are for obtaining such a position?

- What do you think will be the jobs or careers in most demand in the next decade?

Prepare to Read

Preview the article by applying the THIEVES strategy on page 36.

Exercise 1   **Previewing**

Directions: Based on your preview, respond to the following questions:

1. What is the purpose of the *Occupational Outlook Handbook*?
   to make predictions about future job opportunities in different careers and occupations

2. Identify at least three major occupational groups in this country.
   professional, service, management, business and finance, construction and extraction, etc.

3. What two major occupational groups are predicted to have the biggest increase in employment between now and 2016?
   professional and service occupations

4. What is the role of workers in management, business, and financial occupations?
   They plan and direct the activities of business, government, and other organizations.

5. What field is expected to make up almost half of the 20 fastest-growing occupations?
    health care

Check Out the Vocabulary

You will encounter the following words in the reading in bold type. Are you familiar with some of them? Knowledge of these words will help support your comprehension.

Exercise 2   **Checking Out the Vocabulary**

Directions: Complete the following matching exercise *before, during*, or *after* your reading. Be sure to review each word in the context of the selection.

_d_ 1. civilian   a. obtaining something by physical, chemical, or mechanical means

_b_ 2. commercial   b. relating to business or trade

_f_ 3. constitute*   c. pertaining to housing, where people live

_a_ 4. extraction*   d. citizens who are not in the military

_j_ 5. labor*   e. lure, tempt, invite interest

_h_ 6. postsecondary   f. compose, make up

_i_ 7. projections*   g. staying still, not moving or growing

_k_ 8. reliable*   h. after high school, as in training or education

_c_ 9. residential*   i. predictions for the future based on data

_e_ 10. solicit*   j. productive activity for economic gain of people engaged in that activity

_g_ 11. stagnation   k. can be trusted or counted upon

*from the Academic Word List

 as you read

Establish Your Purpose

Now, read and annotate the selection. Focus on the major points of information. Identify the factors that impact employment and the projected changes in the labor force. Identify the major occupational groups, the kinds of jobs offered within each, and the projections for employment in these areas over the next decade.

Actively Process While You Read

Monitor your comprehension as you read. (See Chapter 2, "Monitoring Questions," page 40.) Be sure to stop to reflect at the conclusion of each paragraph, and ask yourself the following questions:

- Did I understand that paragraph?
- What is the main idea?
- Am I ready to continue?

Highlight the most important points. Write your notes in the margins and then move on.

Tomorrow's Jobs

1   Making informed career decisions requires **reliable** information about opportunities in the future. Opportunities result from the relationships between the population, **labor** force, and the demand for goods and services. For example, opportunities for medical assistants and other health care occupations have surged in response to rapid growth in demand for health services.

2   Examining the past and present, and **projecting** changes in these relationships is the foundation of the Occupational Outlook Program. This excerpt presents highlights of Bureau of Labor Statistics' **projections** of the labor force and occupational employment that can help guide your career plans.

Population

3   Population trends affect employment opportunities in a number of ways. Changes in population influence the demand for goods and services. For example, a growing and aging population has increased the demand for health services. Equally important, population changes produce corresponding changes in the size and demographic composition of the labor force.

4   The U.S. **civilian** population is expected to increase by 21.8 million over the 2006–2016 period. Continued growth will mean more consumers of goods and services, spurring demand for workers in a wide range of occupations and industries. The effects of population growth on various occupations will differ.

5   As the baby boomers continue to age, the 55 to 64 age group will grow more than any other group. The 35 to 44 age group will decrease by 5.5 percent, reflecting a slowed birth rate following the baby boom generation, while the youth population, aged 16 to 24, will decline 1.1 percent over the 2006–2016 period.

6   Minorities and immigrants will **constitute** a larger share of the U.S. population in 2016. The number of Asians and people of Hispanic origin are projected to continue to grow much faster than other racial and ethnic groups.

Labor Force

7   Population is the single most important factor in determining the size and composition of the labor force—people either working or looking for work. The civilian labor force is projected to increase by 12.8 million, to 164.2 million over the 2006–2016 period. The number of women will grow at a slightly faster rate than the number of men.

8   The U.S. workforce will become more diverse by 2016. Despite relatively slow growth, white, non-Hispanics will remain the overwhelming majority of the labor force. Hispanics are projected to be the fastest growing ethnic group, growing by 29.9 percent. By 2016, Hispanics will constitute an increased proportion of the labor

force, growing from 13.7 percent to 16.4 percent. Asians are projected to account for an increased share of the labor force by 2016, growing from 4.4 to 5.3 percent. Blacks will also increase their share of the labor force, growing from 11.4 percent to 12.3 percent.

Occupation

9   Expansion of service-providing industries is expected to continue, creating demand for many occupations. However, projected job growth varies among major occupational groups.

10   ***Professional and related occupations***. These occupations include a wide variety of skilled professions. Professional and related occupations will be one of the two fastest growing major occupational groups and will add nearly 5 million new jobs. Professional and related workers perform a wide variety of duties and are employed throughout private industry and government. Almost three-quarters of the job growth will come from computer and mathematics related occupations, health care, and technical, education, training, and library occupations—which together will add 3.5 million jobs.

11   ***Service occupations***. Duties of service workers range from fighting fires to cooking meals. Employment in service occupations is projected to increase by 4.8 million, or 16.7 percent, the second largest numerical gain and tied with professional and related occupations for the fastest rate of growth among the major occupational groups. Food preparation and serving-related occupations are expected to add the most jobs. However, health care support occupations and personal care and service occupations are expected to grow the fastest. Combined, these two occupational groups will account for 2.1 million new jobs.

12   ***Management, business, and financial occupations.*** Workers in management, business, and financial occupations plan and direct the activities of business, government, and other organizations. Their employment is expected to increase by 1.6 million, or 10.4 percent, by 2016. The numbers of social and community service managers and gaming managers will grow the fastest. Construction managers will add the most new jobs—77,000—by 2016. Farmers and ranchers are the only workers whose numbers are expected to see a large decline, losing 90,000 jobs. Among business and financial occupations, accountants and auditors and all other business operation specialists will add the most jobs, 444,000 combined. Financial analysts and personal financial advisors will be the fastest growing occupations in this group.

13   ***Construction and extraction occupations***. Construction and **extraction** workers build new **residential** and **commercial** buildings, and also work in mines, quarries, and oil and gas fields. Employment of these workers is expected to grow 9.5 percent, adding 785,000 new jobs. Construction trades will account for nearly 4 out of 5 of these new jobs. Minor declines in extraction occupations will reflect overall employment **stagnation** in the mining and oil and gas extraction industries.

14   ***Installation, maintenance, and repair occupations***. Workers in installation, maintenance, and repair occupations install new equipment and maintain and repair older

equipment. These occupations will add 550,000 jobs by 2016, growing by 9.3 percent. Automotive service technicians and mechanics and general maintenance and repair workers will account for close to half of all new jobs. The fastest growth rate will be among locksmiths and safe repairers, an occupation that is expected to grow 22.1 percent over the 2006–2016 period.

15   ***Transportation and material moving occupations***. Transportation and material moving workers transport people and materials by land, sea, or air. Employment of these workers should increase by 4.5 percent, accounting for 462,000 new jobs by 2016.

16   ***Sales and related occupations***. Sales and related workers **solicit** businesses and consumers to purchase goods and services. Sales and related occupations are expected to add 1.2 million new jobs by 2016, growing by 7.6 percent. Retail salespersons will contribute the most to this growth.

17   ***Office and administrative support occupations***. Office and administrative support workers perform the day-to-day activities of the office, such as preparing and filing documents, dealing with the public, and distributing information. Employment in these occupations is expected to grow by 7.2 percent, adding 1.7 million new jobs by 2016. Customer service representatives will add the most new jobs, while stock clerks and order fillers will see the largest employment decline.

18   ***Farming, fishing, and forestry occupations***. Farming, fishing, and forestry workers cultivate plants, breed and raise livestock, and rescue animals. These occupations will decline 2.8 percent by 2016. Agricultural workers, including farm workers and laborers, will account for nearly 3 out of 4 lost jobs in this group. The number of fishing and hunting workers is expected to decline by 16.2 percent, while the number of forest, conservation, and logging workers is expected to decline by 1.4 percent.

19   ***Production occupations.*** Production workers are employed mainly in manufacturing, where they assemble goods and operate plants. Production occupations are expected to decline by 4.9 percent, losing 528,000 jobs by 2016. Some jobs will be created in production occupations, mostly in food processing and woodworking. Metal workers and plastic workers; assemblers and fabricators; textile, apparel, and furnishings producers, and other production workers will account for most of the job loss among production occupations.

20   Among all occupations in the economy, those in health care are expected to make up 7 of the 20 fastest growing careers, the largest proportion of any occupational group (Chart A). These 7 health care occupations, in addition to exhibiting high growth rates, will add nearly 750,000 new jobs between 2006 and 2016. Other work groups that have more than one occupation in the 20 fastest growing occupations are computer, personal care and service, community and social services, and business and financial occupations.

21   Declining occupational employment stems from declining industry employment, technological advances, changes in business practices, and other factors. For example, installation of self-checkouts and other forms of automation will increase productivity and are expected to contribute to a loss of 118,000 cashier positions over the 2006–2016 period.

Chart A: Percent Change in Employment in Occupations Projected to Grow Fast (2006–16)

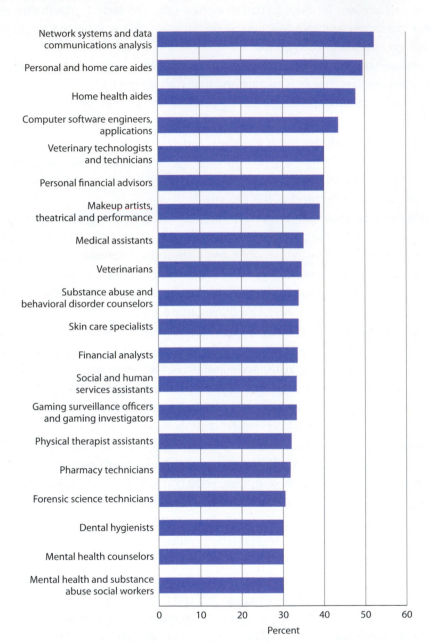

Education and Training

22   For 12 of the 20 fastest growing occupations, an associate degree or higher is the most significant level of **postsecondary** education or training. On-the-job training is the most significant level of postsecondary education or training for another 6 of the 20 fastest growing occupations.

▶ after you read

Review Important Points

Going over major points immediately after you read, while the information is fresh in your mind, will help you to recall the content and record key ideas.

| Exercise 4 | **Reviewing Important Points** |

Directions: Choose the best answer for each of the following questions using information provided in the selection.

_a_ 1. The overall topic of the reading selection is:

    a. job opportunities of the future.
    b. how population trends affect employment.
    c. how to pick the right job.
    d. workforce changes.

_d_ 2. Changes in the population affect employment opportunities by:

    a. influencing the demand for goods and services.
    b. changing the size and background of the workforce.
    c. affecting the demand for workers in various occupations and industries.
    d. all of the above.

_b_ 3. The age group predicted to have the greatest growth in the next decade is:

    a. the youth population.
    b. baby boomers.
    c. the elderly.
    d. the 35- to 44-year-olds.

_c_ 4. Though the workforce will continue to diversify, the largest workforce population in the United States will remain:

    a. Hispanic.
    b. Asian.
    c. white.
    d. African American.

_b_ 5. Paragraphs 10–19 enumerate:

    a. occupations in which people should look for employment.
    b. projected job growth throughout major occupational groups.
    c. the history of job opportunities over the last 10 years.
    d. projections for job growth in the health industry.

_d_ 6. The two fastest-growing occupational groups are within:

    a. management and sales.
    b. construction/extraction and service occupations.
    c. installation and transportation.
    d. professional and service occupations.

_c_   7. **Which occupations within the installation, maintenance, and repair field will grow the fastest?**

    a. automotive technician
    b. air conditioner installer
    c. locksmith and safe repairer
    d. mechanic

_a_   8. **The topic of paragraph 20 is:**

    a. the fastest-growing occupational groups.
    b. computer occupations.
    c. the social service industry.
    d. health care professions.

_d_   9. **The topic sentence of paragraph 20 is:**

    a. the first sentence.
    b. the second sentence.
    c. the third sentence.
    d. the last sentence.

_d_ 10. **In paragraph 21, by identifying factors leading to the decline of certain occupations and providing an example, the author uses the _____ organizational pattern.**

    a. classification
    b. definition
    c. comparison and contrast
    d. cause and effect

_b_ 11. **For the majority of the fastest-growing occupations, the educational degree most often required is:**

    a. a high school diploma.
    b. an associate's degree or better.
    c. a certificate from an accredited adult education program.
    d. on-the-job training.

_a_ 12. **From this selection, you can infer that the best chances of securing employment in the near future would be found in the fields of:**

    a. health care, social assistance, and computer technology.
    b. management, business, and accounting.
    c. farming, fishing, and forestry.
    d. health care and manufacturing.

Organize the Information

Organizing the information shows you have understood it and provides you with a useful study tool. (See Chapter 9.)

| **Exercise 5** | **Organizing the Information** |

A. Directions: Summarize the content found in paragraphs 9–19 by completing the following table. For each major occupational group, identify its general function or purpose. Then list some examples of jobs within that group that are either stated in the text or that you can add based on your own knowledge. Finally, place a check in the positive or negative column under Employment Projections, based on predictions for job growth made in the selection.

Projected Job Growth Among Major Occupational Groups

Occupational Group	Function or Purpose	Jobs	Employment Projections +	Employment Projections −
Professional and related occupations	Skilled professions; variety of duties in private industry and government	Computer and mathe-matical jobs, practitioners, technicians, educators, librarians	✓	
Service occupations	Fighting fires to cooking meals	Food preparation, health care support, personal care/service occupations	✓	
Management, business, financial occupations	Plan and direct activities of business, government, etc.	Social, community, and gaming managers, construction managers (farmers, ranchers), accountants	✓	
Construction and extraction occupations	Build residential and commercial buildings, work in mines, quarries, oil and gas fields	Miners, construction workers, safe repair workers	✓ (Stagnant in extraction)	
Installation, maintenance, and repair occupations	Install new equipment, maintain and repair old equipment	Automotive service technicians, mechanics, locksmiths, safe repair	✓	
Transportation and material moving occupations	Transport people and materials by land, sea, or air	Pilots, train engineers, taxi drivers, ship captains	✓	
Sales and related occupations	Solicit goods and services to businesses and consumers	Retail and door-to-door salespeople, telemarketers	✓	
Office and administrative support occupations	Day-to-day activities of office work; prepare and file documents, distribute information	Customer service representatives, stock clerks	✓	
Farming, fishing, forestry occupations	Cultivate plants, breed and raise livestock, catch animals	Farmers, cattle ranchers, fishing and hunting workers		✓
Production occupations	Manufacturing, assemble goods, operate plants	Factory workers, food processing, wood-working, metal/plastic workers, furnishing		✓

B. Directions: Read through the occupations listed in Chart A on page 414. To better understand the content, reorganize the occupations using the following categories based on the fastest growing occupations: health care, social assistance positions, professional/technical/scientific service jobs, and other. What can you conclude about career opportunities of the future? Are any of these fields interesting to you?

The Fastest Growing Occupations
Classified According to Area

Health Care	Social Assistance Industries	Professional, Scientific, and Technical Service Industries	Other
Personal and home care aides	Substance abuse and behavioral disorder counselors	Network systems and data communications analysts	Makeup artists, theatrical and performance
Home health aides	Social and human service assistants	Computer software engineers, applications	Gaming surveillance officers and investigators
Medical assistants	Mental health counselors	Veterinary technologists and technicians	
Skin care specialists	Mental health and substance abuse workers	Personal financial advisors	
Physical therapist assistants		Veterinarians	
Pharmacy technicians		Financial analysts	
Dental hygienists		Forensic science technicians	

Integrate the Vocabulary

Make the new vocabulary *your* vocabulary.

Exercise 6   **Integrating the Vocabulary**

Directions: On the line provided, write a word, or form of the word, from the vocabulary list at the beginning of the selection that could replace the italicized, boldfaced phrase in the sentence.

1. On the first day of class our professor asked us to identify the qualities that *merge together to make up* a good student.
   constitute

2. The candidate's blog included a section in which she *sought opinions and invited* comments from citizens.
   solicited

3. The workers in the diamond mines labored tirelessly in their effort *to locate and carefully remove* the precious gems from the earth.
   extract

4. Bob's training as an architect focused on creating *private living spaces*, rather than commercial buildings for stores and businesses.
   residential

5. Because the water in the pond had been ***still and unmoving*** for so long, it became murky and filled with sludge and silt.
stagnant

6. Damon had no experience in the stock market, so before making his investments he sought the advice of a broker for ***predictions about the future*** for a variety of companies.
projections

7. As manager of the local fast-food restaurant, Ron was looking for a cashier who would be ***on time, responsible, and able to be counted upon to show up to work when expected.***
reliable

8. The carpenter's ***hard work and effort*** finally paid off when he sold his handcrafted oak cabinet for over $10,000.
labor

9. While apartment hunting, Renee refused to consider any offerings on Cantor Street because he felt the area was overly ***filled with shops, businesses, banks, and clinical*** buildings.
commercial

10. Though he had gained many skills and forged close relationships while in the Marines, Captain Hogan did not regret returning to the life of a ***person not in the armed forces.***
civilian

11. Many opportunities are available as ***educational experiences after high school,*** including vocational school, community college, four-year college, on-the-job training, and the military.
postsecondary

Make Personal Connections Through Writing and Discussion

When you make your new learning relevant to yourself in some way, it becomes more meaningful and long lasting. Whenever you read, try to connect to the content on a personal level. How does it relate to you? How can you apply what you have read to other situations? What else would you like to know?

| **Exercise 7** | **Making Personal Connections** |

Directions: Think about yourself in relation to the article you just read. Apply the information you learned from reading it to respond to the follow-ing questions.

Answers will vary.

1. In which of the major occupational groups do you anticipate pursuing a career or already have a job? What is the job? Is it listed on Chart A? What projections are made for that line of work in the selection? How might these impact your future plans?

2. Paragraph 8 in the selection points to an increasingly diverse workforce. Have you experienced this already? How so? What do you think might

be some of the benefits of having diversity in the workplace? Do you see any problems?

3. Do you know anyone who has recently lost a job because of downsizing? In what major occupational group was the position? Thinking about trends in the economy or business and industry discussed in the selection, what might you identify as the reasons behind the downsizing?

4. What continued postsecondary training are you considering to secure a place in your desired occupational group?

Independent Reading
Textbook Reading Selection: Business

The Interview Process
By Gareth Jones

This selection is an adapted portion of a business textbook chapter titled "Human Resource Management" (Jones 2007). It discusses an important part of the job search process, that of the interview. The interview is often carried out by the Human Resource Management (HRM) system of a company or institution. HRM works to support an organization by recruiting, training, evaluating, and compensating and supporting its employees.

◀ before you read

Answer the following questions before you read the textbook selection, "The Job Interview."

■ Have you ever been interviewed for a job? What was it like? What do you think the interviewer(s) was trying to learn about you?

■ What do you think is the best way to prepare for an interview?

Prepare to Read

Preview the textbook selection using the THIEVES strategy on page 37.

Exercise 1   **Developing Preview Questions**

Directions: Based on your previewing, write *three* questions you anticipate will be answered in the selection.

1. *What is a structured interview?*
2. *What is nondirective interviewing?*
3. *What is quality questioning?*

Check Out the Vocabulary

The following words from this textbook selection appear in academic writing across many disciplines. Be sure you learn their meanings.

Academic Word List

structured	highly organized
scenario	a made up incident or situation
via	by way of
crucial	very important, vital, necessary
scope	the area or range covered
biases	prejudices, preconceived beliefs
team oriented	tendency to collaborate, work in groups
inappropriate	not acceptable or proper for the situation
encounter	run into, meet, come upon

Exercise 2   **Checking Out the Vocabulary**

Directions: Complete each of the following sentences with a word from the preceding Academic Word List.

1. Catherine likes to study in a very _____*structured*_____ manner, while Sharon prefers to vary the way she prepares for class based on her mood on any given day.

2. I'm a very social person, so I was thrilled to have Professor Marin for English. She is well known for teaching _____*team-oriented*_____ classes where students collaborate with one another and always work as part of a small group.

3. It was _____*crucial*_____ that Janet get her paper in on time. If she lost points for lateness, there would be no way in which she could pass the class.

4. After our argument, I wasn't sure how to communicate with Tamara. Should I call her, write her a note, or attempt to connect _____*via*_____ email?

5. Although Roman likes to assert his individuality, I think he was totally _____*inappropriate*_____ when he showed up for his interview with orange spiked hair.

6. As a real estate agent, it is critical that Jerome not reveal any _____*biases*_____ regarding the ethnicity or age of clients to whom he is showing houses.

7. In her training to become a nurse, Michelle was presented with many different potential _____*scenarios*_____ to prepare her for her internship in the Emergency Room.

8. Taking anthropology for the first time, Marina was impressed by the _____*scope*_____ of the class. It covered such a variety of cultures from across the globe.

9. What a glorious vacation! It was wonderful to _____*encounter*_____ such beautiful beaches, fabulous weather, and such friendly hospitality at the hotel.

 **as you read**

Establish Your Purpose

Now, read and annotate the selection. Focus on the major points of information. Identify the various types of interviews described in the selection and the ways in which they can be carried out. Consider what interviewers want to learn through the interview process.

Actively Process While You Read

Monitor your comprehension as you read. Highlight the most important points. Write your notes in the margins and move on.

The Interview Process

By Gareth Jones

1   After the number of applicants for a job has been narrowed down **via** testing, companies generally interview the applicants. Human resource managers, together with the area managers with job openings, look over the remaining pool of applicants and decide which ones to invite for an interview. They may, for example, decide to invite three of the original twenty applicants. Interviewing is expensive because it is very time consuming. HRM's goal is to select the best applicants to interview at the lowest possible cost (least managerial time and effort).

2   Many companies regard interviews as the most **crucial** part of the selection process. The more important the position, the more face to face interviews a candidate is likely to go through. The most common interviewing methods are (1) structured, and (2) nondirective interviewing.

The Structured Interview

3   In **structured** interviews, the job description for the open position is used to create a series of standard questions that all applicants are asked. Because each applicant is asked the same questions, interviewers can make direct comparisons between candidates to choose the best one.

4   To give applicants more **scope** to show their abilities, one technique in structured interviewing is to create a **scenario**: a made up incident about a job-specific event that might occur in the course of that job. Each applicant is then asked how he or she would respond to the event. Applicants for a bank teller's job, for example, might be asked how they would respond to (1) a customer who becomes rude after being informed his or her account is overdrawn, (2) a customer who asks to withdraw all of the funds in his or her account, and (3) a customer who turns out to be a bank robber.

Nondirective Interviewing

5   Structured interviews are most commonly used to select applicants for lower-level jobs. When a company needs to determine if candidates have the skills and qualities necessary to perform complex or demanding jobs, such as those in research or management, nondirective interviews are used. Nondirective interviews do not ask applicants to respond to the same set of predetermined questions. Rather, questions are open ended to give applicants ample opportunity to reveal their skills, abilities, and strengths and weaknesses. In a nondirective interview, the interviewer might ask applicants to describe what they like most about their current job or what problems they seem to **encounter** most on a day-to-day basis. An interviewer might probe into how different applicants prefer to work with other people. For example, does a particular applicant express a preference for a **team-oriented** or a "go-it-alone" work approach? The most appropriate answer depends on the kind of skills needed to do a particular job and the kinds of values and norms a company wants its employees to possess.

6   Some companies involve several people in the interviewing process. Potential co-workers might take applicants out to lunch and use this time to evaluate which person they would most prefer to have on the team. For senior positions, job applicants are interviewed by a series of managers at all levels, so each manager can form an opinion about each applicant. The managers then meet to share their views and debate each candidate's job-related strengths and weaknesses.

Quality Questioning

7   All questions used in the interview should be job related. Companies must be careful that errors or **biases** do not creep into the interview process. Indeed, the interview process needs to be carefully planned so interviewers clearly understand that their questions should focus on the fit between the applicant and the job and company. They also need to know what kinds of questions are **inappropriate** or illegal, like ones about personal characteristics, such as a person's age, religion, or if they are single, married, or have children. Finally, interviewers must be counseled how to prevent their personal biases from affecting their evaluations of job applicants. Questions that are appropriate, inappropriate, or illegal are presented in Table A, which also shows how even general interview questions can be wrongly used.

(Adapted from *Introduction to Business*, Gareth Jones, 2007)

 **after you read**

Think back to the questions you posed after previewing the selection but before your actually read it. Now that you have read the selection, can you answer your initial questions?

Exercise 3   **Answering Your Preview Questions**

Answers will vary.

Directions: If you have discovered the answers to the preview questions you created earlier, write them on the lines provided.

1. _____

   _____

2. _____

   _____

3. _____

   _____

Exercise 4   **Reviewing Important Points**

Directions: Choose the best answer for each of the following questions using information provided in the selection.

_c_ 1. What is the overall topic of the selection?
   - a. bias in job interviewing
   - b. structured interviews
   - c. the job interview
   - d. appropriate interview questions

_a_ 2. The overall purpose of the selection is to:
   - a. inform the reader about the interview process.
   - b. criticize the process of interviewing.
   - c. teach readers how to conduct an interview.
   - d. entertain the reader.

_d_ 3. By identifying the differences between structured and nondirective interviews, the writer is predominantly using the _____ organizational pattern.
   - a. classification
   - b. sequence order
   - c. cause and effect
   - d. comparison and contrast

_a_ 4. The main idea of paragraph 4 is:
   - a. in the first sentence.
   - b. in the fourth sentence.
   - c. in the last sentence.
   - d. unstated.

_c_ 5. An important distinction between structured interviews and nondirective interviews is that:

   a. Structured interviews are reserved for higher-level positions.
   b. In nondirective interviews the questions are the same for all candidates.
   c. In nondirective interviews, questions are open ended and not predetermined.
   d. Structured interview questions are generally more probing.

_d_ 6. In nondirective interviews, the questions put to an applicant are designed to find out whether he or she:

   a. has the skills needed for the job.
   b. shares the values of the company.
   c. works as a team player or alone.
   d. all of the above.

_d_ 7. Which of the following accurately paraphrases the main idea of paragraph 6?

   a. Managers often argue over the best candidate.
   b. Managers form their own opinions about candidates.
   c. One can expect to be taken out to lunch when being interviewed for a high-level position.
   d. Often, several people in an organization are involved in the interview process.

_b_ 8. The topic sentence in paragraph 7 is:

   a. the first sentence.
   b. the second sentence.
   c. the third sentence.
   d. the last sentence.

_d_ 9. Questions about the personal characteristics of applicants, such as their age, ethnicity, marital status, and income are generally considered:

   a. inappropriate.
   b. illegal.
   c. biased.
   d. all of the above.

_b_ 10. The only question from the list below that is likely to be considered appropriate in a job interview is:

   a. How long have you been married?
   b. How long have you been in this line of work?
   c. How long have you been out of high school?
   d. How long have you been a citizen?

_c_ 11. What is the overall main idea of the selection?

   a. Job interviews are difficult.
   b. Asking illegal questions during a job interview is common, though inappropriate.
   c. The style of a job interview varies based on the position, but all interview questions must be appropriate and unbiased.
   d. Scenarios are the best way to find out how people deal with on-the-job situations.

_a_ **12. From this selection, you can infer that:**
  a. Being invited for a job interview is a sign that a company is interested in you more than in some other applicants.
  b. The interview is the first step in the job selection process.
  c. Getting an interview means you have the position.
  d. The higher the position, the less likely it is that you would have to go through many interviews.

| **EXERCISE 6** | **Organizing the Information** |

Directions: Either by using your notes or referring back to the selection, complete the following table to show the differences between structured and nondirective interviews.

The Interview Process

Structured	Nondirective
Standard questions for all candidates	*Questions not predetermined*
Interviewers make direct comparisons between candidates	*Questions open ended*
Interviewers often use scenarios	*Questions designed to reveal skills, abilities, strengths, and weaknesses*
Used for lower- level positions	*Questions designed to determine candidates values and style*
	Used for more complex and demanding jobs

| **EXERCISE 7** | **Using Context Clues** |

Directions: Use context clues in the following sentences to figure out the meaning of the words in bold print. The paragraph in which the sentence appears has been indicated for you in parentheses. A second sentence shows the word used in another context. Underline any clue words that help you define the words or terms. Then write a definition on the line provided.

1. a. Because each applicant is asked the same questions, interviewers can make direct comparisons between **candidates** in order choose the best one. (3)
    b. In order to make their positions clear, the **candidates** for president agreed to hold three debates.

    Candidate means *one who is running for or being considered for a position* .

2. a. Interviewing is very expensive because it is very time **consuming.** (1)
    b. I have **consumed** all the chocolate in this house!

    Consume means *to use, to use up* .

3. a. Nondirective interviews do <u>not</u> ask applicants to respond to the same set of **predetermined** questions. (5)

    b. Nick was reluctant to go out for the softball team, believing that the choices had been **predetermined** <u>before</u> the tryouts.

    Predetermined means *decided upon ahead of time or in advance*   .

4. a. The most appropriate answer <u>depends</u> on the kind of skills needed to do a particular job and the kinds of <u>values</u> and **norms** a company wants its employees to possess. (5)

    b. The **norm** <u>for acceptable behavior</u> in this class includes <u>arriving</u> on time, having the textbook, completing assignments, and participating verbally.

    Norm means *a typical standard or level of performance*   .

Exercise 8	**Making Personal Connections Through Writing and Discussion**

Directions: Think about yourself in relation to the article you just read. Apply the information you learned from reading it to help respond to the following questions.

Answers will vary.

1. Think back to any interviews you may have had in the past. Were they structured or nondirective? How so?

2. How might you prepare differently based upon the type of interview you anticipate will be used by a potential employer?

3. What do you think of the stringent criteria for the kinds of questions that may or may not be asked in an interview? Why do you think these guidelines have been developed? Are interviewers ever biased? Have you ever perceived a bias based on questions you have been asked when applying for a position of any sort?

Synthesizing Your Reading: Reflective Journal Writing

The Job Market

Having read three selections on the topic of the job market, you now have a broader, more scholarly understanding of the subject matter.

Write a reflective journal entry on the topic of the job market demonstrating both your knowledge of the content in the selections and your personal viewpoint on the issue. You should write at least one page.

In the first section of your entry, briefly summarize each article. Include the thesis and a few key points for each.

In the second section, reflect on the topic. Consider any or all of the following: What are your own plans for entering the job market? How do your plans fit in with what you have learned about job opportunities of the future? How can you prepare yourself for the interview process? What are your concerns about entering the job market after finishing your education?

Readings About the Media

Time

Newsweek

Feature Title

Get Acquainted with the Issue

How does the media impact our daily lives?

Media refers to the various methods by which information is communicated and reaches large numbers of people in our society. Media include print materials, such as books, newspapers, magazines, journals, and the broadcast and electronic communication methods, such as radio, television, and, of course, the Internet. Media has had, and continues to have, a large impact on our lives.

In the first reading, "Beauty and Body Image in the Media," a website article discusses the many ways media influences our sense of selves and others on the basis of physical appearance. The second selection, "Adolescents' TV Watching Is Linked to Violent Behavior," is a newspaper article. The last selection, "The Birth of Television," is a textbook excerpt about the early years of television and the impact of television on America during the 1950s and 1960s.

You are likely to find the media discussed in technology, journalism, and communications college textbooks. However, because its impact is so far reaching, the topic of media is likely to appear in other texts that discuss cultural and societal issues, such as sociology, psychology, criminal justice, and history.

Guided Reading
Reading Selection 1

Beauty and Body Image in the Media
Media Awareness Network

The Media Awareness Network, Mnet, is a nonprofit Canadian organization that promotes media literacy. It believes that to be literate in today's world, to "read" messages that we are confronted with daily, we need critical thinking skills. Mnet provides information and tools to help consumers make informed lifestyle choices by promoting awareness of the media's attempts to manipulate or influence consumers. This article, posted on its site, explores the variety of ways the media influences people's sense of beauty, particularly for women.

before you read

It's important to think about what you may already know about a topic before you read. In this way, you will attach your new learning to your background knowledge and more easily understand the new information. (See Chapter 2, "Access Prior Knowledge," page 33.)

Answer the following questions related to appearance.

■ Have you ever considered how your judgments of your own looks or the appearance of others is influenced by what you read in magazines or see on TV and in movies?

- Do you find yourself buying certain products because you think they will make you look better to yourself or others? What products have you been convinced to buy and why?

- What do you think about the emphasis on physical appearance in our society?

Prepare to Read

Now, preview the selection "Beauty and Body Image in the Media" using the THIEVES strategy on page 36.

Exercise 1   Previewing

Complete the following items.

1. Take a look at the selection and check off the items that are available to you for preview.

    X Title

    X Headings

    X Introduction

    X Every first sentence in each paragraph

    X Visuals/vocabulary

    ___ End of chapter questions

    X Summary/concluding paragraph

2. Read and highlight as you preview the selection.

3. Based on your preview, what do you anticipate the reading will be about?

    Answers will vary. Sample responses are provided.

    The article will discuss the standards of beauty that are imposed on women in the media. It will talk about the unhealthy ways college women diet, despite the fact that many of the images they seek are unattainable. It will tell about the ways people are influenced by the media to be believe they have to be thin and the negative impact this has on them.

Check Out the Vocabulary

The following words appear in bold font in the reading. Are you already familiar with some of them? Knowing the meaning of these terms will increase your understanding of the material.

Exercise 2   Checking Vocabulary

Directions: Complete the matching exercise below *before, during,* or *after* your reading. Be sure to review each word in the context of the selection.

a	1. activist	a. a person who acts vigorously to achieve social or political goals
k	2. criterion*	b. to lay upon or thrust upon others
e	3. epidemic	c. to encourage the existence of, advertise

_d_	4. externally*	d.	from the outside or from others
_b_	5. imposed*	e.	the rapid spread of something, affecting many
_h_	6. internalize*	f.	one of a kind, unlike any other
_c_	7. promoted*	g.	to make the same throughout, establish a standard
_g_	8. standardize	h.	to bring inside as one's own thoughts or feelings
_j_	9. stereotype	i.	not able to be reached or achieved
_i_	10. unattainable*	j.	a conventional or typical image accepted by others
_f_	11. unique*	k.	a standard or judgment on which to be evaluated

*from the Academic Word List

as you read

Establish Your Purpose

Now, read and annotate the selection. Focus on the major points of information. Identify the ways the media and advertising has had an impact on the way we define beauty and what we do to attain it.

Actively Process While You Read

Stop and process information as you read.

Exercise 3   **Processing While You Read**

Directions: Answer the following questions at the conclusion of each paragraph. This will help you monitor your reading process and understand the material.

Paragraph 1

1. What is the main idea of the paragraph?
   That there are images of women everywhere that encourage women to lose weight and imply that by doing so they will be happy.

Paragraph 2

2. According to the paragraph, what is the reason for imposing external standards of beauty on women, particularly since most are physically larger and older than the "ideal"?
   The cosmetic and diet product industries want to assure growth of their business and financial profits.

Paragraph 3

3. According to the author, who is likely to be the greatest consumer of beauty products and diet aids?
   Women who are insecure about their bodies.

4. According to the research, what are the results of frequent exposure to images of thin, young, female bodies in the media?

It leads to depression, loss of self-esteem, and unhealthy eating habits in women and girls.

5. What can you infer from the use of the term "air-brushed" to describe the images?

The images are not real but altered to make people appear a certain way.

Paragraph 4

6. What is the main idea of the paragraph?

The main idea is that the pressure to be thin is impacting women of all ages, leading them to be dissatisfied with their bodies and encouraging them to diet and pursue unhealthy methods of weight control.

7. What are the various categories of females cited in the paragraph?

College-aged women, girls 5 and 6 years old, preadolescent girls, girls aged 6–12, women

8. List the unhealthy methods of weight control mentioned in the paragraph?

fasting, skipping meals, excessive exercise, laxative abuse, self-induced vomiting

Paragraph 5

9. Paraphrase the main point made by activist Jean Kilbourne.

Because of the media's heavy emphasis on dieting, prompted by the diet industry, almost all women are made to feel concerned and worried about their weight.

Paragraphs 6–7

10. What is the overall point of these paragraphs? How does the example of Barbie support this point?

The overall point is that most women will never be able to achieve the image that is depicted in the media. Barbie's body is almost a physical impossibility and would lead to chronic illness and death.

Paragraph 8

11. What is compared and contrasted in the paragraph?

The number of weight loss ads and articles written for women compared to those written for men.

Paragraph 9

12. According to the paragraph, how do television and movies reinforce the importance of a thin body as a measure of self-worth?

Most actresses are underweight and only one in twenty are above average in size. Heavier actresses are often put down by male characters because of their weight.

Paragraph 10

13. What is the primary organizational pattern of the paragraph?

listing

What is the topic of the paragraph?

Some of the efforts that have been taken to combat the overemphasis on being thin.

Paragraph 11

14. In contrast, what is the main idea of this paragraph?

Advertisers have a great deal of control, and they believe that thin models sell products.

Efforts to include heavier models were curtailed because advertisers preferred slimmer

models.

Paragraphs 12–13

15. What is the final conclusion of activist Jean Kilbourne? How does the phrase, ". . . real women's bodies have become invisible in the mass media" relate to the quote at the opening of the article, "We don't need Afghan-style burquas to disappear as women. . . ."?

She concludes that, unfortunately, many women internalize the messages put forth by the

media about beauty and judge themselves negatively. They "lose sight" of reality and what

it means to be a real woman, as opposed to the fantasy model of womanhood depicted in

the media.

Beauty and Body Image in the Media
Media Awareness Network

1   Images of female bodies are everywhere. Women—and their body parts—sell everything from food to cars. Popular film and television actresses are becoming younger, taller and thinner. Some have even been known to faint on the set from lack of food. Women's magazines are full of articles urging that if they can just lose those last twenty pounds, they'll have it all—the perfect marriage, loving children, great sex, and a rewarding career.

2   Why are standards of beauty being **imposed** on women, the majority of whom are naturally larger and more mature than any of the models? The roots, some analysts say, are economic. By presenting an ideal difficult to achieve and maintain, the cosmetic and diet product industries are assured of growth and profits. And it's no accident that youth is increasingly **promoted,** along with thinness, as an essential **criterion** of beauty. If not all women need to lose weight, for sure they're all aging, says the Quebec Action Network for Women's Health in 2001. According to the industry, age is a disaster that needs to be dealt with.

3   The stakes are huge. On the one hand, women who are insecure about their bodies are more likely to buy beauty products, new clothes, and diet aids. It is estimated that the diet industry alone is worth anywhere between 40 to 100 billion (U.S.) a year selling temporary weight loss (90 to 95% of dieters regain the lost weight).[1] On the other hand, research indicates that exposure to images of thin, young, air-brushed female bodies is linked to depression, loss of self-esteem and the development of unhealthy eating habits in women and girls.

4   The American research group Anorexia Nervosa & Related Eating Disorders, Inc. says that one out of every four college-aged women uses unhealthy methods of weight

control—including fasting, skipping meals, excessive exercise, laxative abuse, and self-induced vomiting. The pressure to be thin is also affecting young girls: the Canadian Women's Health Network warns that weight control measures are now being taken by girls as young as 5 and 6. American statistics are similar. Several studies, such as one conducted by Marika Tiggemann and Levina Clark in 2006 titled "Appearance Culture in Nine- to 12-Year-Old Girls: Media and Peer Influences on Body Dissatisfaction," indicate that nearly half of all preadolescent girls wish to be thinner, and as a result have engaged in a diet or are aware of the concept of dieting. In 2003, *Teen* magazine reported that 35 per cent of girls 6 to 12 years old have been on at least one diet, and that 50 to 70 per cent of normal weight girls believe they are overweight. Overall research indicates that 90% of women are dissatisfied with their appearance in some way.[2]

5   Media **activist** Jean Kilbourne concludes that, "Women are sold to the diet industry by the magazines we read and the television programs we watch, almost all of which make us feel anxious about our weight."

Unattainable Beauty

6   Perhaps most disturbing is the fact that media images of female beauty are **unattainable** for all but a very small number of women. Researchers generating a computer model of a woman with Barbie-doll proportions, for example, found that her back would be too weak to support the weight of her upper body, and her body would be too narrow to contain more than half a liver and a few centimeters of bowel. A real woman built that way would suffer from chronic diarrhea and eventually die from malnutrition. Jill Barad, president of Mattel (which manufactures Barbie), estimated that 99% of girls aged 3 to 10 years old own at least one Barbie doll.[3]

7   Still, the number of real life women and girls who seek a similarly underweight body is **epidemic**, and they can suffer equally devastating health consequences. In 2006 it was estimated that up to 450,000 Canadian women were affected by an eating disorder.[4]

The Culture of Thinness

8   Researchers report that women's magazines have ten and one-half times more ads and articles promoting weight loss than men's magazines do, and over three-quarters of the covers of women's magazines include at least one message about how to change a woman's bodily appearance—by diet, exercise, or cosmetic surgery.

9   Television and movies reinforce the importance of a thin body as a measure of a woman's worth. Canadian researcher Gregory Fouts reports that over three-quarters of the female characters in TV situation comedies are underweight, and only one in twenty are above average in size. Heavier actresses tend to receive negative comments from male characters about their bodies ("How about wearing a sack?"), and 80 per cent of these negative comments are followed by canned audience laughter.

10   There have been efforts in the magazine industry to buck the trend. For several years the Quebec magazine *Coup de Pouce* has consistently included full-sized women in their fashion pages, and *Châtelaine* has pledged not to touch up photos and not to include models less than 25 years of age. In Madrid, one of the world's biggest fashion capitals, ultra-thin models were banned from the runway in 2006. Furthermore Spain has recently undergone a project with the aim to **standardize** clothing sizes through

using a **unique** process in which a laser beam is used to measure real life women's bodies in order to find the most true to life measurement.[5]

11   However, advertising rules the marketplace and in advertising thin is "in." Twenty years ago, the average model weighed 8 per cent less than the average woman—but today's models weigh 23 per cent less. Advertisers believe that thin models sell products. When the Australian magazine *New Woman* recently included a picture of a heavy-set model on its cover, it received a truckload of letters from grateful readers praising the move. But its advertisers complained and the magazine returned to featuring bone-thin models. *Advertising Age International* concluded that the incident "made clear the influence wielded by advertisers who remain convinced that only thin models spur the sales of beauty products."

Self-Improvement or Self-Destruction?

12   The barrage of messages about thinness, dieting and beauty tells "ordinary" women that they are always in need of adjustment—and that the female body is an object to be perfected.

13   Jean Kilbourne argues that the overwhelming presence of media images of painfully thin women means that real women's bodies have become invisible in the mass media. The real tragedy, Kilbourne concludes, is that many women **internalize** these **stereotypes**, and judge themselves by the beauty industry's standards. Women learn to compare themselves to other women, and to compete with them for male attention. This focus on beauty and desirability "effectively destroys any awareness and action that might help to change that climate."

■ ■ ■

after you read

Review Important Points

Going over major points immediately after you read, while the information is fresh in your mind, will help you to recall the content and record key ideas.

Exercise 4   **Reviewing Important Points**

Directions: Answer the following questions based on the information provided in the selection. You may need to go back to the text and reread certain portions to be sure your responses are correct and can be supported by information in the text.

1. What is the author's overall message or thesis?

    The thesis is that the media sends out messages all the time that women need to be thin, young, and beautiful in order to be valued, by themselves and others.

2. According to the article, what is the most disturbing aspect of media's depiction of beauty?

    It is most disturbing that, no matter how hard a woman tries, she can never really achieve the body type depicted. Much of it is unattainable, based on untruths, air-brushing, and physical impossibilities.

3. List some ways the media has tried to stop sending the message that women need to look a certain way.

They include full-size women in fashion pages. They don't touch up photos. They don't use models under the age of 25. They ban ultra-thin models from fashion shows. They try to find sizes that correspond to the real measurements of women.

Answers will vary.

4. Would you say the article is biased or objective? Support your position.

The article primarily presents one point of view, so in that sense it is biased. It doesn't discuss other reasons why women might have low self-esteem, and blames it all on the media. It also doesn't talk about the benefits of being physically fit rather than obese, including better health, greater energy, and high self-esteem. Many girls and women want to be thinner, but is this all because of the media? Does it always lead to an eating disorder?

Organize the Information

Organizing the information you have learned from a reading selection shows you have understood it and can restate the material in a different way. You may use your reorganization to help you study for exams and prepare for written assignments. (See Chapter 9.)

Exercise 5   **Organizing the Information**

Directions: Refer back to the selection. Generate a comprehensive list of the effects of the media's depiction of beauty on women and girls mentioned throughout the article. Then look over your list. What do you conclude?

Effects of the Media's Depiction of Beauty on Women and Girls

1. *depression*
2. *low self-esteem*
3. *unhealthy eating habits including fasting, skipping meals*
4. *anorexia and other eating disorders*
5. *excessive exercise*
6. *laxative abuse*
7. *self-induced vomiting*
8. *dissatisfaction with one's appearance*
9. *quest for an underweight body*
10. *setting unattainable goals*

Integrate the Vocabulary

Make the new vocabulary presented in the reading *your* vocabulary. Using the terms in other contexts will help them become part of your own spoken and written language.

Exercise 6   **Integrating the Vocabulary**

Directions: Replace the italicized, boldfaced phrase in each of the following sentences with a word, or alternate form of the word, from the vocabulary list at the beginning of the selection on pages 430–431. Write the word in the parentheses. Next, write a sentence of your own on the line provided, in which you use the word in some aspect of your own life.

Answers will vary.

1. Many believe that the Civil Rights Movement in the 1960s began achieving its goals due to the efforts of *those who fervently believed in the cause of political, economic, and social justice* designed to attain equal rights for all people. (_____*activists*_____)

   _____

2. Although Shakira was deeply opposed to the war, she didn't want to *force or push* her viewpoint on the rest of the people in the political action club. (_____*impose*_____)

   _____

3. At the start of the semester, Professor Rice clearly identified all the *standards and requirements* for earning an A in her class. (_____*criteria*_____)

   _____

4. The entrance exams for all the state's colleges were *redesigned at the same level of difficulty and with the same format* so that reliable statistics on college admissions across the state could be gathered. (_____*standardized*_____)

   _____

5. Once the ticket prices were posted for the new stadium, Greg had to admit that his dream of box-seat season tickets was *impossible, and far beyond his reach*. (_____*unattainable*_____)

   _____

6. Fast foods are often blamed for the wave of obesity that is *ever increasing and widespread* across the country. (_____*epidemic*_____)

   _____

7. Professor Chen's class always fills early. Students just love her *unusual, one-of-a-kind* style of teaching. (_____*unique*_____)

   _____

8. Ronnie made such a conscious effort to better manage her time that by the end of the semester she didn't even have to remind herself to use a planner and complete assignments in advance of due dates. These strategies had become *part of her, without a need for reminders and direction from the outside*. (_____*internalized*_____)

   _____

9. The importance of regular exercise and maintaining a healthy diet is *regularly supported and talked about* by the American Medical Association. (_____*promoted*_____)

   _____

10. Ross resented being *thought of in a certain way on the basis of his outward appearance*. Just because he wore thick glasses, had pens protruding from his shirt pocket, and often read while eating lunch, he certainly was not a "geek." He went out dancing three times a week, and partied with his friends every Saturday night! (_____*stereotyped*_____)

    _____

11. Though Janice was a uniquely beautiful woman, her greatest hope was that people would not judge her by her *visible, outside* appearance, but by her intelligence, kindness, and wonderful sense of humor. (____*external*____)

Make Personal Connections Through Writing and Discussion

When you make your new learning relevant to yourself in some way, it becomes more meaningful and long lasting. Whenever you read, try to connect to the content on a personal level. How does it relate to you? How can you apply what you have read to other situations? What else would you like to know?

Exercise 7	**Making Personal Connections**

Directions: Think about yourself in relation to the article you just read. Apply the information you learned from reading it to respond to the following questions.

Answers will vary.

1. Have you been influenced by the media regarding your own physical appearance? How so?

2. Do you agree with the author's point of view that media has had a negative influence on the public's perception of beauty? Why or why not?

3. What regulations, if any, would you impose on the media to curtail the stereotyping of beauty?

Self-Monitored Reading
Reading Selection 2

Adolescents' TV Watching Is Linked to Violent Behavior

By Rosie Mestel

This newspaper article appeared as a feature selection in the Health Section of the Los Angeles Times. It reports on a long-term study of young people that was designed to find out how watching television might relate to future acts of aggression.

⏪ before you read

Think about what you may know, or can predict, about views on television watching and violence. In this way, you will attach your new learning to your background knowledge and more easily understand the new information. (See Chapter 2, "Access Prior Knowledge," page 33.)

Answer the following questions before you read the selection:

- Do you think that watching violence on television leads to hostile or aggressive behavior?

- Would you predict that there is a connection between watching television and violent behavior, regardless of the kinds of shows that are viewed?

- Do you think that the amount of time children watch television should be limited? Why or why not?

Prepare to Read

Preview the article by applying the THIEVES strategy on page 36.

Exercise 1	**Previewing**

Direction: Based on your preview, respond to the following questions:

1. What was the overall finding of the study?
   The study found that there is a link, or relationship, between watching TV as an adolescent and violent behavior later on in life.

2. How were families chosen to participate in the study?
   They were chosen randomly from families in the state of New York.

3. What is at least one criticism of the study?
   The study didn't describe the kinds of TV shows that were being watched.

4. What are some medical groups that believe that violence on TV is a problem?
   the American Academy of Pediatrics, the American Academy of Child and Adolescent Psychiatry, and the American Medical Association

5. What does the study say to parents?
   Free access to television is not good for children.

Check Out the Vocabulary

The following words appear in bold font in the reading. Are you familiar with some of them? Knowing the meaning of all these terms will increase your comprehension of the material.

Exercise 2   **Checking Out the Vocabulary**

Directions: Complete the following matching exercise *before, during,* or *after* your reading. Be sure to review each word in the context of the selection.

_e_ 1. correlation
_h_ 2. counter
_d_ 3. credibility
_j_ 4. emeritus
_g_ 5. hailed
_c_ 6. implication
_a_ 7. randomly*
_b_ 8. significant*
_k_ 9. study
_f_ 10. subsequent*
_i_ 11. unfettered

a. without a plan, order, or predetermined selection
b. of important or meaningful consequence or result
c. something implied or suggested based on data or results
d. capacity to be trusted or believed in
e. causal, parallel, or reciprocal relationship
f. occurring or coming later or after
g. praised publicly
h. to present the opposite point
i. not restrained in any manner
j. retired from activity, but retaining title or rank
k. a detailed examination and analysis of a subject or question, following certain standards and procedures

*from the Academic Word List

as you read

Establish Your Purpose

Now, read and annotate the selection. Focus on the major points of information. Identify the purpose of the study and the most important findings. Also note some criticisms or points that raise questions about the results.

Actively Process While You Read

Monitor your comprehension as you read. (See Chapter 2, "Monitoring Questions," page 40.) Be sure to stop to reflect at the conclusion of each paragraph, and ask yourself the following questions:

- Did I understand that paragraph?
- What is the main idea?
- Am I ready to continue?

Highlight the most important points. Write your notes in the margins and then move on.

Adolescents' TV Watching Is Linked to Violent Behavior

By Rosie Mestel

1   Adolescents who watch more than one hour of television a day are more likely to commit aggressive and violent acts as adults, according to a 17-year **study** reported today in the journal *Science*. The study, which tracked more than 700 adolescents into adulthood, found that young people watching one to three hours of television daily were almost four times more likely to commit violent and aggressive acts later in life than those who watched less than an hour of TV a day. Girls as well as boys exhibited increased aggression, according to the study, which was **hailed** by psychologists and social scientists as more evidence of TV's harmful effects.

2   "It's a very important study and has a great deal of **credibility**—it very niftily isolates television as a causal factor," said George Comstock, a researcher on media violence at Syracuse University in New York. It is also the first study, Comstock said, to clearly link TV viewing among adolescents to later, adult violence.

Gathering the Data

3   The study authors, from Columbia University and Mount Sinai Medical Center in New York, used data from a wide-ranging survey of the behavior of children in 707 New York state families. The families had been selected **randomly**—not because their children had any behavior problems. Over the study's 17 years, the children and their parents were periodically interviewed about TV habits, violence and aggression. Interviews began in 1983, when the children's average age was 14; follow-up interviews were conducted at average ages of 16, 22 and 30.

4   The scientists also examined state and FBI records in 2000 to find out if any of those in the study—who by then had reached an average age of 30—had been arrested or charged with a crime.

The Findings

5   The authors found that 5.7% of those who reported watching less than one hour of TV a day as adolescents committed aggressive acts against others in **subsequent** years—either by their own admission, a parent's report or legal records. Those acts included threats, assaults, fights, robbery and using a weapon to commit a crime. That figure rose to 22.5% of those who watched TV for one to three hours a day and to 28.8% of those who watched more than three hours daily.

6   The size of the effect was surprising, said lead author Jeffrey Johnson, assistant clinical professor of psychology in Columbia University's psychiatry department. He and his coauthors, who conducted the study with federal funds, believe the findings help cement the link between TV and violence. The authors used statistics to rule out other possible causes, such as neglect, poverty and living in a violent neighborhood.

7   The study did not describe the kinds of programs children were watching, drawing criticism from Jonathan Freedman, a professor of psychology at the University of Toronto. He also said such studies don't clearly demonstrate that viewing programs is the cause of **subsequent** violence. "To suggest that because you get this effect that watching two hours a day causes aggressiveness is going so far beyond the data it's shocking," Freedman said.

Historical Concerns

8   Six major medical groups—including the American Academy of Pediatrics, the American Academy of Child and Adolescent Psychiatry and the American Medical Association—have stated that they believe TV violence is a significant problem. Fears about the negative influence of TV have been voiced almost since 1946, when TV broadcasting began in the United States.

9   The study published today is the latest in a string of investigations aimed at figuring out the link. One study in the early 1960s shocked the public by showing that children shown a TV program of adults beating a toy clown were more likely to repeat the behavior. Other studies similarly showed a rise in aggressive attitudes and behaviors after people watched violent programs. Subjects were more likely to fight in the playground or "punish" people with fake zaps of electricity. Other studies have explored the relationship between violent programming and real-life, serious violence—and have also found smaller, although **statistically significant,** links.

11   The effects of such viewing pale, by comparison, with the effect of living in an abusive home or hanging out with delinquent peers. But TV watching is far more prevalent, said Joanne Cantor, professor **emeritus** of the University of Wisconsin in Madison and a longtime media violence researcher.

12   The Motion Picture Association of America declined to comment on the report until staff members had a chance to read it. Association spokesman Rich Taylor said parents have the technology to easily control what their children watch. "The V-chip puts a new level of control into a parent's hands, allowing them to determine and set the level of programming that they wish to allow in their home at any given time," he said.

Implications

13   "The **implications** for parents is that **unfettered** access to television is not good for your child," Cantor said. "It has these negative effects—which affect them personally in terms of feeling more hostile. And it looks like it affects other people too—through expression of that hostility in aggressive behavior towards others."

14   Responding to the study, National Assn. of Broadcasters spokesman Dennis Wharton said, "For every study of this sort that finds a **correlation** between TV violence and real life violence, there are studies that conclude just the opposite."

15   Freedman, meanwhile, said that finding a correlation between TV viewing and violence does not prove TV programs are to blame. Children who are naturally more aggressive may be drawn to watch more violent TV, he said. While this may be true, Johnson **countered,** this study and others show that even-tempered children also became more aggressive after watching a lot of television.

■ ■ ■

 **after you read**

Review Important Points

Going over major points immediately after you have read, while the information is fresh in your mind, will help you to recall the content and record key ideas.

| Exercise 3 | **Reviewing Important Points** |

Directions: Choose the best answer for each of the following questions using information provided in the selection.

_c_ 1. The article reports on:

    a. an experiment on television watching.
    b. the difference between the TV habits of girls and boys.
    c. a study to learn the impact of TV watching on adolescents.
    d. why TV watching leads to aggressive behavior.

_b_ 2. The 700 subjects in the study were looked at:

    a. from birth through adolescence.
    b. from adolescence into adulthood.
    c. during the teenage years.
    d. from youth to old age.

_b_ 3. The overall findings of the study indicate that:

    a. Adolescents who watch from 1–3 hours of TV daily are 10 times more likely to commit violent crime than those who watch less than 1 hour.
    b. Young people who watch television for 1–3 hours a day are about four times more likely to commit aggressive acts later in life than those who watch less.
    c. The more television children watch, the more likely they are to commit murder.
    d. Boys exhibit far more aggression than girls.

_d_ 4. To gather data for their study, the authors:

    a. interviewed parents.
    b. interviewed the children.
    c. examined state and FBI arrest records.
    d. all of the above.

_a_ 5. The adolescent subjects in the study were selected:

    a. randomly within New York state.
    b. on the basis of their criminal records.
    c. because they volunteered to be part of the research.
    d. in order to receive federal funds.

  a   6. **The findings in paragraph 5 support the main idea expressed in:**
- a. paragraph 1.
- b. paragraph 3.
- c. paragraph 4.
- d. paragraph 12.

  b   7. **From the last sentence in paragraph 6, the reader can infer that:**
- a. Television watching is the primary cause of violence today.
- b. Violent behavior has a variety of causes.
- c. Neglect, poverty, and living in a violent neighborhood always lead to violence.
- d. Statistics may be used to get rid of violence.

  c   8. **The main idea of paragraphs 8 and 9 is that:**
- a. Television has been the victim of critics about its violent nature.
- b. Serious violence can usually be traced back to watching television.
- c. Since television broadcasting began, there have been concerns about and investigations into the link between violence on TV and aggressive behavior in viewers.
- d. We will never understand the relationship between TV watching and aggressive behavior.

  a   9. **An accurate paraphrase of paragraph 11 is:**
- a. The impact of growing up as an abused child or with aggressive and violent friends is far greater than watching a lot of TV, but television viewing occurs much more often.
- b. TV watching is much worse than the effects of living in an abusive home or having delinquent friends.
- c. Unfortunately, abuse at home and having friends involved in crime occurs much more often than watching a great deal of television.
- d. Being abused and having delinquent friends is far more prevalent than watching television.

  c 10. **Criticisms of the study mentioned in the text include all of the following *except:***
- a. The study didn't describe the kinds of programs children were watching.
- b. The study didn't clearly demonstrate that watching TV for several hours actually caused the aggressive behaviors and that more aggressive children may be naturally drawn to watch TV that is often violent.
- c. The researchers who ran the study were not truly qualified to conduct such an investigation.
- d. As many studies as there are like this one, there are studies that conclude just the opposite.

  c 11. **A reasonable inference regarding the Motion Picture Association's spokesperson Rich Taylor's comment in paragraph 12 about parents using the V-chip to control their children's TV watching is that:**
- a. He believes parents have been too lenient in raising their children.
- b. He wants technology to do the job of parenting.

c. He would prefer parents to monitor their children's viewing rather than put limits on television broadcasting.

d. He would like people to purchase technology to support the Motion Picture Association.

_d_ 12. **The overall organizational pattern used in reporting the findings of the research mentioned in this selection is:**

a. classification.

b. comparison and contrast.

c. listing or enumeration.

d. cause and effect.

Organize the Information

Organizing information shows that you have understood it and provides you with a useful study tool. (See Chapter 9.)

| **Exercise 4** | **Organizing the Information** |

Directions: Use the information you find throughout the article to complete the outline that follows.

Study Links Adolescents' TV Watching to Violent Behavior

I. Gathering the Data

  A. Researchers are from _Columbia University_ and _Mount Sinai Medical Center_

  B. Subjects in the study were

    1. selected _randomly_, not because children had behavioral problems

    2. from _707_ families located in _New York state_

  C. Research was conducted over _17 years_

    1. funded by the _federal government_

  D. Interviews of _children and parents_ focused on

    1. _TV habits_ and _violence and aggression_

    2. Began in _1983_, when children's average age was _14_

    3. Follow-ups at ages _16, 22, and 30_

  E. FBI records checked to discover _any arrests or criminal charges_

II. _Findings_

  A. 5.7 % who watched less than one hour of TV daily as adolescents committed aggressive acts in subsequent years.

    1. threats

    2. _assaults_

3. *fights*

4. *robbery*

5. *using a weapon to commit a crime*

B. *22.5%* of those watching for 1–3 hours daily committed aggressive acts

C. 28.8% *of those who watched more than three hours daily committed aggressive acts*

D. According to the authors, the results link *TV and violence*

E. Statistics were used to rule out other possible causes of violent behavior

1. *neglect*

2. *poverty*

3. *living in a violent neighborhood*

III. Criticisms of the Study

A. Does not *describe the kinds of programs children are watching*

B. *Such studies don't clearly demonstrate that viewing programs is the cause of the subsequent violence*

1. Children who are naturally more aggressive may be drawn to watch more violent TV.

C. For every study that finds a correlation between TV violence and real life violence, *other studies conclude just the opposite*

Integrate the Vocabulary

Make the new vocabulary *your* vocabulary.

Exercise 5   **Integrating the Vocabulary**

Directions: On the line provided, write a word, or form of the word, from the vocabulary list at the beginning of the selection that could replace the italicized, boldfaced phrase in the sentence.

1. Rather than specifically choosing members for the team, Ralph, *casually, without prior thought or consideration,* designated the players from among the many hopefuls who had gathered at the athletic field.
   randomly

2. Dr. Jenson, the college president *who had retired several years ago but still kept his title,* was honored to be the keynote speaker at our graduation.
   emeritus

3. Rocco thoroughly enjoyed the feeling he got from skydiving; jumping out of the plane so *completely free and unrestrained* made him feel like he was flying through the sky.
   unfettered

4. Lying on the couch in her psychologist's office, Pam recounted her childhood, trying to recall the most *important and meaningful* events in her life to share with her therapist.
   significant

5. After sharing one story after the next as to why he was habitually late for class, Jason lost the *ability to sound truthful and honest* when speaking to his professor.
   credibility

6. After listening to her mother's reasons for why she should stay in and study, Melanie *presented all her opposing viewpoints* loudly and somewhat harshly, in an attempt to go to a party the night before the English exam.
   countered

7. Professor Mason did her best to convince the students in Sociology 101 of the *strong relationship* between practicing good study skills and success in college classes.
   correlation

8. Because I had such a glorious time on my trip to Puerto Rico, I knew that all of my *future* vacations would be somewhere in the Caribbean.
   subsequent

9. Caryn conducted a *detailed review and analysis* of the eating habits of 9- and 10-year-old children living in urban settings in order to fulfill her requirements for a Master's Degree in Diet and Nutrition.
   study

10. We *celebrated and publicly cheered* our football team for getting through the season undefeated.
    hailed

11. Kwanisha and Megan wondered about the *possible meanings* of their landlord's scowling face and shaking head as he moved down the corridor in the direction of their apartment.
    implications

Make Personal Connections Through Writing and Discussion

When you make your new learning relevant to yourself in some way, it becomes more meaningful and long lasting. Whenever you read, try to connect to the content on a personal level. How does it relate to you? How can you apply what you have read to other situations? What else would you like to know?

| **Exercise 6** | **Making Personal Connections** |

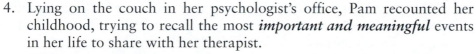

Directions: Think about yourself in relation to the article you just read. Apply the information you learned from reading it to respond to the following questions.

Answers will vary.

1. The study relates watching more than three hours of TV of any kind to violence and aggression. What is your opinion? What do you think of some of the criticisms of the study cited in the article?

2. Have you had any experiences of your own in which you sense a connection with watching something violent on TV and then feeling angry or particularly aggressive? Tell about this.

3. Think of a study you might like to construct to measure the impact of television in some way. What would it be like? What would you like to discover?

4. What are some other implications of the results of this study on other aspects of society? Does it say something about the entertainment industry? Videogames? The criminal justice system? What do you think?

Independent Reading
Textbook Reading Selection: American History

The Birth of Television
By Alan Brinkley

This selection is adapted from an American History textbook chapter called "The Affluent Society" (Brinkley 2007). The chapter talks about the social and economic changes in the United States during the 1950s and early 1960s. This excerpt focuses on the origins and growth of television during that time, its power as a medium, and its impact on American culture.

 ◀◀ **before you read**

Answer the following questions before you read the textbook selection "The Birth of Television."

■ What do you know about society in the United States after World War II? How were things different in the culture then than they are today?

■ Do you know about any television shows from those years? What were they like? Have you seen any in reruns? How do they compare to the TV shows of today?

Prepare to Read

Preview the textbook selection using the THIEVES strategy on page 36.

| Exercise 1 | **Developing Preview Questions** |

Directions: Based on your previewing, write three questions you anticipate will be answered in the selection.

Answers may vary.

1. *Why was the growth of television so phenomenally rapid?*
2. *What were the roots of television?*
3. *How did television present an idealized version of life?*

Check Out the Vocabulary

The following words from the selection appear in academic and scholarly writing across many disciplines. Be sure you learn their meanings.

Academic Word List

emerge	to come forth, develop or evolve
medium	the means of communication
unprecedented	never having occurred before

Other Words Often Found in Scholarly Texts

accentuate	to stress or emphasize
benign	favorable, kindly, not harmful or hurtful
diversion	a distraction, drawing away attention
encounter	run into, meet, come upon
epitomize	to be the ideal version of something
homogeneous	of only one kind, way, or type
inadvertently	unintentionally, without preplanning or intention
pervasive	spreading or found throughout
profound	penetrating deeply, thorough
urban	of or relating to the city

| Exercise 2 | **Checking Out the Vocabulary** |

Directions: Complete each of the following sentences with a word or form of a word from the academic or scholarly word lists.

1. Pamela felt awful when she _____*inadvertently*_____ moved her foot into the aisle and tripped the flight attendant who was carrying a tray of hot coffee.

2. Professor Miller always told his students he couldn't ever _____*accentuate*_____ enough the importance of managing and organizing time effectively.

3. After studying for four hours, Tamika welcomed the _____*diversion*_____ of a phone call from her best friend.

4. The use of cell phones has become so _____*pervasive*_____ that there is a sign up at the library reminding students to turn them off or put them into vibrate mode when entering the reading room.

5. After spending her entire life in the country, Caroline longed for the lights, crowds, and overall stimulation she anticipated in an _____*urban*_____ setting.

6. Although some might consider Jonathan's jokes and insults hurtful and degrading, I know they are just part of his odd sense of humor and are really quite _____*benign*_____.

7. The crowds that appeared at President Obama's campaign speeches were truly _____*unprecedented*_____. No candidate has ever drawn as many people before.

8. While some educators have supported _____*homogeneous*_____ grouping in classes, most agree that having students with varying levels of ability and learning styles is the better way to structure a classroom.

9. The Russian Tea Room _____*epitomized*_____ the romantic restaurant. It had dark velvet seating, private booths, dim lights, candles at every table, and soft music playing in the background.

10. Jacob's visit to New Orleans after the hurricane had a _____*profound*_____ effect on him. After viewing the destruction and numbers of displaced people, he immediately volunteered to spend three months rebuilding homes with Habitat for Humanity.

11. Though it was slow going during the first half of the game, our football team scored three touchdowns in the final quarter and _____*emerged*_____ victorious.

12. Among people in their teens and twenties, the Internet is apparently the most important _____*medium*_____ through which they learn most about the news.

▶ as you read

Establish Your Purpose

Now, read and annotate the selection. Focus on the major points of information. Learn about the early days of television. Understand how the need to attract advertisers impacted programming. Identify the various ways TV stereotyped the culture. Finally, consider how it inadvertently contributed what would become major upheavals in our society.

Actively Process While You Read

Monitor your comprehension as you read. Highlight the most important points. Write your notes in the margins and move on.

The Birth of Television
By Alan Brinkley

1   Television, perhaps the most powerful **medium** of mass communication in history, was central to the culture of the postwar era. Experiments in broadcasting pictures (along with sound) had begun as early as the 1920s, but commercial television began only shortly after World War II. Its growth was phenomenally rapid. In 1946, there were only 17,000 sets in the country; by 1957, there were 40 million sets in use—almost as many sets as there were families. More people had television sets, according to one report, than had refrigerators (a statistic strikingly similar to one in the 1920s that had revealed more people owned radios than bathtubs).

Television's Roots

2   The television industry **emerged** directly out of the radio industry, and all three of the major networks—the National Broadcasting Company, the Columbia Broadcasting Company, and the American Broadcasting Company—had started as radio companies. Like radio, the television business was driven by advertising. The need to attract advertisers determined most programming decisions; and in the early days of television, sponsors often played a direct, powerful, and continuing role in determining the content of the programs they chose to sponsor. Many early television shows bore the names of the corporations that were paying for them: the GE Television Theater, the Chrysler Playhouse, the Camel News Caravan, and others. Some daytime serials were actually written and produced by Procter & Gamble and other companies.

Social Consequences of Television

3   The impact of television on American life was rapid, **pervasive**, and **profound.** By the late 1950s, television news had replaced newspapers, magazines, and radios as the nation's most important vehicle for information. Television advertising helped create a vast market for new fashions and products. Televised athletic events gradually made professional and college sports one of the most important sources of entertainment (and one of the biggest businesses) in America. Television entertainment programming—almost all of it controlled by the national networks and their corporate sponsors—replaced movies and radio as the principle source of **diversion** for American families.

TV's Idealized Portrayal of Life

4   Much of the programming of the 1950s and early 1960s created a common image of American life—an image that was predominantly white, middle-class, and suburban.

This was **epitomized** by such popular situation comedies as *Ozzie and Harriet* and *Leave It to Beaver.* Programming also reinforced the concept of gender roles that most men (and many women) unthinkingly embraced. Most situation comedies, in particular, showed families in which, as the title of one of the most popular put it, *Father Knows Best,* and in which most women were mothers and housewives striving to serve their children and please their husbands.

5   But television also conveyed other images: the gritty, **urban** working-class families in Jackie Gleason's *The Honeymooners;* the childless show-business family of the early *I Love Lucy;* the unmarried professional women in *Our Miss Brooks* and *My Little Margie,* the hapless African Americans in *Amos 'n Andy.* Television not only sought to create an idealized image of a **homogeneous** suburban America—it also sought to convey experiences at odds with that image—but to convey them in warm, unthreatening terms, taking social diversity and cultural conflict and turning them into something **benign** and even comic.

The Seeds of Change

6   Yet television also **inadvertently** created conditions that could **accentuate** social conflict. Even those unable to share in the affluence of the era could, through television, acquire a vivid picture of how the rest of their society lived. Thus at the same time that television was reinforcing the homogeneity of the white middle class, it was also contributing to the sense of alienation and powerlessness among groups excluded from the world it portrayed. And television news conveyed with **unprecedented** power the social upheavals that gradually spread beginning in the late 1950s, and in conveying them helped make more such upheavals likely.

(Adapted from Brinkley, pp. 802–3.)

▶▶ after you read

Go back to the questions you posed after previewing the selection but before you read it. Now that you have read the selection, can you answer your initial questions?

Exercise 3   **Answering Your Preview Questions**

Directions: If you have discovered the answers to the preview questions you created earlier, write them on the lines provided.

Answers will vary.

1. _____
   _____

2. _____
   _____

3. _____
   _____

| Exercise 4 | **Reviewing Important Points** |

Directions: Choose the best answer for each of the following questions using information provided in the selection.

_c_ 1. **What is the overall topic of the selection?**
    a. the impact of advertising on television.
    b. how television stereotyped our lives.
    c. the early days of television.
    d. the social consequences of television.

_d_ 2. **To emphasize the point of television's incredible growth, the author:**
    a. calls the speed of the growth phenomenal.
    b. compares and contrasts the number of sets owned in 1946 and 1957.
    c. compares and contrasts the ownership of sets with the ownership of refrigerators.
    d. all of the above.

_c_ 3. **The three networks that began the television industry emerged from the:**
    a. corporate sector.
    b. advertising industry.
    c. radio industry.
    d. drug companies.

_b_ 4. **The topic sentence of paragraph 2 is stated in the:**
    a. first sentence.
    b. second sentence.
    c. fourth sentence.
    d. last sentence.

_b_ 5. **The primary organizational pattern used by the author to show the social consequences of television in paragraph 3 is:**
    a. definition.
    b. listing or enumeration.
    c. sequence order.
    d. classification.

_a_ 6. **Which of the following is not mentioned in the text as an area impacted by televisions?**
    a. education.
    b. professional and college sports.
    c. fashion.
    d. other forms of media such as radio, newspapers, and magazines.

_b_ 7. **The idealized image of American life created by TV in the 1950s and 1960s included all the following *except:***
    a. women as mothers and housewives.
    b. diverse suburban neighborhoods.
    c. predominately white, middle-class suburban households.
    d. a strong male image.

a   8. According to the author, when TV shows depicted situations with images other than the idealized version, they did so:

    a. in a way that made differences and difficulties appear humorous and unthreatening.

    b. in a biased, insensitive manner.

    c. to mock the working class and unmarried women.

    d. to cover up suffering and hardship.

b   9. The following statement (paragraph 6): "Thus, at the same time that television was reinforcing the homogeneity of the white middle class, it was also contributing to the sense of alienation and power-lessness among groups excluded from the world it created" implies that:

    a. Television was attempting to make the world a better place by portraying an idealized way of life.

    b. By depicting the stereotypical, idealized suburban life, television unknowingly was fueling feelings of discontent and separateness among the less affluent and minority populations.

    c. Television intentionally tried to contribute to the well-being of those groups who were not able to attain the white, middle-class suburban lifestyle.

    d. None of the above.

b 10. Generally speaking, the tone of the selection is:

    a. critical and condemnatory.

    b. informative and straightforward.

    c. biased.

    d. humorous.

b 11. The last sentence in paragraph 6 expresses:

    a. a fact.

    b. an opinion.

    c. a judgment.

    d. a falsehood.

d 12. What is the overall main idea of the selection?

    a. We should be careful in how much television we watch, because its advertisers try to influence our lives in many ways.

    b. Television is big business.

    c. Beginning after World War II, television has had an ongoing neg-ative effect on the nation's social and economic systems.

    d. Since its birth in 1946, television has had a major impact on the economic and social institutions in our country.

Exercise 5   **Organizing the Information**

Directions: Refer back to the selection and complete the following concept map to reflect the major points and important supporting details. Notice how, in this case, the body of the map is organized to correspond to the major headings in the text.

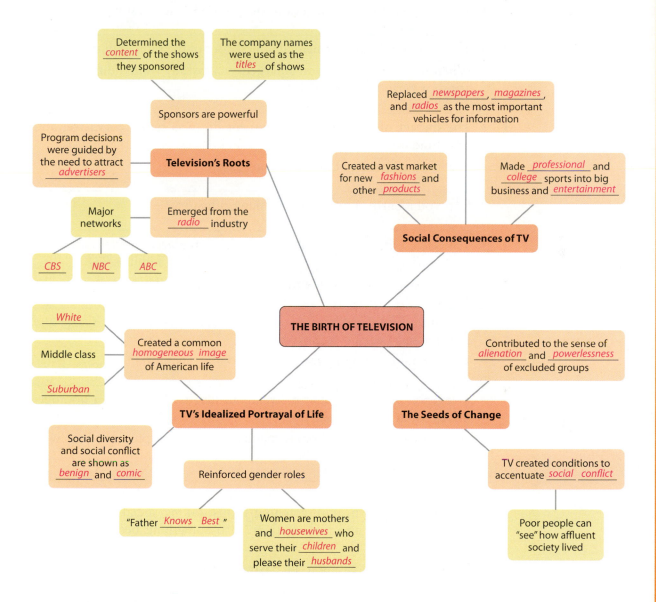

E x e r c i s e 6 **Using Context Clues**

Directions: The words introduced to you before you read the selection are presented again here in the sentences in which they appeared. (The paragraph in which each sentence is found is noted in parentheses, and you may want to reread it to get an even broader context for the word.)

Read each sentence. Then read the question following it that uses the word in a different context. Answer the question in a complete sentence using the boldfaced word in your response.

Answers will vary.

1. • Television, perhaps the most powerful **medium** of mass communication in history, was central to the culture of the postwar era. (1)
   • What is your preferred **medium** for obtaining the latest news?

2. • The television industry **emerged** directly out of the radio industry. . . . (2)
   • When was the last time you **emerged** successfully from a difficult situation or period of your life?

3. • The impact of television on American life was rapid, **pervasive**, and **profound**. (3)
   • What is a **pervasive** activity on your campus?

   • Can you identify a **profound** moment in history?

4. • Television entertainment programming . . . replaced movies and radio as the principle source of **diversion** for American families. (3)
   • After a long day of work and study, what is your favorite **diversion?**

5. • This was **epitomized** by such popular situation comedies as *Ozzie and Harriet* and *Leave It to Beaver*. (4)
   • What would **epitomize** your most relaxing vacation?

6. • Television not only sought to create an idealized image of a **homogeneous** suburban America. (5)
   • Would you prefer a **homogeneous** college campus, or one with diversity?

7. • It also sought to convey experiences at odds with that—but to convey them in warm, unthreatening terms, taking social diversity and cultural conflict and turning them into something **benign** and even comic. (5)
   • Do you consider teasing to be harmful or **benign?**

8. • Yet television also **inadvertently** created conditions that could **accentuate** social conflict. (6)
   • Have you ever **inadvertently** hurt someone's feelings?

   • What could you say to the next generation to **accentuate** the benefits of a college education?

9. • And television news conveyed with **unprecedented** power the social upheavals that gradually spread. . . . (6)
   • What is an event in your lifetime that was **unprecedented?**

| **Exercise 7** | **Making Personal Connections Through Writing and Discussion** |

Directions: Think about yourself in relation to the article you just read. Apply the information you learned from reading it to help respond to the following questions.

Answers will vary.

1. Based on the reading and your own observations, how has television changed since it first began? Do you think that television has changed for the better or for the worse? How so?

2. Were you surprised to learn that commercial television began with three networks that still exist today—CBS, NBC, and ABC? How do these differ from the cable channels you may currently watch?

3. What do you think is the driving force behind television today? Is it still advertising? Are there other elements that determine what is shown on television?

4. What is your medium of choice to stay current or be entertained?

Synthesizing Your Reading: Reflective Journal Writing

The Media

Having read these selections on the topic of media, you now have a broader, more scholarly understanding of the subject matter.

Write a reflective journal entry on the topic of the media demonstrating both your knowledge of the content in the selections and your personal viewpoint on the issue. You should write at least one page.

In the first section of your entry, briefly summarize each selection. Include the thesis and a few key points for each.

In the second section, reflect on the topic. Consider any or all of the following: What is your own assessment of the media today, in regard to its impact on society? Do you think it makes our lives better, or more complicated and difficult? Does the media benefit us? Hurt us? Does media report fairly? Is it objective or biased? If you could make any changes in the way media reports information, what would they be? What are your predictions for the future of media? What will it be like in the next century? Add details and examples to expand and explain your views.

Readings About Social Networks

Get Acquainted with the Issue

Making friends isn't what it used to be.

Finding relationships is an important life goal for most people, and the ways to go about doing this have grown in the new millennium. Online social networking sites allow users to post personal profiles and photos, talk about their lives, and communicate with others. They have become extremely popular and grow and develop almost daily.

The first selection here, "Online Social Networking Issues Within Academia," discusses the impact of social networking sites, such as Facebook, on college campuses. The next magazine article, "We Just Clicked," talks about the expansion of online dating sites as a global phenomenon. The last selection, excerpted from a sociology textbook, identifies the underlying societal factors that influence Americans today as they look for their perfect mate.

You are likely to find reading selections about making connections in business, sociology, law, and communications college textbooks.

Guided Reading

Reading Selection 1

Online Social Networking Issues Within Academia . . .

By Jeff Cain, Ed.D

University of Kentucky College of Pharmacy

The selection that follows was adapted from an article published in the American Journal of Pharmaceutical Education. *The author shares his research on the impact of social networking sites on college campuses. Read it to learn about issues created by the new technology of exchanging information.*

◀◀ before you read

It's important to think about what you may already know about a topic before you read. In this way, you will attach your new learning to your background knowledge and more easily understand the new information. (See Chapter 2, "Access Prior Knowledge," page 33.)

Answer the following questions related to the topic discussed in this article:

- Do you belong to Facebook, MySpace, Twitter, or any other social networking site? If so, who do you contact on these sites? Your college friends? Friends from other schools? Old acquaintances?

- Do any of your professors use social networking sites as part of their course work? If so, in what way?

- What is your opinion about communicating through social networking sites?

Prepare to Read

Now preview the selection "Online Social Networking Issues Within Academia . . ." using the THIEVES strategy on page 36.

| Exercise 1 | **Previewing** |

Directions: Complete the following items.

1. Take a look at the selection and check off the items that are available to you for preview.

   _X_ Title

   _X_ Headings

   _X_ Introduction

   _X_ Every first sentence in each paragraph

   ___ Visuals/vocabulary

   ___ End of chapter questions

   _X_ Summary/concluding paragraph

2. Read and highlight as you preview the selection.

Answers will vary.

3. Based on your preview, what do you anticipate the reading will be about?

   Many people communicate through social networking websites such as Facebook. Although these sites are public, people— frequently students—often post very personal information about themselves, which can cause problems for them. Some students have been suspended or expelled from school because they made threatening or biased remarks on Facebook; others have felt their privacy and safety has been threatened. Colleges are beginning to take action, such as monitoring student activity on this and other sites, in order to protect their students.

Check Out the Vocabulary

The following words appear in bold font in the reading. Are you already familiar with some of them? Knowing the meaning of these terms will increase your understanding of the material.

Exercise 2   **Checking Out the Vocabulary**

Directions: Complete the following matching exercise *before, during,* or *after* your reading. Be sure to review each word in the context of the selection.

h   1. abstract*   a. continuation, staying on, persistence
g   2. articulate   b. lawsuit, legal action
d   3. facilitator*   c. nonprofessional, member of the general public
i   4. foremost   d. one who makes something easy or easier
m   5. inherent   e. the process of reaching out and connecting with others
c   6. lay   f. critical and minute examination
b   7. litigation   g. state clearly, give clarity or distinction
e   8. networking*   h. a summary of a study or research
k   9. persona   i. first in place, order, or rank
l 10. prominence   j. effects or results; a rebound or recoil after an impact
j 11. repercussions   k. appearance for the public; an outside image
a 12. retention*   l. the state of being important, noticeable, or standing out
f 13. scrutiny   m. existing within something permanently and inseparably

*from the Academic Word List

 ## as you read

Establish Your Purpose

Now, read and annotate the selection. Focus on the major points of information. Identify the strengths of social networking sites such as Facebook, as well as the issues. Identify the issues that specifically relate to college students. Identify the repercussions of sharing private information within a public sphere.

Actively Process While You Read

Stop and process information as you read.

Exercise 3   **Processing While You Read**

Directions: Answer the following questions at the conclusion of each paragraph or set of paragraphs. This will help you monitor your reading process and better understand the material.

Paragraph 1

1. Based on your reading of the abstract, what is the focus of this article?

   This article will focus on the positive and negative aspects of online social networking.

Paragraph 2

2. Which technological advance continues to impact the twenty-first century in terms of the way people socialize and communicate and deal with public and private information?

   social networking

3. What is the purpose of social networking software?

   to create online places for people to present themselves, speak to others in their social network, and create and continue connections and interactions with others

4. What are some of the features of popular sites, such as Facebook and MySpace?

   You can post profiles and photos, connect with others who share commonalities, and help establish relationships with others.

Paragraph 3

5. Which is the most popular social networking site among college students? How does the information presented by the author confirm this finding?

   Facebook. It has been reported that 80–90% of U.S. college students use this site. In addition, over one-third of Facebook's users in the United States are between 18–24 and users worldwide are between 17–25 years old.

Paragraph 4

6. What is the only requirement to join Facebook?

   The only requirement is a valid email address.

7. Once you join a specific school network, what kind of information can a student access?

   profiles and photos of anyone on the site

8. What kind of information can one see in a profile?

   work and education history, personal information, and a listing of friends

9. What can prevent someone from viewing your profile?

   an optional privacy feature

Paragraph 5

10. How can the information posted on Facebook, a public site, be used by its viewers?

    It may be recorded, searched, replicated, altered, and accessed by others.

11. Which audiences may misinterpret the messages you intend for a friend or an acquaintance?

    a college professor, a current or future employer, parents

12. According to the article, are college students aware of these multiple audiences? If not, why not?

   No, they are often unaware of the multiple audiences. Very few students use the privacy features that enable the user to control what is seen by the wider Facebook public.

Paragraph 6

13. How does Facebook benefit students?

   It helps students establish who they are and where they fit in within their college community. They can use it to communicate with old and new friends.

14. Which benefit is especially important in helping students stay in school?

   They can make connections on campus, which creates a sense of community and belonging and lessens feelings of isolation.

Paragraph 7

15. What are the greatest issues with social networking?

   privacy, safety, and attitudes about revealing personal information

16. According to incidents reported by newspapers and magazines, what information has contributed to most of the problems with social networking?

   information that is made available through postings, profiles, and photographs

Paragraph 8

17. How has unprofessional, illegal, or disreputable behavior revealed through Facebook by college students been sanctioned or punished?

   suspension, expulsion, being called before the dean of students, losing positions on the school newspaper, and being denied a degree

18. In addition to college students, who else has displayed inappropriate behavior on Facebook?

   a university president

Paragraph 9

19. How have issues with safety, privacy, and social networking made students more vulnerable to abuse?

   Students disclose a lot more personal information about themselves on these sites, so they may become victims of harassment and stalking by users who have learned about them from these sites.

Paragraph 10

20. How can a future employer use information gleaned from a social networking site?

   The employer can use the information to learn more about a potential employee, especially details that are not revealed through a background check.

21. What kind of information might a law enforcement official hope to get from one of these sites?

   learn about any past or current criminal activities that an individual might have shared with a friend

Paragraph 11

22. What are institutions of higher education doing to address the issues related to social networking?

They are educating students about online privacy, the importance of securing personal information, the potential dangers to students, legal ramifications, and school policy on monitoring these sites.

Paragraph 12

23. In what way are some colleges trying to prevent the potential dangers connected to social networking?

Some athletic departments are prohibiting Facebook profiles entirely. Others require that students take great care not to post material that violates codes of conduct or could potentially be used to harm them, invade their privacy, or hurt the university's image.

Paragraph 13

24. Why do college administrators feel compelled to address issues about social networking?

They are afraid of possible legal repercussions if they don't do everything possible to protect students from the dangers of drug abuse and suicide, which may be revealed through social networking sites.

25. Why are some colleges still reluctant to monitor student behavior on these sites?

They feel it infringes on free speech and privacy rights.

Online Social Networking Issues Within Academia . . .

By Jeff Cain, Ed.D
University of Kentucky College of Pharmacy

Abstract

1   Online social **networking** sites such as Facebook and MySpace are extremely popular as indicated by the numbers of members and visits to the sites. They allow students to connect with users with similar interests, build and maintain relationships with friends, and feel more connected with their campus. The **foremost** criticisms of online social networking are that students may open themselves to public **scrutiny** of their online **personas** and risk physical safety by revealing excessive personal information. This review outlines issues of online social networking in higher education by drawing upon articles in both the **lay** press and academic publications.

Introduction

2   The 21st century continues to usher in technological advances that change the nature of communication, socialization, and private versus public information. One such change is the **prominence** that social networking websites currently enjoy, especially among the younger generations. Social networking software has been designed to create "online spaces that allow individuals to present themselves, **articulate** their social networks, and establish or maintain connections with others." While there are numerous types and variations of social networking websites, the two most common are

Facebook and MySpace. Among other things, social networking sites allow members to post personal information and photos, communicate with each other, and connect to users with similar interests, all within an online environment. Generally speaking, online social networking allows for individuals to remain in relatively close contact with others through the use of these websites. These sites have been described as "relationship **facilitators**" that help individuals build connections with others.

Online Social Networking

3   The popularity and growth of social networking websites has been phenomenal. MySpace is the membership leader among social networking sites, but Facebook is adding a reported 100,000 new users per day. While MySpace and Facebook are similar in the features offered, MySpace has been available to the general public while Facebook traditionally required affiliation with an educational institution. Although Facebook has recently expanded membership opportunities to include those outside the education realm, it is reported to be the most preferred social networking site among college students, containing profiles for an estimated 80%–90% of US college students. Since its inception in 2004, Facebook has attracted more than 22 million active users and as of February 2007, Facebook was the sixth most visited website in the United States as measured by average visits per visitor. Over one-third of all unique visits to Facebook.com sites were from users in the 18–24 year old age range, and Facebook was the most frequently visited site in the world for the 17–25 year old demographics. Representatives for Facebook state that the average user signs on to the site 6 times a day. This review will center primarily on Facebook because of its origin within higher education and because of its predominant use among college students.

Facebook Features

4   Facebook and other online social networking sites require users to register themselves online and create a personal profile. A valid email address is the only requirement to join Facebook. Once a user has joined, then he/she can join a regional and/or school network. Valid school email addresses are required to join a specific school network. Users can search for anyone on Facebook and view the user's photo, but by default can only see profiles and photo albums of others users in their own network. Within a profile, users can share interests, list work and education history, post photos, publish notes, share personal details, and communicate with others by posting on "the wall." A news feed section shows all actions such as photos, profile changes, and wall posts of other users that have been added as "friends." "Tagging" the names of other users in photos enables those photos to also show up on the profiles of "tagged" individuals. Facebook also has a set of optional privacy features, which allow the user to restrict access to portions of their profile. These privacy features enable the user to control what is seen by the wider Facebook public.

Private Information in Public Spaces

5   Social networking sites such as Facebook are public sites. The "conversations" may be recorded indefinitely, can be searched, replicated, and altered, and may be accessed by others without the knowledge of those in the conversation. Pictures or comments may be linked with an individual long after the user's attitudes and behaviors have matured. Furthermore, individuals conversing on social network sites imagine their audience and speak to the generally accepted norms of that audience. What they may

not understand is that there may be multiple audiences, including those with some type of power or authority over them. These other audiences may hold completely different views on what is socially acceptable. Facebook profiles are based within a culture and can lend themselves to misinterpretation, partially because of unidentifiable audiences that are **inherent** in online social networking environments. What students perceive as perfectly normal and harmless expressions among friends and classmates (their audience), may be perceived entirely different by parents, faculty members, and current or potential employers. The ability to define the audience through privacy features is an important component of Facebook; however, that ability "does not necessarily imply an understanding about the ways—both good and bad—that the information might be read. Relatively few users invoke the privacy features available to them.

Facebook and Academia Issues

6   Facebook is a tool that aids students in developing their identities and finding their "fit" within a college community. Helping students connect and stay in contact with old and new friends is touted as one of the significant benefits of Facebook. Making connections on campus, which help them feel that they belong, may be an important factor in student **retention.** These capabilities along with the many facets of communicating with their friends make social networking sites very appealing.

7   Although extremely popular, especially among younger generations, social networking sites are not without their issues. Controversy surrounds the use of these sites, specifically in terms of privacy, safety, and attitudes toward revealing personal information to the world. Most of the press concerning these sites has been negative in focus. Newspapers and magazines related to higher education are replete with cases of college students who experienced negative **repercussions** from questionable activities that were made public online. The list of incidents is long and revolves around a myriad of issues related to photos, posts, and/or personal profiles.

8   Students have been suspended or expelled from their respective universities for threats of crime and for racially insensitive remarks posted on Facebook. Other students have been reported or disciplined for alcohol/drug violations that were discovered through Facebook postings. Facebook has been used in investigations of campus brawls and for identifying students who illegally stormed a football field. Students have been expelled from class, called before the dean of students, lost positions on the school newspaper staff, and even been investigated by the Secret Service all because of ill-advised postings on Facebook. One student was refused an education degree with the accompanying teaching certificate because of her MySpace photograph, which was deemed "unprofessional." Issues surrounding Facebook are not limited entirely to students. A university president encountered substantial criticism as a result of a photo taken at an annual Halloween party that was placed on a student's Facebook account.

9   In addition to incidences involving illegal or disreputable acts, other students have suffered due to encroachments upon their personal privacy and/or safety. Students have been harassed and stalked and have encountered uninvited strangers at home. These abuses at least partially resulted from the availability of personal information on Facebook. A new wave of "identity" information is being published on these online social network sites that are different in nature from the classic name, address, and phone number. Vast disclosures of photographs, political views, sexual orientation,

etc. by students warrant further discussion of identity information protection on higher education campuses.

10   Further complicating the situation, many students have difficulty believing that the online expression of information intended for their peers may be viewed and even sought out and used by others. What should be of great concern to students is that employers, law enforcement officials, and administrators are increasingly using these sites to obtain information about individuals that is not necessarily included in resumes or uncovered by general background checks. Some students reject the idea that "outsiders" should be able to use information posted on a social networking website and feel that basing judgments on and making inferences from a user's comments or photographs on Facebook is unfair. The attitude expressed is that Facebook postings are intended for the general audience of other students and that faculty member and administrators should not be viewing them.

Institutional Considerations

11   Online social networking sites are beginning to garner more attention from higher education institutions. Educating students about the risks associated with social networking services was introduced by Educause as a new item in its Current Issues Survey, which addresses the critical information technology issues of 1,785 higher education institutions. Institutions are taking steps to educate students regarding issues of online privacy, potential dangers to students, responsibilities for controlling others, and school policy on monitoring sites. One law school has begun educating students regarding the "public" nature of Facebook postings and the need to project a professional online persona to avoid repercussions in the legal profession.

12   Many other institutions have taken a proactive stance in terms of dealing with student use/abuse of online social networking sites. The number of institutions in which the athletics department has developed policies regarding social networking profiles is growing. Several universities have either mandated "sterile" profiles or banned student athlete Facebook profiles completely for the stated purpose of protecting student identities, privacy, and university image. Advocates for education and communication about online social networks suggest that warnings should address the threat of legal actions against behavior, student safety and identity, violations of codes of conduct, and repercussions from potential employers.

13   Administrators struggle to decide to what extent, if at all, Facebook should be monitored. Some administrators have felt compelled to respond to social networking issues due to the sheer volume of online activity by their students and on their campuses. Colleges are facing increasing pressure and possible **litigation** in proving they have done enough to protect students from drug abuse, suicide, etc. However, the surveillance and/or regulation of students' social networking profiles raises concerns of free speech and privacy, which may simultaneously conflict with schools' commitments to student safety. Differences in rights of students at public and private schools, conflicting laws, and complications related to regulating "cyberspace" blur the boundaries in which schools can and /or should operate. If a college monitors social networking sites to ensure that students abide by codes of conduct or act in accordance with the school's mission, they could be creating a "duty of care" toward the students. In the legal sense, this heightens the responsibility of the school to prevent harm and increases the likelihood of lawsuits.

In respect to the Fourth Amendment and the right to privacy, there has yet to be a clear-cut ruling on the legality of law enforcement officials using Facebook postings for investigations. However, Facebook users would generally have difficulty proving that material posted to a publicly accessible site was intended and expected to be private.

Conclusions

14   Social networking sites provide individuals with a way of maintaining and strengthening social ties, which can be beneficial in both social and academic settings. The same sites, however, also pose a danger to students' privacy, safety, and professional reputations if proper precautions are not taken. Colleges would be advised to consider how these issues might affect their students. At a minimum, schools should take appropriate steps to educate students about these matters.

Source: "Online Social Networking Issues Within Academia and Pharmacy Education," *American Journal of Pharmaceutical Education,* 2008, February 15; 72(1): 10.

■ ■ ■

 **after** **you read**

Review Important Points

Going over major points immediately after you read, while the information is fresh in your mind, will help you to recall the content and record key ideas.

Exercise 4   **Reviewing Important Points**

Directions: Answer the following questions based on the information provided in the selection. You may need to go back to the text and reread certain portions to be sure your responses are correct and can be supported by information in the text.

1. What is the overall message in this selection?
    While online social networking sites have provided many benefits to college students, they also raise issues about privacy and safety.

2. Why are social networking sites so popular?
    They allow individuals the opportunity to maintain contact with others, including old and new acquaintances. They have been described as "relationship facilitators" that help individuals build connections with others.

3. What is a major concern about social networking sites?
    Students are posting personal information on a public site, which is accessible to anyone.

4. How are colleges responding to some of the concerns about social networking sites?
    They are educating students about safety and privacy, and some colleges are creating policies that restrict or even ban the use of online social networking sites.

Organize the Information

Organizing the information you have learned from a reading selection shows you have understood it and can restate the material in a different way. You can use the reorganized information to help you study for exams and prepare for written assignments. (See Chapter 9.)

| Exercise 5 | Organizing the Information |

Directions: Using the reading selection, create a list of the benefits and dangers of social networking. Then, look over your list. Can you identify any additional benefits or risks?

Social Networking and College Students

Benefits	Dangers
1. Students develop their identity	1. Privacy violations: harassment, stalking, revealing of identifying information
2. Students find a "fit" within the college community	2. Safety: threatening remarks can be made
3. Helps students to stay in contact with old and new friends	3. Sanctions: suspension, expulsion, reports to the Dean of Students loss of jobs or campus leadership roles, refusal of a degree
4. Students feel more connected with their campus	4. Investigations by the Secret Service, law enforcement officials, current or future employers

Integrate the Vocabulary

Make the new vocabulary presented in the reading *your* vocabulary. Using the terms in other contexts will help you make them part of your own spoken and written language.

| Exercise 6 | Integrating the Vocabulary |

Directions: Replace the italicized word or phrase in each of the following sentences with a word, or alternate form of the word, from the vocabulary list at the beginning of the selection on page 461. Paraphrase and rewrite the sentence on the line provided, using the new word.

Example

Carlos *reviewed the benefits and disadvantages* of working at the new pharmacy in order to make his decision to accept the job offer.

Carlos assessed whether to work at the new pharmacy to decide if he should take the job he was offered there.

1. Janice did her utmost to be sure everything she wrote on her job application was true. She knew her potential employer would put her application under *critical examination.*

   Janice was careful in completing her job application, knowing it would be reviewed with great scrutiny.

2. Before reporting the results of his experiment in detail, Jonathan wrote *a short paragraph identifying the major procedures he used and the findings of his research.*

   *Jonathan wrote an **abstract** for his research study paper.*

3. Though Clark's *outward appearance* in public was always calm and in control, inside he was often racked with self-doubt and anxiety.
   Even though Clark's public **persona** *was calm and collected, he actually was very anxious and unsure of himself.*

4. Jason was quite concerned he would end up in *a long and complicated court case* when he was pulled over for driving 30 miles above the speed limit and realized he had left his driver's license and insurance paperwork at home.
   Jason was worried about **litigation** *since he was caught speeding and didn't even have his license and proof of auto insurance.*

5. At the start of every semester, Professor Smathers *carefully identified and explained* to his students the requirements and grading standards in his class.
   Professor Smathers **articulated** *the class requirements and standards for grades to his students each semester.*

6. Time management may very well be *the most important* study skill a college student can possess.
   Time management may be the **foremost** *study skill for college students.*

7. Of all the positions at the university, the role of president is the one *of the greatest standing and importance.*
   The role of college president is the one with the greatest **prominence.**

8. It was only after he failed two exams and neglected to complete his research project that Peter began to consider *the impact and results* of his unscholarly behaviors.
   After not doing his work and failing two tests, Peter began to worry about the **repercussions** *of his actions.*

9. The neurosurgeon edited most of the presentation he had given at the hospital for the attendees at the local library program. Otherwise, the *general public* would not have been likely to comprehend the importance of his latest research findings.
   The neurosurgeon had to revise his presentation for the **lay** *public so that that they would understand the significance of his recent work.*

10. Mr. Malone, the advisor for the school newspaper, *makes it easier for us to do our jobs and enables us* to publish the paper each month.
    Mr. Malone **facilitates** *the publication of our school newspaper.*

11. *Built into* Kathleen's personality, *and never wavering*, are the qualities of kindness, concern, and empathy.
    Kindness, concern, and empathy are **inherent** *in Kathleen's personality.*

12. The university administrators are concerned about *keeping* students motivated so that they will *continue* their education and *complete* their degrees.
    The administrators at the college are concerned about student **retention.**

13. Last Spring, Maxwell attended the job fair and distributed over 100 of his business cards with the hope *of meeting and connecting with people in his field* and, hopefully, securing employment.
    Maxwell went to the job fair and **networked** *by handing out about 100 cards in hope of getting a job.*

Make Personal Connections Through Writing and Discussion

When you make your new learning relevant to yourself in some way, it becomes more meaningful and longer lasting. Whenever you read, try to connect to the content on a personal level. How does it relate to you? How can you apply what you have read to other situations? What else would you like to know?

| Exercise 7 | **Making Personal Connections** |

Directions: Think about yourself in relation to the article you just read. Apply the information you learned from reading it to respond to the following questions.

Answers will vary.

1. Having read the selection, what personal concerns, if any, have been raised for you regarding social networking?

   _____

   _____

2. Would you advise other college students to be part of a social networking site? Why? What advice would you offer based on this selection?

   _____

   _____

3. What additional information would you be interested in learning about social networking sites?

   _____

   _____

Self-Monitored Reading
Reading Selection 2

> # We Just Clicked
> By Lisa Takeuchi Cullen and Coco Masters

This article, from Time Magazine, *looks at the business of Internet dating and how American companies are trying to expand internationally. Find out how matchmaking has developed into a global enterprise.*

⏪ before you read

Think about what you may already know about social networking. In this way, you will attach your new learning to your background knowledge and more easily understand the new information. Answer the following questions before you read the selection.

- Do you use social networking sites such as Facebook or Twitter? If so, what do you use them for? To talk to friends? To reconnect with old acquaintances? To meet new people? What is your opinion of these sites?
- Where would you consider meeting people to date? In school? At work?
- Have you ever tried online dating websites such as Match.com or eHarmony.com? What is your viewpoint on Internet dating? Do you think it's a good way to meet a potential partner to date or marry?

Prepare to Read

Preview the article by applying the THIEVES strategy on page 36.

| **Exercise 1** | **Previewing** |

Directions: Based on your preview, respond to the following questions.

1. How has matchmaking, as a means of meeting a prospective dating or a marriage partner, changed over the past 10 years?
   The Internet has made matchmaking both a profitable and international business venture.

2. When did U.S. singles begin to participate in the "traditional" way of meeting a prospective partner through matchmaking that is practiced in many other countries?
   It began about 10 years ago with the arrival of Internet dating sites.

3. Name one popular Internet dating site.
   eHarmony, Match.com, Yahoo! Personals

4. Which countries are already involved in the Internet dating business?
   China and India

5. What challenges might American Internet dating companies encounter in potential international markets, especially China and India?
   American Internet dating companies may have to consider cultural differences before they try to expand their businesses abroad.

Check Out the Vocabulary

The following words appear in bold font in the reading. Are you familiar with them? Knowledge of these words will support your comprehension of the article.

<table>
<tr><td>**Exercise 2**</td><td colspan="2">**Checking Out the Vocabulary**</td></tr>
</table>

Directions: Complete the following matching exercise *before, during,* or *after* your reading. Be sure to review the words in the context of the selection.

_k_ 1. accrued
_f_ 2. bewilder
_j_ 3. bodes
_h_ 4. disdain
_a_ 5. ebbed
_d_ 6. euphemism
_n_ 7. exploit*
_m_ 8. forge
_r_ 9. hurdle
_b_ 10. lucrative
_q_ 11. migrating*
_p_ 12. perusing

_e_ 13. pervasive
_g_ 14. revenue*
_o_ 15. rife
_c_ 16. robust
_l_ 17. temperament
_i_ 18. unscrupulous

a. declined in size
b. profitable, moneymaking
c. strong
d. a nice way of saying something offensive
e. common, general
f. puzzle, mystify
g. income
h. dislike intensely
i. dishonest
j. to give an indication in advance
k. increased in growth
l. manner of behavior, thinking or reactions
m. to form by a concentrated effort
n. use for profit
o. abundant, numerous
p. read through carefully
q. move away and settle elsewhere
r. obstacle or difficult problem to overcome

*from the Academic Word List

 **as you read**

Establish Your Purpose

Now, read and annotate the article. Focus on the major points of information that explain what American Internet dating websites must consider before they expand overseas.

Actively Process While You Read

Monitor your comprehension as you read. (See Chapter 2, "Monitoring Questions," page 40.) Be sure to stop to reflect at the conclusion of each paragraph. Ask yourself the following questions:

- Did I understand that paragraph?
- What is the main idea?
- Am I ready to continue?

Highlight the most important points. Write notes in the margin, and move on.

from the pages of

TIME

> ## We Just Clicked
> By Lisa Takeuchi Cullen and Coco Masters

1   At the global headquarters of eHarmony in Pasadena, Calif., one blue wall is papered with testimonies of love: snapshots of couples who met on the Internet matchmaking site and subsequently got hitched. There are older couples, military couples, kissing couples, couples with physical disabilities, couples dressed in wedding whites. Soon, if all goes as planned, there will be Chinese couples, Indian couples, European couples, many dressed in the brilliant matrimonial hues of their cultures. They're going to need a new wall.

2   Once a practice as provincial as it was personal, the art of pairing up people for marriage has become an increasingly international and technology-driven business. As young people all over the world move far from home for school and work, even those from tradition bound cultures can no longer rely solely on the resources of crafty aunties to find them suitable mates. Enter the Internet, where marriage and dating sites began to appear a decade ago and have multiplied rapidly over the past several years. In the U.S. alone, there are close to 1,000 such sites, led by Match.com, eHarmony and Yahoo! Personals. The industry rang up $649 million in **revenues** in 2006, according to Jupiter Research, a market-research firm. With growth slowing in the U.S., Web matchmaking giants are eyeing fertile potential markets such as China and India. But an international match presents **hurdles** in business as in love: differing societal attitudes, wily competition and cultural quirks to **bewilder** the most sophisticated suitor. Love, it turns out, isn't the same in every language—not even close.

3   Love is, however, a **lucrative** and recession-proof business, and that makes translating it worth the effort. As far back as the Paleolithic Era, arranged marriages served to **forge** networks between family groups, writes Stephanie Coontz in *Marriage, a History*. Families exchanged daughters and sons for labor, land, goods and status. These matches were so important that, in almost every society, a community member eventually set up shop in setting up unions; in northern India, it was the barber's wife, the nayan. "Be a matchmaker once," goes the Chinese saying, "and you can eat for three years."

4   In the U.S., matchmaking took off as an industry only in this decade, with the arrival of Internet dating sites. Suspicion and **disdain** eased into acceptance as more Americans found a partner—or at least a date and not a nut—on the sites. Of the 92 million unmarried Americans 18 and older counted by the Census last year, about 16 million have tried online dating, according to the Pew Internet & American Life Project. In 2003 online daters increased 77%. With sites charging $35 a month on average, **revenues** popped accordingly. Growth has **ebbed** of late to about 10% a year, say analysts, partly because of the competing popularity of social-networking sites. You can flirt on Facebook, too—and for free.

5   If a country with little tradition of matchmaking can embrace a version of it online, then it follows that cultures long used to a third party's hand in love affairs would do the same. That's what many Western companies seem to believe anyway, judging by their expansion strategies. Match.com, the leading online dating site in the U.S.,

began **exploiting** first-mover advantage through international acquisitions in 2002. Now in 35 countries, the Dallas-based company says 30% of its 1.3 million members live outside the U.S., accounting for 30% of its $350 million 2007 **revenues** (the bulk of its 15 million members just browse for free).

6   But it has learned along the way that its model does not always translate. On Match, users post personal profiles and photos, attracting and **perusing** potential mates in what resembles a colossal bar scene. While many Americans like the freedom and convenience, single women in Japan felt threatened by the lack of privacy. Plus, parts of the profiles weren't culturally appropriate, as Match CEO Thomas Enraght-Moony learned over lunch in a Tokyo restaurant with his country manager. "He pointed to the women there and said, 'We really don't need to ask for hair color. We all have the same,'" says Enraght-Moony. In Scandinavia, on the other hand, the 2.2 million Web-savvy singles were long used to dating online. To differentiate itself from local competitors when it launched there in 2003, Match toned down its window-shopping aspect and played up the promise of long-term love. "The dream here is not to marry a millionaire prince," says Johan Siwers, vice president of Northern Europe. "The dream is to live a good life in the countryside and be happy." Match now rules the Scandinavian market, with 1.5 million members.

7   One way U.S. online matchmakers seek to set themselves apart from local competitors is science. Match hired Rutgers University anthropologist Helen Fisher to devise a compatibility test for a spin-off called Chemistry.com. As Chemistry prepares to launch abroad, Fisher is confident that the test—56 questions that place users in four **temperament** categories—is applicable to any culture. The societal trends that drive online matchmaking in the U.S. apply in much of the world, after all: women going to work, young people **migrating** far from home and, perhaps most important, a newly **pervasive** insistence on love as an essential ingredient of marriage. Fisher cites a study that asked 10,000 people of 36 cultures about their No. 1 criterion for marriage. "Everywhere, the answer was love," she says.

8   That **bodes** well for the international hopes of eHarmony, the leader among compatibility focused sites in the U.S. Started in 2000 by Neil Clark Warren, the folksy clinical psychologist who starred in the company's ads, eHarmony poses 436 questions to users in order to find them the best match. It has since **accrued** 17 million members, 230 employees, $200 million in annual **revenues** and 30% yearly growth. That's not to mention marriages at a rate of 90 a day, unions that so far have produced 100,000 children (a disproportionate number of them named Harmony).

9   But rather than dive quickly into promising markets, eHarmony has remained devoted—some would say slavishly—to its research-based model. In China, that means commissioning researchers at Beijing University to find out whether its model— in which 29 "dimensions" such as humor and spirituality are mined for compatibility— applies to the culture. Kaiping Peng, a professor of psychology at the University of California, Berkeley, who is assisting eHarmony, is unsure. "What is the best match might not be about matching exactly," he says. "Maybe it's complementary—like the yin and the yang." Americans are drawn to eHarmony's deeply probing questionnaires because as a culture we seek to know ourselves. "That probably is not necessarily the teaching of Asian philosophies and religions. Buddha used to talk

about diminishing self—don't look at yourself; look at others for information and for guidance."

10   Perhaps those cultural differences explain why no Western company has yet won the Chinese single's hand. And what a hand: 46% of those 35 and younger are unmarried, according to a university study, and that percentage is increasing. Sixty million Internet users are of marrying age, according to Shanghai-based market-research company iResearch, a population that will grow about 20% a year, to 128 million in 2010. In Beijing alone, there are more than 2 million marriage-age singles. Local competition is **rife.** Chinese matchmaking sites had 14 million registered users in 2006, a number iResearch says will triple by 2010.

11   China should be a natural haven for online matchmaking. Up until a century ago, marriage-registration forms required the seal of an "introducer." Young, educated professionals seem open-minded. Even today, the off-line matchmaking business remains **robust;** there are a reported 20,000 agencies, many run by local governments and bearing such dreamy names as the Beijing Military and Civilian Matchmaking Service and the Tianjin Municipal Trade Union Matchmakers' Association. The imbalance of genders brought on by the single-child rule (many parents opted to keep only a male baby) has also led to a desperate demand for matchmakers among rural men, opening the door to **unscrupulous** brokers who con women into unions.

12   Western online matchmakers, however, do face challenges in gaining a foothold in the Chinese matchmaking market. Of the 14 million Chinese Internet daters, only 500,000 pay subscription fees; thus industry revenues are estimated at just $24 million, according to iResearch. Paying users are expected to rocket to 3 million by 2010, **generating** sales of at least $160 million. But fees are minimal compared with the $59 per month charged by the likes of eHarmony. "In China, if you charge money, you'll die fast," says Gong Haiyan, CEO and founder of the leading Web dating site, Jiayuan (formerly Love21cn). Chinese sites rely instead on online advertising and ticket sales from events such as speed-dating mixers that charge about $13 for admission (parents who tag along have to pay too). Another popular dating site, 915915.com.cn—in Chinese, the numbers sound like "only want me"—set up a "love cruise" in 2006 on the Huangpu River near Shanghai to introduce men worth at least 2 million yuan ($274,000) to attractive women. Edward Chiu, CEO of ChinaLoveLinks, says his free websites steer users to his 30 off-line matchmaking offices, where they can pay fees totaling up to $6,000. Both eHarmony and Match say they have yet to decide how to adjust their subscription-based models to the market.

13   Like China, India has a long history of and cultural comfort with matchmaking; as many as 90% of weddings are arranged, says Patricia Oberoi, a Delhi-based sociologist. There are 60 million singles ages 20 to 34, and 71% believe arranged marriages are more successful than "love" marriages. But with so many moving to cities or even abroad—up to a third of the population, according to the latest census—the Internet is proving preferable to the services of the village nayan. So-called matrimonial sites first appeared 10 years ago and today make up half the world's matchmaking sites. Like U.S. sites, they offer free viewing but charge about $40 to subscribe for three months. BharatMatrimony, a leading site, claims 10 million members and, in its 10 years, a million marriages. Another, named Shaadi,

boasts 800,000 matches. Industry growth in India could be even more explosive than in China; users have doubled every year. Sales are growing 50% annually and reached $30 million in 2006. "Online matrimony has become a mainstream activity, like checking email," says Uday Zokarkar, business head of BharatMatrimony.

14   Partly because India's matrimonial sites have already succeeded in wooing the nation, Western companies have hesitated at the door. "India is a very different business, and we just haven't got there yet," says Match's Enraght-Moony. For instance, sites there make matches on the basis of factors unfamiliar to outsiders, including caste, language and "character"—a **euphemism** for chastity. About 15% of pro-files are filled in not by the prospective bride or groom but by their parents. And now Indian

sites are challenging Western matchmaking companies on their own turf. Shaadi CEO Vibhas Mehta says 30% of its business comes from the U.S., Europe, Australia and the Middle East. Perhaps love needs no translation after all.

■ ■ ■

▶ after you read

Review Important Points

Going over major points immediately after you read, while the information is fresh in your mind, will help you recall the content and record key ideas.

Exercise 3   **Reviewing Important Points**

Directions: Choose the best answer for each of the following questions using information provided in the selection.

_c_ 1. The topic of this selection is:
   a. many people have found their perfect match online.
   b. online sites are popular in China and India.
   c. the expansion of Internet dating into the international market.
   d. finding a date, an activity partner, or a marriage partner.

_c_ 2. The thesis of this article can be found in:
   a. paragraph 1.
   b. paragraph 2.
   c. paragraph 3.
   d. paragraph 4.

_b_ 3. **The numbers of Internet dating websites have increased worldwide because:**
   a. People are moving back home.
   b. People are moving away from home because of educational and job opportunities.
   c. Traditional matchmakers are no longer practicing their craft.
   d. It's a multimillion-dollar business.

_d_ 4. **How does the marketing of online dating sites differ outside the United States?**
   a. There are fewer markets in the United States.
   b. In other countries, there is competition from traditional matchmakers.
   c. More questions are asked by online dating services.
   d. There are cultural differences regarding the meaning of love.

_c_ 5. **The main idea of paragraph 4 is:**
   a. The business of arranged marriages is short-lived.
   b. Arranged marriage dates back to the Paleolithic Era.
   c. Since arranged marriages have always played an important role in society, matchmaking is a solid business venture.
   d. Once you become a matchmaker, you will eat for three years.

_c_ 6. **In the United States, the popularity of online dating sites has:**
   a. caused suspicion and disdain amongst consumers.
   b. increased the number of marriages nationally.
   c. decreased because of free social networking sites.
   d. spread to other countries.

_d_ 7. **In its expansion abroad, Match.com, a popular U.S. online dating site, has learned that:**
   a. Single women in Japan prefer more privacy online than their American counterparts.
   b. In Japan, it is not necessary to provide information about hair color because all Japanese have black hair.
   c. In Scandinavia, long-term love and happiness is most important.
   d. All of the above.

_a_ 8. **According to a recent study of 10,000 people in 36 countries, the number one criterion for marriage is:**
   a. love.
   b. happiness.
   c. spirituality.
   d. humor.

_b_ 9. **eHarmony, the leader among compatibility focused sites in America, has learned that in China:**
   a. People seek to know themselves as deeply as possible.
   b. People look to others for information and direction rather than at themselves.
   c. People are unsure what compatibility means.
   d. People turn to Buddha for guidance and information.

_d_ 10. **According to paragraph 11, the main reason why the United States has not made inroads into China is because of:**
   a. the large number of competing Chinese companies.
   b. the differences between the U.S. and Chinese cultures.
   c. there being a small percentage of unmarried people in China.
   d. A and B.

_d_ 11. **In paragraph 12, we can infer that the reference to "dreamy" names means:**
   a. The Chinese have selected names that are romantic sounding.
   b. The Chinese have named matchmaking sites after heavenly bodies.
   c. The matchmaking sites are run by the government.
   d. The authors are being ironic; they do not believe the names are romantic.

_a_ 12. **Chinese matchmaking sites generate most of their revenue from all of the following *except*:**
   a. charging high membership fees.
   b. inviting online daters to speed-dating mixers.
   c. promotion of online advertising.
   d. setting up "love cruises."

_b_ 13. **China and India are similar because:**
   a. They share the belief that arranged marriages are better than "love" marriages.
   b. Both have a long history and level of cultural comfort with matchmaking.
   c. Ninety percent of their marriages are arranged.
   d. Both have a large amount of subscribers.

_d_ 14. **The United States is having difficulty entering the Indian market because:**
   a. In India, matches are based on caste, language, and chastity.
   b. Fifteen percent of profiles are filled out by the parents of prospective marriage partners.
   c. Indian online dating sites are themselves entering the global market.
   d. All of the above.

_b_ 15. **The overall main idea of this article is that:**
   a. Both China and India, with a long history of matchmaking, are entering the online dating services.
   b. American online dating sites are facing challenges as they attempt to expand their markets abroad.
   c. The U.S. is afraid that cultural differences will prevent them from entering the Chinese market.
   d. Matchmaking has a long tradition in the United States, China, and India.

_b_ 16. **The overall pattern of organization in this selection is:**
   a. cause and effect.
   b. comparison and contrast.
   c. enumeration or listing.
   d. classification.

<u>*d*</u> **17. What is the tone of this article?**

   a. concerned
   b. humorous
   c. objective
   d. ironic

Organize the Information

Organizing information shows that you have understood it and provides you with a useful study tool. (See Chapter 9.)

| **Exercise 4** | **Organize the Information** |

Directions: Complete the following summary using details from the article.

   U.S. matchmaking sites began as an industry only <u>*10*</u> years ago. In 2006, the industry earned more than <u>*$649 million*</u> in revenues. However, the growth began to slow down partly because of the competing popularity of social-networking sites, like <u>*Facebook*</u>, which doesn't charge memberships fees. Consequently, matchmaking giants, such as Match.com and eHarmony, began searching for potential markets in <u>*China and India*</u>.

   Both of these countries have a long tradition of matchmaking. Up until a century ago in China, marriage registration forms required the seal of an <u>*"introducer"*</u>. Like China, India has a long history and cultural comfort with matchmaking. Even today, ninety percent of marriages are <u>*arranged*</u>. Nevertheless, American companies are facing <u>*hurdles*</u> in trying to capture these markets. For example, unlike U.S. companies that charge at least $35 per month, the Chinese charge <u>*minimal fees*</u> to their online subscribers. Both eHarmony and Match.com do not as yet know how they will adjust their subscription-based models to that market. American companies have also learned that their models do not always translate well in other cultures; that is, what constitutes a match in the U.S. may be quite different in <u>*other cultures*</u>. In India, for example, matches are made based on <u>*caste*</u>, <u>*language*</u>, and even chastity, while in the U.S. matches are based on personal and probing questions about such matters *as* <u>*humor*</u> and <u>*spirituality*</u>. While the U.S. matchmaking sites continue to explore these fertile markets, sites in India are already challenging Western matchmaking companies by expanding their markets to <u>*the U.S., Europe, Australia, and the Middle East*</u>.

Integrate the Vocabulary

Make the new vocabulary *your* vocabulary.

| Exercise 5 | Integrating the Vocabulary |

Directions: Replace the italicized, boldfaced word or phrase in each sentence with a word, or form of the word, from the vocabulary list at the beginning of the selection. Then paraphrase and rewrite the sentence using the new word.

Answers may vary. Sample answers provided.

1. The students were told **to read through** the directions **carefully** before tackling their final test.

   Prof. Green instructed his students to **peruse** *the directions before beginning the exam.*

2. At the beginning of each semester, the bookstore manager orders **numerous** quantities of notebooks, college calendars, and daily planners.

   The bookstore is **rife** *with supplies that will enhance student success and promote good time-management skills.*

3. As students begin their freshman year in college, it is important that they try hard to **form** new friendships so they will feel more comfortable in a new and unfamiliar setting.

   As students transition from high school to college, it is important that they **forge** *new friendships.*

4. By the end of the second semester, Dr. Hallows said the new social work program had **grown** from 12 to 50 students.

   Dr. Hallows proudly announced that the new degree program in social work had already **accrued** *fifty students.*

5. Nowadays, more students are going into computers, so programs like electrical engineering are **declining in size**.

   Since the introduction of the computer engineering program, the number of students in the electrical engineering program has **ebbed from** *125 to 35.*

6. The nursing department said the applicant pool was very **strong** even though students knew there were very few openings.

   Applicants for programs in allied health science programs, such as nursing, remain **robust** *in spite of limited openings.*

7. One of the greatest **obstacles** to achieving academic success in college is juggling my job with my schoolwork; however, I need the money to support my family.

   Since I must work, the greatest **hurdle** *I face in college is trying to find time to do my schoolwork.*

8. It's fairly **common** for students to have to balance a job with attending classes on either a full- or part-time basis.

   Problems managing work and school schedules are **pervasive** *: almost everyone in my biology class works full- or part-time.*

9. Five students in my business law class **moved from** Korea *to* the United States.

   The numbers of Asian students **migrating** *from Korea have increased over the past ten years.*

10. Byeong came to the United States because he felt there would be more *profitable* opportunities to start his own business here.

    *One reason for increased immigration is to pursue **lucrative** business opportunities that would otherwise not be possible in one's native country.*

11. The first English lesson that Byeong learned was *a polite way to say* "toilet."

    *Byeong learned that a **euphemism** for "toilet" or "bathroom" is Men's or Ladies' Room.*

12. At first, Byeong was *puzzled* by the friendly dialogue between students and their teachers. In Korea, it was unusual to interact so informally with professors.

    *Byeong was **bewildered** by the informal way in which college students engaged with their instructors and professors.*

13. Byeong *disliked intensely* the American way of teaching; he expected all his teachers to lecture the way they had done so in Korea. Instead, they often conducted discussions or asked students to work in groups.

    *Byeong **disdained** the instructional approach used in the United States, which required students to work in small groups and participate in discussions.*

14. Because of Lisa's nervous *nature,* she was ill at ease when she had to give a speech in her public speaking class.

    *Because of Lisa's nervous **temperament,** she was anxious about the oral presentation she had to give in her communications course.*

15. With the *money* the college had *taken in* from extracurricular activities, it was able to build a new computer lab in the library.

    *The **revenue** raised through charging a fee for extracurricular activities funded the new computer lab.*

16. The college was careful not to *take advantage of* adjunct faculty, and so the administration did not require them to hold office hours. This presented a dilemma to students who wanted to meet with these part-time professors.

    *The college's policy not to **exploit** adjunct faculty left students with little opportunity to conference with these instructors.*

Make Personal Connections Through Writing and Discussion

When you make new learning relevant to yourself in some way, it becomes more meaningful. Whenever you read, try to connect to the content on a personal level. How does it relate to you? How can you apply what you have read to another situation? What else would you like to know about the topic or issue?

EXERCISE 6   **Making Personal Connections**

Directions: Think about yourself in relation to the article you have just read. Apply the information you learned from reading it to respond to the following questions.

Answers will vary.

1. After reading this article, would you be willing to use an Internet dating site or recommend one to a friend as a way of meeting a prospective partner? Explain.

2. Devise your own compatibility test for finding a partner/mate. Write at least 10 questions. Then ask your classmates to respond to your questions and see if you find a match.

3. In your opinion, what are some advantages and disadvantages to online dating?

Independent Reading
Textbook Reading Selection: Sociology

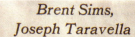

John Brullo

Brent Alan Sims and Dr. Joseph Robert Taravella celebrated their partnership last evening at the Waldorf-Astoria in New York. The Rev. Dr. Susan Corso, a nondenominational Christian minister, led a ceremony of commitment.

Mr. Sims (above, left), is 36. He works in New York as the vice president for finance and administration in the national advertising sales division of Fox television stations. He graduated from the University of Texas and received an M.B.A. from Southern Methodist University. Mr. Sims uses the surname of his mother and stepfather, Sandra and Loyd Sims of Lindale, Tex., who retired as the owners of a Western Auto store in Dumas.

Dr. Eva Marya Ogielska and Dr. Paul Cameron Zei were married yesterday at the Compass Rose Gardens in Bodega Bay, Calif. The Rev. Nancy Hargis, a non-denominational minister, performed the ceremony.

The couple, both 32, met at Stanford University, where the bride earned a Ph.D. in neuroscience and the bridegroom a medical degree and a Ph.D. in molecular and cellular physiology.

The bride is to become an associate in September at Foley Hoag, a Boston law firm. She graduated cum laude from Brandeis and received a law degree from the University of California at Berkeley.

She is the daughter of Sophia and Andrew Ogielski

Controlling Love: American Mate Selection
By J. John Palen

This excerpt is adapted from a sociology textbook chapter called "Ties that Bind: The Changing Family." In the context of exploring the changing American family in the twenty-first century, it identifies and discusses the factors that influence how people search for and select life partners in the United States.

 **before you read**

Answer the following questions before you read the textbook selection "Controlling Love: American Mate Selection."

- What criteria have you considered when searching for a potential partner? What factors do you think would contribute to compatibility and the chances for a successful long-term relationship or marriage?

- Have you ever been advised by your parents or others in selecting a mate? What have they expressed?

Prepare to Read

Preview the textbook selection using the THIEVES strategy on page 37.

| Exercise 1 | **Developing Preview Questions** |

Directions: Based on your previewing, write *three* questions you anticipate will be answered in the selection.

Answers vary.

1. *What is endogamy?*
2. *What five factors do norms for endogamy in North America focus on?*
3. *What is socioeconomic status?*

Check Out the Vocabulary

The following words from this textbook selection appear in academic and scholarly writing across many disciplines. Be sure you learn their meanings.

Academic Word List

assumption	the act of taking for granted, a supposition
enhance	raise to a higher degree in value or quality
ethnicity	racial or national background
norms	typical standards or expected ways to behave
residing	living in or inhabiting
unconstitutional	violating rights guaranteed in the U.S. Constitution

Other Words Often Found in Scholarly Texts

bulwark	protection against external danger
compulsory	mandatory, obligatory, required
encounter	run into, meet, come upon
impediment	something that impedes, interferes with
inappropriate	not acceptable or proper for the situation
interracial	between two or more different races
sanctions	legal measures that force compliance
subtly	finely, delicately, faint not forceful
whims	sudden, fanciful, idle wishes or notions

| **E x e r c i s e 2** | **Checking Out the Vocabulary** |

Directions: Complete each of the following sentences using a word from the academic or scholarly word lists.

1. Though the rule doesn't apply worldwide, attending school through the age of 16 is ___compulsory___ in the United States.

2. Just because Ryan is earning a good salary at his new job, do not make the ___assumption___ that he is willing to spend over $100.00 on dinner at the French restaurant that just opened in town.

3. In order to vote in the next election, it's required that citizens must have been ___residing___ at the same address for at least six months.

4. Having transferred from a large, urban community college, it took a while for Francis to learn the new social ___norms___ of a small, private school.

5. Citing his right to free speech, Max said it was ___unconstitutional___ when the campus security guards ordered him to stop shouting about the poor quality of food in the cafeteria.

6. Caroline bought several new age CDs, hoping their soothing tones would ___enhance___ the quality of her daily yoga and meditation sessions.

7. Sensing the presence of strangers, the mother cat placed herself as a ___bulwark___ in front of her kittens as visitors entered the animal shelter.

8. Constance finally had to acknowledge that listening to rock music while studying for her exams was actually more of an ___impediment___ than a support. After studying several hours that way for her Criminal Justice exam, she failed the test.

9. Students enjoyed the ___whims___ of Professor Raddock, who, seemingly without thought, would break into a song, tell a joke, or even pass out candy on any given day in the classroom.

10. It is illegal to demand that prospective home buyers identify their age or ___ethnicity___ on information forms they complete in the real estate broker's office.

11. Growing up in a happy home with a Chinese father and a Dominican mother, Carolina's views on ___interracial___ marriage were very positive.

12. To stop the surge of graffiti appearing on buildings across the campus, the administration imposed harsh and severe ___sanctions___ on anyone who was caught defacing college property.

13. Rather than come on too strong, Matthew decided to approach Mariel more ___subtly___; he simply and casually mentioned he had tickets for a jazz club and would really enjoy some company should he go.

14. It was <u>*inappropriate*</u> to speak at the meeting without being recognized by the committee chairperson.

15. The politician <u>*encountered*</u> resistence to her new tax proposal.

▶ as you read

Establish Your Purpose

Now, read and annotate the selection. Focus on the major points of information. Identify the factors in U.S society that influence Americans in choosing, dating, and selecting their mates. Notice how these have changed over time.

Actively Process While You Read: Independent Reading

Highlight the most important points. Write your notes in the margins and move on.

> ## Controlling Love: American Mate Selection
> By J. John Palen

1   Because romantic love is potentially disruptive, most cultures attempt to prevent socially undesirable marriages. The establishment of new families is felt to be too important to be left totally to chance or the **whims** of the young. Every society has **norms**, or unwritten social standards, to restrict marriage choices; American society is no exception.

2   There is less social control over the American dating-mating system than in the past, but there are still clear norms, favoring marriage within one's own religious or social class group. The custom of marrying within one's own group, often applied in terms of religion and social class, is called *endogamy*. Marriages that violate these norms are still often viewed as a "problem," both for the families involved and for the larger society. Societal norms also can be used as a means of predicting risks of divorce. Even where people are expected to marry for love, they are most definitely *not* expected to fall in love with just anyone. The norms for endogamy in North America focus on **ethnicity,** religion, socioeconomic status, age, and race.

Ethnicity

3   Marriage endogamy within one's own ethnic group was virtually **compulsory** among first-generation immigrants to America, and it was expected to be the same in the second generation. With the passage of time, ethnic differences have become far less important as an **impediment** to marriage. However for today's new immigrant groups, ethnicity is an important factor in partner selection. For those of European ancestry, a new general European ethnic group is being formed based on ancestry from anywhere in Europe.

Religion

4   With ethnicity declining in importance, religion sometimes serves as the next **bulwark** against marriage outside the group. For most of the twentieth century, America had a triple melting pot, with separate Catholic, Protestant, and Jewish marriage pools. However, even these broad divisions are breaking down and there is an increasing amount of marriage between people within different religions. The highest level of endogamy may still be found within Jewish populations.

Socioeconomic Status

5   Love may be blind, but it is not expected to bypass the barriers of social status. One is expected to marry someone of roughly similar occupation level and educational background. The basic **assumption** is that such couples are most likely to have much in common and to share similar attitudes, values, and goals. The norms against cross-status marriages are strongest where there are large class and education differences between spouses. Where differences do exist, it still remains more socially acceptable that the male have the higher economic or educational background. Historically, the term *husband* referred not to a married man but to one who had "husbanded" enough resources to marry.

Age

6   Every society specifies "suitable" ages for marriage. In America, spouses are expected to be relatively close in age. The 1995 average age for first marriage was 26.5 for males and 24.5 for females. These are the oldest average ages for first marriages in America's history. (It shocks today's students to learn that in the early 1960s, most women had completed their childbearing by age 25.) Where ages do differ, the male is expected to be the older partner. Among those remarrying, there is a greater age difference between spouses.

Race

7   Of all the endogamy rules, race has been the most persistent. Fifty years ago, **interracial** marriage was illegal in 28 southern and western states, and not until 1967 did the Supreme Court rule antimiscegenation laws (laws prohibiting cross racial marriage) **unconstitutional**. Even with legal **sanctions** removed, however, racial endogamy still remains a major factor in mate selection. While marriages between whites and Asians are now more accepted, black-white marriages still meet disapproval from within both groups.

8   The strength of the norms against cross-racial marriages can be seen in the fact that until the 1970s the proportion of black marriages that involved whites was less than 1 percent. Since that time, interracial black-white marriages increased four times to 246,000 marriages a year, or about 2.2 percent of all marriages. The most common interracial marriage is between an African American male and a Caucasian female. Census data indicate that 6 percent of black men and 2 percent of black women have spouses who are not African American. Outside the South, the percentage of black men marrying a white woman is over 10 percent, while under 2 percent of black women marry white men.

9   The low interracial marriage rate for black females is showing signs of increasing. With the number of black women attending college double that of black men, some African American women say that to find a compatible mate, they are **compelled** to marry outside their race.

Overview

10   Students are frequently unaware of the degree to which the factors of socio-economic status, ethnicity, religion, and race have **subtly** influenced their lives. For instance, their family may have moved to a different school district in order to send adolescents to a "more appropriate" high school. Also, parents may urge children to attend a particular college, for more than academic reasons. The parents are aware that by controlling the college environment, they can partly control the marriage market for their children. As expressed by the director of public relations for a small Mormon college, "Families want kids to meet people with values similar to their own." Peer pressures often do the rest. (At this small Mormon college, 20 percent of the students married other students last year.) Students are also aware that attending a particular college or **residing** in a certain neighborhood **enhances** one's social opportunities. Only the workplace is a better place than college for meeting a potential partner.

(Adapted from *Social Problems for the Twenty-First Century,* J. John Palen, 2001)

■ ■ ■

 **after you read**

Think back to the questions you posed after previewing the selection but before you read it. Now that you have read the selection, can you answer your initial questions?

EXERCISE 3   **Answering Your Preview Questions**

Directions: If you have discovered the answers to your preview questions, write them on the lines provided.

Answers will vary.

1. _____
   _____

2. _____
   _____

3. _____
   _____

EXERCISE 4   **Reviewing Important Points**

Directions: Choose the best answer for each of the following questions using information provided in the selection.

b 1. **What is the central thesis of the selection?**

   a. Socioeconomic status is important in mate selection.
   b. Norms still exist in American society that favor endogamy in dating and marriage.
   c. Race is the most persistent rule in endogamy.
   d. Families want their children to marry within their same ethnic group.

a 2. **The overall purpose of the selection is to:**

   a. inform the reader about factors contributing to mate selection in the United States.
   b. criticize the biased nature of the mate selection process in the United States.
   c. convince people to marry "their own kind" of people.
   d. compare and contrast mate selection in different cultures.

d 3. **The norms of *endogamy:***

   a. encourage marriage within one's own social class and religion.
   b. can be used as a means of predicting risks of divorce.
   c. are still widely applied in America.
   d. all of the above.

b 4. **According to the selection, factors that influence mate selection in the United States include all of the following *except:***

   a. race and ethnicity.
   b. political views.
   c. age.
   d. socioeconomic status.

d 5. **Paragraph 3 tells, in general, how ethnic endogamy norms have changed among immigrants to America. The primary organizational patterns used by the author are:**

   a. definition and classification.
   b. cause and effect and classification.
   c. process and spatial order.
   d. time order and comparison and contrast.

a 6. **Paragraph 6 can be paraphrased in the following way:**

   a. Although religion is still a factor in mate selection, it has become less important over the years as more Americans marry outside their faith.
   b. Over time, religion has become a factor for endogamy only for those of the Jewish faith in the United States.
   c. Catholic, Protestant, and Jewish people increasingly are marrying people of their own faith, since ethnicity is less of a factor.
   d. All of the above.

_b_   7. **Based on the information in paragraph 5, we can infer that socio-economic status is based upon:**

    a. age, education, and job.
    b. schooling, occupation level, and income.
    c. economic level, religion, and profession.
    d. ethnic background, occupation, and earnings.

_c_   8. **In paragraph 6, when the author says, "It shocks today's students to learn that in the early 1960s, most women had completed their childbearing by the age of 25," we can conclude that he means the following:**

    a. By today's standards, that age is very high.
    b. Women today are more immature than women of the 1960s.
    c. By today's standards, that age is very low.
    d. None of the above.

_b_   9. **According to the author, which norm of endogamy in America has been the most consistent?**

    a. religion
    b. race
    c. age
    d. ethnicity

_b_   10. **To support the main idea that cross-racial marriage between African Americans and Caucasians are still contrary to the norm, the author presents:**

    a. his opinions.
    b. facts and statistics.
    c. expert testimony.
    d. personal anecdotes.

_b_   11. **The author implies that the rate of African American women marrying outside their race is increasing because:**

    a. The number of available African American men is decreasing.
    b. As more and more African American women are attending college, their social network includes a greater number of men of different races.
    c. African American men prefer to socially network outside of their race.
    d. They prefer mates of a different ethnicity.

_b_   12. **The main idea of paragraph 10 is expressed in the:**

    a. first and second sentence.
    b. third and fourth sentence.
    c. fifth and sixth sentence.
    d. last sentence.

_c_   13. We can conclude that the most likely places for finding a potential mate include all of the following *except:*

    a. your college.
    b. your neighborhood.
    c. your shopping center.
    d. your workplace.

Exercise 5   Organizing the Information

Directions: Using your notes and referring back to the selection, complete the following map to identify the major norms for endogamy in North America today. Fill in important details for each factor.

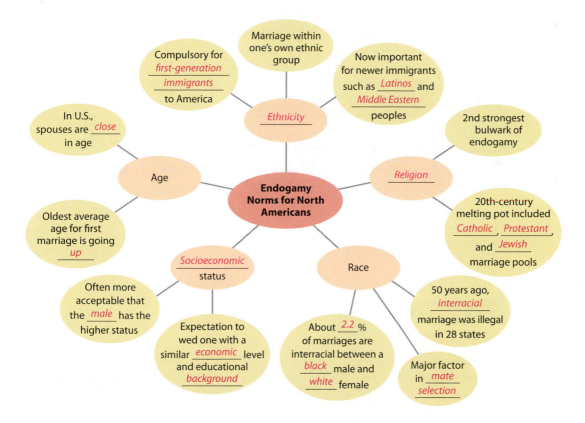

Exercise 6   Using Context Clues

Directions: Use context clues to complete the following letter from Fernando to his friend Malia, using words from the Academic Word List located at the beginning of the selection.

Dear Malia,

Since _residing_ in the United States, I have come to better understand the _norms_ of behavior here, especially for dating. Although it is _unconstitutional_ to limit prospective mates, and there are no written _sanctions_ that stop people from asking others out, I have learned that there are many _subtle_ rules. One of these is about staying within one's own _ethnicity_ and avoiding _interracial_ dating. However, I do see more and more connections developing between people of different races as they socialize with each other on campus, at least as friends.

I guess that I shouldn't make the _assumption_ that anyone will go out with me simply because I am so handsome! Although my good looks do _enhance_ my chances and surely are not an _impediment_, it isn't _compulsory_ that everyone I approach must accept my advances!

There are many personal liberties here in the United States, and opportunities to interact with people from many cultures. I think this freedom acts as a _bulwark_ against bias and prejudice. It's nice to know that, even on a _whim_, and even if it doesn't lead to romance, I can still say hello to someone different than me and become their friend. The social networking process here for dating definitely has its unwritten rules, but I think things are changing every day.

Your friend always,
Fernando

Exercise 7   **Making Personal Connections Through Writing and Discussion**

Directions: Think about yourself in relation to the article you just read. Apply the information you learned from reading it to help respond to the following questions.

Answers will vary.

1. Has endogamy played a role in your social networking? Which of the norms discussed in the selection, if any, are important to you?

2. In the last portion of the selection, the author presents ways in which parents have a hand in "controlling" the educational environment of their children "for more than academic reasons." What do you think of this? Does it sound caring or manipulative? How have your parents or family impacted your choice of a life partner?

3. What other criteria do you believe are important in selecting a person to date or even marry?

Synthesizing Your Reading: Reflective Journal Writing

Social Networks

Having read three selections on the topic of social networks you now have a broader, more scholarly understanding of the subject matter.

Write a reflective journal entry on the state of making social connections today, demonstrating both your knowledge of the content in the selections and your own viewpoints on the issue. You should write at least one page.

In the first section of your entry, briefly summarize each selection. Include the thesis and a few key points for each.

In the second section, reflect on the topic. Consider any or all of the following: How would you, or do you, set out to generate social connections in your life? What would you want people to know about you through social networking? Do you think social networking helps people find others with their same needs and values? How should issues of privacy be dealt with? What do you see as the future of social networking and finding relationships?

Readings About the Environment

Get Acquainted with the Issue

Everything is going green!

We are in the midst of a "green" revolution. People worldwide are engaging in behaviors and taking actions to sustain the environment and conserve energy now and for future generations. However, ways to create consumer awareness and efforts to implement sound environmental practices are not always that simple.

In the first article, "The Green Mirage," you will read about how consumers and businesses feel about environmental issues. In the second article, "The Green Campus," you will discover that even colleges are getting into the act of adopting *green* policies. Finally, in the excerpt from an environmental science textbook, you will learn what consumers really need to know when they purchase environmentally friendly products.

You will encounter the topic of the environment in a number of college textbooks. The disciplines of environmental science, biology, chemistry, physical sciences, sociology, and business all deal with this topic.

Guided Reading
Reading Selection 1

> ## The Green Mirage
> ### By Rick Newman

In this selection from U.S. News & World Report, *Rick Newman interviews the president of Yankelovich, a market research firm, about what American consumers say about the environment.*

◀◀ before you read

It's important to think about what you already know about a topic before you read. In this way, you attach new learning to your background knowledge and more easily understand the new information. (See Chapter 2, "Access Prior Knowledge," page 33.)

- Do you purchase green products? Which ones?
- Do you use any green services?
- Do you believe that a majority of Americans are concerned about the environment?

Prepare to Read

Now preview the selection "The Green Mirage" using the THIEVES strategy. (See Chapter 2, page 37.)

Exercise 1   **Previewing**

Directions: Complete the following items.

1. Take a look at the selection and check off the items that are available to you for preview.

    <u>X</u> Title

    <u>   </u> Headings

    <u>X</u> Introduction

    <u>X</u> Every first sentence in each paragraph

     _X_   Visuals/vocabulary

     ___   End of chapter questions

     _X_   Summary/concluding paragraph

2. Read and highlight to preview the selection.

Answers will vary.   3. Based on your preview, what do you anticipate the reading will be about?

A small percentage of consumers are really concerned about the environment, while others

would probably respond more to this issue if they could save money. Some businesses

are concerned about the environment, including car manufacturers like Toyota, yet other

businesses, such as financial institutions, are not.

Check Out the Vocabulary

The following words appear in bold font in the reading. Are you already familiar with them? Knowing the meaning of these terms will increase your understanding of the material.

| **Exercise 2** | **Checking Out the Vocabulary** |

Directions: Complete the following matching exercise *before, during,* or *after* your reading. Be sure to review the word in the context of the selection.

_e_   1. abstract*

                     a. special area of demand; specific market segment

_h_   2. debunk

_b_   3. disproportionately   b. not evenly, unequally

_i_   4. mainstream   c. relating to wealthy consumers

                                    d. having a negative connotation; tendency to belittle or show disapproval

_e_   5. mirage   e. an illusion, something without substance or reality

_a_   6. niche   f. not representing something specific

_d_   7. pejorative   g. being almost the same, in essence

_c_   8. upscale   h. expose as a false or exaggerated claim

_g_   9. virtually*   i. prevailing current activity, direction, or influence

*from the Academic Word List

as you read

Establish Your Purpose

Now, read and annotate the selection. Focus on major points of information presented in Newman's interview that deal with how consumers and businesses feel about environmental concerns.

Actively Process While You Read

Stop and process information as you read.

Exercise 3   **Processing While You Read**

Directions: Answer the following questions at the conclusion of each paragraph. This will help you monitor your reading process and comprehend the material.

Paragraph 1

1. How do most consumers feel about buying environmentally friendly products?

   Most are unwilling to pay the higher prices these products cost.

2. How do businesses view environmentally friendly products?

   They see them as an opportunity to make more money.

Paragraph 3

3. According to the interview, how can businesses get consumers more interested in buying *green* products?

   Show consumers how they can economize by purchasing these "green" products, not focus on saving the environment

Paragraph 5

4. What is the profile of people who feel strongly about environmental issues?

   upscale, live in Northeast or on West Coast

5. Why are so many people indifferent about environmental issues?

   because they see it as an abstract issue rather than a real or practical issue

Paragraph 7

6. What questions do big businesses have about the environment?

   Should they pay attention to the environment and if so, how?

Paragraph 9

7. Why are industries that manufacture consumer packaged goods beginning to think about the environment?

   to see if there are possible ways to use green in marketing and if the health angle would sell more products

8. Which industries are least likely to care about environmental issues?

   financial service companies, retailers, grocery retailers, and the fashion industry

Paragraph 11

9. What were the conclusions of the survey? How did these conclusions differ from what was previously believed about green consumerism?

   The majority of the American public are not concerned about the environment. Prior to this survey, it was believed that most consumers were interested in preserving the environment.

Paragraph 13

10. What are some eco-friendly behaviors in which Americans are willing to engage?

buying products with Energy Star ratings, turning out lights, doing things that will save them money

11. What is a *tree-hugger*? Why don't people want to be described in that way?

It is a person who is passionate about environmental issues. This term has a negative connotation because it suggests that they are going overboard by preaching or being excessive about their willingness to engage in or promote green activities.

Paragraph 15

12. What is the traditional marketing model?

Change attitudes to change behaviors.

13. How can companies get the public to preserve the environment without getting them to change the way they think about environmental issues?

Don't talk about the environment; talk about how consumers can save money. For example, instead of trying to sell people a car that is good for the environment, tell them how the car can help them save money.

Paragraph 16

14. Which company has the best environmental image?

Toyota

Paragraph 20

15. How do their customers feel about paying higher prices?

They are willing to pay higher prices because they feel strongly about the environment.

The Green Mirage
By Rick Newman

1   We're in the midst of a green revolution, right? Actually, no. Despite Al Gore's Nobel Peace Prize and the green-branding of products from toothpaste to toilet paper, most consumers are unwilling to pay extra or make sacrifices to be more environmentally friendly. A recent study by the market research firm Yankelovich found that only 13 percent of Americans are passionate about environmental issues—while 29 percent have **virtually** no interest. For most companies, green products represent only a **"niche"** opportunity, according to the report. *U.S. News* spoke recently with Yankelovich President J. Walker Smith about consumer attitudes and behavior:

2   *So consumers still don't respond strongly to environmental concerns?*

3   Public opinion about the environment is pretty mushy. If you want to get people to act greener, the best thing to do is talk to them about saving money, not about saving the environment. Also talk to them about health concerns. That gets their attention.

4   *How do attitudes vary by region?*

5   Thirteen percent of Americans are passionate about the environment. They're more **upscale** and tend to live in the Northeast or West Coast. Most people are indifferent about the environment. That shows up **disproportionately** among white males in the South. There's a strong lack of personal connection to the environment. In the U.S., people understand it as an **abstract** issue.

6   *Your clients include some big corporations. What's their interest?*

7   Our clients want to know if this is an issue they should pay attention to. And if so, how should they pay attention. It's not just about green products; it could be about green manufacturing. Some of our clients just come out and say, it's not the issue for me.

8   *In what industries does this matter the most and the least?*

9   Industries where there's concern include home builders, autos, consumer packaged goods. . . . The last one, they're looking very strongly but haven't yet decided how to deal with green. It could be areas where there's a connection between green and wellness.

10   Financial services companies are largely uninterested. Retailers, there are a lot who couldn't care less—probably a majority. Most grocery retailers, they're not making a big push. The fashion industry is at the bottom of the list, unless you tag lifestyle concerns.

11   *Still, your numbers don't show that people don't care; they just show that it's not a huge trend, right?*

12   A lot of the publicity surrounding green makes it sound like a **mainstream** concern. It's not. It's a pretty big number, but not the majority of Americans. Our priority is to **debunk** the notion that green is a priority among a majority of Americans. It's not.

13   *So what are some of the things people are willing to do to be environmentally correct, or whatever the right term is?*

14   Green behaviors are things people tend to do when it can save them money, like turn out the lights when you leave the room. But people don't like to be characterized as a tree-hugger. There are still some **pejorative** connotations with that. For most Americans green is nice, but don't go overboard. People tend to buy products with Energy Star ratings, for instance, because it saves them money.

15   *So most companies are free not to worry about environmental concerns? Or should they still be doing something?*

16   The traditional marketing model is, you change attitudes in order to change behavior. But you might be able to change behavior here without changing attitudes, as opposed to the tree-hugger route, where you're preaching an environmental message. So if you come out with a hybrid car, why are you talking about the environment? Why don't you talk about saving money on gas instead? If you have environmentally friendly building materials, why not talk about the savings?

17   *Some companies, like Toyota, have developed a very strong environmental image. Does your research show whether that translates into business success? Whether it actually helps them make money?*

18   Toyota is our top-rated company in terms of environmental image, with 23 percent of consumers giving it a favorable rating. But if I were Toyota, I'd be concerned that 75 percent of people gave me a moderate score.

19   *Even if the percentage of Americans who are passionate about the environment is fairly low, that's a pretty desirable group of consumers, right? And that's got to be likely to grow.*

20   As for the 13 percent, they really, really care. They think that paying more is the right price. And 13 percent is a good strong part of the consumer market. I believe the 13 percent will continue to grow and will draw people.

Source: Rick Newman, "The Green Mirage," *U.S. News & World Report,* 10/30/07.

after you read

Review Important Points

Going over the major points immediately after you read, while the information is fresh in your mind, will help you to recall the content and record key ideas.

| **Exercise 4** | **Reviewing Important Points** |

Directions: Answer the following questions based on the information provided in the selection. You may need to go back to the text and reread certain portions to be sure your responses are correct and can be supported by information in the text.

1.   Which paragraph contains the main idea? Paraphrase it here.
      The first paragraph contains the main idea. For most Americans, the environment is not a major issue, and they are unwilling to spend more on eco-friendly products, and business mostly sees environmental issues as an opportunity to benefit from an eco-market.

2.   What are the demographics of those who are passionate about the environment and those who show no personal connection and are indifferent?
      Passionate—more affluent, living mostly in the Northeast or West Coast. Indifferent—mostly white males in the South

3.   List examples of industries that are involved in environmental issues and those that are not.
      Involved in environmental issues—home builders, autos, consumer-packaged goods. Not involved—financial services, retailers, including grocers, and the fashion industry

4.   What advice does J. Walker Smith give about enlisting public support for environmental concerns?
      Focus on changing behaviors, not attitudes. Show consumers that they can save money by purchasing green products and using green services.

5. Based on the findings from the survey, what conclusions can be drawn about public opinion on the environment?

The majority of American consumers are not concerned about environmental issues.

Organize the Information

Organizing the information you have learned from a reading shows that you have understood it and can restate the material in a different way. You may use this reorganized material to help you study for exams and prepare for written assignments. (See Chapter 9.)

| **Exercise 5** | **Organizing the Information** |

Directions: Complete the following summary about American consumers' attitudes toward environmental issues. Fill in the blanks with details from the article.

According to a recent _____*study*_____ by a market research firm, only _____*13 percent*_____ of American consumers feel strongly about _____*issues related to the environment*_____. This group tends to be more _____*upscale*_____ and resides in _____*the Northeast or West Coast*_____. Most Americans, however, do not feel _____*passionate*_____ about the environment and see it as an _____*abstract*_____ concern. In fact, according to the findings, _____*29 percent*_____ have almost no interest in the environment. They only see _____*green*_____ behavior as a way of saving _____*money*_____. They are unwilling to pay extra, and they do not want to make _____*sacrifices*_____.

Integrate the Vocabulary

Make the new vocabulary presented in the reading *your* vocabulary. Using the terms in other contexts will help you make them part of your own spoken and written language.

| **Exercise 6** | **Integrating the Vocabulary** |

Directions: Replace the italicized word or phrase in each of the following sentences with a word, or alternate form of the word, from the vocabulary list at the beginning of the selection on page 496. Paraphrase and rewrite the sentence on the line provided, using the new word.

1. Last month, I went on a field trip with my botany class. We ran out of water after a few hours. I was so thirsty that *I imagined I saw* a water fountain among the clearing of trees.

I was so thirsty while I was on a field trip with my botany professor that I could have sworn I saw a water fountain. To my disappointment, it was only a **mirage.**

2. I wish I had taken notes on the chapters in my textbook. *In essence*, I had to read over every chapter of my biology book to be prepared for my finals.

Because I hadn't annotated my textbook, I **virtually** *had to reread the entire biology textbook in preparation for my final exam.*

3. When the new cafeteria opens, the vendors to the college will be able to provide a *special market situation* where fast-food concessions are going to be replaced by healthier food establishments.

*The opening of a new cafeteria on campus will provide a **niche** opportunity for the health-food vendors to replace some of the fast-food chains.*

4. There are no parking lots near my college because it is in the middle of a *wealthy* residential community.

*Since my college is located in the middle of an **upscale** residential neighborhood, there are no public parking facilities nearby.*

5. Students really don't understand what topic and main idea mean if they do not apply these concepts to something *specific*, like a paragraph or longer selection.

*Some concepts in reading, such as topic and main idea, remain **abstract** unless you have the opportunity to apply them to brief passages and longer selections.*

6. Nowadays, the *prevailing current activity* for colleges is finding ways of keeping students from dropping out of school.

*It appears that the **mainstream** concern of colleges today is retention.*

7. Many colleges are requiring their liberal arts students to undertake course work in diversity so that they can learn to *expose false and exaggerated claims* about different ethnic groups.

*Requiring course work in diversity and pluralism will serve to **debunk** myths about multiethnic groups in American society.*

8. Barth College is made up of students from many different backgrounds and with many different needs; nevertheless, there *are far more* male students and *only about* 25% female students.

*Although my college contains a diverse group of students, the school is **disproportionately** made up of male students.*

9. Cynthia was *insulted* when her boyfriend William *called her a "jerk"* for not going over her class notes before the midterm.

*Although Cynthia knew she should have reviewed her class notes before the midterm examination, she did not appreciate her boyfriend's use of **pejorative** language.*

Make Personal Connections Through Writing and Discussion

When you make your new learning relevant to yourself in some way, it becomes more meaningful and long lasting. Whenever you read, try to connect to the content on a personal level. How does it relate to you? How can you apply what you have read to other situations? What else would you like to know?

> **Exercise 7**   **Making Personal Connections**

Directions: Think about yourself in relation to the article you have just read. Apply the information you learned from reading it to respond to the following questions.

Answers will vary.

1. Look through the products in your home. Make a list of products that contain a "green" label. How many did you find? Did you purchase these products because they were environmentally safe?

2. How could grocery retailers or the fashion industry promote green products that would be safer for the environment?

3. Write a letter to a local retailer you shop from regularly urging the business to become more eco-friendly.

4. Design a slogan that will encourage consumers to become environmentally conscious.

Self-Monitored Reading
Reading Selection 2

The Green Campus: How to Teach New Respect for the Environment?
The 3 R's: Reduce Your Carbon Footprint, Reuse, and Recycle

By Anne Underwood

In this article from Newsweek, *the author explains in what ways colleges are getting involved with environmental issues.*

 before you read

It's important to think about what you may already know about a topic before you read. In this way, you will attach your new learning to your background knowledge and more easily understand the new information. (See Chapter 2, "Access Prior Knowledge," p. 33.)

- Does your college cafeteria serve organically grown fruits and vegetables?
- Have you ever taken any courses that address environmental issues?
- Have you ever been involved in college activities that promote environmental awareness?

Prepare to Read

Preview the article by applying the THIEVES strategy on page 36.

| **Exercise 1** | **Previewing** |

Directions: Based on your preview, respond to the following questions:

1. Why are some colleges changing what they serve in cafeterias and at college events?
   To not only reduce energy consumption and waste but also to prepare college students for careers in environmental studies

2. What does the author mean when she says, ". . . sustainability is no longer an elective"?
   All students at colleges need to be aware of and involved in the importance of preserving the environment.

3. How is Harvard going green?
   Students are urged to buy only energy-efficient appliances and purchase compact fluorescent bulbs.

4. How are some other colleges going green?
   They are building new structures that use ecodesigns.

5. How has environmental awareness impacted the courses of study at colleges?
   Colleges have expanded their majors and programs to include more formal study about the environment.

6. What are students doing to promote their colleges' involvement in preserving the environment?
   They are urging colleges to purchase renewable energy.

Check Out the Vocabulary

The following words appear in bold font in the reading. Are you familiar with them?

| **Exercise 2** | **Checking Out the Vocabulary** |

Directions: Complete the following matching exercise *before*, *during*, or *after* your reading. Be sure to review the words in the context of the selection.

_c_	1. coveted	a. advanced or forward-thinking idea or method
_f_	2. generating	b. trying to influence the actions of others in favor of a specific action
_h_	3. iconic	c. desired enviously
_e_	4. initiative	d. distinctive part or section
_a_	5. innovative	e. an introductory act or step
_i_	6. linchpin	f. creating, making
_b_	7. lobbying	g. to nudge, to get someone's attention
_g_	8. prodding	h. representative of, symbolic
_d_	9. sector*	i. a central element that holds things together

*from the Academic Word List

Understanding Discipline-Specific Vocabulary: Environmental Science

In this reading, you are introduced to many words that deal specifically with the subject of environmental science. Some you may already know. For example, you probably know what the words *pollution* and *emissions* mean. **Pollution** is the introduction of harmful substances or products into the environment. **Emissions** are substances discharged from your car's engine that pollute the environment. In fact, many states require a periodic motor vehicle inspection to check the level of emissions. Does your state require such an inspection?

Exercise 3   Using Word Parts

Directions: In this reading, you are introduced to many words that deal specifically with the subject of environmental science, such as *pollution* and *emissions*. Using your knowledge of word parts, write definitions of the following discipline-specific words.

Prefixes	Roots	Suffixes
de- (remove)	*bio* (life)	*-able* (capable of)
di- (two)	*eco* (habitat, home)	*-ed* (characteristic of)
	grad (step, walk, degree)	*-ity* (state, condition)
	vers (turn)	*-ly* (in the manner of)
		-ology (the study of)

1. **biodegradable**
   capable of decaying through the actions of living organisms, such as biodegradable paper or detergent

2. **biodiversity**
   the variation of life forms often used as a measure of the health of biological systems

3. **ecology**
   the study of the interactions of organisms and their environment

   In this reading, many compound and hyphenated words contain the root *eco-*. See how many of these words from the reading selection you can define using the word part *eco-*. Then write their definitions in the spaces provided.

4. **ecodesign**
   an approach to the design of a product with special consideration for the environmental impacts of the product during its whole life cycle

5. **ecothemed**
   a theme that highlights a natural environment

6. **ecofriendly**
   refers to goods and services considered to inflict minimal or no harm on the environment

7. **eco-oriented**
   an integrated set of attitudes and beliefs about the environment

Answers will vary. 8. Do you know any other words that contain the root *eco*? List them.
   ecosystem, ecoterrorism, ecotourism, ecophobia, ecotoxic, eco-consultant

   You may need to know other important words before you read this selection. Below you will find the definitions of these words.

- **carbon footprint** (para. 6) Your carbon footprint is the sum of all the CO^2 (carbon dioxide) produced as a result of your activities (driving a car, flying in a plane, using a lawn mower, etc.) and the production of goods or services you used (food, clothing, appliances, electricity, etc.) within a given time-frame.

- **stewardship** (para. 3) responsible care taking, based on the premise that we do not own natural resources but are managers of them and therefore responsible to future generations for maintaining and preserving them.

- **sustainability** (para. 2) living within the bounds of nature based on renewable resources used in ways that do not harm essential ecological services or limit the ability of future generations to meet their own needs; using methods, systems and materials that won't deplete resources or harm natural cycles.

 **as you read**

Establish Your Purpose

Now, read and annotate the article. Focus on the major points of information. Read to discover what colleges are doing to promote a safe environment for the students of today and for future generations.

Actively Process While You Read

Monitor your comprehension as you read. (See Chapter 2, "Monitoring Questions," page 40.) Be sure to stop and reflect at the conclusion of each paragraph. Ask yourself the following questions:

- Did I understand that paragraph?
- What is the main idea?
- Am I ready to continue?

Highlight the most important points. Write notes in the margin, and move on.

The Green Campus: How to Teach New Respect for the Environment?

The 3 R's: Reduce Your Carbon Footprint, Reuse, and Recycle

By Anne Underwood

---

1   If you attended this year's commencement at Williams College in western Massachusetts, you probably sampled the fresh cinnamon gelato made from locally produced, hormone-free milk. You might have tried the organic greens with edible chive blossoms (purple, of course, the Williams color) or sampled the fresh asparagus—all from nearby farms. These dishes not only tasted better than standard fare but also saved fossil fuels normally used to ship food long distances. Disposable plates and cutlery were nowhere to be found, reducing trash by 80 percent. And the rare disposable items were ecofriendly. "We used compostable paper napkins and biodegradable straws," says Stephanie Boyd, who helped organize the "green commencement" as part of her job as chair of Williams's climate-action committee.

2   It was not a stunt to impress parents. More and more colleges are getting serious about going green. In June, 284 university presidents representing some of the nation's most influential schools announced an agreement pledging to make their campuses "carbon neutral." The message was clear. "We're saying that sustainability is no longer an elective," says Cornell president David Skorton.

3   Their motivation wasn't merely to reduce energy consumption and waste. As a $315 billion **sector** of the economy—and one that will train future leaders—higher education has a special responsibility to encourage environmental stewardship. The university presidents hope that even students who don't pursue increasingly popular majors in environmental studies will learn simply from being on a green campus, living in green buildings, eating sustainable food and absorbing everyday messages of conservation. And who knows? Far-reaching environmental programs may create an air of excitement that attracts applicants. "In the long run, students will say, 'Why would I want to go to a school that doesn't care about this?'" says Michael Crow, president of Arizona State University, which has made a major commitment to sustainability.

4   At Harvard, going green starts before students even arrive on campus, when freshmen receive mailings urging them to buy only energy-efficient refrigerators for their dorm rooms and purchase compact fluorescent bulbs, which use an average of 18 watts apiece instead of 75. But some of the most effective **lobbying** comes from students themselves. Harvard pays 20 undergraduates to help get the green message out to fellow students in a fun way. That might mean whipping up a competition between residential houses to win the **coveted** Green Cup for the greatest energy reductions and biggest increases in recycling. Or it could be organizing trash-free dances or green movie nights ("Who Killed the Electric Car?") with free ice cream for anyone who brings a recyclable bowl. One day a year, students collect trash from Harvard Yard and pile it into a single heap, dubbed "Mount Trashmore." The giant mound reminds students how much they are throwing away—and how much waste they could avoid by recycling. Students even compete to come up with the best eco-themed cartoons. This year's second-place winner showed Marilyn Monroe with her **iconic** billowing skirt under the caption, "Wind does great things." The fun adds up to serious savings. "Energy use in the dorms has decreased 15 percent over the past few years, and recycling has risen 40 percent," says Leith Sharp, head of the Harvard Green Campus **Initiative.**

5   At many schools, the construction of a new building is another chance to push green solutions. "What message does a conventional campus send?" asks David Orr, who teaches environmental studies at Oberlin. "It sends the message that energy is cheap and plentiful." At Oberlin and other colleges, administrators are seeking to reverse that message with energy-efficient buildings. The Lewis Center at Oberlin, opened in 2000, was one of the first. It's powered entirely by solar arrays, which produce 30 percent more energy than the building consumes—and this is in cloudy Ohio. Sensors throughout the building monitor energy use. And all wastewater is purified on site in a "living machine," an artificial wetland with carefully selected tropical plants and microorganisms that filter the water. Located in the building's lobby, the living machine looks like a greenhouse. "You'd have no clue it's a wastewater system," says Orr. It even includes an indoor waterfall, powered by the sun, with 600 gallons of water flowing across a rocky surface. As long as the sun is shining, the water flows. Orr credits the building with having helped to inspire hundreds of Oberlin students to choose professions in ecodesign, architecture and related fields—including Sadhu Johnston, class of 1998, who joined other students in brainstorming ideas for the new building and who now works as environment commissioner of Chicago.

6   If buildings can influence people, so can something as profound as the food we eat. Melina Shannon-DiPietro of the Yale Sustainable Food Project says she tries to "seduce students into the sustainable-food movement" with tasty dishes. Favorites include grass-fed-beef burgers from a nearby farmers' cooperative and pizzas made with organic flour, heirloom tomatoes and organic basil. In all, 40 percent of the university's menu items now come from local organic farms. "Most food travels 1,500 miles before we eat it," she says. "It doesn't taste fresh, and transporting it long distances adds to the university's carbon footprint." Eating locally and organically solves those problems. And, as students learn from placards in the dining halls, the benefits don't stop there. "Connecticut loses farmland at the rate of 8,000 to 9,000 acres

a year," says Shannon-DiPietro. "Supporting local farmers helps maintain a working agricultural landscape."

7   For those who want to go the extra carbon-neutral mile and formally study the environment, the possibilities are expanding. Sustainability has become a multi-disciplinary field that goes beyond ecology and biodiversity to embrace architec-ture, engineering, urban planning, economics and public health. Arizona State has just opened an entire School of Sustainability that will start taking undergradu-ates in the fall of 2008, drawing faculty from 25 departments. "Sustainability is the **linchpin,**" says Oberlin's Orr. "If you get it right, it reduces dependence on Middle East oil, cuts carbon emissions, takes care of pollution, reduces health-care costs associated with pollution, and creates jobs." ASU is now working on the employment aspect, set-ting up a high-tech business park to draw **innovative,** eco-oriented businesses from around the world—and to provide internships and, ultimately, employment for stu-dents. Early occupants include a Chinese water-purification company and a firm mak-ing lenses that focus more sunshine onto solar panels, **generating** added power for less money.

8   As vigorously as colleges are encouraging students to research environmental problems, students are **prodding** colleges to purchase renewable energy and set ambitious carbon targets. In part because of student lobbying, Middlebury Col-lege in Vermont adopted a goal of carbon neutrality by 2016, says Nan Jenks-Jay, dean of environmental affairs. "Students were telling us, 'You're not doing enough,'" she says. Undergrads at dozens of schools have gone so far as to vote for increases in their activities fees to help finance green initiatives. At St. Mary's College of Maryland, for example, 93 percent of students voted last spring for a $25 annual increase in fees, which will raise approximately $45,000 a year for the purchase of renewable energy.

9   There is, of course, room for improvement. "Not a single campus is even close to achieving sustainability at this point," says Richard Olson of Kentucky's Berea College, which aims to reduce its energy consumption 45 percent below 2000 levels by 2015. "Colleges need to get out ahead and model truly sustainable behavior to society."

10   Many students are helping to do just that. This June, a group of 11 Dartmouth students struck out across the country in a big green school bus fueled by waste oil from fast-food restaurants. The bus itself contains the filters that make the french-fry grease usable. Stopping at parks and music festivals, the vehicle became "a sci-ence fair on wheels," says senior Brent Butler. But for sheer creativity, few top Allison Rogers, Harvard class of 2004. After wrestling with her feminist principles, she ran for and won the 2006 Miss Rhode Island title on a green platform and spent the next year delivering a version of Al Gore's slide show to schools and civic groups. It may be an inconvenient truth—but her post gave Rogers a very convenient way to spread the word.

 **after you read**

Review Important Points

Going over major points after you read, while the information is fresh in your mind, will help you to recall the content and record key ideas.

| **Exercise 3** | **Reviewing Important Points** |

Directions: Choose the best answer for each of the following questions using information provided in the selection. You may need to go back to the text and reread certain portions to be sure your responses are verifiable and accurate.

d 1. **Williams College has adopted an eco-friendly policy:**
  a. because it wants to impress parents.
  b. to comply with parents' insistence that the college serve more organic foods.
  c. since students prodded the administration to become more mindful of the environment.
  d. as part of the work of the climate-action committee.

d 2. **In paragraph 3, the article states that colleges are motivated to adopt environmentally friendly policies for all of the following reasons** *except:*
  a. to train future leaders for environmental careers.
  b. to help students learn about the importance of conservation.
  c. to attract applicants to environmental programs of study.
  d. to create an air of excitement about living in green buildings.

c 3. **What do selected students at Harvard do to promote respect for the environment?**
  a. send out mailings to freshmen
  b. offer sums of money to fellow students as an incentive
  c. design green competitions and programs
  d. give out free ice cream on movie night

b 4. **What is the main idea of paragraph 5?**
  a. Colleges are restoring old structures on campuses.
  b. Many colleges are constructing energy-efficient buildings.
  c. Oberlin College was one of the first colleges to build an energy-efficient structure.
  d. Many students are majoring in ecodesign, architecture, and related fields.

d 5. **What is one of the benefits of eating organically grown food?**
  a. Students will become healthier.
  b. Students will learn to like organic food.

c. Colleges will no longer have to pay to transport food.

d. Colleges will be able to cut back on fuel or energy consumption.

_d_ 6. **Why is Arizona State University designing courses that address sustainability?**

a. They want to create awareness about the environment.

b. They want to expand their major offerings to students.

c. They want to reduce pollution.

d. They want to prepare students for all kinds of employment opportunities.

_c_ 7. **Formal study of the environment includes all of the following *except*:**

a. majors in engineering, architecture, urban planning, economics, and public health.

b. courses in ecology and biodiversity.

c. employment opportunities at a Chinese water-purification company and in the Middle East.

d. opportunities for internships.

_c_ 8. **In addition to collegewide efforts, what are students doing to protect the environment?**

a. purchasing renewable energy products

b. conducting research on environmental problems

c. voting to raise activity fees to help finance green initiatives

d. raising funds for their college's green initiatives

_d_ 9. **Off campus, a former student is continuing to spread the green message by:**

a. purchasing cars that use waste oil.

b. singing songs about the environment.

c. displaying slide shows at parks and music festivals.

d. speaking publicly about the importance of preserving the environment.

_c_ 10. **What is the overall main idea of this selection?**

a. Colleges are now beginning to focus on the importance of buying locally produced, organic food.

b. Colleges are not truly serious about going green.

c. Colleges and college students are making an increasing commitment to sustainable environmental practices.

d. Colleges are now offering programs and courses in environmental studies.

_a_ 11. **The overall pattern of organization is _____.**

a. cause and effect

b. comparison and contrast

c. definition

d. listing or enumeration

   c **12. The purpose of this article is to:**

      a. persuade.
      b. instruct.
      c. inform.
      d. illustrate.

   d **13. Who is the intended audience for this article?**

      a. college presidents
      b. college students
      c. parents
      d. the general public

Organize the Information

Organizing the information you have discovered in a reading selection shows you have understood it and provides you with a useful study tool. (See Chapter 9.)

> **Exercise 4**   **Organizing the Information**

Directions: In paragraphs 5–13, the author discusses what some colleges have done to demonstrate their concern about the environment and also create awareness about the importance of sustainability. Use the details from the reading to complete the following table.

The Green Campus

	Examples of Green Solutions	How the Solution Saves Energy
Food	____*Organic*____ and locally grown	Saves ____*fossil fuel*____
Products	____*Disposable*____ plates and cutlery, ____*compostable*____ napkins and ____*biodegradable*____ straws	____*Reduces*____ trash by 80%
	Compact florescent bulbs	Uses ____*18 watts*____ instead of 74 watts
Construction	____*Energy-efficient*____ buildings	Uses ____*solar*____ energy and purify ____*wastewater*____

Integrate the Vocabulary

Make the new vocabulary *your* vocabulary.

Exercise 5   **Integrating the Vocabulary**

Directions: On the line provided, write a word or a form of the word from the vocabulary list at the beginning of the selection that could replace the italicized, boldfaced word or phrase in the sentence.

1. The ***introduction of a new program*** to serve the needs of working students is the "Weekend College"; all the classes are held Friday evening through Sunday afternoon.

   initiative

2. The Office of Student Activities offered a scholarship of $500 to any student who developed an ***advanced or forward thinking*** way to promote environmental awareness on campus.

   innovative

3. Prof. Ash ***nudged*** his students to hand in extra assignments to increase their final grade by five points.

   prodded

4. The Center for Academic Success is the ***central point*** for all help centers and tutorial services at the college.

   linchpin

5. Brandon Jones was honored to receive the ***much desired*** "Student Leadership Award" for all of his work on student activities.

   coveted

6. The Spanish Language Club ***made*** enough money from its latest bake sale to bring in an international dance troupe for the upcoming Multicultural Fair.

   generated

7. Some of the professors in the marketing department worked in the private ***segment*** of the business industry prior to teaching at the college.

   sector

8. The Student Advocacy Group tried ***to influence*** the administration to get a greater voice in college policies that impact students, such as registration procedures.

   lobby

Make Personal Connections Through Writing and Discussion

When you make new learning relevant to yourself in some way, it becomes more meaningful and long lasting. Whenever you read, try to connect to the content on a personal level. How does it relate to you? How can you apply what you have read to other situations? What else would you like to know?

Exercise 6   **Making Personal Connections**

Directions: Think about yourself in relation to the article you have just read. Apply the information you learned from reading it to respond to the following questions.   *Answers will vary.*

1. Work with a group of students and collaborate on one of the following projects:

   ■ Create an ecofriendly poster.

   ■ Write an ecothemed poem, song or slogan.

   ■ Generate a list of ways to increase student awareness of the importance of environmental issues on your campus.

2. Take a tour of your college campus. Make a list of eco-oriented initiatives you would introduce at your college. Make recommendations for how these plans should be instituted.

3. Write a 250-word argumentative essay in which you defend your response to the following statement:

   All college students should be required to take a course in environmental studies.

Independent Reading
Textbook Reading Selection: Environmental Science

What Can Individuals Do?

"Green Washing" Can Mislead Consumers

By William P. Cunningham and Mary Ann Cunningham

This selection is from an environmental science textbook chapter titled "What Can Individuals Do?" The excerpt focuses on the impact of business and marketing on the consumer.

◀◀ before you read

Answer the following questions before you read the textbook selection on consumers and the environment.

- Think about the food and products you purchase in the supermarket. Do you read the labels on the products you buy?

  _____

  _____

- If you are checking to see if a product is environmentally friendly, which words or phrases do you look for? Check off the words or terms that apply.

  - nontoxic   _____
  - biodegradable   _____
  - recyclable   _____
  - reusable   _____
  - compostable   _____
  - natural   _____
  - organic   _____

- After you've made your purchase, are you confident that you are helping the environment? What other information would you want to know about the product you have bought?

  _____

  _____

  _____

Prepare to Read

Preview the textbook selection using the THIEVES strategy on page 37.

Exercise 1   **Developing Preview Questions**

Directions: Based on your preview, write *three* questions you anticipate will be answered in the selection.

1. *What is green washing and how can this mislead consumers?*

2. *What are the limitations of green consumerism?*

3. *In addition to green consumerism, what else can be done to effect a change in the environment?*

Check Out the Vocabulary

The following words from this textbook selection are likely to appear in academic writing across many disciplines. Be sure you know their meanings.

> ### Academic Word List
>
> **accessible**   easy to approach, use, or enter
>
> **consumer**   a person who purchases a product or service for personal use
>
> **institution**   an organization, foundation, or establishment devoted to a particular cause
>
> **range**   to vary within limits, cover, encompass
>
> **sustainable**   meeting the needs of the present without compromising the needs of future generations

Exercise 2   **Checking Out the Vocabulary**

Directions: Complete each of the following sentences with a word from the preceding Academic Word List.

1. Contrary to popular belief, the number of ____consumers____ who are concerned about the environment is actually quite low.

2. The number of people in the United States who are seriously worried about the environment ____ranges____ from between 13 to 16 percent.

3. One of the reasons that consumers do not buy "green" products is that they are often not easily ____accessible____.

4. By eating foods that are produced locally, which do not require fuel to transport them, we can participate in the ____sustainable____ food movement that helps promote the environment.

5. As ____institutions____ of higher education, colleges have the obligation to prepare students for important careers in environmental studies, such as engineering, urban planning, and architecture.

 **as you read**

Establish Your Purpose

Now, read and annotate the selection. Focus on major points of information and important supporting details.

 ## Actively Process While You Read

Highlight the most important points as you read. Write your notes in the margins and move on.

What Can Individuals Do?
"Green Washing" Can Mislead Consumers
By William P. Cunningham and Mary Ann Cunningham

1   Although many people report they prefer to buy products and packaging that are socially and ecologically **sustainable,** there is a wide gap between what **consumers** say in surveys about purchasing habits and the actual sales data. Part of the problem is **accessibility** and affordability. In many areas, green products aren't available or are so expensive that those on limited incomes . . . can't afford them. Although businesses are beginning to recognize the size and importance of the market for "green" merchandise, the variety of choices and the economies of scale haven't yet made them as accessible as we would like.

2   Another problem is that businesses, eager to cash in on this premium market, offer a great deal of confusing and often misleading claims about the sustainability of their offerings. Consumers must be wary to avoid "green scams" that sound great but are actually only overpriced standard items. Many terms used in advertising are vague and have little meaning. For example:

- "Nontoxic" suggests that a product has no harmful effects on humans. Since there is no legal definition of the term, however, it can have many meanings. How non-toxic is the product? And to whom? Substances not poisonous to humans can be harmful to other organisms.

- "Biodegradable," "recyclable," "reusable," or compostable" may be technically cor-rect but not signify much. Almost everything will biodegrade *eventually*, but it may take thousands of years. Similarly, almost anything is potentially recyclable or reusable; the real question is whether there are programs to do so in your com-munity. If the only recycling or composting program for a particular material is half a continent away, this claim has little value.

- "Natural" is another vague and often misused term. Many natural ingredients—lead or arsenic, for instance—are highly toxic. Synthetic materials are not necessarily more dangerous or environmentally damaging than those created by nature.

- "Organic" can connote different things in different places. There are loopholes in stan-dards so that many synthetic chemicals can be included in "organics." On items such as shampoos and skin-care products, "organic" may have no significance at all. Most detergents and oils are organic chemicals, whether they are synthesized in a laboratory or found in nature. Few of these products are likely to have pesticide residues anyway.

- "Environmentally friendly," "environmentally safe," and "won't harm the ozone layer" are often empty claims. Since there are no standards to define these terms, anyone can use them. How much energy and nonrenewable material are used in manu-facture, shipping, or use of the product? How much waste is generated, and how will the item be disposed of when It Is no longer functional? One product may well be more environmentally benign than another, but be careful who makes this claim.

Certification Identifies Low-impact Products

3   Products that claim to be environmentally friendly are being introduced at 20 times the normal rate for consumer goods. To help consumers make informed

choices, several national programs have been set up to independently and scientifically analyze environmental impacts of major products. Germany's Blue Angel, begun in 1978, is the oldest of these programs. Endorsement is highly sought after by producers since environmentally conscious shoppers have shown that they are willing to pay more for products they know have minimum environmental impacts. To date, more than 2,000 products display the Blue Angel symbol. They **range** from recycled paper products, energy-efficient appliances, and phosphate-free detergents to refillable dispensers.

4   Similar programs are being proposed in every Western European country as well as in Japan and North America. Some are autonomous, nongovernmental efforts like the United States' Green Seal program (managed by the Alliance for Social Responsibility in New York). Others are quasigovernmental **institutions** such as the Canadian Environmental Choice programs.

5   The best of these organizations attempt "cradle-to-grave" life-cycle analysis that evaluates material and energy inputs and outputs at each stage of manufacture, use, and disposal of the product. While you need to consider your own situation in making choices, the information supplied by these independent agencies is generally more reliable than self-made claims from merchandisers.

Green Consumerism Has Limits

6   To quote Kermit the Frog, "It's not easy being green." Even with the help of endorsement programs, doing the right thing from an environmental perspective may not be obvious. Often we are faced with complicated choices. . . .

7   When the grocery store clerk asks you, "Paper or plastic?" you probably choose paper and feel environmentally virtuous, right? Everyone knows that plastic is made from synthetic chemical processes from nonrenewable petroleum or natural gas. Paper from naturally growing trees is a better environmental choice, isn't it? Well, not necessarily. . . . Paper-making consumes water and causes much more water pollution than does plastic manufacturing. Paper mills also can release air pollutants, including foul-smelling sulfides and captans, as well as highly toxic dioxins. . . . The best choice of all is to bring your own reusable cloth bag.

8   Complicated, isn't it? We often must make decisions without complete information, but it's important to make the best choices we can. Don't assume that your neighbors are wrong if they reach conclusions different from yours. They may have valid considerations of which you are unaware. The truth is that simple black and white answers often don't exist.

9   Taking personal responsibility for your environmental impact can have many benefits. Recycling, buying green products, and other environmental actions not only set good examples for your friends and neighbors, they also strengthen your sense of involvement and commitment in valuable ways. There are limits, however, to how much we can do individually through our buying habits and personal actions to bring about the fundamental changes needed to save the earth. Green consumerism generally can do little about larger issues of global equity, chronic poverty, oppression, and the suffering of millions of people in the developing world. There is a danger that exclusive focus on such problems as whether to choose paper or plastic bags, or to sort recyclables . . . will divert our attention from the greater need to change basic institutions.

(Adapted from *Environmental Science: A Global Concern*, Cunningham, 2008)

after you read

Think back to the questions you posed after previewing the selection but before you actually read it. Now that you have read the selection, can you answer your initial questions?

| **Exercise 3** | **Answering Your Preview Questions** |

Directions: If you have discovered the answers to the preview questions you created earlier, write them on the lines provided.

1. _____   *Answers will vary.*
   _____

2. _____
   _____

3. _____
   _____

| **Exercise 4** | **Reviewing Important Points** |

Directions: Choose the best answer for each of the following questions using information provided in the selection.

_c_ 1. **What is one reason consumers do not buy green products?**
   a. They are inferior products.
   b. There are too many products on the shelves.
   c. The labeling of these products is confusing.
   d. Advertisers do not promote green products.

_a_ 2. **In paragraph 2, the author discusses different advertising terms used in green advertising in order to:**
   a. warn consumers about the nature of these claims.
   b. get consumers to feel confident these products help the environment.
   c. let consumers know they should not buy these overpriced products.
   d. inform consumers that all these claims are true.

_c_ 3. **In paragraph 2, we can infer that a product that claims to be "recyclable" but for which there are no recycling facilities nearby:**
   a. can still be sustainable.
   b. may take a thousand years to biodegrade.
   c. will require fuel to transport it to a recycling facility and thereby waste energy.
   d. can be more expensive to transport.

_d_ 4. **What information do certification programs provide to consumers?**
   a. They help them to make informed choices.
   b. They evaluate the material and energy inputs and outputs at every stage of production of an item.
   c. They provide cradle-to-grave analysis.
   d. All of the above.

_c_ 5. In paragraph 6, "It's not easy being green" means:

    a. It is difficult to find green products in supermarkets.

    b. Consumers have to sacrifice a great deal to be environmentally conscious.

    c. Consumers have to question the sustainability of the food and products they buy.

    d. Consumers have to spend a lot of money when buying green products.

_c_ 6. **Why does the author recommend using reusable cloth bags to carry groceries?**

    a. They are the least expensive.

    b. They are made of synthetic material.

    c. They don't pollute the environment.

    d. They are usually the most readily available.

_d_ 7. **According to the author, green consumerism:**

    a. is the only way to save the environment.

    b. can lead to solving other issues, such as global inequities and world poverty.

    c. can help reduce oppression.

    d. is one way to promote environmental awareness.

_c_ 8. **In the final paragraph, we can infer that the real problem with the environment is related to:**

    a. false advertisements.

    b. poor buying habits.

    c. larger social issues.

    d. basic institutions.

_a_ 9. **The overall pattern of organization of this reading is _____.**

    a. cause and effect

    b. definition

    c. comparison and contrast

    d. listing or enumeration

Exercise 5   **Organizing the Information**

Directions: Use your annotations of the reading to complete the following outline of paragraphs 1–5.

Limits to Green Consumerism

I. Factors that prevent people from buying green products

    A. *Inaccessibility:* _____ products are not available

    B. Affordability

        1. Too *expensive* _____

        2. People on limited incomes can't afford these products

C. *Confusing and misleading claims by advertisers*

    1. Green Scams—sound great but are really overpriced standard items

    2. Vague terms with little meaning

       a. *nontoxic*

       b. *biodegradable*

       c. *natural*

       d. *organic*

       e. *environmentally friendly*

II. Programs that help consumers make informed choices

    A. Blue Angel, U.S. Green Seal, and Canadian Environmental Choice

    B. Programs should provide life cycle analysis

       1. *evaluate raw materials*

       2. measure energy *inputs and outputs* at each stage of manufacture

       3. consider use

       4. look at *disposal* of product

Exercise 6   **Using Context Clues**

Directions: Use context clues or the meaning of word parts to discern the meaning of the words or phrases in bold print in the following sentences. Underline any clue words or phrases that help you define the words or terms. The paragraph in which the sentence appears has been indicated for you in parentheses.

Word Parts

auto-   self

bene-   good

co-, com-   together, in conjunction with

equi-   equal

syn-   along with, together

1. If the only recycling or **composting** program for a particular material is a half a continent away, this claim has little value. (2)

   Composting means *recycling of waste material to lessen the burden of landfills and provide benefits to the soil*

2. Most detergents and oils are organic material, whether they are **synthesized** in a laboratory or found in nature. (2)

   Synthesized means *produced*   .

3. **Synthetic** materials are not necessarily more dangerous or environmentally damaging than those created by nature. (2)

   Synthetic means *manufactured, not created by nature*   .

4. "Organic" can **connote** different things in different places. (2)

   Connote means *to suggest or indicate as additional; to designate by implication; to include in the meaning; to imply*   .

5. One product may well be more environmentally **benign** than another, but be careful who makes this claim. (2)

   Benign means *harmless*   .

6. **Endorsement** is highly sought after by producers since environmentally conscious shoppers have shown that they are willing to pay more for products that they know have minimum environmental impacts. (3)

   Endorsement means *approval*   .

7. Some are **autonomous,** nongovernmental efforts like the United States Green Seal Program . . . (4)

   Autonomous means *self-governing*   .

8. When the grocery store clerk asks you, "Paper or plastic?" you probably choose paper and feel environmentally **virtuous,** right? Everyone knows that plastic is made from synthetic chemical processes from nonrenewable petroleum or gas. (7)

   Virtuous means *conforming to ethical principles*   .

9 and 10. Green consumerism generally can do little about larger issues of global **equity,** chronic poverty, **oppression,** and the suffering of millions of people in the developing world. (9)

   Equity means *fairness or equality*   .

   Oppression means *arbitrary and cruel use of power or authority*   .

Exercise 7   **Making Connections Through Writing and Discussion**

Directions: Think about yourself in relation to the article you just read. Apply the information you learned from reading this selection to respond to the following questions.

Answers will vary.

1. If you were to limit your consumption of products and services whose production is causing serious harm to the environment, what would you omit? Which things could you do without, and which things must you keep?

2. List five things you can do to reduce your environmental impact.

3. Write an argumentative essay in which you respond to one of the following topics:

- Poverty causes environmental degradation.
- Businesses are engaging in misleading marketing of green products and services.
- Overreliance on green consumerism cannot protect the environment.
- Activism is crucial to the environmental movement.

Synthesizing Your Reading: Reflective Journal Writing

Environmental Science

Having read three selections on the topic of the environment, you now have a greater understanding and appreciation of what you can do as an individual, a consumer, and as a student to protect and maintain it.

Write a reflective journal entry on the topic of the environment, demonstrating both your knowledge of the content in the selections and your personal viewpoint on the issue. You should write at least one page.

In the first section, briefly summarize each reading selection. Include the thesis and a few key points for each.

Then, in the next section, reflect on what you've learned about environmental issues. What has been the most influential point that has shaped your attitude about sustainability?

Working with Word Parts and Compound Words

Word Parts

Using context clues is one way to discover the meaning of an unfamiliar word. Another method for unlocking its meaning is to analyze word parts.

Word parts—roots, prefixes, and suffixes—make up the words we use every day. In English, many words are formed by adding to the **root** word, the part that contains the basic meaning or definition of the word. Parts that are attached to the beginning of a word are called **prefixes**. They add meaning to the **root** word. Parts that come after the root are called **suffixes**; they can indicate the part of speech or change the meaning of the word. A **compound word** is made when two words are joined to form a new word. Academic disciplines commonly use compound words, often hyphenating them.

The process of **previewing** a selection or textbook chapter is the first step to effective college reading. The word *previewing* can be divided into the following word parts:

Prefix	Root	Suffix
pre-	*view*	*-ing*

The meaning of the prefix *pre-* is *before*.
The meaning of the root *view* is *see*.
The suffix *-ing* means *the act of doing something*.

From studying the word parts, we can understand that **previewing** means *the act of seeing something before*. An actual dictionary definition for the word **previewing** is *an introductory message or overview*. As you can see, a simple analysis of the word parts may lead you to a pretty good understanding of an unfamiliar word.

Prefixes

Prefixes are located at the beginning of words. They change the meaning of root words. For example, when the prefix *pre-* is added to the root word *view*, the word **preview** is formed, meaning *viewing before*. However, if you add the prefix *re-* (again) to the root *view,* the word becomes **review** and the meaning changes to *view again*.

Prefix	Root	Meaning
pre- (before)	*view*	see before
re- (again)	*view*	see again

Answers will vary. Possible answers provided.

Can you think of any other words that contain the prefix *re-*? List them on the lines provided.

1. *revisit*
2. *readjust*
3. *reinforce*
4. *reconsider*
5. *rebuild*

Here are two lists of prefixes: common academic prefixes and number prefixes.

Common Academic Prefixes

Prefix	Meaning	Example	Definition
ante-	before	antebellum	before the war
anti-	against	antifreeze	liquid used to guard against freezing
auto-	self	automatic	self-acting or self-regulating
bene-	good	benefit	an act of kindness; a gift
circum-	around	circumscribe	to draw a line around; to encircle
contra-	against	contradict	to speak against
de-	reverse, remove	defoliate	remove the leaves from a tree
dis-	apart	dislocate	to unlodge
dys-	bad	dysfunctional	not functioning
ecto-	outside	ectoparasite	parasite living on the exterior of animals
endo-	within	endogamy	marriage within the tribe
equi-	equal	equidistant	equal distance
ex-	out	excavate	to dig out
extra-	beyond	extraterrestrial	beyond the earth
hyper-	over	hypertension	high blood pressure
hypo-	under	hypotension	low blood pressure
in-	in	interim	in between
inter-	between	intervene	come between
intra-	within	intramural	within bounds of a school
intro-	in, into	introspect	to look within, as one's own mind
macro-	large	macroscopic	large enough to be observed by the naked eye
mal-	bad	maladjusted	badly adjusted

Prefix	Meaning	Example	Definition
micro-	small	microscopic	so small that one needs a microscope to observe
multi-	many	multimillionaire	one having two or more million dollars
neo-	new	neolithic	new stone age
non-	not	nonconformist	one who does not conform
pan-	all	pantheon	a temple dedicated to all gods
poly-	many	polygonal	having many sides
post-	after	postgraduate	after graduating
pre-	before	precede	to go before
pro-	for	proponent	a supporter
proto-	first	prototype	first or original model
pseudo-	false	pseudonym	false name; esp., an author's pen-name
re-, red-	back again	rejuvenate	to make young
re-, red-	together	reconnect	to put together again
retro-	backward	retrospect	a looking back on things
semi-	half	semicircle	half a circle
sub-	under	submerge	to put under water
super-	above	superfine	extra fine
tele-	far	telescope	seeing or viewing afar
trans-	across	transalpine	across the Alps

(Pauk, Walter. *How to Study in College,* 4th ed., 1989.)

Number Prefixes

uni-	one	*quad-*	four	*sept-*	seven
mono-	one	*tetra-*	four	*hept-*	seven
bi-	two	*quint-*	five	*oct-*	eight
duo-	two	*pent-*	five	*nov-*	nine
di-	two	*sex-*	six	*dec-*	ten
tri-	three	*hex-*	six		

The best way to learn prefixes is to study them in groups based on their meaning. In the following exercise, you will practice using prefixes that mean *not*.

USING PREFIXES I

Directions: The prefixes that mean *not* are: *in-, il-, im-* and *ir-*. They appear in words such as **inactive** (not active), **illegal** (not legal), **improper** (not proper), and **irregular** (not regular). Match the words in the column on the left with their definitions in the column on the right, and write your answers in the spaces provided.

Column 1	Column 2
_g_ 1. illiterate	a. not by one's own choice
_e_ 2. illogical	b. deprived of reason and sound judgment
_h_ 3. immature	c. not following a set of manners
_d_ 4. immoral	d. not conforming to the patterns of socially acceptable behavior
_c_ 5. improper	e. contrary to the rules of logic
_f_ 6. inarticulate	f. lacking the ability to express oneself in clear and effective speech
_j_ 7. inconclusive	g. unable to read or write
_a_ 8. involuntary	h. emotionally underdeveloped
_b_ 9. irrational	i. not reliable or trustworthy
_i_ 10. irresponsible	j. without final results or outcome

Caution: Sometimes a word will contain a prefix such as *in-*, but it will have a different meaning from *not*. For example, the word **inflammable** does not mean *not* flammable; on the contrary, it means capable of being set on fire. **Inflammable** and **flammable** are actually synonyms.

A helpful hint for checking the meaning of a prefix is to see how the word is used in the sentence. Look at the sentences below.

> Most clothing and household textiles are **inflammable.** For example, if you leave a hot iron on a cotton shirt too long, the heat will scorch the shirt and can start a fire.

Here the example in the second sentence tells us that **inflammable** means capable of being set on fire. Materials that *cannot* be set on fire are called **nonflammable.**

USING PREFIXES II

Directions: In this exercise, you will practice using prefixes that are opposite in meaning to each other. Look at the meanings of the prefixes in the following textbox. Then, write the words that follow the box next to their correct definitions.

Prefix	Meaning
bene-	good
mal-	bad
hyper-	over
hypo-	under
ante-	before
post-	after
sub-	below
over-	more
inter-	between
intra/intro-	within

antecedent   hypochondria   maltreatment   subconscious
benevolent   intervention   overanalyze
hypersensitive   introverted   postoperative

1. *hypersensitive* excessive or highly sensitive
2. *maltreatment* treat in a rough and cruel way
3. *antecedent* one that comes before, precursor
4. *overanalyze* to devote an extreme amount of time to researching a situation
5. *benevolent* expressing goodwill or kindly feelings
6. *introverted* concentrated upon oneself, shy or reserved
7. *hypochondria* chronic or abnormal anxiety about a physical symptom
8. *postoperative* period of time following surgery
9. *intervention* care provided to improve a situation such as when a doctor prescribes treatment for his patient
10. *subconscious* operating in the mind beneath the consciousness level

Roots

A **root** or stem is the basic part of a word to which other parts are added. The meaning of a word changes by the addition of prefixes and/or suffixes.

Examples

Root	Meaning	Example	Definition
script	write	**in**scribe	engrave or dedicate a book to someone
		manuscript	document
		postscript	P.S., an afterthought in a correspondence
		prescribe (verb)	write a recommendation for medication
		prescript**ion** (noun)	medicine
		transcript**ion**	record or copy
dic, dict	say, tell	**bene**dic**tion**	blessing
		dict**ator**	tyrant
		dict**ionary**	list of vocabulary with definitions
		indict	accuse, charge with a crime
		predict	expect something to happen

Becoming familiar with common roots will help you to figure out the meanings of many new and unfamiliar words and terms.

The root *spec* means *to see*. It appears in words like **inspect** (to look at carefully) and **spectacular** (showy or amazing). Can you define the following words that contain this root? Write the meanings in the spaces provided. Check your dictionary if you are unsure.

1. aspect   *way something looks or appears*
2. inspector   *someone who looks at something closely and critically*
3. perspective   *the appearance of something as determined by the position of the viewer*
4. spectacles   *eyeglasses*
5. spectator   *a close observer*

Following is a list of common root words and their meanings.

Common Word Roots

Root	Meaning	Example	Definition
agri	field	agronomy	field-crop production and soil management
anthropo	man	anthropology	the study of man
astro	star	astronaut	one who travels in interplanetary space
bio	life	biology	the study of life
cardio	heart	cardiac	pertaining to the heart
cede	go	precede	to go before
chromo	color	chromatology	the science of colors
demos	people	democracy	government by the people
derma	skin	epidermis	the outer layer of skin
dyna	power	dynamic	characterized by power and energy
geo	earth	geology	the study of the earth
helio	sun	heliotrope	any plant that turns toward the sun
hydro	water	hydroponics	growing of plants in water reinforced with nutrients
hypno	sleep	hypnosis	a state of sleep induced by suggestion
ject	throw	eject	to throw out
magni	great, big	magnify	to enlarge, to make bigger
man(u)	hand	manuscript	written by hand
mono	one	monoplane	airplane with one wing
ortho	straight	orthodox	right, true, straight opinion
pod	foot	pseudopod	false foot
psycho	mind	psychology	study of the mind in any of its aspects
pyro	fire	pyrometer	an instrument for measuring temperatures
script	write	manuscript	hand written
terra	earth	terrace	a raised platform of earth
thermo	heat	thermometer	instrument for measuring heat
zoo	animal	zoology	the study of animals

(From Walter Pauk, *How to Study in College,* 4th ed. [Orlando, FL: Houghton Mifflin Harcourt, 1989].)

USING ROOTS

Directions: Look at the meanings of the common roots in the following textbox. Then, write the words that follow the box next to their correct definitions. Use the lists of prefixes and suffixes on pages A-2 and A-9 if you need additional help decoding the meaning of the words.

Prefix	Meaning
aud-	hear
cred-	believe
cephal-	head
graph-	write
log-	study
neuro-	nerve
spec-	see
vent-	come

auditory	inconspicuous	introspective	retrospective
electroencephalograph	incredulous	neurology	
grapheme	intervention	neuropsychology	

1. _retrospective_ looking back, contemplating past experiences

2. _intervention_ interference or involvement; care provided to improve a situation, an action intended to relieve an illness

3. _incredulous_ expressing disbelief

4. _neurology_ medical science that deals with the nervous system and disorders affecting it

5. _auditory_ perceived through and resulting from a sense of hearing

6. _inconspicuous_ readily not noticeable

7. _electroencephalograph_ an instrument for measuring or recording brain activity

8. _introspective_ to consider one's own internal state or feeling

9. _neuropsychology_ a branch of psychology that deals with the relations between the brain and mental functions

10. _grapheme_ a minimal unit in a system of writing

Suffixes

Suffixes added to the end of a verb can change the verb tense. When you add -d or -ed to the end of a verb, the verb is changed to the simple past.

Examples

discuss+ed: Yesterday, we *discussed* the impact of Sigmund Freud on the science of psychology.

develop+ed, define-d: Late in the nineteenth century, Freud *developed* the theory of psychoanalysis, which he *defined* as the analysis of internal and mostly unconscious forces.

Suffixes also change a word's part of speech. For example, adding *-ion* or *-tion* (the action of doing something) to the verbs *discuss* and *define*, changes them to nouns.

discuss (verb), to talk about, + *-ion* → **discussion** (noun), talking about, sharing views with others

define (verb), to make clear or distinct + *-tion* → **definition** (noun), a statement of the meaning of a word, as given in a dictionary for instance.

Other examples:

alert (verb) + *-ness* = **alertness** (noun)

sick (adjective) + *-ly* = **sickly** (adverb)

weak (adjective) + *-en* = **weaken** (verb)

Look at the verbs in column A of the following list. In column B, add the suffixes *-d* or *-ed,* and write the simple past tense form. In column C, add *-ion, -sion, -ation,* or *-tion* (action) to the verbs in column A and write the noun forms. You may want to check the dictionary for correct spellings.

A	B	C
Verbs	**Past Tense**	**Nouns**
1. add	added	addition
2. culminate	culminated	culmination
3. decide	decided	decision
4. educate	educated	education
5. explain	explained	explanation
6. inform	informed	information
7. initiate	initiated	initiation
8. organize	organized	organization
9. revise	revised	revision
10. saturate	saturated	saturation

Other suffixes provide meaning. For example, the suffix *-or* means *a person that does something,* so the word **instructor** means *a person who instructs or teaches.* The suffixes *-an, -ar, -er, -ist* also mean *a person who does something.* Look at the following examples and try to think of additional words that contain the same suffix.

-or   instructor   _____, _____, _____

-an   librarian   _____, _____, _____

-ar   scholar   _____, _____, _____

-er   philosopher   _____, _____, _____

-ist   chemist   _____, _____, _____

Following are several lists of common suffixes with examples of how they are used to form nouns, adjectives, adverbs, and verbs.

Common Suffixes

Suffix	Meaning	Example
Used to Form Nouns		
-age, -ance, -cy, -ence, -ion, -ism, -ity, -ment, -ness, -tion, -tude, -ure	state, condition, act, quality	action, adjustment, assistance, attitude, bankruptcy, communism, conversation, intelligence, kindness, mixture, percentage, sanity
-an, -ar, -er, -ist, -or	a person or thing that does something	librarian, liar, scholar, dispatcher, dispenser, cartoonist, administrator
-cle, -cule	small	corpuscle, molecule
-ology	study of	sociology
Used to Form Adverbs		
-ly	in the manner of	slowly, unlikely
Used to Form Nouns or Adjectives		
-ful	full of	teaspoonful, helpful
-ant, -ary, -ent, -ery, -ory	one who, quality of, place for	assistant, adversary, recipient, robbery, advisory
Used to Form Adjectives		
-able, -ible	able to be	memorable, flexible
-ac, -al, -an, -en, -em, -ic, -eous, -ious, -ous	like, having the quality related to	democratic, minimal, American, brazen, western, Islamic, courteous, anxious, boistrous
-ive	one who is, that which is	additive, aggressive
-less	full of	useless, worthless
Used to Form Verbs		
-ate, -en, -ify, -ize	to make	liberate, weaken, magnify, criticize

(Adapted from www1.fccj.edu/lchandouts/communicationshandouts/vocabularyhandouts/V-3.doc)

USING SUFFIXES

Directions: The suffixes in the following textbox convey a special meaning. Use your knowledge of word parts to write the definition or meaning of each of the words below it in the spaces provided. Check your dictionary for more complete definitions.

Suffix	Meaning	Example
-or, -er,	a person or one who	teacher, professor
-ist	one who does or practices	psychologist
-ist	one who believes, supports or studies an idea	conformist
-ism	doctrine, system	behaviorism
-ology	the study of	psychology
-ogy		

1. behaviorism *system of studying behavior as a way to understand human psychology*
2. collector *someone who collects things, usually as a hobby, like paintings and stamps*
3. egocentrism *self-centered, regarding oneself as the center of everything*
4. interpreter *someone who interprets or translates from one language to another*
5. negativism *behavior characterized by a refusal to follow the suggestions of others without any logical reasons*
6. nonconformist *someone who does not adhere to the attitudes and customs of others*
7. pathology *the examination of tissues and performance of laboratory study to diagnose disease*
8. perfectionist *a belief that everything has to be perfect*
9. psychiatrist *a doctor who specializes in the diagnosis and treatment of mental, emotional, or behavioral disorders*
10. radiology *the study of diseases through the use of x-rays and other forms of radiant energy*

USING WORD PARTS

Directions: The words in this exercise come from a psychology textbook. Look at the meanings of the word parts located in the textbox. Then match the words that follow the box with their correct meanings on the lines provided.

Prefixes		Roots		Suffixes	
anti-	against	cogn	know	-al	adjective: pertaining to
as-	toward	gen	race, kind	-ar	adjective: related to
bi-	two	path	feeling	-ate	verb: to make
em-	in	sim	like		
in-	not	soc	join	-ic	adjective: quality or state quality
poly-	many	somus	sleep	-ive	adjective: having the
post-	after			-y	noun: characteristic of

antisocial	cognitive	insomnia	sociocultural
assimilate	empathy	polygraph	
bipolar	genotype	posttraumatic	

1. _genotype_ a sum total of all the genes passed on from parent to child

2. _polygraph_ an instrument that is used to record heart beat, blood pressure and respiration, usually used as a lie detector test

3. _antisocial_ behavior in which the rights of others are persistently violated

4. _sociocultural_ combination of social and cultural elements

5. _empathy_ identifying or understanding of another's situation or feelings

6. _cognitive_ pertaining to the mental processes of thinking as opposed to emotion

7. _bipolar_ a major psychological disorder characterized by episodes of mania and depression

8. _insomnia_ sleeplessness

9. _posttraumatic_ something occurring after a physical or psychological shocking situation

10. _assimilate_ to be absorbed to a prevailing culture or to incorporate as if your own

Compound Words

A compound word is made when two words are joined to form a new word. You are already familiar with many compound words used in spoken and written language—for example, *freshman, course work*, and *textbook*. Academic disciplines commonly use this type of word, often hyphenating them. Understanding the separate words can assist you in your quest for just the right meaning of an unfamiliar word or term.

Examples

eyewitness   eye + witness = a person who actually sees an act and can give an account of what he or she saw

wholehearted   whole + hearted = fully sincere, enthusiastic and energetic

self-awareness   self + awareness = awareness of oneself, including behaviors and feelings

DECODING COMPOUND WORDS

Directions: Match the following compound words with their definitions. Remember to consider the meaning of each part of the compound word to find the correct definition.

daydream	fantasy-prone	long-term memory	underachiever
drug-induced	flashback	self-conscious	
extraordinary	framework	sleepwalker	

1. _sleepwalker_ a person who performs actions while sleeping
2. _drug-induced_ a state caused by the introduction of drugs
3. _long-term memory_ a system of unlimited capacity to remember information
4. _self-conscious_ excessively aware of how others see you
5. _underachiever_ one who achieves below what is expected
6. _flashback_ recurrent memories of a traumatic experience
7. _framework_ the basis of viewing reality
8. _daydream_ to dream while you are awake
9. _fantasy-prone_ characterized by engaging in fantasies
10. _extraordinary_ exceptional, beyond what is normal or usual

Appendix 2

Working with Resources and Strategies to Improve Vocabulary

You can use many resources and strategies to help you read effectively and build your college vocabulary. Consult a **dictionary** to find the exact meaning of new words, search for related word forms, and find synonyms for new vocabulary. Use a **glossary,** an alphabetical list of words that relate to specialized topics or specific disciplines, to locate the meaning of new and unfamiliar terminology. Go to a thesaurus to discover **synonyms** or **antonyms.**

Using Dictionaries

If using context clues or the other strategies discussed in Chapter 3 does not provide you with a complete enough understanding of unfamiliar words, you might want to consult a dictionary. A good collegiate dictionary, such as *Merriam-Webster's Collegiate Dictionary,* or an electronic one, such as *Franklin's Dictionary & Thesaurus,* are helpful tools.

*A word of caution: B*ecause many words have multiple meanings, you will still need to consider the context of the word you are looking up. As you look at the listing of definitions, locate the one that seems to fit best and substitute for the word in the sentence. If it makes sense, you have probably selected the best definition. Also, consider the parts of speech, because many words can be used in different forms.

Parts of Speech

noun (n) a word indicating a person, place or thing

verb (v) a word that expresses action or existence

adjective (adj.) a word that is used to qualify (describe) or limit the meaning of a noun

adverb (adv.) a word that is used to qualify or limit a verb or adjective or another adverb

pronoun (pron.) a word that replaces a noun that was previously stated

preposition (prep.) a word that shows the relationship between nouns, pronouns, or phrases

Now look at the following example:

> B.F. Skinner's work increased society's attention to the **broad** issue of motivation. A **key** behaviorist assumption is that poor performance should not be attributed to laziness or bad attitude.
>
> (*Psychology*, Passer & Smith)

Here is the dictionary entry for the word **broad** taken from *The Merriam-Webster Online Dictionary*.

---

¹**broad** adjective 1 **a:** having ample extent from side to side or between limits <*broad* shoulders> **b:** having a specified extension from side to side <made the path 10 feet *broad*> 2: extending far and wide: SPACIOUS <the *broad* plains> 3 **a:** OPEN, FULL <*broad* daylight> **b:** PLAIN, OBVIOUS <a *broad* hint> 4: dialectal especially in pronunciation 5: marked by lack of restraint, delicacy, or subtlety: **a:** *obsolete*: OUTSPOKEN **b:** COARSE, RISQUÉ <*broad* humor> 6: *of a vowel*: OPEN—used specifically of *a* pronounced as in *father* 7 **a:** LIBERAL, TOLERANT <*broad* views> **b:** widely applicable or applied: GENERAL <a *broad* rule> 8: relating to the main or essential points <*broad* outlines>
²**broad** noun 1 *British*: an expansion of a river—often used in plural 2 *often offensive*: WOMAN
³**broad** adverb: in a broad manner: FULLY <*broad* awake>

(Definition of "broad." By permission. From *Merriam-Webster's Collegiate® Dictionary*, 11th Edition ©2010 by Merriam-Webster, Incorporated [www.Merriam-Webster.com].)

In the sample sentence, the word **broad** is used as an adjective to describe the word *issue*, so you can eliminate the meanings that pertain to nouns and adverbs. Now, look at the list of meanings for the adjective form of *broad*, and choose the one that best fits the context of the sentence.

The meaning *general* is the best choice. Now substitute it in the sentence to see if it makes sense.

> B.F. Skinner's work increased society's attention to the **general** issue of motivation.

Now take a look at the dictionary entry for **key.** Read through the definitions and synonyms and decide which definition fits in the context of this sentence.

> A **key** behaviorist assumption is that poor performance should not be attributed to laziness or bad attitude.

---

key *(key) n.* 1. an instrument for opening and closing a lock, valve, circuit, etc. 2. a control lever operated by the fingers, as on a telegraph, typewriter, piano, horn. 3. something explanatory; a translation of cipher, symbols, problems, perplexities, etc. 4. *(Music)* the tonic note or name of a scale; a signature; the tonality implied by a sequence of chords 5. pitch; degree of intensity; tone or mood. 6. a reef or or low island near the coast; cay. –*adj.* principal; fundamental. –*v.t.* provide with a key or reference system.

(*The New American Webster Handy College Dictionary,* 3rd ed., prepared by Philip D. Morehead, a Signet Book, August 1995.)

In this case, **key** is used as an adjective. A good synonym for **key** is *principal* or *fundamental.*

The web has a wide range of online dictionaries, too. At www.Merriam-Webster.com and www.dictionary.com you can find definitions, synonyms, word origins, and even pronunciation sound cues. Many online dictionaries also provide the etymology of words so that you can learn the word origin and understand the word parts.

Here is the entry from www.Merriam-Webster.com about the etymology of the word ***dictionary:***

Origin: Medieval Latin *dictionarium,* from Late Latin *diction-, dictio* word, from Latin, speaking. First Known Use: 1526

(Etymology of "dictionary." By permission. From *Merriam-Webster's Collegiate® Dictionary,* 11th Edition ©2010 by Merriam-Webster, Incorporated [www.Merriam-Webster.com].)

From the etymology of this word, you learn that the root **dictio** means *words,* so when you see this root in words like *diction, dictation, predict,* and *indication,* you will have a clue to the meanings of these words. The suffix -ary means a place as in *glossary* and *library.*

Using Textbook Glossaries

Glossaries contain alphabetical listings of words that relate to specific disciplines or specialized topics. In most college textbooks, you can locate them in the back of the book. Many times, they contain the same words that are in bold print and/or are defined in the margins of the text. The benefit of using a glossary instead of a dictionary is that the definitions relate directly to the subject you are studying, and you do not have to search for a meaning that seems to fit the context of the word you are unfamiliar with.

Following are two examples taken from the glossary of a psychology textbook. These terms may not be found in a traditional dictionary.

deep structure   A linguistic term that refers to an underlying meaning of a spoken or written sentence; the meanings that make up a deep structure are stored as concepts and rules in long-term memory.

long-term memory   Our vast library of more durable stored memories.

(*Psychology,* Passer & Smith)

Using a Thesaurus

Whereas a dictionary assists you in reading and understanding academic language and college-level vocabulary, and a glossary defines the terminology used in a specific discipline, a **thesaurus** is more useful when you are looking for a synonym. **Synonyms** are words that have similar meanings to each other. A **thesaurus** is a book of synonyms (usually organized alphabetically), which often also contain **antonyms,** or words that have opposite meanings. You may find a thesaurus useful in putting ideas into your own words or when you are writing a summary of an article or assignment you have read. Just remember that you will still need to use context clues before you select a synonym or antonym for an unfamiliar word!

Roget's 21st Century Thesaurus, Franklin's Electronic Dictionary, word-processing programs, or online dictionaries can be consulted for synonyms and antonyms. These words will add interest and variety to your writing assignments. Instead of repeating the same word throughout a piece of writing, a thesaurus will provide you with many words that have the same or similar meaning.

The following sentence appears in the selection "The Bilingual Brain."

> In general, it appears that when people **acquire** a second language early in life or learn it to a high degree of proficiency later in life, both languages use a common neural network.

> (*Psychology,* Passer and Smith)

To locate a synonym for the word **acquire,** using a thesaurus, look at this entry:

acquire: come by, gain, get, obtain, procure, secure, win. (Informal) land, pick up, develop, form

(From AHD Staff. *Roget II Thesaurus* 3e 2003. © 2003 Heinle/Arts & Sciences, a part of Cengage Learning, Inc. Reproduced by permission. www.cengage.com/permissions.)

The only word that seems to fit the context about language learning is **develop.** Now confirm your choice by placing the word in the sentence.

> In general, it appears that when people **develop** a second language early (as in learning a new language) in life or learn it to a high degree of proficiency later in life, both languages use a common neural network.

The word **develop** fits the context here, and so it is a good synonym for **acquire.**

Learning synonyms is also a great way to increase your vocabulary. Look at the following entry for the word **language.** See how many words have similar meanings.

Main Entry:	*language*
Part of Speech:	*noun*
Definition:	system of words for communication
Synonyms:	accent, argot, articulation, brogue, cant, communication, conversation, dialect, diction, dictionary, discourse, doublespeak*, expression, gibberish, idiom, interchange, jargon, lexicon, lingua franca, palaver, parlance, patois, phraseology, prose, signal, slang, sound, speech, style, talk, terminology, tongue, utterance, verbalization, vernacular, vocabulary, vocalization, voice, word, wording
Notes:	Don't use "**language**" when you mean "**writing system**"—Chinese is a spoken language with no characters; the Chinese writing system uses thousands of characters

(Roget's 21st Century Thesaurus, 3rd ed. Copyright © 2010 by the Philip Lief Group, Inc. All rights reserved.)
* = informal or slang

Techniques for Learning Vocabulary

1. **Use index cards or flash cards.**

    ■ List new terminology on an index card for easy review and study.

    ■ Write the new term on the blank side of the card and the definition on the lined side.

    ■ For vocabulary words, write synonyms and original sentences using the word. For terminology, provide examples, their context or source, and a picture or diagram that helps you remember the meaning of the word.

    ■ Review these words right after you write them down. Then review them regularly until you have mastered them.

    Here are some examples for learning terminology through the use of index cards:

Side 1

psychological

Side 2

Part of Speech: adjective
Related form: psychology
Pronunciation: si-ko-log-ic-al
Meaning: relating to the mind
Root: *psych-* mind, soul, spirit
Ex. Psychiatry, psychosis, psychopath, psychic, psychobiography
Sentence: I am taking a course in <u>psychology</u> because I am interested in how people think and act.

Side 1

---

physiological

Side 2

(adjective) phys *(fiz)* I o log I cal

Root: *phys-* nature, normal functioning of living things, relating to the body

Ex: physical, physician

Sentence: The nurse checked my <u>physiological</u> signs, such as my heartbeat and blood pressure.

---

2. **Create a split page for new vocabulary words or terms.**
   - Write the new word or term in the left-hand column and its definition on the right.
   - Include additional information that will help you retrieve and remember this word, such as examples, your own sentences, or pictures.

Here is an example of a split page entry:

mnemonic device	a study or technique that aids in remembering, e.g., THIEVES, a previewing technique for textbook reading (title, heading, introduction, every first sentence, vocabulary or visuals, end of chapter questions and summary) or ROY G. BIV (colors: red, orange, yellow, green, blue, indigo and violet)

3. **Make a Personal Vocabulary Journal of new words or terminology.**
   - Use a spiral notebook.
   - Label it "Personal Vocabulary Journal."
   - Date each page.
   - From your lecture notes or textbook reading, compile a list of words you need to learn.
   - Include definitions, examples, sentences, etc.
   - Review these words and terms regularly.

4. **Store new words in an electronic folder.**
   - In your word-processing program, create a file for new vocabulary and/or terminology.
   - Include definitions, sentences, sources, examples, etc. to help you remember these words.

Active Textbook Reading

Learn about different ways people connect in groups and organizations in society as you complete activities in Chapter 2, Are You Ready to Read? Active Reading Strategies for Managing College Texts. The chapter in this Appendix is from *Sociology: A Brief Introduction* by Richard Schaefer.

chapter

GROUPS AND ORGANIZATIONS

Understanding Groups

Understanding Organizations

Case Study: Bureaucracy and the Space Shuttle *Columbia*

The Changing Workplace

Social Policy and Organizations: The State of the Unions

Boxes

SOCIOLOGY IN THE GLOBAL COMMUNITY: Amway the Chinese Way

RESEARCH IN ACTION: Pizza Delivery Employees as a Secondary Group

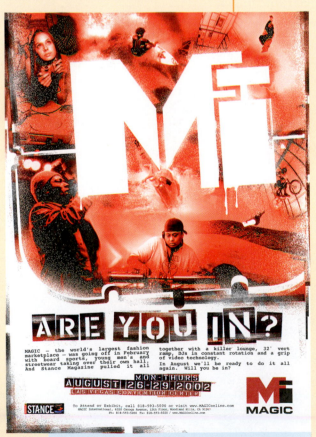

Groups come in all sizes and cover a broad array of interests. This poster is directed to a group of people interested in a marketplace featuring fashions for young men. It asks: "Are you in?"

Ray Kroc (1902–1984), the genius behind the franchising of McDonald's restaurants, was a man with big ideas and grand ambitions. But even Kroc could not have anticipated the astounding impact of his creation. McDonald's is the basis of one of the most influential developments in contemporary society. Its reverberations extend far beyond its point of origin in the United States and in the fast-food business. It has influenced a wide range of undertakings, indeed the way of life, of a significant portion of the world. And in spite of McDonald's recent and well-publicized economic difficulties, that impact is likely to expand at an accelerating rate.

However, this is *not* a book about McDonald's, or even about the fast-food business. . . . I devote all this attention to McDonald's . . . because it serves here as the major example of, and the paradigm for, a wide-ranging process I call *McDonaldization.* . . . As you will see, McDonaldization affects not only the restaurant business but also education, work, the criminal justice system, health care, travel, leisure, dieting, politics, the family, religion, and virtually every other aspect of society. McDonaldization has shown every sign of being an inexorable process, sweeping through seemingly impervious institutions and regions of the world.

Other types of business are increasingly adapting the principles of the fast-food industry to their needs. Said the vice chairman of Toys "R" Us, "We want to be thought of as a

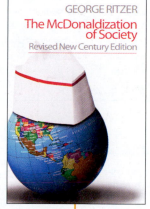

GEORGE RITZER
The McDonaldization of Society
Revised New Century Edition

sort of McDonald's of toys." . . . Other chains with similar ambitions include Gap, Jiffy Lube, AAMCO Transmissions, Midas Muffler & Brake Shops, Great Clips, H&R Block, Pearle Vision, Bally's. . . .

Other nations have developed their own variants of this American institution. . . . Paris, a city whose love for fine cuisine might lead you to think it would prove immune to fast food, has a large number of fast-food croissanteries; the revered French bread has also been McDonaldized. India has a chain of fast-food restaurants, Nirula's, that sells mutton burgers (about 80% of Indians are Hindus, who eat no beef) as well as local Indian cuisine. Mos Burger is a Japanese chain with over fifteen hundred restaurants that in addition to the usual fare, sells Teriyaki chicken burgers, rice burgers, and "Oshiruko with brown rice cake." . . .

McDonald's is such a powerful model that many businesses have acquired nicknames beginning with Mc. Examples include "McDentists" and "McDoctors," meaning drive-in clinics designed to deal quickly and efficiently with minor dental and medical problems; "McChild" care centers, meaning child care centers such as KinderCare; "McStables," designating the nationwide race horse-training operation of Wayne Lucas; and "McPaper," describing the newspaper *USA TODAY.* (Ritzer 2004a:1–4, 10–11) ■ 🌐

Additional information about this excerpt can be found on the Online Learning Center at **www.mhhe.com/schaefer6.**

130   Chapter 6

In this excerpt from *The McDonaldization of Society,* sociologist George Ritzer contemplates the enormous influence of a well-known fast-food organization on modern-day culture and social life. Ritzer defines ***McDonaldization*** as "the process by which the principles of the fast-food restaurant are coming to dominate more and more sectors of American society as well as of the rest of the world" (Ritzer 2004a:1). In his book, he shows how the business principles on which the fast-food industry is founded—efficiency, calculability, predictability, and control—have changed not only the way Americans do business and run their organizations, but the way they live their lives. Today, busy families rely on the takeout meals served up by fast-food establishments, and McDonald's has become a regular meeting place for social groups from adolescents to senior citizens.

Despite the runaway success of McDonald's and its imitators, and the advantages these enterprises bring to millions of people around the world, Ritzer is critical of their effect on society. The waste and environ-mental degradation created by billions of disposable containers and the dehumanized work routines of fast-food crews are two of the disadvantages he cites in his critique. Would the modern world be a better one, Ritzer asks, if it were less McDonaldized?

This chapter considers the impact of groups and organizations on social interaction. Do we behave differently in large groups than in small ones? How do we make large organizations manageable? What effect are current social changes having on the structure of groups? We'll begin by noting the distinctions between various types of groups, with particular attention to the dynamics of small groups. We'll examine how and why formal organizations came into existence and describe Max Weber's model of the modern bureaucracy. In a case study of the loss of the space shuttle *Columbia,* we'll see how NASA's bureaucratic culture contributed to the ship's disastrous accident. Finally, we'll look at recent changes in the workplace, some of which are designed to counteract the failures of bureaucracies. The social policy section at the end of the chapter focuses on the status of organized labor today. ■

UNDERSTANDING GROUPS

Most of us use the term *group* loosely to describe any collection of individuals, whether three strangers sharing an elevator or hundreds attending a rock concert. However, in sociological terms a ***group*** is any number of people with similar norms, values, and expectations who interact with one another on a regular basis. College sororities and fraternities, dance companies, tenants' associations, and chess clubs are all considered examples of groups. The important point is that members of a group share some sense of belonging. This characteristic distinguishes groups from mere *aggregates* of people, such as passengers who happen to be together on an airplane flight, or from *categories* of people—those who share a common feature (such as being retired) but otherwise do not act together.

Consider the case of a college a cappella singing group. It has agreed-on values and social norms. All members want to improve their singing skills and schedule lots of performances. In addition, like many groups, the singing ensemble has both a formal and an informal

structure. The members meet regularly to rehearse; they choose leaders to run the rehearsals and manage their affairs. At the same time, some group members may take on unofficial leadership roles by coaching new members in singing techniques and performing skills.

The study of groups has become an important part of sociological investigation because they play such a key role in the transmission of culture. As we interact with others, we pass on our ways of thinking and acting—from language and values to ways of dressing and leisure activities.

Types of Groups

Sociologists have made a number of useful distinctions between types of groups—primary and secondary groups, in-groups and out-groups, and reference groups.

Primary and Secondary Groups

Charles Horton Cooley (1902) coined the term ***primary group*** to refer to a small group characterized by intimate, face-to-face association and cooperation. The members of a street gang constitute a primary group; so do mem-

Research in Action

6-1   PIZZA DELIVERY EMPLOYEES AS A SECONDARY GROUP

What is it like to deliver pizzas for a living? Most of us give little thought to this question, but sociologists Patrick Kinkade and Michael Katovich did a scientific study of it. For 18 months, one of them worked on delivery crews at three different restaurants in Fort Worth, Texas. Taking an interactionist perspective, this participant observer explored the social relationships that developed among drivers as they worked, waited for orders, or hit the bars after work. Through observation and interview, the two researchers found that drivers formed a tight network based on shared experience—both the ordinary transactions and the occasional dangerous encounters that were part of the job.

Within their culture, the pizza delivery drivers take risks and receive minimal rewards. While attacks on them are usually publicized, they are not documented statistically. But the drivers themselves are well aware of the possible dangers and talk to one another a great deal about them. During the observation period, two drivers were robbed and eight others were "tailed," resulting in four automobile accidents.

The researchers found that the world of this secondary group is "hypermasculine," with racist and sexist overtones. The drivers uniformly characterized the dangers to their safety as coming from members of racial and ethnic communities, even when there was no evidence of their assertion. The drivers also regularly boasted of their sexual prowess, and told and retold accounts of sexual favors they received from customers.

Among the 106 drivers studied by the researchers, five types emerged:

- *The comedian.* This individual uses humor to neutralize or trivialize the anxiety of making runs into neighborhoods perceived as high-risk.
- *The adventurer.* The adventurer claims to invite problems, and actu-

> *Within their culture, the pizza delivery drivers take risks and receive minimal rewards.*

   ally looks forward to testing himself in dangerous situations.
- *The denier.* This individual attempts to neutralize anxiety by suggesting that a problem does not exist or has been exaggerated.
- *The fatalist.* This person recognizes and admits the risk of danger, but simply accepts it without making any effort to neutralize it.
- *The pro.* The pro generally has had a long history in the delivery busi-

ness, having worked for several pizza services, and perhaps served as an assistant manager, if not a manager, at one of the other stores.

While on the job, members of the delivery crew may have seemed like "family" (a primary group), but their interaction was limited strictly to the job. Still, membership in the secondary group was important to the drivers. They accepted their identity as delivery persons and assumed whichever role type they felt most comfortable with. Kinkade and Katovich found that in general, crew members derived more satisfaction from their occupational camaraderie than from the job's monetary rewards. The study shows how, especially in urban environments, people use membership in secondary groups to carve out a niche in the larger social world.

Let's Discuss

1. Think about a secondary group to which you belong. Can you identify any common role types? If so, describe them.
2. If you were to do research like that of Kinkade and Katovich, what group would you choose to study? What research techniques would you use?

Source: Kinkade and Katovich 1997.

bers of a family living in the same household, as do a group of "sisters" in a college sorority.

Primary groups play a pivotal role both in the socialization process (see Chapter 4) and in the development of roles and statuses (see Chapter 5). Indeed, primary groups can be instrumental in a person's day-to-day existence. When we find ourselves identifying closely with a group, it is probably a primary group.

We also participate in many groups that are not characterized by close bonds of friendship, such as large college classes and business associations. The term *secondary group* refers to a formal, impersonal group in which there is little social intimacy or mutual understanding (see Table 6-1, page 132). The distinction between primary and secondary groups is not always clear-cut. Some social clubs may become so large and impersonal that they no longer function as primary groups.

Secondary groups often emerge in the workplace among those who share special understandings about their occupation. Almost all of us have come into contact with people who deliver pizzas. Using observation research, two sociologists have given us a new

132   Chapter 6

understanding of the secondary group ties that emerge in this occupation (see Box 6-1, page 131).

In-Groups and Out-Groups

A group can hold special meaning for members because of its relationship to other groups. For example, people in one group sometimes feel antagonistic to or threatened by another group, especially if that group is perceived as being different either culturally or racially. To identify these "we" and "they" feelings, sociologists use two terms first employed by William Graham Sumner (1906): *in-group* and *out-group*.

An **in-group** can be defined as any group or category to which people feel they belong. Simply put, it comprises everyone who is regarded as "we" or "us." The in-group may be as narrow as a teenage clique or as broad as an entire society. The very existence of an in-group implies that there is an **out-group** that is viewed as "they" or "them." An out-group is a group or category to which people feel they do *not* belong.

In-group members typically feel distinct and superior, seeing themselves as better than people in the out-group. Proper behavior for the in-group is simultaneously viewed as unacceptable behavior for the out-group. This double standard enhances the sense of superiority. Sociologist Robert Merton (1968) described this process as the conversion of "in-group virtues" into "out-group vices." We can see this differential standard operating in worldwide discussions of terrorism. When a group or a nation takes aggressive actions, it usually justifies them as necessary, even if civilians are hurt and killed. Opponents are quick to label such actions with the emotion-laden

"So long, Bill. This is my club. You can't come in."

An exclusive social club is an in-group whose members consider themselves superior to others.

term of *terrorist* and appeal to the world community for condemnation. Yet these same people may themselves retaliate with actions that hurt civilians, which the first group will then condemn.

Conflict between in-groups and out-groups can turn violent on a personal as well as a political level. In 1999 two disaffected students at Columbine High School in Littleton, Colorado, launched an attack on the school that left 15 students and teachers dead, including themselves. The gunmen, members of an out-group that other students referred to as the Trenchcoat Mafia, apparently resented taunting by an in-group referred to as the Jocks. Similar episodes have occurred in schools across the nation, where rejected adolescents, overwhelmed by personal and family problems, peer group pressure, academic responsibilities, or media images of violence, have struck out against more popular classmates.

In-group members who actively provoke out-group members may have their own problems, including limited time and attention from working parents. Sociologists David Stevenson and Barbara Schneider (1999), who studied 7,000 teenagers, found that despite many opportunities for group membership, young people spend an

Table 6-1	Comparison of Primary and Secondary Groups	
Primary Group	**Secondary Group**	
Generally small	Usually large	
Relatively long period of interaction	Relatively short duration, often temporary	
Intimate, face-to-face association	Little social intimacy or mutual understanding	
Some emotional depth in relationships	Relationships generally superficial	
Cooperative, friendly	More formal and impersonal	

summingUP

George Clooney in the motion picture *The Perfect Storm*. Warner Brothers changed the movie's final scene when focus groups reacted negatively to the original ending, which featured the doomed fisherman's final thoughts.

average of three and a half hours alone every day. While youths may claim they want privacy, they also crave attention, and striking out at members of an in-group or out-group, be they the wrong gender, race, or friendship group, seems to be one way to get it.

Use Your Sociological Imagination   www.mhhe.com/schaefer6

Try putting yourself in the shoes of an out-group member. What does your in-group look like from that perspective?

Focus Groups

Another type of group includes people who do not interact on a regular basis. A ***focus group*** is composed of 10 to 15 people assembled by a researcher to discuss a predetermined topic, such as a new consumer product or community needs. Guided by a moderator, the members, who are selected to be representative of the general public, offer their own opinions on the topic and react to other members' views. Focus group members are usually paid for their participation and realize that their views are being recorded.

Focus groups were first developed by Robert Merton (1987) and his colleagues at Columbia University in the early 1940s, to evaluate the relative effectiveness of radio advertising. Today, advertisers and corporations rely heavily on this research method, which Merton called

the *focused interview*. While the corporate world has been the principal user of focus groups over the last six decades, sociologists have recently returned to the method to investigate community opinion and workplace morale. They use the information they receive from the groups to design more extensive qualitative or quantitative research.

Reference Groups

Both in-groups and primary groups can dramatically influence the way an individual thinks and behaves. Sociologists call any group that individuals use as a standard for evaluating themselves and their own behavior a ***reference group***. For example, a high school student who aspires to join a social circle of hip-hop music devotees will pattern his or her behavior after that of the group. The student will begin dressing like these peers, listening to the same tapes and CDs, and hanging out at the same stores and clubs.

Reference groups have two basic purposes. They serve a normative function by setting and enforcing standards of conduct and belief. The high school student who wants the approval of the hip-hop crowd will have to follow the group's dictates at least to some extent. Reference groups also perform a comparison function by serving as a standard against which people can measure themselves and others. An actor will evaluate himself or herself against a reference group composed of others in the acting profession (Merton and Kitt 1950).

Reference groups may help the process of anticipatory socialization. For example, a college student majoring in finance may read the *Wall Street Journal*, study the annual reports of corporations, and listen to midday stock market news on the radio. Such a student is using financial experts as a reference group to which he or she aspires.

Often, two or more reference groups influence us at the same time. Our family members, neighbors, and co-workers all shape different aspects of our self-evaluation. In addition, reference group attachments change during the life cycle. A corporate executive who quits the rat race at age 45 to become a social worker will find new reference groups to use as standards for evaluation. We shift reference groups as we take on different statuses during our lives.

134 Chapter 6

Groups come in all types and sizes. The members of this Manchester, Vermont, group belong to a national club of antique bicycle buffs called the Wheelmen. They take their Victorian-era bicycles out for rides and often dress in period costume from the late 1800s, as shown here.

Studying Small Groups

Sociological research done on the micro level and research done from the interactionist perspective usually focus on the study of small groups. The term *small group* refers to a group small enough for all members to interact simultaneously—that is, to talk with one another or at least be well acquainted. Certain primary groups, such as families, also may be classified as small groups. However, many small groups differ from primary groups in that they do not necessarily offer the intimate personal relationships characteristic of primary groups. For example, a manufacturer may bring together its seven-member regional sales staff twice a year for an intensive sales conference. The salespeople, who live in different cities and rarely see one another, constitute a small secondary group, not a primary group.

We may think of small groups as being informal and unpatterned; yet, as interactionist researchers have revealed, distinct and predictable processes are at work in the functioning of small groups. A long-term ethnographic study of street gangs in Chicago revealed an elaborate structure resembling that of a family business. A street gang there is composed of several geographically based units called sets, each of which possesses a leader, lower-ranking officers, and a rank-and-file membership. Besides staffing the economic network of the drug trade, gang members develop relationships with tenant leaders in public housing projects and participate in nondelinquent so-

cial activities important to the maintenance of their authority in the neighborhood (Venkatesh 2000).

Size of a Group

At what point does a collection of people become too large to be called a small group? That is not clear. In a group with more than 20 members, it is difficult for individuals to interact regularly in a direct and intimate manner. But even within a range of 2 to 20 people, group size can substantially alter the quality of social relationships. For example, as the number of group participants increases, the most active communicators become even more active relative to others. Therefore, a person who dominates a group of 3 or 4 members will be relatively more dominant in a 15-person group.

Group size also has noticeable social implications for members who do not assume leadership roles. In a larger group, each member has less time to speak, more points of view to absorb, and a more elaborate structure to function in. At the same time, an individual has greater freedom to ignore certain members or viewpoints than he or she would in a smaller group. It is harder to disregard someone in a 4-person workforce than someone in an office with 30 employees, harder to disregard someone in a string quartet than someone in a college band with 50 members.

The German sociologist Georg Simmel (1858–1918) is credited as the first sociologist to emphasize the importance of interactive processes within groups and to note how they change as the group's size changes. The simplest of all social groups or relationships is the *dyad,* or two-member group. A wife and a husband constitute a dyad, as does a business partnership or a singing duo. The dyad offers a special level of intimacy that cannot be duplicated in larger groups. However, as Simmel ([1917] 1950) noted, a dyad, unlike any other group, can be destroyed by the loss of a single member. Therefore, the threat of termination hangs over a dyadic relationship perhaps more than over any other.

Obviously, the introduction of one additional person to a dyad dramatically transforms the character of the small group. The dyad becomes a three-member group, or *triad.* The third member has many ways of interacting with and influencing the dynamics of the group. The new person may play a *unifying* role in the triad. When a married couple has their first child, the baby may serve to bind the group closer together. A newcomer also may play a *mediating* role in a three-person group. If two roommates are perpetually sniping at each other, the third roommate may attempt to remain on good terms with both and to arrange compromise solutions to problems. Finally, a member of a triad can choose to employ a *divide-and-rule* strategy. Such is the case, for example, with a coach who tries to gain greater control over two assistants by making them rivals (Nixon 1979).

Coalitions

As groups grow to the size of triads or larger, coalitions begin to develop. A **coalition** is a temporary or permanent alliance geared toward a common goal. Coalitions can be broad-based or narrow and can take on many different objectives. Sociologist William Julius Wilson (1999b) has described community-based organizations in Texas that include Whites and Latinos, working class and affluent, who have banded together to work for improved sidewalks, better drainage systems, and comprehensive street paving. Out of this type of coalition building, Wilson hopes, will emerge better interracial understanding.

Some coalitions are intentionally short lived. Short-term coalition building is a key to success in popular TV programs like *Survivor*. In *Survivor I*, broadcast in 2000, the four members of the "Tagi alliance" banded together to vote fellow castaways off the island. The political world is also the scene of many temporary coalitions. For example, in 1997 big tobacco companies joined with anti-smoking groups to draw up a settlement for reimbursing states for tobacco-related medical costs. Soon after the settlement was announced the coalition members returned to their decades-long fight against each other (Pear 1997).

The effects of group size and coalitions on group dynamics are but two of the many aspects of the small group that sociologists have studied. Another aspect, conformity and deviance, is examined in Chapter 8. Although it is clear that small-group encounters have a considerable influence on our lives, we are also deeply affected by much larger groups of people, as we'll see in the next section.

Survivor: All-Stars featured 18 former champions of the popular reality TV series. Short-term coalition building has been one of the keys to success in the mock struggle for survival.

UNDERSTANDING ORGANIZATIONS

Formal Organizations and Bureaucracies

As contemporary societies have shifted to more advanced forms of technology and their social structures have become more complex, our lives have become increasingly dominated by large secondary groups referred to as *formal organizations*. A **formal organization** is a group designed for a special purpose and structured for maximum efficiency. The U.S. Postal Service, McDonald's, the Boston Pops orchestra, and the college you attend are all examples of formal organizations. Though organizations vary in their size, specificity of goals, and degree of efficiency, they are all structured to facilitate the management of large-scale operations. They also have a bureaucratic form of organization, described in the next section.

In our society, formal organizations fulfill an enormous variety of personal and societal needs and shape the lives of every one of us. In fact, formal organizations have become such a dominant force that we must create organizations to supervise other organizations, such as the Securities and Exchange Commission (SEC) to regulate brokerage companies. While it sounds much more exciting to say that we live in the "computer age" than to say that ours is the "age of formal organization," the latter is probably a more accurate description of our times (Azumi and Hage 1972; Etzioni 1964).

136   Chapter 6

Whistle-blower Colleen Rowley, an FBI agent, tried unsuccessfully to bring her superiors' attention to a French Moroccan who had signed up for pilot training at a local flight school, keen to operate a 747. The man later used his training to crash a hijacked jet into the World Trade Center. Rowley was photographed as she testified before the Senate Judiciary Committee in June 2002.

Ascribed statuses such as gender, race, and ethnicity can influence how we see ourselves within formal organizations. For example, a study of women lawyers in the nation's largest law firms found significant differences in the women's self-images, depending on the relative presence or absence of women in positions of power. In firms in which fewer than 15 percent of partners were women, the female lawyers were likely to believe that "feminine" traits were strongly devalued, and that masculinity was equated with success. As one female attorney put it, "Let's face it: this is a man's environment, and it's sort of Jock City, especially at my firm." Women in firms where female lawyers were better represented in positions of power had a stronger desire for and higher expectations of promotion (Ely 1995:619).

Characteristics of a Bureaucracy

A ***bureaucracy*** is a component of formal organization that uses rules and hierarchical ranking to achieve efficiency. Rows of desks staffed by seemingly faceless people, endless lines and forms, impossibly complex language, and frustrating encounters with red tape—all these unpleasant images have combined to make *bureaucracy* a dirty word and an easy target in political campaigns. As a result, few people want to identify their occupation as "bureaucrat," despite the fact that all of us perform various bureaucratic tasks. Elements of bureaucracy enter into almost every occupation in an industrial society.

Max Weber ([1913–1922] 1947) first directed researchers to the significance of bureaucratic structure. In an important sociological advance, Weber emphasized the basic similarity of structure and process found in the otherwise dissimilar enterprises of religion, government, education, and business. Weber saw bureaucracy as a form of organization quite different from the family-run business. For analytical purposes, he developed an ideal p. 11 type of bureaucracy that would reflect the most characteristic aspects of all human organizations. By ***ideal type*** Weber meant a construct or model for evaluating specific cases. In actuality, perfect bureaucracies do not exist; no real-world organization corresponds exactly to Weber's ideal type.

Weber proposed that whether the purpose is to run a church, a corporation, or an army, the ideal bureaucracy displays five basic characteristics. A discussion of those characteristics, as well as the dysfunctions of a bureau- p. 14 cracy, follows. Table 6-2 (opposite) summarizes the discussion.

1. Division of labor.   Specialized experts perform specific tasks. In your college bureaucracy, the admissions officer does not do the job of registrar; the guidance counselor doesn't see to the maintenance of buildings. By working at a specific task, people are more likely to become highly skilled and carry out a job with maximum efficiency. This emphasis on specialization is so basic a part of our lives that we may not realize that it is a fairly recent development in Western culture.

The downside of division of labor is that the fragmentation of work into smaller and smaller tasks can divide workers and remove any connection they might feel to the overall objective of the bureaucracy. In *The Communist Manifesto* (written in 1848), Karl Marx and Friedrich Engels charged that the capitalist system reduces workers to a mere "appendage of the machine" (Feuer 1989). Such a work arrangement, they wrote, produces extreme ***alienation***—a condition of estrangement or dissociation from the surrounding society. According to both Marx and conflict theorists, restricting workers to very small tasks also weakens their job security, since new employees can be easily trained to replace them.

Although division of labor has certainly enhanced the performance of many complex bureaucracies, in some cases it can lead to ***trained incapacity;*** that is, workers become so specialized that they develop blind spots and fail to notice obvious problems. Even worse, they may not care about what is happening in the next

summingUP

Table 6-2	**Characteristics of a Bureaucracy**		
		Negative Consequence	
Characteristic	**Positive Consequence**	**For the Individual**	**For the Organization**
Division of labor	Produces efficiency in a large-scale corporation	Produces trained incapacity	Produces a narrow perspective
Hierarchy of authority	Clarifies who is in command	Deprives employees of a voice in decision making	Permits concealment of mistakes
Written rules and regulations	Let workers know what is expected of them	Stifle initiative and imagination	Lead to goal displacement
Impersonality	Reduces bias	Contributes to feelings of alienation	Discourages loyalty to company
Employment based on technical qualifications	Discourages favoritism and reduces petty rivalries	Discourages ambition to improve oneself elsewhere	Fosters Peter principle

department. Some observers believe that such developments have caused workers in the United States to become less productive on the job.

In some cases, the bureaucratic division of labor can have tragic results. In the wake of the coordinated attacks on the World Trade Center and the Pentagon on September 11, 2001, Americans wondered aloud how the FBI and CIA could have failed to detect the terrorists' elaborately planned operation. The problem, in part, turned out to be the division of labor between the FBI, which focuses on domestic matters, and the CIA, which operates overseas. Officials at these intelligence-gathering organizations, both of which are huge bureaucracies, are well known for jealously guarding information from one another. Subsequent investigations revealed that they knew about Osama bin Laden and his al-Qaeda terrorist network in the early 1990s. Unfortunately, five federal agencies—the CIA, FBI, National Security Agency, Defense Intelligence Agency, and National Reconnaissance Office—failed to share their leads on the network. Although the hijacking of the four commercial airliners used in the massive attacks may not have been preventable, the bureaucratic division of labor definitely hindered efforts to defend against terrorism and actually undermined U.S. national security.

2. Hierarchy of authority. Bureaucracies follow the principle of hierarchy; that is, each position is under the supervision of a higher authority. A president heads a college bureaucracy; he or she selects members of the administration, who in turn hire their own staff. In the

Roman Catholic Church, the pope is the supreme authority; under him are cardinals, bishops, and so forth.

3. Written rules and regulations. What if your sociology professor gave your classmate an A for having such a friendly smile? You might think that wasn't fair, that it was against the rules.

Rules and regulations, as we all know, are an important characteristic of bureaucracies. Ideally, through such procedures, a bureaucracy ensures uniform performance of every task. Thus your classmate cannot receive an A for a nice smile, because the rules guarantee that all students will receive essentially the same treatment.

Through written rules and regulations, bureaucracies generally offer employees clear standards for an adequate (or exceptional) performance. In addition, procedures provide a valuable sense of continuity in a bureaucracy. Individual workers will come and go, but the structure and past records of the organization give it a life of its own that outlives the services of any one bureaucrat.

Of course, rules and regulations can overshadow the larger goals of an organization to the point that they become dysfunctional. What if a hospital emergency room physician failed to treat a seriously injured person because he or she had no valid proof of U.S. citizenship? If blindly applied, rules no longer serve as a means to achieving an objective, but instead become important (and perhaps too important) in their own right. Robert Merton (1968) used the term *goal displacement* to refer to overzealous conformity to official regulations.

138 Chapter 6

4. Impersonality. Max Weber wrote that in a bureaucracy, work is carried out *sine ira et studio,* "without hatred or passion." Bureaucratic norms dictate that officials perform their duties without giving personal consideration to people as individuals. Although this norm is intended to guarantee equal treatment for each person, it also contributes to the often cold and uncaring feeling associated with modern organizations. We typically think of big government and big business when we think of impersonal bureaucracies. In some cases, the impersonality that is associated with a bureaucracy can have tragic results, as the case study of the *Columbia* space shuttle disaster on pages 141–142 shows. More frequently, it produces frustration and disaffection. Today, even small firms screen callers with electronic menus.

5. Employment based on technical qualifications. Within the ideal bureaucracy, hiring is based on technical qualifications rather than on favoritism, and performance is measured against specific standards. Written personnel policies dictate who gets promoted, and people often have a right to appeal if they believe that particular rules have been violated. Such procedures protect bureaucrats against arbitrary dismissal, provide a measure of security, and encourage loyalty to the organization.

In this sense, the "impersonal" bureaucracy can be considered an improvement over nonbureaucratic organizations. College faculty members, for example, are ideally hired and promoted according to their professional qualifications, including degrees earned and research published, rather than because of whom they know. Once they are granted tenure, their jobs are protected against the whims of a president or dean.

Although any bureaucracy ideally will value technical and professional competence, personnel decisions do not always follow this ideal pattern. Dysfunctions within bureaucracy have become well publicized, particularly because of the work of Laurence J. Peter. According to the *Peter principle,* every employee within a hierarchy tends to rise to his or her level of incompetence (Peter and Hull 1969). This hypothesis, which has not been directly or systematically tested, reflects a possible dysfunctional outcome of advancement on the basis of merit. Talented people receive promotion after promotion, until, sadly, some of them finally achieve positions that they cannot handle with their usual competence (Blau and Meyer 1987).

The five characteristics of bureaucracy, developed by Max Weber more than 80 years ago, describe an ideal type rather than precisely defining an actual bureaucracy. Not every formal organization will possess all five of Weber's characteristics. In fact, wide variation exists among actual bureaucratic organizations.

Bureaucratization as a Process

Have you ever had to speak to 10 or 12 individuals in a corporation or government agency just to find out which official has jurisdiction over a particular problem? Ever been transferred from one department to another until you finally hung up in disgust? Sociologists have used the term *bureaucratization* to refer to the process by which a group, organization, or social movement becomes increasingly bureaucratic.

Normally, we think of bureaucratization in terms of large organizations. But bureaucratization also takes place within small-group settings. Sociologist Jennifer Bickman Mendez (1998) studied domestic houseworkers employed in central California by a nationwide franchise. She found that housekeeping tasks were minutely defined, to the point that employees had to follow 22 written steps for cleaning a bathroom. Complaints and special requests went not to the workers, but to an office-based manager.

Oligarchy: Rule by a Few

Conflict theorists have examined the bureaucratization of social movements. The German sociologist Robert Michels (1915) studied socialist parties and labor unions in Europe before World War I and found that such organizations were becoming increasingly bureaucratic. The emerging leaders of these organizations—even some of the most radical—had a vested interest in clinging to power. If they lost their leadership posts, they would have to return to full-time work as manual laborers.

Through his research, Michels originated the idea of the *iron law of oligarchy,* which describes how even a democratic organization will eventually develop into a bureaucracy ruled by a few (called an oligarchy). Why do oligarchies emerge? People who achieve leadership roles usually have the skills, knowledge, or charismatic appeal (as Weber noted) to direct, if not control, others. Michels argued that the rank and file of a movement or organization look to leaders for direction and thereby reinforce the process of rule by a few. In addition, members of an oligarchy are strongly motivated to maintain their leadership roles, privileges, and power.

Michels's insights continue to be relevant today. Contemporary labor unions in the United States and Western Europe bear little resemblance to those organized spontaneously by exploited workers. Conflict theorists have pointed to the longevity of union leaders, who are not always responsive to the needs and demands of the membership, and seem more concerned with maintaining their own positions and power. (The social policy section at the end of this chapter focuses on the status of labor unions today.)

Sociology in the Global Community

6-2   AMWAY THE CHINESE WAY

Amway began in 1959, when two young men in Michigan began a person-to-person merchandise marketing system. Today, more than 3.6 million individuals in 80 countries distribute Amway cosmetics, food supplements, and home care products. Distributors will often gather friends and neighbors at a party designed to persuade them to buy the company's products, or better yet, to become distributors themselves. Distributors' ability to line up customers who become distributors themselves, and in turn line up still more customers and distributors, has been critical to the company's success. Thus, primary group ties have become the tool of a large, bureaucratic business organization.

Amway entered China in 1995, followed closely by rival direct sellers like Avon and Mary Kay. China's more than 1 billion residents, combined with its growing acceptance of capitalistic business practices, made it an attractive market for these Western merchandisers. And Amway's emphasis on building sales networks through relatives and friends seemed a perfect fit for Chinese culture, in which personal recommendations are considered especially persuasive. After

just two years, Amway had 80,000 distributors in China. But in 1998, the Chinese government suddenly outlawed Amway's operation, accusing the company of fostering "weird cults, triads, superstitious groups, and hooliganism."

What had happened? Apparently Amway's success had produced a host of copycats, some of them con artists peddling dubious merchandise. Government officials complained, too, about the pro-

> To do business globally, Amway has successfully reinvented its business model.

motional hoopla at Amway's sales meetings, which featured songs, sloganeering, and other Western-style activities designed to encourage organizational bonding. To the Chinese, these innocuous activities suggested a cult-like fervor.

Facing the loss of their Chinese investments, Amway and other direct marketers asked the U.S. trade representative to intervene. After intense pressure, the Chinese government agreed to a partial

reversal of the ban on direct selling. Under new regulations issued in 1998, Amway, Avon, and Mary Kay are permitted to sell their products through conventional retail outlets. They can also employ salespeople to go door to door, but those salespeople cannot receive any income from signing up new distributors. Despite this handicap, China is now Amway's fourth largest market worldwide. In 2002 sales were four times what they were before the government ban on direct selling. To do business globally, Amway has successfully reinvented its business model.

Let's Discuss

1. Have you ever bought merchandise from a direct seller like Amway, perhaps at a party? If so, who introduced you to the organization? Were you comfortable with its merchandising methods? Explain.
2. Can you think of another kind of bureaucratic organization, other than a business, that exploits its members' ties to primary groups in order to grow? Analyze the organization and its operating methods from a sociological point of view.

Sources: Amway 1999, 2003; L. Chang 2003; C. Hill 2003; Wonacott 2001.

Bureaucracy and Organizational Culture

How does bureaucratization affect the average individual who works in an organization? The early theorists of formal organizations tended to neglect this question. Max Weber, for example, focused on the management personnel within bureaucracies but had little to say about workers in industry or clerks in government agencies.

According to the ***classical theory*** of formal organizations, also known as the ***scientific management approach,*** workers are motivated almost entirely by economic rewards. This theory stresses that only the physical constraints on workers limit their productivity. Therefore, workers may be treated as a resource, much like the

machines that began to replace them in the 20th century. Under the scientific management approach, management attempts to achieve maximum work efficiency through scientific planning, established performance standards, and careful supervision of workers and production. Planning involves efficiency studies but not studies of workers' attitudes or job satisfaction.

Not until workers organized unions—and forced management to recognize that they were not objects—did theorists of formal organizations begin to revise the classical approach. Along with management and administrators, social scientists became aware that informal groups of workers have an important impact on organizations (Perrow 1986). An alternative way of considering bureaucratic dynamics, the ***human relations approach,***

140   Chapter 6

The AARP is a voluntary association of people ages 50 and older, both retired and working, that advocates for the needs of older Americans. A huge organization, it has been instrumental in maintaining Social Security benefits to retirees. Here AARP volunteers staff a phone bank in an effort to get out the vote in Des Moines, Iowa.

menter's expectations. The major focus of the Hawthorne studies, however, was the role of social factors in workers' productivity. One aspect of the research concerned the switchboard-bank wiring room, where 14 men were making parts of switches for telephone equipment. The researchers discovered that these men were producing far below their physical capabilities. The discovery was especially surprising because the men would have earned more money if they had produced more parts.

What accounted for such an unexpected restriction of output? The men feared that if they produced switch parts at a faster rate, their pay rate might be reduced, or some of them might lose their jobs. As a result, this group of workers had established their own (unofficial) norm for a proper day's work and created informal rules and sanctions to enforce it. Yet management was unaware of these practices and actually believed that the men were working as hard as they could (Roethlisberger and Dickson 1939).

emphasizes the role of people, communication, and participation in a bureaucracy. This type of analysis reflects the interest of interactionist theorists in small-group behavior. Unlike planning under the scientific management approach, planning based on the human relations perspective focuses on workers' feelings, frustrations, and emotional need for job satisfaction.

The gradual move away from a sole focus on the physical aspects of getting the job done—and toward the concerns and needs of workers—led advocates of the human relations approach to stress the less formal aspects of bureaucratic structure. Informal groups and social networks within organizations develop partly as a result of people's ability to create more direct forms of communication than under the formal structure. Charles Page (1946) used the term *bureaucracy's other face* to refer to the unofficial activities and interactions that are such a basic part of daily organizational life. As Box 6-2 (page 139) shows, some direct merchandising companies have capitalized on the existence of informal groups and social networks to build their organizations—though in China they have run into trouble with the formal government bureaucracy.

A series of classic studies illustrates the value of the human relations approach. The Hawthorne studies alerted sociologists to the fact that research subjects may ◀ p. 39 alter their behavior to match the experi-

Today, research on formal organizations is following new avenues. First, the proportion of women and minority group members in high-level management positions is still much lower than might be expected, given their numbers in the labor force. Researchers are now beginning to look at the impact this gender and racial/ethnic imbalance may have on managerial judgment, both formal and informal. Second, a company's power structure is only partly reflected in its formal organizational charts. In practice, core groups tend to emerge to dominate the decision-making process. Very large corporations—say, a General Electric or a Procter & Gamble—may have hundreds of interlocking core groups, each of which plays a key role in its division or region (Kleiner 2003).

Voluntary Associations

In the mid-19th century, the French writer Alexis de Tocqueville noted that people in the United States are "forever forming associations." By 2003, there were more than 444,000 voluntary associations in a U.S. national database. *Voluntary associations* are organizations established on the basis of common interest, whose members volunteer or even pay to participate. The Girl Scouts of America, the American Jewish Congress, the Kiwanis Club, and the League of Women Voters are all considered voluntary associations; so, too, are the American Association of Aardvark Aficionados, the Cats on Stamps Study Group, the Mikes of America, the New York Corset Club, and the William Shatner Fellowship (Gale Group 2003).

The categories of "formal organization" and "voluntary association" are not mutually exclusive. Large voluntary associations such as the Lions Club and the Masons have structures similar to those of profit-making corporations. At the same time, certain formal organizations, such as the Young Men's Christian Association (YMCA) and the Peace Corps, have philanthropic and educational goals usually found in voluntary associations. The Democratic Party and the United Farm Workers union are considered examples of voluntary associations. Even though membership in a political party or union can be a condition of employment and therefore not genuinely voluntary, political parties and labor unions are usually included in discussions of voluntary associations.

Participation in voluntary associations is not unique to the United States. This textbook's author attended a carnival in London featuring bungee-jumping, at which participants were expected to jump from a height of 180 feet. Skeptics were given assurances of the attraction's safety by being told that the proprietor belonged to a voluntary association: the British Elastic Rope Sports Association. An analysis of 15 industrial nations, including the United States, showed that active memberships in voluntary associations typically increased during the 1980s and 1990s. Only relatively inactive memberships in religious organizations and labor unions have showed a decline. On the whole, then, voluntary associations are fairly healthy (Baer et al. 2000).

Voluntary associations can provide support to people in preindustrial societies. During the post–World War II period, migration from rural areas of Africa to the cities was accompanied by a growth in voluntary associations, including trade unions, occupational societies, and mutual aid organizations developed along old tribal lines. As people moved from the *Gemeinschaft* of the countryside to the [p. 118] *Gesellschaft* of the city, these voluntary associations provided immigrants with substitutes for the extended groups of kinfolk in their villages (Little 1988).

Voluntary associations in the United States are largely segregated by gender. Half of them are exclusively female, and one-fifth are all-male. Because the exclusively male associations tend to be larger and more heterogeneous, in terms of the background of members, all-male associations hold more promise for networking than all-female groups. Although participation varies across the population of the United States, most people belong to at least one voluntary association (see Figure 6-1), while more than one-fourth maintain three or more memberships.

The importance of voluntary associations—and especially of their unpaid workers (or volunteers)—is increasingly being recognized. Traditionally, society has devalued unpaid work, even though the skill levels, experience, and training demands are often comparable with those of wage labor. Viewed from a conflict perspective, the critical difference has been that women perform a substantial amount of volunteer work. Feminists and conflict theorists agree that like the unpaid child care and household labor of homemakers, the effort of volunteers has too often been ignored by scholars—and awarded too little respect by the larger society—because it is viewed as "women's work." Failure to recognize women's volunteerism obscures a critical contribution women make to a society's social structure (Daniels 1987, 1988).

FIGURE 6-1

Membership in Voluntary Associations in the United States

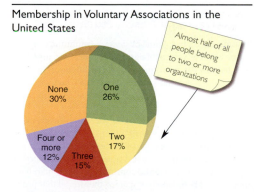

Almost half of all people belong to two or more organizations

Source: J. Davis and Smith 2001:347.

Think About It
How many voluntary associations do you belong to? What functions do they serve?

CASE STUDY: BUREAUCRACY AND THE SPACE SHUTTLE *COLUMBIA*

In February 2003, the space shuttle *Columbia* disintegrated as it reentered the earth's atmosphere. Seven astronauts died in the accident, which was blamed at first on a piece of foam weighing less than two pounds that had struck the spacecraft's wing during liftoff. But by August, the *Columbia* Accident Investigation Board (2003) had identified a second cause: NASA's bureaucratic organizational culture.

142   Chapter 6

The board's blistering report cited NASA's emphasis on bureaucratic rules and regulations at the expense of astronauts' safety. Though engineers had voiced safety concerns over the years, especially after the shuttle *Challenger*'s explosion in 1986, their memos rarely reached the top of NASA's hierarchy, where costs and scheduling were considered paramount. In fact, the organization's culture discouraged the expression of safety concerns (Vaughan 1996, 1999). When engineers tried to obtain special images of the *Columbia*'s wing during its last flight, so they could check for damage, managers denied their request. Aside from cost concerns, officials may have been unwilling to admit that something had gone wrong. In general, hierarchical organizations tend to encourage the concealment of mistakes.

Another part of the problem was that over the years, foam debris had fallen during liftoff in about 10 percent of NASA's launches, without disastrous results. Officials had come to expect that a shower of debris might occur, and to speak of it as an "acceptable risk." Rather than treating it as a safety issue, they labeled it a maintenance problem. Thus, bureaucratic rules and regulations that were meant to highlight such a serious risk may have had the unintended consequence of obscuring it.

Investigators had condemned the "acceptable risk" attitude following the *Challenger* explosion in 1986, but NASA's organizational culture had not changed. In a bureaucratic organization, bringing about real change can be extremely difficult. Thus, in the wake of the second disaster, members of the *Columbia* Accident Investigation Board (2003:13) predicted, "The changes we recommend will be difficult to accomplish—and will be internally resisted."

In a hangar at the Kennedy Space Center, members of the team charged with reconstructing the space shuttle *Columbia* examine what remains of the front landing gear. Damage to the ship's protective tiles, which might have been prevented by stricter adherence to safety standards, caused the disaster. Historically, insufficient attention to safety hazards has been a problem at NASA, a huge government bureaucracy with an emphasis on cost and efficiency.

THE CHANGING WORKPLACE

Weber's work on bureaucracy and Michels's thinking on oligarchy are still applicable to the organizational structure and culture of the workplace. But today's factories and offices are undergoing rapid, profound changes unanticipated a century or more ago. Besides the far-reaching impact of technological advances such as computerization, workers must cope with organizational restructuring. This section will detail the dramatic changes evident in today's workplace.

Organizational Restructuring

To some extent, individual businesses, community organizations, and government agencies are always changing, if only because of personnel turnover. But since the late 20th century, formal organizations have been experimenting with new ways of getting the job done, some of which have significantly altered the workplace.

Collective decision making, or the active involvement of employee problem-solving groups in corporate management, first became popular in the United States in the 1980s. Management gurus had noted the dazzling success of Japanese automobile and consumer products manufacturers. In studying these companies, they found that problem-solving groups were one key to success. At first, such groups concentrated on small problems at specific points in the production line. But today, these groups often cross departmental and divisional boundaries to attack problems rooted in the bureaucratic division of labor. Thus, they require significant adjustment by employees long used to working in the bureaucracy (Ouchi 1981).

Another innovation in the workplace, called *minimal hierarchy,* replaces the traditional bureaucratic hierarchy of authority with a flatter organizational structure. Minimal hierarchy offers workers greater access to those in authority, giving them an opportunity to voice concerns that might not be heard in a traditional bureaucracy. This new organizational structure is thought to minimize the potential for costly and dangerous bureaucratic oversights. Clearly, hierarchical barriers to the expression of workers' concerns contributed to the *Challenger* and *Columbia* disasters.

Finally, organizational *work teams* have become increasingly common, even in smaller organizations. There are two types of work team. *Project teams* address ongoing issues, such as safety or compliance with the Americans with Disabilities Act. *Task forces* pursue nonrecurring issues, such as a major building renovation. In both cases, team members are released to some degree from their regular duties in order to contribute to the organizationwide effort (W. Scott 2003).

The common purpose of work teams, minimal hierarchy, and collective decision making is to empower workers. For that reason, these new organizational structures can be exciting for the employees who participate in them. But these innovations rarely touch the vast numbers of workers who perform routine jobs in factories and office buildings. The 22 million part-time workers and 1 million full-time workers who earn the minimum wage or less know little about organizational restructuring (Bureau of Labor Statistics 2004b).

Work teams are becoming an increasingly common form of organizational restructuring. Members of this team are brainstorming ways to address the needs of the disabled.

Telecommuting

Increasingly, in many industrial countries, workers are turning into telecommuters. *Telecommuters* are employees who work full-time or part-time at home rather than in an outside office, and who are linked to their supervisors and colleagues through computer terminals, phones, and fax machines (see Chapter 16). One national survey showed that next to on-site day care, most office workers want virtual offices that allow them to work off-site. Not surprisingly, the number of telecommuters increased from 8.5 million in 1995 to 28 million in 2001 (Donald B. Davis and Polonko 2001).

What are the social implications of this shift toward the virtual office? From an interactionist perspective, the workplace is a major source of friendships; restricting face-to-face social opportunities could destroy the trust that is created by "handshake agreements." Thus, telecommuting may move society further along the continuum from *Gemeinschaft* to *Gesellschaft.* On a more positive note, telecommuting may be the first social change that pulls fathers and mothers back into the home rather than pushing them out. The trend, if it continues, should also increase autonomy and job satisfaction for many employees (Castells 2001; DiMaggio et al. 2001).

Use Your Sociological Imagination

If your first full-time job after college involved telecommuting, what do you think would be the advantages and disadvantages of working out of a home office? Do you think you would be satisfied as a telecommuter? Why or why not?

Electronic Communication

Electronic communication in the workplace has generated some heat lately. On the one hand, e-mailing is a convenient way to push messages around, especially with the CC (carbon copy) button. It's democratic, too:

144   Chapter 6

lower-status employees are more likely to participate in e-mail discussion than in face-to-face communications, giving organizations the benefit of their experience and views (DiMaggio et al. 2001).

But e-mail doesn't convey body language, which in face-to-face communication can soften insensitive phrasing and make unpleasant messages (such as a reprimand) easier to take. It also leaves a permanent record, which can be a problem if messages are written thoughtlessly. In an antitrust case that the federal government brought against Microsoft in 1998, the prosecutors used as evidence e-mail sent to and from Microsoft's CEO Bill Gates. Finally, as will be discussed in detail in Chapter 16, companies can monitor e-mail as a means of "watching" their employees. Dartmouth professor Paul Argenti advises those who use e-mail, "Think before you write. The most important thing to know is what not to write" (Gwynne and Dickerson 1997:90).

SOCIAL POLICY and ORGANIZATIONS	The State of the Unions

The Issue

How many people do you know who belong to a labor union? Chances are you can name a lot fewer people than someone could 50 years ago. In 1954, unions represented 39 percent of workers in the private sector of the U.S. economy; in 2002 they represented only 13 percent. What has happened to diminish the importance of organized labor today? Have unions outlived their usefulness in a rapidly changing global economy that is dominated by the service sector (AFL-CIO 2001; Bureau of Labor Statistics 2004a)?

Members of the South Florida Carpenters union join together to support one another and demonstrate their strength. In recent decades economic change has eliminated many union jobs, reducing unions' membership and weakening their bargaining power.

The Setting

Labor unions consist of organized workers who share either the same skill (as in electronics) or the same employer (as in the case of postal employees). Unions began to emerge during the Industrial Revolution in England, in the 1700s. Groups of workers banded together to extract concessions from employers (e.g., safer working conditions, a shorter workweek), as well as to protect their positions. They frequently tried to protect their jobs by limiting entry to their occupation based on gender, race, ethnicity, citizenship, age, and sometimes rather arbitrary measures of skill levels. Today we see less of this protection of special interests, but individual labor unions are still the target of charges of discrimination, as are employers.

The power of labor unions varies widely from country to country. In some countries, such as Britain and Mexico, unions play a key role in the foundation of governments. In others, such as Japan and Korea, their role in politics is very limited, and even their ability to influence the private sector is relatively weak. Unions in the United States can sometimes have a significant influence on employers and elected officials, but their effect varies dramatically by type of industry and even region of the country (see Figure 6-2) (M. Wallerstein and Western 2000).

FIGURE 6-2

Union Membership in the United States

Mapping Life NATIONWIDE

W States with "right to work" laws

High level of union membership (15 percent and more)

Average level (8–14.9 percent)

Low level (8 percent and less)

Note: Right to work means that legally, workers cannot be required to join a union or pay union dues.

Source: Developed by the author based on data from Bureau of Labor Statistics 2003; National Right to Work Legal Defense Foundation 2004.

Think About It

What is the relationship between the level of union membership in a given state and the presence of right-to-work laws?

Few people today would dispute the fact that union membership is declining. What accounts for this decline? Among the reasons offered are the following:

1. Changes in the type of industry. Manufacturing jobs, the traditional heart of the labor union, have declined, giving way to postindustrial service jobs.

2. Growth in part-time jobs. Between 1982 and 1998 the number of temporary jobs in the United States rose 577 percent, while total employment increased only 41 percent. Only in 2000 did laws governing collective bargaining allow temporary workers to join a union.

3. The legal system. The United States has not made it particularly easy for unions to organize and bargain, and some government measures have made it more difficult. A dramatic example was President Ronald Reagan's firing of 11,000 air traffic controllers in 1981, when their union threatened they would walk off the job while seeking a new contract.

4. Globalization. The threat of jobs leaving the country has undercut the ability of union leaders to organize workers at home. Some say that labor union demands for wage increases and additional benefits have themselves spurred the exodus of jobs to developing nations, where wages are significantly lower and unions are virtually nonexistent.

5. Employer offensives. Increasingly hostile employers have taken court action to block unions' efforts to represent their members.

6. Union rigidity and bureaucratization. Labor has been slow to embrace women, minorities, and immigrants. Furthermore, in some unions the election of leaders seems to dominate the organization's activity (AFL-CIO 2001; Clawson and Clawson 1999; Cornfield 1991; S. Greenhouse 2000a; *Migration News* 2001).

Perhaps as a result of all these factors, confidence in unions is low. Only 1 out of 10 persons in the United

146   Chapter 6

States expresses a great deal of confidence in unions—more than for major corporations and government, but far less than for educational and religious institutions and the military (Bureau of the Census 2001a:249).

Sociological Insights

Both Marxists and functionalists would view unions as a logical response to the emergence of impersonal, large-scale, formal, and often alienating organizations. This view certainly characterized the growth of unions in major manufacturing industries with a sharp division of labor. However, as manufacturing has declined, unions have had to look elsewhere for growth (Cornfield 1991).

Today labor unions in the United States and Europe bear little resemblance to those early unions organized spontaneously by exploited workers. In line with the oligarchic model developed by Robert Michels (see page 138), unions have become increasingly bureaucratized under a self-serving leadership. Conflict theorists would point out that the longer union leaders are in office, the less responsive they are to the needs and demands of the rank and file, and the more concerned they are with maintaining their own positions and power. Yet research shows that under certain circumstances, union leadership can change significantly. Smaller unions are vulnerable to changes in leadership, as are unions whose membership shifts in composition from predominantly White to African American or Latino (Cornfield 1991; Form 1992).

Many union employees encounter role conflict. For example, they may agree to provide a needed service and then organize a strike to withhold it. Role conflict is especially apparent in the so-called helping occupations: teaching, social work, nursing, law enforcement, and firefighting. These workers may feel torn between carrying out their professional responsibilities and enduring working conditions they find unacceptable (Aronowitz and Di Fazio 1994).

◀ p. 109

Policy Initiatives

U.S. law grants workers the right to self-organize via unions. But the United States is unique among industrial democracies in allowing employers to actively oppose their employees' decision to organize (Comstock and Fox 1994).

A major barrier to union growth exists in the 21 states that have so-called right-to-work laws (see Figure 6-2, page 145). In these states, workers cannot be *required* to join or pay dues or fees to a union. The very term *right to work* reflects the anti-union view that a worker should not be forced to join a union, even if the union may negotiate on his or her behalf and achieve results that benefit the worker. This situation is unlikely to change. That is, right-to-work states will remain so; those without such laws typically have a strong union tradition or restrict union activities in other ways.

On the national level, union power is waning. In the security buildup that followed the terrorist attacks of September 11, 2001, federal officials created many new jobs and reorganized existing agencies into the Department of Homeland Security. In doing so, they specified that some 170,000 workers would not have collective bargaining rights, and that 56,000 newly federalized airport security screeners could not be unionized. Though these stipulations may or may not stand up to legal challenges, many observers see them as another sign of increasingly anti-union sentiment at all levels of government (Borosage 2003).

Yet some unions, such as the Hotel and Restaurant Employees Union, have been managing to grow by pursuing new strategies. In their recruitment efforts, these unions stress the desirability of diversity, regardless of workers' race or citizenship status. Organizers supplement their efforts to improve members' wages and working conditions by developing alliances within the broader community and by addressing social issues such as immigration (Voss and Fantasia 2004).

In Europe, labor unions tend to play a major role in political elections. (The ruling party in Great Britain, in fact, is called the Labour Party.) Although unions play a lesser political role in the United States, they have recently faced attacks for their large financial contributions to political campaigns. Debate over campaign finance reform in Congress in 2001 raised the question of whether labor unions should be able to use dues to support a particular candidate or promote a position via "issue ads" that favor one party, usually the Democrats.

Let's Discuss

1. What unions are represented on your college campus? Have you been aware of union activity? Has there been any opposition to the unions on the part of the administration?

2. Do you think nurses should be allowed to strike? Why or why not? What about teachers or police officers?

3. If a union is working on behalf of all the workers of a company, should all the employees be required to join the union and pay dues? Why or why not?

GETTING INVOLVED

www.
mhhe.com
/schaefer6

To get involved in the debate over the labor movement, visit this text's Online Learning Center, which offers links to relevant websites. Check out the Social Policy section on the Online Learning Center as well; it provides survey data on U.S. public opinion regarding this issue.

CHAPTER RESOURCES

Summary

Social interaction among human beings is necessary to the transmission of culture and the survival of every society. This chapter examines the social behavior of *groups, formal organizations,* and *voluntary associations.*

1. When we find ourselves identifying closely with a group, it is probably a *primary group.* A *secondary group* is more formal and impersonal.
2. People tend to see the world in terms of *in-groups* and *out-groups,* a perception often fostered by the very groups to which they belong.
3. *Reference groups* set and enforce standards of conduct and serve as a source of comparison for people's evaluations of themselves and others.
4. Interactionist researchers have noted distinct and predictable processes in the functioning of *small groups.* The simplest group is a *dyad,* composed of two members. *Triads* and larger groups increase the ways of interacting and allow for *coalitions* to form.
5. As societies have become more complex, large *formal organizations* have become more powerful and pervasive.
6. Max Weber argued that in its ideal form, every *bureaucracy* has five basic characteristics: division of labor, hierarchical authority, written rules and regulations, impersonality, and employment based on technical qualifications.
7. Bureaucracy can be understood both as a process and as a matter of degree. Thus, an organization may be more or less bureaucratic than other organizations.
8. When leaders of an organization build up their power, the result can be *oligarchy* (rule by a few).
9. The informal structure of an organization can undermine and redefine official bureaucratic policies.
10. People join *voluntary associations* for a variety of purposes—for example, to share in joint activities or to get help with personal problems.
11. Organizational restructuring and new technologies have transformed the workplace through innovations such as *collective decision making* and *telecommuting.*
12. *Labor unions* are on the decline because of major shifts in the economy.

Critical Thinking Questions

1. Think about how behavior is shaped by reference groups. What different reference groups have shaped your outlook and your goals at different periods in your life? How have they done so?
2. Are primary groups, secondary groups, in-groups, out-groups, and reference groups likely to be found within a formal organization? What functions do these groups serve for a formal organization? What dysfunctions might occur as a result of their presence?
3. Max Weber identified five basic characteristics of bureaucracy. Select an actual organization familiar to you (for example, your college, a workplace, or a religious institution or civic association you belong to) and apply Weber's five characteristics to that organization. To what degree does it correspond to Weber's ideal type of bureaucracy?

148   Chapter 6

Key Terms

Alienation   A condition of estrangement or dissociation from the surrounding society. (page 136)

Bureaucracy   A component of formal organization that uses rules and hierarchical ranking to achieve efficiency. (136)

Bureaucratization   The process by which a group, organization, or social movement becomes increasingly bureaucratic. (138)

Classical theory   An approach to the study of formal organizations that views workers as being motivated almost entirely by economic rewards. (139)

Coalition   A temporary or permanent alliance geared toward a common goal. (135)

Dyad   A two-member group. (134)

Focus group   A group of 10 to 15 people assembled by a researcher to discuss a predetermined topic, guided by a moderator. (133)

Formal organization   A group designed for a special purpose and structured for maximum efficiency. (135)

Goal displacement   Overzealous conformity to official regulations of a bureaucracy. (137)

Group   Any number of people with similar norms, values, and expectations who interact with one another on a regular basis. (130)

Human relations approach   An approach to the study of formal organizations that emphasizes the role of people, communication, and participation in a bureaucracy and tends to focus on the informal structure of the organization. (139)

Ideal type   A construct or model for evaluating specific cases. (136)

In-group   Any group or category to which people feel they belong. (132)

Iron law of oligarchy   A principle of organizational life under which even democratic organizations will eventually develop into bureaucracies ruled by a few individuals. (138)

Labor union   Organized workers who share either the same skill or the same employer. (144)

McDonaldization   The process by which the principles of the fast-food restaurant are coming to dominate more and more sectors of American society as well as of the rest of the world. (130)

Out-group   A group or category to which people feel they do not belong. (132)

Peter principle   A principle of organizational life according to which every employee within a hierarchy tends to rise to his or her level of incompetence. (138)

Primary group   A small group characterized by intimate, face-to-face association and cooperation. (130)

Reference group   Any group that individuals use as a standard for evaluating themselves and their own behavior. (133)

Scientific management approach   Another name for the classical theory of formal organizations. (139)

Secondary group   A formal, impersonal group in which there is little social intimacy or mutual understanding. (131)

Small group   A group small enough for all members to interact simultaneously—that is, to talk with one another or at least be well acquainted. (134)

Telecommuter   An employee who works full-time or part-time at home rather than in an outside office, and who is linked to supervisor and colleagues through computer terminals, phone, and fax machines. (143)

Trained incapacity   The tendency of workers in a bureaucracy to become so specialized that they develop blind spots and fail to notice obvious problems. (136)

Triad   A three-member group. (134)

Voluntary association   An organization established on the basis of common interest, whose members volunteer or even pay to participate. (140)

Groups and Organizations   **149**

TECHNOLOGY RESOURCES

Internet Connection

Note: While all the URLs listed were current as of the printing of this book, these sites often change. Please check our website (www.mhhe.com/schaefer6) for updates, hyperlinks, and exercises related to these sites.

1. The website of the Illinois Labor History Society (**www.kentlaw.edu/ilhs/index.html**) contains extensive information on labor unions, strikes, and disasters past and present in that state. Visit the site for an overview of labor history in Illinois.

2. The Advocacy Project (**www.advocacynet.org**) is a nonprofit organization that provides support to other organizations working for peace and human rights. Examine this site to better understand the often complex interrelationships among organizations.

Online Learning Center with PowerWeb

The focus of this chapter has been groups and organizations. Everyone is a member of an "in-group," and most people have been members of an "out-group." Visit the student center in the Online Learning Center (**www.mhhe.com/schaefer6**) and link to the first Interactive Activity, called "In-Groups, Out-Groups, and Un-words." In this activity, you will be asked to discuss your experiences as a member of an in-group and an out-group. You also can do the word scramble, which contains key words or phrases from this chapter.

Reel Society Interactive Movie CD-ROM 2.0

Reel Society 2.0 can be used to spark discussion about the following topic from this chapter:

- Understanding Groups

Appendix 4

Applications of Skills

The pages that follow include four-part worksheets to guide you through the process of applying many of the skills you have learned in this textbook. Use the cover sheet to monitor your progress. You may photocopy these pages and use them in your subject area courses or as part of an assignment in your reading class.

Target a course in which you are currently enrolled that has an assigned textbook to which you can apply the exercises. If you are not taking such a class, you may practice your skills on the textbook chapter in *Environmental Science*, "What Then Shall We Do?" that follows the worksheets. You may also apply the strategy to the complete textbook chapter on "Groups and Organizations" found in Appendix 3 of this book.

Application of Skills: Active Textbook Reading

Cover Sheet

Name: _____ Semester: _____

Targeted Course: _____ Instructor: _____

Author: _____ Textbook Title: _____

Enter the due dates for each part and check each as you complete it.

Part I: Survey the Text.

- **Worksheet I**   **Date Due** _____   **Completed** _____
- **Evaluation**   **Date Due** _____   **Completed** _____

Part II: Preview a Chapter of your choice from your text.

- **Worksheet II**   **Date Due** _____   **Completed** _____
- **Evaluation**   **Date Due** _____   **Completed** _____

Part III: Read Actively, Highlight, and Annotate your text.

- **Worksheet III**   **Date Due** _____   **Completed** _____
- **Evaluation**   **Date Due** _____   **Completed** _____

Part IV: Recite, Review, Rehearse to enhance your knowledge and recall.

- **Worksheet IV**   **Date Due** _____   **Completed** _____
- **Evaluation**   **Date Due** _____   **Completed** _____

Application of Skills: Active Textbook Reading

Name: _____   Targeted Course: _____

Author: _____   Textbook Title: _____

Part I Worksheet: Survey the Text (See Chapter 2)

This worksheet will guide you through evaluating the organization of one of your textbooks. Being familiar with each of your texts will help you use them efficiently to access information and to understand the content. So select a text and get acquainted!

I. IDENTIFY TOPICS FOR READING AND STUDY

A. **Consult the *Table of Contents*.** Copy the titles of the first five chapters, and <u>briefly state</u> what you expect to learn from each chapter.

Chapter 1: _____
I expect to learn: _____

_____

Chapter 2: _____
I expect to learn: _____

_____

Chapter 3: _____
I expect to learn: _____

_____

Chapter 4: _____
I expect to learn: _____

_____

Chapter 5: _____
I expect to learn: _____

_____

B. Which topics, if any, have you already studied? _____

_____

C. Did you find any topics that you knew nothing about? Identify these.

_____

_____

D. How are the chapters arranged: *sequentially*, *chronologically* or *topically*?

What does this organization tell you about the topics of study?

_____

_____

II. TEXTBOOK FEATURES:

A. **Look through your textbook**. Check off any of the features that are included in your textbook.

_____ **Title Page**

_____ **Table of Contents**

_____ **Preface**

_____ **Index**

_____ **Glossary**

_____ **Appendix**

_____ **Bibliography**

_____ **Webliography**

_____ **Acknowledgments**

_____ Other: _____

B. If there is an appendix, list the items included:

_____

C. **Look through a chapter**. Check off the features that will support your reading and study.

_____ **Introduction**

_____ **Chapter objectives**

_____ **Chapter outline**

_____ **Vocabulary word lists** (terminology)

_____ **Headings and subheadings**

_____ **Marginal notes**

_____ **Text boxes**

_____ **Graphic organizers** (outlines, maps, charts)

_____ **Visual aids** (diagrams, photos, drawings, maps)

_____ **End of chapter questions**

_____ **Chapter summary or key points**

_____ **Resources or suggested readings**

_____ Other: _____

III. ADDITIONAL FEATURES:

A. Which **supplemental materials** are available for your text? Check below.

_____ study guides   _____ companion website

_____ supplemental readings   _____ computer CD-ROMs

_____ workbooks   _____ other: _____

B. Which of the indicated supplemental materials might you use in your course work? Explain.

_____

_____

Now evaluate the process for surveying the text:

Do you think this strategy is worthwhile? How do you think this technique will help you to improve your performance in your targeted course? Write at least one paragraph in which you answer these questions and explain your responses.

_____

_____

_____

_____

_____

_____

Application of Skills: Active Textbook Reading

Name: _____ Targeted Course: _____

Author: _____ Textbook Title: _____

Part II Worksheet: Preview a Chapter (See Chapter 2)

Prepare for reading. This worksheet will guide you through the previewing process. You will determine the topic and general organization of a textbook chapter, access your prior knowledge, and plan your reading and study time.

Photocopy the first three pages of your selected chapter and present them with this sheet. Complete the following questions based on *previewing the entire chapter.*

1. Why will you be reading this chapter at this time? (homework, test preparation, research, report writing)

   _____

2. What is the title of the chapter? _____

3. What do you already know about the topic? _____

   _____

   _____

4. Is there an introduction? _____ On what page(s)? _____ How many paragraphs? _____

   What do you learn about the chapter from the introduction?

   _____

   _____

5. Read and highlight the major headings and subheadings of the chapter.

6. Read and underline the first sentence in each paragraph.

7. List and briefly describe any illustrations, charts, diagrams, or tables or other visual aids presented.

   _____

   _____

   _____

   _____

   _____

8. Are any vocabulary words presented? _____ How? _____

9. Is there a chapter summary? _____ On what page? _____ How many paragraphs? _____

10. Based on your preview, how much time do you think you will need to devote to reading this chapter? _____

11. Based on all you have previewed, briefly describe what this chapter will be about; what it will discuss, and what you *predict* you will learn. You may use the back of this page if needed.

_____

_____

_____

_____

_____

_____

_____

_____

Now evaluate the process for previewing a chapter:

Do you think this strategy is worthwhile? How do you think this technique will help you to improve your performance in your targeted course? Write at least one paragraph in which you answer these questions and explain your responses.

_____

_____

_____

_____

_____

_____

_____

_____

_____

_____

_____

Application of Skills: Active Textbook Reading

Name: _____   Targeted Course: _____

Author: _____   Textbook Title: _____

Part III Worksheet: Read Actively, Highlight, and Annotate (See Chapter 2)

Using the chapter you previewed, photocopy pages that include at least five headings or subheadings. Then, read with a purpose. First, turn each heading into a question, and write it here. Next, read, highlight, and annotate to target the answers to your questions and to identify main ideas and important details. Finally, return to this page and paraphrase the answers to the questions you asked. Attach your annotated pages to this sheet.

Question 1 _____

_____

Answer _____

_____

_____

_____

Question 2 _____

_____

Answer _____

_____

_____

_____

Question 3 _____

_____

Answer _____

_____

_____

_____

Question 4 _____

_____

Answer _____

Question 5 _____

_____

Answer _____

_____

_____

_____

Now evaluate the process of reading actively, highlighting, and annotating:

Do you think this strategy is worthwhile? How do you think this technique will help you to improve your performance in your targeted course? Write at least one paragraph in which you answer these questions and explain your responses.

Application of Skills: Active Textbook Reading

Name: _____   Targeted Course: _____

Author: _____   Textbook Title: _____

Part IV Worksheet: Recite, Review, Rehearse (See Chapter 9)

To successfully prepare for exams, you need to make a final review of all of the material, rehearse it, write it, recite it, and test yourself. In preparation for writing, you need to understand the content and be able to present it in an organized fashion.

A. Using a chapter you are currently studying in one of your classes, choose a section of several pages, photocopy, read, and annotate them, and then complete *one* of the following review activities:

Develop an outline
or
Create a map
or
Write a comprehensive summary

Attach your annotated photocopies and outline, map, or summary to this sheet.

B. Using your outline, map, or summary of the material, create five study questions that might appear on an exam. These questions should address the most important concepts and information in the material and be narrative in nature. Do *not* write short-answer questions or multiple-choice questions. Write questions that cover broad areas of content and require short essay-type answers. (See Chapter 11.)

Study Questions

Textbook: _____   **Chapter:** _____

1. _____

   _____

   _____

   _____

2. _____

   _____

   _____

   _____

3. _____

_____

_____

_____

4. _____

_____

_____

_____

5. _____

_____

_____

_____

C. Choose two of the questions you wrote previously and write complete answers for them on a separate sheet of paper.

Attach your essay answers to this sheet.

Now evaluate the process to recite, review, rehearse:

Do you think this strategy is worthwhile? How do you think this technique will help you to improve your performance in your targeted course? Write at least one paragraph in which you answer these questions and explain your responses.

_____

_____

_____

_____

_____

_____

_____

_____

_____

Ecotourism and whale watching provide jobs for local people and help protect the Laguna San Ignacio.

C H A P T E R

25

What Then Shall We Do?

You must be the change you wish to see in the world.
—Mahatma Gandhi—

LEARNING OUTCOMES

After studying this chapter, you should be able to:

16.1 Explain how we can make a difference.

16.2 Summarize environmental education.

16.3 Evaluate what individuals can do.

16.4 Review how we can work together.

16.5 Investigate campus greening.

16.6 Define the challenge of sustainability.

Case Study Saving a Gray Whale Nursery

At first glance, the Laguna San Ignacio may merely look like a shallow bay surrounded by a barren, rocky desert. But to many people, this lagoon on the west coast of Mexico's Baja Peninsula is a biological treasure. It's the last relatively pristine place where gray whales congregate each winter to mate, give birth, and nurse their calves. Pacific gray whales (*Eschrichtius robustus*) make a round trip of about 16,000 km (10,000 mi) every year between their summer feeding grounds north of the Arctic Circle and the Baja (fig. 25.1). The warm, salty water of bays like San Ignacio give calves extra buoyancy that helps them swim and nurse, while also sheltering them from predators and winter storms.

In the nineteenth century, a whaling captain named Scammon discovered the winter calving areas in Baja. The enclosed bays that once protected the whales became killing grounds. In a short time, the Pacific population was reduced from an estimated 25,000 animals to only a few thousand. Whaling bans have allowed the species to rebound to nearly its prehunting population, a great success story in endangered species protection. In 1994, Pacific gray whales were removed from the U.S. endangered species list.

In 1954, the same year that Mexico banned commercial whaling, a sea salt extraction facility was built in Guerro Negro bay (formerly Scammon's Lagoon) and the nearby Ojo de Liebre just north of Laguna San Ignacio. These saltworks, which are now operated by Expotadora de Sal and jointly owned by the Mitsubishi Company and the Mexican government, are the largest in the world, producing 6.5 million metric tons of salt per year. Concern about the effects of this huge industrial development on both the whales and the surrounding desert caused Mexican President Miguel de La Madrid to establish the Vizcaino Biosphere Reserve in 1988, including all three lagoons plus 2.4 million ha (6 million acres) of surrounding desert.

In 1994, however, Expotadora de Sal announced intentions to build an even bigger saltworks at Laguna San Ignacio. Plans called for 300 km² (116 mi²) of salt evaporation ponds carved out of the shoreline and filled by diesel engines that would pump 23,000 l (nearly 6,000 gal) of seawater per second. A 1.6 km (1 mi) long concrete pier built across the lagoon would transport the salt to an offshore loading area that would fill more than 120 salt tankers per year. The threat to whale survival from this immense operation was evident.

One of Mexico's leading environmental groups, el Grupo de los Cien (the Group of 100) started a campaign to stop this huge industrial development. They joined with other nongovernmental groups (NGOs), including the Natural Resources Defense Council (NRDC) and the International Fund for Animal Welfare (IFAW), to raise public awareness and to lobby the Mexican government. The campaign took a number of different approaches. One of these was to organize whale-watching trips featuring movie stars, such as Glenn Close and Pierce Brosnan, to gain attention and educate the public about the issue. Newspaper ads and magazine articles criticized the industrialization of San Ignacio. One of these, entitled "An Unacceptable Risk," presented the scientific value of the lagoon and was signed by 33 of the world's most famous scientists, including several Nobel laureates.

Environmentalists also lobbied Mitsubishi directly, threatening to boycott their cars, TVs, electronics, and other products. A 1998 UN World Heritage Conference in Kyoto, Japan, provided an excellent opportunity to meet face-to-face with company leaders. Activists said to Hajime Koga, manager of Mitsubishi's "Salt Team," "You would never contemplate such a project in a World Heritage site in Japan. Why would you destroy one in another country?" The company was amazed to receive more than 1 million petitions, letters, and emails from all over the world, criticizing their expanded saltworks. Although the environmental NGOs weren't successful in obtaining "In Danger" designation for the biosphere reserve at the conference in Kyoto, they did get this classification at the next meeting of the World Heritage Committee in Marrakech, Morocco, in 2000.

In 2002, Expotadora de Sal announced that it was abandoning plans for Laguna San Ignacio. Mitsubishi said it was the first time in its history that it had changed its policy because of environmental concerns. Simply blocking development isn't enough; long-term solutions need to be economically sustainable as well as scientifically sound and socially just. The 35,000 Mexicans who live within the biosphere reserve need to make a living. In 2005, local residents and environmental NGOs signed an agreement to preserve 50,000 ha (124,000 acres) of land around Laguna San Ignacio. The Ejido Luis Echeverria, a land cooperative, which owns the land, will limit development in exchange for a $25,000 annual payment to be used for low-impact projects, such as ecotourism and whale watching. Eventually, conservationists hope to reach a similar agreement with five other *ejidos* to extend protection to 4,000 km² (1 million acres) of the Vizcaino Biosphere Reserve. This will cost about $10 million.

This case study demonstrates some of the steps in influencing public policy. First, you have to gather information and understand the science that informs your issue. You should recognize how, and by whom, policy is made. You must evaluate which of the many techniques for educating the public and shaping opinion can be effective. And you need to learn how to work with other groups, and to reason with those whose opinions you hope to sway. In this chapter, we'll study how individuals and groups can work to affect this process.

FIGURE 25.1 Gray whale migration route from Alaska to Baja, California.

25.1 MAKING A DIFFERENCE

Throughout this book you have read about environmental problems, from climate change to biodiversity to energy policy debates. Biodiversity is disappearing at the fastest rate ever known; major ocean fisheries have collapsed; within 50 years, it is expected that two-thirds of countries will experience water shortages, and 3 billion people may live in slums. You have also seen that, as we have come to understand these problems, many exciting innovations have been developed to deal with them. New irrigation methods reduce agricultural water use; bioremediation provides inexpensive methods to treat hazardous waste; new energy sources, including wind, solar, and even pressure-cooked garbage, offer strategies for weening our society from its dependence on oil and gas. Growth of green consumerism has developed markets for recycled materials, low-energy appliances, and organic foods. Population growth continues, but its rate has plummeted from a generation ago.

Stewardship for our shared resources is increasingly understood to be everybody's business. The environmental justice movement (chapter 23) has shown that minority groups and the poor frequently suffer more from pollution than wealthy or white people. African Americans, Latinos, and other minority groups have a clear interest in pursuing environmental solutions. Religious groups are voicing new concerns about preserving our environment (chapter 2). Farmers are seeking ways to save soil and water resources (chapter 9). Loggers are learning about sustainable harvest methods (chapter 12). Business leaders are discovering new ways to do well by doing good work for society and the environment (chapter 21). These changes are exciting, though many challenges remain.

Whatever your skills and interests, you can contribute to understanding and protecting our common environment. If you enjoy science, there are many disciplines that contribute to environmental science. As you know by now, biology, chemistry, geology, ecology, climatology, geography, demography, and other sciences all provide essential ideas and data to environmental science. Environmental scientists usually focus on one of these disciplines, but their work also serves the others. An environmental chemist, for example, might study contaminants in a stream system, and this work might help an aquatic ecologist understand changes in a stream's food web.

You can also help seek environmental solutions if you prefer writing, art, working with children, history, politics, economics, or other areas of study. As you have read, environmental science depends on communication, education, good policies, and economics as well as on science.

In this chapter, we will discuss some of the steps you can take to help find solutions to environmental problems. You have already taken the most important step, educating yourself. When you understand how environmental systems function—from nutrient cycles and energy flows to ecosystems, climate systems, population dynamics, agriculture, and economies—you can develop well-informed opinions and help find useful answers (fig. 25.2).

FIGURE 25.2 What lives in a tide pool? Learning to appreciate the beauty, richness, and diversity of the natural world is important if we are to protect it.

25.2 ENVIRONMENTAL EDUCATION

In 1990 Congress recognized the importance of environmental education by passing the National Environmental Education Act. The act established two broad goals: (1) to improve understanding among the general public of the natural and built environment and the relationships between humans and their environment, including global aspects of environmental problems, and (2) to encourage postsecondary students to pursue careers related to the environment. Specific objectives proposed to meet these goals include developing an awareness and appreciation of our natural and social/cultural environment, knowledge of basic ecological concepts, acquaintance with a broad range of current environmental issues, and experience in using investigative, critical-thinking, and problem-solving skills in solving environmental problems (fig. 25.3). Several states, including Arizona, Florida,

FIGURE 25.3 Environmental education helps develop awareness and appreciation of ecological systems and how they work.

TABLE 25.1

Outcomes from Environmental Education

The natural context: An environmentally educated person understands the scientific concepts and facts that underlie environmental issues and the interrelationships that shape nature.

The social context: An environmentally educated person understands how human society is influencing the environment, as well as the economic, legal, and political mechanisms that provide avenues for addressing issues and situations.

The valuing context: An environmentally educated person explores his or her values in relation to environmental issues; from an understanding of the natural and social contexts, the person decides whether to keep or change those values.

The action context: An environmentally educated person becomes involved in activities to improve, maintain, or restore natural resources and environmental quality for all.

Source: *A Greenprint for Minnesota,* Minnesota Office of Environmental Education, 1993.

TABLE 25.2

The Environmental Scientist's Bookshelf

What are some of the most influential and popular environmental books? In a survey of environmental experts and leaders around the world, the top 12 best books on nature and the environment were:

A Sand County Almanac by Aldo Leopold (100)[1]
Silent Spring by Rachel Carson (81)
State of the World by Lester Brown and the Worldwatch Institute (31)
The Population Bomb by Paul Ehrlich (28)
Walden by Henry David Thoreau (28)
Wilderness and the American Mind by Roderick Nash (21)
Small Is Beautiful: Economics as if People Mattered by E. F. Schumacher (21)
Desert Solitaire: A Season in the Wilderness by Edward Abbey (20)
The Closing Circle: Nature, Man, and Technology by Barry Commoner (18)
The Limits to Growth: A Report for the Club of Rome's Project on the Predicament of Mankind by Donella H. Meadows, et al. (17)
The Unsettling of America: Culture and Agriculture by Wendell Berry (16)
Man and Nature by George Perkins Marsh (16)

[1]Indicates number of votes for each book. Because the preponderance of respondents were from the United States (82 percent), American books are probably overrepresented.

From Robert Merideth, *The Environmentalist's Bookshelf: A Guide to the Best Books,* 1993, by G. K. Hall, an imprint of Macmillan, Inc. Reprinted by permission.

Maryland, Minnesota, Pennsylvania, and Wisconsin, have successfully incorporated these goals and objectives into their curricula (table 25.1).

A number of organizations have been established to teach ecology and environmental ethics to elementary and secondary school students, as well as to get them involved in active projects to clean up their local community. Groups such as Kids Saving the Earth or Eco-Kids Corps are an important way to reach this vital audience. Family education results from these efforts as well. In a World Wildlife Fund survey, 63 percent of young people said they "lobby" their parents about recycling and buying environmentally responsible products.

Environmental literacy means understanding our environment

Speaking in support of the National Environmental Education Act, former Environmental Protection Agency administrator William K. Reilly called for broad **environmental literacy** in which every citizen is fluent in the principles of ecology and has a "working knowledge of the basic grammar and underlying syntax of environmental wisdom." Environmental literacy, according to Reilly can help establish a stewardship ethic—a sense of duty to care for and manage wisely our natural endowment and our productive resources for the long haul. "Environmental education," he says, "boils down to one profoundly important imperative: preparing ourselves for life in the next century. When the twenty-first century rolls around, it will not be enough for a few specialists to know what is going on while the rest of us wander about in ignorance."

You have made a great start toward learning about your environment by reading this book and taking a class in environmental science. Pursuing your own environmental literacy is a life-long process. Some of the most influential environmental books of all time examine environmental problems and suggest solutions (table 25.2). To this list we'd add some personal favorites: *The Singing Wilderness* by Sigurd F. Olson, *My First Summer in the Sierra* by John Muir, and *Encounters with the Archdruid* by John McPhee.

Citizen science encourages everyone to participate

While university classes often tend to be theoretical and abstract, many students are discovering they can make authentic contributions to scientific knowledge through active learning and undergraduate research programs. Internships in agencies or environmental organizations are one way of doing this. Another is to get involved in organized **citizen science** projects in which ordinary people join with established scientists to answer real scientific questions. Community-based research was pioneered in the Netherlands, where several dozen research centers now study environmental issues ranging from water quality in the Rhine River, cancer rates by geographic area, and substitutes for harmful organic solvents. In each project, students and neighborhood groups team with scientists and university personnel to collect data. Their results have been incorporated into official government policies.

Similar research opportunities exist in the United States and Canada. The Audubon Christmas Bird Count is a good example (Exploring Science p. 570). Earthwatch offers a much smaller but more intense opportunity to take part in research. Every year hundreds of Earthwatch projects each field a team of a dozen or so volunteers who spend a week or two working on issues ranging from loon nesting behavior to archaeological digs. The American River Watch organizes teams of students to measure water quality. You might be able to get academic credit as well as helpful practical experience in one of these research experiences.

FIGURE 25.4 Many interesting, well-paid jobs are opening up in environmental fields. Here an environmental technician takes a sample from a monitoring well for chemical analysis.

Environmental careers range from engineering to education

The need for both environmental educators and environmental professionals opens up many job opportunities in environmental fields. The World Wildlife Fund estimates, for example, that 750,000 new jobs will be created over the next decade in the renewable energy field alone. Scientists are needed to understand the natural world and the effects of human activity on the environment. Lawyers and other specialists are needed to develop government and industry policy, laws, and regulations to protect the environment. Engineers are needed to develop technologies and products to clean up pollution and to prevent its production in the first place. Economists, geographers, and social scientists are needed to evaluate the costs of pollution and resource depletion and to develop solutions that are socially, culturally, politically, and economically appropriate for different parts of the world. In addition, business will be looking for a new class of environmentally literate and responsible leaders who appreciate how products sold and services rendered affect our environment.

Trained people are essential in these professions at every level, from technical and clerical support staff to top managers. Perhaps the biggest national demand over the next few years will be for environmental educators to help train an environmentally literate populace. We urgently need many more teachers at every level who are trained in environmental education. Outdoor activities and natural sciences are important components of this mission, but environmental topics such as responsible consumerism, waste disposal, and respect for nature can and should be incorporated into reading, writing, arithmetic, and every other part of education.

Green business and technology are growing fast

Can environmental protection and resource conservation—a so-called green perspective—be a strategic advantage in business? Many companies think so. An increasing number are jumping on the environmental bandwagon, and most large corporations now have an environmental department. A few are beginning to explore integrated programs to design products and manufacturing processes to minimize environmental impacts. Often called "design for the environment," this approach is intended to avoid problems at the beginning rather than deal with them later on a case-by-case basis. In the long run, executives believe this will save money and make their businesses more competitive in future markets. The alternative is to face increasing pollution control and waste disposal costs—now estimated to be more than $100 billion per year for all American businesses—as well as to be tied up in expensive litigation and administrative proceedings.

The market for pollution-control technology and know-how is also expected to be huge. Many companies are positioning themselves to cash in on this enormous market. Germany and Japan appear to be ahead of America in the pollution-control field because they have had more stringent laws for many years, giving them more experience in reducing effluents.

The rush to "green up" business is good news for those looking for jobs in environmentally related fields, which are predicted to be among the fastest growing areas of employment during the next few years. The federal government alone projects a need to hire some 10,000 people per year in a variety of environmental disciplines (fig. 25.4). How can you prepare yourself to enter this market? The best bet is to get some technical training: Environmental engineering, analytical chemistry, microbiology, ecology, limnology, groundwater hydrology, or computer science all have great potential. Currently, a chemical engineer with a graduate degree and some experience in an environmental field can practically name his or her salary. Some other very good possibilities are environmental law and business administration, both rapidly expanding fields.

For those who aren't inclined toward technical fields, there are many opportunities for environmental careers. A good liberal arts education will help you develop skills such as communication, critical thinking, balance, vision, flexibility, and caring that should serve you well. Large companies need a wide variety of people; small companies need a few people who can do many things well. There are many opportunities for planners (chapter 22), health professionals (chapter 8), writers, teachers, and policymakers.

Exploring SCIENCE

Citizen Science and the
Christmas Bird Count

Every Christmas since 1900, dedicated volunteers have counted and recorded all the birds they can find within their team's designated study site (fig. 1). This effort has become the largest, longest-running, citizen-science project in the world. For the 100th count, nearly 50,000 participants in about 1,800 teams observed 58 million birds belonging to 2,309 species. Although about 70 percent of the counts in 2000 were made in the United States or Canada, 650 teams in the Caribbean, Pacific Islands, and Central and South America also participated. Participants enter their bird counts on standardized data sheets, or submit their observations over the Internet. Compiled data can be viewed and investigated online, almost as soon as they are submitted.

Frank Chapman, the editor of *Bird-Lore* magazine and an officer in the newly formed Audubon Society, started the Christmas Bird Count in 1900. For years, hunters had gathered on Christmas Day for a competitive hunt, often killing hundreds of birds and mammals as teams tried to outshoot each other. Chapman suggested an alternative contest: to see which team could observe and identify the most birds, and the most species, in a day. The competition has grown and spread. In the 100th annual count, the winning team was in Monte Verde, Costa Rica, with an amazing 343 species tallied in a single day.

The tens of thousands of bird-watchers participating in the count gather vastly more information about the abundance and distribution of birds than biologists could gather alone. These data provide important information for scientific research on bird migrations, populations, and habitat change. Now that the entire record for a century of bird data is available on the BirdSource website (www.birdsource.org), both professional ornithologists and amateur bird-watchers can study the geographical distribution of a single species over time, or they can examine how all species vary at a single site through the years. Those concerned about changing climate can look for variation in long-term distribution of species. Climatologists can analyze the effects of weather patterns such as El Niño or La Niña on where birds occur.

FIGURE 1 Citizen-science projects, such as the Christmas Bird Count, encourage people to help study their local environment.

One of the most intriguing phenomena revealed by this continent-wide data collection is irruptive behavior: that is, appearance of massive numbers of a particular species in a given area in one year, and then their move to other places in subsequent years following weather patterns, food availability, and other factors.

In 2005 the 105th Christmas Bird Count, collected data on nearly 70 million birds from 2,019 volunteer groups. This citizen-science effort has produced a rich, geographically broad data set far larger than any that could be produced by professional scientists (fig. 2). Following the success of the Christmas Bird Count, other citizen-science projects have been initiated. Project Feeder Watch, which began in the 1970s, has more than 15,000 participants, from schoolchildren and backyard bird-watchers to dedicated birders. The Great Backyard Bird Count of 2005 collected records on over 600 species and more than 6 million individual birds. In other areas, farmers have been enlisted to monitor pasture and stream health; volunteers monitor water quality in local streams and rivers; and nature reserves solicit volunteers to help gather ecological data. You can learn more about your local environment, and contribute to scientific research, by participating in a citizen-science project. Contact your local Audubon chapter or your state's department of natural resources to find out what you can do.

How does counting birds contribute to sustainability? Citizen-science projects are one way individuals can learn more about the scientific process, become familiar with their local environment, and become more interested in community issues. In this chapter, we'll look at other ways individuals and groups can help protect nature and move toward a sustainable society.

Black-capped chickadee

Christmas Bird Count

2002-03

> 500
100–500
50–100
10–50
< 10
0

FIGURE 2 Volunteer data collection can produce a huge, valuable data set. Christmas Bird Count data, such as this map, are available online. Data from Audubon Society.

25.3 WHAT CAN INDIVIDUALS DO?

Some prime reasons for our destructive impacts on the earth are our consumption of resources and disposal of wastes. Technology has made consumer goods and services cheap and readily available in the richer countries of the world. As you already know, we in the industrialized world use resources at a rate out of proportion to our percentage of the population. If everyone in the world were to attempt to live at our level of consumption, given current methods of production, the results would surely be disastrous. In this section we will look at some options for consuming less and reducing our environmental impacts. Perhaps no other issue in this book represents so clear an ethical question as the topic of responsible consumerism.

How much is enough?

A century ago, economist and social critic, Thorstein Veblen, in his book, *The Theory of the Leisure Class,* coined the term **conspicuous consumption** to describe buying things we don't want or need just to impress others. How much more shocked he would be to see current trends. The average American now consumes twice as many goods and services as in 1950. The average house is now more than twice as big as it was 50 years ago, even though the typical family has half as many people. We need more space to hold all the stuff we buy. Shopping has become the way many people define themselves (fig. 25.5). As Marx predicted, everything has become commodified; getting and spending have eclipsed family, ethnicity, even religion as the defining matrix of our lives. But the futility and irrelevance of much American consumerism leaves a psychological void. Once we possess things, we find they don't make us young, beautiful, smart, and interesting as they promised. With so much attention on earning and spending money, we don't have time to have real friends, to cook real food, to have creative hobbies, or to do work that makes us feel we have accomplished something with our lives. Some social critics call this drive to possess stuff "affluenza."

A growing number of people find themselves stuck in a vicious circle: They work frantically at a job they hate, to buy things they don't need, so they can save time to work even

longer hours. Seeking a measure of balance in their lives, some opt out of the rat race and adopt simpler, less-consumptive lifestyles. As Thoreau wrote in *Walden,* "Our life is frittered away by detail . . . simplify, simplify."

We can choose to reduce our environmental impact

Marketers and trend spotters have noticed that an increasing number of people in affluent countries are becoming concerned about the effects of pollution and social inequity. There's a name for consumers who worry about the environment, want products to be produced in a fair, sustainable way, and use purchasing power to express their values. They're called Lohas, an acronym for "lifestyles of health and sustainability." Encompassing things like organic food, energy-efficient appliances and automobiles, natural home care and health products, active vacations and eco-tourism, the total market for this group represents $230 billion per year, according to Natural Business Communications, a company in Colorado that publishes *The Lohas Journal* and is credited with coining the term. Altogether, 68 million Americans—about one-third of the adult population—qualify as Lohas, consumers who take environmental and social issues into account when they make purchases. Ninety percent of this group say they prefer to make purchases from companies that share their values, and many say they are willing to pay a premium for products and services they consider healthier for themselves, their families, society, and the environment. Merchants flock to annual Lohas business conferences to learn how to tap into this important market.

Another name for people who are deeply concerned about nature and want to be involved in creating a new and better way of life is **cultural creatives,** a term introduced by Paul Ray and Sherry Ruth Anderson in a book by the same title. Ray and Anderson describe this group as socially conscious, involved in improving communities, and willing to translate values into action. They are strongly aware of environmental problems and want to do something to remedy them. Most cultural creatives place great importance on helping other people, care intensely about psychological or spiritual development, and volunteer for

MODERNE MAN

FIGURE 25.5 Is this our highest purpose?

one or more good causes. They dislike the modern emphasis on wealth, consumerism and power, and enjoy learning about new places and people and alternative ways of life.

Neither cultural creatives nor Lohas are defined by particular demographic characteristics. They work at all sorts of jobs and occupy every economic level. The majority are mainstream in their religious beliefs and are no more liberal or conservative than the U.S. average. One important trait is that about two-thirds of them are women, and many of the values most important to them—relationships, family life, children, education, and responsibility—are traditionally thought of as women's issues. Because women now do a majority of family shopping as well as hold more than half of all personal wealth in America, both businesses and non-profits are beginning to pay attention to these concerns.

Recognizing that making people feel guilty about their life-styles and purchasing habits isn't working, many organizations are now attempting to find ways to make sustainable living something consumers will adopt willingly. The goal is economically, socially, and environmentally viable solutions that allow people to enjoy a good quality of life while consuming fewer natural resources and polluting less. A good example of this approach is a British automaker that provides a mountain bike with every car it sells, urging buyers to use the bike for short journeys. Another example cited by UNEP is European detergent makers who encourage customers to switch to low-temperature washing liquids and powders, not just to save energy but because it's good for their clothes.

Although each of our individual choices may make a small impact, collectively they can be important. The What Can You Do? box on p. 572 offers some suggestions for reducing waste and pollution.

"Green washing" can mislead consumers

Although many people report they prefer to buy products and packaging that are socially and ecologically sustainable, there is a wide gap between what consumers say in surveys about purchasing habits and the actual sales data. Part of the problem is accessibility and affordability. In many areas, green products either aren't available or are so expensive that those on limited incomes (as many living in voluntary simplicity are) can't afford them. Although businesses are beginning to recognize the size and importance of the market for "green" merchandise, the variety of choices and the economies of scale haven't yet made them as accessible as we would like.

Another problem is that businesses, eager to cash in on this premium market, offer a welter of confusing and often misleading claims about the sustainability of their offerings. Consumers must be wary to avoid "green scams" that sound great but are actually only overpriced standard items. Many terms used in advertising are vague and have little meaning. For example:

- "Nontoxic" suggests that a product has no harmful effects on humans. Since there is no legal definition of the term, however, it can have many meanings. How nontoxic is the product? And to whom? Substances not poisonous to humans can be harmful to other organisms.

What Can You Do?

Reducing Your Impact

Purchase Less

Ask yourself whether you really need more stuff.

Avoid buying things you don't need or won't use.

Use items as long as possible (and don't replace them just because a new product becomes available).

Use the library instead of purchasing books you read.

Make gifts from materials already on hand, or give nonmaterial gifts.

Reduce Excess Packaging

Carry reusable bags when shopping and refuse bags for small purchases.

Buy items in bulk or with minimal packaging; avoid single-serving foods.

Choose packaging that can be recycled or reused.

Avoid Disposable Items

Use cloth napkins, handkerchiefs, and towels.

Bring a washable cup to meetings; use washable plates and utensils rather than single-use items.

Buy pens, razors, flashlights, and cameras with replaceable parts.

Choose items built to last and have them repaired; you will save materials and energy while providing jobs in your community.

Conserve Energy

Walk, bicycle, or use public transportation.

Turn off (or avoid turning on) lights, water, heat, and air conditioning when possible.

Put up clotheslines or racks in the backyard, carport, or basement to avoid using a clothes dryer.

Carpool and combine trips to reduce car mileage.

Save Water

Water lawns and gardens only when necessary.

Use water-saving devices and fewer flushes with toilets.

Don't leave water running when washing hands, food, dishes, and teeth.

Based on material by Karen Oberhauser, Bell Museum Imprint, University of Minnesota, 1992. Used by permission.

- "Biodegradable," "recyclable," "reusable," or "compostable" may be technically correct but not signify much. Almost everything will biodegrade *eventually,* but it may take thousands of years. Similarly, almost anything is potentially recyclable or reusable; the real question is whether there are programs to do so in your community. If the only recycling or composting program for a particular material is half a continent away, this claim has little value.

http://www.mhhe.com/cunningham10e

- "Natural" is another vague and often misused term. Many natural ingredients—lead or arsenic, for instance—are highly toxic. Synthetic materials are not necessarily more dangerous or environmentally damaging than those created by nature.
- "Organic" can connote different things in different places. There are loopholes in standards so that many synthetic chemicals can be included in "organics." On items such as shampoos and skin-care products, "organic" may have no significance at all. Most detergents and oils are organic chemicals, whether they are synthesized in a laboratory or found in nature. Few of these products are likely to have pesticide residues anyway.
- "Environmentally friendly," "environmentally safe," and "won't harm the ozone layer" are often empty claims. Since there are no standards to define these terms, anyone can use them. How much energy and nonrenewable material are used in manufacture, shipping, or use of the product? How much waste is generated, and how will the item be disposed of when it is no longer functional? One product may well be more environmentally benign than another, but be careful who makes this claim.

Certification identifies low-impact products

Products that claim to be environmentally friendly are being introduced at 20 times the normal rate for consumer goods. To help consumers make informed choices, several national programs have been set up to independently and scientifically analyze environmental impacts of major products. Germany's Blue Angel, begun in 1978, is the oldest of these programs. Endorsement is highly sought after by producers since environmentally conscious shoppers have shown that they are willing to pay more for products they know have minimum environmental impacts. To date, more than 2,000 products display the Blue Angel symbol. They range from recycled paper products, energy-efficient appliances, and phosphate-free detergents to refillable dispensers.

Similar programs are being proposed in every Western European country as well as in Japan and North America. Some are autonomous, nongovernmental efforts like the United States' Green Seal program (managed by the Alliance for Social Responsibility in New York). Others are quasigovernmental institutions such as the Canadian Environmental Choice programs.

The best of these organizations attempt "cradle-to-grave" **life-cycle analysis** (fig. 25.6) that evaluates material and energy inputs and outputs at each stage of manufacture, use, and disposal of the product. While you need to consider your own situation in making choices, the information supplied by these independent agencies is generally more reliable than self-made claims from merchandisers.

Green consumerism has limits

To quote Kermit the Frog, "It's not easy being green." Even with the help of endorsement programs, doing the right thing from an environmental perspective may not be obvious. Often we are faced with complicated choices. Do the social benefits

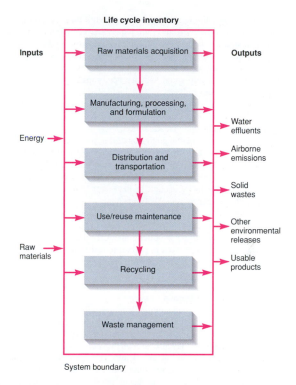

Life cycle inventory

FIGURE 25.6 At each stage in its life cycle, a product receives inputs of materials and energy and produces outputs of materials or energy that move to subsequent phases and wastes that are released into the environment.

of buying rainforest nuts justify the energy expended in transporting them here, or would it be better to eat only locally grown products? In switching from Freon propellants to hydrocarbons, we spare the stratospheric ozone but increase hydrocarbon-caused smog. By choosing reusable diapers over disposable ones, we decrease the amount of material going to the landfill, but we also increase water pollution, energy consumption, and pesticide use (cotton is one of the most pesticide-intensive crops grown in the United States).

When the grocery store clerk asks you, "Paper or plastic?" you probably choose paper and feel environmentally virtuous, right? Everyone knows that plastic is made by synthetic chemical processes from nonrenewable petroleum or natural gas. Paper from naturally growing trees is a better environmental choice, isn't it? Well, not necessarily. In the first place, paper making consumes water and causes much more water pollution than does plastic manufacturing. Paper mills also release air pollutants, including foul-smelling sulfides and captans as well as highly toxic dioxins.

Furthermore, the brown paper bags used in most supermarkets are made primarily from virgin paper. Recycled fibers aren't strong enough for the weight they must carry. Growing, harvesting, and transporting logs from agroforestry plantations can be as environmentally disruptive as oil production. It takes a great deal of energy to pulp wood and dry newly made paper. Paper is also heavier and bulkier to ship than plastic. Although the polyethylene used to make a plastic bag contains many calories, in the end, paper bags are generally more energy-intensive to produce and market than plastic ones.

If both paper and plastic go to a landfill in your community, the plastic bag takes up less space. It doesn't decompose in the landfill, but neither does the paper in an air-tight, water-tight landfill. If paper is recycled but plastic is not, then the paper bag may be the better choice. If you are lucky enough to have both paper and plastic recycling, the plastic bag is probably a better choice since it recycles more easily and produces less pollution in the process. The best choice of all is to bring your own reusable cloth bag.

Complicated, isn't it? We often must make decisions without complete information, but it's important to make the best choices we can. Don't assume that your neighbors are wrong if they reach conclusions different from yours. They may have valid considerations of which you are unaware. The truth is that simple black and white answers often don't exist.

Taking personal responsibility for your environmental impact can have many benefits. Recycling, buying green products, and other environmental actions not only set good examples for your friends and neighbors, they also strengthen your sense of involvement and commitment in valuable ways. There are limits, however, to how much we can do individually through our buying habits and personal actions to bring about the fundamental changes needed to save the earth. Green consumerism generally can do little about larger issues of global equity, chronic poverty, oppression, and the suffering of millions of people in the developing world. There is a danger that exclusive focus on such problems as whether to choose paper or plastic bags, or to sort recyclables for which there are no markets, will divert our attention from the greater need to change basic institutions.

25.4 How Can We Work Together?

While a few exceptional individuals can be effective working alone to bring about change, most of us find it more productive and more satisfying to work with others.

Collective action multiplies individual power (fig. 25.7). You get encouragement and useful information from meeting regularly with others who share your interests. It's easy to get discouraged by the slow pace of change; having a support group helps maintain your enthusiasm. You should realize, however, that there is a broad spectrum of environmental and social action groups. Some will suit your particular interests, preferences, or beliefs more than others. In this section, we will look at some environmental organizations as well as options for getting involved.

FIGURE 25.7 Working together with others can give you energy, inspiration, and a sense of accomplishment.

As the opening case study for this chapter shows, individuals and organizations can bring about major changes in governmental and corporate policy. Mitsubishi had already invested a great deal of money planning for the salt works at Laguna San Ignacio. Their potential profits could have been millions of dollars per year. But the persuasive moral arguments of environmental groups, plus the risk of international embarrassment made them rethink their position. This example shows the power of persistence and organization.

National organizations are influential but sometimes complacent

Among the oldest, largest, and most influential environmental groups in the United States are the National Wildlife Federation, the World Wildlife Fund, the Audubon Society, the Sierra Club, the Izaak Walton League, Friends of the Earth, Greenpeace, Ducks Unlimited, the Natural Resources Defense Council, and The Wilderness Society. Sometimes known as the "group of 10," these organizations are criticized by radical environmentalists for their tendency to compromise and cooperate with the establishment. Although many of these groups were militant—even extremist—in their formative stages, they now tend to be more staid and conservative. Members are mostly passive and know little about the inner workings of the organization, joining as much for publications or social aspects as for their stands on environmental issues. Collectively, these groups grew rapidly during the 1980s (fig. 25.8), but many of their new members had little contact with them beyond making a one-time donation.

Lack of progress over the past decade in important areas, such as global climate change, despite millions of dollars spent by major environmental organizations has led some critics to discuss the "death of environmentalism." They charge that professional staff have become more concerned about protecting their jobs and access to corridors of power in Washington than in bringing about change. Some observers argue that we need to abandon established structures and ways of thinking to come up with new approaches and new coalitions to protect our environment.

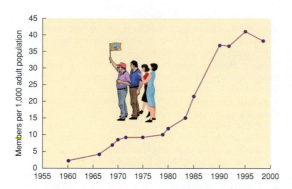

FIGURE 25.8 Growth of national environmental organizations in the United States.

FIGURE 25.9 The Nature Conservancy buys land with high biodiversity or unique natural values to protect it from misuse and development.

Still, the established groups are powerful and important forces in environmental protection. Their mass membership, large professional staffs, and long history give them a degree of respectability and influence not found in newer, smaller groups. The Sierra Club, for instance, with about half a million members and chapters in almost every state, has a national staff of about 400, an annual budget over $20 million, and 20 full-time professional lobbyists in Washington, D.C. These national groups have become a potent force in Congress, especially when they band together to pass specific legislation, such as the Alaska National Interest Lands Act or the Clean Air Act.

In a survey that asked congressional staff and officials of government agencies to rate the effectiveness of groups that attempt to influence federal policy on pollution control, the top five were national environmental organizations. In spite of their large budgets and important connections, the American Petroleum Institute, the Chemical Manufacturers Association, and the Edison Electric Institute ranked far behind these environmental groups in terms of influence.

Although much of the focus of the big environmental groups is in Washington, Audubon, Sierra Club, and Izaak Walton have local chapters, outings, and conservation projects. This can be a good way to get involved. Go to some meetings, volunteer, offer to help. You may have to start out stuffing envelopes or some other unglamorous job, but if you persevere, you may have a chance to do something important and fun. It's a good way to learn and meet people.

Some environmental groups, such as the Environmental Defense Fund (EDF), The Nature Conservancy (TNC), the National Resources Defense Council (NRDC), and the Wilderness Society (WS), have limited contact with ordinary members except through their publications. They depend on a professional staff to carry out the goals of the organization through litigation (EDF and NRDC), land acquisition (TNC), or lobbying (WS). Although not often in the public eye, these groups can be very effective because of their unique focus. TNC buys land of high ecological value that is threatened by development. With more than 3,200 employees and assets around $3 billion, TNC manages 7 million acres in

what it describes as the world's largest private sanctuary system (fig. 25.9). Still, the Conservancy is controversial for some of its management decisions, such as gas and oil drilling in some reserves, and including executives from some questionable companies on its governing board and advisory council. The Conservancy replies that it is trying to work with these companies to bring about change rather than just criticize them.

Radical groups capture attention and broaden the agenda

A striking contrast to the mainline conservation organizations are the direct action groups, such as Earth First!, Sea Shepherd, and a few other groups that form either the "cutting edge" or the "radical fringe" of the environmental movement, depending on your outlook. Often associated with the deep ecology philosophy and bioregional ecological perspective, the strongest concerns of these militant environmentalists tend to be animal rights and protection of wild nature. Their main tactics are civil disobedience and attention-grabbing actions, such as picketing, protest marches, road blockades, and other demonstrations. Some of these actions are humorous and lighthearted, such as street theater that gets a point across in a nonthreatening way (fig. 25.10). Many of these techniques are borrowed from the civil rights movement and Mahatma Gandhi's nonviolent civil disobedience. While often more innovative than the mainstream organizations, pioneering new issues and new approaches, the tactics of these groups can be controversial.

Greenpeace, for example, is notorious (or famous, depending on your perspective) for attention-grabbing actions, such as draping protest signs from buildings, bridges, and other tall structures,

FIGURE 25.10 Street theater can be a humorous, yet effective, way to convey a point in a nonthreatening way. Confrontational tactics get attention, but they may alienate those who might be your allies and harden your opposition.

or pursuing whaling vessels in small rubber runabouts. Some people regard these tactics as meaningless stunts that contribute little to a constructive dialog on how to solve real problems. Others see them as useful tools in gaining public attention to serious problems. Is civil disobedience dangerous and counterproductive, or is it brave and constructive? Remember that many major social movements—from the slavery abolition, labor rights, and women's suffrage movements of the eighteenth and nineteenth centuries to civil rights and anti-war movements of the twentieth century gained much of their momentum from mass demonstrations and protests that many contemporaries regarded as unjustified and inexcusable. Nevertheless, these actions resulted in crucial social change.

How far you can go in disobeying rules and customs to influence public opinion and change public policy remains a difficult question. Is it better to try to overturn society or to work for progressive change within existing political, economic, and social systems? Is it more important to work for personal perfection or collective improvement? There may be no single answer to these questions: it's good to have people working in many different ways to find solutions.

International nongovernmental organizations mobilize many people

As the opening Case Study in this chapter shows, international **nongovernmental organizations (NGOs)** can be vital in the struggle to protect areas of outstanding biological value. Without this help, local groups could never mobilize the public interest or financial support for projects, such as saving Laguna San Ignacio.

The rise in international NGOs in recent years has been phenomenal. At the Stockholm Conference in 1972, only a handful of environmental groups attended, almost all from fully developed countries. Twenty years later, at the Rio Earth Summit, more than 30,000 individuals representing several thousand environmental groups, many from developing countries, held a global Ecoforum to debate issues and form alliances for a better world.

Some NGOs are located primarily in the more highly developed countries of the north and work mainly on local issues. Others are headquartered in the north but focus their attention on the problems of developing countries in the south. Still others are truly global, with active groups in many different countries. A few are highly professional, combining private individuals with representatives of government agencies on quasi-government boards or standing committees with considerable power. Others are on the fringes of society, sometimes literally voices crying in the wilderness. Many work for political change, more specialize in gathering and disseminating information, and some undertake direct action to protect a specific resource.

Public education and consciousness-raising using protest marches, demonstrations, civil disobedience, and other participatory public actions and media events are generally important tactics for these groups. Greenpeace, for instance, carries out well-publicized confrontations with whalers, seal hunters, toxic waste dumpers, and others who threaten very specific and visible resources. Greenpeace may well be the largest environmental organization in the world, claiming some 2.5 million contributing members.

In contrast to these highly visible groups, others choose to work behind the scenes, but their impact may be equally important. Conservation International has been a leader in debt-for-nature swaps to protect areas particularly rich in biodiversity. It also has some interesting initiatives in economic development, seeking products made by local people that will provide livelihoods along with environmental protection (fig. 25.11).

FIGURE 25.11 International conservation groups often initiate economic development projects that provide local alternative to natural resource destruction.

25.5 Campus Greening

Colleges and universities can be powerful catalysts for change. Across North America, and around the world, students and faculty are studying sustainability and carrying out practical experiments in sustainable living and ecological restoration.

Organizations for secondary and college students often are among our most active and effective groups for environmental change. The largest student environmental group in North America is the **Student Environmental Action Coalition (SEAC).** Formed in 1988 by students at the University of North Carolina at Chapel Hill, SEAC has grown rapidly to more than 30,000 members in some 500 campus environmental groups. SEAC is both an umbrella organization and grassroots network that functions as an information clearinghouse and a training center for student leaders. Member groups undertake a diverse spectrum of activities ranging from politically neutral recycling promotion to confrontational protests of government or industrial projects. National conferences bring together thousands of activists who share tactics and inspiration while also having fun. If there isn't a group on your campus, why not look into organizing one?

Another important student organizing group is the network of Public Interest Research Groups active on most campuses in the United States. While not focused exclusively on the environment, the PIRGs usually include environmental issues in their priorities for research. By becoming active, you could probably introduce environmental concerns to your local group if they are not already working on problems of importance to you. Remember that you are not alone. Others share your concerns and want to work with you to bring about change; you just have to find them. There is power in working together.

Environmental leadership can be learned

One of the most important skills you are likely to lean in SEAC or other groups committed to social change is how to organize. This is a dynamic process in which you must adapt the realities of your circumstances and the goals of your group, but there are some basic principles that apply to most situations (table 25.3). Using communications media to get your message out is an important part of the modern environmental movement. Table 25.4 suggests some important considerations in planning a media campaign.

It's probably not a surprise to anyone that the Internet is changing our world. You may not have thought, however, about how it can effect an environmental crusade. In 2007, author Bill McKibben worked with a small group of recent college graduates to organize the "Step it Up" campaign to demand national action to combat global climate change. They realized that they didn't have the financial or organizational muscle to mount a conventional campaign, so they turned to the Internet. Reaching other students through blogs and online journals, such as Grist, they built a huge, grassroots environmental protest movement.

With hardly any attention from the conventional press, they organized nearly 1,500 events involving thousands of individuals across the United States. Instead of a massive march on Washington

---

TABLE 25.3

Organizing an Environmental Campaign

1. What do you want to change? Are your goals realistic, given the time and resources you have available?
2. What and who will be needed to get the job done? What resources do you have now and how can you get more?
3. Who are the stakeholders in this issue? Who are your allies and constituents? How can you make contact with them?
4. How will your group make decisions and set priorities? Will you operate by consensus, majority vote, or informal agreement?
5. Have others already worked on this issue? What successes or failures did they have? Can you learn from their experience?
6. Who has the power to give you what you want or to solve the problem? Which individuals, organizations, corporations, or elected officials should be targeted by your campaign?
7. What tactics will be effective? Using the wrong tactics can alienate people and be worse than taking no action at all.
8. Are there social, cultural, or economic factors that should be recognized in this situation? Will the way you dress, talk, or behave offend or alienate your intended audience? Is it important to change your appearance or tactics to gain support?
9. How will you know when you have succeeded? How will you evaluate the possible outcomes?
10. What will you do when the battle is over? Is yours a single-issue organization, or will you want to maintain the interest, momentum, and network you have established?

Source: Based on material from "Grassroots Organizing for Everyone" by Claire Greensfelder and Mike Roselle from *Call to Action,* 1990 Sierra Book Club Books.

(and the time, expense, and greenhouse gas emissions required to get huge numbers of people to a single location), they encouraged small groups to gather in their local communities to hike, bike, climb, walk, swim, kayak, canoe, or simply sit or stand with banners proclaiming a commitment to action (fig. 25.12). Calling this electronic environmentalism, they showed how it's now possible to link many local systems into a virtual network. Another important example of this is the dramatic change in political campaigns in recent years, ranging from fundraising by web organizations, such as MoveOn.org, or the rapid spread of information through blogs, YouTube, and MySpace.

Schools can be environmental leaders

Colleges and universities can be sources of information and experimentation in sustainable living. They have knowledge and expertise to figure out how to do new things, and they have students who have the energy and enthusiasm to do much of the research, and for whom that discovery will be a valuable learning experience. At

TABLE 25.4

Using the Media to Influence Public Opinion

Shaping opinion, reaching consensus, electing public officials, and mobilizing action are accomplished primarily through the use of the communications media. To have an impact in public affairs, it is essential to know how to use these resources. Here are some suggestions:

1. *Assemble a press list.* Learn to write a good press release by studying books from your public library on press relations techniques. Get to know reporters from your local newspaper and TV stations.

2. *Appear on local radio and TV talk shows.* Get experts from local universities and organizations to appear.

3. *Write letters to the editor, feature stories, and news releases.* You may include black and white photographs. Submit them to local newspapers and magazines. Don't overlook weekly community shoppers and other "freebie" newspapers, which usually are looking for newsworthy material.

4. *Try to get editorial support from local newspapers, radio, and TV stations.* Ask them to take a stand supporting your viewpoint. If you are successful, send a copy to your legislator and to other media managers.

5. *Put together a public service announcement and ask local radio and TV stations to run it* (preferably not at 2 A.M.). Your library or community college may well have audiovisual equipment that you can use. Cable TV stations usually have a public access channel and will help with production.

6. *If there are public figures in your area who have useful expertise, ask them to give a speech or make a statement.* A press conference, especially in a dramatic setting, often is a very effective way of attracting attention.

7. *Find celebrities or media personalities to support your position.* Ask them to give a concert or performance, both to raise money for your organization and to attract attention to the issue. They might like to be associated with your cause.

8. *Hold a media event that is photogenic and newsworthy.* Clean up your local river and invite photographers to accompany you. Picket the corporate offices of a polluter, wearing eye-catching costumes and carrying humorous signs. Don't be violent, abusive, or obnoxious; it will backfire on you. Good humor usually will go farther than threats.

9. *If you hear negative remarks about your issue on TV or radio, ask for free time under the Fairness Doctrine to respond.* Stations have to do a certain amount of public service to justify relicensing and may be happy to accommodate you.

10. *Ask your local TV or newspaper to do a documentary or feature story about your issue or about your organization and what it is trying to do.* You will not only get valuable free publicity, but you may inspire others to follow your example.

FIGURE 25.12 Protests, marches, and public demonstrations can be an effective way to get your message out and to influence legislators.

more than 100 universities and colleges across America, graduating students have taken a pledge that reads:

> "I pledge to explore and take into account the social and environmental consequences of any job I consider and will try to improve these aspects of any organization for which I work."

Could you introduce something similar at your school?

Campuses often have building projects that can be models for sustainability research and development. More than 110 colleges have built, or are building structures certified by the U.S. Green Building Council. Some recent examples of prize-winning sustainable design can be found at Stanford University, Oberlin College in Ohio, and the University of California at Santa Barbara. Stanford's Jasper Ridge building will provide classroom, laboratory, and office space for its biological research station. Stanford students worked with the administration to develop *Guidelines for Sustainable Buildings,* a booklet that covers everything from energy-efficient lighting to native landscaping. With 275 photovoltaic panels to catch sunlight, there should be no need to buy electricity for the building. In fact, it's expected that surplus energy will be sold back to local utility companies to help pay for building operation.

Oberlin's Environmental Studies Center, designed by architect Bill McDonough, features 370 m² of photovoltaic panels on its roof, a geothermal well to help heat and cool the building, large south-facing windows for passive solar gain, and a "living machine" for water treatment, including plant-filled tanks in an indoor solarium and a constructed wetland outside (see figs. 18.27 and 20.10).

UCSB's Bren School of Environmental Science and Management looks deceptively institutional but claims to be the most environmentally state-of-the-art structure of its kind in the United States (fig. 25.13). It wasn't originally intended to be a particularly green building, but planners found that some simple features like having large windows that harvest natural light and open to let ocean breezes cool the interior make the building both more functional and more appealing. Motion detectors control light levels and sensors monitor and refresh the air when there is too much CO_2 putting students to sleep. More than 30 percent of interior materials are recycled. Solar panels supply 10 percent of

many colleges and universities, students have undertaken campus audits to examine water and energy use. waste production and disposal, paper consumption, recycling, buying locally produced food, and many other examples of sustainable resource consumption. At

FIGURE 25.13 The University of California at Santa Barbara claims its new Bren School of Environmental Science and Management is the most environmentally friendly building of its kind in the United States.

the electricity, and the building exceeds federal efficiency standards by 30 percent. "The overriding and very powerful message is it really doesn't cost any more to do these things," says Dennis Aigner, dean of Bren School.

These facilities can become important educational experiences. At Carnegie Mellon University in Pittsburg, students helped design a green roof for Hamershlag Hall. They now monitor how the living roof is reducing storm water drainage and improving water quality. A kiosk inside the dorm shows daily energy use and compares it to long-term averages. Classrooms within the dorm offer environmental science classes in which students can see sustainability in action. Green dorms are popular with students. They appreciate natural lighting, clean air, lack of allergens in building materials, and other features of LEED-certified buildings. One of the largest green dorms in the country is at the University of South Carolina, where more than 100 students are on a waiting list for a room.

A recent study by the Sustainable Endowments Institute evaluated more than 100 of the leading colleges and universities in the United States on their green building policies, food and recycling programs, climate change impacts, and energy consumption. The report card ranked Dartmouth, Harvard, Stanford, and Williams as the top of the "A list" of 23 greenest campuses. Berea College in Kentucky got special commendation as a small school with a strong commitment to sustainability. It's "ecovillage" has a student-designed house that produces its own electricitiy and treats waste water in a living system. The college has a full-time sustainability coordinator to provide support to campus programs, community outreach, and teaching. Some other campuses with academic programs in sustainability include Arizona State in Tempe, and Northern Arizona University in Flagstaff.

Your campus can reduce energy consumption

The Campus Climate Challenge, recently launched by a coalition of nonprofit groups, seeks to engage students, faculty, and staff at 500 college campuses in the United States and Canada in a long-term campaign to eliminate global warming pollution. Many campuses have invested in clean energy, set strict green building standards for new construction, purchased fuel-efficient vehicles,

and adopted other policies to save energy and reduce their greenhouse gas emissions. Some examples include Concordia University in Austin, Texas, the first college or university in the country to purchase all of its energy from renewable sources. The 5.5 million kilowatt-hours of "green power" it uses each year will eliminate about 8 million pounds of CO_2 emissions annually, the equivalent of planting 1,000 acres of trees or taking 700 cars off the roads. Emory University in Atlanta, Georgia, is a leader in green building standards, with 11 buildings that are or could become LEED certified. Emory's Whitehead Biomedical Research Building was the first facility in the Southeast to be LEED certified. Like a number of other colleges, Carleton College in Northfield, Minnesota, has built its own windmill, which is expected to provide about 40 percent of the school's electrical needs. The $1.8 million wind turbine is expected to pay for itself in about ten years. The Campus Climate Challenge website at http://www.energyaction.net contains valuable resources, including strategies and case studies, an energy action packet, a campus organizing guide, and more.

At many schools, students have persuaded the administration to buy locally produced food and to provide organic, vegetarian, and fair trade options in campus cafeterias. This not only benefits your health and the environment, but can also serve as a powerful teaching tool and everyday reminder that individuals can make a difference. Could you do something similar at your school? See the Data Analysis box at the end of this chapter for other suggestions.

25.6 SUSTAINABILITY IS A GLOBAL CHALLENGE

As the developing countries of the world become more affluent, they are adopting many of the wasteful and destructive lifestyle patterns of the richer countries. Automobile production in China, for example, is increasing at about 19 percent per year, or doubling every 3.7 years. By 2030 there could be nearly as many automobiles in China than the United States. What will be the effect on air quality, world fossil fuel supplies, and global climate if that growth rate continues? Already, two-thirds of the children in Shenzhen, China's wealthiest province, suffer from lead poisoning, probably caused by use of leaded gasoline. And, as chapter 8 points out, diseases associated with affluent lifestyles—such as obesity, diabetes, heart attacks, depression, and traffic accidents—are becoming the leading causes of morbidity and mortality worldwide.

We would all benefit by helping developing countries access more efficient, less-polluting technologies. Education, democracy, and access to information are essential for sustainability (fig. 25.14). It is in our best interest to help finance protection of our common future in some equitable way. Maurice Strong, chair of the Earth Charter Council, estimates that development aid from the richer countries should be some $150 billion per year, while internal investments in environmental protection by developing countries will need to be about twice that amount. Many scholars and social activists believe that poverty is at the core of many of the world's most serious human problems: hunger, child deaths, migrations, insurrections, and environmental

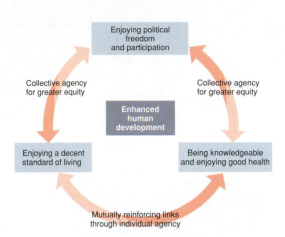

FIGURE 25.14 Human development, democracy, and education are mutually reinforcing.
Source: UN, 2002.

FIGURE 25.15 A model for integrating ecosystem health, human needs, and sustainable economic growth.

degradation. One way to alleviate poverty is to foster economic growth so there can be a bigger share for everyone.

Strong economic growth already is occurring in many places. The World Bank projects that if current trends continue, economic output in developing countries will rise by 4 to 5 percent per year in the next 40 years. Economies of industrialized countries are expected to grow more slowly but could still triple over that period. Altogether, the total world output could be quadruple what it is today.

That growth could provide funds to clean up environmental damage caused by earlier, wasteful technologies and misguided environmental policies. It is estimated to cost $350 billion per year to control population growth, develop renewable energy sources, stop soil erosion, protect ecosystems, and provide a decent standard of living for the world's poor. This is a great deal of money, but it is small compared to over $1 trillion per year spent on wars and military equipment.

While growth simply implies an increase in size, number, or rate of something, development, in economic terms, means a real increase in average welfare or well-being. **Sustainable development** based on the use of renewable resources in harmony with ecological systems is an attractive compromise to the extremes of no growth versus unlimited growth (fig. 25.15). Perhaps the best definition of this goal is that of the World Commission on Environment and Development, which defined sustainable development in *Our Common Future* as "meeting the needs of the present without compromising the ability of future generations to meet their own needs." Some goals of sustainable development include:

- A demographic transition to a stable world population of low birth and death rates.
- An energy transition to high efficiency in production and use, coupled with increasing reliance on renewable resources.

- A resource transition to reliance on nature's "income" without depleting its "capital."
- An economic transition to sustainable development and a broader sharing of its benefits.
- A political transition to global negotiation grounded in complementary interests between North and South, East and West.
- An ethical or spiritual transition to attitudes that do not separate us from nature or each other.

Notice that these goals don't apply just to developing countries. It's equally important that those of us in the richer countries adopt these targets as well. Supporting our current lifestyles is much more resource intensive and has a much greater impact on our environment than the billions of people in poorer countries. Many environmental scientists prefer to simply use the term **sustainability** to describe the search for ways of living more lightly on the earth because it can include residents of both the developed and developing world.

In 2000, United Nations Secretary-General Kofi Annan called for a **millennium assessment** of the consequences of ecosystem change on human well-being as well as the scientific basis for actions to enhance the conservation and sustainable use of those systems. More than 1,360 experts from around the world worked on technical reports about the conditions and trends of ecosystems, scenarios for the future, and possible responses.

TABLE 25.5

Millennium Development Goals

Goals	Specific Objectives
1. Eradicate extreme poverty and hunger.	1a. Reduce by half the proportion of people living on less than a dollar a day.
	1b. Reduce by half the proportion of people who suffer from hunger.
2. Achieve universal primary education.	2a. Ensure that all boys and girls complete a full course of primary schooling.
3. Promote gender equality and empower women.	3a. Eliminate gender disparity in primary and secondary education by 2015.
4. Reduce child mortality.	4a. Reduce by two-thirds the mortality rate among children under five.
5. Improve maternal health.	5a. Reduce by three-quarters the maternal mortality ratio.
6. Combat HIV/AIDS, malaria, and other diseases.	6a. Halt and begin to reverse the spread of HIV/AIDS.
	6b. Halt and begin to reverse the spread of malaria and other major diseases.
7. Ensure environmental sustainability.	7a. Integrate the principles of sustainable development into policies and programs; reverse the loss of environmental resources.
	7b. Reduce by half the proportion of people without sustainable access to safe drinking water.
	7c. Achieve significant improvement, in the lives of 100 million slum dwellers by 2020.
8. Develop a global partnership for development.	8a. Develop further an open trading and financial system that is rule-based, predictable, and nondiscriminatory, including a commitment to good governance, development, and poverty reduction.
	8b. Address the least-developed countries' special needs. This includes tariff- and quota-free access for their exports; enhanced debt relief for heavily indebted poor countries.

The findings from the millennium assessment serve as a good summary for this book. Among the key conclusions are:

- All of us depend on nature and ecosystem services to provide the conditions for a decent, healthy, and secure life.
- We have made unprecedented changes to ecosystems in recent decades to meet growing demands for food, fresh water, fiber, and energy.
- These changes have helped improve the lives of billions, but at the same time they weakened nature's ability to deliver other key services, such as purification of air and water, protection from disasters, and the provision of medicine.
- Among the outstanding problems we face are the dire state of many of the world's fish stocks, the intense vulnerability of the 2 billion people living in dry regions, and the growing threat to ecosystems from climate change and pollution.
- Human actions have taken the planet to the edge of a massive wave of species extinctions, further threatening our own well-being.

- The loss of services derived from ecosystems is a significant barrier to reducing poverty, hunger, and disease.
- The pressures on ecosystems will increase globally unless human attitudes and actions change.
- Measures to conserve natural resources are more likely to succeed if local communities are given ownership of them, share the benefits, and are involved in decisions.
- Even today's technology and knowledge can reduce considerably the human impact on ecosystems. They are unlikely to be deployed fully, however, until ecosystem services cease to be perceived as free and limitless.
- Better protection of natural assets will require coordinated efforts across all sections of governments, businesses, and international institutions.

As a result of this assessment, the United Nations has developed a set of goals and objectives for sustainable development (table 25.5). From what you've learned in this book, how do you think we could work—individually and collectively—to accomplish these goals?

CONCLUSION

All through this book you've seen evidence of environmental degradation and resource depletion, but there are also many cases in which individuals and organizations are finding ways to stop pollution, use renewable rather than irreplaceable resources, and even restore biodiversity and habitat. Sometimes all it takes is the catalyst of a pilot project to show people how things can be done differently to change attitudes and habits. In this chapter, you've learned some practical approaches to living more lightly on the world individually as well as working collectively to create a better world.

Public attention to issues in the United States seems to run in cycles. Concern builds about some set of problems, and people are willing to take action to find solutions, but then interest wanes and other topics come to the forefront. For the past decade, the American public has consistently said that the environment is very important, and that government should pay more attention to environmental quality. Nevertheless, people haven't shown this concern for the environment to be a very high priority, either in personal behavior or in how they vote.

Recently, however, the whole world seems to have reached a tipping point. Countries, cities, companies, and campuses all are vying to be the most green. This may be a very good time to work on social change and sustainable living. We hope that you'll find the information in this chapter helpful. As the famous anthropologist Margaret Mead said, "Never doubt that a small group of thoughtful, committed people can change the world. Indeed, it is the only thing that ever has."

REVIEWING LEARNING OUTCOMES

By now you should be able to explain the following points:

25.1 Explain how we can make a difference.

25.2 Summarize environmental education.
- Environmental literacy means understanding our environment.
- Citizen science encourages everyone to participate.
- Environmental careers range from engineering to education.
- Green business and technology are growing fast.

25.3 Evaluate what individuals can do.
- How much is enough?
- We can choose to reduce our environmental impact.
- "Green washing" can mislead consumers.
- Certification identifies low-impact products.
- Green consumerism has limits.

25.4 Review how we can work together.
- National organizations are influential but sometimes complacent.
- Radical groups capture attention and broaden the agenda.
- International nongovernmental organizations mobilize many people.

25.5 Investigate campus greening.
- Environmental leadership can be learned.
- Schools can be environmental leaders.
- Your campus can reduce energy consumption.

25.6 Define the challenge of sustainability.

PRACTICE QUIZ

1. Describe four major contexts for outcomes from environmental education.
2. Define *conspicuous consumption.*
3. Describe Lohas and cultural creatives.
4. Give two examples of green washing.
5. List five things that you can do to reduce your environmental impact.
6. List six stages in the Life Cycle Inventory at which we can analyze material and energy balances of products.
7. Identify the ten biggest environmental organizations.
8. List six goals of sustainable development.
9. Identify two key messages from the UN millennium assessment that you believe are most important for environmental science.
10. Identify two goals or objectives from the UN millennium goals that you believe are most important for environmental science.

CRITICAL THINKING AND DISCUSSION QUESTIONS

1. What lessons do you derive from the case study about protecting Laguna San Ignacio. If you were interested in protecting habitat and resources somewhere else in the world, which of the tactics used in this effort might you use for your campaign?
2. Reflect on how you learned about environmental issues. What have been the most important formative experiences or persuasive arguments in shaping your own attitudes. If you were designing an environmental education program for youth, what elements would you include?
3. How might it change your life if you were to minimize your consumption of materials and resources? Which aspects could you give up, and what is absolutely essential to your happiness and well-being. Does your list differ from that of your friends and classmates?

4. Have you ever been involved in charitable or environmental work? What were the best and worst aspects of that experience? If you haven't yet done anything of this sort, what activities seem appealing and worthwhile to you?

5. What green activities are now occurring at your school? How might you get involved?

6. In the practice quiz, we asked you to identify two key messages from the millennium assessment and two goals and objectives that you believe are most important for environmental science. Why did you choose these messages and goals? How might we accomplish them?

DATA analysis   Campus Environmental Audit

How sustainable is your school? What could you, your fellow students, the faculty, staff, and administration do to make your campus more environmentally friendly? Perhaps you and your classmates could carry out an environmental audit of your school. Some of the following items are things you could observe for yourself; other information you'd need to get from the campus administrators.

1. *Energy* How much total energy does your campus use each year? Is any of it from renewable sources? How does your school energy use compare to that of a city with the same population? Could you switch to renewable sources? How much would that cost? How long would the payback time be for various renewable sources? Is there a campus policy about energy conservation? What would it take to launch a campaign for using resources efficiently?

2. *Buildings.* Are any campus buildings now LEED certified? Do any campus buildings now have compact fluorescent bulbs, high-efficiency fans, or other energy-saving devices? Do you have single-pane or double-pane windows? Are lights turned off when rooms aren't in use? At what temperatures (winter and summer) are classrooms, offices, and dorms maintained? Who makes this decision? Could you open a window in hot weather? Are new buildings being planned? Will they be LEED certified? If not, why?

3. *Transportation.* Does your school own any fuel-efficient vehicles (hybrids or other high-mileage models)? If you were making a presentation to an administrator to encourage him or her to purchase efficient vehicles, what arguments would you use? How many students commute to campus? Are they encouraged to carpool or use public transportation? How might you promote efficient transportation? How much total space on your campus is devoted to parking? What's the cost per vehicle to build and maintain parking? How else might that money be spent to facilitate efficient transportation? Where does runoff from parking lots and streets go? What are the environmental impacts of this storm runoff?

4. *Water use.* What's the source of your drinking water? How much does your campus use? Where does wastewater go? How many toilets are on the campus? How much water does each use for every flush? How much would it cost to change to low-flow appliances? How much would it save in terms of water use and cost?

5. *Food.* What's the source of food served in campus dining rooms? Is any of it locally grown or organic? How much junk food is consumed annually? What are the barriers to buying locally grown, fair-trade, organic, free-range food? Does the campus grow any of its own food? Would that be possible?

6. *Ecosystem restoration.* Are there opportunities for reforestation, stream restoration, wetland improvements, or other ecological repair projects on your campus. What percentage of the vegetation on campus is native? What might be the benefits of replacing non-native species with indigenous varieties? Have gardeners considered planting species that provide food and shelter for wildlife?

What other aspects of your campus life could you study to improve sustainability? How could you organize a group project to promote beneficial changes in your school's environmental impacts?

For Additional Help in Studying This Chapter, please visit our website at www.mhhe.com/cunningham10e. You will find additional practice quizzes and case studies, flashcards, regional examples, place markers for Google Earth™ mapping, and an extensive reading list, all of which will help you learn environmental science.

(From Ch. 25 of William P. Cunningham and Mary Ann Cunningham, *Environmental Science*, 10th ed. McGraw-Hill, 2008.)

Credits

Text and Line Art Credits

CHAPTER 1

Pages 4–5: From *Success is a Choice* by Rick Pitino. Copyright © 1997 by Rick Pitino. Used by permission of Broadway Books, a division of Random House, Inc., and by permission of Vigliano Associates, Rick Pitino, 10/13/10. **Fig. 1.1:** *Dunn and Dunn Learning Style Model* graphic, designed and developed by Dr. Rita Dunn and Dr. Kenneth Dunn. Copyright © 2008-Graphic Design by Susan M. Rundle. Used with permission. **Pgs. 20–23:** *Dunn and Dunn Learning Style Model*, developed by Dr. Rita Dunn and Dr. Kenneth Dunn, adapted from Learning Styles Network site. Used with permission. **Pgs. 25–27:** Adapted from Mark Moring, "This Is Not Your High School English Class," *Campus Life*, Feb. 2001. pg. 84. Copyright © 2001 Christianity Today International/ Campus Life. Used with permission.

CHAPTER 3

Pages 57–71: Adapted from Michael W. Passer and Ronald E. Smith, *Psychology: The Science of Mind and Behavior*, 3rd ed. Copyright © 2007 The McGraw-Hill Companies. Used with permission of The McGraw-Hill Companies. **Pg. 63:** Brenda Wegmann and Miki Knezevic, *Mosaic Two, Reading*, 5th ed. McGraw-Hill, 2006. **Pgs. 67, 69:** Saundra Hybels & Richard L. Weaver, *Communicating Effectively*, 9th ed. McGraw-Hill, 2009. **Pg. 76:** H. Jackson Brown, quoted in H. Jackson Brown, Jr., *A Father's Book of Wisdom*, pg. 103. Thomas Nelson, Inc., 1999.

CHAPTER 4

Pages 86–99, 101–106: Adapted from Dale B. Hahn, Wayne A. Payne, and Ellen B. Lucas, *Focus on Health*, 8th ed. Copyright © 2007 The McGraw-Hill Companies. Used with permission of The McGraw-Hill Companies.

CHAPTER 5

Pages 113, 116–129, 131: Adapted from Dale B. Hahn, Wayne A. Payne, and Ellen B. Lucas, *Focus on Health*, 8th ed. Copyright © 2007 The McGraw-Hill Companies. Used with permission of The McGraw-Hill Companies.

CHAPTER 6

Page 157: www.prisonstudies.org. Publisher: The International Centre for Prison Studies, author: Director of the World Prison Brief, Roy Walmsley Permission given by the Director of the Centre, Professor Andrew Coyle. **Pgs. 137, 139–148, 150–151, 154–155, 158–161:** Excerpts from Robert M. Bohm and Keith N. Haley, *Introduction to Criminal Justice*, 4th ed. McGraw-Hill, 2007. Copyright © The McGraw-Hill Companies. Used with permission of The McGraw-Hill Companies.

CHAPTER 7

Pages 167–172, 176–189: Excerpts from Stanley J. Baran, *Introduction to Mass Communication*, 5th ed. Copyright © 2008 The McGraw-Hill Companies. Used with permission of The McGraw-Hill Companies. **Pg. 172, 177:** Adapted from Cecily Hall and Emily Kaiser, "The Power of Persuasion," *WWD*, Thursday, January 19, 2006. **Pg. 174:** Excerpt adapted from Joe Saltzman, "Media Overkill Is More Frightening Than the Real Thing." Reprinted with permission from *USA Today Magazine*, Nov. 2002. Copyright © 2002 by the Society for the Advancement of Education, Inc. All Rights Reserved. **Pg. 176:** Excerpts from Julius Lester, "Carved Runes In a Clearing: The Place of the Book In Our Lives," *UMassMag*, Spring 2002. **Pg. 190:** *Anchorage Daily News* editorial.

permission of The McGraw-Hill Companies.

Copyright © 2000 by McClatchy Company. Reproduced with permission of McClatchy Company in the format Textbook and Other Book via Copyright Clearance Center. **Pgs. 192–196:** Ariel Gore, "TV Can Be a Good Parent." Article first appeared in *Salon.com* at http:// www.salon.com. An online version remains in the Salon archives. Reprinted with permission.

CHAPTER 8

Page 203: Screenshot of Business Training Media, Inc.™ home page. Used with permission.

CHAPTER 9

Pages 214–216, 218–221, 226–227, 231–236: Adapted from Conrad Phillip Kottak, *Anthropology: The Exploration of Human Diversity*, 12th ed. Copyright © 2008 The McGraw-Hill Companies. Used with permission of The McGraw-Hill Companies. **Pgs. 228–230:** D. Applegate, CAL Learning Strategies Database, www.muskingum.edu/~cal/ database/general/organization.html.

CHAPTER 10

Page 240: Alan Brinkley, *American History: A Survey*, 12e. Copyright © 2007 The McGraw-Hill Companies. Used with permission of The McGraw-Hill Companies. **Pgs. 245–246:** Excerpt from Michael Pollan, "Unhappy Meals," 1/28/2007. Reprinted by permission of International Creative Management, Inc. Copyright © 2007 by Michael Pollan. **Pg. 248:** Abstract for article Meryl Davids, "Ray Kroc 1902–1984: Flipping Over Efficiency," *Journal of Business Strategy*, 9/1/99. Used with permission. **Pgs. 248–250:** Meryl Davids, "Ray Kroc 1902–1984: Flipping Over Efficiency," *Journal of Business Strategy*, 9/1/99. © Meryl Davids, 1999. Used with permission of the author. **Pgs. 252, 254:** Primary

Source Investigator CD accompanying Alan Brinkley, *American History: A Survey*, 12e. Copyright © 2007 The McGraw-Hill Companies. Used with permission of The McGraw-Hill Companies. **Pg. 253:** Adapted from Alan Brinkley, *American History: A Survey*, 12e. Copyright © 2007 The McGraw-Hill Companies. Used with permission of The McGraw-Hill Companies. **Pgs. 256–257:** Excerpts from jacket cover of *The Kite Runner* by Khaled Hosseini. Riverhead Books, 2003. **Pgs. 257–258:** "December 2001", from *The Kite Runner* by Khaled Hosseini. Copyright © 2003 by Khaled Hosseini. Used by permission of Riverhead Books, an imprint of Penguin Group (USA) Inc., and by permission of Bloomsbury Publishing Plc.

CHAPTER 11

Pages 278–279: Penn State Learning, "Dealing with Physical Tension," http://pennstatelearning.psu.edu/resources/study-tips/test-anxiety/anxiety#tension. Used with permission.

MODULE 1

Pages 289–290: Katherine Hobson, "A Plateful of Myths," *U.S. News & World Report*, 142.3 (Jan 22, 2007). Used with permission. **Pgs. 297–299:** Stephen Clapp, "Japanese Food Pyramid Revised to take Account of Eating Out," FoodChemicalNews.com (Sept 19, 2005). **Pg. 298:** Japanese Food Guide Spinning Top (English version), http://www.mhlw.go.jp/bunya/kenkou/pdf/eiyou-syokuji4.pdf. Used with permission of the Ministry of Health, Labour and Welfare, Japan. **Pgs. 307–309:** Dale B. Hahn, Wayne A. Payne, and Ellen B. Lucas, *Focus on Health*, 8th ed. Copyright © 2007 The McGraw-Hill Companies. Used with permission of The McGraw-Hill Companies.

MODULE 2

Pages 318–322: Terri D'Arrigo, "Stress and Diabetes," Copyright © 2000 American Diabetes Association. From *Diabetes Forecast*, April 2000. Modified with permission from The American Diabetes Association. **Pgs. 328–330:** Adapted from Dale B. Hahn, Wayne A. Payne, and Ellen B. Lucas, *Focus on Health*, 8th ed. Copyright © 2007 The McGraw-Hill Companies. Used with permission of The McGraw-Hill Companies. **Pgs. 337–338:** Robert M. Bohm and Keith N. Haley, *Introduction to Criminal Justice*, 4th ed. McGraw-Hill, 2007. Copyright © The McGraw-Hill Companies. Used with permission of The McGraw-Hill Companies.

MODULE 3

Pages 365–366: George Johnson and Jonathan Losos, "Ethical Issues Raised by Gene Therapy," *The Living World*, 5th ed. Copyright © 2008 The McGraw-Hill Companies. Used with permission of The McGraw-Hill Companies.

MODULE 4

Pages 377–378: Candy Tymson, "Business Communication: How to Bridge the Gender Gap," *The Journal of Banking and Financial Services*, June 2001. Reprinted with permission of the author, www.tymson.com.au. **Pgs. 386–389:** Excerpted from *Communication World* by Anne E. Beall. Copyright © 2004 by International Association of Business Communicators (IABC). Reproduced with permission of International Association of Business Communicators (IABC) in the format Textbook and Other Book via Copyright Clearance Center. **Pgs. 397–399:** John Stewart, *Bridges Not Walls: A Book About Interpersonal Communication*, 10th ed. Copyright © 2009 The McGraw-Hill Companies. Used with permission of The McGraw-Hill Companies. **Pg. 397:** "Something," Words and Music by George Harrison. Copyright © 1969 Harrisongs Ltd., Copyright Renewed 1998. All Rights Reserved. Reprinted by permission of Hal Leonard Corporation.

MODULE 5

Pages 428–429: Gareth Jones, "The Interview Process" from *Introduction to Business: How Companies Create Value for People*. Copyright © 2007 The McGraw-Hill Companies. Used with permission of The McGraw-Hill Companies.

MODULE 6

Pages 439–441: *Beauty and Body Image in the Media*, Media Awareness Network, © 2010 Media Awareness Network, www.media-awareness.ca, reproduced with permission. **Pgs. 447–448:** Adapted from Rosie Mestel, "Adolescents' TV Watching Is Linked to Violent Behavior," *Los Angeles Times*, 3/29/2002. Copyright © 2002 Los Angeles Times. Reprinted with Permission. **Pgs. 457–458:** Alan Brinkley, *American History: A Survey*, 12e, pg. 802–803. Copyright © 2007 The McGraw-Hill Companies. Used with permission of The McGraw-Hill Companies.

MODULE 7

Pages 469–473: Jeff Cain, "Online Social Networking Issues Within Academia and Pharmacy Education," *American Journal of Pharmaceutical Education*, 2008 February 15; 72(1): 10. Used with permission. **Pgs. 492–494:** J. John Palen, "Controlling Love: American Mate Selection," adapted from *Social Problems for the 21st Century*. Copyright © 2001 The McGraw-Hill Companies. Used with permission of The McGraw-Hill Companies.

MODULE 8

Pages 504–506: Excerpted from Rick Newman, "The Green Mirage," *U.S. News & World Report*, 10/30/07. Used with permission. **Pgs. 522–524:** William PG. Cunningham and Mary Ann Cunningham, "What Can Individuals Do? 'Green Washing' Can Mislead Consumers," *Environmental Science: A Global Concern*, ppg. 571–576. Copyright © 2008 The McGraw-Hill Companies. Used with permission of The McGraw-Hill Companies.

APPENDIX 1

Pages A-2–A-3, A-6: From Pauk. *How to Study in College*, 4E. © 1989 Wadsworth, a part of

Cengage Learning, Inc. Reproduced by permission. www.cengage.com/permissions. **Pgs. A-9–A-10:** Suffixes, adapted from Communications Lab, Florida State College at Jacksonville, http://www1.fccj.org/lchandouts/communicationshandouts/vocabularyhandouts/V-3.doc. Used with permission.

APPENDIX 2

Pages A-14–A-16: Adapted from Michael W. Passer and Ronald E. Smith, *Psychology: The Science of Mind and Behavior*, 3rd ed. Copyright © 2007 The McGraw-Hill Companies. Used with permission. **Pg. A-14:** Definition of "key" from *New American Webster's Handy College Dictionary* by Philip D. Morehead and Andrew T. Morehead, copyright 1951 (renewed), © 1955, 1956, 1957, 1961 by Albert H. Morehead, 1972, 1981, 1985, 1995 by Philip D. Morehead and Andrew T. Morehead. Used by permission of Dutton Signet, a division of Penguin Group (USA) Inc. **Pg. A-16:** Entry for "language," from *Roget's 21st Century Thesaurus* © 2010 The Philip Lief Group, Dell Publishing. Used with permission. **Pg. A-20:** H. Jackson Brown, quoted in H. Jackson Brown, Jr., *A Father's Book of Wisdom*, pg. 103. Thomas Nelson, Inc., 1999.

APPENDIX 3

Pages A-26–A-47: Richard Schaefer, Ch. 6 from *Sociology: A Brief Introduction*, 6th ed. Copyright © 2006 The McGraw-Hill Companies. Used with permission. **Pg. A-27:** *McDonaldization of Society (Paper)* by George Ritzer. Copyright © 2004 by Sage Publications Inc. Books. Reproduced with permission of Sage Publications Inc. Books in the format Textbook and Other Book via Copyright Clearance Center.

APPENDIX 4

Pages A-59–A-77: William PG. Cunningham and Mary Ann Cunningham, *Environmental Science: A Global Concern.* Copyright © 2008 The McGraw-Hill Companies. Used with permission of The McGraw-Hill Companies. **Pg. A-62:**

From *Environmentalist's Bookshelf.* Copyright © 1993 Gale, a part of Cengage Learning, Inc. Reproduced by permission. www.cengage.com/permissions. **Pg. A-65:** Moderne Man cartoon, "We Need to Consume" by b. von alten, 1990. Used with permission. **Pg. A-66:** "What Can You Do?" by Karen Oberhauser. Based upon material originally published by the Bell Museum of Natural History, University of Minnesota. Used with permission.

Photo Credits

CHAPTER 1

Pages 2–3: © Somos/Veer/Getty Images; **pg. 9:** © Ingram Publishing/AGE Fotostock; **pg. 13:** © Moodboard/Corbis; pg. 14: © BananaStock/PictureQuest; **pg. 16:** © Digital Vision/Getty Images; **pg. 23:** © The McGraw-Hill Companies, Inc./John Flournoy, photographer; **pg. 24:** © Gaetan Bally/Keystone/Corbis; **pg. 26:** © BananaStock/JupiterImages

CHAPTER 2

Pages 28–29: © Dynamic Graphics/JupiterImages; **pg. 31:** © Rubberball/Getty Images; **pg. 36:** © Image Source/Getty Images; **pg. 39:** © Graham Bell/Corbis; **pg. 44:** © Digital Vision/Getty Images

CHAPTER 3

Pages 50–51: © Lifesize/Getty Images; **pg. 53:** Image Source; **pg. 55:** © Rodney Brindamour/Contributor; **pg. 53:** © Alix Minde/PhotoAlto/Getty Images; **pg. 66:** © Stockbyte/Getty Images; **pg. 71:** © Doug Menuez/Getty Images

CHAPTER 4

Pages 78–79: © Floresco Productions/OJO Images /Getty Images; **pg. 83:** © Image Source/Getty Images; **pg. 85:** © Stockdisc/PunchStock; **pg. 90:** © Lifesize/Getty Images; **pg. 96:** © Getty Images; **pg. 102:** © Ingram Publishing/AGE Fotostock

CHAPTER 5

Pages 104–105: © Corbis; **pg. 111:** © RubberBall Productions; **pg. 114:** © Ryan McVay/Getty Images;

pg. 119: © Jupiterimages / Thinkstock/Alamy; **pg. 122:** © Janis Christie/Getty Images; **pg. 125:** © Royalty-Free/Corbis

CHAPTER 6

Pages 128–129: © Brand X Pictures; **pg. 133:** © David R. Frazier Photolibrary, Inc.; **pg. 137:** © David R. Frazier Photolibrary, Inc.; **pg. 144:** © 1998 Image Ideas, Inc.; **pg. 151:** © Dynamic Graphics Group/PunchStock; **pg. 156:** © Thinkstock Images /Getty Images

CHAPTER 7

Pages 160–161: © Digital Vision Ltd. / SuperStock; **pg. 163:** © RubberBall Productions; **pg. 171:** © Andersen Ross/Age Fotostock; **pg. 179:** © Petrified Collection / Getty Images; **pg. 182:** © AFP/Getty Images; **pg. 190:** © C Squared Studios/Getty Images

CHAPTER 8

Pages 194–195: © Mike Clarke/AFP/Getty Images; **pg. 196:** © Ingram Publishing / Fotosearch; **pg. 201:** © Digital Vision/Getty Images; **pg. 204:** © Mike Segar/Reuters/Corbis

CHAPTER 9

Pages 206–207: © Adam Woolfitt/Corbis; **pg. 209:** © Khaled Desouki/AFP/Getty Images; **pg. 213:** © Jo Prichard/epa/Corbis; **pg. 220:** © Kim Kaminski / Alamy; **pg. 225:** © Rob Melnychuk/Getty Images; **pg. 229:** © Soul/Getty Images

CHAPTER 10

Pages 232–233: © Dynamic Graphics Group/PunchStock; **pg. 234:** © Jay Laprete/Bloomberg via Getty Images; **pg. 243:** © Bohemian Nomad Picturemakers/Corbis; **pg. 246:** © Bichon/photocuisine/Corbis; **pg. 248:** © Ewing Galloway

CHAPTER 11

Pages 256–257: © Image Source/Getty Images; **pg. 258:** © Rubberball/Getty Images; **pg. 263:** © Fuse/Getty Images; **pg. 269:** © Ingram Publishing/Alamy; **pg. 270:** © Iain Crockart /Digital Vision/Getty Images; **pg. 271:** © Stockbyte/Getty Images

MODULE 1

Page 278: © Jose Luis Pelaez, Inc./ Blend Images/Corbis; **pg. 279:** © Qilai Shen/epa/Corbis; **pg. 284:** © Photodisc/Getty Images; **pg. 288:** © McGraw-Hill Companies; **pg. 289:** © Markus Altmann/Corbis

MODULE 2

Page 308: © Bob Thomas/Stone/ Getty Images; **pg. 309:** © Royalty-Free/Corbis; **pg. 313:** © Somos Photography/Veer; **pg. 315:** Photo #1 from U.S. Dept of Commerce photoset Hawaii Volcanism: Lava Forms; **pg. 317:** © Will & Deni McIntyre / Photo Researchers, Inc.; **pg. 320:** © Jocelyn Augustino/ FEMA; **pg. 328:** © Hill Street Studios/Blend Images/Getty Images

MODULE 3

Page 338: © Getty Images; **pg. 339:** © AP Photo /ashleytreatment.spaces. live.com/ blog; **pg. 348:** © AP Photo/ Jean-Marc Bouju; **pg. 351:** © Karen Kasmauski/Corbis; **pg. 356:** © Adam Gault/Getty Images; **pg. 359:** © Science Photo Library RF/Getty Images

MODULE 4

Page 366: © Zave Smith/Corbis; **pg. 367:** © Eric Audras/Photoalto/ PictureQuest; **pg. 374:** © Comstock Images/JupiterImages; **pg. 377:** © Noel Hendrickson/Getty Images; **pg. 382:** © Mike Kemp/Getty

Images; **pg. 388:** (top) © Stockdisc/ PunchStock, (bottom) © Sigrid Olsson/PhotoAlto/Corbis; **pg. 392:** © Kerry-Edwards 2004, Inc./Sharon Farmer, photographer

MODULE 5

Page 398: (top left) © Jamie Grill/ Iconica/Getty Images, (top right) © Rubberball/Getty Images, (bottom left) © DreamPictures/Stone/Getty Images, (bottom right) © Bob Handelman/Stone/Getty Images; **pg. 399:** © Keith Brofsky/Getty Images; **pg. 403:** © Keith Brofsky/Getty Images; **pg. 408:** © James Leynse/ Corbis; **pg. 412:** © Ingram Publishing/ Alamy; **pg. 420:** © Digital Vision

MODULE 6

Page 428: © John Gress/Getty Images; **pg. 435:** © Ryan McVay/ Lifesize/Getty Images; **pg. 438:** © Kakimage / Alamy; **pg. 448:** (left) © Photo by CBS Photo Archive/ Getty Images, (middle) © Photo by Leonard Mccombe//Time Life Pictures/Getty Images, (right) © MPI/Getty Images; **pg. 451:** © Photodisc

MODULE 7

Page 458: © The Image Works; **pg. 459:** © The McGraw-Hill Companies, Inc./John Flournoy, photographer; **pg. 471:** © Jerry Cooke/Corbis; **pg. 477:** © Erica

Simone Leeds 2007; **pg. 483:** © The Photo Works / Alamy

MODULE 8

Page 494: © Doug Sherman/Geofile; **pg. 499:** © Ralph Orlowski/Getty Images; **pg. 503:** © Jeff Greenberg/ The Image Works; **pg. 508:** © Blend Images/Getty Images; **pg. 514:** © David Young-Wolff/Getty Images

APPENDIX 3

Page A-20: Courtesy of MAGIC International; **Pg. A-25:** © Warner Bros/The Kobal Collection/Claudette Barius; **Pg. A-26:** © AP Photo; **Pg. A-27:** CBS Photo Archive; **Pg. A-28:** © AP Photo; **Pg. A-32:** © Kenneth Jarecke/Woodfin Camp & Associates; **Pg. A-34:** © AP Photo; **Pg. A-35:** © Peter Hvizdak/ The Image Works; **Pg. A-36:** © Jeff Greenberg/PhotoEdit, Inc.

APPENDIX 4

Page A-53: © Robert Sobol; **Pg. A-55:** (top & bottom) © William P. Cunningham; **Pg. A-57:** © William P. Cunningham; **Pg. A-58:** © William P. Cunningham; **Pg. A-62:** © William P. Cunningham; **Pg. A-63:** David L. Hansen, University of Minnesota Agricultural Experiment Station; **Pg. A-64:** (top & bottom) © William P. Cunningham; **Pg. A-66:** © William P. Cunningham; **Pg. A-67:** © William P. Cunningham

Index